FIFTH EDITION

NorthWestNet's Guide to Our World Online

NorthWestNet

Prentice Hall PTR
Englewood Cliffs, New Jersey 07632

Library of Congress Cataloging-in-Publication Data
NorthWestNet
The Internet passport : NorthWestNet's guide to our world online—5th ed.
    p. cm.
Includes bibliographical references and index.
ISBN 0-13-194200-X
1. Internet (Computer network)
I. NorthWestNet. II. Title.
TK5105.875.I57R63   1995
025.04--dc20   94-43394
                                       CIP

NortWestNet Production Staff

Contributing authors: *Jonathan Kochmer, David F.W. Robison, Lawrence E. Gales* ("Using Supercomputers")
Editor and production supervisor: *Jan Eveleth*
Executive editor: *Eric S. Hood*
Technical editor: *Dan L. Jordt*
Assistant editor: *Anthony C. Naughtin*

Prentice Hall Staff

Editorial/production supervision and interior design: *Patti Guerrieri, Ann Sullivan, Camille Trentacoste*
Manufacturing manager: *Alexis R. Heydt*
Acquisitions editor: *Mary Franz*
Editorial assistant: *Noreen Regina*
Cover design: *Anthony Gemmellaro, Singer Design*
Cover art: *Telegraph Colour Library/FPG*

Published by Prentice Hall PTR
Prentice-Hall, Inc.
A Simon & Schuster Company
Englewood Cliffs, New Jersey 07632

The publisher offers discounts on this book when ordered in bulk quantities. For more information, contact:
Corporate Sales Department   Phone: (800)382-3419 or (201)592-2498
PTR Prentice Hall   Fax: 201-592-2249
113 Sylvan Avenue   E-mail: dan_rush@prenhall.com
Englewood Cliffs, NJ 07632

NorthWestNet   e-mail: passport@nwnet.net
15400 SE 30th Place, Suite 202   voice: (206)562-3000
Bellevue, WA 98007   fax: (206)562-4822

Printed in the United States of America
10 9 8 7 6 5 4 3 2 1

ISBN 0-13-194200-X

Prentice-Hall International (UK) Limited, *London*
Prentice-Hall of Australia Pty. Limited, *Sydney*
Prentice-Hall Canada Inc., *Toronto*
Prentice-Hall Hispanoamericana, S.A., *Mexico*
Prentice-Hall of India Private Limited, *New Delhi*
Prentice-Hall of Japan, Inc., *Tokyo*
Simon & Schuster Asia Pte. Ltd., *Singapore*
Editora Prentice-Hall do Brasil, Ltda., *Rio de Janeiro*

Contents

■■■

■■■

SECTION II • BASIC INTERNET TOOLS

■■■

Contents

Contents

Contents

SECTION III • COMMUNITY FORUMS

9 • USENET   121
DISCUSSIONS IN THE CAFES OF THE GLOBAL VILLAGE

■■

SECTION IV • TEXTS AND DATA

12 • ELECTRONIC JOURNALS AND NEWSLETTERS   169

13 • ELECTRONIC BOOKS   175

14 • LIBRARIES ON THE INTERNET   183
ONLINE PUBLIC ACCESS CATALOGS (OPACs)

SECTION V • RESOURCE DISCOVERY AND RETRIEVAL TOOLS

16 • ARCHIE   271
THE FTP ARCHIVE GURU

Contents

18 • WAIS (WIDE AREA INFORMATION SERVER)   311
EASY ACCESS TO INTERNET DATABASES

19 • CAMPUS WIDE INFORMATION SYSTEMS (CWIS)   325

20 • WORLD WIDE WEB   337
A HYPERTEXT-BASED VIEW OF THE INTERNET

21 • A BIG BLACK BOOK   357
DIRECTORIES OF INTERNET USERS AND HOSTS

Section VI • Targeted Interests

22 • Becoming an Information Provider

387

Contents

Contents

Contents

Contents

■■■

■■■

SECTION VII • APPENDICES

■■■

Contents

■ ■■■ ■

Contents

Preface

*O*nce you get started, you'll start to understand...

—Overheard in a crowd

Until very recently, using computer networks was like using a car at the beginning of the 20th century. Charlie Chaplin and Buster Keaton made comedies featuring wrestling matches with temperamental cars. It was funny because everybody knew you couldn't drive to the next town without getting greasy up to your elbows at least once. The technology was still being perfected, and sometimes it was hard to get where you were going.

It was also hard to figure out how to find the places you were looking for.

There's an old joke in New England about a city slicker asking for directions from a farmer sitting on his front porch. The farmer says, "You can't get there from here." As a person who grew up in a rural area, I've always thought this was short for saying, "well, I can give you directions, but unless you grew up in these parts, you probably won't understand anyway..."

But things have changed with automobiles, and they're beginning to change with computer networks.

Most of us use complex technologies like automobiles, televisions, or telephones every day without knowing exactly how they work. We take it for granted that when we turn on a radio we'll hear news or music, and that when we start a car we'll get to where we want to go.

Computer networks have jumped the first hurdle on the path which all technologies must run. They are now usually very reliable. Most of the time, you can press a few buttons and know that your message will be received by someone thousands of kilometers away, maybe even in a few seconds. Today, global computer networks like the Internet are being used by millions of people who don't know much more about computers than the average person knows about the inner workings of a television set.

The purpose of *The Internet Passport* is to help network users get over the second great hurdle of new technologies: now that computer networks are reliable, what can they be used for? And once you know what can be done, you'll learn "how to get there from here." You can think of *The Internet Passport* as a set of basic driving lessons, and a glove compartment full of "road maps" to the many interconnected routes and valuable services that together comprise a worldwide network of networks known as "The Internet."

HOW TO USE YOUR *INTERNET PASSPORT*

...a book is more than a verbal structure, or a series of verbal structures; a book is the dialogue with the reader, and the peculiar accent he gives to its voice, and the changing and durable images it leaves in his memory. That dialogue is infinite.

—Jorge Luis Borges
"For Bertrand Russell"

The Internet Passport is for anyone who uses or wants to use the Internet: from elementary school teachers at small and isolated rural schools, to the most sophisticated supercomputer users at major urban research institutions. Throughout, every attempt has been made to keep the text simple without being simplistic, and thorough without being thoroughly overwhelming.

No single book can provide complete documentation about the Internet, so your *Passport* is meant to be a generic framework upon which to build a collection of materials suiting your level of expertise and particular sets of interests. This book will have succeeded in one of its primary goals if each *Passport* user creates their own unique library of Internet documentation, just like everybody's glove compartment contains a different collection of road maps. Most of the on-line documents referred to throughout the book can be obtained, for free, from any computer connected to the Internet.

Every Internet user is different, but most network activities depend on the mastery of three basic skills: using electronic mail to communicate with other Internet users, logging in to remote computers with a service called Telnet, and obtaining on-line documents, software, and other materials via FTP. It is also a good idea to have an overview of the Internet as a whole. So you are encouraged to read through the chapters on the Internet, electronic mail, Telnet, and FTP first. Once you've mastered the basic "Internet-working" skills and concepts you should be able to use the remaining chapters in any order that suits your needs.

Most chapters have the following structure (where "x" is the topic of the chapter):

What is x?

What is x used for?

What do I need to know before I start using x?

How do I access x?

A sample session using x, with step-by-step explanations

For more information on x

Because the Internet is able to support a tremendous diversity of hardware and software, it is sometimes impossible to present examples guaranteed to work for everyone. For instance, there are dozens of software packages for electronic mail. In such cases, a generic example using a "lowest common denominator" implementation is presented to illustrate the essential features of a particular Internet topic. When necessary, you should obtain appropriate documentation from your instructor or user services staff on how a particular application is used at your site.

The Internet is also a rapidly changing realm. Although every on-line resource and example in *The Internet Passport* was tested and checked repeatedly during the writing and editing, you may find that a few of the resources listed here have changed, moved, or maybe even no longer exist by the time you use this book.

Stylistic Conventions

Throughout this book, a number of typographic conventions are used to communicate what happens (or should happen!) during your Internet sessions.

Sample Internet sessions, or information which appears on a computer screen, will appear in boxes:

```

```

Inside such boxes, you will see characters that have been sent to your screen by a computer—either your computer, or a remote Internet computer to which you've connected. Such messages will be in a typeface known as `courier`:

```
Welcome to the Internet!
```

This font has also been used in tables for names of Internet computers or on-line files we may encourage you to obtain.

```
FTP host:      nis.nsf.net
directory:     /internet/documents/rfc
filename:      rfc1000.txt
```

Of course, computers aren't of much value unless you can send commands or ask questions. Because what we as computer users want is often of the *utmost* urgency, a font called "*courier italic*" is used to indicate commands which you will type:

```
telnet answer.library.net
```

Sometimes, what the computer sends to your screen and what you enter as a reply may appear on the same line. In such cases, the computer's message will be in `courier` and what you type in response will be in *courier italic*:

```
Display what topic(s)?: all
```

In the screen snapshot above, you've been shown exactly what to type. At other times, you need to supply information of your choosing. Such user-supplied information is presented in `courier`, surrounded by angle brackets:

```
Display what topic(s)?: <a topic of your choice>
```

This doesn't mean that you should literally type "<a topic of your choice>", but rather, that you should type the name of a topic.

When some explanation about a command or its consequences might help you understand what is happening on your screen, you will see parenthetical comments on the screen (**in courier bold**):

```
telnet answer.library.net
(followed by login messages from answer.library.net)
```

Finally, there will be cases where several of these conventions may appear in a single, extended screen snapshot, as in the following:

```
Display what topic(s)?: all          (display all topics)
  1. Aeronautics and Aerospace
  2. Afro-American Studies
  3. Agriculture
  4. Algebra
  5. American Studies
  6. Ancient History
     ...
 20. Arabic Studies
 21. Archery
 22. Arctic Studies
 23. Art History

Select 1-23, n for next page, or q to quit:

20
            Welcome to the Arabic Studies Database
            --------------------------------------

Begin search, Display datasets, Help:

<enter a number, b, d or h>
```

As you may see, the "20" that our hypothetical computer user typed is in italics, but it's a little hard to spot. So when you see a screen like this, you may have to squint every now and then to distinguish between what you will type, and what will be sent by the computer. Also note the ellipses ("...") in the middle of the screen. These will often be used when what the computer will display may be much longer than is convenient to include in the screen snapshot. In this case, you can assume that on-line resources for other topics have been displayed on your screen.

Your Comments and Suggestions

This document will be most effective if it is a continuing dialogue, between you, the Internet, and NorthWestNet User Services. If you have any comments or suggestions about *The Internet Passport*, feel free to drop us a line.

NorthWestNet
Attn: The Internet Passport
15400 SE 30th Place, Suite 202
Bellevue, WA 98007 USA

e-mail: `passport@nwnet.net`
voice: (206) 562-3000
fax: (206) 562-4822

Acknowledgments

ACKNOWLEDGMENTS FOR THE FIFTH EDITION

Working on a follow-up edition of someone else's work presents special challenges. The first is to learn the material and the second is to get into the mind of the original author. I have attempted here to update and expand on the excellent work of my predecessor, Jonathan Kochmer, in a way that will not jar the reader with two voices. Although I have only met Jonathan once, and briefly, I do feel that I know quite a bit about him now. I am glad that I have had the opportunity to work with him, even if indirectly.

I also wish to acknowledge the other NorthWestNet User Services staff, Carol Brand, Stefan Kramer, and Mike Showalter, who have supported me and the effort of producing another edition of the *Passport* over the last six months. Jan Eveleth receives special notice as the forever-upbeat editor and comma commander who has kept my spirits up when the task seemed endless. Thanks also goes to Eric Hood and Dan Jordt for editing the new chapters of this edition. The Technical Services staff has helped both in terms of offering specific information needed for this book, as well as making sure that the computers we use are running. The rest of the NorthWestNet staff cannot go unmentioned since each member of the organization contributes to the environment in which this edition was completed.

Finally, I wish to thank Jeff Gaisford for making Seattle an even better place to live.

—David Feiner Willard Robison

Seattle, Washington
April, 1994

ACKNOWLEDGMENTS FOR THE FOURTH EDITION

It is perhaps appropriate that this book, which is meant to teach you how to use the extraordinary wealth of information on the Internet, was written using the Internet itself as the main source of information. Only a very small number of traditional printed books were consulted during the preparation of this document. Therefore, primary thanks go to the Internet itself, for being such a treasure trove of documentation!

Most of the research and writing was done from my home, which became an "electronic cottage" in the global village by virtue of a personal computer connected to the Internet by a modem. *The Internet Passport* is proof of the ease with which the wealth of Internet resources can be accessed with minimal hardware and software requirements.

Snippets of information were collected from tens of thousands of postings in many Internet community forums, including Usenet, LISTSERV discussion groups, and Internet mailing lists. I thank everyone who so willingly shares their knowledge with the Internet community. Reading and answering typical questions from new Internet users posted in these forums was also invaluable for helping to determine what should be included in an entry-level Internet guide. Another useful source of information was existing, on-line Internet documentation written by Internet User Services staff around the world, and a large number of helpful documents about the Internet written by individuals on their own initiative, and freely distributed through the Internet. A rich collection of K-12 Internet resources prepared by Jim Flanagan of the Glenview School District in Illinois is just one of many such documents which made this manual possible.

The Internet Passport has benefited from reviews of the previous edition of this book; comments and suggestions made by John S. Quarterman were of particular value.

A number of my friends and housemates with no prior Internet experience—Martin Gaspe, Peter Marks, Spain McMillan and Sarah Scott—read and commented on the earliest drafts, and gave insight into how best to present this material to new Internet users. Almost as importantly, these and other friends eased the decompression process during re-entries from cyberspace to reality. And without the friendship of Cynthia Walcker, I may never have survived the weaving of this epic.

Like Vergil in his telling of *The Aeneid*, Jan Eveleth, NorthWestNet's new Director of User Services, joined this project *in media res* and steered this book to completion.

I am very thankful for the expertise of Larry Gales of the University of Washington, who wrote the chapter on Supercomputer Access, and to user services staff at the super-computer sites for providing up-to-date descriptions of their state-of-the-art sites.

Preliminary drafts of chapters of *The Internet Passport* received thorough and expert review by User Services staff from a number of NorthWestNet member institutions: we would like to thank Marilyn Bushway (Oregon Health Sciences University), Thomas Bremer (North Dakota State University), Betsy Draper (North Dakota State University), Jessica Dubey (Reed College), Marvin Dunn (Reed College), Marty Hoag (North Dakota State University), Dick Jacobson (North Dakota State University), David McMullen (North Dakota State University), Tim Preuss (North Dakota State University), and Marty Zimmerman (University of Idaho). Kudos to Sheryl Erez of the University of Washington for thoroughly reviewing some of the materials not just once, but twice!

Every page of the penultimate (and antepenultimate!) draft of this book was vastly improved by the reviews and revisions by NorthWestNet staff: Carol Brand (Educational Services Specialist), Jan Eveleth, Eric Hood (Executive Director) and Dan Jordt (Director of Technical Services). And in our pursuit of perfection, a final proof was made by Eric Hood and Tony Naughtin (Manager of Member Relations). Any errors in the final copy were of course caused by cosmic rays corrupting the diskettes we carried to the printer. :-)

Yale University and my dissertation committee have graciously allowed an extended leave of absence from my research in evolutionary biology to work with North-WestNet on Internet documentation. Rick Harrison (now at Cornell University) and Rob DeSalle (now at the American Museum of Natural History) have been particularly under-standing, and I genuinely look forward to working with them again now that I am newly invigorated by my travels through the Internet.

Finally, I owe special and personal gratitude to my parents, Anne and Kenneth Kochmer, MD, and my brother, Casey, for a childhood suffused by a love of language and learning, and a familial belief that being a renaissance person is still possible and even desirable in the information age. Thanks to a number of Internet databases I learned about while writing this book, my father was able to develop a treatment for a frequently fatal disease he had contracted. I am delighted to report that he is still alive, and is now enthu-siastically pursuing his own second career as a photographer. So in closing, as in opening, I must thank the Internet for being an invaluable resource.

—Jonathan Patrick Kochmer

The Cottage
Seattle, Washington
December, 1992

Acknowledgments

■■■

SUPPORTERS

■■■

NorthWestNet wishes to acknowledge and express appreciation for the financial support provided for this project by the Directorate for Computer and Information Science and Engineering through the Division of Networking and Communications Research and Infrastructure of the National Science Foundation under Grant No. NCR-9100415.

Acknowledgments

Trademarks and Copyrights

NOTE

▪▪▪

Courier is a registered trademark of Smith Corona.

Cray X-MP, Cray Y-MP, and Cray 2 are trademarks of Cray Research, Inc.

DEC, DECNET, TOPS-20, Ultrix, VAX, VAXcluster, VAXstation, VAX/VMS and VMS are registered trademarks of the Digital Equipment Corporation.

DYNIX is a trademark of Sequent Computer Systems Inc.

Dow Jones News/Retrieval is a registered trademark of Dow Jones and Company, Inc.

The Electronic Newsstand is a trademark of the Internet Company.

Ethernet is a registered trademark of the Xerox Corporation.

Fido and FidoNet are trademarks of Tom Jennings.

Geographic NameServer is a copyright of Merit, Inc.

Hewlett-Packard is a trademark of the Hewlett-Packard Corporation.

IBM, IBM PC, PC/XT, PC/AT and OS/2 are registered trademarks of the International Business Machines Corporation.

IEEE is a trademark of the Institute of Electrical and Electronics Engineers, Inc.

Intel is a trademark of the Intel Corporation.

K12Net is a trademark and servicemark of Jack Crawford.

Knowbot is a trademark of the Corporation for National Research Initiatives.

Microsoft, Microsoft Excel, Microsoft Windows, Microsoft Word, and MS-DOS are trademarks of the Microsoft Corporation.

Lotus 1-2-3 is a trademark of the Lotus Corporation.

The National Research and Education Network (NREN) is a registered trademark of the National Science Foundation.

NFS, Sun, SunOS are trademarks of Sun Microsystems, Inc.

PINE and UWIN are trademarks of The University of Washington.

QUIPU is a trademark of NYSERNet, Inc.

SAS is a trademark of SAS Institute, Inc.

Telenet and TELE-MAIL are trademarks of the GTE Telenet Communications Corporation.

UNIX is a registered trademark of AT&T Bell Laboratories.

VT100 is a registered trademark of the Digital Equipment Corporation.

WordPerfect is a trademark of the WordPerfect Corporation.

Xerox is a registered trademark of the Xerox Corporation.

About NorthWestNet

Providing digital communications and computer networking services to clients throughout six states, NorthWestNet is the most experienced, reliable provider of Internet access, related information resources, and support services in the region. Established in 1987 to link researchers and scholars at the region's nine leading universities and The Boeing Company, NorthWestNet has since expanded to serve a diverse clientele from a variety of industries and markets.

Today NorthWestNet provides Internet services to over 145 organizations—universities, colleges, commercial businesses, primary and secondary schools and school districts, government agencies, hospitals and clinics, libraries, and other not-for-profit entities—across Alaska, Idaho, Montana, North Dakota, Oregon, and Washington. NorthWestNet delivers a comprehensive suite of Internet connectivity and value-adding information services including:

- Exceptionally reliable, high performance Internet access delivered using path diverse and switch redundant architectures, "state-of-the-art" network components, and "round-the-clock" network monitoring and management;

- "Real-time" access to advanced computing and information systems including specially-licensed databases (e.g., MEDLINE) and on-line electronic library resources (e.g., CARL);

- Tools that allow users to access and share information in an interactive, convenient, integrated, and easy-to-learn manner (e.g., NorthWestNet's *Members Only* gopher service);

- *The Internet Passport: NorthWestNet's Guide to Our World Online,* a premier, annually updated Internet user's manual and resource guide, available in both hard copy and online electronic formats to our members;

- Training in the use of a variety of Internet services and applications ranging from electronic mail (e-mail) to high-performance computing systems and networked information resources;

- Electronic distribution services and discussions lists facilitate communication among participants in our technical committees and user groups;

- Technical and user documentation, network planning guides, training materials, resource bibliographies, networking policies, and working papers available from NorthWestNet's information server;

- Technical seminars, training courses, and workshops on a variety of topics delivered by NorthWestNet network engineers, communications technicians, and user services specialists.

Today, our member/clients enjoy the significant competitive advantages afforded by NorthWestNet's value-adding services. Enhanced by these services, NorthWestNet clients discover that the Internet can truly be a productivity tool enabling research, education, and commerce.

In our region's rapidly growing, technology-based economy, the demand for computing, electronic communications, and information services is ever increasing. With our expanded and enhanced Internet service offerings, NorthWestNet will continue to support the growing, internationally competitive Pacific Northwest region through the 1990s.

For further information contact:

NorthWestNet
15400 SE 30th Place, Suite 202
Bellevue, WA 98007 USA
voice: (206) 562-3000
fax: (206) 562-4822
e-mail: **info@nwnet.net**

June 1994

SECTION

I

Introduction

INTERNET

PASSPORT

@

CHAPTER 1

Introducing the Internet

The Internet is a worldwide network of networks which interconnects computers ranging from the simplest personal computers to the most sophisticated mainframes and supercomputers. This network of networks is used for an extraordinary range of purposes—long distance collaborations, retrieving free software and documents, accessing library catalogs, logging in to supercomputers—the list of current Internet activities and services is large and the range of possible future applications is as unlimited as our imagination.

The Internet is huge. No one is exactly sure just how huge, but there are over two million connected computers. Because it is in direct communication with satellites far above us, it could even be said that the Internet is already bigger than the Earth. And because the Internet is incredibly complex, there probably isn't a single person who understands everything about it. Remember this if you get confused and you'll probably feel better!

This chapter will give you a basic orientation to the world of the Internet, and the rest of this book will help you go where you want to go and meet who you want to meet.

WHAT IS A NETWORK?

The Internet is comprised of networks, but what's a network?

Every one of us, every moment, is surrounded by, embedded in, and in fact made up of networks.

As you read this page, light passes through your eyes into your nervous system, a complex network of cells that somehow allows you to make sense of the patches of light and dark on the page, and turns these words into meaning. In turn, the page you are reading was brought to you by a complex network of networks made up of people, vehicles, buildings, and more people. And when you travel to another country, you travel on networks of roads, buses, airline routes, and sea lanes.

Almost everything you see around you is part of or made possible by networks of networks. In both the human and natural worlds, networks provide communication, sharing of resources, and collaboration of many distinct parts as one big system, greater than the sum of its parts.

WHAT IS A COMPUTER NETWORK?

You have probably seen or used simple computer networks made up of a few identical computers in an office or a store. Such simple networks may allow files to be transferred between computers, sharing of centralized hard disks, printers, and other services, and can be very useful in situations where all users are performing the same tasks.

But just as a small organism comprised of only a few types of nerve cells may be limited to a few simple behaviors, a network made up of computers using only one kind of operating system can only be used by people using that kind of computer, and can only offer a limited variety of applications.

What Is an "Internet"?

An internet (note the lower case "i") is a computer network which allows computers with distinctive software and hardware to communicate, or "internetwork." Many kinds of computers can be connected to an internet, and each computer can serve a specialized role, allowing an internet to offer a wide variety of services to its users. For example, you could use one internet computer designed to perform complex calculations and then send the output to another internet computer designed to display colorful graphs.

What Is "The Internet"?

The Internet is a specific kind of internet. In *The Internet Passport*, the Internet will be defined as the network of networks which follow a set of rules known as the "Internet Protocol (IP) suite."

But what does this mean to you? It means that any computer which is connected to the Internet can communicate with any other Internet computer thanks to the rules of IP, and that a message sent from one Internet computer to another will get to the intended destination. From the user's perspective, this works much the way the telephone system works. You can dial from your phone to any other phone on the system no matter what kind of telephone you have; you only need to know the phone number of the person you want to reach.

Two related terms you might encounter are "The Net," which among Internet users is shorthand for the Internet but may sometimes refer to whatever network that person happens to use, and "The Matrix," which is often used to refer to the Internet, as well as all other networks to which Internet computers may communicate. And finally, you should note that other sources may define the Internet more or less restrictively.

What Is the Internet Used for?

The Internet contains the electronic equivalents of conference rooms and cafes, libraries and bookstores, post offices and telephones, radio and television stations, newspapers and magazines, and a growing variety of services that have no counterparts in "the real world."

Accessing Computer Resources

No matter how humble your own computer might be, if it is connected to the Internet you can access the resources of thousands of computers throughout the world. With an Internet connection you can:

- access online library catalogs,
- copy computer files or software from archives,
- access databases for teaching or research,
- obtain free electronic books,
- use educational and information services,
- use directory services to find Internet users, and
- access supercomputer sites.

Although the Internet is made up of many diverse computers, together they work like one worldwide computer system.

Communicating with Other People

People communicating with people is the essence of the Internet. Using the Internet you can:

- exchange electronic mail,
- find people throughout the world who share your interests, and
- engage in discussions and collaborations with other Internet users.

These services have created a truly global village where people communicate with each other not because they happen to live in the same place, but because they share the same interests. This simple fact has profound consequences for everyone no matter where they live.

Who Uses the Internet?

The Internet is a global community of communities: as of November 1994, it is estimated that there are 30 million Internet users in over 80 countries. These millions of people from all walks of life count on the Internet as an integral part of their day-to-day activities. When you use the Internet, you will be able to communicate with:

- researchers and students at universities,
- senior citizens,
- government officials,
- K-12 students and teachers,
- business people,
- librarians,
- health care service providers,
- agricultural extension agents,
- and other people who share your interests, whatever they may be.

■■

How Does the Internet Work?

■■

This section is meant to give you just a brief overview of the nuts and bolts of the Internet. If you don't really care about nuts and bolts, feel free to skip this section. As a network user, you really don't need to know much about these details, just like you don't need to understand particle physics to use a toaster. If you want more detailed and technical descriptions about how the Internet actually works, you should consult the references listed in the bibliography of Internet protocols and standards at the end of this chapter.

The Internet Protocol Suite (IP)

An early precursor of today's Internet was the ARPANET, supported by the Advanced Research Projects Agency (ARPA), now known as the Defense Advanced Research Projects Agency (DARPA). Research on the ARPANET led to the development of today's Internet Protocol suite, or IP. But what is a protocol suite?

In international affairs, diplomatic protocols are established to allow people from distinct cultures to negotiate and come to agreement; similarly, each computer that is part of the Internet must use software conforming to a collection (or suite) of rules, namely IP, in order to communicate with other Internet computers.

The need to develop shared protocols is of special importance because of the diversity of computer software and hardware. All of these computers need to have a shared language to communicate! If software conforming to IP is installed in a computer, it can participate in the Internet.

About Packet Switching

To understand how information is moved through the Internet, it's often useful to draw analogies with postal mail. Although the following examples all deal with mail and electronic mail, the principles described apply to other forms of communication on the Internet.

Suppose you have written a letter to a friend in Brazil. Your letter is taken to a local postal office and sorted on the basis of the address information on its envelope. To get to Brazil, your letter may now be put into a truck carrying completely unrelated packages going to many other destinations. The particular routes chosen by the postal service to deliver your letter might vary depending upon the volumes of letters passing through different intermediate stations, or the availability of vehicles.

All of this is similar to what happens when a message enters the Internet, except everything happens much more quickly. When you send a message or command from your computer to another Internet computer, the circuits carrying your message might contain messages sent from other users of your Internet computer to many other locations. Depending upon conditions within the network between here and there, a message you send to a friend on the other side of the continent might go by a northern route one

■■■

day, or a southern route another day. To you, it doesn't really matter, as long as the message gets to its intended destination in a timely fashion.

Returning to the postal mail analogy, suppose a furniture company wanted to mail a very large object to Brazil, such as a desk. They would have to disassemble it into units which were lighter in weight and smaller in size than the limits set by the postal service. Each package would require addressing information, as well as information about how the contents of this particular package were associated with the contents of the other packages, so that a fully functional desk could be reassembled at the destination. Each of the packages might get to Brazil by different routes, some by land, some by air, some through Texas, and some through California. It doesn't really matter as long as they all end up in Brazil at approximately the same time. And if one or more parts are missing, the client in Brazil would write a letter saying, "please send another front panel for the left bottom drawer."

Again, this is similar to what happens when you send a file or message through the Internet. The file is broken into smaller parts, called "packets," each of which has addressing information and the information needed to reassemble the complete file at its destination. Each packet may take a separate route, and the packets are reassembled at the destination.

A network or service which works in this way is referred to as a "packet switched network." A message is broken up into component packages ("packets") which can travel by different routes (by being "switched"), and then be reassembled at the destination.

In contrast, the telephone networks of the world are mostly "circuit switched" networks. When you are having a telephone conversation with someone else, the circuit between you and the other party is set up specifically for, and then dedicated solely to your conversation. If a word of the conversation is lost because of static interference, it is lost forever.

But in the Internet, the circuit carrying your message might be carrying messages and signals bound for multiple locations, yet gives the appearance, at the end points, of a dedicated line. And if something is lost in transmission, it can be sent again. All of this is possible because of the activities of the Transmission Control Protocol/Internet Protocol (TCP/IP).

Transmission Control Protocol (TCP)

TCP, the Transmission Control Protocol, is what is referred to as an "upper layer protocol" used in conjunction with IP (written as TCP/IP). "Upper layer" means that TCP relies upon IP; other protocols could be (and sometimes are) placed atop IP for other purposes.

TCP guarantees that the packets sent through the Internet are properly packaged and transmitted in a reliable fashion. In Internet communications, individual files or messages are packaged into smaller units called "datagrams," each containing a portion of the actual data being transmitted, the relationship of the datagram to other datagrams derived from the same file or process, and all information required to send the data to a destination independently of other, associated datagrams. After being transmitted through the Internet by IP, the datagrams are then reassembled by TCP at the destination into an exact copy of the original data stream.

Internet Hardware (Router Rooters: "Go Internet Go!")

Physically, the Internet is composed of computers using software conforming to the rules of IP, and the transmission media, bridges, and routers that allow data to be moved between these computers.

The transmission media may be physical wires, such as telephone lines or twisted pair cables, or through the air, as in the case of microwaves or infrared light signals. But once computers are linked together by transmission media, how does information get to the right locations? This is the role of routers, which are responsible for moving the packets through a packet switched network such as the Internet.

A router receives packets of data and then forwards each packet toward its destination. By reading the packet's address information and using its internal "routing tables" to determine which path is optimal, a router will pass the packet on to the next router, which will repeat the performance until the packet has arrived at its final destination.

This relay race approach may strike you as slow and cumbersome, but in fact transmission of packets through the Internet can be remarkably speedy and efficient. For example, I have just run a command called "traceroute" from my computer here at NorthWestNet, in Seattle, Washington, to determine what path a message would take to reach a computer at the Artificial Intelligence Labs at MIT, in Cambridge, Massachusetts. The path reported goes south to San Francisco, then due east to Chicago, Cleveland, and Hartford, involving 11 routers along the way. Using another network diagnostic tool called "ping," I found that the total round-trip time for the transmission of packets to Cambridge and back (involving 26 routers!) averaged less than 1/10th of a second.

Bon Appétit at the Information Diner: Internet Applications

The tremendous diversity of services described throughout the rest of this book are referred to as Internet applications. Unlike computer applications with which you may already be familiar, such as the word processor on your personal computer, Internet applications and the computers on which they are located are usually designed to be used by many people simultaneously. For this and other reasons, most Internet applications follow what is known as the "client-server" model.

Clients and Servers

In the old days (e.g., a couple of years ago), terminals and personal computers connected to mainframes and networks usually acted as "dumb terminals" which simply accessed and displayed the services provided by the mainframe. Most of the actual processing of information was done on the remote machine.

Today, many Internet applications are built from two interrelated components that have complementary and active functions: "clients" and "servers." The concept is very simple if you think in terms of human clients and servers. A client makes a request and a server fulfills that request.

For example, when you sit down at a restaurant, you are a client. At your table, you will find a menu displaying what sorts of foods are available. You think about your choices, and then you tell the person waiting on you what you want to eat. Your request is passed on to the kitchen, and the cook prepares the meal. (Note that in this example, there are actually two servers: the waiter and the cook.)

Similarly, the client-server model involves client software installed on your local computer that performs basic functions such as displaying menus or negotiating connections to a remote computer, and a server that performs tasks such as searching databases and sending the results back to you. And just like the restaurant example above, one server may pass your request on to yet other servers before your request is fulfilled.

The client-server model has several advantages. Client software is often designed to let you work with the features of your computer that you know and love, such as pull-down menus, a mouse, or familiar commands. Since the client and server software are separate, developers can change the client and server software independently. And because the client software may handle a significant portion of the data processing of your request, the load on those computers (which many people access) may be reduced: the client-server model is intended to spread the computational load of the network more evenly among all the computers on the network.

PEOPLE AND PLACES, NAMES AND DOMAINS

To send a letter to someone or get to their home, you follow a set of rules used to read and write addresses. Similarly, to communicate and travel within the Internet global village, you need to know how to read and write Internet names and addresses.

Understanding Internet Addresses

Continuing the postal mail analogies, let's start with a typical postal address for a house in the U.S.:

> 11 Maple Street
> Seattle,
> Washington, 98103
> USA

You may not have thought of this before, but such postal addresses follow a precise set of rules. Each line provides increasingly general information about a location, from street to country. (Since streets are in cities, cities are in states, and states are in countries, this is called a hierarchical addressing scheme.) Let's call this the official address—the address a postal service actually uses to deliver a letter to the building.

■■■

Internet Protocol (IP) Addresses

To be a part of the Internet, a computer must be assigned an "Internet Protocol (IP) address." A computer used by people that has been assigned an IP address is known as "an Internet host." Like the postal addresses or telephone numbers whose rules you take for granted, IP addresses follow a specific set of rules: an IP address is made up of four numbers, separated by dots. For example, an Internet host at the University of Washington might be assigned the following IP address:

128.95.10.207

This is the kind of address by which hosts and routers on the Internet "find" each other. When you need to read IP addresses, use the word "dot" for the periods: "one-twenty-eight dot ninety-five..." If such addresses look and sound forbidding and unfriendly, don't worry; the "Domain Name System" offers an easier alternative.

Domain Name System Addresses

Luckily for humans, who remember series of words more easily than series of numbers, the official IP addresses used in the Internet can be represented by words instead of numbers. This is one of the tasks of "Domain Name System" software which allows numeric IP addresses to be represented in more nearly human-readable "domain names." The Internet host with the IP address 128.95.10.207 might have the following domain name:

my-mac.biology.washington.edu

Domain names for Internet hosts are much like postal addresses. They are hierarchical, but the parts are separated by dots, instead of being on separate lines. Here's what our hypothetical domain name might mean:

`my-mac`	a particular Internet host (probably a Macintosh!)
`biology`	within the biology department
`washington`	within the University of Washington domain
`edu`	within the education-oriented domain of the U.S. Internet

So when you use the Internet, a domain name that you type ("norman.nwnet.net") is translated by Domain Name System software into the host's corresponding Internet address (192.35.180.15). (Although IP addresses are hierarchical from right to left, there is not a part-to-part correspondence between the domain name and Internet address.)

It's important to note that although the numeric IP address is the official Internet address, people often refer to domain names as Internet addresses as well. Though not strictly correct from a technical perspective, this usage is widespread and is sometimes used in *The Internet Passport* as well.

The Domain Name System is a method used for the management of parts of the Internet called "domains." The Internet host "my-mac" is in the domain called "biology." So someone, probably in this biology department, is responsible for keeping track of host names within this domain. Similarly, the domain "biology" is one of many domains within the domain "washington," and again, someone is responsible for those domains. Once a name has been used within a domain, it can still be used in other domains: there is nothing to prevent a domain administrator in the english department from assigning the name "my-mac.english.washington.edu".

Using an IP Address

It is rare to use an IP address instead of the domain name but there are times when it is needed. If you try and connect to a remote computer with the domain name and the local domain name server is down the translation cannot be made. Instead of connecting, you will get a message saying "unknown host." In this case, use the IP address if it is available. If the host is reachable, you should be able to connect. It is not advisable to use IP addresses as a matter of practice for two reasons. First, they are much harder to remember than domain names, and second, they change more frequently than domain names.

Electronic Mail Addresses

Perhaps there will be a time when you could use a person's real name when you send messages to them over the Internet, but at the present, people on the Internet are known by their "userid," short for USER IDentification. (At your site, the userid may be known as "login name," "account id," or something similar.) Associated with most userids is an electronic mailbox, which is where messages to a person are received at an Internet host. Just like there may be many mailboxes in an apartment building there may be hundreds or even thousands of mailboxes on an Internet host, each assigned a unique name.

Userids can be constructed in many ways; this will be discussed in more detail in Chapter 2. But let's suppose that we have a friend "Sue D. Nimh" who has a mailbox named "sue" at the Internet host my-mac.biology.washington.edu. Her electronic mail address would be written as

sue@my-mac.biology.washington.edu

where "@" simply means "at."

Notice that when someone says, "my Internet address is joe@ibmpc.school.edu," this is informal shorthand for saying the more technically correct, "I have a mailbox named 'joe' which is on a computer with the domain name 'ibmpc.school.edu'." So again, be aware that the term "Internet address" has yet another common meaning!

There are occasions when what is to the left of the "@" sign may serve roles other than a simple mailbox name. It could be an "alias" which means that messages sent to this address would be distributed to many mailboxes, or it could be forwarding information needed to send messages to networks beyond the Internet. Because the person administering each Internet host can locally set up mailboxes, aliases, and gateways at that host, whatever is to the left of the "@" sign is referred to as "the local part." So although "something@a.domain.name" usually means "a mailbox named 'something' at a host named 'a.domain.name'," it could have other meanings as well.

The Major Domains of the Internet

Just like the real world is divided into countries containing smaller units, the addresses found in the Internet world are divided into "top level domains" which contain "subdomains."

Consider the following three addresses:

`cascade.nwnet.net`	(host.subdomain.domain)
`stis.nsf.gov`	(host.subdomain.domain)
`cnri.reston.va.us`	(host.subdomain.subdomain.domain)

The first part of each of these DNS addresses is the name of an individual computer, or host. The rest of the address represents subdomains within domains, just like postal addresses represent streets within cities, and cities within states.

Sometimes domains and subdomains correspond to "real world" political boundaries; for example "cnri.reston.va.us" is an address for the Corporation for National Research Initiatives in Reston, Virginia, USA.

But more often than not, domains and subdomains reflect the naming structure of the Internet more than the structure of the world. Unlike political boundaries, boundaries of domains can overlap partially or entirely. To make this clear, let's look first at domain names which correspond to political boundaries, and then domain names which are based on categories of organizations.

International First Level Domains

Here's a list of the top level domain names of countries and territories which had Internet connectivity in February 1994. This information was gathered from statistics supplied by the Merit Network Information Center and is available via anonymous FTP from `nic.merit.edu` as the file `nets.by.country` in the directory `/nsfnet/statistics`.

AE	United Arab Emirates		IT	Italy
AO	Antarctica		JP	Japan
AR	Argentina		KE	Kenya
AT	Austria		KR	Korea, South
AU	Australia		KW	Kuwait
BE	Belgium		KZ	Kazakhstan
BG	Bulgaria		LB	Lebanon
BR	Brazil		LI	Lichtenstein
CA	Canada		LU	Luxembourg

(Continued)

CH	Switzerland	LV	Latvia
CL	Chile	MX	Mexico
CM	Cameroon	MY	Malaysia
CR	Costa Rica	NL	Netherlands
CY	Cyprus	NO	Norway
CZ	Czech Republic	NZ	New Zealand
DE	Germany	PE	Peru
DK	Denmark	PL	Poland
EC	Ecuador	PR	Puerto Rico
EE	Estonia	PT	Portugal
EG	Egypt	RO	Romania
ES	Spain	RU	Russian Federated Republic
FI	Finland	SE	Sweden
FJ	Fiji	SG	Singapore
FR	France	SI	Slovenia
GH	Ghana	SK	Slovakia
GL	Greenland	TH	Thailand
GR	Greece	TN	Tunisia
GU	Guam	TR	Turkey
HK	Hong Kong	TW	Taiwan
HR	Croatia (local name: Hrvatska)	UA	Ukraine
HU	Hungary	UK	United Kingdom
ID	Indonesia	US	United States
IE	Ireland	VE	Venezuela
IL	Israel	VI	Virgin Islands
IN	India	ZA	South Africa
IS	Iceland		

Within each national top level domain, there might be several distinct networks that are physically and administratively separate. Within Japan, both the JUNET and WIDE networks are part of the "jp" domain.

Similarly, a network may span several domains. NORDUnet, the Nordic Academic and Research Network, serves Iceland (is), Norway (no), Sweden (se), Finland (fi), and Denmark (dk).

First Level Domains in the U.S.

Although there is a top level domain for each country, there are also top level domains based on kinds of organizations, instead of geographical location:

COM	Commercial organizations
EDU	Educational and research institutions
GOV	Government agencies
INT	International organizations
MIL	Military agencies
NET	Major network support centers
ORG	Other organizations

Any Internet network within the U.S. might have hosts in two or more of these domains. For example, NorthWestNet has hosts in the com, edu, gov, net, and org domains.

THE STRUCTURE OF THE INTERNET

The Internet is not just one network. In fact it is currently more than 20,000 networks, each of which may contain thousands or tens of thousands of computers!

In general, the boundaries between these many Internet networks are invisible to the average Internet user, just like the existence of regional phone companies is usually not apparent to you when you make a long distance phone call.

Kinds of Internet Networks

To give you a general understanding of how the Internet is structured, let's go through the major classes of Internet networks.

Government Sponsored National Networks

Many countries have government sponsored national Internet networks. For example, within the U.S., there are several distinct nationwide networks operated by various U.S. government agencies. The most widely used network of this sort in the U.S. is the National Science Foundation Network (NSFNET). Other examples include the NASA Science Internet (NSI) and the Department of Energy's Energy Science Network (ESNET).

Government Sponsored Regional Networks

Within national government sponsored networks, there may be government sponsored regional networks to serve specific geographic areas. In the U.S., there are nearly two dozen NSF-funded regional networks, each of which is connected to NSFNET at a "backbone site." For example, NorthWestNet is a regional network serving the six northwestern states, including Alaska, and is linked to NSFNET at the University of Washington in Seattle.

Supercomputer Access Networks

Several Internet networks are dedicated to providing local access to supercomputer sites. Examples within the U.S. include the Los Alamos National Laboratory network (LANL), the National Center for Supercomputer Applications Network (NCSANet), the Pittsburgh Supercomputer Network (PSCNET), and the San Diego Supercomputer Center Network (SDSCnet).

Statewide Networks

Within the U.S. many states currently have active statewide networks. Some, but not all state networks, use the TCP/IP protocols. Similarly, there are provincial or district networks in other countries which may serve particular administrative regions within that country.

Metropolitan Area Networks (MANs)

Metropolitan Area Networks (MANs) are a more recent entry to the network world. As the name suggests, these networks are designed to provide network services to geographically-restricted metropolitan regions, for example, NCFN in Beijing, China. MANs are frequently used for local communications among government and other public service communities, including libraries, hospitals, and educational institutions.

Commercial Networks

There has been a rapid proliferation of commercial Internet networks in the past several years. Some of these commercial networks are "spin-offs" from pre-existing regional or international networks.

WHO RUNS THE INTERNET?

No one person or organization runs the Internet. Instead it is a collective effort of many organizations each responsible for some subset of the Net with the shared goal of providing global communications and network services. Quarterman (1990) and Marine et al. (1992) provide more thorough descriptions of the specific activities of Internet administrative and standards bodies.

Administrative Bodies and Organizations

Much of the research, development, and planning upon which the Internet is based is handled and coordinated by a variety of organizations.

The Internet Architecture Board (IAB) and specific task forces within the IAB such as the Internet Engineering Task Force (IETF) and the Internet Research Task Force (IRTF) play technical, engineering, and administrative roles throughout the worldwide Internet.

The activities and overall administration of these groups is coordinated by an organization called The Internet Society (ISOC).

Standards Bodies

The IAB, and its various, related task forces, are seen by many as the body guiding the development of Internet standards. A number of other organizations also help to create or participate in the evolution of related computing or networking standards. These standards bodies may be international, national, or regional groups of people from government, business, and educational institutions.

Among the standards bodies that you will most frequently hear about are the American National Standards Institute (ANSI), the Comite Consultatif International de Telegraphique et Telephonique (CCITT), the International Organization for Standardization (ISO), and the National Institute for Standards and Technology (NIST).

Internet NICs and NOCs

The day-to-day running and caring for specific Internet networks and their users are handled by Network Operations Centers (NOCs) and Network Information Centers (NICs).

A network's NOC deals with the operational aspects of running the network, including installation and maintenance of the network's hardware and software; monitoring and troubleshooting of the network's activity; and establishing connections to new network sites. A NOC staff may also field questions from technical representatives from member institutions and from institutions which are contemplating connecting to the network.

A network's NIC provides centralized support for users and user services staff throughout their network. Typical NIC activities can include preparing, distributing, and maintaining documentation for network users; publication of newsletters; maintenance of a central computer archive of information files or other resources; directory services for users of the network; and educational training classes for the users and network staff of member institutions.

In addition to local NICs, there is also the InterNIC, a Federally-supported NIC "of first and last resort." The InterNIC provides information services, directory services, and domain name registration services for the entire network.

NICs and NOCs may be actual parts of the network's administration, or they may be services provided by third-party organizations.

OTHER NETWORKS

There are a number of widely used computer networks which do not use the TCP/IP protocols, and thus are not technically part of the Internet. Services offered by these networks are usually limited to electronic mail and file exchange. In particular, it is not usually possible to do "remote logins," one of the special features of the Internet, to computers on such networks.

Nonetheless, you can communicate with users and computers on many non-Internet networks via e-mail messages sent to electronic mail "gateways." (See Chapter 5.) These e-mail gateways are responsible for translating messages between networks using different protocols.

Here are a few additional networks which you might hear about, and what they have to offer Internet users.

Corporation for Research and Educational Networking (CREN)

CREN is an umbrella organization which was responsible for two national networks, BITNET and CSNET. As of October 1991, CSNET was no longer operational. BITNET, however, is still a provider of educational networking.

BITNET—"Because It's Time Network"

This is a multi-disciplinary network designed to facilitate electronic communications among universities. Like the Internet, BITNET has associated networks such as EARN, the European Academic and Research Network, GULFNet in Saudi Arabia and Kuwait, and NetNorth in Canada.

BITNET is of interest to Internet users mainly because of a variety of valuable services such as mail servers and discussion lists. (See LISTSERV described in Chapter 10.) Although many computers in the world are on both BITNET and the Internet, there are computers which are only on BITNET, and you may want to communicate with users on these BITNET-only computers.

Users and services of BITNET are readily accessible to Internet users through mail gateways at several sites which are connected to both the Internet and to BITNET. For more information about electronic mail gateways, refer to Chapter 5.

FidoNet

FidoNet is an international network with more than 10,000 electronic "Bulletin Board Systems" (BBS's) in more than 50 countries. It is a grassroots, decentralized, not-for-profit network operated entirely through volunteer effort and it is based on simple technology. FidoNet is mainly used by networking hobbyists and in lesser developed nations. In several cases, e.g., in South Africa, FidoNet networks have been invaluable for demonstrating the value of networking and thereby have helped to create full-fledged Internet networks.

K12Net

K12Net is a spin-off of FidoNet designed specifically for K-12 students and teachers. Although K12Net offers more limited services than the Internet, many K-12 schools have found K12Net to be an effective way to start networking. Like FidoNet, K12Net may, in some cases, be a valuable stepping stone to the use of full service Internet networks.

Institute for Global Communications (IGC)

Joining any one of the IGC networks offers access to all three of their networks (PeaceNet, EcoNet, and ConflictNet), as well as e-mail gateways to the Internet. The three IGC Networks offer users a forum for social, political, and environmental issues.

UUCP

The UUCP network is a set of computers that exchange e-mail messages with the UUCP protocols. While using the Internet, you will encounter messages to discussion groups which have come from the UUCP network. The major UUCP networks are UUNET in the United States, EUnet in Europe, and ERNET in India. Many UUCP hosts are also part of the Internet and offer valuable archives of software and documents for Internet users. Addresses in UUCP are gradually being changed into a format that conforms with the Internet addresses.

The Future of the Internet

No one knows what the future of the Internet is, but some things are known. In the last few years, the rate of growth of the Internet has been astounding, with the number of users doubling approximately every eight months! There are also rapid changes in other types of global communications, and most see a "convergence" of voice communications, video transmission, and data communications. Among all of this growth and activity is the U.S. government's National Information Infrastructure (NII) initiative which intends to stimulate the development of a privately owned information infrastructure that offers Americans ubiquitous access to digital communications and information services (often referred to as the "information superhighway"). The proposal is driven by five basic principles: to promote investment, to provide and protect competition, to secure open access, to provide for universal service, and to ensure that government regulation itself is flexible and adaptable. The initiative is still in the early stages of development and legislation related to various aspects of it is currently pending in Congress. The administration has also created the Information Infrastructure Task Force (IITF) within the Commerce Department to serve as the coordinating group for Federal activities related to the information infrastructure.

Conclusion

Now that you have a general understanding of the Internet world, you are ready to begin your journeys.

Welcome to the Internet. You are now a citizen of the global village!

■■■

FOR MORE INFORMATION
■■■

Online Resources

The U.S. Commerce Department National Telecommunications and Information Administration's (NTIA) Information Infrastructure Task Force (IITF) Secretariat has an information server covering the NII and related issues. Included at this site is the administration's paper, "National Information Infrastructure: Agenda for Action."

Gopher:	**iitf.doc.gov**
Telnet:	**iitf.doc.gov**
login:	**gopher**
modem:	(202) 501-1920
	setting: data=8, parity=N, stop=1

Contact: e-mail: **ddavis@ntia.doc.gov**

IITF Gopher
Dr. Dan Davis
U.S. Department of Commerce/NTIA
14th & Constitution Ave., N.W., Room 4888
Washington, DC 20230 USA

voice: (202) 482-1835
fax: (202) 482-0979

e-mail: **cfranz@ntia.doc.gov**

IITF Secretariat
Charles Franz
U.S. Department of Commerce/NTIA
14th & Constitution Ave., N.W., Room 4892
Washington, DC 20230 USA

voice: (202) 482-1835
fax: (202) 482-0979

Bibliography

Non-Technical Bibliography on the Internet and Related Topics

Aboba, B. *The BMUG Guide to Bulletin Boards and Beyond.* Berkeley, CA: BMUG, Inc., 1992.

Brand, S. *The Media Lab: Inventing the Future at MIT.* New York: Viking, 1987.

Braun, E. *The Internet Directory.* New York: Fawcett Columbine, 1994.

Brownrigg, E. B. "The Internet as an external economy: The emergence of the invisible hand." *Library Administration and Management*; 5(2):95-97. 1991.

■■■

Corbin, R. A. "The development of the National Research and Education Network." *Information Technology and Libraries*. 10(3):212-220. 1991.

Dern, D. *The Internet Guide for New Users*. New York: McGraw-Hill, Inc., 1994.

Engst, A. *Internet Starter Kit for Macintosh*. Indianapolis: Hayden Books, 1993

Estrada, S. *Connecting to the Internet: A Buyer's Guide*. Sebastopol, CA: O'Reilly and Associates, 1993.

Fraase, M. *The Mac Internet Tour Guide: Cruising the Internet the Easy Way*. Chapel Hill: Ventana Press, 1993.

Frey, D. and R. Adams. *!%@:: A Directory of Electronic Mail Addressing and Networks*. Sebastopol, CA: O'Reilly and Associates, 1993.

Gilster, P. *The Internet Navigator*. New York: John Wiley, 1993.

Hafner, K. and J. Markoff. *Cyberpunk: Outlaws and Hackers on the Computer Frontier*. New York: Simon and Schuster, 1991.

Hahn, H. and R. Stout. *The Internet Complete Reference*. Berkeley: Osborne McGraw-Hill, 1993.

Holbrook, J. P. and C. S. Pruess. *CICNet Resource Guide*. Ann Arbor, MI: CICNet, Inc., 1992.

Kahin, B. "Information policy and the Internet." *Government Publications Review*. 18(5):451-72. 1991.

Kahin, B. (ed.) *Building Information Infrastructure: Issues in the Development of the National Research and Education Network*. McGraw Hill. 1992.

Kalin S. W and R. Tennant. "Beyond OPACs: the Wealth of Information Resources on the Internet." *Database* 14(4):28-33. 1991.

Kehoe, B. *Zen and the Art of the Internet: A Beginner's Guide to the Internet*. Englewood Cliffs, NJ: Prentice Hall, 1992.

Krol, E. *The Whole Internet User's Guide and Catalog*. Sebastopol, CA: O'Reilly and Associates, 1992.

LaQuey, T. *The User's Directory of Computer Networks*. Bedford, MA: Digital Press, 1990.

LaQuey, T., and J. Ryer. *The Internet Companion: A Beginner's Guide to Global Networking*. Addison-Wesley, Inc.: Reading, MA, 1992.

Levy, S. *Hackers: Heroes of the Computer Revolution*. Garden City, NY: Anchor Press, 1984.

Malamud, C. *Exploring the Internet: A Technical Travelogue*. Englewood Cliffs, NJ: Prentice Hall, 1992.

Marine, A., S. Kirkpatrick, V. Neou, and C. Ward. *Internet: Getting Started*. Menlo Park. CA: SRI International, Network Information Systems Center, 1992.

McClure, C. R., J. Ryan, D. Lauterbach, and W.E. Moen. *Public Libraries and the Internet/NREN: New Challenges, New Opportunities*. Syracuse, NY: School of Information Studies, Syracuse University, 1992.

■■

National Education and Technology Alliance. *NetPower: The Educator's Resource Guide to Online Computer Services.* Lancaster, PA: NETA, 1992.

Perry, A. *New User's Guide to Useful and Unique Resources on the Internet,* version 2.0. Syracuse, NY: NYSERNet, 1991.

Quarterman, J. S. *The Matrix: Computer Networks and Conferencing Systems Worldwide.* Bedford, MA: Digital Press, 1990.

Sachs, D. and H. Stair. *Hands-On Internet: A Beginning Guide for PC Users.* Englewood Cliffs, NJ: Prentice Hall, 1994.

Stockman, B. "Current status of networking in Europe." *ConneXions: The Interoperability Report* 5(7):10-14. 1991.

Stoll, C. *The Cuckoo's Egg: Tracking a Spy Through the Maze of Computer Espionage.* New York: Doubleday, 1989.

Vallee, J. *The Network Revolution: Confessions of a Computer Scientist.* Berkeley, CA: And/Or Press, 1982.

Bibliography of Internet Protocols and Standards

Comer, D. E. *Internetworking With TCP/IP.* Volume 1: *Principles, Protocols, and Architecture.* Englewood Cliffs, NJ: Prentice Hall, Inc.,1991.

Garcia-Luna-Aceves, J. J., M. K. Stahl, and C. A. Ward. *Internet Protocol Handbook: The Domain Name System (DNS) Handbook.* Menlo Park, CA: SRI International, Network Information Systems Center, 1989.

Lynch, D. C. and M. T. Rose (editors). *Internet System Handbook.* Addison-Wesley Inc.: Reading, MA. 1992.

Quarterman, J. S., and S. Wilhelm. *UNIX, POSIX, and Open Systems: The Open Standards Puzzle.* Addison-Wesley, Inc.: Reading, MA. 1992.

Stallings, W. *Handbook of Computer-Communications Standards* Volume 1: *The Open System (OSI) Model and OSI-Related Standards*; Volume 2: *Local Area Network Standards*; Volume 3: *The TCP/IP Protocol Suite.* New York: Macmillan, 1990.

Online Documentation of Internet Protocols and Standards

There are thousands of online documents that explain just about everything about the Internet. Appendix A explains how and where to obtain the "Requests For Comments" (RFCs) which define and explain many of the protocols upon which the Internet is based.

SECTION II

Basic Internet Tools

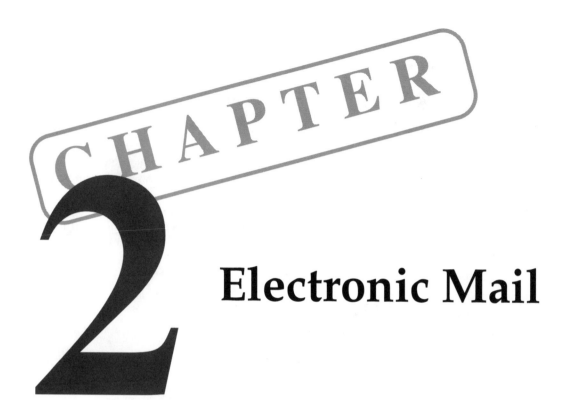

Electronic Mail

In the sixth century B.C., a postal system for government correspondence was established by King Cyrus of the Persian Empire. It took another 2,500 years until basic postal services became generally available to the average person. Today, we take postal mail for granted and feel indignant when a birthday card gets to a relative a week late. But when you think about the tremendous volume of letters that are currently handled and shuffled throughout the world each day, it's amazing that anything gets anywhere at such a low cost.

But technology marches on: in the last 20 years a service called "e-mail" (electronic mail) has evolved. E-mail provides many of the same services as postal mail, but transmits messages in minutes or even seconds instead of days or weeks. In fact, many e-mail users refer to regular mail as "snail mail." What would have seemed unimaginably fast to King Cyrus, seems quaint and slow to e-mail users!

WHAT IS ELECTRONIC MAIL?

Like postal mail, e-mail is used to exchange messages or other information with people or services. Instead of being delivered by a postal service to your postal mailbox, e-mail is delivered by Internet software through a computer network to your computer mailbox.

E-mail is so quick, versatile, and easy to use that Internet users often avoid using postal mail, fax services, or even telephone calls except when they have to do so. Once you've gotten the hang of using e-mail, you'll find that you use it almost every day that you use the Internet.

E-mail can be used for the same purposes as postal mail:

- exchange correspondence with friends
- transfer documents
- obtain (electronic) books
- subscribe to (electronic) news services or journals
- get computer software
- obtain just about anything that can be stored on a computer

Internet users can even exchange sounds, graphics, and animations via e-mail, which is much like mailing cassettes or videos. About the only things you can't send through e-mail are physical objects, like carnations or chocolate chip cookies.

Electronic Mail Compared to Postal Mail

Because you probably already know how to write and send letters, it's easy to learn about e-mail by comparing it step by step to regular postal mail.

Suppose you wanted to write a letter to your aunt Susan Rose Allen to ask if you could stay at her farm the second week of July. You would simply:

1. write your letter;
2. put her name and address on an envelope; and,
3. give your letter to the post office. (See Example 1.)

   Using e-mail is just as simple and involves exactly the same three steps:

1. write your e-mail message on a computer;
2. include the person's e-mail address; and,
3. send your e-mail message! (See Example 2.)

Instead of using pen and paper to write your letters, you need to use an e-mail software package (technically known as a "mail user agent") to compose and read your messages. Instead of being handled by postal workers, e-mail messages are moved electronically by computer throughout the Internet.

Example 1: A Postal Mail Letter on Paper

James T. Allen
NE 47th Ave.
Seattle, Washington
June 1, 1992

Susan Rose Allen
Idaho Creek High School
Apple Tree Lane
Idaho Creek, Idaho USA

Dear Aunt Susan,

Do you think I could visit you the second week of July?
I promise to help pick cherries from your orchard! Well,
I'd better put down my pen and stop writing, the mail truck
is coming by in a few minutes. Please write back soon!

Sincerely yours,

James

■■I

Example 2: An E-mail Message Viewed in an E-mail Software Package (Pine)

```
PINE 3.03    VIEW MAIL    Folder:inbox   Message 1 of 3    100%

Date:     Mon, 6 June 92 14:22 PST
From:     jtallen@jrhs.lakeside.washington.edu
To:       sra@hs.idacrk.idaho.edu
Subject:  My first e-mail message!
----- Message Text -----
Dear Aunt Susan,

Thanks for letting me know I could visit starting July 15th.
When I'm there do you think your friend the geology teacher,
Bill Diaz, could take me prospecting again in the mountains?

Please send me a computer message back soon. This is my
*first* time using e-mail, and I want to be sure this gets
to you! I can't believe that it's so easy to use this
computer to send a message to you all the way in Idaho!

James


? Help M Main Menu P Prev Msg - Prev Page F Forward D Delete
O OTHER I Index N Next Msg SPACE Next Page R Reply S Save
```

INTERPRETING E-MAIL ADDRESSES

■■I

Postal mail addresses probably seem commonsensical to you: there's a person's name followed by an address. In this section, you'll learn that e-mail addresses follow the same rules. Basically, an e-mail address like "sra@hs.idacrk.idaho.edu" means "a mailbox at an Internet host."

Anything to the left of the "@" sign is more technically known as the "local part" which can contain other kinds of information besides the name of a mailbox. For example as described in Chapter 5, the local part could contain information about gateways needed to send e-mail messages beyond the Internet. But in this chapter, we will be dealing only with mailbox names.

The Userid

Before you mail a regular letter, the first thing you should know is to whom it will be sent. Usually, you'll put that person's regular name on the envelope.

If you want to send e-mail to someone, you need to know both their "userid" and their host computer's Internet address. Userid is an abbreviation for USER IDentification,

■■■

and is pronounced "user eye dee." At your Internet site, userids might be known as "login names," "user names," or "account names."

Userids may be assigned by the people who run your Internet host, or you may be able to pick your own. Susan Rose Allen's userid is "sra", which is made from the initials of her real name; this is one of many ways in which userids are constructed. Here are some typical kinds of userids Susan might have at other Internet hosts and how they were constructed.

`allsusr`	(ALLen, SUSan, Rose)
`srallen`	(Susan, Rose, ALLEN)
`IdahoRose`	(a userid Susan picked for herself)
`nrg1234t`	(an arbitrary userid assigned to Susan)

So just because you know someone's regular name doesn't mean you can guess their userid. Chapter 21 explains how to get e-mail addresses from various Internet directory services, which is like using a phone book to get a phone number.

Let's look again at the beginning of the second and third lines of the simple e-mail message in Example 2. (We'll get to the "@hs.idacrk.idaho.edu" part in just a little bit.)

```
From: jtallen
To:   sra
```

The first line means that the message is from "jtallen" (James Trevor Allen) and the second line means that the message is going to the "mailbox" of the person with userid "sra" (Susan Rose Allen).

The Mailbox

An electronic mailbox is where incoming e-mail messages are stored, just like your real mailbox is a place for the postal service to put your mail.

Note that both postal and electronic mailboxes might be for one person or many people.

When an electronic mailbox is assigned to a person, it will usually have the same name as that person's userid.

When a mailbox is assigned to a group of people, it will often have a longer, descriptive name which indicates what these people have in common, like "idaho-fossil-hunters". Such mailboxes are often used for Internet mailing lists. (See Chapter 11.)

And when a mailbox is assigned to a computer program, it will usually have a name that describes what service the program provides, like "archive-server" or "whois."

■■■

Okay, now you understand that "sra" in Susan's e-mail address is her userid and the name of her Internet mailbox. But what in the world does "@hs.idacrk.idaho.edu" mean? It tells where the "sra" mailbox is located in the Internet world!

"@" an Internet Address

If you want to send a postal letter to somebody, knowing their name is not enough. You also need to know their address.

The same is true for e-mail: you need to know the Internet address for the mailbox if you really want your message to get delivered.

Luckily, Internet addresses (or more properly, domain names) are put together in almost the same way as postal mail addresses. Let's look at Susan Allen's postal mail address again.

> Idaho Creek High School
> Apple Tree Lane
> Idaho Creek, Idaho
> USA

There are four lines in this address, starting with the most local information (a school) and ending with the most general (a country). This standard way of writing an address helps the postal service find the right person in the right town, in the right state, in the right country. After all, there might be 10 Susan Allens in Idaho, 100 Susan Allens in the U.S., and 1,000 Susan Allens in the world.

The same is true of Susan's mailbox name, "sra." There might be many mailboxes with this name, but a full Internet address uniquely identifies Susan's.

Put Susan's complete postal and Internet addresses into the same format and compare them.

> Internet: `sra@hs.idacrk.idaho.edu`
>
> Postal: SusanAllen at HighSchool.IdahoCreek.Idaho.USA

Makes sense now, doesn't it!

Decoding Internet Addresses

Internet addresses usually follow a few simple rules similar to the rules of postal addresses.

- An Internet address has several parts separated by periods instead of being on separate lines.
- Many parts will be abbreviations, like "cs" for computer science.
- You read a computer's Internet address left to right; the first part is usually the name of a computer (a host), and the last part is an abbreviation for a geographic or administrative domain, like "au" for AUstralian hosts on the Internet, or "edu" for the EDUcational domain in the Internet.

- The particular words in each part of an Internet address may have no particular geographic significance, just like there may be no good reason why a street is called "Oak Street." Internet addresses may include arbitrary names like cartoon characters, famous persons, or brands of soda.
- Internet addresses may have various parts just like full postal addresses might have fewer or more lines than Susan's. But in general, you'll rarely encounter full addresses with more than five or less than two parts.

For more detailed information about Internet addresses throughout the world, see "Internet Addresses" in Chapter 1.

ELECTRONIC MAIL SOFTWARE (MAIL USER AGENTS)

When you write a letter, you might use a pen, a pencil, or a typewriter, and a piece of paper. The editor you use with your e-mail software is all of these things. However, when you write and receive e-mail messages, you use an e-mail software program, technically known as a "mail user agent." The mail user agent lets you see incoming e-mail messages and provides an editor for composing outgoing messages.

There are many kinds of e-mail software programs ranging from simple "line-at-a-time" packages, to full featured word processing interfaces. Your computer support staff should be able to help you get started with one of the e-mail software packages used on your Internet host computer.

If you're the self-starting kind of person (or if you just can't wait to use e-mail), you could try the online help system on your Internet host. Here are some general hints on finding mail software on some common types of Internet hosts.

Unix	The basic Unix mail software is called "mail." Common full screen mail software includes "elm" and "pine." Type "man mail", "man elm", or "man pine" for the "manual pages" of these mail packages. Manual pages are help files for Unix commands; at the Unix prompt, type "man man" for manual pages about the man command.
CMS or VMS	Try typing "help mail". You should get some basic information on the locally installed mail software.

If you're working from a personal computer such as a Mac or an IBM PC, there might be one of many different mail software packages installed. Contact your local computer support staff for help in identifying the Mac or PC mail resources that might be available to you.

FOR BEGINNERS, A FEW WORDS OF ADVICE

If you've read this far, you now know enough to start using e-mail!

No matter what kind of e-mail software you will be using, you should try sending your first few e-mail messages to yourself so you can get the hang of sending and receiving e-mail. You might also consider asking a friend who uses the Internet to be an electronic pen pal while you practice your e-mail skills. A little bit of practice locally will make using e-mail globally much easier!

E-MAIL MESSAGES FROM STEM TO STERN

Now that you understand that e-mail addresses contain a mailbox name and the Internet address of a computer, let's take a quick look at e-mail "envelopes" and e-mail "letters."

Your country's postal service has rules and regulations about how postal mail should be addressed and packaged. For example, the U.S. States Postal Service employs a cartoon character named Speedy Zip who urges you to "remember to use ZIP codes!"

Similarly, in order to guarantee that e-mail messages can get anywhere in the Internet, a set of rules have been established for the format of e-mail messages. These rules are spelled out in "Request For Comments" (RFCs) documents, especially RFC822. (See Appendix A for more information about RFCs.)

RFC822 states that all Internet e-mail messages must be divided into two parts: a "message header" which, like a postal envelope, displays address and delivery information, and the e-mail "message body," which is like a postal letter's contents.

The E-mail Message Header

The RFC822 document also defines the rules which all message headers must follow. Let's take another look at the message header of Example 2.

```
Date:    Mon, 6 June 92 14:22 PST
From:    jtallen@jrhs.lakeside.washington.edu
To:      sra@hs.idacreek.idaho.edu
Subject: My first e-mail message!
```

This message header shows some of the delivery information specified by RFC822: "Date," "From," and "To." "Date" is when the e-mail message was sent and it works like a postmark on a postal envelope; "From" is the Internet e-mail address from which the message was sent; and "To" contains one or more Internet e-mail addresses to which the message is being sent.

■■■

More about "To" and "From"

Most Internet e-mail software packages know the RFC822 rules and take care of the "Date" and "From" information for you. All you really have to worry about is supplying the right address(es) in the right format(s) in the "To" field.

Although the basic "To" field should contain a full Internet address, there are times when you can get away with less and times when you might want to add more.

Sending Mail within a Host

If you are sending e-mail to people with mailboxes on the same Internet host as your mailbox, you usually need only the mailbox name in the address. Suppose Susan sends an e-mail message to Bill Diaz at Idaho Creek High School. She might use only his mailbox name (wt_diaz) instead of his entire Internet e-mail address (wt_diaz@hs.idacrk.idaho.edu).

Sending Mail within a Domain

Similarly, you can sometimes type in just part of an Internet address if the destination host is in the same domain as your host. For example, at the University of Washington here in Seattle, there are a large number of hosts in the domain "u.washington.edu", including "milton.u.washington.edu" and "byron.u.washington.edu". A person using the host "milton" can send mail to someone using "byron" by using "mailbox@byron", instead of "mailbox@byron.u.washington.edu".

Customized Address Fields

You will often see e-mail addresses which look like these:

```
Susan Allen <sra@hs.idacreek.idaho.edu>, or
"S. R. Allen, Geode Crusher!" <sra@hs.idacreek.idaho.edu>
```

If you want to add a person's name or other information to a mail header, you can put the text on the "To" line, before their e-mail address, but be sure that the real e-mail address is surrounded by angle brackets (< and >)! If the text you are adding has anything but letters in it—for example, periods, commas, or numbers—then the text must be surrounded by quotes, as in the second example above.

Optional Message Header Fields that You Can Add

The following message header fields can be added in most mail software packages.

Subject: The subject line should capture the essence of the message in a few words, for example "Subject: Does Santa Claus Exist??" If you don't write a subject, your outgoing message will say "Subject: (none)." Informative "Subject" lines make handling and storing e-mail much easier when other people check their mailboxes. Furthermore, when you've used the subject field, replies to your message will have the same subject line preceded by "Re:", for example, "Subject: Re: Does Santa Claus Exist??"

(Continued)

CC: (Carbon Copy) Sending someone a "CC" of a message is like saying to them, "I wanted you to know I sent this material."

BCC: (Blind Carbon Copy) A form of "CC" that is invisible to the people named in the "To" and "CC" (and "BCC") fields, i.e., they won't see who, or if anyone, receives the BCC.

Reply-to: If you want replies to be sent to a different e-mail address, put that e-mail address in this field.

Keywords: Extra information about the contents of an e-mail message, that can be used later for classifying, sorting, and searching messages in very large message databases.

Message Header Fields Added by Mail Delivery Agents

Other message header fields may be added by mail delivery agents as the message is passed around the Internet.

Resent-< >:   The "<>" could be "From", "To", "Date", or "CC." These fields are added when a received message is forwarded to another person. Original message headers are left untouched, so the recipient of a forwarded message knows who the original sender was and when it was originally sent.

Received: When an e-mail message has passed through a number of mail delivery agents on its way to a destination, their Internet addresses and date of handling are put into "Received" fields, much like international postal mail might get postmarked repeatedly on its way from Peoria to Bora Bora.

Message-ID: A unique number is assigned by a mail delivery agent to a message which it has handled, for example:

`<36476234.AA583@ica.beijing.canet.cn>.`

Message-ID and Received fields are often used by postmasters to figure out why rejected e-mail messages have been "bounced." (See "Bounced Mail.")

The E-mail Message Body

The message body contains the actual message being sent. This could be regular text, like the message James sent to his Aunt Susan, or it might be computer code for software, graphics, or sounds. A blank line separates the message header from the body.

How Long Can My E-mail Messages Be?

The Internet itself has no limit on the size of e-mail messages, but just as postal services cannot transport arbitrarily large or heavy packages, some Internet hosts won't accept e-mail messages above a certain size. A common limit currently is 100 Kilobytes, which is about 25 pages of printed text. When you need to transfer *really* big files, you'll use another basic Internet service called "FTP." (See Chapter 7.)

The Signature

E-mail users often include a brief file called a signature, or "sig," at the end of their e-mail messages. The sig usually contains a few lines of contact information and, depending on preference, nuggets of personal philosophy, pithy quotes, or simple pictures. For information on how to include a sig in your e-mail messages, ask savvy e-mail users or a computer consultant at your Internet host. Please refer to Chapter 4 before you launch your sig into the world.

SHIPPING E-MAIL

Beyond here there be daemons and dragons

—Numerous Medieval Maps of the Unknown

The actual nuts and bolts (or more correctly, sockets and packets) of e-mail delivery are tremendously complicated, but this little summary should give a feeling of what's going on behind the scenes. The main players are the diligent SMTP, the ever vigilant mail daemons, your most wise Postmaster—and yes, even Elvis Presley plays a role.

Mail Delivery Agents

SMTP and BSMTP

Most of the handling of e-mail is done automatically by "mail delivery agents," special software programs and protocols such as SMTP (Simple Mail Transfer Protocol) which must be installed at every Internet host. When you are reading e-mail messages, you will occasionally see header information containing the terms SMTP or BSMTP. These are messages from the mail delivery agents, working diligently day and night to deliver your e-mail messages. ("Neither snow, nor rain, nor heat, nor gloomy night stays their couriers from the swift completion of their appointed rounds.")

Bounced Mail: "Return to Sender; Uh-ddress Uhn-known!"

If you have supplied an incorrect address in an e-mail message, or if there is a problem with the mail delivery agents on the way to the destination mailbox, your message may be returned to your mailbox. This is called "bounced mail."

Mail Daemons Are Your Friends

When you catch bounced mail in your mailbox, you may see added information from a "mail daemon." A "daemon" is software programmed to respond to specific events in a computer, so a mail daemon is a software program that lies dormant until it detects a mail message coming through. Bounced mail may originate from other sources as well.

The information provided by mail daemons may help you figure out what's gone wrong when e-mail messages get returned to you. For example "user unknown likely means that you've given an incorrect mailbox name in your mail header; "host unknown" likely means that you've given an incorrect Internet address, and so forth.

Most e-mail users don't need to know much more than this, but if your curiosity is piqued, references to the technical documents describing these protocols are provided at the end of this chapter.

Postmasters

Most Internet hosts or domains also have a person assigned to take care of any serious problems that may occur with e-mail at those sites. This person is usually assigned the mailbox name "postmaster@a.local.internet.address". (On the BITNET network, which is discussed in Chapters 1 and 10, the postmaster's userid is usually "POSTMAST@HOST".)

When you have e-mail problems, save the messages and show them to your local user services staff. If they are unable to figure out your problem, they may pass the information on to the postmaster.

SAMPLE E-MAIL SESSION WITH UNIX "MAIL"

Let's step through a sample e-mail session using Unix "mail", which is one of the most "bare-bones" mail software packages around. Although these particular instructions won't work for all e-mail software packages, the general steps will probably be the same no matter what e-mail software you use.

Sending an E-mail Message

In this example, you'll send a mail message to yourself.

Start the Mail Software

Type "mail" and your own full e-mail address on the same line. Even though your message would probably be delivered if you just entered your userid, this gives you some practice typing full e-mail addresses.

```
% mail <you>@<your.internet.host>
```

■■■

Enter a Subject

Most e-mail software gives you a chance to enter a subject for your message. Enter something short and informative to get in the habit of using subject lines.

```
Subject: My first e-mail!!!
```

Type a Message

Now you can type a message. How you do this will vary, depending upon what software you are using. Sophisticated mail editors will let you move around with arrow keys and "wrap" text to a new line while you're typing. As you can read in this sample message, others may be less sophisticated.

```
Okay, I'm in the editor. To end each line I pres thee return
key. Dang! I can't fix my spelling errors on the previous
line! Oh well, that's okay, I'm mailing this to myself
anyway. (I'll have to ask the compter consultant if we have
a full screen mail package I can use?). To send my message,
I have to type a period on a line by itself and then press
the return key. Let's see if this works:
.
```

Send Your Message!

Type a period on a line by itself and press enter. (If a period doesn't work, try <ctrl-d>–"d" for done–on a line by itself.) This sends your message and you should now be back at your Unix prompt. No matter what mail software you use, when you send your message it is transferred to your host's mail delivery agent.

Receiving E-mail Messages

Check Your Mailbox

Wait a little while (maybe get away from your computer to stretch your legs or eat a chocolate chip cookie) and then check your mailbox.

To look at the contents of your mailbox from Unix mail, type "mail" at the Unix prompt. This lets you use Unix mail as a mail reader. Typically, you will see messages from your mailbox in a list that shows the e-mail addresses of the senders, the subject lines, and other, optional information. Even if you haven't used mail before, there may be messages in your mailbox. And if you followed the last example and all went well, you'll find at least the one you've just sent.

```
% mail

Mail version 5.3 2/18/88. Type ? for help.

"/usr/spool/mail/user-id": 4 messages 4 new

N 1 friend@another.host    Mon Jun  1 09:15 17/356  "Long time no see!"
N 2 friend@another.host    Wed Jul 15 16:26 13/59   "Reply pleeeese!"
N 3 friend@another.host    Wed Aug 26 18:01 12/120  "Helllllooooooo!!"
N 4 you@your.internet.host Thu Aug 27 14:42 17/564  "My First email!!!"
```

Read Messages in Your Mailbox

Type a message number at the "&" prompt and that message will be displayed on your screen.

```
& 4
Message 4:

Date: Thu, 27 Aug 92 04:42:56 -0700
From: you@your.internet.host
Sender: you@your.internet.host
To: you@your.internet.host
Subject: My first e-mail!!!

Okay, I'm in the editor. To end each line I pres thee return

(etc.)
```

Even though you only entered a destination e-mail address and a subject, the mail software filled in the "Date," "Sender," and "From" fields for you.

If you want to reply to your message, you can type "R" (on some Unix systems the plain reply key is "r"), and you will be put back into the simple line-at-a-time mail editor. You would then repeat the steps you went through when writing your original message.

Getting Help While Using Mail

Most e-mail software packages have some sort of help available. In Unix mail, type "?" at the "&" prompt and you'll see a list of commands. More sophisticated mail software packages may have an on-screen help menu.

Quit Your Mail Software

To quit Unix mail, just type "x" or "q" at the "&" prompt.

```
& x

Held 1 messages in /usr/spool/mail/you

%
```

If you're using another kind of mail user agent, check the help for that package. If you're stuck, try "quit", "exit", or "end".

Managing Your E-Mail

Organizing Your Mail

In addition to checking your mail box on a regular basis, there are other steps you can take so that e-mail does not become a burden. (After all, it is intended to make your life, easier, more pleasant, and completely fulfilling.) Most mailers offer the option of saving mail messages to folders. If this feature is available on your system, make use of it, but be sure to set up enough folders so that you can store messages in logical places. Even if folders are not available, you should be able to save messages as files separate from the system's mail program. By setting up various subdirectories, you can create a filing system to suit your needs.

How to Keep Your Mailing Lists Under Control

Mailing lists are a way that groups of people communicate using electronic mail. The number of people on a list, and the number of messages that appear on a list in a given period of time varies widely. As many people have found, e-mail lists can be both a boon and a curse. For more detailed information on e-mail lists, see Chapters 10 and 11.

Depending on the amount of activity on the lists you subscribe to, and the number of lists you subscribe to, you may need to take serious action to prevent e-mail mayhem. First, don't bother saving messages from an archived mailing list (unless it's really crucial) since you can always get a copy from the archive. Of course, you will need to remember which list you saw the message on to retrieve it. There are also a number of prophylactic measures to cut down the number of mailing list messages you receive, short of simply ending your subscription entirely:

- Subscribe to mailing lists in digest format, when available;
- Monitor Usenet newsgroup versions of mailing lists instead (for more on Usenet, see Chapter 9);
- Make a deal with a colleague to read different lists and share the information in which the other would be interested.

E-Mail and Your Organization

The Eyes Have It

If you are using an e-mail account for your job that is provided by your employer, find out what e-mail policies are in place. You'll want to know if it's OK to use your e-mail account for personal correspondence. If it is, and you do use it for personal communication, find out if your files can be reviewed by persons outside of your organization. In the case of some government agencies, e-mail falls under the Freedom of Information Act. Do you mind if a gossip columnist reads the explicit details of your recent haircut and nightmare dye job that you sent to your old college roommate?

Even if the details of your haircut are free from the eyes of a local reporter, consider who else might have access to your e-mail. Minimally, the staff members managing the mail system at your site will have the ability to read your mail. While this access is rarely abused, valid instances can occur in which your e-mail is scanned or read by others at your site. At some companies, managers may reserve the right to review your e-mail. Are you informed each time someone at your organization reads or accesses your mail? At other sites e-mail policy only allows access to an individual's account if a search warrant has been served and the individual has been informed to this effect. In this extreme case, there is likely to be some strong evidence that the e-mail is being used in conjunction with illegal activities.

Needless to say, don't use your e-mail for compromising activities. Think "postcard." Would you be willing to send the details of your haircut and dye job in an e-mail message if that same message were being sent by postcard? If not, then don't send it by e-mail. If you don't mind having the postal carrier read the details of your really bad hair day, then go for it. Here's another question you need to answer: if your message were accidentally sent to a shared office printer or forwarded to 10 other people (that you may or may not know), what would the consequences be? If embarrassment is the worst, then it's no big deal. If you would find yourself open for a libel or slander suit, think again! Think "postcard."

What's in a Name?

Because of its structure, the domain portion of an Internet e-mail address provides direct information about the organization from which the message originated. If you use an account provided by your employer, they may view any mail you send from your e-mail address as business correspondence on organization letterhead with your signature. If this is the case, you should know in advance. Other organizations are content to allow personal use of the e-mail account so long as a disclaimer (e.g., "the views expressed are my own and in no way should be construed as a representation of the ACME Bird Seed Corp.") is appended to the message. This usually provides an opportunity for people involved in research to carry on scholarly discussions about bird seed ingredients without running the risk of adversely affecting the organization. Of course, using a disclaimer does not absolve you of all responsibility. It still won't look good to disclose the latest secret in bird seed fortifiers.

■■■

Making the Most of ASCII and a Blank Screen

The vast majority of e-mail exchanged is plain old, bare-bones ASCII text. Old-time Internet users have become comfortable and familiar with this stark and limited medium. Apart from offering you the perfect opportunity to hone your writing skills (no exotic fonts to hide bad grammar and spelling here), plain ASCII doesn't have much to offer. But there are some things you can do to help make the best of the situation.

Your group or organization may choose to set standards for out-going mail messages much the way they do for outgoing letters. For example, they may ask that you set line width to 65 characters, leave blank lines between paragraphs, and have everyone in the organization use the same template for their sig files so that your messages are distinct and clearly identifiable. Whether your organization uses a standard or not, you should be consistent in the format and appearances of your e-mail messages. And when you break from your traditional format, make it mean something. Since you don't have much freedom to make a visual impression with your work, make every bit count.

Who's Got Your Number?

Remember this image from the movies? At the back of a smoky bar room, the protagonist speaks with urgency into the phone and adds yet another name and number to the hundreds already scribbled onto the nearby wall. In movies of the future, will this image be replaced by the pay terminal surrounded by scribbled names and e-mail addresses? Come to think of it, just where does your e-mail address end up? You've asked the same thing about your phone number and have partially answered your own question when you discover that telemarketing groups all over the country want to sell you the "most perfect and exquisite bird-seed-of-the-day," usually while you're eating dinner.

While unwanted e-mail is not nearly as intrusive as a ringing telephone at 7pm, it can become a problem. In order to escape from the potential of unsolicited contacts, be as judicious about giving out your e-mail address as you would your telephone number. If you work for a company, there may even be policies about giving out the e-mail addresses of all or some of the employees. Ask first.

"Parting Can Be Such Sweet Sorrow"

People move on—they graduate from school and they change jobs. Either of these events may mean a discontinuity in your Internet access and e-mail access. But wait! What about those 500 ASCII graphics files you've collected via e-mail for the past two years? What will happen to this esteemed and prized collection when you leave? While your friends and associates may find sweetness in your sorrow at losing this collection ("Hey, look at this one!"), you may find it a bitter experience.

If you are leaving your organization find out: 1) can your e-mail be forwarded to your new e-mail account and if yes, for how long? 2) will you have access to your account after you've left for some transition period and if yes, for how long? If there is no grace period and your account will be deactivated shortly after you leave, you'll want to plan ahead and schedule time to transfer files as well as pack your desk. If you will have an Internet account at your new location and you can have that account activated early, you should be able to transfer your important files to your new account by e-mail and by FTP (see Chapter 7). If you won't have an account and access to the Internet after leaving, then you may need to find a way to transfer your important files and correspondence to a diskette so that you can take the files with you.

FOR MORE INFORMATION

Mail Software Programs (Mail User Agents)

For more information about using specific electronic mail software, consult your local users service staff or your computer support staff. If you are using a mainframe computer, you may also be able to get help by typing "man mail" (on Unix computers), or "help mail" (on most other mainframes).

Bibliography

Quarterman's book offers one of the best semi-technical discussions of electronic mail on the Internet (especially Chapters 1-7, but the rest of the book is chock full of useful general information as well). Comer's book focuses on the technical details of e-mail format and delivery. Sproul and Kiesler provide an informative and well reasoned analysis of the effects of e-mail in organizational and personal behavior.

Comer, D. E. *Internetworking With TCP/IP.* Volume 1: *Principles, Protocols, and Architecture.* Englewood Cliffs, NJ: Prentice Hall, Inc., 1991.

Frey, D. and R. Adams. *!%@:: A Directory of Electronic Mail Addressing and Networks.* Sebastopol, CA: O'Reilly & Associates, 1993.

Lane, G. *Communications for Progress: A Guide to International E-mail.* London: Environment and Development Resource Center, 1990.

Quarterman, J. S. *The Matrix: Computer Networks and Conferencing Systems Worldwide.* Bedford, MA: Digital Press, 1990.

Sproul, L. and S. Kiesler. *Connections: New Ways of Working in the Networked Organization.* Cambridge, MA: MIT Press, 1992.

Technical Information about Internet Mail Protocols

Many of the technical details about how e-mail is packaged and handled on the Internet are specified in the following Requests for Comments (RFCs):

RFC821	Simple Mail Transfer Protocol
RFC822	Standard for the format of ARPA Internet text messages
RFC886	Proposed standard for message heading munging
RFC934	Proposed standard for message encapsulation

RFC974	Mail routing and the domain system
RFC1047	Duplicate messages and SMTP
RFC1049	Content-type header field for Internet messages
RFC1056	PCMAIL A distributed mail system for personal computers
RFC1082	Post Office Protocol Version 2 Extended service offerings
RFC1113	Privacy enhancement for Internet electronic mail Part I - message encypherment and authentication procedures
RFC1114	Privacy enhancement for Internet electronic mail Part II - certificate-based key management
RFC1115	Privacy enhancement for Internet electronic mail Part III - algorithms, modes, and identifiers
RFC1122	Requirements for Internet Hosts -- Communication Layers
RFC1123	Requirements for Internet Hosts -- Application and Support
RFC1153	Digest Message Format
RFC1154	Encoding header field for Internet messages
RFC1176	Interactive Mail Access Protocol Version 2
RFC1225	Post Office Protocol: Version 3

These and all other RFCs can be obtained from mail servers and many FTP archives (Chapters 3 and 7). One currently authoritative FTP archive for RFCs is:

FTP host:	`ds.internic.net`	
directory:	`rfc`	
filenames:	`rfc-index.txt`	(index of RFCs)
	`rfc-retrieval.txt`	(information on retrieving the RFCs)
	`rfc1000.txt`	(each RFC is named rfcXXXX,
	`rfc1001.txt`	where "XXXX" is the RFC number,
	`rfc1002.txt`	e.g., rfc822)
	etc...	

Usenet Newsgroups about Internet Mail and Mail User Agents

The following newsgroups deal with various technical aspects of Internet mail and mail user agents. (For more on Usenet, see Chapter 9.)

Note: These newsgroups are not good places to ask beginning questions about using e-mail! For such questions, try the following in this order: local documentation, friends at your Internet site, your local user services staff. If all else fails, post a note to the newsgroup "news.newusers.questions".

If you do wish to post a question to a newsgroup, first read Chapter 9. Pay special attention to issues of Usenet etiquette, and be sure to indicate what mail package you are running, what version, your operating system, and a detailed description of what is going wrong. (Questions like "My e-mail package is not working. Why not?" are not appropriate in these forums.)

Newsgroup Name	General Areas of Discussion
`bit.listserv.cw-email`	Discussion about using e-mail for intra-campus communications.
`bit.listserv.mailbook`	Discussion about the Rice mail user agent for VM/CMS.
`comp.mail.elm`	General discussion about the elm mailer for Unix.
`comp.mail.headers`	Technical discussion of Internet mail headers.
`comp.mail.maps`	Posting of "maps" for UUCP mail routing.
`comp.mail.mh`	Discussion of the Rand Mail Handler.
`comp.mail.misc`	Miscellaneous discussion about Internet mail.
`comp.mail.multi-media`	Discussion about multi-media in Internet mail.
`comp.mail.mush`	Discussion about the "mail user shell" package for Unix.
`comp.mail.sendmail`	Discussion about Unix sendmail utility (not a mail package).
`comp.mail.uucp`	General discussion about UUCP mail.
`de.admin.mail`	Discussion of administration of e-mail in Germany (in German).
`fj.mail`	Discussion about e-mail issues peculiar to Kanji character sets but you must be able to display Kanji characters to read the "fj" newsgroups.

CHAPTER

3

Electronic Mail Servers

Retrieving Files via E-mail

■ ■

WHAT IS A MAIL SERVER?

In addition to exchanging messages with people, you can use e-mail to retrieve files from software programs on the Internet. Such services are sometimes called "mail servers," or more formally, "mail archive servers." You will also encounter the generic term "file servers."

Mail servers are similar to mail-order catalogs. Instead of ordering the latest Shill-Co slicer-dicer or a subscription to *Pork Belly Digest*, you can get shareware graphics packages, libraries of sophisticated mathematical algorithms from AT&T Laboratories, and even daily updates on agricultural markets.

HOW DO MAIL SERVERS WORK?

A mail server is a software program that has been assigned a mailbox at an Internet address just like an Internet user. Because it is just a software package and not a person, it handles your requests with robot-like and humorless precision.

To use a mail server, you send an e-mail message to the mail server's e-mail address and put precisely worded requests in the body of your mail message. Some mail servers accept commands placed in the Subject: line, but don't do this unless you are certain it's O.K. Like the people who work for mail-order catalogs, mail server software packages aren't interested in reading long, personal letters. They are efficient order-processors which expect certain precise commands in your e-mail message, like "get super-dooper.graf" or "send eigen-vector.corrector.c".

To get started using a particular mail server, you should send an e-mail message with the word "help" in the body of your message. Essentially, this is asking for an order form. Within a short time—often minutes, but sometimes as long as a day—you will receive a message in your electronic mailbox with a description of commands used by that mail server. Sometimes, detailed descriptions of what files are available (or at least instructions on how to order a catalog of files) will also be included.

Mail servers perform most of the same functions as the anonymous FTP hosts described in Chapter 7. In fact, most mail servers simply facilitate access to FTP archives by e-mail. This is great for people who only have e-mail access to the Internet. You will probably use FTP more frequently than mail servers, but there *are* times when using a mail server is preferable, or when it may be your only option.

TABLE OF MAIL SERVERS

Here's a potpourri of mail servers in the U.S., Europe, and Australia to help get you started. There's something for nearly everyone here. This information is derived from a

■■

comprehensive and frequently updated list of mail servers maintained by Jonathan Kamens of MIT's Project Athena. In a nicely self-referential twist, his list is obtainable from a mail server as described in "For More Information" at the end of this chapter.

E-mail Address	Partial Description of Mail Server's Contents
`almanac@oes.orst.edu`	Information on agriculture, IBM PCs, electronic books, and more.
`archive-server@ames.arc.nasa.gov`	NASA and space related files.
`archive-server@ncsa.uiuc.edu`	National Center for Supercomputer Applications: Telnet, TCP/IP, Mosaic software for personal computers and other NCSA software.
`mailserv@ds.internic.net`	InterNIC Directory Services: performs search of directories of people and network resources.
`mailserv@is.internic.net`	InterNIC Information Services: Large archive of network directories, guides, bibliographies, RFCs, and FYIs.
`mail-server@pit-manager.mit.edu`	Many files useful for new Internet users, such as "FAQ" (Frequently Asked Questions) files, for many Usenet newsgroups.
`netlib@research.att.com`	U.S. AT&T Netlib: Large archive of sophisticated mathematical source code and algorithms.
`netlib@draci.cs.uow.edu.au`	Australian AT&T Netlib server.
`netlib@nac.no`	European (non-UK) AT&T Netlib server.
`netlib@ukc.ac.uk`	UK netlib AT&T server.
`netlib@uunet.uu.net`	Not to be confused with AT&T Netlib—a large general purpose collection including software for most kinds of personal computers, archives of Usenet newsgroups, and much more.
`ps-file-server@adobe.com`	PostScript software for software developers.
`statlib@lib.stat.cmu.edu`	Statistical software.

SAMPLE MAIL SERVER SESSION USING ALMANAC

In this example, we'll use e-mail to retrieve files from an unusually versatile and speedy mail server called Almanac, that is operated by the Oregon Extension Service. Part of this exercise is to teach you how to use mail servers, but it is also an exercise in using e-mail.

Getting Started with Almanac

As with most mail servers, the first thing you should do is to send e-mail with a message for help.

```
mail:      almanac@oes.orst.edu
subject:   (none needed)
message:   help
```

(With the InterNIC mail servers, send the message "send help".)

Handling the Reply from Almanac

The mail you get back from Almanac should be the *Almanac Users Guide*, which explains Almanac's many features. Here's what the first page looks like in the mail software, PINE.

```
PINE 3.89   MESSAGE TEXT   Folder: INBOX Message 23 of 27    1%
Date: Wed, 23 Feb 94 15:04:10 -0800
From: Almanac Information Server <almanac@oes.orst.edu>
Reply to: owner-almanac@oes.orst.edu
To: David Robison <robison@nwnet.net>
Subject: RE: (null)
--------
## Regarding your request:
   help
                        Almanac Users Guide
                      Oregon State University
                        Extension Service
                  Last Updated: March 26, 1992


0. Table of Contents

You may move directly to any section of this guide by using your text
viewer's search option to locate the upper-case search string for that
section. The list below shows the search strings for each section.
                        Section           Search String
                1    Introduction
                2    Mail Addresses        -ADDR-
                3    Receiving Help        -HELP-

? Help M Main Menu P Prev Msg - Prev Page F Forward D Delete
O OTHER I Index N Next Msg SPACE Next Page R Reply S Save
```

You can read your copy in your mail reader, save it to a file, or print it (or any combination of these three) depending on your system's capabilities.

Requesting Specific Files from Almanac

Here's one last Almanac exercise for the road.

```
mail:      almanac@oes.orst.edu
subject:   (none needed)
message:   send quote
           send market-news wafv281
```

"Send quote" will send you a pithy little quotation, a network version of a Chinese fortune cookie; "send market-news wafv281" will send you information on last week's international arrivals of fruits and vegetables into the U.S. Here's how Almanac responded to my "send quote" and market news requests:

```
## Regarding your request: send quote

              "Those who can't write, write manuals."
                                        - anonymous

## Regarding your request: send wafv281

Date: Wed, 23 Feb 94 08:53:44 AM

AVAILABLE DOMESTIC SHIPMENTS AND IMPORTS OF ORNAMENTAL CROPS
(AMTS SHOWN ARE IN UNITS OF 1,000 STEM COUNT UNLESS OTHERWISE DESIGNATED)

                      FEB 6    FEB 14   TOT THIS   TOT LAST   TOTAL
                      FEB 12   FEB 20   SSN THRU   SSN THRU   LAST
                      1994       1993   FEB 1994   FEB 20 93  SEASON

CARNATIONS
  CALIF CENT          2214     1258     11521      12810      90375
  CALIF SOUTH         68       81       226        838        3146
  BOLIVIA             45       -        62         244        557
  CHILE               -        -        -          34         52
  COLOMBIA            22916    20293    173873     232094     1213506
  COSTA RICA          -        -        181        212        664
  DOMIN REPUBLIC      -        -        -          -          18
  ECUADOR             436      98       2457       3537       18487
  FRANCE              -        -        -          -          7
  GUATEMALA           20       77       433        862        4759
  ISRAEL              -        -        -          32         683
  ITALY               -        -        -          2          11

(etc., for many pages)
```

I *wish* this were a cute and contrived example, but this is really what Almanac sent when I submitted my requests. Oh well, what does Almanac know anyway?!? It's just a computer program! But how *polite* and *sweet* of it to send me carnations... :-)

FTP MAIL SERVERS

The nooks and crannies of the Internet are full of useful and interesting files and computer programs. Usually these are accessed by using File Transfer Protocol (FTP). (See

Chapter 7.) But some people do not have access to FTP so innovative mail servers have been set up to help these people get these files and programs.

FTP mail servers use e-mail messages to perform all the commands of an FTP session. By sending a message with each FTP command, you can see directory listings and get files from any anonymous FTP site through the mail. The following lists some FTP mail server addresses.

E-mail Address	Comments
`ftpmail@decwrl.dec.com`	Not a fully supported service, outages may occur.
`ftpmail@src.doc.ic.ac.uk`	
`ftpmail@cs.uow.edu.au`	
`ftpmail@grasp.insa-lyon.fr`	For use by Europeans getting files from European FTP sites. No help file available on this server.

SAMPLE FTP MAIL SERVER SESSION

Again, the best way to get started is to send a message requesting help.

```
mail:     ftpmail@decwrl.dec.com
subject:  (none needed)
message:  help
```

In the following example, we will get a recipe for cauliflower with mushrooms and parmesan cheese from an FTP site in Germany using the FTP mail server.

```
mail:     ftpmail@decwrl.dec.com
subject:  (none needed)
message:
open gmdzi.gmd.de
cd recipes
get cauliflower-1
quit
```

The response is an e-mail message containing the recipe and a second message detailing the activity of the actual FTP session. If your request is put into a queue, you will be sent a message indicating so, along with the number assigned to your job. This message also includes instructions on canceling your job if you want. If you make an error in your original request, you will receive an e-mail message that contains a log of the FTP session. With this log, you can analyze what went wrong with your request. If you see nothing wrong with the commands you issued and there are no typos, it may be that the file you requested no longer exists at that site. In this case you should see a message "No such file or directory."

USING AN FTP MAIL SERVER TO LOCATE AND RETRIEVE FILES

In the example above, we already knew the filename (cauliflower-1) and the directory (recipes) used to retrieve the message, but in many instances you'll need to find this information using the FTP mail server. Since these servers allow you to issue all FTP commands, you can scrounge around FTP archives by issuing the directory listing commands ("dir" and "ls") and then the change directory command ("cd") in successive e-mail messages. Each of these messages will build upon the last, using the new information as a new command (or sometimes just changing an old one) before the "quit" statement.

Once you've established the exact location of a file, you can send a final message with the "get <filename>" command inserted before the quit statement and the file will be sent to you. While it may take three, four, or even more messages to establish the location of a desired file and then retrieve it, for those without access to FTP or who want to avoid spending the time trying to login to busy FTP hosts directly, FTP mail servers can be a life-saver.

FOR MORE INFORMATION

General Information

Jonathan Kamens of MIT maintains two very useful files relating to mail servers.

`"How To Find Sources"`	Includes comprehensive listing of electronic mail servers; this file is packed with good advice on finding network sources.
`"Mail Archive Server Software List"`	An invaluable resource containing a list of mail server software with useful summary information for folks who want to set up a mail server.

You can get these files by mail server or by FTP.

■■

By Mail Server

To get these files by mail server, send one of the following e-mail messages:

```
mail:     mail-server@pit-manager.mit.edu
subject:  (none needed)
message:
send usenet/comp.sources.wanted/How_to_find_sources_(READ_THIS_BEFORE_POSTING)
```

   or

```
mail:     mail-server@pit-manager.mit.edu
subject:  (none needed)
message:
send usenet/comp.mail.misc/Mail_Archive_Server_(MAS)_software_list
```

Be sure to type the messages EXACTLY as shown above. If you miss a single "/" or "_" you won't get the file. (As I said, mail servers are humorless robots.)

By FTP or Usenet Newsgroup

Both files are also available via anonymous File Transfer Protocol (FTP) and periodically posted to the newsgroups "comp.sources.wanted" and "comp.mail.misc". (For more on FTP and Usenet, see Chapters 7 and 9.) As above, when you retrieve these files from the FTP host, be sure to enter the filenames exactly as shown below:

```
FTP host:      pit-manager.mit.edu
directory:     /pub/usenet/comp.sources.wanted
filenames:     How_to_find_sources_(READ_THIS_BEFORE_POSTING)
               Mail_Archive_Server_(MAS)_software_list
```

4

Electronic Mail
Etiquette
"How to Talk Internet"

Many travellers take little phrase books to help them communicate in foreign lands. Such books may offer invaluable tidbits like "How do I get to the 'Islands of the Dreadful Hummingbirds?'" or "I collect paperclips. Do you have a hobby?" Apart from a selection of phrases, the best of these books also alert you to the unspoken nuances of etiquette and behavior that are woven into the fabric of a culture. Abiding by some simple rules can make your visit more pleasant and can help you avert a cultural faux pas.

This is equally true when travelling the world online.

There are a number of generally agreed upon do's and dont's you should understand before you enter the world online. After reading many mail messages from many other people—in other words, after becoming encultured to the ways of the Net—you will probably understand why these principles make good sense.

First, consider two examples of e-mail messages.

Example 1 illustrates the intelligent and tasteful use of e-mail rules of etiquette and style. It is easy to read, written in an informative manner, and generally is an example of e-mail etiquette.

Example 1: E-mail Following Suggested Etiquette Guidelines

```
Date:   Wed 8 June 92 10:45 MST
From:   Bill Diaz <wt_diaz@hs.idacrk.idaho.edu>
To:     Jim Allen <jtallen@jrhs.lkside.wash.edu>
CC:     Susan Allen <sallen@hs.idacrk.idaho.edu>
Subject: Prospecting in Ponderosa Canyon? You Bet!

Jim,

I'm *delighted* to hear you're visiting this summer! You wrote:

> When I'm there, do you think that geology teacher Bill Diaz
> could take me prospecting again in the mountains?

You bet, I'd be glad to have you come along!  I've planned a trip
from July 24-27, if that fits with your plans. Here's a few things
to get ahold of before you visit:

        a geological hammer, and plastic sunglasses
        a good field guide for rocks and minerals
        a *light* sleeping bag (remember how HOT
           you were in that down bag last summer? :-)
        a sturdy pair of hiking boots

If you need advice, feel free to contact me!  Take care,

Bill
```

Example 2 may seem extreme, but as everyone who has used the Internet can attest, messages such as this *do* occur! The text of Example 1 was carefully contorted into Example 2 by violating nearly every rule of etiquette espoused in this chapter.

Example 2: E-mail Violating Suggested Etiquette Guidelines

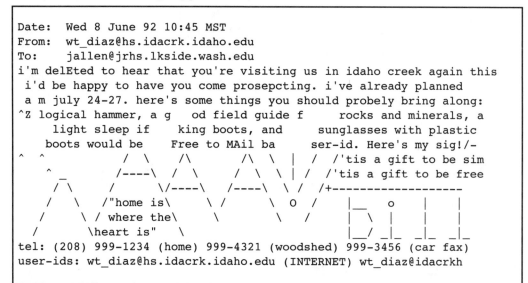

```
Date:  Wed 8 June 92 10:45 MST
From:  wt_diaz@hs.idacrk.idaho.edu
To:    jallen@jrhs.lkside.wash.edu
i'm delEted to hear that you're visiting us in idaho creek again this
 i'd be happy to have you come prosepcting. i've already planned
 a m july 24-27. here's some things you should probely bring along:
^Z logical hammer, a g  od field guide f     rocks and minerals, a
     light sleep if   king boots, and      sunglasses with plastic
     boots would be      Free to MAil ba     ser-id. Here's my sig!/-
 ^  ^            / \   /\        /\ \  |  / /'tis a gift to be sim
      ^ _       /----\ / \     / \ \ | /  /'tis a gift to be free
   / \      /       \/----\  /----\  \ /  /+-------------------
  /    \   /"home is\    \ /       \ o /   |__   o   |  |
 /      \ / where the\    \        \ /    |  \   |   |  |
/         \heart is"   \               |__/ _|_  _|_  _|_
tel: (208) 999-1234 (home) 999-4321 (woodshed) 999-3456 (car fax)
user-ids: wt_diaz@hs.idacrk.idaho.edu (INTERNET) wt_diaz@idacrkh
```

The Format of E-mail Messages

Many e-mail etiquette principles arise from the current state of terminal technology in networks. Although some lucky people have extraordinarily powerful graphics workstations that can display characters and graphics of varying fonts, sizes, and colors, most folks on the Internet still eke by with simple, text-only displays limited to 80 columns and 24 rows of text.

Screen Size

Be brief. What you need to communicate can usually fit in a screen of text.

Try to keep your e-mail messages narrower than 65 characters and/or spaces wide; short lines are easier to read on a computer screen, and other people's terminals may not be able to display longer lines. This also leaves room for text to be moved to the right when it is quoted by others. (This point is described in greater detail below.)

Blank spaces between paragraphs or other logical units of text make it easier to read the message. Along the same lines, keep your paragraphs short; in general, fewer than 15 lines should be about right. Large blocks of text can make it difficult to keep one's place within a screen or when moving between screens. (Unfortunately blocks of text that are proportioned correctly for a computer screen often seem disjointed when printed.)

Stylistic Conventions of Text-Only Messages

Using standard capitalization and mixed-case text is preferable in both written and electronic communication. messages in all lower case can cause problems. it creates a halting, uncertain reading pattern. on the other hand, USING ALL UPPER CASE IN A MAIL MESSAGE IS LIKE SHOUTING WHEN YOU SPEAK!

Emphasis can be subtle and effective. For example, use asterisks, underlines, or other special characters around words or phrases, like *this*, or like _this_, or >>even<< like that!

Control Characters and "The Sorcerer's Apprentice" Phenomenon

Avoid using control sequences (like "ctrl m") or special keys (like "tab"). Even if they seem to work fine while you are editing your mail document, such special characters may do really bizarre things to your file when someone else reads it with their e-mail software. (Using control characters is in fact how the weird slanted columns were generated in Example 2.)

THE CONTENT OF E-MAIL MESSAGES

Strive to be concise, clear, and polite in your own writing and flexible in your interpretation of the mail you receive from other people. This conforms to an old networking axiom: "Be precise in what you send, and forgiving of what you receive."

The following set of points deals with stylistic considerations that are based on the often neglected fact that the readers of e-mail messages are actually real people!

Of Relevance to All Outbound Messages

These guidelines should be used for all messages you send out whether originally written or forwarded by you. How closely you follow them depends to a certain extent on the level of formality of the message. A note to your best friend may look different from a memo to your boss. While the list may seem long for a mode of communications that is often characterized as spontaneous and informal, they will quickly become second nature.

Clarity

Use short, informative subject lines. In most cases, software for receiving e-mail displays only the first 15 or 20 characters. Since your subject line is the first impression your message makes on your recipient, be sure to distill the essence of your message into a few choice words that hit the proverbial nail on the head.

Sending Your Message to the Right People

Most mail software packages have a CC (Carbon Copy) option allowing your mail to be sent to those who are at least marginally interested in what you have sent to the person indicated in the "To" field. This might be a boss you are trying to impress with your unending torrent of high-quality, work-related memos, or it might be yourself, if you need a reminder in your mailbox to "MEET THE DEADLINE!"

Greetings and Salutations

Begin your message with the name of the person to whom you are writing. Even though the person's e-mail address is in the mail header, starting your text with their real name makes your message more personal. Similarly, many mail software packages allow you to add a person's real name to the "To" field (see Chapter 2). Most people prefer to be known by their real names rather than by a userid. If you've never met the person to whom you're sending e-mail, a more formal title (Ms. Allen) or more generic salutation (Hello!) may be appropriate.

For some unknown reason, e-mail messages rarely begin with "Dear <insert name here>." Although this salutation is standard practice in regular letters, it is conspicuously absent in e-mail exchanges. (This is one of the *many* peculiarities of computer mediated communication that is worthy of analysis. If anybody takes this on, please let me know!)

Non-Verbal Communications

In face-to-face conversation, subtle body language and intonation let us know how our speech affects the other person. These cues are completely absent when using e-mail.

Since e-mail doesn't contain direct physical cues, a number of conventions peculiar to e-mail have taken hold. In particular, the classic "smiley" is used to indicate that the previous statement was meant in a lighthearted or humorous way. Smileys, when looked at sideways, look vaguely like stick drawings of human faces. There are hundreds of smileys that can be made with the basic characters of a keyboard, each of which conveys a different emotion. Here's a small audience of smileys and their less fortunate relatives, dubbed "weepies," "frownies," or "anti-smileys":

:-)	the basic smiley	:-(	the basic frowney
;-)	the winking smiley	:-o	"OH NO!"
;^}	a more sinister winking smiley	>:-/	Sick of smileys

You get the idea. Hundreds of such ASCII glyphs are possible and there are in fact smiley hunters prowling through the Net with collecting jars in hand. Although smileys serve a purpose, as with all things, moderation is best.

In addition to smileys, there are other ways to suggest the tone of a message, or more usually, the tone of part of a message. By enclosing words in angle brackets, you can tell your readers how you want them to "hear" your message. For example, "Coffee? <sarcasm on> Nobody in Seattle drinks coffee! <sarcasm off>." If you notice that your own message seems to be a rant, you may want to reconsider sending it. If you do choose to send it, surround the appropriate text with <rant on/off> or <on/off soapbox> markers to let others know that you know it's an emotionally stated point of view. (The term "on soapbox" refers to the action of getting up on your soapbox to declare your view of the world, your opinions, or your ideas.) These bracketed cues act like stage directions in a play. People will also include such directions as, <guffaw>, <laugh>, and so on. In an informal message, these non-verbal assists can really help you express yourself in the manner that you intend. However, be advised that these are not likely to be constructive additions to a business report!

Etc.

There are also a number of abbreviations common in e-mail messages that make life on the Net a little easier:

IMHO	"in my humble opinion" (with or without sarcasm)	OTOH	"on the other hand"
BTW	"by the way"	WRT	"with respect to"

Signing Off

As a courtesy, always end your message with your name. You may also want to include your first name, nickname, e-mail address, organization—whatever seems appropriate to the context.

Never forget that your e-mail is read by another human being—someone whose feelings and beliefs may be very different from yours! This is always important, but especially now as the Internet becomes a global community. The underlying humanity of the Net can be easy to forget when you are sitting at a computer terminal writing a mail message to someone you have never met in person and about whom you may know virtually nothing—except that they are human.

The Infamous Signature: *John Hancock* Lives to See the Internet

With some mail software, you can automatically append a file called a "signature" (or "sig") to every outgoing mail message you send. As people grew weary of always typing their names, e-mail addresses, and other information at the end of every message, it seemed reasonable to automate the process. Thus, the signature file was born.

If you use a sig, remember the following:

- Keep your sig short, fewer than five lines is enough. Simple is best.

- Don't include ASCII graphics made of letters and characters (like a 24 row map of the Indian Ocean) or lists of all possible telephone numbers, postal, and e-mail addresses at which you can be contacted. At the very least, they take up space in other people's computers.

Of Relevance to Replies and Forwarded Messages

With most mail software, the reply and forward features allow you to automatically include someone else's mail message in your outgoing message. Pare the original text down to the minimum needed to establish context.

There are some stylistic conventions used when replying to e-mail messages. Symbols such as ">" or "|" are commonly added by the mail software in the first column of the message to which you are replying. This is sometimes referred to as "quoting." Where the message you received contained quoted material as well, these symbols may become layered.

```
>>> When did Henry IV of England live?
>> Henry IV lived in a flat near Shrewsbury in 1934.
> Are you sure? Last I checked with British Telecom, he was
> living in Nottingham.

Close, but not quite. Henry IV lived from 1366-1413 in
Bolingbroke and London!
```

True e-mail artists have a way of efficiently interspersing their comments with the original message, as in the following hypothetical e-mail reply (derived from W. Shakespeare, "*Henry IV, Part 1*", Scene III, Act 2):

```
On Wed, 16 Nov. 1402, The Earl of Worcester wrote:

> But, for mine own part, my lord, I could be well contented
> to be there, in respect of the love I bear your house.

You could be contented, why are you not then?

> The purpose you undertake is dangerous.

Why, that's certain: 'tis dangerous to take a cold, to
sleep, to drink: but I tell you, out of this nettle,
danger, we pluck this flower, safety.

> the friends you have named uncertain; the time itself
> unsorted; and your whole plan too light for the
> counterpoise of so great an opposition.

Say you so, say you so? I say unto you again, you are a
```

(Continued)

```
shallow, cowardly hind, and you lie. What a lack brain is
this! By the Lord, our plan is a good plan as ever was
laid; our friends true and constant: a good plan, good
friends, and full of expectation; an excellent plan, very
good friends. ;-)

Your cool-headed friend
Hotspur
```

Do *not* include the entire original message unless you absolutely have to. This wastes resources used for transmitting and storing mail and, more importantly, the time of the person who has to locate the single word at the end of the message wherein you so eloquently doth declaim "NOT!"

Be careful when forwarding someone else's mail to a third party, especially if that third party is a 3,000 member discussion group! Something someone writes to you as a private message was probably not intended for a wide audience. If you are unsure whether or not the originator would appreciate having their message forwarded, always ask.

Before sending off your e-mail message:
- Review what you have written and correct grammar and spelling errors.
- Make sure you've said everything you needed to say.
- Make sure you haven't said things you didn't need to say.
- Check the "To", "CC", and "BCC" fields to be sure you are sending the mail to the person or people you intend.

And finally, finally, finally, make shure you've yewsed korrect speling and grammer, splling errers end bad grammers make it harder for uther peeple to reed what you wrought. :^) Here's my sig!:

✗ THE BASIC RULES OF E-MAIL ETIQUETTE

Be brief.

Keep line lengths to less than 65 columns.

Use blank spaces between paragraphs to help the reader's eyes.

Use mixed upper and lower case.

Use capitals AND special characters for *emphasis*!

(Continued)

Keep your paragraphs short. Fewer than 15 lines is best.

Avoid using control characters or special keys.

Begin text with the real name of the person to whom you're writing.

If useful, include parts of the mail message to which you are replying.

End the text of your message with your real name.

If you use a "sig," keep it short and simple.

Review what you've written BEFORE you send it.

If possible, include the person's real name in the "To" line of the header.

Use the CC option if available and appropriate.

Read through your message and be sure it conveys the tone you intend.

FOR MORE INFORMATION

Online Information

The following articles appear in the newsgroup "news.announce.newusers" as "periodic postings." Although written with Usenet in mind, many of the principles they espouse are relevant to all electronic mail communication. For more on Usenet, see Chapter 9.

Offutt, A. J., and G. Spafford. "Hints on Writing Style for Usenet." 1992.

Templeton, B., and G. Spafford. "Emily Postnews Answers Your Questions on Netiquette." (A tongue-in-cheek, very funny, but very informative essay on what not to do in electronic mail, especially in Usenet postings.) 1992.

Von Rospach, C. and G. Spafford. "A Primer on How to Work With the Usenet Community." 1992.

Bibliography

Goode, J. and M. Johnson, "Putting Out the Flames: The Etiquette and Law of E-mail." *Online* 15(6) (1991):61-65.

Quarterman, J. S. "Etiquette and Ethics." *ConneXions*—The Interoperability Report. (Advanced Computing Environments, Mountain View, CA.) 3(4) (1989):12-16.

Shapiro, N. Z., and R. H. Anderson. "Towards an Ethics and Etiquette for Electronic Mail." Santa Monica, CA: Rand Corporation, 1985.

5

Electronic Mail Gateways

Sending Messages to the Great Beyond

Although the Internet connects many countries and millions of people, there is a wide variety of non-Internet networks as well. Even though these other networks use a different communications protocol, many of them provide Internet e-mail service for their users. This aggregate group of networks, which can communicate in one way or another, is often referred to as the "matrix."

You may want to exchange e-mail messages with people using these networks or to access services those networks provide. This chapter explains how you can communicate with people or services on many non-Internet networks by using electronic mail gateways.

WHAT ARE ELECTRONIC MAIL GATEWAYS?

Mail gateways are computers that allow e-mail messages to be transmitted between networks that use differing methods of addressing and packaging information.

Many computer networks are not part of the Internet and do not use the Internet Protocols (IP). Recall that if you want to send an e-mail message anywhere in the Internet you would use the standard Internet address format.

`mailbox@an.Internet.host.address`

Addresses on other networks may use very different formats. Consider the format of an MCI e-mail address.

`Firstname Lastname (123-4567)`

Internet mailers cannot read an address like this, because it contains information and symbols that are not part of an Internet address; likewise your postal service would be baffled by a letter with an Internet address. Furthermore, the actual way in which mail messages are packaged in other networks may be considerably different.

Mail gateways are able to resolve differences in both addressing and packaging when transmitting information between networks.

HOW TO USE ELECTRONIC MAIL GATEWAYS

You need to know four things to send mail to users and computers on other networks:

1. the addressing convention of the network to which you are sending mail;

2. how to present the foreign network's address in your mail header so the Internet mailers won't reject it;

3. the Internet address of a gateway computer connected to the other network; and,

4. the e-mail address of the person or computer on the other network.

■■■

All of the information you need to answer questions 1-3 for many of the more commonly used non-Internet networks is provided in the table in the next section. It's up to you to supply the destination e-mail address.

The basic strategy used by mail gateways to transmit messages from the Internet to other networks is very simple:

* the Internet address of the appropriate e-mail gateway is put in the Internet address field;

* and sometimes, address information from the alien network is put in the userid field of an Internet e-mail address.

For example, suppose you want to send an e-mail message to a friend in France who uses the EARN network (a portion of the BITNET network). The typical e-mail address within the BITNET network looks like this:

`user@host`

To send an e-mail message to our friend from a computer on the Internet, some people just need to add ".bitnet" to the address, while many others also need to include the whole e-mail address and the Internet address of an Internet-BITNET gateway.

Here's a general example of the e-mail address you would enter.

`user%host.bitnet@An.Interbit.Gateway.Address`

where "An.Interbit.Gateway.Address" is one of the several computers providing Internet gateway services to both the Internet and to BITNET. (See the table in the next section for a listing of these gateways.)

"C'est tres facile, non?" "You betcha!"

Table of Mail Gateways from the Internet to Other Networks

This table summarizes the information you need to send e-mail messages to some of the many non-Internet networks. It is derived from a more complete guide originally created by John Chew and now maintained by Scott Yanoff. (Refer to the end of this chapter for information on obtaining the "Inter-Network Mail Guide.")

For each network:

1. the first row contains the electronic mail address syntax used in each non-Internet network;

2. the second row shows how you modify that network's native electronic mail address syntax to send mail from the Internet to that network.

America Online	1) userid
	2) userid@aol.com
Applelink	1) userid
	2) userid@applelink.apple.com

BITNET	1) `userid@site`
	2) `userid@site.bitnet`
	At many Internet sites, you can address mail to BITNET users with the syntax above. If this doesn't work, try the following syntax:
	`userid%host.bitnet@An.Interbit.Gateway.Address`
	where "`An.Interbit.Gateway.Address`" is one of the following:
	`CORNELLC.CIT.CORNELL.EDU`
	`CUNYVM.CUNY.EDU`
	`MITVMA.MIT.EDU`
	`VM1.NODAK.EDU`
CompuServe	1) `7xxxx,yyy`
	2) `7xxxx.yyy@CompuServe.Com`
EASYnet/ DECNET	1) `host::user`
	2) `user@host.enet.dec.com`
FidoNet	1) `Firstname Lastname at 1:2/3.4`
	2) `Firstname.Lastname@p4.f3.n2.z1.fidonet.org`
JANET	1) `userid@A.Janet.Domain.Address` (e.g., `"uk.ac.ox.vax"`)
	2) `userid@Address.Domain.Janet.A` (e.g., `"vax.ox.ac.uk"`)
MCI	1) `FirstName LastName (123-4567)`, where `123-4567` is an MCI phone id #
	2) `1234567@mcimail.com`
PeaceNet	1) `userid`
	2) `userid@cdp.igc.org`
Prodigy	1) `userid`
	2) `userid@prodigy.com`
Sprintmail	1) `Firstname Lastname at AnOrganization`
	2) `/G=Firstname/S=Lastname/O=AnOrganization/ADMD=TELEMAIL/C=US/@Sprint.Com`

Using the Mail Gateways Table

As the previous example demonstrates, you need to know the Internet addresses of gateways which are appropriate for sending e-mail to users on non-Internet networks. Suppose you wanted to send an e-mail message to a friend who has an account on the FidoNet network. They've told you that their FidoNet address is the following:

Kelley Meithisson at 3:56/67.4

First make sure that you, and they, have got everything in this address right. Simple transcriptional errors are one of the more frequent causes of Inter-gateway mail problems.

Look in the first column to find Fidonet. Read across to the line labeled "1)." This shows a typical FidoNet userid and address which corresponds to your friend Kelley's address information above. Now look at the next line labeled "2)." This shows how Kelley's FidoNet address should be translated by an Internet user so that an e-mail message will be successfully sent to her. According to line 2, Kelley's FidoNet address should be translated to:

`Kelley.Meithisson@p4.f67.n56.z3.fidonet.org`

This address is now acceptable to mailers that conform to the Internet standards. When it arrives at the Internet-Fidonet gateway, it will be translated to a FidoNet address format and delivered within the FidoNet network to Kelley.

FOR MORE INFORMATION

Online Table of Gateways

"The Inter-Network Mail Guide," originally by John Chew and now updated by Scott Yanoff, is a comprehensive and usually up-to-date table of gateways between the Internet and many other networks available by anonymous FTP. (For more on FTP, see Chapter 7.)

FTP host:	`csd4.csd.uwm.edu`
directory:	`/pub`
filename:	`internetwork-mail-guide`

This document is also posted periodically to the following newsgroups, which are good forums for asking and answering questions about gateway problems.

`news.newusers.questions`	a good newsgroup for simple gateway problems
`comp.mail.misc`	a good newsgroup for obstinate gateway problems

It is also available from the following LISTSERV list:

mail:	`listserv%unmvm.bitnet@cunyvm.cuny.edu`
subject:	**(none needed)**
message:	`get network guide`

(For more on Usenet and LISTSERV, see Chapters 9 and 10.)

RFCs about Gateways

The following RFCs give some insight into the nuts and bolts of some gateway protocols:

RFC987	Mapping between X.400 and RFC822
RFC1026	Addendum to RFC987: (mapping between X.400 and RFC-822)
RFC1137	Mapping between full RFC 822 and RFC 822 with restricted encoding
RFC1148	Mapping between X.400 (1988) / ISO 10021 and RFC 822
RFC1168	Intermail and commercial mail relay services

Bibliography

The following three reference books are invaluable resources for understanding the intricacies of electronic mail gateways specifically and intercommunication between networks generally:

Frey, D., and R. Adams. *!%@:: A Directory of Electronic Mail Addressing and Networks*. Sebastopol, CA: O'Reilly and Associates, 1993.

LaQuey, T. L. *The User's Directory of Computer Networks*. Bedford, MA: Digital Press, 1990.

Quarterman, J. S. *The Matrix: Computer Networks and Conferencing Systems Worldwide*. Bedford, MA: Digital Press, 1990.

CHAPTER

6

Telnet

Using Computers throughout the Internet

Telnet allows you to use Internet computers throughout the world as if they were on your own desktop. Note that Telnet is not a network; it is one of the TCP/IP applications that makes the Internet possible and useful.

Some of the many services that Telnet allows you to access include:

- library catalogs;
- databases;
- supercomputers;
- directories of e-mail addresses;
- and a huge variety of information services.

When you run a Telnet session with a computer thousands of kilometers away, the activities of that computer seem to be unfolding in real time right on your computer's screen. It's really quite amazing!

Telnet that supports 3270 terminal emulation (usually called "tn3270") is required for remote sessions to and from IBM mainframes. For the time being, assume that what applies to Telnet applies equally to tn3270. But as you'll find out later in this chapter, effective use of tn3270 often requires special attention and preparation.

TELNET BASICS

Most Internet computers already have Telnet software installed. When you use Telnet, your local software (i.e., the Telnet "client") communicates with the remote software (i.e., the Telnet "server") on the computer whose services you want to access. All of this happens behind the scenes. What you see on your screen is the computer service you have requested.

Levels of Telnet Access

In practice, there are two levels of Telnet access.

- "Guest Telnet" allows you to login to an Internet host to use special, publicly available service(s) on the remote computer.
- With "full privilege Telnet" you can login to any other Internet computer on which you have an account.

Telnet Etiquette

All Telnet etiquette derives from one simple fact: somebody, somewhere, has been generous enough to let people on the Internet use their computer. In exchange for this generosity, these systems should be used with the utmost consideration and respect.

Some services request that you not use them during specific hours of the day, usually during standard business hours. If this is the case, honor this request and remember to take into consideration any difference in time zones between you and the site to which you would like to telnet.

■■

Using Telnet

■■

Getting Started

From most hosts on the Internet, starting a Telnet session is fairly straightforward.

Typically you just type "telnet" followed by the Internet address of a computer to which you want to connect.

```
telnet an.internet.host.address
```

If you are working from a computer with a graphical user interface such as the Apple Macintosh, a DOS machine running Windows, or a specific workstation, you might start Telnet by clicking an icon.

If you can't figure out how to start Telnet, try your local online help system or get help from your user services staff. Here are some of the more common requests you might use to get online help.

Unix	`man telnet`
VMS, VM/CMS, some Unix machines	`help telnet` or `help tcpip`

Command Mode

When you type telnet without a host address, you may find yourself in Telnet command mode. The prompt "telnet >" usually appears. This may also happen if you've misspelled the host's name or the host is unreachable. In the following example, I attempted to telnet to a (so far as we know) nonexistent host and was presented with the telnet prompt.

```
telnet alpha.centuri.gov
alpha.centuri.gov: host unknown
telnet>
```

From this prompt, you can issue a variety of Telnet commands, of which the most commonly needed are "open" and "quit".

Open is used to open a telnet connection to a remote host.

```
telnet> open <an.internet.host.address>
```

Not surprisingly, quit is used to end any current remote sessions and exit Telnet, returning you to your operating system's prompt.

For more on what commands are available in command mode, see the sections "Ending a Telnet Session" and "Help!" later in this chapter.

A Sampler of Destinations

Here's a list of a few of the many Telnet sites on the Internet that offer valuable and interesting services. Enjoy!

Service Type and Name	Internet Address	Login Name
Internet Front Ends		
University of North Carolina's laUNChpad	bbs.oit.unc.edu	launch
Services	library.wustl.edu	none needed
Library Catalogs		
CARL	pac.carl.org	none needed
MELVYL	melvyl.ucop.edu	none needed
Directory and Information Services		
Library of Congress Information	locis.loc.gov	none needed
Library of Congress Gopher	marvel.loc.gov	marvel
InterNIC Gopher	ds.internic.net	gopher
Paradise	hypatia.umdc.umu.se	de
Databases		
U.S. Department of Agriculture Economic and Statistics Service	usda.mannlib.cornell.edu	usda
FEDIX (Grants, Scholarships)	fedix.fie.com	new
Spacelink (NASA and Space Sciences)	spacelink.msfc.nasa.gov	newuser

Login Name and Password

One usually uses Telnet to engage in an interactive session with a Telnet host or service. In such cases, you have to supply a login name and maybe a password much as you would with your own computer account.

Sometimes a login screen displays information needed to use the service. For example, users of the University of North Carolina "laUNChpad" (whose Internet address is "bbs.oit.unc.edu") see the following message when they login:

```
telnet bbs.oit.unc.edu

Trying...
Connected to lambada.oit.unc.edu.
Escape character is '^]'.

ULTRIX V4.3 (Rev. 44) (lambada)

         *** ATTENTION laUNChpad USERS ***
        Type 'launch' at the login prompt.

login: launch
```

In this case you would simply type "launch" at the "login:" prompt. But you will often need to know these login instructions before you access the service. Most reference lists of Telnet sites will give you this information.

Telnet Troubleshooting

If you type "telnet <an.internet.host.address>" and you don't get connected, read the error message that has appeared on your screen.

- "unknown host"—Most likely you have misspelled the computer's domain name, or the domain name might have changed, or the host may simply no longer exist.
- "foreign host not responding" and related messages—There's probably too much traffic somewhere on the Internet between you and the host, or the host is temporarily disabled in some way. Try again later.
- "maximum number of users exceeded" or something to that effect—This is likely to happen during the business hours of the site you are trying to reach, or on a system that has internally limited the number of simultaneous users accessing a specific service. Try again later.

About Terminal Emulation

When you want to use Telnet to access another Internet host, that host will often ask you for your "terminal type." You might be shown a list of options. Here is a terminal type list from pac.carl.org, an Internet host providing library catalog services:

```
telnet pac.carl.org

Trying...
Connected to pac.carl.org.
Escape character is '^]'.
Welcome to the CARL system

Please identify your terminal. Choices are:
1.ADM (all)
2.APPLE,IBM
3.TANDEM
4.TELE-914
5.VT100
6.WYSE 50
7.ZENTEC
8.HARDCOPY
9.IBM 316x

Use HARDCOPY if your terminal type isn't listed

SELECT LINE #:
```

Terminal type does not mean, "Is your computer a Macintosh SE or a Cray Y-MP?" but rather "What kind of terminal is your computer software emulating?"

Early on in the history of computers, each major computer company designed special terminals for particular purposes. For example, the Digital Electronics Corporation (DEC) developed the VT series of terminals (VT52, VT100, etc.) for accessing DEC computers; Tektronix terminals were developed for displaying graphics; and IBM developed the 3270 terminal for accessing IBM mainframes.

Today, you can use communications software that allows your computer to emulate one or more of these terminal types. The most commonly used terminal type on the Internet is VT100.

For more information about terminal emulation, ask a local user services person for help. The right answers to your questions depend heavily on the software and hardware installed at your site.

About tn3270

As alluded to above, 3270 refers to a special kind of terminal designed to interface with IBM mainframes, and tn3270 refers to software that emulates (or acts like) a 3270 terminal. Why is this important? Because you value your sanity.

The 3270 terminal implements the full-screen interface necessary for most IBM mainframe applications and relies heavily upon special features such as input areas and protected fields (areas where you can and cannot type, respectively), program function keys (the infamous "PF" keys), and other command keys ("PA," "clear") not employed by the standard VT100 emulation.

What this means to Internet users is that if you want to telnet to a 3270 based system, you must use a version of Telnet which emulates the 3270 terminal.

For users of IBM mainframes, this is usually no problem: you will typically use a program called "telnet" (which is actually 3270 based), and your remote IBM mainframe session will probably be just like your host mainframe session. So, "PF 12! PA1!" and "More...'" to your heart's content.

However, things are a bit trickier going between IBM mainframes and non-3270 based sites.

If you are going from a non-IBM mainframe to an IBM mainframe, you will need to use a version of Telnet called tn3270. Much of the time, tn3270 functions just the way your telnet software does. Simply type "tn3270" followed by the IBM host name. For example, "tn3270 orbis.ycc.yale.edu" would connect you to Yale's online library catalog, ORBIS.

However, even if you connect successfully, you may become confused or have trouble during your session; when prompted for "PF2", you may in fact have to type "esc 2" or some other initially nonintuitive incantation or permutation. And if your screen freezes (often accompanied by the word "HOLDING" in the lower right corner), and nothing will let you proceed, you either need to use a "clear" key if it has been assigned, or break your session ungracefully by using your Telnet escape command to quit the session.

To melt icy screens and resolve other quirks of the tn3270 world in future sessions, you may have to invoke special keymap files. For example, Unix users may be able to avail themselves of a file called "map3270" which allows tn3270 functions to be "mapped" to the keyboards of VT100 or other terminal types.

And if you telnet from an IBM mainframe to a service requiring VT100 emulation, the remote host may present you with an unintelligible, nonfunctional display, if it is not able to understand 3270 emulation.

Don't feel badly if this discussion has you confused—we are not alone. As with all issues that are site-related, your best bet is to talk with your local computer support staff.

What Is a Telnet Session Like?

What happens during your Telnet session from this point on depends upon the software and services of the computer you are accessing. It could be anything from an easy to use menu driven system giving information about the Internet to arcane, highly specialized programs designed to help you with very specific tasks like determining the locations of all telecommunications satellites within a 736.15 kilometer radius of Papete, Bora Bora.

Most all Telnet accessible services have some sort of online help system. If you don't see anything on screen about how to get help, try typing "help", "info", or "?". Commands like, "How does this thing work?" usually don't.

Ending a Telnet Session

Most Telnet services have a correct way of ending the session, usually a command like "logout", "logoff", "exit", "quit", or "bye". If the command to end is not obvious, try checking online help.

However, some services simply don't offer a way to exit. Or, for a variety of reasons, your session may suddenly display gibberish and not respond to commands.

If you must bail out of a Telnet session for some reason, try the "escape character" command. The most common version of this command is "control right bracket," symbolized as "^]". To issue this command, hold the key marked "ctrl" while pressing the "]" key. The Telnet escape character puts you in Telnet command mode and invokes the Telnet prompt ("telnet>") at which you can enter the command "quit". (Standard disclaimer: the procedure described here may not work with all Telnet software. Talk to your local computer support staff for more information.)

Help!

With most Telnet software, you can get help. Try starting Telnet without supplying an Internet host address, and then type "help" at the "telnet>" prompt. Most people never use the advanced Telnet commands, but you might as well know that they are available.

```
telnet

telnet> help

Commands may be abbreviated. Commands are:

close      close current connection
display    display operating parameters
mode       try to enter line-by-line or character-at-a-time
           mode
open       connect to a site
quit       exit telnet
send       transmit special characters ('send ?' for more)


set        set operating parameters ('set ?' for more)
status     print status information
toggle     toggle operating parameters ('toggle ?' for more)
z          suspend telnet
?          print help information
```

■■■

For more detailed information about these commands, you can type the command name followed by a "?"

```
telnet> toggle ?

autoflush    toggle flushing of output when sending
             interrupt characters
autosynch    toggle automatic sending of interrupt
             characters in urgent mode
binary       toggle sending and receiving of binary data
crlf         toggle sending carriage returns as telnet
             <CR><LF>
crmod        toggle mapping of received carriage returns
localchars   toggle local recognition of certain control
             characters
debug        (debugging) toggle debugging
netdata      (debugging) toggle printing of hexadecimal
             network data
options      (debugging) toggle viewing of options
             processing
?            display help information
```

If this process doesn't work for you, ask your local computer support staff to assist you in finding help for your Telnet software.

Telnet Ports

Just like there may be many doors leading into a building, there are many different "ports" leading into most Internet hosts. Each of these ports is assigned a name, number, and purpose. The default Telnet port is usually assigned to TCP port number 23. When you type "telnet an.internet.host.address" the Telnet protocol assumes you mean "telnet an.internet.host.address 23". This gives you a screen where you are usually requested to provide a userid and password to continue.

However, some Telnet services may be assigned to other ports in which case you will be required to add a port number or name after an Internet address when you use Telnet. Here's an example of a very simple service available on port 13 of many Internet hosts called "daytime." (Try using the Internet address of your own Internet host.)

```
telnet <an.internet.host.address> 13

Trying...
Connected to an.internet.host.address.
Escape character is '^]'.

Mon Jan  3 15:19:59 PST 1994

Connection closed by foreign host.
```

(Note that the exact syntax used to issue a port number may vary between Telnet software packages.)

A wide variety of Internet services, many of which are described throughout *The Internet Passport*, require specifying a port number. Some examples include the University of Michigan Weather Underground and the Knowbot Information Server.

WHAT HAPPENS BEHIND THE SCENES?

When you telnet to an Internet host, the Telnet program at your host and the Telnet program at the other host send messages back and forth to each other, in effect negotiating how they will communicate.

Some of the negotiations concern simple matters like how many columns of text your screen can display; others are more complicated issues dealing with exactly how information will be coded.

If the negotiations were conversations on which you could eavesdrop, you'd hear something like the following:

```
telnet <an.internet.host.address>

Trying...

Local Telnet:    "Hello 'an.internet.host.address'! Are you
                    there?"
Remote Telnet:   "You bet! Pleased to meet you. Let's talk."

Local Telnet:    "Will you put a carriage return and a line
                    feed at the end of every line that is sent
                    to Jonathan's screen?"
```

■■

(Continued)

```
Remote Telnet:    "Yes, I will do that."
Local Telnet:     "Will you display output in 124 columns?"
Remote Telnet:    "No, I won't do that! Sorry."

...               ... more questions and answers

Both Telnets:     "Okay, we've come to an agreement and have
                  created a 'virtual terminal' for Jonathan's
                  Telnet session. Let's tell him that we're
                  ready!"

Connected to <an.internet.host.address>
Escape character is '^]'.

login:
```

Now that a method of communicating has been established, your screen displays the commands that you type and the responses from the computer to which you have connected. Throughout your Telnet session, the local and remote Telnet programs continue to send information back and forth across the Internet.

FOR MORE INFORMATION
■■

Lists of Telnet Accessible Resources

Many of the chapters of *The Internet Passport* give information about Telnet accessible resources. In particular, try the chapters covering OPACs, Databases, Gopher, CWISs, WAIS, World Wide Web, and Directory Services.

Special Internet Connections

A frequently updated list of Internet resources that includes many Telnet accessible sites is maintained by Scott Yanoff. You can obtain this list in at least the three following ways:

1. From the newsgroup "alt.internet.services": The list is posted once or twice a month to this newsgroup. (For more on using Usenet, see Chapter 9.)

2. Via FTP:

   FTP host: `csd4.csd.uwm.edu`
   directory: `/pub`
   filename: `inet.services.txt`

For more on FTP see Chapter 7.

3. By subscribing to the "special Internet connections" mailing list: Send the following e-mail message:

```
mail:     yanoff@csd4.csd.uwm.edu
subject: inet
message: (none needed)
```

If your host has the "finger" program, you can get up-to-date information about Yanoff's list by issuing the command "finger yanoff@csd4.csd.uwm.edu".

Technical Descriptions

Authoritative sources for technical information about Telnet (and most anything else about the Internet) can be found in Request for Comments (RFCs) documents.

Here's a partial list of relevant RFCs on Telnet:

RFC854	Telnet Protocol specification
RFC855	Telnet Option specifications
RFC856	Telnet binary transmission
RFC857	Telnet echo option
RFC858	Telnet Suppress Go Ahead option
RFC859	Telnet status option
RFC860	Telnet timing mark option
RFC861	Telnet extended options: List option
RFC1184	Telnet linemode option

Although RFCs are available from many other sources on the Internet (see Appendix A for a longer list of access methods), here are instructions on how to obtain RFCs from a definitive RFC repository using three methods of access.

1. Via electronic mail messages to the InterNIC's Information Service automated mail server:

```
mail:            mailserv@ds.internic.net
subject:         (none needed)
message:
file rfcxxxx.yyy (where xxxx is the RFC number and yyy is
                 "txt" or "ps" for the text or PostScript
                 version when appropriate)
```

■■■

2. Via FTP:

FTP host:	`ds.internic.net`	
directory:	`/rfc`	
filename:	`rfcxxxx.txt`	(where xxxx is the RFC number)
	`rfcxxxx.ps`	(for the PostScript version when available)

3. Via Telnet:

Telnet:	`ds.internic.net`
login:	`gopher`
menus:	`InterNIC Directory and Database Services (AT&T)/Internet Documentation (RFC's, FYI's, etc.)/RFC's (Request For Comments)/`

TCP/IP Packages That Include Telnet

Although it dates from 1990, a document that may be useful is the "Network Protocol Implementations and Vendors Guide," which contains more than 300 pages of description of TCP/IP hardware and software. It is available at no charge via FTP and electronic mail. (Be aware that the mail server method of obtaining the file will return it in 35 separate pieces.)

FTP host:	`archive.cis.ohio-state.edu`
directory:	`/pub/netinfo`
filename:	`vendors-guide.doc`

```
mail:      service@nic.ddn.mil
subject:   netinfo vendors-guide.doc
message:   (none needed)
```

CHAPTER

7

Moving Files with File Transfer Protocol (FTP)

FTP is a method used to transfer files between computers connected to the Internet. You can move your own files with FTP, but even better, you can copy files from numerous FTP archives throughout the world. By using FTP, the worldwide Internet becomes like a huge disk drive attached to your computer; the big difference is that you have millions of files to choose from! With FTP you have the ability to establish a special connection to any one of over 1,500 computers world wide and to transfer files. This has become so popular that FTP has literally transformed the software publication business.

FTP can be daunting to the new user. With a little practice and a bit of guidance, however, it can become as easy as using an automated teller machine to move money from your checking account to your savings.

WHAT IS FTP USED FOR?

Getting Files from Anonymous FTP Archives

The most common use of FTP is to get files from Internet computers containing "anonymous FTP archives."

What kinds of files are in anonymous FTP archives? You name it!
* Software for most computers and for most purposes
* Informative documents (e-texts, e-journals, e-newsletters, archived discussions from LISTSERVs and more)
* Graphics
* Data
* MIDI music sequences
* And much more!

There are more files in anonymous FTP hosts than any one person could ever use.

It is estimated that there are over 2,000,000 files in more than 1,500 anonymous FTP hosts. It is also estimated that all together these files occupy more than 100 billion bytes of computer space. That's a lot of floppies!

Like most services on the Internet, FTP archives and the files they contain continue to grow in number daily. In Chapter 16, you will learn about a program called "archie" that allows you to keep track of this growing, ever changing wealth of files.

Full Privilege FTP

If you have full access privileges on two or more Internet hosts (e.g., your desktop computer and a mainframe) you can use FTP to copy files between these computers no matter where they are located.

Anonymous FTP Archives

Because most people on the Internet use FTP primarily for accessing anonymous FTP archives, most of this chapter will focus on the use of anonymous FTP. Almost everything described here applies equally well to the use of full privilege FTP, except you would need a userid and password.

The Organization of Anonymous FTP Hosts

Most FTP hosts are organized as directories and subdirectories of files. This hierarchical file system can be illustrated as an upside-down tree.

Here's a diagram of part of a typical FTP host, ftp.nwnet.net.

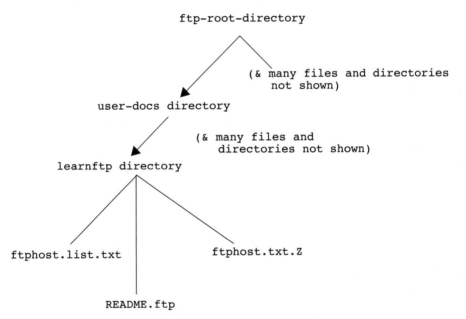

The "root" of this tree is the FTP root directory, which is where you start when you enter an FTP host. Directories are like the branching limbs of an apple tree and files are like the apples you pick.

To get to a file, you go down the tree (remember, it's upside-down and the root is at the top) along a "directory path." For example the directory path leading to "README.ftp" in the illustration above is "/user-docs/learnftp". Other paths lead to other files on the FTP host. Because the root is not a named directory, all path names are presented on the assumption that you proceed from the root.

Keep this image of an upside down tree in mind whenever you use FTP hosts, and navigating through FTP directories should be much easier. If you move onto one branch and want to look at another, you need to back up the tree until you reach a trunk common to both branches.

Some people prefer to think of directories and files in terms of folders and papers: folders can hold individual documents (files), or even other folders, and so on. For example, you might have a folder in your desk called "Letters." Inside this folder, you might have folders labeled "Amie," "Doug," and "Sarah," holding letters to and from these friends.

Case Sensitivity

Case sensitivity means that upper and lower case characters are treated differently by a program or operating system. And as you might infer, to a case insensitive system "a rose, is a 'Rose,' is a 'ROSE,' is a 'rose.'"

As a general rule, FTP hosts on Unix or Macintosh computers are case sensitive, while FTP hosts on DOS, VM/CMS, or VMS are not case sensitive. In a case sensitive FTP host, what you see is what you should type, UPPER.&.lower.case, exactly as displayed.

If you don't know an FTP host's operating system, how can you tell if it's case sensitive? Well, as Yogi Berra may have said, "you can observe a lot just by looking." If the directory listing of an FTP host shows mixed case in the file names, the host is case sensitive and you must type filenames exactly as shown. If all you see is lower case, the host is still probably case sensitive but there just aren't any mixed case filenames in sight. And finally, if everything you see on the screen is in upper case letters, the site is probably case insensitive.

Where's My File?

When you FTP a file to your computer, you are transferring it to the computer where you have your Internet account. For most people, this is not the computer on their desktop, but a host computer elsewhere. The file will be located in the same directory you were in when you started FTP, unless you issued the lcd command during the FTP session, changing the local directory.

BEFORE USING ANONYMOUS FTP, "README.FIRST"!

Anonymous FTP hosts can contain a huge amount of material. Luckily, the folks who maintain FTP hosts often provide three kinds of files that can help you understand an FTP host's structure and contents: "README," "INDEX," and "ls-lR" files.

README Files

Well organized FTP hosts often have filenames containing the word "readme" in many of their directories. Readme files usually contain understandable and informative descriptions about what's in a directory, and possibly even subdirectories within that directory. Typical names are "Readme," "READ.ME," "READ_ME," "README.1st," "00README," "$README," and so forth. These names are chosen so that they will appear conspicuously when you display the contents of a directory.

INDEX Files

INDEX files usually list the names of the files contained in an FTP host directory, sometimes with a very brief description of the contents of each file.

"ls-lR" Files

An ls-lR file is a drawing of an FTP host "tree" complete with branches (directories) and apples (files). "ls-lR" is the Unix command for a recursive directory listing. When executed, this command lists all the files and sub-directories in a directory, followed by all the files and sub-directories within each sub-directory. (Do not attempt to run this command on an FTP server! Because there are typically so many directories and files available, it may take an inordinate amount of time to process the command.)

Some of the really gargantuan FTP hosts like wuarchive.wustl.edu may have so many files that the ls-lR file from their root directory may be megabytes in size! In addition to being great reference material for the serious FTP user, these seemingly endless lists of filenames in ls-lR files make great reading for insomniacs.

Anonymous FTP Etiquette

There are a few very important rules of etiquette when using FTP just as there are when using e-mail. FTP etiquette is based on the fact that you are using another institution's computer that has been generously made available to the Internet community.

Life always involves tradeoffs. In the case of FTP, you need to consider tradeoffs of space and time—how far the FTP site is from your host and what the local time is at the FTP site.

When to FTP

Although you should feel free to FTP from your Internet host, any time day or night, you should avoid using anonymous FTP hosts between 8am to 5pm *their* local time, since the computer is probably being used by folks at that institution for work activities. Heavy anonymous FTP activity can interfere with the functioning of a host computer for its primary tasks, which do not usually include the running of anonymous FTP. For your convenience, many FTP hosts will display the local time at the host site when you first login. Of course, if you are aware of any explicit time restrictions on access to an anonymous FTP host different than the 8am to 5pm exclusion rule, honor them.

It may sometimes be difficult for you to avoid using FTP during your own working hours, especially if you are using FTP for work-related activities and the site you want to FTP to is in your time zone. But since the Internet makes it easy to access computers anywhere in the world, you may be able to find an FTP site in a different time zone that has what you need. Query the archie service to see what FTP host options you might have. (To learn more about archie, see Chapter 16.)

Where to FTP

You might think that this means you should use the most distant FTP host possible when you're working during the day. But this is not true for a number of reasons. U.S. and Canadian users in general should not need to access FTP hosts outside of North America since most of the world's FTP files still originate from North America. On the other hand, choosing an FTP archive at a remote site does add to the amount of traffic on the network, as your data will be on the network for a longer distance. In addition, some sites, notably Australia, have somewhat limited networking off-continent, so FTP'ing a large file from such an archive is not encouraged.

FTP users from outside North America can often use FTP hosts in their countries that duplicate the contents of U.S. FTP hosts.

Is an Anonymous User Really Anonymous?

When you access an anonymous FTP host, you will login as "anonymous" when you are asked for an access name. Does this mean that you are truly an "anonymous" user? No, not really.

After you've entered "anonymous," you will be asked for "your ident" or "your real ident" as a password. Many sites may ask you to respond by typing in your userid, <you>@<your.internet.address>. Providing your e-mail address voluntarily is a demonstration of your willingness to be forthright and honest about who you are while using the resources of the FTP host. In fact, some FTP hosts automatically get your host's Internet domain address when you first login and will compare it with the address you entered.

Transfer logs containing the e-mail addresses of people who have transferred files from an FTP site are sometimes used to notify folks who have transferred a file that is later found to have problems. And on rare occasions, an FTP host administrator may have to track down a person (not you, of course!) who is abusing FTP privileges in some way.

GETTING STARTED WITH ANONYMOUS FTP

On most mainframes, workstations, and many personal computers, you should be able to start an FTP session simply by typing "ftp <FTP.host.address>".

If you are using a computer with a graphical user interface, such as the Apple Macintosh, DOS machines running Windows, and some workstations, you might be able to start FTP by clicking an icon.

▪▪

If you don't know if FTP is available or don't know how to access it, ask your user services staff.

You can also try your local online help system. Here are some of the more common forms of help syntax you might use.

Unix	`man ftp`
VMS, CMS, some Unix machines	`help ftp` or `help tcpip`
Macintosh (from a pull down menu)	`find telnet` or `find tcp`

The Essential FTP Commands

The following FTP commands are sufficient for most FTP sessions:

Command	Meaning or Action
`ftp <FTP.host.address>`	start an FTP session
`cd <directory.name>`	change directories down
`cdup`	move up one directory level
`dir`	display the contents of a directory with full information, in alphabetical order
`ls`	display list of files and subdirectories in directory
`ascii`	prepare FTP for a text-only transfer (default setting)
`binary`	prepare FTP for a binary file transfer (usually used for getting program files)
`get <filename>`	copy a file from FTP host to your computer
`quit`	end your FTP session

Simple Sample Anonymous FTP Session

In this sample session, you will log into an anonymous FTP host and then copy files to your own Internet computer. The exercise assumes you are using a Unix system. If you aren't, you may need to vary some of the commands to suit your system.

■ ■

The same sample session is presented in two formats. On the first page, the commands, and what they do, are explained step by step. On the second page, you see what the session looks like on-screen.

While you are connected to the FTP host, explore! There are many computer files on this FTP host, probably many more than you could fit into your own computer. You will encounter files with name endings such as ".Z," ".tar," ".exe," ".bin," but you may not want to retrieve them until you've read Chapter 8, which explains how to handle such files. After you quit you should have on your computer copies of the files README.ftp, ftphost.list.txt, or any other files you copied during your FTP session. Please note that the file ftphost.list.txt has not been updated since 1991 as the maintainer of the list was unable to continue working on it. Instructions for accessing a more up-to-date list can be found at the end of this chapter. For the most up-to-date information on FTP sites, it is best to use the archie service (Chapter 16).

What you want to do:	What you type:
1) Start the FTP program with the host address:	`ftp ftp.nwnet.net`
2) Identify yourself:	
type an FTP login name	`anonymous`
type a password	`<your e-mail address>`
3) Move to the "learnftp" directory	`cd user-docs/learnftp`
4) List the contents of the "learnftp" directory	`dir` (or `ls`)
5) Copy the files "README.ftp" and "ftphost.list.txt" to your computer (They will be copied to the directory from which you started FTP.)	`get README.ftp`
	`get ftphost.list.txt`
6) Explore an FTP host:	
a) Go back to "root" ("/") directory	`cd /`
b) Display contents of root directory	`dir` (or `ls`)
c) Enter a directory	`cd <directory-name>`
d) Display contents of that directory	`dir` (or `ls`)
e) Get another file	`get <filename>`
7) Repeat any of these steps in any order as desired!	
8) Quit an FTP session (use at any time)	`quit`

What You May See On-Screen During Your FTP Session

```
ftp ftp.nwnet.net

Connected to dns2.nwnet.net.
220 dns2.nwnet.net FTP server (ULTRIX Version 4.1 Tue Mar 19 00:38:17
EST 1991)ready.

Name (ftp.nwnet.net:<you>): anonymous

331 Guest login ok, send ident as password.

Password: <you>@<your.internet.address>

230 Guest login ok, access restrictions apply.

ftp> cd user-docs/learnftp
250 CWD command successful.

ftp> dir
200 PORT command successful.
150 Opening data connection for /bin/ls (192.80.13.50,1614) (0 bytes).

total 207
-rw-r--r--  1 1264      55              2824 Jun 10  1993 README.ftp
-rw-r--r--  1 1264      55            148620 Nov  9 16:58 ftphost.list.txt
-rw-r--r--  1 1264      55             44242 Nov  9 17:00 ftphost.txt.Z

226 Transfer complete.
218 bytes received in 0.1 seconds (2.1 Kbytes/s)

ftp> get README.ftp

200 PORT command successful.
150 Opening data connection for README.ftp (ascii mode) (1863 bytes).
226 Transfer complete.
local: README.ftp remote: README.ftp
1886 bytes received in 0.086 seconds (21 Kbytes/s)

(You can explore the FTP host by using commands like "cd ..",
 "cd <directory-name>", "dir", "ls", and other commands, as described
 in the rest of this chapter.)

ftp> quit
221 Goodbye.
```

A Sample List of FTP Hosts

The ftphost.list.txt file you may have gotten from the host ftp.nwnet.net contains a comprehensive list of anonymous FTP hosts throughout the world.

Because this huge list can be slightly intimidating for beginners, a very brief list of some of the more useful, well organized, voluminous, or interesting anonymous FTP hosts in North America, Europe, Asia, and Australia is provided below. Try a site near you, and try the /pub directory first.

And please, don't forget: in the immortal words of Jon Granrose, "anonymous FTP is a privilege, not a right."

Internet Address (and Country)

archive.cis.ohio-state.edu(USA)	nis.nsf.net	(USA)
ftp.sura.net (USA)	pit-manager.mit.edu	(USA)
ftp.uni-kl.de (Germany)	plaza.aarnet.edu.au	(Australia)
ftp.uu.net (USA)	src.doc.ic.ac.uk	(United Kingdom)
ftp.nwnet.net (USA)	ftp.cso.uiuc.edu	(USA)
gatekeeper.dec.com (USA)	wuarchive.wustl.edu	(USA)

FULL PRIVILEGE FTP

If you have computer accounts on two or more computers on the Internet, you can use full privilege FTP to move the files between these Internet hosts. Some anonymous sites also allow users to put files into their "incoming" directory.

Using full privilege FTP is essentially just like using anonymous FTP with one big exception: since you are working with your own accounts, you have the privileges needed to actually add, delete, and reorganize files on that remote host. You can put files into your account on the remote machine with the "put" command ("put <filename>"), make directories ("mkdir <directory-name>"), and even delete files on the remote computer ("delete <filename>").

To use full privilege FTP, from your system prompt simply type "ftp" followed by the Internet address of a computer on which you have an account.

```
ftp <your.host.internet.address>
```

Next, enter the userid and password for your account on the remote Internet host.

```
Name (your.host.internet.address): <your userid>
Password required for YOUR-USERID.
PASSWORD: <your password>
230 User YOUR-USERID logged in.
```

■■■

MORE DETAILS ABOUT FTP COMMANDS
■■■

The information presented up to this point is the bare minimum you need to use FTP, and with what you've learned so far, you could probably fill enough diskettes to overload the springs of a medium-sized automobile. But if you're interested in quality rather than quantity, please read on. You are encouraged to work through these examples while actually exploring any FTP host of your choice. Here we go!

```
ftp any.old.FTP.host

Connected to any.old.FTP.host.
220 an FTP server (Version 4.191 Thu Feb 14 17:09 PST 1991) ready.

Name (any.old.ftp.host:yourname): anonymous
331 Guest login ok, send ident as password.

Password: <you>@<your.internet.address>
230 Guest login ok, access restrictions apply.

ftp>
```

Now you should be at the root directory of "any.old.FTP.host." What does it have to offer? Most FTP hosts support two commands to display listings of a directory's contents: "ls" and "dir."

"ls": A Quick Peek at What's in a Directory

"ls" is good for a quick peek at the contents of a directory. It is an abbreviation for the command "list." (But you could think of it as short for "look see"!) Only the names of the files and directories are listed.

```
ftp> ls
README.NOW
doc
etc
ls-lR
nic
pub
zebra.jokes
```

■■

Notice that ls doesn't show whether an entry is a file or a directory. If you tried to "get pub", you'd probably get a message saying something like "550: pub: not a plain file."

"dir": More Detailed Information about the Contents of a Directory

You should use dir when you want a better view of what's in a directory. In addition to the file and directory names, dir also lets you know which entries are files or directories, the size of the files, and the date the files were most recently changed.

The file size is an especially important piece of information. You need to be certain you have enough space on your computer to receive the files you want to transfer. Some files, particularly graphics, can take several megabytes of disk space.

The format in which all this information is presented depends upon the operating system used by the FTP host computer. Although many FTP hosts are Unix based, you will encounter some that are based on VMS and VM/CMS, so a brief comparison of what these dir listings would look like in these three operating systems is given to save you future headaches. Each example has an explanatory key at the top to help you figure out how each operating system presents the information.

"dir" Display from a Typical Unix FTP Host

```
                                  File Size
File System Information            in Bytes    Date Info.     File or Dir
============================      =========   ===========    ===========

ftp> dir
-rw-r--r-- 1  20800  system          7463    Sep 21  2:01   README.NOW
drwxr-xr-x 1  bin    system          2048    Oct 23  4:02   doc
drwxr-xr-x 1  bin    staff            512    Feb 29  1991   etc
-rw-r--r-- 1  20800  system       1458364    Oct 14  1:30   ls-lR
drwxr-xr-x 1  bin    system          1024    Jun 23  1989   nic
drwxr-xr-x 1  bin    system           512    Apr 22  1990   pub
drwxr-xr-x 1  bin    system           512    Apr 01 00:01   zebra.jokes
```

In the very first column, a "-" means that the entry in that line is a file, a "d" means that the entry is a directory. So "doc" is a directory, and "README.NOW" is a file. (The rest of the file system information is beyond the scope of this document.)

Notice that directories have an entry in the file size column. This does not mean that the directory only contains that amount of information! In fact, a directory showing a file size of 512 might have many megabytes of files within it.

■■

"dir" Display from a VMS FTP Host

File or Dir Name;Version	File Size in Kbytes	Date Info.	File System Info.
===============	=========	================	========================
ftp> *dir*			
README.NOW;10	7	15-SEP-1992 2:01	[274,164] (RWED,RWE,,)
DOC.DIR;1	0	23-OCT-1992 4:02	[274,164] (RWED,RWED,,)

In a VMS FTP host, a directory is indicated by a name ending with "dir," e.g., "DOC.DIR." Note that the file sizes are given in Kilobytes instead of bytes. ("7" here corresponds to "7,463" in the Unix dir display!)

"dir" Display from a VM/CMS FTP Host

			File Size Info.				
			=====================				
filename, type, mode			# cols	# lines	Kb	Date Modified	Disk
=====================			======	=======	==	=================	======
ftp> *dir*							
$README	NOW	V	1	156	7	9/15/92 02:01:50	DSK191
A	FILE	V	1	8	1	11/09/91 14:00:50	DSK191
ANOTHER	FILE	V	1	8	1	1/09/91 14:00:50	DSK191

VM/CMS doesn't use a hierarchical file structure, so there are no directories to see. Instead, there will be a long list of files in one "flat" directory. Like VMS, VM/CMS displays file size in kilobytes.

Directing the Output from "dir" or "ls" to a Local File

If the FTP host you are using does not have INDEX or ls-lR files, you may find it useful to send directory listings to your local computer for local browsing or printing.

Move to the directory above the one you want to list (cdup), then type "dir <name.of.directory.to.list>" followed by a name for an output file on your local host. For example, at the "ftp>" prompt, you could type:

```
ftp> dir <name.of.directory.to.list> <local.filename>
```

The dir display will be sent to your local host, and stored using the filename you provided.

■■■

"cd": Changing Directories

In order to move around an anonymous FTP host, you need to go up and down the directory tree. This is done with various forms of the "cd" command. If you are still in an FTP host, try some of the following versions of cd to get a feeling for how they work.

All FTP Hosts

Three forms of cd should work on most any FTP host.

`cd <directory name>`	Moves you "down" into the directory you have named.
`cdup`	Moves you up in the directory tree to the directory immediately above.
`cd <directory path>`	Lets you move down multiple directories with one cd command. The exact syntax used for <directory path> depends upon the syntax of the operating system. In an earlier example on a Unix host, we used the directory path user-docs/learnftp.

Unix FTP Hosts

In addition to the universally available cd commands described above, Unix FTP hosts support the following cd commands:

`cd ..`	Moves you "up" to the parent directory
`cd ../..`	Moves you "up" two levels in the FTP host
`cd /`	Moves you back to the FTP host's root directory (Really handy if you're feeling a bit disoriented in a big FTP host!)
`cd ../../<directory name>`	Moves you "up" two levels in the FTP host, and then down into a directory

VMS FTP Hosts

In addition to the universally available cd commands described above, certain implementations of FTP on VMS systems support the following cd commands:

`cd [-]`	Move back to a parent directory (like the Unix "cd ..")
`cd [-.-]`	Move up two levels in the directory (like Unix "cd ../..")

VM/CMS Hosts

Because VM/CMS does not have a hierarchical file structure, you can't really move up and down directories! However, you can sometimes move between minidisks (which are loosely analogous to directories) with the following command:

`cd [username.minidisk]` E.g., "cd anonymou.191".

"get": Variations on a Theme

Basic Syntax

The basic syntax of the "get" command is "get <filename>". This will copy the file named <filename> to your computer maintaining the same name. For example:

```
ftp> get README.FIRST
```

The file "README.FIRST" has now been copied to your computer and has been put into your computer as a file with the same name in the directory from which you started FTP.

Creating Informative and Functional Filenames

You can also change the name of a file by typing the desired new name after the file's original name.

```
ftp> get README.FIRST topic.readme
```

In this example, FTP would transfer the file "README.FIRST" to your Internet host with the new name "topic.readme".

This ability to rename while copying is very handy for a number of reasons.

Although files stored in FTP archives usually have informative and easy to use names, you will inevitably encounter some extremes. Some FTP archive maintainers prefer cryptic filenames. For example, a hypothetical software packaged called MAUS-GRAF could be called "mg" in one FTP archive. Other FTP archive maintainers may go to an expository extreme and store the same file as "Before_You_Copy_This_MAUS-GRAF.exe_file_FEED_YOUR_KATZ".

Strive to create concise and meaningful names for files you've ftp'ed. If the operating system of your Internet host uses a hierarchical file system with directories, thoughtful organization and naming of directories can help tremendously by providing positional information. I personally might store the above file with the filename "MausGraf.exe" in the directory path "Katz/fed".

Of course, you must be aware of the file naming conventions used by your computer's operating system. For example, IBM PCs running DOS require that filenames fit the following format: "A:filename.ext" where "A:" indicates a disk drive and path, "filename" is a name no longer than eight characters in length, and "ext" is a filename extension no more than three characters long. Consider the following example:

```
ftp> get <a.file.with.a.long.name> <a:tinyname.doc>
```

This would result in a file on your A: disk drive with a suitable DOS name. Other operating systems, such as Unix and Macintosh, are less restrictive about filename lengths, but may still prohibit the use of certain characters in filenames.

Previewing a File's Contents with the "get" Command

When you access a Unix FTP site, you may be able to preview a file before actually copying it to your own computer. For example, when connected to a UNIX based FTP site from a UNIX host, you can use the following nifty trick:

```
ftp> get <filename> |more
```

The contents of the file will then appear on your screen, one page at a time. To display the next page, press the space bar on your keyboard. (You have piped your get command to the "more" program on your local Unix host, so the information is being sent to "more" instead of being written to your disk.) If you want to stop previewing the file before you get to the end, type "q" to quit. While you are using |more on a file, you can search for text in the document by typing a "/" then the exact pattern you want to match, followed by the return key. But be aware that |more only works with text files. If you accidently or unintentionally try |more on a non-text file, you are likely to get some garbage on the screen and beeps from the speaker. To get out of the file, hit the q key to quit as usual. You can use the |more trick to check whether a file is binary or text before you get it.

"mget" and "mput": Moving Multiple Files

There may be times when you want to move several files to or from an FTP host. Depending upon the version of FTP installed on your Internet host, you may be able to use the "mget" command. Similarly, "mput" can be used to put multiple files in a full privilege FTP session. (Although all examples in this section use mget, the instructions apply equally to mput.)

To use mget and mput to their fullest potentials, you should learn a little about wildcards, and the FTP commands "verbose" and "prompt."

■■

Wildcards

Most FTP software supports "wildcards," special symbols that mean "any character or string of characters might be in this place." There are two main wildcards in the FTP world: "?" is a place holder for a single character in that location, and "*" can stand for one or more characters.

Using "?" is straightforward: "wor?" could stand for anything from "wora" to "worZ", "wor1" to "wor9", and depending upon other special characters available to the FTP host, "wor!", "wor." and so forth.

Using "*" is a little more complicated and takes a bit more attention and foresight on your part. For example, "*ism" might mean anything from "prism" to "intro.to.antidis-establishmentarianism", and "cat*" might stand for anything from "cats" to "cata-log.of.all.stars.dimmer.than.magnitude2". A further complication is that the "*" does not necessarily reach beyond the file delimiter symbol (".") in DOS based FTP hosts. So "cat*" would not represent "cats.doc" from a DOS host; you would have to use "cat*.*" to represent the file.

So how about some practical applications of wildcards? Suppose that you are a xylophone buff, and after reading the README.first file for a "xylophone.history" directory you've decided you want to get every single file in the directory. If you are in the "xylophone.history" directory, at the FTP prompt just issue mget with a wildcard.

```
ftp> mget *
```

All the files from that directory will be copied to your Internet host.

You can also use the wildcard to help specify a subset of files, for example, only those which contain the word "marimba" in the filename.

```
ftp> mget *marimba*
```

You can also use mget and mput by listing multiple filenames after the command ("mget file1 file2 file3").

Before you try the mget command, be sure that you have enough room on your Internet host to accommodate the incoming files. Also, if your host has restrictions on filenames, you may have trouble using mget if the filenames in the FTP archive are not in the correct format.

"verbose" and "prompt" Commands

When you issue the mget command, your FTP session will usually provide a prompt before getting each file, at which you must type "y" or "n".

```
ftp> mget cat*

mget catalog.of.all.stars.dimmer.than.magnitude2? n
mget cats.and.aardvarks? y

200 PORT command successful.
150 Opening data connection for cats.and.aardvarks
226 Transfer complete.
local: cats.and.aardvarks: remote: cats.and.aardvarks
4987 bytes received in 0.031 seconds (1.6e+02 Kbytes/s)

mget cats.and.abalones? y
```

If there are many files, from "cats.and.aardvarks" to "cats.and.zoot.simms", this could be a long session spent typing "y" after each prompt. Furthermore, the FTP session is being "verbose": it is displaying the results of your request, the speed of the transfer, and other information which you may not be interested in seeing.

When you are confident that your mget or mput request is well specified and won't involve many unwanted files, you can toggle the "prompt" mode off.

```
ftp> prompt
Interactive mode off.
```

For the rest of your session, you will not be prompted about each file when you use mget or mput. If you want prompts to reappear, just enter "prompt" again.

Similarly, you can toggle FTP verbosity: typing "verbose" at the FTP prompt will suppress the informative messages that during a long FTP session may be more annoying than helpful.

"ascii", "binary", and "image"

"ascii", "binary", and "image" are commands that specify how the requested files should be transferred. File formats you may encounter during an FTP session are explained in more detail in Chapter 8.

*   "ascii" is used for text-only files, such as standard text documents and other formats that use ASCII, such as PostScript.
*   "binary" (or "image") is used for non-text files, such as software, graphics, and executable files.

■■■

When you want to get a file in one of these formats, you should specify the proper transfer mode at the FTP prompt.

```
ftp> ascii
200 Type set to A.
ftp> get <an.ascii.file>

ftp> binary
200 Type set to I.
ftp> get <a.binary.file>
```

Help!

If you want more information on FTP, you will generally find that the best online help is available from your computer's regular help system, e.g., "help ftp", or on Unix hosts, "man ftp".

Local Online Help

For a listing of all the commands available to you, type help at the command prompt while using FTP.

```
ftp> help
Commands may be abbreviated. Commands are:

!             cr          ls          prompt       runique
$             delete      macdef      proxy        send
account       debug       mdelete     sendport     status
append        dir         mdir        put          struct
ascii         disconnect  mget        pwd          sunique
bell          form        mkdir       quit         tenex
binary        get         mls         quote        trace
bye           glob        mode        recv         type
case          hash        mput        remotehelp   user
cd            help        nmap        rename       verbose
cdup          image       ntrans      reset        ?
close         lcd         open        rmdir
ftp>
```

(The exact commands available to you will depend on the FTP software your system is running.)

Now type help for any command, and you'll see a concise definition of what the command does.

```
ftp> help cd
cd                     change remote working directory
```

But in general this help is terse and primarily useful as a reminder about what you've learned elsewhere.

Remote Online Help

If the FTP host you are accessing is using a different version of FTP, there might be more or fewer FTP commands at your disposal. These are displayed by using the "remotehelp" command, available from some Internet host systems. Say you were using FTP from a Unix Internet host to a remote FTP site running VM/CMS. Here's what you'd see:

```
ftp> remotehelp

214-The server-FTP commands are:
214-ABOR, ACCT,*ALLO, APPE,  CWD, DELE, HELP, LIST, MODE
214-NLST, NOOP, PASS, PASV, PORT,  PWD, QUIT, REIN, RETR
214-RNFR, SITE, SYST, STAT, STOR, STOU, STRU, TYPE, USER
214-The commands preceded by  '*'  are unimplemented
214-Data representation type may be ASCII EBCDIC or IMAGE.

214-For information about a particular command, type
214 HELP SERVER command.
```

Even if you know the remote commands, actually using them can be tricky. For example, to get help on one of the commands above, you would not literally type "help server <command>" as is suggested, but rather "remotehelp <command>".

FTP VIA E-MAIL

If your only access to the Internet is via e-mail, you can still get files from FTP servers. There is a mail server program called FTPmail that will retrieve files and send them to you as mail messages. The server listed below is designed for use by users in the United Kingdom.

The commands for using FTPmail are listed in a help file that you can order via e-mail to the mail server as follows:

```
mail:     ftpmail@src.doc.ic.ac.uk
subject:  (none needed)
message:  help
```

For more information on FTP via e-mail and a more complete list of servers, see Chapter 3.

FOR MORE INFORMATION

List of Anonymous FTP Sites

Perry Rovers (Perry.Rovers@kub.nl) maintains a very useful "List of Anonymous FTP Sites" that is available for anonymous FTP and via mail server.

FTP host:	`rtfm.mit.edu`
directory:	`/pub/usenet/news.answers/ftp-list`
filename:	`faq`
directory:	`/pub/usenet/news.answers/ftp-list/sitelist` (many or all)
FTP host:	`oak.oakland.edu`
directory:	`/pub/msdos/info`
filename:	`ftp-list.zip` (Zipped version)

Via mail server:

```
mail:       mail-server@rtfm.mit.edu
subject:    (none needed)
message:
send usenet/news.answers/ftp-list/faq
send usenet/news.answers/ftp-list/stelist/part1
send usenet/news.answers/ftp-list/stelist/part2
send usenet/news.answers/ftp-list/stelist/part3
send usenet/news.answers/ftp-list/stelist/part4
send usenet/news.answers/ftp-list/stelist/part5
send usenet/news.answers/ftp-list/stelist/part6
send usenet/news.answers/ftp-list/stelist/part7
```

If you worked through the FTP example to ftp.nwnet.net, you have already retrieved one version of this file (ftphost.list.txt). The best way to find files though is through the archie service. (See Chapter 16.)

Usenet Newsgroups

The following Usenet newsgroups deal with anonymous FTP archives and FTP from administrative and technical perspectives:

`comp.archives`	Announcements about new and updated FTP files
`comp.archives.admin`	Discussion about FTP archives, access, administration, etc.
`comp.protocols.tcp-ip`	Discussion about TCP/IP protocols, including FTP
`comp.protocols.tcp-ip.misc`	Discussion about TCP/IP protocols, including FTP, under various operating systems
`comp.protocols.tcp-ip.ibmpc`	Discussion about TCP/IP protocols, including FTP, on IBM PC computers

Read Chapter 9 for details on Usenet.

Mailing Lists

A number of the larger FTP hosts have mailing lists for people interested in the maintenance and activity of that particular FTP host. In general, information about such mailing lists will be displayed when you access the FTP host.

See Chapter 11 on how to locate and use mailing lists.

Technical References

The following documents are essential reading for anyone who wants a detailed understanding of the nuts and bolts of how FTP works:

Comer, D.E. *Internetworking With TCP/IP.* Volume 1: *Principles, Protocols, and Architecture.* Chapter 23. Prentice Hall, Inc., Englewood Cliffs, NJ. 1991.

The following RFCs contain specifications for the File Transfer Protocol:

RFC783	TFTP Protocol
RFC913	Simple File Transfer Protocol
RFC959	The File Transfer Protocol
RFC1068	Background File Transfer

You can obtain RFCs by FTP from many anonymous FTP hosts throughout the Internet, or by e-mail from a mail server.

Via FTP (this is only one of many anonymous FTP sources of RFCs):

FTP host: `nis.nsf.net`
directory: `/document/rfc`
filename: `rfcxxxx.txt`   (where xxxx is the RFC number. e.g., "rfc0913.txt" or "rfc1068.txt")

Via electronic mail messages to nic.ddn.mil's automated mail server:

```
mail:    service@nic.ddn.mil
subject: rfc xxx
message: (none needed)
```

Bibliography

Jul, E. "FTP: Full-Text Publishing?" *Computers in Libraries* 12(5) (May 1992):41-42.

Tomer, C. "Anonymous FTP Resources" *Academic and Library Computing* 9(10) (November/December 1992):8-12.

7 • Moving Files with File Transfer Protocol (FTP)

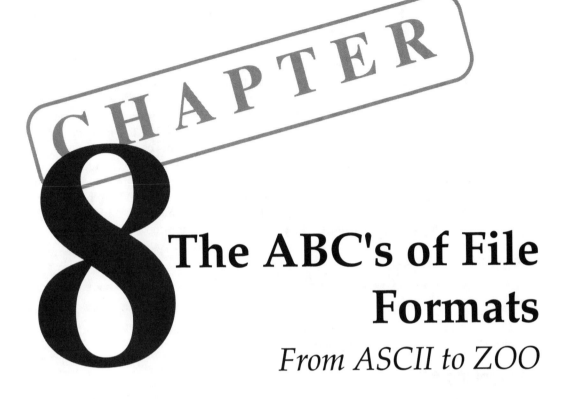

CHAPTER

8

The ABC's of File Formats

From ASCII to ZOO

Electronic information can be stored in a variety of formats many of which require special handling or processing before the file can be used. It is often important to know about these formats when you are getting files from anonymous FTP archives.

Most FTP users at one time or another will obtain files from anonymous FTP archives that just don't seem to work as expected. Chances are that the files were compressed, archived, or in one of the special formats described in this chapter.

This chapter is by no means meant to be comprehensive, but it does provide a quick overview of some of the main formats in which files are stored on the Internet, along with an introductory table that gives information on how to handle them. While the information presented here is specifically relevant to Internet FTP, it may also be appropriate for telecommunications and file transfer packages on personal computers.

ASCII FILES

Many documents on the Internet are in a text-only format called "ASCII." ("ASCII" stands for American Standard Code for Information Interchange.) ASCII format files can be read on most computers without any special handling.

Recognizing ASCII Files

Typically, but not always, ASCII files in FTP archives will have a filename that ends with ".doc" or ".txt" such as "manual.txt". Sometimes, there may be no special ending as in the case of a "README" file.

Transferring ASCII Files

When retrieving ASCII files with FTP, set the transfer type, or "mode," to ASCII before you begin. (ASCII is the default FTP setting, but just to be sure, you may want to specific it.) Simply type "ascii" at the FTP prompt. The system will respond "Type set to A."

```
ftp> ascii
200 Type set to A.
ftp> get manual.txt
```

BINARY FILES

When people speak of "binary files" or "binaries," they typically mean executable or non-text files such as computer programs or graphical bitmaps.

8 • The ABC's of File Formats

Recognizing Binary Files

Binary files can have a wide variety of endings for their filenames. These endings depend, in large part, upon the operating system in which the binary is meant to work. For example, ".exe" (short for "executable") is a common filename ending for binary files meant to run in DOS. There is also a chart below which lists file extensions and their types.

In general you need to know ahead of time whether a file is binary or not. README files in FTP archives will often give you this information.

Transferring Binary Files

Not surprisingly, you must use the binary transfer type (or binary "mode") when transferring binary files with FTP. Otherwise your computer may try to translate the file into text format and the file will no longer function as a binary program. On the other hand, when you're not sure what format a file is in and both your local host computer and the remote computer are using the same operating system, try transferring it using binary mode. While ASCII mode will not allow you to successfully transfer binary files, binary mode can usually transfer both successfully.

You put FTP into binary mode by typing the word "binary" at the FTP prompt. The system will respond "Type set to I."

```
ftp> binary
200 Type set to I.
ftp> get <filename>
```

ARCHIVED FILE GROUPS

When several files are logically related in some way, they are sometimes put together and stored as one archived file. Combining several files into one archived file makes it easier for you to copy the information to your computer. (An archived file should not be confused with a file archive. The former is a file that contains many files in it and the latter is a collection of files put on an FTP server. So an FTP archive may contain many archived files!) You only need to use the FTP "get" command once to transfer the whole archive file to your computer. Once retrieved, you can execute a program on your local computer that will "unpack" the archive into its component files.

Recognizing Archived Files

There are many archive programs, each of which adds a special suffix to the file's name. Refer to Lemson's table for more information. (A portion of this table, "Table of

Archive and Compression Programs," and instructions for retrieving the complete Lemson table are provided at the end of this chapter.)

Note that archived files are often compressed as well, so be sure to read the section on compressed files before wrestling with archived files.

"tar" (Tape ARchive) Files

The most commonly encountered archive format on the Internet is called "tar," an abbreviation for "tape archive." These tar archives are created and unpacked using the tar program on Unix computers.

Files which have been archived with tar usually contain the word "tar" at or towards the end of their filename.

On most Unix systems, you can type "tar -xf filename" to extract a tarred file. Type "man tar" for more detailed information on the tar program. Refer to the "Table of Archive and Compression Programs" at the end of this chapter for information on handling tarred files in other operating systems.

Self-Extracting Archives

Self-extracting archives are most commonly encountered with Mac software and typically have a filename ending in ".sea". Use binary mode when transferring these files with FTP. Once the file is transferred to your Mac, double-click on the icon of the self-extracting archive and it will unpack into all its component files and folders.

"shar" (SHell ARchive) Files

The concept of a "shell archive" evolves from the Unix community where the intent was to bundle multiple files within a Unix shell command file that is self-extracting. Usually, the author of the shell archive has provided comments and instructions at the beginning of the file. These instructions typically ask the recipient to delete the comment lines up to a marked point in the file, and then begin the extraction of the archive by invoking "sh" (on Unix).

Alternatively, your machine may have a program that automates this process even further. Refer to the "Table of Archive and Compression Programs" found later in this chapter for more information.

COMPRESSED FILES

■ ■

As the name suggests, compressed files are files which have been made smaller so that they take up less space on a computer disk or other storage media. Because they are smaller than the original file, compressed files are also transferred more quickly over the Internet.

When you encounter a file whose name ends with ".Z" (for example, "really.big.doc.Z"), you're probably looking at a file which has been compressed with the Unix "compress" utility. You will also come across files whose names end with ".tar.Z". These files have been compressed and archived. To work with such a file, you would first uncompress it and then untar the archive.

There are many other compression programs for Unix and other operating systems, and each will add a particular suffix to the file's name. Refer to Lemson's table for more information. (Instructions for retrieving this table are provided at the end of this chapter.)

Compressed files, like archived files, should be transferred in binary mode during an FTP session.

GIF Files

"GIF" stands for "Graphical Interchange Format," which is a special format used for encoding graphical images. These filenames typically end with ".gif", for example, "mars-scape.gif" might be a GIF file displaying the surface of Mars. There are several FTP archives on the Internet specializing in GIF files. But be forewarned—many of these files are huge and can be time consuming to transfer and process. GIF files should be transferred in binary mode. They require special software to view them and can only be printed on some kinds of printers.

PostScript Files

PostScript, developed by Adobe Systems, Inc., is a programming language with powerful graphics and coding capabilities. Many Internet documents are distributed in both ASCII and PostScript format.

On the Internet, files which are in PostScript format conventionally have filenames that end with ".ps", for example, "rfc1125.ps".

To use Postscript files, you must have access to a printer with PostScript printing capabilities (typically a laser printer) or a PostScript previewing program. You should also be aware that some PostScript files may use special character sets (or fonts) that may not be available on your printer. If you're lucky, those fonts will translate to an available font. On rare occasions, a PostScript file may cause your printer to gag ungracefully. If this happens, ask your local user services staff for help. They may be able to change some of the code in the PostScript file so it will work with your printer.

PostScript files should be transferred in ASCII mode, as they are made up of ASCII text. If the translation, or rendering, does not work, use a text editor to open the file and be sure that the first two characters are a "%!". If there is some other character first, delete it and try rendering or printing again. If this still fails, try transferring the file a second time using binary mode.

▪▪

TABLES OF ARCHIVE AND COMPRESSION PROGRAMS AND OTHER FILE FORMATS

▪▪

Tables 8-1 and 8-2 are derived from a comprehensive listing of compression and archiving programs maintained by David Lemson of the University of Illinois, Ubrana-Champaign. (We have added a few formats not covered by Lemson.) You may already have some of these programs installed on your Internet host or personal computer. If not, you can obtain Lemson's master list, which gives instructions on which anonymous FTP archives have copies of the archive and compression packages. Be aware that in some cases, a single file may have more than one extension, for instance, PostScript file may also be compressed (.ps.Z). To use the file, it must first be uncompressed, then rendered or printed. Many FTP hosts have copies of these archive and compression programs, or you can use archie, as described in Chapter 16, to search for them.

Table 8-1: Compression for DOS and Mac systems

Archive or Compression Program Name	Added File Extension	Transfer Mode (Binary or ASCII)	Name of program *you* use to process this file on your computer's operating system	
			DOS	Mac
ARC	.ARC	B	arc602	ArcMac
BinHex	.hqx	A	xbin23	BinHex
compress	.Z	B	u16	MacCompress
GIF (Graphical Interchange Format)	.gif	B	cshow	JPEGView
DOS executable	.exe	B	run the program	-
JPEG (Joint Photographic Experts Group	.jpeg	B	cshow	JPEGView
PackIt	.pit	B	UnPackIt	PackIt
PKZIP	.ZIP	B	pkz204g	UnZip
Portable Display Format	.pdf	A	Adobe Acrobat	Adobe Acrobat

■■ ■

Table 8-1: Compression for DOS and Mac systems (Continued)

Archive or Compression Program Name	Added File Extension	Transfer Mode (Binary or ASCII)	Name of program *you* use to process this file on your computer's operating system	
			DOS	**Mac**
PostScript	.ps	A	PostScript printer or rendering program	PostScript printer or rendering program
SHellARchive	.shar	A	toadshr1	UnShar
StuffIt	.Sit	B	unsit30	StuffItLite
tar	.tar	B	tar	UnTar
TIFF (Tagged Image File Format)	.tif	B	cshow	JPEGView
uuencode	.uu	A	toaduu20	uutool
ZOO	.ZOO	B	zoo210	MacBooz

Table 8-2: Compression for UNIX and VM/CMS systems

Archive or Compression Program Name	Added File Extension	Transfer Mode (Binary or ASCII)	Name of program *you* use to process this file on your computer's operating system	
			Unix	**VM/CMS**
ARC	.ARC	B	arc521	arcutil
BinHex	.hqx	A	mcvert	binhex
compress	.Z	B	uncompress	compress
DOS executable	.exe	B	-	-
GIF (Graphical Interchange Format)	.gif	B	xv	-
gzip	.z, .gz	B	gunzip	-

■■■

Table 8-2: Compression for UNIX and VM/CMS systems (Continued)

Archive or Compression Program Name	Added File Extension	Transfer Mode (Binary or ASCII)	Name of program *you* use to process this file on your computer's operating system	
			Unix	**VM/CMS**
JPEG (Joint Photographic Experts Group)	.jpeg	B	xv	-
PackIt	.pit	B	unpit	-
PKZIP	.ZIP	B	unzip41	-
Portable Display Format	.pdf	A	Adobe Acrobat (not yet available)	-
PostScript	.ps	A	PostScript printer or rendering program	-
SHellARchive	.shar	A	sh	-
StuffIt	.Sit	B	unsit	-
Tape ARchive	.tar	B	tar	-
TIFF (Tagged Image File Format)	.tif	B	xv	-
uuencode	.uu	A	uudecode	arcutil
ZOO	.ZOO	B	zoo210	zoo

FOR MORE INFORMATION

A comprehensive table of nearly 100 programs for handling compress and archived files is maintained by David Lemson. His document also gives detailed information on where all listed programs can be obtained.

FTP host:	**ftp.cso.uiuc.edu**
directory:	**/doc/pcnet**
filename:	**compression**

This file is available on other FTP hosts as well.

Usenet Newsgroups

Two newsgroups deal specifically with the theory and practice of file compression. (Chapter 9 explains how to use Usenet.)

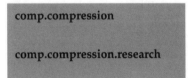

comp.compression	General discussion about compression
comp.compression.research	High tech discussions about compression

There are several newsgroups devoted to the distribution of binary files for a variety of operating systems. Note that some of the newsgroups are for discussion, and some are solely for posting of binary files, so be sure to monitor the newsgroups first before posting inappropriately! Here's a sampling of some newsgroups which may be of interest to you:

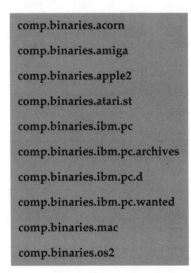

comp.binaries.acorn

comp.binaries.amiga

comp.binaries.apple2

comp.binaries.atari.st

comp.binaries.ibm.pc

comp.binaries.ibm.pc.archives

comp.binaries.ibm.pc.d

comp.binaries.ibm.pc.wanted

comp.binaries.mac

comp.binaries.os2

fj.binaries.mac

fj.binaries.misc

fj.binaries.msdos

fj.binaries.msdos.d

fj.binaries.x68000

alt.binaries.multimedia

alt.binaries.sounds.misc

(to use the fj newsgroups, you
need to be able to handle files
with Kanji characters)

Bibliography

Delfino, E. "The Internet Toolkit: File Compression and Archive Utilities" *Online* 17(6) (November 1993):90-92.

Simmonds, C. "Painless File Extraction: The A(rc)-Z(oo) of Internet Archive Formats" *Online* 17(6) (November 1993):60-65.

SECTION

III

Community
Forums

CHAPTER

9

Usenet

Discussions in the Cafes
of the Global Village

Whether it's over Darjeeling in Djibouti or maté in Montevideo, the cafe has traditionally been a place for people to share ideas, argue politics, engage in pleasant conversation, and generally enjoy camaraderie and communication. At one table, Gyorgi from the Crimea may be passionately debating farm policy with Pauletta from Italy while at another table, Nancy and Xiabo may be drinking in the banter and chatter as quietly as they sip their tea.

In some ways, a service called Usenet has become like a cafe for the electronic global village—and not just one cafe, but thousands, each with its own Gyorgis and Paulettas debating fine points of some arcane topic, plain folks chatting about whatever interests them, and Nancys and Xiabos, unheard and unseen, who are listening, learning, and loving every minute of it.

WHAT IS USENET?

The term "Usenet," also sometimes called "netnews," refers to several things simultaneously:

- Usenet is a collection of thousands of topically organized "newsgroups," covering everything from supercomputer design to bungee cord jumping, and ranging in distribution from the whole world to single institutions.

- Usenet is a loosely defined worldwide network of computers, not all on the Internet, that receive Usenet newsgroups.

- But most importantly, Usenet is a collection of worldwide and local communities of *people* who communicate with other people.

As you will eventually discover, Usenet is also much more. But let's cover the basics, one by one: Usenet newsgroups, newsfeeds, and newsreader software.

USENET BASICS: NEWSGROUPS, NEWSFEEDS, AND NEWSREADERS

Newsgroups

The term "Usenet newsgroups" might suggest that Usenet is mainly concerned with news, but Usenet newsgroups are also forums for information, debates, questions and answers, and just plain chatting. They are very similar to the bulletin board rooms, special interest groups, or conference rooms provided by Bulletin Board Systems or various commercial network services.

■ ■

Names

Each newsgroup has a distinct name that describes the topics discussed in the group. Here are the names of a few newsgroups to give you a sense of the diversity of topics and how newsgroups' names are put together.

`alt.dreams`	`misc.jobs.offered`
`alt.sport.bungee`	`news.newusers.questions`
`bionet.genome.arabidopsis`	`rec.bicycles.rides`
`bit.listserv.history`	`rec.food.recipes`
`biz.comp.services`	`sci.environment`
`comp.binaries.ibm.pc.wanted`	`sci.math.research`
`comp.robotics`	`soc.college`
`k12.chat.elementary`	`soc.culture.nepal`
`k12.lang.francais`	`talk.politics.guns`
`misc.activism.progressive`	`talk.rights.human`

Newsgroup names look similar to, but should not to be confused with, Internet addresses.

Newsgroup names contain a string of words or abbreviations separated by periods. Unlike Internet addresses however, the words and abbreviations of newsgroup names are usually painstakingly designed by members of the Usenet community to be informative in some way. The newsgroup named "sci.physics.fusion" is exactly what the name says it should be: a group for discussion about physics of fusion.

Newsgroup names are hierarchical. For example, "k12.chat.elementary" is a group in the main hierarchy created for pre-college (k12) users oriented towards casual discussion (chat) among elementary school students.

The Main Categories

Newsgroups are organized into a few top-level categories, within which may be hundreds of specific newsgroups.

There are seven "traditional" categories distributed through most of the Usenet world:

`comp`	computer hardware, software, and languages
`misc`	topics not easily pigeonholed into other categories
`news`	newsgroups about Usenet newsgroups and administration

▪▪▪

`rec`	recreational activities and hobbies
`sci`	discussion about science ranging from popular to research levels
`soc`	discussions about cultures and current events around the world
`talk`	debates on controversial topics (e.g., abortion, Mideastern politics)

In addition, there are a rapidly growing number of top-level "alternative" hierarchies which may or may not be distributed globally:

`alt`	tentative, frivolous, or highly controversial topics
`bionet`	learned discussions among research biologists
`bit.listserv`	a wide variety of LISTSERV lists "gatewayed" to Usenet
`biz`	business and commercial topics
`cern`	CERN high energy physics laboratory
`de`	German Usenet newsgroups
`embnet`	European molecular biologists
`fj`	Japanese Usenet newsgroups
`gnu`	discussion about Free Software Foundation software
`ieee`	newsgroups relating to the IEEE
`k12`	newsgroups for pre-college students and educators
`vmsnet`	newsgroups for discussion of the VMS operating system

Many topics could fit comfortably in two or more main level categories. Consider the following music related newsgroups:

`alt.exotic-music`

`comp.music`

`k12.ed.music`

`rec.music.makers`

Although all these newsgroups deal with music, they are each aimed at distinct audiences.

Regional and Local Newsgroups

Most of the main level categories mentioned above are distributed globally, but Usenet also contains regional or local hierarchies which range in distribution from institutions to continents.

Institutions	`uw`	University of Washington
	`yale`	Yale University
Cities	`pdx`	Portland
	`tor`	Toronto
States or provinces	`ab`	Alberta
	`or`	Oregon
Regions	`pnw`	Pacific Northwest
	`ne`	New England
Countries	`fnet`	France
	`nz`	New Zealand
Continents	`eunet`	Europe
	`na`	North America

Regional newsgroups provide forums for articles that probably wouldn't interest users elsewhere in the world, such as where the Yale Macintosh Users Group will meet next week, or a listing of bicycle parts stores in New Zealand.

Usenet Articles

Within newsgroups are the actual articles that have been "posted" by Usenet users. Usenet articles are much like e-mail messages with header information used for sending the article through Usenet, address information about the person who wrote the article, and the message body containing information submitted by a Usenet subscriber.

Unmoderated and Moderated Newsgroups

Most newsgroups are "unmoderated," i.e. open for anyone to post messages as they see fit. But some newsgroups are "moderated," meaning that a person (the moderator) screens postings before they are released to the newsgroup. Here are some examples of moderated newsgroups:

Newsgroup Name	Moderator	Moderator's Address
`news.announce.newgroups`	David Lawrence	`tale@uunet.uu.net`
`news.announce.newusers`	Mark Moraes	`netannounce@deshaw.com`
`news.answers`	Jonathan I. Kamens	`news-answers-request@mit.edu`

Newsfeeds

Usenet news is received through "newsfeeds." A Usenet site's newsfeed is handled by news transfer software and Usenet news administrators.

Newsfeed Software

Within the Internet, Usenet news is usually distributed among Usenet hosts by the Network News Transfer Protocol (NNTP). The tens of thousands of Usenet postings which may be received daily in a newsfeed are stored on one computer that thousands of users can access. NNTP on the main newsfeed computer keeps track of the message-ids of articles currently in storage and can selectively retrieve only those articles that are new. Because of this selectivity and screening, NNTP also allows an Internet Usenet site to have dozens of Usenet newsfeeds. Since Usenet articles can come from all over the world, this means that newsfeeds can propagate in a web-like fashion.

Usenet was originally developed within the UUCP network using the Unix to Unix CoPy protocol suite for communications instead of TCP/IP. In contrast to the multidirectional distribution flow of Usenet articles in the Internet, UUCP based sites receive articles from an "upstream" site. If that upstream site did not receive certain newsgroups or articles then neither would your site.

A given Usenet article might bounce around between UUCP and NNTP propagation as it makes its way around the world to your site.

The News-Admin

Each site that receives Usenet news has a news-administrator (or "news-admin") who is ultimately responsible for what newsgroups a site receives and how the newsfeed is operated. Depending upon the particular situation, the news-administrator may make independent decisions about what newsgroups to display or they may only execute the policies of an institutional board. Usenet sites may choose to restrict the flow of news to a trickle of carefully selected newsgroups, or may choose to let their Usenet users "drink from the firehose" and receive every conceivable (and some inconceivable) newsgroups.

Newsreader Software

Just like you use an electronic mail software program to read your personal e-mail messages in your electronic mailbox, you use newsreader programs to read Usenet articles. However, the big difference between the two is that a newsgroup is like a mailbox which anyone with newsreader software and a Usenet newsfeed can contribute to or read from. You might read a posting by someone from South Africa responding to a previous posting by someone in Saskatoon and your reply to their exchange may well be read by people in Stockholm, Singapore, and Sao Paulo.

Locating Newsreader Software at Your Internet Host

Before diving into Usenet, find out what newsreader software, if any, is available at your Internet host. There are many newsreader packages for both mainframes and personal computers. If you're not sure of the name or even the existence of newsreader software on your computer, ask your local user services staff or computer support staff for help.

Sample Usenet Session with "rn"

This sample Usenet session uses "rn," a basic but widespread newsreader for Unix computers. Currently, this is a "lowest common denominator," workhorse newsreader—one that just about everyone with a Unix account can probably access. Even if you can use a spiffier, workstation-based newsreader with windows and widgets, working through this rn example with your newsreader should give you a feeling for what a typical Usenet session involves.

Regardless of the newsreader software you use, a typical Usenet session often involves the following steps:

Step 1	Start the newsreader software.
Step 2	Select or subscribe to a newsgroup.
Step 3	Scan the titles of articles in that newsgroup.
Step 4	Read, save, or print articles you find particularly interesting.
Step 5	Send e-mail to another Usenet user or post an article to the newsgroup.
Step 6	Clear all remaining articles in the newsgroup so they won't appear in your next Usenet session.
Step 7	Select or subscribe to another newsgroup.
Step 8	Repeat steps 3 through 8 as desired.
Step 9	End your Usenet session.

Starting a Newsreader

To start the rn newsreading software, simply type "rn". (If your newsreader is on a personal computer or workstation with a graphical user interface, like the Mac or PC's with Windows, you might launch your newsreader by double clicking on an icon.)

Here's what happens when you issue the rn command in Unix.

```
rn

Trying to set up a ".newsrc" file--running newsetup...
Creating .newsrc
Done.

If you have never used the news system before, you may find
```

(Continued)

```
the articles in news.announce.newusers to be helpful. There
is also a manual entry for rn.

To get rid of newsgroups you aren't interested in, use the
'u' command. Type h for help at any time while running rn.

(Revising soft pointers--be patient.)
```

Since the newsreader is asking us to be patient, let's look at what's happened so far.

If this is the first time you are running a Usenet newsreader, a news resources file may be constructed for you from the master list of newsgroups subscribed to by your site. In the case of rn, this resource file is called ".newsrc."

This news resource file will be used by your newsreader in future sessions to keep track of which newsgroups you want to read, and which articles you have already read thus preventing duplicated efforts in future Usenet sessions.

Most newsreaders will respond with a series of informative messages and a list of a few basic commands including how to get online help. Depending upon your newsreader, this ranges from a simple list that appears when you start the software, to on-screen menus and icons. For rn, "h" will get you help.

After a short while, you should see something like the following on your screen:

```
Unread news in news.announce.newusers          35 articles
Unread news in news.newusers.questions         85 articles

 ...etc.

35 articles in news.announce.newusers--read now? [ynq]
```

We are now entering the newsgroup selection level.

Selecting and Subscribing to Newsgroups

Depending upon what newsreader you are using, you may be presented with lists of newsgroups from which you can choose or you may be asked to "subscribe" to newsgroups you want to read.

The term "subscription" refers to the fact that your newsreader will keep a record of the newsgroups in which you are interested and which articles in those newsgroups have been read. Note that when using newsreaders that maintain a subscription file, you would need to "unsubscribe" to newsgroups you no longer want to read.

■■■

Because this is our first time using rn, we have been presented with a newsgroup that all new Usenet users should read: "news.announce.newusers."

```
35 articles in news.announce.newusers--read now? [ynq]
```

The last line in the startup screen is asking if we want to read articles in the newsgroup "news.announce.newusers." As a newuser, reading these articles would probably be advisable. Note that in rn, selecting the newsgroup is equivalent to subscribing.

The "[ynq]" at the end of the line indicates that we can type "y" for "yes, I want to read this newsgroup," "n" for "no," and "q" for "I want to quit the newsgroup selection level."

(Note that other newsreader software may not start you at this particular newsgroup. You can work with whatever newsgroup happens to pop up on your screen and much of the rest of this session will probably still be relevant.)

Help at the Newsgroup Selection Level

By typing "h", we can see what commands are available at the newsgroup selection level. Using these commands would allow us to jump to other newsgroups in which we might be interested.

```
35 articles in news.announce.newusers--read now? [ynq] h

y,SP      Do this newsgroup now.
.cmd      Do this newsgroup, executing cmd as first command.
=         Start this newsgroup, list subjects before reading articles.
u         Unsubscribe from this newsgroup.
c         Catch up (mark this newsgroup all read).
n         Go to the next newsgroup with unread news.
N         Go to the next newsgroup.
p         Go to the previous newsgroup with unread news.
P         Go to the previous newsgroup.
-         Go to the previously displayed newsgroup.
1         Go to the first newsgroup.
^         Go to the first newsgroup with unread news.
$         Go to the last newsgroup.
g name    Go to the named newsgroup. Subscribe to new newsgroups this way too.
/pat      Search forward for newsgroup matching pattern.
?pat      Search backward for newsgroup matching pattern. (Use * and ?
          style patterns. Append r to include read newsgroups.)
l pat     List unsubscribed newsgroups containing pattern.
m name    Move named newsgroup elsewhere (no name moves current newsgroup).

[Type space to continue]
```

Scanning Articles within a Newsgroup

Displaying Article Subject Lines

In rn and many other newsreaders, we can use the "=" command at the newsgroup selection level to display the subjects of articles in the current newsgroup. This is much more efficient than reading through the contents of every message in order.

Sample article listing

```
    437 Regional Newsgroup Hierarchies, Part II
    438 Regional Newsgroup Hierarchies, Part III
    440 Regional Newsgroup Hierarchies, Part I
    448 How to become a USENET site
    449 Publicly Accessible Mailing Lists, Part I
    450 Publicly Accessible Mailing Lists, Part II
    451 Publicly Accessible Mailing Lists, Part III
    452 Introduction to news.announce
    453 Rules for posting to Usenet
    454 What is Usenet?
    455 A Primer on How to Work With the Usenet Community
    456 Answers to Frequently Asked Questions
    457 USENET Software: History and Sources
    458 Hints on writing style for Usenet
    459 Emily Postnews Answers Your Questions on Netiquette
    460 List of Active Newsgroups, Part I
    461 List of Active Newsgroups, Part II
    462 Alternative Newsgroup Hierarchies, Part I
    463 List of Moderators for Usenet
    464 How to Get Information about Networks
    465 Alternative Newsgroup Hierarchies, Part II
    466 How to Create a New Usenet Newsgroup
    467 A Guide to Social Newsgroups and Mailing Lists

[Type space to continue]
```

Whoever has been posting these messages really seems to know how to make informative subject lines! In fact, the articles in news.announce.newusers are written by folks who have been using Usenet almost since it was born, back in 1979. As you can see, just about everything that has been discussed in this chapter can be researched in more detail simply by reading the messages in "news.announce.newusers".

Selecting an Article You Want to Read

The numbers in the left column of the previous screen show the article numbers. To read an article whose title interests you, simply type the article's number instead of pressing the space bar.

```
rn> What next? [^Nnpq]
456
```

Reading a Usenet Article

The Structure of a Usenet Article: "It's Just Like an E-mail Message!"

A Usenet article begins with a header much like a standard e-mail header: there are the familiar, "From," "Subject," and "Date" lines, and the "Newsgroups" and "Followup-To" lines are analogous to the "To" and "Reply-To" lines of e-mail headers. The remaining Usenet header lines are peculiar to Usenet articles. In rn, even more header information can be displayed by typing "v", for "verbose header."

```
Article 456 (34 more) in news.announce.newusers (moderated):

From:          spaf@cs.purdue.EDU
Newsgroups:    news.announce.newusers,news.answers
Subject:       Answers to Frequently Asked Questions
Date:          4 Sep 92 03:52:07 GMT
Followup-To:   news.newusers.questions
Organization:  Dept. of Computer Sciences, Purdue Univ.
Lines:         786
Supersedes:    <spaf-questions_711614923@cs.purdue.edu>

Archive-name: usenet-faq/part1
Original-author: jerry@eagle.UUCP
Last-change: 19 Jul 1992 by mvac23!thomas@udel.edu

                  Frequently Submitted Items

This document discusses some questions and topics that occur
repeatedly on USENET. They frequently are submitted by new
users, and result in many followups, sometimes swamping
groups for weeks. The purpose of this note is to head off
these annoying events by...--
MORE--(3%)
```

Also, just like e-mail messages, the actual message is contained in the body.

■■■

The article has now filled up the screen. If you wanted to see the next screen, you would press the space key. To display the next article, type "n", or use "q" to exit from the article.

Help while Viewing Articles

In most all newsreaders, you should be able to get help for commands that can be used when viewing articles. In rn and many other newsreaders, just type "h".

Posting a Message to the Newsgroup

There are two reasons to post a message to a newsgroup: to introduce a topic and to respond to someone else's posting. Before you do either of these, be sure to read the FAQ for the newsgroup to find out something about the culture of that group. It is also highly recommended that you read *Suggestions for First Time Usenet Readers* and *Suggestions for First Time Usenet Posters,* later on in this chapter for more details on getting started with Usenet. That said, you can begin a posting using the "f" (for "follow up") command. This will only work from the article selection level, not when you are choosing newsgroups. When you start, you will be prompted for a prepared file (you don't need one), and a text editor. Then you're into the message.

```
Newsgroups: alt.off-world.visitors           <system-supplied>
Subject: Re: Reply to B. Cisco                <system-supplied>
Summary:
Expires:
References: <1994Feb10.239.@quarks.org>       <system-supplied>
Sender:
Followup-To:
Distribution:
Organization: Station Security.              <system-supplied>
Keywords:

Please rest assured that all public areas have been
secured in anticipation of the arrival of our visitors.
Certain gambling establishments have been closed for the
occasion.
(I can assure you that the protests of one proprietor
were loud and protracted.)
```

Just as with e-mail, you need to fill in the header. A number of defaults will be filled in for you, but you can change these manually. Before you send the message you have the option of aborting, editing, or reviewing the article (list). These instructions are not meant to make you a Usenet posting expert, but merely to give you a sense of how things work.

■■■

Finding Newsgroups You REALLY Want to Read

You're probably just itching to dive right into those exciting, exotic, and educational newsgroups that you've heard about. Here's how to find the newsgroups you want to read.

Listing All Available Newsgroup Names

This is a good strategy if you're just starting to use Usenet and you aren't yet sure what's available, or how newsgroups are named. Some newsreaders show you all the newsgroup names right away, while in other newsreaders, you have to explicitly ask for a complete list of available newsgroups. In rn, you would use the "l" command (list) when at the newsgroup selection level.

```
l

Completely unsubscribed newsgroups:
alt.znet.fnet
alt.znet.pc
[Type return to continue]

Unsubscribed but mentioned in .newsrc:
alt.3d
alt.activism
alt.alien.visitors
alt.amateur-comp
alt.angst
alt.aquaria
alt.archery
alt.astrology
alt.atheism
alt.bbs
alt.bbs.internet
alt.bbs.lists
alt.beer
alt.books.technical
alt.boomerang
alt.brother-jed
alt.callahans
alt.cd-rom
alt.censorship
alt.child-support
alt.chinese.text
alt.co-ops--
More--
```

■ ■

Searching Newsgroups' Names for Keywords

You may be able to use your newsreader to search through the newsgroups' names for a particular word which you think might be in the names of groups you'd like to read.

In rn, one could search for all the newsgroups whose names contained the word "mac," using the "/" command followed by the word "mac" in order to identify newsgroups dealing with Apple Macintosh Computers.

```
/mac

bit.mailserv.word-mac
comp.binaries.mac
comp.emacs
comp.lang.forth.mac
comp.os.mach
comp.sources.mac
comp.sys.mac
comp.sys.mac.announce

... (many more "comp.sys.mac" groups)

gnu.emacs.announce

... (many more "gnu.emacs" groups)
```

If you use this method to search for newsgroups, try to use the shortest likely abbreviation for a topic (like "bio" instead of "biology") and/or scan the master list of newsgroups to get an idea of what a likely abbreviation might be. However, some abbreviations may be redundant and refer to two or even multiple discussion groups. In this example, the word "mac" is also contained in newsgroup names which have nothing to do with Macintosh computers, like "comp.os.mach," and newsgroups dealing with the "emacs" editor.

SUGGESTIONS FOR FIRST TIME USENET READERS

■ ■

Usenet is a huge, sprawling collection of thousands of newsgroups containing megabytes of articles and used by millions of people worldwide. If you dive into Usenet carelessly, it's easy to get overwhelmed and frustrated. But if you follow a few simple rules you can learn to love Usenet without having to attend the college of hard knocks.

Start Simply!

As was mentioned in the introduction, each Usenet site may subscribe to thousands of newsgroups. There are a number of steps you can take to make your introduction to Usenet encouraging instead of intimidating. Most importantly:

Start simply. Don't try to read everything. Be selective.

First, issue a newsreader command which gives the names of all newsgroups available at your site in a list format. You can then start exploring Usenet by subscribing to one or a small number of groups that look really interesting to you.

Try reading a few articles to become familiar with the folkways of each newsgroup. These can vary from polite, deferential discussion to contentious free-for-alls.

Read Periodic Postings and Frequently Asked Questions (FAQs)

Newsgroups often feature periodic postings that contain useful information for new and intermediate readers. Such postings usually appear once a month.

Periodic postings include:

*   Frequently Asked Questions (FAQs)—these are questions which newcomers to a particular newsgroup often ask and which are better answered in periodic postings than in repeated individual answers;
*   things to keep in mind before posting articles to that particular newsgroup;
*   and suggestions about where to find commonly needed information about the Internet generally, or Usenet specifically.

You'll get a lot more out of Usenet if you make a point of reading the periodic postings of the newsgroups to which you subscribe.

Periodic Postings from FTP Archives

You can also obtain periodic postings from an FTP archive of FAQs at MIT. The main archives are in the "/pub/usenet" directory, in subdirectories named for each of the newsgroups. For example, the subdirectory "news.announce.newusers" contains a file "Answers_to_Frequently_Asked_Questions_ about_Usenet". Note that not all newsgroups' FAQs have this filename!

> FTP host: `pit-manager.mit.edu`
> directory: `/pub/usenet/news.announce.newusers`
> filename: `Answers_to_Frequently_Asked_Questions_about_Usenet`

If you want to explore these FAQ archives, just cd to the /pub/usenet directory, and examine the names of the subdirectories, then cd to the directory of a newsgroup whose FAQs you would like to obtain.

If you do not have access to FTP, you can also access the archive via electronic mail. When accessing these FAQs by e-mail, include the parts of the directory path and filename to the right of "/pub/", as in the following example:

```
mail:      mail-server@pit-manager.mit.edu
subject:  (none needed)
message:  (include the following text exactly as it appears)

send usenet/news.announce.newusers/Answers_to_Frequently_Asked_Questions
```

You can also use the send command in your e-mail messages to this mail server to obtain help about how to use the service. For example, the following requests will solicit help and index information:

> send help
>
> send index
>
> send usenet/index
>
> send usenet/news.announce.newusers/index

Read Introductory Newsgroups

There are several newsgroups which every new user should read.

news.announce.newusers

This newsgroup contains informative articles which are posted every month to help explain the workings of Usenet.

news.newusers.questions

As the name suggests, this is a question and answer forum for new Usenet users. If you read this newsgroup for several months, most basic questions you have about Usenet that are not answered by this chapter will be asked by new users and answered by Usenet experts.

news.newusers.answers

FAQ files from many Usenet groups are collected into this newsgroup.

news.announce.important

This newsgroup contains announcements about Usenet which are likely to be of interest to all Usenet users. This newsgroup is *not* for political, commercial, or other non-Usenet related announcements, no matter how important you think they may be!

news.announce.newgroups

If you become an active Usenet reader, you should read this newsgroup to keep up-to-date on announcements of the creation of new Usenet newsgroups.

Selective Reading within Newsgroups

Following Threads of Discussion

You will often find that there may be only a subset of articles you want to read in each newsgroup. Many newsreaders support an automated process for following "threads" of discussion. Threads are articles on the same topic; they can be located either by scanning the subjects, the articles, or even the contents of the articles. (Refer to the help files in your newsreader on how to use thread feature.)

Catching Up

When you first enter the Usenet world, you may encounter a backlog of hundreds of articles which you may not have time to read. Most newsreaders include commands which will erase these backlogged articles. Usually a command such as "catch-up," "clear," or "mark all read," will leave you with a clean and manageable slate with which to start. And don't worry, there will be plenty more articles pouring in to take the place of the cleared materials!

Kill Files

Say you are reading "talk.environment" and you are interested in everything discussed except postings about nuclear waste. You can avoid articles that have "nuclear waste" in the subject line by creating a "kill file." Similarly, if you are consistently annoyed by the postings of a user "space-alien@alpha.centuri.gov", the kill file prevents the display of articles coming from this e-mail address.

Strings upon which you want your kills to be based can often be entered from within your newsreader, or you can manually edit a kill file. For more information about kill files, refer to your newsreader's documentation.

SUGGESTIONS FOR FIRST TIME USENET POSTERS

The most important thing to keep in mind when sending messages to Usenet is that your message may be sent to tens of thousands of machines and read by hundreds of thousands of people. This translates to a significant quantity of computer resources and a substantial accumulation of person hours.

All of the principles of e-mail etiquette discussed in Chapter 4 apply equally well to Usenet. You are strongly encouraged to review that chapter and the following information before you become an active part of the Usenet community.

Learn Usenet's Folkways

Try not to post until you've become familiar with the folkways of Usenet. Making a premature posting to Usenet is an extraordinarily efficient way to embarrass yourself (and perhaps your organization) in front of tens of thousands of people at the stroke of a single key!

Learn How to Respond

If you are responding to someone else's posting, it is often more appropriate to reply directly to that person with an e-mail message. Use your newsreader's command (often called "reply") that sends mail *directly* to that user and not to the newsgroup. If your newsreader doesn't have such a feature, identify the person's userid and e-mail address on the "From" line of their message or in the information at the end of their posting. You can then use your computer's mail software to send them a message directly without sending the message to the many readers of the newsgroup.

Get the FAQs First

Before you post a question, try your local resources including reference books and manuals, local User Service staff, and friends. If you think your question might be a "Frequently Asked Question," check either news.newusers.answers, or the newsgroup's FAQ posting, if available.

How to Followup

If you want to send a "followup" to a posting (i.e., an article responding to an existing article), scan the rest of the submitted articles in the newsgroup before sending mail or posting. You will often find that one posting may elicit a large number of followups and duplicate answers in a few days or even hours! After you have read the thread of discussion which the original posting prompted, you may find that what you wanted to say has already been said, or that the discussion has wandered off to another point. Of course, if your followup is different or if you believe you have something valuable to contribute, go ahead and send the followup.

Provide Context

If you are responding to someone else's posting, whether by e-mail or in a Usenet posting, include enough of their original message to provide a context for your response. Most newsreaders and e-mail programs provide a feature to automate such "quoting." However, try to include only that part of their posting needed to get their point across.

Send Your Message No Further than Necessary

No matter what you're posting, be sure you have specified an appropriate "distribution."

Distribution refers to how widely your posting is propagated. For example, distributions available at the University of Washington include "world," "na" for North America, "pnw" for the Pacific Northwest, "seattle," and "uw" for the University of Washington. If your posting is only of local interest, only post it locally. For more information about distributions, read the FAQ article "Frequently Submitted Items" in news.announce.newusers.

Crosspost Only if Necessary

Sometimes it may be appropriate to post a message to more than one newsgroup. If you are trying to locate economics simulation software for your Atari ST, you could include the names of an economics newsgroup and an Atari newsgroup in the "Newsgroups" field of a single message. This is known as "crossposting."

If you do crosspost, it is considered good network etiquette to include a newsgroup in the "Followup-to" field of the header. This is the newsgroup to which replies will be sent, regardless from which newsgroup they had been submitted. You can also put "poster" in the "Followup-to" field, in which case the messages will be sent to your mailbox, and not to any of the newsgroups. If you've used the poster option, send a summary of the answers you have received if you feel that it would be of interest to the newsgroups. Sharing is a two way street!

Sometimes, a message to which you are responding has been crossposted inappropriately to many newsgroups. For example, someone may have posted a question about how to keep raccoons out of their orchard to "misc.rural," "comp.protocols.tcp-ip," "alt.fan.monty-python," and "sci.space." Whenever you submit a followup, examine the newsgroups named in the "Newsgroups" field in the header of your response and trim it down to those you feel are most appropriate. In this case, "misc.rural" and maybe "alt.fan.monty-python."

Specifically Prohibited Usenet Activities

Although the Usenet community may best be described as a semi-anarchic democracy, there are two explicitly prohibited activities in most newsgroups.

Usenet Is Not for Commercial Communication

This does not mean that you can't discuss commercial products on Usenet. In fact, objective descriptions and comparisons of commercial computer products is a very useful Usenet activity. But, if you represent a company, don't even think of posting commercial advertisements on Usenet. At the very least, you will probably be flooded with complaints from outraged Usenet users.

Do Not Violate Copyright or Any Other U.S. or International Laws

Feel free to reproduce short extracts of a copyrighted work for critical purposes in your postings, but reproduction of copyrighted works in whole or substantial part is forbidden by U.S. and international copyright law, except where it constitutes "fair use." Respect the hard work of copyrighted authors. Similarly, engaging in or communicating about illegal activities on Usenet is forbidden and could endanger your site's Usenet feed.

WHAT TO DO IF SOMETHING GOES WRONG

There are three common problems you may encounter when using Usenet: you might make a mistake, someone else might submit rude or insulting postings, or newsreader software might mess up distribution of Usenet articles. Here's what to do in each case.

Cancelling a Posting

Suppose you've just submitted a posting but realize you've just made a big mistake: "Oh no, I've sent my question about Nepali culture to rec.sport.football by mistake!"

Luckily, most newsreaders allow you to cancel a submission. Make sure you know your newsreader's command for cancellation before you post. Your submission might still get to a few sites, but you can usually squelch a mistaken submission if you act quickly. In general, it's not a good idea to post a second message retracting or apologizing for a posting unless you sincerely feel you've made a most grievous mistake.

Dealing with Flame Wars

If someone posts an article that obviously violates Usenet etiquette, it's usually best not to get involved. There are plenty of Usenet old-timers that can deal with the situation in a sagacious way.

Unfortunately, there are also a few hot-headed individuals who sometimes turn such situations into "flame wars," which is Usenet slang for a rude, disputatious, and inappropriate argument that shouldn't be carried out in a newsgroup.

Always resist the temptation to get involved in or start flame wars; there are no winners. And, in the very unlikely event that someone attacks you personally in a posting, simply ignore it; they'll usually stop. Even the most obnoxious flamers will usually desist when they feel that no one is paying attention. And if you keep your peace, it will be apparent to anyone reading such a posting that it is the flamer, and not you, who is of dubious character.

Dealing with Usenet Malfunctions

If you think that your local newsreader or your Usenet feed is malfunctioning, contact your local user services staff. If something is genuinely wrong, they will pass the information on to the news-admin at your site. Unless you are a Usenet administrator you shouldn't post messages about your local Usenet problems.

CONCLUSION

The Usenet world is inhabited by people from all walks of life, from many cultures, and with wildly varying temperaments. You will at turns be charmed, annoyed, or uplifted by what you read in newsgroups.

You may opt never to post to a newsgroup. Some people quietly lurk in newsgroups, reading the collective wisdom and folly of people throughout the world. Or you may find yourself becoming an active and vocal participant in one or more newsgroups.

However you choose to use Usenet, you will probably find numerous newsgroups which become essential resources for your research, work, or amusement.

Like the world at large, Usenet has something for everyone. Enjoy!

FOR MORE INFORMATION

The best source of information about Usenet is Usenet itself. Be sure to follow the suggestions for first time Usenet users in this chapter!

Bibliography

Nickerson, G. "Effective Use of Usenet" *Computers in Libraries* 12(5) (May 1992):38-40.

Notess, G. R. "Reading Usenet News: Using the rn and trn Newsreader" *Online* 17(5) (September 1993):94-98.

Offutt, A. J., G. Spafford, and M. Moraes. "Hints on Writing Style for Usenet." 1992-Posted regularly on news.announce.newusers and available via FTP.

    FTP host: `pit-manager.mit.edu`
    directory: `/pub/usenet/news.announce.newusers`
    file: `Hints_on_writing_style_for_Usenet`

Quarterman, J. S. *The Matrix: Computer Networks and Conferencing Systems Worldwide.* (Especially Chapter 10.) Bedford, MA: Digital Press, 1990.

Stadnyk, I., and R. Kass. "Modelling Users' Interests in Information Filters," *Communications of the ACM* 35(12) (December 1992). pp.49-50.

Templeton, B., G. Spafford, and S. Summit. "Emily Postnews Answers Your Questions on Netiquette." (A tongue-in-cheek, very funny, but very informative essay on what not to do in electronic mail, especially in Usenet postings.) 1992- Posted regularly on news.announce.newusers and available via FTP.

    FTP host: `pit-manager.mit.edu`
    directory: `/pub/usenet/news.announce.newusers`
    file: `Emily_Postnews_Answers_Your_Questions_on_Netiquette`

Todino, G. and D. Dougherty. *Using UUCP and Usenet*. Sebastopol, CA: O'Reilly and Associates, 1991.

Von Rospach, C. and G. Spafford. "A Primer on How to Work With the Usenet Community." 1992- Posted regularly on news.announce.newusers and available via FTP.

FTP host:	`pit-manager.mit.edu`
directory:	`/pub/usenet/news.announce.newusers`
file:	`A_Primer_on_How_to_Work_With_the_Usenet_Community`

CHAPTER

10 LISTSERV

INTERNET · PASSPORT

LISTSERV, a BITNET service, provides discussion forums and database management covering a huge variety of topics. These lists are often called "online conferences" because they mimic real conferences where people with a shared interest gather to discuss papers and various topics related to their interest. To give you a taste of what's available through LISTSERV, here are 10 of the more than 3,000 currently active LISTSERV discussion lists:

Subject	List Name and Address
Albert Einstein's Writings	EPP-L@BUACCA.BU.EDU
Apple-II Computer	APPLE2-L@BROWNVM.BROWN.EDU
Comics Magazine in Turkish	VM-SHOW@VM3090.EGE.EDU.TR
Ecology and the Biosphere	BIOSPH-L@UBVM.CC.BUFFALO.EDU
Fly Fishing	FLYFISH@UMAB.UMD.EDU
Folklore Discussion	FOLKLORE@TAMVM1.TAMU.EDU
Gaelic Language	GAELIC-L@IRLEARN.UCD.IE
Hospital Computer Networking	HSPNET-L@ALBNYDH2.BITNET
Ocean Drilling	ODP-L@TAMVM1.TAMU.EDU

You might be the only person in your city who would want to read a newspaper or carry on a conversation every day about ocean drilling or fly fishing. But there are many people around the world interested in these topics. Thanks to LISTSERV discussion lists, they can share their interests by communicating electronically.

After you have subscribed to a discussion list, LISTSERV sends news and articles from the list to your electronic mailbox. As a subscriber to a discussion list, you usually can contribute messages which will be distributed to all the (other) subscribers to that list.

The LISTSERV application described in this chapter operates primarily on BITNET connected hosts. Be aware that not all commands work for all LISTSERVs. Also note that some of the information provided in this chapter may not apply to the "listserv" or "list-server" service which offers many of the same functions as BITNET LISTSERV. This other "listserv" service is found mostly on UNIX systems; the command structure and syntax, and the services available, will be somewhat different from those for LISTSERV.

ESSENTIAL POINTS ABOUT LISTSERV

■ ■

List Managers and LISTSERV Software

Every LISTSERV list has a manager in charge of the list, but day to day list operations are managed by the LISTSERV software program. This software handles subscription and unsubscription requests, and related "official" list management business. Because it is a computer program, it only understands certain precise commands. A table of the most common of these commands is provided later in this chapter.

LISTSERV Addresses

The discussion list and the LISTSERV program that manages it will usually be at the same network address but will have different mailbox names. The mailbox name of the LISTSERV program is usually "LISTSERV@address," and the discussion list itself will have the name "listname@address," where "listname" is a descriptive name, eight or fewer characters in length, and "address" can mean one of several things.

Within the BITNET network, "address" simply refers to the name of the BITNET host machine, so LISTSERVers and discussions lists have addresses of the format "LISTSERV@host" and "listname@host".

For some Internet users, "address" may be replaced by "host.bitnet". The format host.bitnet is a pseudo domain format that your Internet host may understand. If your Internet host does not understand the host.bitnet pseudo domain, you must use the format "listname%host.bitnet@an.interbit.gateway", where "an.interbit.gateway" is replaced by one of the following interbit gateways:

```
cornellc.cit.cornell.edu
cunyvm.cuny.edu
mitvma.mit.edu
vm1.nodak.edu
```

For example, if the pseudo domain format "listname@BITNIC.BITNET" did not work from your host, the format "listname%bitnic.bitnet@cunyvm.cuny.edu" might.

LISTSERVers on Internet Hosts

A growing number of LISTSERVers are on hosts connected to both BITNET and the Internet. In such cases, you can send messages to a LISTSERVer's Internet address directly without having to go through a gateway. For example, the LISTSERVer at the University of Washington, which is known in the BITNET world as "LISTSERV@UWAVM," is also on the Internet where it is known as "LISTSERV@uwavm.u.washington.edu." In order to reduce the load on the gateways, it is advisable that you use the direct Internet address whenever it is available.

Moderated and Unmoderated Groups

Some LISTSERV discussion groups are managed by a moderator. In moderated lists, all material contributed to the LISTSERV is reviewed for appropriateness before being distributed to the group subscribers. Moderators sometimes provide the additional service of organizing submitted materials so that all related discussions are packaged into a few mail messages before distribution. In contrast, messages submitted to unmoderated groups are automatically distributed to all subscribers.

Depending on what you want from your LISTSERV subscription and how much time you have to read the mail from the list (some produce hundreds of messages each week), moderated vs. unmoderated may be an important criterion when selecting the groups to which you will subscribe.

WHAT DISCUSSION LISTS ARE AVAILABLE?

Getting the Global List

You might have encountered references to specific LISTSERV lists in other chapters of *The Internet Passport* or in other network documentation. But if you want a comprehensive list of all lists, you should consult the LISTSERV "global list." You can obtain the global list from a LISTSERVer, via FTP, or you can use online Internet resources such as WAIS. (See Chapter 18.)

Via LISTSERV

Using LISTSERV, just send the following simple e-mail request to any LISTSERVer. This example is addressed to a BITNET host (BITNIC) via its Internet address.

```
mail:     listserv@bitnic.cren.net
subject:  (none needed)
message:  list global
```

In a few minutes, the LISTSERVer will acknowledge your request and send a copy of the global list as one long message.

Via FTP

```
          FTP host:   sri.com
          directory:  /netinfo
          filename:   interest-groups      (plain text version)
                      interest-groups.Z    (compressed plain text version)
```

Understanding the Global List

Each line in the global list has a list's name, the BITNET address of the LISTSERVer which manages that list, and a brief description of the topics discussed in that list. Here are five lines from the global list:

■■■

Listname	Address	Brief Description
AGRIC-L	AGRIC-L@UGA	Agriculture Discussion
ALF-L	ALF-L@YORKVM1	Academic Librarian's Forum
ALLMUSIC	ALLMUSIC@AUVM	Discussions on Music
ALTLEARN	ALTLEARN@SJUVM	Approaches to Learning
APPLE2-L	APPLE2-L@BROWNVM	Apple II List

Searching the Global List for Particular Topics

If you want to search the global list for discussion groups on a particular subject, you can add the option "/<topic>" to the list global command, where <topic> is one or more words describing the subject in which you are interested. Since this involves a computer search, this is a good opportunity to think about search strategies.

Say you wanted to retrieve the information for discussion groups about Latin America. You might think that using the search string "Latin America" would be just right. However, many LISTSERV discussion groups are multilingual, so there might be groups whose descriptions contain non-English words or phrases, like "Latinoamericano." Try "Latin" instead.

```
mail:    listserv@bitnic.cren.net
subject: (none needed)
message: list global /Latin
```

Notice that in the sample below, there are a few discussion groups dealing with Latin, but also a few that the string "Latin America" would not have retrieved.

```
Excerpt from the LISTSERV lists known to LISTSERV@BITNIC

Search string: LATIN

Network-
wide ID  Full address        List title
-------- ----------------    -----------------------------------

CANALC-D  CANALC-D@YORKVM1   Latin American and Caribbean Diges+
CH-LADB   CH-LADB@UNMVMA     Latin America Data Base
CLASSICS  CLASSICS@UWAVM     Classical Greek and Latin Discussi+
COURTSHP  COURTSHP@TAMVM1    For discussion or research and ide+
CREAD     CREAD@YORKVM1      Latin American and Caribbean Elect+
EDULAC    EDULAC@ENLACE      EDULAC: Educadores Latinoamericano+
LALA-L    LALA-L@UGA         Latin Americanist Librarians' Anno+
```

■■■

(Continued)

```
LATAMMUS   LATAMMUS@ASUACAD   Discussion of all aspects of music
OLADE-L    OLADE-L@UNALCOL    Organizacion Latinoamericana de En+
REDALC     REDALC@FRMOP11     Reseau Amerique Latine et Caraibes+
TML-L      TML-L@IUBVM        Thesaurus Musicarum Latinarum Data
```

Many LISTSERV Groups Are Available through Usenet

A growing number of lists are available through Usenet in the hierarchy "bit.list-serv." For example, the LISTSERV group "POLITICS" is distributed to Usenet as "bit.list-serv.politics."

One advantage of accessing lists through Usenet is that you can read many LIST-SERV groups without having the messages clog up your mailbox. However, when you post a message to the "bit.listserv" newsgroup, the message may not be distributed to folks who subscribe to the list via a LISTSERVer. This is of course a real problem if you are responding to a message from someone whose message was originally posted to the group from LISTSERV!

For more on Usenet, refer to Chapter 9.

USING LISTSERV TO SUBSCRIBE TO DISCUSSION LISTS

■■■

Subscribing to LISTSERV discussion lists is very simple:

* to subscribe, unsubscribe, or perform other administrative business, you send messages to the e-mail address of a LISTSERVer (LISTSERV@<address>);
* to participate with the discussion list, you send messages to the e-mail address of the discussion list (<listname>@<address>).

To make this clear, think about newspapers. You send subscription requests to the subscription department, never to the people who read the newspaper. Imagine how upset newspaper readers would be if half the articles in the daily paper were letters saying "I would like to subscribe..." or "I would like to cancel my subscription."

LISTSERV Etiquette

All of the issues of e-mail and Usenet etiquette discussed in Chapters 4 and 9 apply equally well in the culture of LISTSERV lists. If you have forgotten the main points, please review those passages before entering the LISTSERV world. Take special care that the messages you send to the LISTSERV are appropriate to the topic and the group. As always, personal messages should remain so: send these to the individual for whom they are intended, not to the group. Be especially careful when using your e-mail's automatic reply function so that you don't accidentally send a personal message to the entire group.

▪▪

Example LISTSERV Subscription Process

Send Your Subscription Request to the LISTSERVer

If you wanted to subscribe to the ALLMUSIC discussion list, you would send the following e-mail message to the LISTSERVer at node AUVM which happens to be at the American University:

```
mail:     listserv@auvm.bitnet
subject:  (none needed)
message:  subscribe allmusic <your name>
```

Or, if you need to use the full interbit gateway format and you didn't know the Internet address, send the message as follows:

```
mail:     listserv%auvm.bitnet@cunyvm.cuny.edu
subject:  (none needed)
message:  subscribe allmusic <your name>
```

In a short while, you should receive an acknowledgment of your subscription from the LISTSERVer by e-mail. Please take the time to read this subscription notice and save it for future reference! It will contain useful information to help you make the most of your subscription to the discussion list, including instructions on how to unsubscribe.

You may receive a notice saying that "subscription to this list is not automatic." In such cases, a list manager reviews the subscription requests which have been received by the LISTSERV program and then manually adds names to the subscription list.

Send Only Discussion Messages to the Discussion List

Once you are subscribed to a LISTSERV list, you can send messages to the list. Messages which you want to be read by list subscribers must be sent to <listname>@<address> not to LISTSERV@<address>!

Some LISTSERV acknowledgments request that you introduce yourself to the list when you have subscribed. If ALLMUSIC requested such an introduction (in fact, it doesn't), you might send a mail message like the following:

```
mail:     allmusic@auvm.american.edu
subject:  Introduction from a new ALLMUSIC subscriber

Greetings! I have just subscribed to the ALLMUSIC discussion
list and would like to introduce myself. My name is <your
name>, and I am particularly interested in the influences of
Gregorian chants and Balinese Gamelan in the post-punk
aesthetic of Dutch underground music...(etc.)

<your contact information>
```

Use the Reply Function Cautiously

Most mailers allow you to use a one or two keystroke function to reply to messages. While this may be very handy, it can lead to problems when responding to messages received from the list. If you don't want your message to go to the entire list, don't use the respond function unless you are sure the mail is going only to those intended. There have been many instances where private mail has gone to an entire list of people causing quite a bit of embarrassment. Some mailers will distinguish types of reply allowing you to specify whether you want the reply to go to the original sender or the list. To figure out how this works on your system and with the lists you are subscribed to, try both types of reply and compare the addresses in the "to" field before sending anything. Remember: when in doubt, stop, check the header, and consider addressing the reply manually.

LISTSERV Subscriptions Can Become Overwhelming

Unlike a newspaper that is delivered once a day, with all the articles in a neat, single package, most lists are distributed as individual messages. Some lists are very active and can send 10's if not 100's of messages to your electronic mailbox every day.

If you've ever subscribed to two or more newspapers, you know how quickly last week's and last month's issues can pile up. Now imagine that instead of a single issue of each newspaper each day, you had to separately handle every single article from every newspaper every day!

This is one of the main drawbacks to the LISTSERV system. If you're subscribed to several LISTSERV lists and don't check your electronic mailbox for a couple of days, you might find several hundred mail files from LISTSERVers waiting for you when you return. Reading all of these files, or even deleting them all, can take hours of your time.

Some lists offer a digest feature, allowing you to set your subscription so that you only receive a collection of messages on a periodic basis (once a day, once a week, etc.), while other lists send their messages only appear as digests. In a variation of the digest format, some lists distribute messages grouped or combined according to topic.

If you prefer more control over your messages from a LISTSERV you have another option. Using the "set index" command (see the section entitled *Basic LISTSERV Commands*) you could set the LISTSERV to send only a list of subject lines and message numbers. When you see a topic that interests you, you could then retrieve the message by using the listserver features of LISTSERV (see the section entitled *Using LISTSERV as an Information Server*). This tactic can make it possible for you to monitor more lists than would otherwise be reasonable.

Cancel a Subscription by Sending a Message to the LISTSERVer

When you want to cancel a subscription to a discussion list, send your request to the LISTSERV, not to the discussion list. Sending cancellation requests directly to a discussion list is a major faux pas in the LISTSERV world.

For example, suppose you accidentally subscribed to AXOLOT-L@AMPHBIAN and are receiving hundreds of messages about paedomorphic Mexican salamanders which you really don't want to read.

Simply send your cancellation to LISTSERV@AMPHBIAN, and the barrage of messages should desist.

```
mail:     listserv@amphbian.bitnet
subject:  (none needed)
message:  signoff axolot-l
```

USING LISTSERV AS AN INFORMATION SERVER

As you will see from the table of LISTSERV commands in *Basic LISTSERV Commands*, in addition to handling subscription and unsubscription requests to discussion lists, LISTSERV is also a very powerful software tool for retrieving files and searching LISTSERV file archives, much like the mail servers described in Chapter 3.

You usually don't have to be subscribed to a LISTSERV discussion list to use the information services of the hundreds of LISTSERVers around the world.

Retrieving Files from a LISTSERVer

Many discussion lists have archives of previous discussions which you can retrieve from the LISTSERVers. These discussion list archives frequently have the filename format of "listname logYYMM," where "YY" is a year and "MM" is a month. For example "axolot-l log9209" would be the log of discussions which took place in AXOLOT-L in September, 1992. Note that LISTSERV filenames are comprised of two words (the filename and the filetype) with a space between them.

Searching LISTSERV Databases with LISTDB

LISTDB is a program within the LISTSERV software that allows you to search through files in a LISTSERVer's archives. To use LISTDB effectively, you should have a copy of the global list-of-lists handy so you know which LISTSERV and which lists you might want to search.

For example, suppose you wanted to find out about the latest software and computer techniques for teaching Russian. Since there is a LISTSERV list devoted to technology in language education called LLTI, let's give it a shot!

A LISTDB request should be in a precise format, though the search itself is case insensitive. The following message should serve as a useful template for most LISTDB requests; simply change the destination LISTSERV address, the keyword after the word "SEARCH," the name of the database (in this case replacing "LLTI"), and how far back into the database you want LISTDB to search. In this case we used a cut off date of January 1, 1994 (94/01/01) since we want the very latest information:

```
mail:    listserv@dartcms1.dartmouth.edu
subject: (none needed)
message:

//
Database Search DD=Rules
//Rules DD    *
Search russian in LLTI since 94/01/01
Index
/*
```

In a short while, you would receive an e-mail message with the results from your search request.

```
> Search russian in LLTI since 94/01/01
--> Database LLTI, 13 hits.

> Index
Item #   Date      Time    Recs    Subject
------   ----      ----    ----    -------
001693 94/01/03  21:13      68     #697 US/Russian Teleconferencing
001782 94/01/21  15:36     100     Re: #707.6 Apples and/or IBMs in labs
001804 94/01/25  08:14     232     #749 EW-ED'94 Conference in Crimea
001826 94/01/27  10:08     126     Re: #754 Seeking ideas for Computer +
001872 94/02/04  08:18     162     #781 East-West Conference on Multime+
001883 94/02/04  16:24     328     #784 SCOLA Schedule/Deutsche Welle
001886 94/02/07  08:07     174     #785 Deutsche Welle: EST
001915 94/02/14  16:29      50     #799 job opening -- Haverford College
001939 94/02/18  08:20      26     #812 Translation Software
001979 94/02/24  16:57      68     Re: #824.2 Language Houses
001982 94/02/25  08:52      28     #827.3 about that teleconference... +
001983 94/02/25  15:28     268     #828 SCOLA updates for LLTI
002001 94/03/02  16:50      34     #836 Job Opening
```

To actually retrieve any of these items, you would send the following request. It is almost exactly like the original, except that you change the last line from "INDEX" to "PRINT", followed by the item numbers from the left column of the response.

■■

```
mail:     listserv@dartcms1.dartmouth.edu
subject: (none needed)
message:

//
Database Search DD=Rules
//Rules DD    *
Search russian in LLTI since 94/01/01
Print 001782 001826 001872 001939
/*
```

LISTDB will then send you via e-mail the requested articles from the LLTI discussion list.

At this point you are probably saying, "You expect me to use this search command? It looks too complicated." A good way to handle the arcane job language of the LISTSERV search command is to write it once, save it as a text file, then edit and reuse it. For each new search, all you need to change is the listname, the search terms themselves, and the command on the second to last line (index or print item), then address your message containing the revised search to the correct LISTSERV.

For more information about the database features of LISTSERV, send the request "info database" to any LISTSERVer.

BASIC **LISTSERV** COMMANDS

■■

LISTSERV is a computer program so it only understands certain commands. Everything you send to a LISTSERVer must fit a precise syntax if you expect meaningful responses. (Avoid including a signature file on the messages sent to the LISTSERV program as it will attempt to process these "commands" and then report to you that it was unable to fill your request.)

You can put multiple requests in a single e-mail message, but they must each be on a separate line. The LISTSERVer sends a response to you by e-mail.

Here's a summary of some of the most useful commands that you can send to a LISTSERVer in an e-mail message.

List Subscription Commands	Result
subscribe <listname> <your-name>	Subscribes you to a list
signoff <listname> or unsub <listname>	Cancels your subscription to a list

(Continued)

LISTSERV Set Commands	Result
`set <listname> nomail`	Suspends mailing of materials from that list (Very useful if you don't want hundreds of messages accumulating in your mailbox while you're on vacation.)
`set <listname> mail`	Resumes mailing of materials to your account after a "nomail" request
`set <listname> digest`	Changes your subscription to digest format (All mail to the list is collected into a single message and sent to you on a regular basis.)
`set <listname> index`	Changes subscription to index format (Just a list of subject lines and message numbers is sent.)

General Purpose LISTSERV Commands	Result
`help`	Receive a brief list of LISTSERV commands
`info`	Receive a catalog of available topics
`info <topic>`	Receive a particular file from the list of info topics (For example, "info refcard" retrieves the LISTSERV "reference card" summarizing all LISTSERV commands.)
`list global`	Receive a list-of-lists that is available from all LISTSERVers
`list global /<topic>`	Receive a list of only those discussion groups which have the specified topic word(s) in their name or description

LISTSERV Information Server Commands	Results
`index <listname>`	Receive an index of the files which have been archived for a particular list
`rev <listname>`	Receive a list of the public subscribers with their full name and e-mail address–a great way to find someone's e-mail address!
`get <filename filetype>`	Receive a particular file named in the index list (The files' names have two parts in this format—filename and filetype.)

(Continued)

`info filelist`	Receive a list of all LISTSERV files on that LISTSERVer that contain LISTSERV help (Note that you can use the "info" command for each of the files reported by the "info filelist" request.)
`info database`	Receive information about the LISTDB program which can be used to search LISTSERV log files for information

More about LISTSERV

LISTSERV Is a BITNET Service

LISTSERV is one of the notable services of BITNET, a network devoted to networking of educational institutions. Even though BITNET is not based upon the IP protocol like the Internet, LISTSERV is available to Internet users thanks to interbit gateways that allow e-mail messages to pass between the two networks.

As with other freely available resources on the Internet, use of a LISTSERVer should be viewed as a special privilege, not a right.

Conclusion

Many Internet users only know about LISTSERV groups by way of those that are gatewayed to the "bit.listserv" hierarchy in Usenet. Even though BITNET only offers e-mail, it merits appreciative use by Internet users because of the abundance of LISTSERV groups and the quality of the LISTSERV software. As this chapter hopefully demonstrates, LISTSERVs and their lists are great resources, both as active forums for discussion and storehouses of files and list archives.

For More Information

The best information about LISTSERV is from LISTSERVers. Use the commands in the "LISTSERV COMMANDS" table to explore LISTSERV's help files. You can also post general questions to LISTSERV lists to which you are subscribed and perhaps some other generous subscriber will help you out.

For general information about LISTSERV you can subscribe to LSTSRV-L@uga.cc.uga.edu or use the archives of this discussion for LISTDB requests. For informative discussion about LISTDB, subscribe to LDBASE-L@ukanvm.cc.ukans.edu.

For more information on lists-of-lists, see Chapter 11.

Bibliography

Association of Research Libraries. *Directory of Electronic Journals, Newsletters and Academic Discussion Lists*. Washington, DC: The Association, 1991-

Hardie, E. T. L. and V. Neou. *Internet: Mailing Lists*. Updated 1993 ed. Englewood Cliffs: PTR Prentice Hall, 1994.

CHAPTER

11

Internet Mailing
Lists

Internet mailing lists (also known as Internet interest groups) create forums for people to exchange electronic mail messages on topics of common interest. Mailing lists cover a dizzying variety of subjects: from comic books to works by James Joyce, from hang gliding to spelunking, from viral biology to cosmology. Mailing lists are an easy way to exercise your curiosity and share knowledge.

A mailing list performs two main tasks: it stores a list of the e-mail addresses of people who share an interest in a topic and distributes messages among these individuals quickly and easily. In this way it is like LISTSERV (described in Chapter 10).

Because mailing lists are distributed by e-mail, these services are available to users of other networks that maintain mail gateways to the Internet.

While you're subscribed to a mailing list, messages sent to that list will be forwarded directly to your electronic mailbox. Similarly, messages you send to the list will be distributed to all the other subscribers. You don't need to know their individual e-mail addresses because the mailing list takes care of this for you.

A mailing list transforms e-mail from a one-to-one exchange of messages, to a community in which you can ask questions, give answers, or simply sit back and learn from the conversations that are passed to you through the network. Mailing lists help network users become part of a community defined by interests, not location.

USING INTERNET MAILING LISTS

Mailing List Names and Addresses

By convention, an Internet mailing list is usually assigned two e-mail addresses. A mailing list with the e-mail address

```
listname@an.internet.address
```

would typically have a companion address for subscription or cancellation requests called

```
listname-request@an.internet.address
```

Messages sent to "listname" are distributed to all subscribers of the list while messages sent to "listname-request" are received only by the list manager.

Unlike LISTSERV listnames, mailing list names are often long and informative. It's not unusual to encounter names like "indo-malaysian.archaeology."

Subscribing to Mailing Lists

Here's an example of a subscription request to a hypothetical mailing list, musica-neuva, for discussion of contemporary Brazilian music.

■■■

```
mail:        musica-nueva-request@venera.brasilia.br
subject:     subscription request
message:     Please subscribe me to musica-nueva. Thanks!


             Kristina Sadia
             ksadia@a.network.address
        (additional gateway information if needed)
```

Notice that the subscriber included her name and network address in the message text. This is very useful for the list manager if you are subscribing from a network outside of the Internet or if the header of your subscription request happened to be corrupted en route.

Sometimes subscription or cancellation requests are sent to the e-mail address of the person who maintains the list, for example, "sarah@an.internet.address." And subscriptions to some lists may be performed by a software package that expects requests in a precise syntax (much like LISTSERV lists). When in doubt, consult one of the lists-of-lists referred to at the end of this chapter for more information. The comprehensive lists-of-lists gives information and correct subscription addresses for hundreds of lists.

After you have submitted your subscription request, you will usually receive an acknowledgment from the list manager containing useful information about the group, such as how to quit the list, or how to obtain related files such as archives of the list's previous discussions. Save such information for future reference so you can get the most out of your membership!

Some lists have a collegial approach to their membership and the list manager may ask you to submit a brief introduction of yourself to the list.

Once your e-mail address has been added to a subscription list, you will begin receiving copies of all messages mailed to the list.

Kinds of Mailing Lists

Mailing lists can be set up and run in a variety of ways. They range in size, from a few individuals within an organization to thousands of people worldwide; in topic, from the highly specialized to the mundane; in activity, from a message once every couple of weeks to volumes of messages daily; and in tone of discussion, from a polite and deferential English tea to a rough and tumble free-for-all.

Moderated and Unmoderated Lists

Unmoderated lists accept and transfer all submissions. Other lists have a moderator who selects and/or edits the messages before distribution to the subscribers. Moderation helps reduce the number of messages that list subscribers don't want to read, (e.g., requests to unsubscribe, which are often erroneously sent to "listname" instead of "list-name-request").

■■■

Digests

Some list maintainers will collect submitted messages into a single file, or digest. Instead of receiving separate files, you receive these digests on a periodic basis. This creates work for the list maintainer but makes mail management easier for list subscribers.

Private and Public Lists

Although most Internet mailing lists are public and can be subscribed to by anyone, other lists are private and intended for restricted distribution. The restriction might be due to limits on the amount of time and computer resources of a list manager, or it might be that the list manager and its subscribers want a restricted community. Unlike Usenet newsgroups, it is easy to set up a private list, if so desired.

Specialization of Mailing Lists

Internet mailing lists often deal with highly specialized, cutting-edge, or sensitive topics which may not be appropriate now, or ever, for the more general Usenet newsgroups.

Autonomy of Mailing Lists

Unlike LISTSERV discussion groups that require the willing participation of a BITNET site or Usenet newsgroups that require discussion and voting by the Usenet community, Internet mailing lists do not necessarily require local or network-wide approval to be started. This means that Internet mailing lists can have whatever properties their managers and participants want them to have.

FINDING MAILING LISTS

■■■

Lists of Mailing Lists

There are several catalogs, or lists-of-lists, which are essential references for helping you track down mailing lists of interest.
• Dartmouth Special Interest Groups List of Lists
• Directory of Scholarly Electronic Conferences
• Publicly Accessible Mailing Lists

Each of these catalogs has a slightly different emphasis. They provide you with some or all of the following information about mailing lists and other types of discussion groups: name and e-mail address; a brief description of the topics discussed; whether the list is considered private or public; information about the folkways of the group; the mechanism of distribution (will you receive individual files, or periodic digests?); the location, and organization of archives of past discussions contact names and e-mail addresses of group owners/managers; and most importantly, the particular syntax used to subscribe or unsubscribe.

Information on how to access these lists-of-lists can be found in the section "For More Information about Internet Mailing Lists" at the end of this chapter.

Network "Word of Mouth"

If all else fails, you might be able to locate mailing lists of interest by posting a request to related Usenet or LISTSERV discussion groups. Sometimes the information about such lists will be included in a discussion group's FAQ (Frequently Asked Questions) file.

MAILING LIST ETIQUETTE AND ETHICS

Of course, all issues of etiquette and ethics which apply to e-mail and Usenet also apply to mailing lists. (See Chapter 4 for a detailed discussion of these general issues.) If you think of a mailing list as an electronic version of a few good friends in a living room, talking passionately about some topic near and dear to their hearts, you'll pretty much understand the issues of etiquette and ethics that pertain to such lists.

Get to Know the People in the Group

It's generally a good idea to sit back and read a mailing list for awhile before you submit messages, just as you would listen to a conversation before chiming in. Turnover in mailing lists is often much lower than in typical newsgroups which tend to have a constant parade of visitors just popping in for a brief look. Also keep in mind that mailing lists can be heavily influenced by the personalities of a few key subscribers.

Address Your Messages to the Appropriate Destination!

Is the message you're mailing of interest to all the list subscribers? Then by all means, send it to the list. To only a single list subscriber? Then send e-mail directly to that subscriber. Is it a request to subscribe to or quit the group? Then please send it to "list-name-request" or the list manager, as appropriate. (Sending unsubscription requests to the group is like constantly interrupting a conversation by asking, "Hey guys, can you let me out the room? I can't open the door!")

Avoid sending the same message to multiple lists. Never send a message to all mailing lists! Such actions are inconsiderate—the initial and response mail volume can overwhelm networks.

Handle Rejection of a Subscription Request Gracefully

You might encounter a list which, for one reason or another, does not accept your subscription request. In such a case, there's no point in making a fuss; mailing lists can be restricted by a list manager and its subscribers in any way they see fit, just like you have the right to decide who to invite into your home for a chat.

Respect a Group's Request for Privacy

Although it is technically true that anything sent via e-mail is public information, some mailing lists would prefer that you not redistribute discussions from the group to the global electronic village. Remember too, material sent to lists is subject to copyright protection.

STARTING AN INTERNET MAILING LIST

Although setting up a mailing list is not difficult, maintenance and management can be a real time consumer. So think before you leap and do some preliminary research to avoid duplicating others' efforts. Talk with your system administrator or the network support group at your site to get advice and help.

Suppose you wanted to start a mailing list about the use of solar ovens in rural areas.

Is there already a mailing list or newsgroup that covers the topic in part or in whole? Examine the lists-of-lists described at the end of this chapter. You can also ask around the net by posting a query to the LISTSERV discussion group "new-list@vm1.nodak.edu". This group publishes list searches in digest form every few weeks. You might also try topically related Usenet, LISTSERV, mailing lists, or BBSs.

If a search of available resources doesn't uncover an existing forum for an in-depth discussion of solar ovens, you may decide to become a list manager. Consider this carefully, as it could become a serious commitment.

If you have already been exchanging e-mail with others about solar ovens and related topics, you have the first part of a mailing list: a list of potential subscribers. When you send out messages to all of these people about your shared interest, you would then have a one-way mailing list, which is sometimes referred to as a "distribution list." To make multiple mailings easier, most mail software packages allow you to use an "alias" or "nickname" for two or more e-mail addresses. You might set up the nickname "solar-ovens" for the e-mail addresses of this set of people.

To turn this private distribution list into a mailing list to which others on the Internet can subscribe and send mail for redistribution, ask your system administrator to set up two new mailboxes—one named "solar-ovens" and the other "solar-ovens-request." The mailbox solar-ovens would be an alias for the list of your subscribers' e-mail addresses. Mail sent to solar-ovens would automatically be distributed to all persons on this list. The mailbox solar-ovens-request would be an alias pointing to your e-mail address. Mail sent to solar-ovens-request would come to your personal mailbox and you would need to handle these administrative requests (e.g., to subscribe and unsubscribe) when you receive them.

If you wish to moderate the discussion and review all submitted messages before they are sent to the group, then the solar-ovens mailbox should be aliased only to your personal account. All mail sent to solar-ovens would come to your mailbox. In this case, you would also need to maintain a separate list of subscribers' e-mail addresses which would be aliased to a third e-mail address such as "solar-ovens-send." Any message you approve will be distributed to the group when you send it to solar-ovens-send.

If you don't wish to handle messages and subscriptions, you may want to ask other list managers for recommendations about software to handle some or all of the administrative duties of the list. Alternatively, a group that already handles mailing lists, or is otherwise related to or interested in the proposed topic, might consider setting up and managing your list.

If you want to broadly announce your mailing list, you should advertise its existence to the LISTSERV discussion group new-list@vm1.nodak.edu, to the maintainers of the lists-of-lists, and to related forums.

For further information on starting your own mailing list and other options for sharing and publishing information electronically, see Chapter 22.

FOR MORE INFORMATION

Lists-of-Lists

No one of these lists-of-lists is complete, but together, they contain useful information about most public Internet mailing lists and LISTSERV discussion groups. In addition, these references often include information about functionally similar services such as COMSERVE, MAILSERVE, and MAILBASE.

Dartmouth Special Interest Groups list-of-lists (SIGLISTS)

This general purpose list contains a fair number of special interest group (SIG) mailing lists and many LISTSERV lists updated on a monthly basis. It is maintained by David Avery of Dartmouth College. Get the READ.ME file first! This list-of-lists is a huge file which is most easily used with the software programs designed to help you format, display, and search these files on Unix, Macintosh, VMS, and CMS computers.

FTP host:	`dartcms1.dartmouth.edu`
directory:	`/SIGLISTS`
filename:	`READ.ME`

Directory of Scholarly Electronic Conferences

An academically oriented list of nearly 800 Internet mailing lists, LISTSERV discussion groups, and other kinds of topically oriented lists, this directory is maintained by Diane Kovacs of Kent University and organized by academic discipline.

FTP host:	`ra.msstate.edu`
directory:	`/pub/docs/words-l/Net-Stuff`
filenames:	`acadlist.readme`
	`acadlist.file1`
	`acadlist.file2`
	`acadlist.file3`
	`acadlist.file4`
	`acadlist.file5`
	`acadlist.file6`

```
acadlist.file7
acadlist.file8
acadlist.file9
acadlist.indexa
cadlist.announce
```

This list also appears in the print publication, *Directory of Newsletters, Journals and Academic Discussion Lists* published annually by the Association of Research Libraries. For ordering information, send a request to osap@cni.org. Of course, since this is a printed version, it won't be as up-to-date as the electronic one.

Publicly Accessible Mailing Lists

A general purpose list of Internet mailing lists originally begun by Chuq Von Rospach and first maintained by Gene Spafford. The list is now maintained by Stephanie DaSilva. This list is organized alphabetically by list name. Updated versions are posted periodically to several newsgroups (news.lists, news.answers, and news.announce.newusers). The list is also available via anonymous FTP and World Wide Web.

```
FTP host:    rtfm.mit.edu
directory:   /pub/usenet/news.answers/mail/mailing-lists
filenames:   part1
             part2
             part3
             part4
             part5
             part6
             part7
             part8

WWW:         http://www.ii.uib.no/~magnus/paml.html
```

SRI International List-of-Lists

This is a general purpose list-of-lists maintained by Steven Bjork of the Network Information Systems Center at SRI International and it is organized alphabetically by list name.

```
FTP host:       sri.com
directory:      /netinfo
filenames:      interest-groups
```

Searchable List-of-Lists on Gopher

Two lists, "Publicly Accessible Mailing Lists" and "List of Lists," are available as searchable indexes via Gopher.

```
Gopher:      cs1.presby.edu
menus:       Internet Resources/Lists of Mailing Lists
             and Discussion Groups/
```

Other Sources of Mailing List Information

Usenet Newsgroups

Periodic updates of *Publicly Accessible Mailing Lists*, and many other useful lists-of-lists for other Internet resources, are posted to the following newsgroups:

```
news.announce.newusers

news.answers

news.lists
```

For more on Usenet, see Chapter 9.

Mailing List about Mailing Lists

Updates and general information about the SRI lists-of-lists can be received by subscribing to the mailing list about a mailing list, interest-groups@nisc.sri.com.

To subscribe, send a message to interest-groups-request@nisc.sri.com.

LISTSERV List about Mailing Lists

When new lists are created, new-list@vm1.nodak.edu is one of the main forums in which they are announced. (For more on using LISTSERV, see Chapter 10.) To subscribe to new-list, send e-mail as follows:

```
mail:      listserv@vml.nodak.edu
subject:   (none needed)
message:   sub new-list <your-full-name>
```

Bibliography

Association of Research Libraries. *Directory of Electronic Journals, Newsletters and Academic Discussion Lists*. Washington, DC: The Association, 1991-

Hardie, E. T. L. and V. Neou. *Internet: Mailing Lists*. Updated 1993 ed. Englewood Cliffs: PTR Prentice Hall, 1994.

SECTION

IV Texts and Data

CHAPTER

12

Electronic Journals and Newsletters

Electronic journals and newsletters are the computer network equivalent of their printed counter parts. For the purposes of this book, an electronic journal or newsletter is a publication where the process of submitting articles and distributing final publications is performed over the network.

Some electronic journals and newsletters are also distributed in hardcopy. For example, NorthWestNet produces a newsletter called "NodeNews" that is available in both printed and electronic forms.

The content of electronic journals and newsletters ranges from the mainstream to the esoteric. Most electronic journals focus on topics of academic interest and many are really indistinguishable from formal, scholarly, printed journals. These journals are published only after the articles have undergone rigorous peer review with an emphasis on the leading concerns of established academic disciplines. Other electronic journals are considerably more informal.

The articles comprising an electronic newsletter are usually shorter than journal articles and the topics typically focus on news and announcements. Information in electronic journals tends to be more timely than that in print publications, due largely to the short lead time that the electronic publications have. The lead time in producing electronic publications is shorter because the three main components of production, editing, peer review, and final production, are all accelerated by the electronic distribution.

USING ELECTRONIC JOURNALS AND NEWSLETTERS

Locating Electronic Journals and Newsletters of Interest

The documents listed in the "For More Information" section provide comprehensive and up-to-date listings of the available electronic journals and newsletters.

It is also possible to use information resources such as WAIS, Gopher, CWISs, and World Wide Web to locate (and access) electronic journals.

Subscribing to Electronic Journals and Newsletters

To get regular printed magazines, you can subscribe and have each issue sent to you by mail or you can go to a newsstand to pick up each issue individually. Obtaining electronic journals works in essentially the same way, except everything is done from a computer on the Internet.

- You send a subscription request and receive each issue via electronic mail
- or, you obtain current or old issues via FTP, LISTSERVers, mail servers, Gopher, WAIS, or World Wide Web.

Here's an example of how to subscribe to an electronic journal known as "The Electronic Journal of Communication/La Revue Electronique de Communication," a bilingual, quarterly journal devoted to communication theory, research, practice, and policy.

Compose an e-mail message as follows:

```
mail:      comserve@vm.ecs.rpi.edu
subject:   (none needed)
message:   join ejcrec <your name>
```

To cancel a subscription to *this particular* e-journal, send the following:

```
mail:      comserve@vm.ecs.rpi.edu
subject:   (none needed)
message:   dropout ejcrec
```

These requests, as with many subscription requests, will be processed by a mail server—a computer program that only understands a limited and specific set of commands. To learn about this particular mail server, you would send an e-mail message with "help" in the body of the message. For a more detailed description of using mail servers generally, refer to Chapter 3.

Note: The exact syntax used to subscribe or unsubscribe to various e-journals will differ. The information you will need to subscribe to or obtain back issues of specific electronic journals is provided in the lists of electronic journals and newsletters described below.

Electronic Journal and Newsletter Etiquette

It is sometimes possible to subscribe others to an electronic journal. This of course should be done only with that other person's permission.

Sample List of E-Journals

This list of electronic journals represents only a small portion of the total number available. The intent is to provide an overview of the range of subjects that are covered in this medium. You may view any or all of these e-journals by gophering to gopher.cic.net and choosing "Electronic Serials."

Journal Name	General Information	Subscription Information
Academe This Week	Events in academia; issued weekly.	Available via Gopher at gopher.cic.net.
Health Info-Com Network Medical Newsletter	Issued bi-weekly.	Send an e-mail message to david@stat.com requesting a subscription.
Post Modern Culture	Issued three times a year; online discussion at PMC-TALK at the same LISTSERV.	Send e-mail to LISTSERV@ncsuvm.cc.edu with the message: SUB PMC <your name>. To cancel your subscription, send mail to the LISTSERV with the message: UNSUB PMC.
Quanta	Science fiction and fantasy; issued almost each month.	Send an e-mail message asking for a subscription to quanta+request-ascii@andrew.cmu.edu for the ASCII version, or to quanta+request-postscript@andrew.cmu.edu for the PostScript version.
Radio Free Europe/Radio Liberty	News from Russia, Transcaucasia and Central Asia, and Central and Eastern Europe; issued daily (Monday-Friday).	Send e-mail to LISTSERV@ubvm.cc.buffalo.edu with the message: SUB RFERL-L <your name>. To cancel your subscription, send mail to the LISTSER

FOR MORE INFORMATION

The CICNet (Committee on Institutional Cooperation Network) Gopher server contains archives of, and information about, a wide variety of electronic journals and newsletters. All of this material is currently located in "Electronic Journals" found in the root directory. For more on using Gopher, see Chapter 17.

```
Gopher:   gopher.cic.net
menu:     Electronic Journals/
items:    (many or all)
```

Lists of Electronic Journals and Newsletters

The best bet for an up-to-date list of electronic journals and newsletters is a printed volume maintained by the Association of Research Libraries titled *Directory of Electronic Journals, Newsletters and Academic Discussion Lists*. The latest printed version of the directory (1994) catalogs 443 journals and newsletters along with specific instructions for obtaining each publication by mail or FTP. In addition, the directory includes listings for almost 1800 academic discussion lists. The online list of electronic journals, compiled by

Michael Strangelove and upon which the ARL directory was based, is not currently being updated.

Electronic Journal List in Print

If you want to purchase a bound version of *Directory of Electronic Journals, Newsletters and Academic Discussion Lists* (combining Strangelove's list of electronic journals with Diane Kovacs' list of academic discussion lists) contact:

> Office of Scientific and Academic Publishing
> Association of Research Libraries
> 21 Dupont Circle
> Washington, DC 20036 USA
>
> e-mail: osap.cni.org
> voice: (202) 296-2296
> fax: (202) 872-0884

From LISTSERVs

Electronic copies of Strangelove's Directory of Electronic Journals and Newsletters are currently available from the following LISTSERV. (Note carefully the spellings of the filenames!). The latest version of Strangelove's directory is from July 1992.

```
mail:     listserv@acadvm1.uottawa.ca
subject:  (none needed)
message:  get ejournl1 directry
          get ejournl2 directry
```

Electronic Journal List via FTP and Gopher

> FTP host: dewey.lib.ncsu.edu
> directory: /pub/stacks/guides
> filename: ejournals.txt
>
> Gopher: dewey.lib.ncsu.edu
> menus: NCSU's "Library Without Walls"/Reference Desk/Guides (to
>   subject literature, to Internet Resources, etc.)/
> item: Directory of Electronic Journals and Newsletters (2nd ed.)

LISTSERV List

The following LISTSERV list is devoted to discussion about electronic journals, including announcements of new journals and the relationship of electronic journals to traditional publication:

VPIEJ-L@vtvm1.cc.vt.edu1V with the message: UNSUB RFERL-L.

Bibliography

Because electronic journals and newsletters cannot be kept in or accessed from a library collection in the same manner as their printed counterparts, librarians and academics have engaged in a lively debate about their future and their utility. The following articles should give you a taste of the many issues that have been raised:

Alexander, A.W. and J. S. Alexander. "Intellectual Property Rights and the 'Sacred Engine': Scholarly Publishing in the Electronic Age." *Advances in Library Resource Sharing* 1 (1990):176-192.

Gardner, W. "The Electronic Archive: Scientific Publishing for the 1990s." *Psychological Science* 1 (1990):333-341.

Harnad, S. "Scholarly Skywriting and the Prepublication Continuum of Scientific Inquiry." *Psychological Science* 1 (1990):342-344.

Krumenaker, Larry. "Virtual Libraries, Complete with Journals, Get Real." *Science* 260(5111) (May 21, 1993):1066-1067.

Litchfield, C. "Local Storage and Retrieval of Electronic Journals: Training Issues for Technical Services Personnel." *Serials Review* 17 (4)(1991):83-84.

Lucier, R.E. "Knowledge Management: Refining Roles in Scientific Communication." *EDUCOM Review* 25 (Fall 1990):21-27.

McMillan, G. "Embracing the Electronic Journal: One Library's Plan." *The Serials Librarian* 21 no. 2/3 (1991):97-108.

McMillan, G. "Technical Services for Electronic Journals Today." *Serials Review* 17 no. 4 (1991):84-86.

Metz, P. "Electronic Journals from a Collection Manager's Point of View." *Serials Review* 17 no. 4 (1991):82-83.

Metz, P. and P.M. Gherman. "Serials Pricing and the Role of the Electronic Journal." *College and Research Libraries* 52 (July 1991):315-327.

Neavill, G.B. "Electronic Publishing, Libraries, and the Survival of Information." *Library Resources and Technical Services* 28 (January/March 1984):76-89.

Okerson, A. "With Feathers: Effects of Copyright and Ownership on Scholarly Publishing." *College and Research Libraries* 52 (September 1991):425-438.

Piternick, A.B. "Electronic Serials: Realistic or Unrealistic Solution to the Journal 'Crisis'?" *The Serials Librarian* 21 no. 2/3 (1991):15-31.

Savetz, Kevin M. "Magazines Without Paper." *Byte* 18(10) (September 1993):108.

CHAPTER

13

Electronic Books

In the broadest sense, an electronic book is any document which is lengthy enough to be considered a book and is stored on diskette, hard drive, magnetic tape, or compact disk (CD). You can read electronic books at your computer screen, print them out in plain text or, if you have access to the right hardware and software, print them out in elegant formats on a laser printer. Note that electronic books are also sometimes referred to by the more general term "e-texts."

By this definition, the many computer-related manuals which are available by FTP can also be thought of as electronic books. However this chapter will focus on a special class of electronic books that include classical texts of world literature such as *The Declaration of Independence*, *The Great Gatsby*, the *Bible*, the *Koran*, the *Oxford English Dictionary*, and even *Hikayat Indraputra*, the notable Malay romance.

OBTAINING ELECTRONIC BOOKS

In general, you can access electronic books via FTP or by downloading them from Bulletin Board Services (BBSs). You may also order electronic books on diskettes or other storage media from electronic book providers. Not all electronic books are free and costs can vary depending on the provider.

Many of the services described throughout *The Internet Passport* allow you to search through the text of books. In particular, Gopher, WAIS, CWISs, BBSs, and World Wide Web, allow access to some of the texts described in this chapter, though it is sometimes more time-consuming to obtain entire book-length documents using these services than by FTP.

ELECTRONIC BOOK PROVIDERS

There are currently hundreds of sources of electronic books, and the number of providers and texts will probably continue to grow significantly for years to come. This chapter introduces you to the main Internet providers of electronic books and provides instructions on how to use a catalog service for finding electronic books. The entries in this section are listed alphabetically by name.

Freedom Shrine

The Freedom Shrine project concentrates on e-texts of short documents which have been of crucial importance in the history of democracy, primarily in the U.S.

All Constitutional Amendments	*German Surrender Documents*
Annapolis Convention	*Gettysburg Address*
Articles of Confederation	*Japanese Surrender Documents*
Bill of Rights	*Jefferson's First Inaugural Address*

Charlotte Town Resolves	*Lincoln's Second Inaugural Address*
Constitution of the Iroquois Nations	*M.L. King's: "I Have a Dream" Speech*
Constitution of the United States	*Magna Carta*
Constitutional Transmittal Letter	*Mayflower Compact*
Declaration and Resolves of the 1st Continental Congress	*Monroe Doctrine*
Declaration of Independence	*Northwest Ordinance of 1787*
Declaration of the Causes and Necessity of Taking up Arms	*Paris Peace Treaty, 1783*
Emancipation Proclamation	*Proclamation of Neutrality*
First Thanksgiving Proclamation	*Treaty of Greenville*
French Declaration of Rights	*Virginia Declaration of Rights*
Fundamental Orders of 1639	*Washington's Farewell Address*

The authoritative site for Freedom Shrine documents is the Cleveland Free-Net BBS. Telnet to one of the following hosts and login as a visitor or apply for an account:

freenet-in-a.cwru.edu
freenet-in-b.cwru.edu
freenet-in-c.cwru.edu

Once you have read the Free-Net introductory materials, select "The Library" from the main menu to access the Freedom Shrine and other electronic book holdings of the Cleveland Free-Net.

Online Book Initiative

The Online Book Initiative is a project of The World, a commercial Internet services provider. It contains an interesting variety of e-texts including classics of English literature, political science, archives of electronic journals, and standard computer-related materials such as operating system documentation.

A Christmas Caroll	Nerd Humor archives
BSD Unix Documentation	NREN documents
Civil Disobedience	*Seven Voyages of Sinbad*
DOD *Orange Book*	Shakespeare's Complete Works
Five Orange Pips	SunFlash documents
Flatland	Supreme Court Decisions
Grimm's Fairy Tales	Usenet Cookbook
Japanese Technical Reports	William Butler Yeats' Poetry
New Hacker's Dictionary	*Wuthering Heights*

The authoritative site for Online Book Initiative documents is the following:

FTP host:	`ftp.std.com`
alternate host:	`world.std.com`
directory:	`/obi`
filenames:	(many or all)
Gopher:	`world.std.com`
menu:	`OBI The Online Book Initiative/`

Oxford Text Archives

The Oxford Text Archives (OTA) are oriented towards e-texts in many different languages of special interest to literary scholars. Many of the e-texts contained in OTA either have to be purchased or have restrictions on their distribution and use.

As of February 1994, there are over 1,300 titles in 28 languages, comprising about 1.2 Gigbytes of data. Here is a very brief excerpt from OTA's large holdings to give you a feel for the wealth and variety of materials available from this source.

A la Recherche du Temps Perdu	*Hamlet*
Arabic Prose Samples	*Hikayat Indraputra* (a Malay Romance)
Aristotle, Complete Works (in Greek)	*Homer, Complete Works* (in Greek)
Beowulf	*Hyckerscorner, Wynkyn de Worde*
Blues Lyric Poetry: An Anthology	*Il paradiso, Il purgatorio, L'Inferno*
British Columbian Indian Myths	*Llyr gwyn Rhydderch: Ronabwy*
Call of the Wild	*MRC Psycholinguistic Database*
Chinese Telegraphic Code Character Set	*Origin of Species*
Das Nibelungenlied	Orwell's "1984" (in Croatian)
Etymological Dictionary of Gaelic Language	*Paradise Lost*
Genji Monogatari	*Plato, Collected Works* (in Greek)

Another service of OTA is a database of information about e-texts available from other archives around the world.

Accessing the Oxford Text Archives

Currently, the majority of these texts are only available on magnetic tape and disks. However, some files are available for FTP, and the managers of OTA are investigating the possibility of distributing their texts over the network.

For More Information about the Oxford Text Archives

You can get more detailed information about OTA from their FTP host:

```
FTP host:    ota.ox.ac.uk
directory:   /ota
filenames:   textarchive.list   (current catalog)
             textarchive.info   (current information on the archive)
```

You can also contact OTA by postal mail or e-mail.

Oxford Text Archive
Oxford University Computing Service
13 Banbury Road, Oxford OX2 6NN UK

```
e-mail:   archive@ox.ac.uk
voice:    + 44 865 273238
fax:      + 44 865 273275
```

Project Gutenberg

Project Gutenberg is a not-for-profit organization whose goal is to prepare electronic editions of more than 10,000 English language books by the year 2001. All documents are available as text-only files, but many can be obtained in PostScript or troff formats. The only exception to this rule so far is Beethoven's 5th Symphony in c-minor, presented as a MIDI binary sound file.

As of January 1994, there are over 100 e-texts distributed by Project Gutenberg, including:

1990 U.S. Census Information	*King James Bible*
Aesop's Fables	*Moby Dick*
Alice in Wonderland	*Night Before Christmas*
As You Like It	*Oedipus Trilogy*
Book of Mormon	*Peter Pan*
CIA World Fact Book	*Red Badge of Courage*
Complete Works of William Shakespeare	*Roget's Thesaurus*
Declaration of Independence	*Scarlet Letter*
Far From the Madding Crowd	*Song of Hiawatha*
Federalist Papers	*Tale of Two Cities*
Frankenstein	*Through the Looking Glass*
Frederick Douglass	*Time Machine*
Her Land	*U.S. Constitution*
Holy Koran	*War of the Worlds*
Hunting of the Snark	*Zen and the Art of the Internet*

Obtaining Project Gutenberg E-Texts

Electronic books from Project Gutenberg can be obtained most easily by FTP or mail server. If you don't have access to the Internet, you can purchase floppy disk versions by postal mail. Please note that because of copyright restrictions some of the texts are only available for U.S. citizens.

FTP Hosts for Project Gutenberg E-Texts

Project Gutenberg files could be retrieved from the following authoritative FTP host.

FTP host:	`mrcnext.cso.uiuc.edu`
directories:	`/etext/etext91`
	`/etext/etext92`
	`/etext/etext93`
	`/etext/etext94`
	`/etext/usonly` (documents for distribution only within the United States)
filenames:	(many or all)

For More Information about Project Gutenberg

Project Gutenberg is a not-for-profit effort that relies on volunteers to submit and proof electronic texts and research copyrights. For more information, contact:

Michael S. Hart, Director Project Gutenberg
405 West Elm St.
Urbana, IL 61801 USA
hart@vmd.cso.uiuc.edu

CATALOGS OF ELECTRONIC BOOK PROVIDERS

■■

American Philosophical Association Subcommittee on Electronic Texts in Philosophy

A catalog of e-texts of interest to philosophers (as well as some of the texts themselves) is maintained on the Gopher of the American Philosophical Association.

Gopher:	`apa.oxy.edu`
menu:	`Books and Journals/Electronic Texts/`

CPET: Catalogue of Projects in Electronic Text

The Center for Text and Technology (CTT) in collaboration with the Academic Computer Center at Georgetown University compiles a catalog of electronic text projects of interest to researchers in the humanities. The focus is on projects producing electronic versions of primary texts and does not currently include information about encyclopedias, dictionaries, or concordances.

For each project in the catalog, CTT attempts to compile the following information:

- identifying acronym or short reference;
- name and affiliation of operation;
- references to any published descriptions;
- contact person and/or vendor with addresses;
- primary disciplinary focus (and secondary interests);
- focus of the materials—time period, geographical area, or individual;
- language(s) of texts;
- intended use(s) and size (number of works, or entries, or citations);
- file format(s);
- mode(s) of access (online, tape, diskette, CD-ROM, etc.);
- source(s) of the archival holdings—encoded in-house, or obtained from elsewhere.

The catalog contains information on more than 300 e-text projects in over 30 countries.

Accessing CPET

The CPET catalog is accessible via Telnet or modem calls and features an interactive front end that allows you to locate information on texts of interest.

Telnet:	`guvax3.georgetown.edu`
username:	`CPET`
modem:	(202) 687-2616
connect:	`Esc +`
dial:	`guvax`
local>	`connect guvax3`
username:	`CPET`

A user's manual is available via FTP as well as a customized version of Kermit that you may need to use this service effectively by modem.

FTP host:	`guvax.georgetown.edu`	
directory:	`/cpet`	
filenames:	`cpet.man`	(user's manual)
	`ibm-kermit.exe`	(Kermit for DOS)
	`mac-kermit.sit`	(Kermit for Macintosh)

For More Information about CPET

An illustrated *User's Guide to the Catalogue of Projects in Electronic Text* is available free of charge through surface mail.

Margaret Friedman, Project Assistant
The Center for Text and Technology
Academic Computer Center
238 Reiss Science Building
Georgetown University
Washington, DC 20057 USA

e-mail: `mfriedman@guvax.georgetown.edu`
voice: (202) 687-6096

FOR MORE INFORMATION

Discussion Groups

The following discussion group focuses mostly on Project Gutenberg, but it is also a forum for discussion about many issues (legal, pedagogical, etc.) concerning e-texts.

To subscribe to the LISTSERV discussion group:

```
mail:    listserv@vmd.cso.uiuc.edu
subject: (none needed)
message: subscribe gutnberg <your name>
```

The LISTSERV discussion is also gatewayed to the following Usenet newsgroup:

bit.listserv.gutnberg

Bibliography

Basch, R. "Books Online: Visions, Plans, and Perspectives for Electronic Text" *Online* 15(4) (July 1991):13-23.

Collis, B. A. "The Evaluation of Electronic Books, Educational and Training." *Technology International* 28(4) (1991):355-63.

Gabriel, M. R. *A Guide to the Literature of Electronic Publishing.* Greenwich, CT: Joi Press. 1989.

Hockey, S. "Developing Access to Electronic Texts in the Humanities" *Computers in Libraries* 13(2) (February 1993):41-43.

Lowry, C. B. "Converging Information Technologies: How Will Libraries Adapt." *CAUSE/EFFECT* 13(3) (1990):35-42.

Saffo, P. "Hot New Medium: Text" *Wired* 1(2) (May/June 1993):48.

Seiler, L. H. "The Concept of Book in the Age of the Digital Electronic Medium." *Library Software Review* 11(1) (1992):19-29.

CHAPTER

14

Libraries on the Internet

Online Public Access Catalogs (OPACs)

For over two decades, libraries throughout the world have been transferring their card catalogs into computer databases called "online public access catalogs," or "OPACs." Many of these libraries in turn have made their OPACs accessible to anyone using the Internet.

Using an OPAC over the Internet is essentially like using a card catalog. The main difference is that instead of going to the library, pulling drawers, and riffling through cards, you access the OPAC from a computer terminal. From your home, school, or office, information about millions of books and articles from around the world is now at your fingertips. Although the first OPACs focused primarily on providing electronic access to the bibliographic records for books and serial publications, second-generation OPACs are now available that provide access to:

- indexes of journal, magazine, and newspaper articles;
- specialized databases of information (directories, facts, reference works, bibliographies, etc.)
- gateways to other networked resources, such as the Internet itself

And although university and research libraries were among the first to open their catalogs to the Internet, a growing number of public libraries are now doing the same.

WHAT CAN BE DONE WITH OPACS?

The primary use of today's OPACs is to obtain the kinds of information stored in the traditional card catalog. Searching the OPAC of a library other than your own has a number of possible advantages:

- access to information that may not be available elsewhere;
- easier or better search capabilities;
- strengths in specific subject areas of interest to you.

Because the number of OPAC software packages and implementations is substantial, you will be required to learn commands specific to these systems. Online help is usually available to get you started.

Searching for References by Subject, Author, and Title

From a patron's perspective, the primary use of a traditional card catalog is to search for documents by subject, author, and title. And although some of us old fashioned academic types get an ineffable enjoyment from the physical rhythm of working with a card catalog, this process takes significant time. The movement of directed swarms of electrons through computers and networks is substantially faster than the most skilled bibliophile's hand. In short, a search that could take hours with a regular card catalog can take seconds with an OPAC.

In addition to author, title, and subject searches, a growing number of OPACs include searches based on call numbers, keyword, year of publication, language, ISSN and ISBN numbers, media type, and organizational information. Such additional search fields can be a blessing when doing a highly specialized search. For example, I just searched an OPAC and requested all books that were written in Hindi, published since 1985, and dealt with education. The search retrieved 75 documents. (Not that I can actually *read* Hindi, but if I could, this would be handy indeed.) It should be noted, however, that OPACs do not necessarily include a complete catalog of a library's holdings.

Obtaining Detailed Bibliographic Information

The amount of information contained on the typical card in a card catalog is often limited, in part by the physical size of a card, and by the amount of person power required to prepare and update the cards. In contrast, electronic bibliographic records contained in an OPAC are easily updated, and can potentially display much more information than a single piece of paper. Some OPACs give you the option of viewing the entire bibliographic record, which in some cases can be several screens long.

Browsing

Many an academic has wandered through library stacks and serendipitously stumbled upon a book or section that proved to be a gold mine for their research. While an OPAC can't show you what's between the covers of the books, some will let you browse. For example, a number of OPAC software packages let you wander forwards and backwards through authors, subjects, titles, or call numbers, which is almost like browsing in the stacks.

Saving Search Results

Recording information from a regular card catalog can be time consuming and frustrating. (Remember wrestling with a drawer of cards with one hand while trying to transcribe information with the other?) If your goal is to assemble a bibliography, you may then have to go through the extra step of entering the information into a word processor.

In contrast, you can usually save the results of OPAC searches to your own computer with a few keystrokes. Some OPACs feature a built-in service that will send the results of your search via e-mail. Even when using OPACs that do not have this capability, you can almost always capture your session into a local file. For example, the "script" command in Unix will save what appears as screen output to a file. Similar commands or programs exist for most operating systems and communications software packages. If you are running a communications program with windowing software, you should be able to "cut" and "paste" the data from the communications screen into your word processor.

Catalogs of Special Collections

A growing number of OPACs include the bibliographic records of videos, movies, photographs, maps, microfilm, phonographs, CDs, and other non-book materials. And manuscript and archive collections across the country are beginning to offer access to their indexes and finding aids. These references may be fully incorporated into the main databases or you may have to specifically request a database of these items once connected to an OPAC service.

Materials Available for Circulation or Interlibrary Loan

Most OPACs are tied into the databases that handle circulation, so you might find out immediately if an item is available for checkout. If the book is already checked out there will usually be an indication of the date it is due back at the library. Some libraries even let you submit requests for materials electronically, either through an OPAC feature or e-mail. Thus you may be able to search for a title, request it, and receive it at your office or home without ever going to the library itself.

OPACs are often used by librarians and patrons to identify potential sources for interlibrary loans. Some library systems have even linked their entire interlibrary loan systems to the Internet so that paperwork is transmitted electronically instead of being sent by postal mail. Of course, most interlibrary loan materials are still sent by postal mail or fax, but who knows what the future holds!

WHAT CAN'T BE DONE WITH OPACS (YET)

Opportunities to read library books from your computer are practically nonexistent due to technical and legal complications. Manual entry of text into computers is extremely time consuming. Many features of printed materials, such as pictures, tables, charts, or even the number and variety of fonts, challenge today's best scanning equipment and software. Furthermore, there are many copyright issues centering on electronic distribution of texts that must be hashed out by legal experts, publishing companies, and authors. It is not likely that OPAC services will grow to supplant physical access to libraries in the very near future. However, a few libraries are beginning to offer the full text of journals and magazines through their OPACs, either directly of via an order-and-fax feature.

Chapters 12 and 13 describe a number of sources for electronic books and electronic journals respectively. Although the number of available electronic texts is expanding, it will probably be some time before they equal the number and diversity of materials held in a typical small college library.

■■■

Effective Use of OPACs

■■■

As the previous sections pointed out, OPACs are more than card catalogs, but they aren't full service libraries either. So your approach to selecting and using an OPAC will be different than the approach you take when selecting and using a traditional library.

Selecting the Right OPAC

Every OPAC has unique strengths and weaknesses. This is due to inherent differences in the quality, depth, and breadth of the collections they serve; disparities in the capabilities of the many OPAC software platforms; and varying goals of the administrations and library staffs at these institutions. So finding the OPAC that suits your needs merits careful study.

Internet users often select the biggest, nearest, most prestigious, most exotic, or most familiar OPAC. Here are some general hints on how to pick the right OPAC for the right job.

Essential Guides for Using OPACs

There are a number of high quality, frequently updated lists of OPACs, some of which are geographically or topically oriented. These lists also include information on the particular strengths of each OPAC's holdings or helpful instructions about the peculiarities of using or accessing each. Online sources for the major lists of OPACs are provided at the end of this chapter under "For More Information."

Define Your Quest

If you're looking for the Holy Grail, then maybe you do want to use a major university's OPAC that has a million or more titles. Others may be satisfied with the local public library's 150,000 titles, particularly if they are looking for popular literature. Smaller research libraries may also have specialized collections.

Ask Your Local Librarians and Peers

For general advice on selecting OPACs, consult the librarians at your Internet site. You might also ask your Internet-savvy peers. If your OPAC needs are for a specialized class of library holdings, you could post a note to an appropriate Usenet newsgroup, LISTSERV list, or Internet mailing list to find out which OPACs are best for searches in particular topics. (For more on Usenet, LISTSERV, and mailing lists, refer to Chapters 9, 10, and 11 respectively.)

Using a Gopher

There are a number of subject-oriented Gophers (see Chapter 17) available which include access to online catalogs. These catalogs will describe collections that are especially strong in the designated subject. You can also use the Internet-Accessible Libraries

■■■

Gopher available through Yale University (see "For More Information"). Not only can you search the list by keywords, but you can then connect directly to the OPAC from the list.

WAIS Databases

If you are looking for a library with especially strong holdings in a particular area, you might also try doing a keyword search in the WAIS database versions of the St. George-Larsen and Barron OPAC lists, which are known as "online-libraries-st-george" and "online-libraries" respectively. For example, searching in these WAIS databases for "entomology" revealed that Cornell and the University of California both have particularly strong holdings in this topic. This is no surprise to professional bug hunters, but may not be apparent to the larval researcher. For more on WAIS, refer to Chapter 18.

How to Think Like an OPAC

Dealing with an Embarrassment of Riches

If you've never used an OPAC before, you're in for a big surprise. OPAC searches can yield hundreds or even thousands of citations if you didn't select your search terms carefully. Most of us are capable of separating the wheat from the chaff when handling actual texts, but even experienced library users sometimes suffer a sense of vertigo when faced with an OPAC screen that announces "7,546 Titles Were Found."

Searches for individual authors tend to yield manageable results, but keyword or subject searches may spew screen-fulls of information to your terminal. I just typed "education" as a keyword search at the University of Washington OPAC, and was told in a matter of seconds that there were 53,216 items in the catalog with that keyword!

Dealing with an Implicit Structure

On the other hand, searches on keywords may lead to a puzzling dearth of results. Most OPACs use Library of Congress Subject Headings (LCSH) or other precise and highly structured classifications system. Subject headings which are intuitively sensible to *you* may not yield any search results, if they do not correspond precisely to an entry in the OPACs list of subject headings. For example, "learning" seems synonymous with "education," but when searching for the keyword "learn" in the same OPAC, only 502 citations were reported—a mere 1% of the documents retrieved with the keyword "education."

Although some OPACs will display subject classifications on your terminal, it can be useful to consult your local reference librarian before beginning a large-scale OPAC search. Reference books on the Library of Congress subject headings or specialized medical subject headings may also be valuable. Some libraries have begun including an online listing of the LCSH, but be aware, it is a very big list!

Precision Searches with Boolean, Adjacency, and Other Operators

Many OPACs allow you to use special operators when you do your searches. Boolean operators such as "and," "or," "nand" ("not and"), and "nor" ("not or") are particularly widespread.

Another class of operators are called "adjacency operators." For example, you can sometimes specify that two search terms be immediately adjacent to each other, in the same search field, or in one or more search fields in order to be counted as a valid item.

If you use such operators, be sure you understand how they work and how they interact. They may have varying priority (one operator in a string is acted upon before others), non-transitivity (the order in which operators are placed affects how they are acted on), or other special rules of use. Versions of "not" (such as "not" and "nand") are particularly slippery.

Special Characters or Parts of Speech in Search Terms

If terms you are searching for contain special symbols such as hyphens, apostrophes, commas, numbers, or scientific symbols, understand how the OPAC handles them before including them in a search. They may be forbidden or require special syntaxes to be recognized by the OPAC. Also be aware that certain parts of speech such as prepositions may be ignored or problematic when used in keyword or subject searches and are usually best left out except in title searches.

Wildcards: Truncation, Stems, and Reverse Stems

"Wildcard" operators allow you to specify any words containing a certain string. Similar operators called "stem" and "reverse stem" allow one to search for prefixes and suffixes. For example, in OPACs using BRS software, "map$" would search for all citations containing any words beginning with "map."

Such operators are extremely useful when used intelligently. As an extreme example of an ill-conceived use of wildcards, suppose you wanted to do a search for the discovery of the principles of genetics. Possibly interesting forms of the word "genetics" might include "gene," "genetics," "genetical," "pangenesis," and so forth. In a rush to be clever, the person who earnestly specifies a search for "disc$ and gene$" is likely to retrieve as many citations about "discourses on Genesis" and "the disco generation" as it is to retrieve citations about Mendel and DNA. Other truncation symbols include?, *, and #.

The use of wildcards can significantly increase the number of "hits" you get on a search. Some OPACs will automatically cut off a search when it reaches a certain number of matches, so you should use wildcards judiciously.

Displaying a History of Your Search Requests

Most OPACs allow you to view a list of the search requests you have made during your session. This can be extraordinarily useful for combining distinct searches into one. For example, on reviewing your history of searches, you may find that search query #17 built up from six tedious steps, and search query #29 created by another eight steps, can be combined for exactly the search you need by typing "17 and 29".

Recording Successful Searches as a Search Strategy

Suppose that you need to do exactly the same literature search every several months, and that it requires many steps to achieve the desired result. A few advanced OPACs allow you to record a search strategy that you can later recall by issuing a single command. However, this service is not likely to be available if you are a guest user of an OPAC.

Tailoring the Display of Search Results

Almost all OPACs allow you to tailor the type and amount of information shown when the results of a search are displayed, ranging from a single line per document, to full bibliographic citations each taking up one or two screens. Take advantage of this flexibility! For quick scans of results, use some form of short or review display. To uncover possible terms that will refine your search, pull up every bit of detail you can from relevant documents.

Summary

By keeping these points in mind, your OPACs experience should be remarkably rewarding. If you spend some time improvising, you'll likely hit upon unique strategies that work well for you.

ACCESSING OPACs

Since OPACs are among the most popular services of the Internet, it's not surprising that there are probably more paths to OPACs than most any other Internet service. Each access method has its peculiar advantages or target audiences.

If you are at a college, university, or other institution with a local OPAC, you may be able to enter a command from your Internet host that will connect you directly to that OPAC. The OPAC is also likely to be available on the campus Gopher (if there is one). Consult your online documentation or ask your local user services staff for help.

Most OPACs on the Internet can be accessed using Telnet, or if they are run on an IBM mainframe, with tn3270. You can get their Internet addresses from the catalogs of OPACs listed at the end of this Chapter or from online lists of OPACs like Catalist or Hytelnet (described below).

Internet Front Ends

Gopher

Gopher is a front end to online documents and services including OPACs. Yale University maintains a Gopher listing and index of library OPACs on the Internet. There is an ongoing effort to add information on the subject specialties of the various library collections described by these OPACs.

> Gopher: `yaleinfo.yale.edu 7000`
> item: `Libraries/`

For a thorough overview of using Gopher, refer to Chapter 17.

■■■

WAIS

A number of specialized library catalogs have been put into the WAIS database format, such as the Columbia University Law Library general catalog and Spanish Law collections, and several French libraries. The number of libraries accessible through WAIS is likely to grow in the coming years, especially as library software incorporating the Z39.50 protocol upon which WAIS is based becomes more widespread.

Other Internet Front Ends

Several other Internet front ends can be used to access OPACs. For example, you can get to many OPACs by telnetting to the following multipurpose services:

Internet Address	Access	Choose
liberty.uc.wlu.edu	login as "lawlib"	"to Libraries"
library.wustl.edu	login as "services"	"Remote Libraries on the Internet"

OPAC Access Software

Hytelnet

Hytelnet is a very easy to use and customize software package developed at the University of Saskatchewan. It contains a list of many Telnet accessible resources and when installed on an Internet host can automate logins to these sites. Hytelnet includes a great selection of OPACs from around the world as well as exceptionally thorough coverage of CWISs and BBSs.

If you want to try out the Hytelnet software, check with your local computer support services to see if it's installed at your local site. Or if you're feeling adventurous, you can obtain a copy of Hytelnet for your local computer. It is moderately difficult to install and may prove too challenging for the novice network user. There are currently versions of Hytelnet which will work under the VMS, DOS, Mac, Amiga, and most Unix operating systems. To try out the Hytelnet system, telnet to the public-access client:

```
Telnet:  access.usask.ca
login:   hytelnet
```

Or, get Hytelnet (and instructions on installation and customization) via FTP from:

```
FTP host:     ftp.usask.ca
directories:  /pub/hytelnet/amiga
              /pub/hytelnet/mac
              /pub/hytelnet/pc
              /pub/hytelnet/unix
              /pub/hytelnet/vms
filenames:    (many or all)
```

14 • Libraries on the Internet

■■■

Libtel

Libtel is an OPAC access program. If you want to try Libtel, it is accessible via Telnet through the University of North Carolina's CWIS, bbs.oit.unc.edu (login "bbs"). The source code for Libtel is available via FTP.

FTP host:	`rohan.sdsu.edu`	
directory:	`/pub/unix`	
filename:	`libtel.unix`	(Unix)
directory:	`/pub/vax`	
filename:	`libtel.com`	(VAX)

LIBS

LIBS is a VAX/VMS front end developed at Sonoma State University that allows users to connect to library catalogs on the Internet. You may try out the version available via Telnet, but only for evaluation purposes. If you want to use it regularly, you should download and run your own copy.

Telnet:	`vax.sonoma.edu`	(for evaluation purposes only)
login:	`LIBS`	
FTP host:	`sonoma.edu`	
directory:	`/pub`	
filename:	`libs.com`	

Catalist

Catalist is an OPAC catalog program for MS Windows. You can have Catalist running in one window displaying OPAC access information and a terminal emulation program running in another. Catalist does not automate Telnet sessions like the other services in this list. It is available via FTP from:

FTP host:	ftp.sunet.se
directory:	`/pub/library/catalist`
filenames:	(many or all)

A Starter Kit for OPAC Exploration

Here is a sample of Internet accessible OPACs throughout the world to get you started.

Internet Address	Institutional Affiliation	Login name
`library.anu.edu.au`	Australian National University	`library`
`melvyl.ucop.edu`	University of California, USA	none
`pac.carl.org`	Colorado Alliance of Research Libraries, USA	none
`ram2.huji.ac.il`	Hebrew University, Israel (features multilingual user interface!)	`aleph`

▪▪▪

There are hundreds of other OPACs on the Internet, so don't make these your default sites! If you decide to make extensive use of OPACs, be sure to get on of the catalogs listed at the end of this chapter so you can choose those OPACs which most nearly suit your needs.

SAMPLE OPAC SESSION

▪▪▪

The Diversity of OPAC Software

OPACs run on a wide variety of platforms. More than 20 OPAC software packages are commonly used and each has different syntaxes and capabilities. To further complicate matters, some of the most widely used packages can be modified heavily once implemented at a site. Some sites rely on home grown packages that may have very peculiar features and behaviors, especially when used from remote locations via Telnet.

However, there are enough similarities between OPACs that a sample session from one robust site should give you a fair indication of what using most other OPACs is like.

About this Sample Session

This section presents a session using the University of California's MELVYL system. Note that the on-screen displays have been edited slightly to make it easier to read in this text.

This sample session is somewhat long and convoluted; this is by design. It would have been simple to present a quick and easy session which immediately produced references to thousands of citations. But as you probably know from your experience with regular card catalogs, effective use of a library often requires careful consideration and reconsideration of how you define your literature search. This OPAC session is meant to reflect this reality. The first search in this example yields no results, but by modifying the search slightly and by following suggestions from MELVYL a very similar search yields more than 600 citations!

Access an OPAC

You should be able to use any one of the access methods described in "Accessing OPACs." But, to make this example as generic as possible, we'll enter MELVYL using a standard Telnet command.

```
telnet melvyl.ucop.edu

Trying 192.35.222.222...
Connected to melvyl.ucop.edu.
Escape character is '^]'.
```

■■■

Identify Your Terminal Type

You will be prompted to provide some information about your computer's terminal emulation.

```
DLA LINE 583 (TELNET) 09:17:43 01/25/94    (MELVYL.UCOP.EDU)

Please Enter Your Terminal Type Code or Type ? for a List of Codes.

TERMINAL?
```

As with many Internet services, you will usually have the option of asking what terminal types are available. In MELVYL, type "?" for this information.

```
TERMINAL? ?
Please enter the Terminal Type Code for your terminal.
Supported Terminal Types and their character codes are:


TERMINAL   TERMINAL              TERMINAL   TERMINAL
CODE                            CODE

TTY33     Teletype 33 (TTY)      BANTAM    Perkin Elmer Bant
ESPRIT    Hazeltine Esprit       ADM3A     ADM 3a
PE1100    Perkin Elmer 1100      HAZ1500   Hazeltine 1500
HARDCOPY  Decwriter/Gencom       HAZ2000   Hazeltine 2000
VT100     IBM PC (VT100)         VT100     Apple MAC (VT100)
HEATH     Heathkit H19           VT100     Dec VT100
ACT5A     Microterm Act5a        ADDS      ADDS/NCR
HP2621    Hewlett Packard HP2621 BITGRAPH  BBN Bitgraph
TI700     TI Silent 700          TTY40     Teletype 40 (TTY)
TELE920   Televideo 910, 912, 920 DISPLAY  IBM Displaywriter
TANDEM    Tandem 635X            OTHER     All Others

Please Enter Your Terminal Type Code or Type ? for a List
of Codes.

TERMINAL? vt100
```

VT100 is a commonly used terminal emulation. If selecting VT100 produces gibberish on your screen, try to logout of the session. If you can't logout, type "^]" (control right bracket), or whatever command gets you to the "telnet>" prompt, then type "quit". Find out what your terminal emulation is, then try again with this information.

■■■

Welcome to the OPAC!

Assuming all is well with your terminal emulation, MELVYL will display an introductory screen with system news and a brief orientation to the system.

```
              Welcome to the University of California's

                       MELVYL* LIBRARY SYSTEM

-------------------- =>> SYSTEM NEWS <<= --------------------
Eureka available--Type SHOW DLA
FirstSearch available--Type SHOW DLA1
TULIP now linked to some INSPEC and Current Contents
     citations. Type SHOW DLA6


------------------------------------------------------------


(c)1984. *Registered trademark of The Regents of the
University of California.
============================================================
OPTIONS:  Choose an option, or type any command to enter the
CATALOG database.

     HELP          - For help in getting started.

     [return]      - Press RETURN to choose a database
                     for searching.

     START <db>    - Type START <database name> to begin
                     searching in a database.
->
```

The "->" prompt at the bottom left corner of the screen above, is where we type our commands to MELVYL.

In case you want to exit MELVYL before completing this exercise, here's what you need to do. From any prompt type "end". This command moves you to a simple "->" prompt. Following the instructions at the top of your screen, type "logoff". This will terminate your MELVYL session.

■■■

Request a Listing of Available Services

Many OPACs contain more than one kind of service. In MELVYL, pressing the return key at the welcome screen displays the first of two pages of services, some of which are restricted for use by the University of California community.

```
                     MELVYL SYSTEM DATABASES

Library databases:
    TEN  For faster searches, type TEN;
              Ten-Year MELVYL Catalog - materials published
                   from 1983 - 1993
    CAT  Full MELVYL Catalog - UC libraries and the
                   California State Library
    PE   Periodical Titles  - California Academic Libraries
                   List of Serials

Indexes to recent articles:(for UC users only; password may be needed)

    MAGS Magazine & Journal- 1,500 magazines and journals
    NEWS Newspaper Articles- five major U.S. newspapers
    CC   Current Contents  - 6,500 scholarly journals
    CCT  Current Contents  - tables of contents of 6,500 scholarly
                             journals
    INS  INSPEC            - 4,000 physics, electronics & computing
                             journals
    MED  MELVYL MEDLINE    - 4,000 medical and life sciences journals
    COMP Computer Articles - 200 computer-related magazines and journals
    PSYC PsycINFO          - 1,300 psychology journals and publications

                                   (continued on next screen)
-----------------------------------------------------------------
Type the code for an option (for example TEN), type HELP, or type any
command.
-> TEN
```

■■■

Selecting a Database within the OPAC

For this session, we've selected the MELVYL Ten-Year database which only includes materials published in the last 10 years. Even for this brief period, MELVYL's holdings include more than 1.6 million distinct titles!

```
            Welcome to the MELVYL TEN-YEAR Catalog Database

    Contents: As of 1/25/94, approximately 1,603,698 titles representing
              3,478,900 holdings for materials in the University of
              California libraries, and the California State Library,

    Coverage: Publication dates 1984 through 1994.

                        --=>> NEWS <<=--



-----------------------------------------------------------------
OPTIONS:        Type an option and press RETURN, or type any command.

    HELP      - For help in getting started.
    E GUIDE   - For a brief guide to using the Ten-Year database.
    START     - To start over or change databases.
    END       - To end your session.
TEN-> help
```

Investigate the Online Help

It's always a good idea to investigate online help when using a new Internet service. Typing "help" in the previous screen displays a list of the basic commands in the TEN database of MELVYL.

```
You can use the TEN-YEAR database with two basic commands:

    FIND [index] [search words]to begin a search
    DISPLAY                     to display the results of a search.

For example: FIND SUBJECT JOB STRESS

For more information, type EXPLAIN FIND or EXPLAIN DISPLAY.

For a list of indexes in the TEN-YEAR database, type EXPLAIN INDEXES.
For a list of commands in the TEN-YEAR database, type EXPLAIN COMMANDS.
------------------------------------------------------------------
    OPTIONS:       Type an option and press RETURN.

                   EXP TEN      - For an explanation of database contents.
                   EXP GUIDE    - For a guide to searching the database.
                   START        - To start over or change databases.
                   END          - To end your session.

    Or type any command.


TEN->
```

Starting a Search

Now we can try a catalog search. Let's do a subject search on the topic "extinction of species" which we'll abbreviate as "species extinction." (Recall that articles and prepositions are usually not worth including in search terms unless one is doing a title search.)

```
TEN-> find su species extinction

 Search request: FIND SU SPECIES EXTINCTION
 Search result: 0 records in the TEN-YEAR Catalog database

 You may get results by redoing your search in the Title
 Word index, i.e., F TW <search words>. Type HELP for more information

TEN->
```

■■■

No Search Results!? Time to Think!

No books were found using "species extinction" as our subject. But don't give up yet! MELVYL now allows the option of doing another search by several other fields, including a title word search (TW). Let's try digging up books that have both the words "species" and "extinction" in their titles.

```
TEN-> find tw species extinction

Search request: FIND TW SPECIES EXTINCTION
Search result: 16 records in the TEN-YEAR Catalog database

Type D to display results, or type HELP.
```

Obtaining Help for Specific OPAC Options

The search string "species extinction," which did not find anything during a subject search, locates 16 titles with a title word search. We've entered "help" to obtain a brief list of display options.

```
TEN-> help

Your search request,

    FIND TW SPECIES EXTINCTION

resulted in 16 retrievals at all libraries.


You can now:                              For more information, type:
    Type D to display your search result  EXPLAIN DISPLAY

    Limit your retrievals by library      EXPLAIN AT
    Broaden or narrow your search result  EXPLAIN ADD ON
    Begin a new search                    EXPLAIN FIND
    Begin a browse                        EXPLAIN BROWSE
    Use any other command                 EXPLAIN COMMANDS

    Type SHOW SEARCH to see other current searches available for display.
    Type SHOW HISTORY to see your search history.
    Type END to end your session.

TEN->
```

▪▪▪

Displaying a Successful Search: Abbreviated Mode

We can review all of the titles retrieved by a search request. When we type "display rev" or "d rev", the display looks like this:

```
TEN -> display rev

Search request: FIND TW SPECIES EXTINCTION
Search result:  16 records in the TEN-YEAR Catalog database

Type HELP for other display options.
 1. AUSTRALIA. Endangered Species Advisory Committee.
        An Australian national strategy for the conservation of
        species...1989
 2. Australia's endangered species : the extinction dilemma. 1990
 3. Australia's endangered species : the extinction dilemma. 1990
 4. Balancing on the brink of extinction : the Endangered Species
Act...1991
 5. COHN, Jeffrey P.  The politics of extinction :...1990
 6. DELGADO-MENDOZA, Suzzette.  Extinction in the enchanted isle :... 1990
 7. ELDREDGE, Niles.  Fossils : the evolution and...1991
 8. ERICKSON, Jon, 1948-  Dying planet : the extinction of... 1991
 9. Extinction in paradise : protecting our Hawaiian species. 1989
10. KELLY, Donald M.  Near extinction : California's...1990
11. LABASTILLE, Anne.  Mama Poc : an ecologist's account...1990
12. MYERS, Norman.  Tackling mass extinction of species... 1986
13. The Road to extinction : problems of categorizing the status of...1987
14. The Road to extinction : problems of categorizing the status of...1987
15. Tropical deforestation and species extinction. 1992

Press RETURN to see the next screen.
TEN->
```

Displaying a Successful Search: Expanded Mode

Now let's ask for a "long" display of item number 1 and see if it provides any clues about how to refine the search.

```
TEN-> d long

Search request: FIND TW SPECIES EXTINCTION
Search result: 16 records in the TEN-YEAR Catalog database

Type HELP for other display options.

1.
Author:        Australia. Endangered Species Advisory
               Committee.
Title:         An Australian national strategy for the
               conservation of species and habitats
               threatened with extinction. [Canberra, ACT]:
               Australian National Parks and Wildlife
               Service, c1989.
Description:   28 p. : col. ill. ; 30 cm.
Notes:         "Draft for public comment."
Subjects:      Wildlife conservation -- Government policy --
               Australia. Nature conservation -- Government
               policy -- Australia. Endangered species --
               Australia.
Other entries: Australian National Parks and Wildlife
               Service.
Call numbers:  CAS   Mailliard QH77.A8 A85 1989 Biodiv

TEN->
```

As you can see by looking at the subject line, this book is cataloged under a number of subjects, of which "endangered species" seems to be the closest fit.

Refining a Search Based on a Partially Successful Search

So judging by the other titles associated with this particular document, it appears that a subject search for "endangered species" will very likely be fruitful.

```
TEN-> f su endangered species
   The MELVYL system is working on your request...

   Search request: F SU ENDANGERED SPECIES
   Search result:  732 records in the TEN-YEAR Catalog database

   Type D to display results, or type HELP.

TEN->
```

■■

Hitting Pay Dirt...

MELVYL responded with 732 titles!

```
TEN-> d rev

Search request: F SU ENDANGERED SPECIES
Search result:  732 records in the TEN-YEAR Catalog database

Type HELP for other display options.

 1. The 5 sea turtle species of the Atlantic and Gulf Coast of the...1991
 2. 1000 points of life, every species counts : threatened, ... 1991.
 3. 1986 IUCN red list of threatened animals. 1986
 4. 1988 IUCN red list of threatened animals. 1988
 5. 1990 IUCN red list of threatened animals. 1990
 6. AAZPA manual of Federal wildlife regulations. 1985
 7. Action plan for African primate conservation: 1986-90. 1985
 8. Action plan for Asian primate conservation, 1987-91. 1987
 9. ADAMS, Douglas, 1952-  Last chance to see. 1991
10. Alaska wildlife week unit : wildlife for the future. Endangered...1985
11. ALLEN, William B. 1928-  State lists of endangered and...1988
12. ALMENDINGER, John C.  Natural communities and rare species :
        Washington County,...1990. MAP
13. ALTENBURG, Wibe.  Etude ornithologique preliminaire... 1989
14. ALTENBURG, Wibe.  Ornithological importance of..1991
15. Amended listing of endangered wildlife of New Mexico. 1990

Press RETURN to see the next screen.
TEN->
```

...Is Just the Beginning of Effective OPAC Use!

This is where the real power of using an OPAC starts. Now that you've established a profitable search strategy, you can easily branch off to other related subject or title searches.

Ending an OPAC Session

To leave the database, type "end" followed by "logoff" to terminate your Telnet connection. MELVYL also accepts other commands to end the session, like, "quit", "adios", "ciao", and "shalom".

```
TEN -> end

Thanks for using the MELVYL Online Catalog.
Type LOGOFF and press RETURN to terminate your TELNET
session. Press RETURN for the MELVYL catalog.

-> logoff

ELAPSED TIME = 0:11:53
END OF SESSION
Connection closed by foreign host.
```

FOR MORE INFORMATION

Worldwide Lists of OPACs

The following lists provide worldwide coverage of OPACs. Although there is considerable overlap between the lists, they have different formats and emphases, so you might want to obtain all three and determine which most nearly suits your needs. Since the Gopher version is the most up-to-date, and will be kept so, it is the best choice by far.

 "University of North Texas' Accessing Online Bibliographic Databases" by Billy Barron

Gopher:	gopher.utdallas.edu *INTERNET SERVICES & INFORMATION*
menu:	Library On-Line Catalogs/
FTP host:	ftp.utdallas.edu
directory:	/pub/staff/billy/libguide
filenames:	libraries.intro
	libraries.instructions
	libraries.africa
	libraries.americas
	libraries.asia
	libraries.europe
	libraries.contacts (list of Gopher sites with this information)

"Internet Accessible Library Catalogs and Databases" by Art St. George and Ron Larsen

FTP host:	`ariel.unm.edu`
directory:	`/library`
filenames:	`internet.library`

(text only)
(Apple PostScript)
(generic PostScript)

`library.apple`
`library.ps`

(Last updated May 1992)

"Internet Libraries" by Dana Noonan

FTP host:	`sunsite.unc.edu`
directory:	`/pub/docs/about-the-net/libsoft`
filenames:	`guide1.txt`
	`guide2.txt`

(Last updated June 1992)

Topically Oriented Lists of OPACs

General

The collection of Internet-accessible OPACs maintained on the Yale University Gopher includes an index-searchable list of OPACs with subject information.

Gopher:	`yaleinfo.yale.edu 7000`
item:	`Libraries/`

Agriculture

"Not Just Cows: A Guide to Internet/Bitnet Resources in Agriculture and Related Sciences," by Willfred Drew. Contains a list of OPACs with particularly strong holdings in agricultural topics and many non-OPAC resources of interest to agricultural researchers. Available via FTP from:

FTP host:	`ftp.sura.net`
directory:	`/pub/nic`
filename:	`agricultural.list`

Medicine and Health Science

Among other things, Lee Hancock's *Internet/Bitnet Health Sciences Resources* contains information on online medical libraries. His list can be accessed in a number of ways:

FTP host:	`ftp.sura.net`	
directory:	`/pub/nic`	
filename:	`medical.resources.MM-YY`	(where MM-YY indicate the month and year of the last update)
Telnet:	`ukanaix.cc.ukans.edu`	(use VT100 emulation)
login:	`kufacts`	
select:	`Reference Shelf/ Internet Health Science Resources`	(use cursor controls to move through the screen, press "?" for help)
Gopher:	`sluava.slu.edu`	(St. Louis University)
menu:	`Library Services/SLU Health Sciences Center Library/Health Sciences Center Library/Guides to Internet Resources`	
item:	`Lee Hancock's Health Sciences Resources (Hancock List)`	

FTP Archives Specializing in OPAC Related Materials

The following FTP sites have a wealth of archived materials about OPACs. Although there is some overlap in their contents, it is worthwhile becoming familiar with each of these resources if you are an active user of OPACs.

FTP host:	`hydra.uwo.ca`
directory:	`/libsoft`
filenames:	(many or all)
FTP host:	`ftp.unt.edu`
directory:	`/pub/library`
filenames:	(many or all)

Online Discussion Groups and Lists via FTP

There are many online discussion groups dealing with OPACs and library information sciences. They range in coverage from discussion on a specific site's OPAC installation to general discussion of present and future OPAC technology. The main forum for general discussion of OPACs is PACS-L, which can be accessed via LISTSERV or as a Usenet newsgroup. The PACS-L archives are also available for searching as a WAIS database.

LISTSERV:	`PACS-L@UHUPVM1.UH.EDU`
WAIS database:	`bit.listserv.pacs-l`
Usenet newsgroup:	`bit.listserv.pacs-l`

A comprehensive and up-to-date list of most OPAC related groups is included in the "Directory of Scholarly Electronic Conferences," by Diane K. Covets of Kent State University. It is available via FTP from many sites throughout the Internet including the following:

FTP host:	`ra.msstate.edu`
directory:	`/pub/docs/words-l/Net-Stuff`
filenames:	`acadlist.readme`
	`acadlist.file1`
	`acadlist.file2`
	`acadlist.file3`
	`acadlist.file4`
	`acadlist.file5`
	`acadlist.file6`
	`acadlist.file7`
	`acadlist.file8`

As of January 1994, the "Libraries and Information Sciences" section of the list can be found in the file "acadlist.file2." However, you might want to get all of these files. This is a tremendous resource that pieces together information from many sources and makes it available in one easy to use document.

Bibliography

Rather than duplicate the efforts of others, you are encouraged to obtain a copy of one of the following references, which contain very useful bibliographies on OPACs.

Farley, L. (Ed.). "Library Resources on the Internet: Strategies for Selection and Use." August 1991. Available via FTP from:

FTP host:	`dla.ucop.edu`
directory:	`/pub/internet`
filename:	`libcat-guide`

Kalin, S. W. "Support Services for Remote Users of Online Public Access Catalogs" *RQ* 31(2) (Winter, 1991):197-213.

Stanton, D. E. "Libraries and Information Resources Networks: A Bibliography." 1991. Available via FTP from:

FTP host:	`sunsite.unc.edu`
directory:	`/pub/docs/about-the-net/libsoft`
filename:	`stanton.bib`

For more general information on libraries and the Internet, see:

Nielsen, B. "Finding it on the Internet: the Next Challenge for Librarianship." *Database* 13(5) (October 1990):105-107.

Saunders, L. M. "The Virtual Library Today" *Library Administration & Management* 6(2) (Spring 1992):66-70.

CHAPTER

15
Databases and Bibliographies

A database is a collection of information that is structured to allow easy searching and retrieval of particular items.

One of the tasks at which computers excel is the storage and retrieval of vast quantities of information such as research databases. Until recently, access to computer databases was limited. Now that a growing number of the world's computers are accessible on the Internet, a wide variety of databases are available to anyone using the Internet.

This efficient access to networked databases has also spurred an increase in the number of databases available, the types of databases available, the ways in which they can be accessed, and the demand for more. This is only the beginning!

DATABASE ACCESS

The resources described in this chapter range from relatively small, specialized datasets that you can copy to your own computer by e-mail or FTP, to huge databases with gigabytes of data that must be accessed with sophisticated database software using a Telnet, Gopher, or other connection. A few databases are easily accessible and contain information of interest to the average Internet user, while others are likely to interest only trained specialists.

A few repositories of databases have been included which are not yet on the Internet. They are described either because they are likely to be accessible though the Internet soon, or because their wealth of holdings are too extraordinary to ignore. But in many such cases, you can make inquiries about their data holdings by e-mail through the Internet and may then order CD or magnetic tape copies of the datasets of interest.

ONLINE BIBLIOGRAPHIES? WHY NOT JUST USE AN OPAC?

This chapter also includes pointers to bibliographic databases containing extensive literature citations. These bibliographies are often the product of a labor of love on the part of someone who genuinely cares about and intimately knows the literature in a particular field. Such experts have an ability to separate the wheat from the chaff and may also know about citations that would never show up in a purely mechanical search. So if there is already an authoritative, freely-available bibliography compiled by a world expert, it would be silly to spend your own money and time recreating the wheel.

DATABASE ETIQUETTE

Although these are all publicly accessible resources, you should not use them trivially. Many scholars count on these services for research activities, and excessive use for random or meaningless searches done purely "for kicks" would place a strain on the computational resources of the host computers.

■■ ■

Related Resources
■■ ■

There are many more databases on the Internet than are described in this chapter!

- Many Online Public Access Catalogs of libraries, described in Chapter 14, allow access to the kinds of databases described in this chapter.
- The archie program maintains a catalog of most of the world's anonymous FTP sites (which can themselves be thought of as databases), and is described in Chapter 16.
- Gopher (Chapter 17), WAIS (Chapter 18), CWISs (Chapter 19), and World Wide Web (Chapter 20) offer access to databases, including many that are described in this chapter.
- Databases of e-mail and other addresses are described in Chapter 21.
- Databases related to subjects covered in detail in other chapters: K-12 (Chapter 23) and health and medical sciences (Chapter 24).

Only a few commercial database services are included in this chapter. However, the bibliography at the end of this chapter gives many citations to references describing such services.

General Interest "Databases"
■■ ■

About These "Databases"
The following group of resources are not databases, strictly speaking. However, they contain a great deal of organized information that is of interest to many current and potential Internet users. If you haven't used databases before, these resources are a good starting point. They give you an accessible and immediately rewarding preview of the immense quantities of information you will encounter when using Internet databases.

X
Clearinghouse for Subject-Oriented Internet Resource Guides

Contents: Guides to Internet resources related to specific topics. As new guides are created, they are loaded onto the server and made available via anonymous FTP and Gopher. There are currently 62 guides available.

Comments: This is an ongoing project of the University of Michigan's University Library and School of Information and Library Studies (SILS) to create subject-oriented guides to resources on the Internet. Guides are produced by SILS students and other members of the Internet community. The Gopher and WWW versions include an index of the full text of all the guides.

(Continued)

Access: Gopher: una.hh.lib.umich.edu
               menu: inetdirs/

               FTP host: una.hh.lib.umich.edu
               directory: /inetdirs
               filenames: (many or all)

               WWW: http://www.lib.umich.edu/chhome.html

Contact: e-mail: i-guides@umich.edu

               Clearinghouse for Subject-Oriented Internet Resource Guides
               c/o School of Information and Library Studies
               University of Michigan
               550 East University
               Ann Arbor, MI 48109-1092 USA

               voice: (313) 747-3581
               fax: (313) 764-2475

 ## The Electronic Newsstand

Content: Electronic versions of complete issues and excerpts of over 70 magazines and
               journals, including such titles as *Discover, The Economist, Foreign Affairs, Internet
               World, Maclean's, The New Republic, The New Yorker,* and *The Times Literary
               Supplement.*

Comments: All of the materials in this service are copyrighted by their respective magazines.
               International law allows individuals to make copies of these materials for their
               own personal use. Further distribution of these materials is strictly forbidden. The
               Electronic Newsstand is not responsible for the content presented herein. Content
               is the sole responsibility of the individual publisher.

Access: Gopher: internet.com
               menu: Magazines, Periodicals, and Journals (all titles)/
               items: (many or all)

Contact: e-mail: comments@enews.com

Free-Nets and Community Nets

Contents:	Many informative files and discussion groups on health, education, politics, recreation, technology, and other topics of general interest.
Comments:	Free-Net is best described as an "open access community electronic information system" which, for registered users, also allows easy access to discussion groups including Usenet. Free-Net uses a novel interface in which the user wanders through an "electronic city." Files are in "buildings," so for example, to get information on politics and government, one would enter City Hall. This is a rather extraordinary open access system which could be set up at other sites at very little cost. Many Free-Net sites are being established around the world as part of a not-for-profit cooperative network called "The National Public Telecomputing Network" (NPTN). A Community Net is similar in concept and function, except that it may not by free of access charges. Typically, though, these charges are very reasonable.
Access:	Several Telnet accessible sites. When you first log in, you will be asked if you want to visit or register. Follow the instructions. As a visitor, your privileges in Free-Net are restricted. If you register, you will be sent a registration packet through the mail which you must fill out and return.

Telnet:	`freenet-in-a.cwru.edu`	(Cleveland)
	`freenet-in-b.cwru.edu`	
	`freenet-in-c.cwru.edu`	
	`freenet.lorain.oberlin.edu`	(Oberlin, OH; login as "guest")
	`yfn.ysu.edu`	(Youngstown, OH; login as "visitor")
	`tso.uc.edu`	(Cincinnati, OH; login as "visitor")
	`heartland.bradley.edu`	(Peoria, IL; login as "visitor")
	`cap.gwu.edu`	(Washington, DC; login as "guest"; password is "visitor")
Gopher:	`gopher.neoucom.edu 1070`	(Akron, OH)
menu:	`"Free World" Free-Nets`	(access to other Free-Nets)
	`Theme Park/Free-Nets`	
	`Transporter Room/`	
Gopher:	`golem.wcc.govt.nz`	(Wellington, New Zealand)
Contact:	e-mail: `info@nptn.org`	

(Continued)

T.M. Grundner, Ed.D
Director, National Public Telecommunication Network
Box 1987
Cleveland, Ohio 44106 USA
voice: (216) 247-5800
fax: (216) 247-3328

More info: LISTSERV list: COMMUNET@uvmvm.uvm.edu

INFO: University of Maryland Database

Contents: Gopher and FTP archive that include data and files on the following topics:
              computers, economics, literature, political science, meteorology, area studies, and
              electronic journals.

Access: Gopher: `info.umd.edu`

              Telnet: `info.umd.edu`

              FTP host: `info.umd.edu`
              directory: `info`
              filenames: (many or all)

Contact: `consult@umail.umd.edu`

              Consulting Lab at the Computer Science Center
              voice: (301) 405-1500

WUARCHIVE (Washington University Public Domain Archives)

Contents: An immense quantity of documents, Graphical Interchange Files (GIFs), and
              public domain and shareware software for the Amiga, Apple II, Atari, CP/M,
              DOS, GNU, Macintosh, Sun, TeX, Unix, VAX/VMS, and X Windows operating
              environments. This server "mirrors" a number of other FTP hosts around the
              world. When mirrored archives receive new information, it is sent also to
              wuarchive. The archive also contains files besides computer software, but
              software is its main strength.

Comments: This is a gargantuan archive. A simple listing of just the *filenames* contained in wuarchive is over 15 megabytes in size! To use this resource effectively, it is crucial that you get the README files for each directory whose contents you want to explore. We recommend that you follow the suggestions provided in these README files. There is currently a limit of 250 simultaneous users. Be patient, and keep trying.

Access: FTP host: `wuarchive.wustl.edu`
            directories: (hundreds!)

Contact: e-mail: `archives@wugate.wustl.edu`

            Washington University
            Office of the Network Coordinator
            One Brookings Drive
            Campus Box 1048
            St. Louis, MO 63130-4899 USA
            voice: (314) 935-7390

AGRICULTURE

PENpages

Contents: Online articles and brochures on agriculture, careers, health, consumer issues, weather, and other topics from the Pennsylvania State Department of Agriculture, Pennsylvania State University College of Agriculture, and Rutgers University.

Comments: Very accessible, general information of interest to almost anyone; vt100 terminal emulation recommended.

Access: Telnet: `psupen.psu.edu`
            login: <your state's 2 letter code>   (from within USA)
                      `world`   (from outside USA)
            choose: `(1) PENpages`

Contact: e-mail: `ppmenu@psupen.psu.edu`

            PENpages Coordinator
            405 Agricultural Administration Building
            The Pennsylvania State University
            University Park, PA 16802 USA
            voice: (814) 863-3449

More Info: PENpages *User Guide* available online or by request from above address.

QUERRI (Questions on University Extension Regional Resource)

Contents: A bibliographic database and catalog of information on more than 12,000 agricultural publications, abstracts, and catalogs of audio-visual materials. The North Central Region Educational Materials Project (NCREMP) does not produce or distribute the resources, but you can get full ordering instructions.

Comments: The information in this database is primarily of relevance to the north central U.S.

Access: Telnet: `isn.rdns.iastate.edu`
             dial: `querri`

Contact: e-mail: `j2.ncr@isumvs.iastate.edu`
             North Central Region Educational Materials Project
             B-10 Curtiss Hall
             Iowa State University
             Ames, IA 50011 USA
             voice: (515) 294-8802
             fax: (515) 294-4517

AREA STUDIES

INFO-SOUTH Latin American Information System

Contents: Extensive listings of citations and abstracts on a wide variety of Latin America issues.

Access: You may order hardcopy or CD versions of the datasets; to access online (via Telnet or DIALOG), you must establish an account to use this fee-based system.

             Telnet: `sabio.ir.miami.edu`

Contact: e-mail: `msgctr@sabio.ir.miami.edu`
             INFO-SOUTH
             North-South Center
             1500 Monza, P.O. Box 248014
             Coral Gables, FL 33124-3027 USA
             voice: (305) 284-4442 or (800) 752-9567
             fax: (305) 284-5089

■■■

LADB (Latin American Data Base)

Contents:	More than 10,000 articles from 1987 to the present organized under the following titles: "Chronicle of Latin American Economic Affairs," "Central America Update," and "SOURCEMEX—Economic News and Analysis on Mexico." Hundreds of articles are added each month, mostly current information originating directly from Latin America.
Comments:	You must contact LADB to arrange access.
Access:	After contacting LADB, access is via the Internet or by a modem call to an 800 number.
Contact:	To establish access, contact:

e-mail: `ladbad@bootes.unm.edu`

Roma Arellano
Latin American Institute
University of New Mexico
801 Yale NE
Albuquerque, NM 87131-1016 USA

voice: (505) 277-6839

More Info:	There is a LISTSERV list devoted to discussion about this database.

`ch-ladb@unmvma.unm.edu`

■■■

ARTIFICIAL INTELLIGENCE

■■■

✗

Bibliographic Mail Server
for Artificial Intelligence Literature

Contents: Bibliography of more than 26,000 references in artificial intelligence.

Comments: Most appropriate for researchers already very familiar with artificial intelligence.

Access: Via a mail server. To get a basic orientation to this service, send the following e-mail message. You can specify that the output should be sent to you in English, as shown below:

```
mail:     lido@cs.uni-sb.de
subject:  lidosearch info english
message:  (none needed)
```

Contact: e-mail: bib-l@cs.uni-sb.de

Dr. Alfred Kobsa
Department of Information Science
University of Konstanz
D-W-7750 Konstanz 1 Germany
voice: + 49 75 31 88 1

✗

University of California at Irvine Repository of Machine
Learning Databases and Domain Theories

Contents: Databases and domain theories useful for evaluating learning algorithms.

Comments: The dataset files come in pairs: "<filename>.data" contains raw data and "<filename>.names" contains documentation about the dataset file. Some of the files in the archive are not datasets, but in fact are used to generate datasets. If you have datasets of possible interest, you are encouraged to submit them!

Access: FTP host: ics.uci.edu
             directory: /pub/machine-learning-databases
             filenames: (many or all)

Via mail server:

```
mail:     archive-server@ics.uci.edu
subject:  (none needed)
message:  help
```

Contact: e-mail: `ml-repository@ics.uci.edu`
                          or
                          `aha@insight.cs.jhu.edu`
                  Patrick M. Murphy
                  Department of Information and Computer Science
                  University of California, Irvine
                  Irvine, CA 92717-3425 USA
                  voice: (714) 856-5011

Astronomy / Space Science

 ### Lunar and Planetary Institute Gazetteer of Planetary Features and Planetary Bibliography

Contents: Information about most major physiographic features of the planets and satellites
                   of our solar system, and references to maps on which they may be located. If
                   you've ever wanted to know about a particular crater on the backside of Titan, this
                   is the database for you. Also includes access to the *Electronic Lunar and Planetary
                   Information Bulletin (ELPIB)*.

Comments: Part of a larger information system run by LPI which also contains an online
                   catalog of monographs, documents, and journals with over 28,000 references.

Access: Telnet: `lpi.jsc.nasa.gov`
                   username: `LPI`

Contact: Lunar and Planetary Institute
                   3600 Bay Area Boulevard
                   Houston, TX 77058-1113 USA

■■■ ■ ı

NED (NASA/IPAC Extragalactic Database)

Contents: Extensive information on over 200,000 extragalactic objects (galaxies, quasars, infrared and radio sources) and database software to search raw data, associated bibliographies, and literature abstracts. Much of the software and some of the data are available from the FTP host for copying. Includes online tutorial.

Comments: X-windows interface is available for those directly connected to the Internet.

Access: Telnet: `ned.ipac.caltech.edu`
               login: `ned`

Contact: e-mail: `ned@ipac.caltech.edu`
               NED c/o IPAC
               MS 100-22
               California Institute of Technology
               Pasadena, CA 91125 USA
               voice: (818) 397-9503

More Info: FTP host: `ipac.caltech.edu`
               directories: `/ipac-docs`
                            `/ipac-sw`
                            `/ned`

NODIS (NSSDC's (National Space Science Data Center) Online Data & Information Service)

Contents: Official clearinghouse for NASA data; contains a directory of publicly available data. Datasets referenced by this service include: global change datasets, Nimbus-7 GRID TOMS data, Interplanetary Medium Data (OMNI), Geophysical Models, International Ultraviolet Explorer Data, Astronomical Data Center, Voyager and other planetary images, Earth observation data, and star catalogs. The Telnet front end also allows access to the Standards and Technology Information System, back issues of CANOPUS newsletters, etc.

Comments: The data can be purchased in CD-ROM, diskette, or magnetic tape formats. You can set up an official account with userid and password if you plan to use NODIS regularly.

Access: Telnet: `nssdca.gsfc.nasa.gov`
               login: `NSSDC or NODIS`

Contact: e-mail: `request@nssdca.gsfc.nasa.gov`
                National Space Science Data Center
                Request Coordination Office
                NASA Goddard Space Flight Center
                Code 633
                Greenbelt, MD 20771 USA
                voice: (301) 286-6695

SDDAS (Southwest Research Data Display and Analysis System)

Contents: Space, magnetosphere, and atmospheric data collected from a number of
                satellites—currently, Dynamic Explorers 1 and 2, UARS Partial Environment
                Monitor, and TSS-1 ROPE.

Comments: This service can only be accessed through an X-windows terminal. Although you
                can "take it for a spin" without establishing an account, substantial use requires
                authorization from the contact person listed below. The service is menu driven,
                easy to use, and provides extraordinary visual display of the datasets.

Access: Telnet: `espsun.space.swri.edu 10000`   (X-windows only!)

Contact: e-mail: `sddas-help@pemrac.space.swri.edu`

                Dr. J. D. Winningham
                Southwest Research Institute
                Division of Instrumentation and Space Sciences
                P.O. Drawer 28510
                San Antonio, TX 78228-0510 USA
                voice: (512) 522-3259

More Info: *User's Guide* mailed to authorized users; detailed listing of data holdings can be
                requested from sddas-help@pemrac.space.swri.edu.

SEDS (Students for the Exploration and Development of Space)

Contents: GIF and TIFF images or planets, eclipses, and other astronomical objects and
                events; animated movies in a number of formats (software to play the movies is
                also available in the same directory); information about spacecraft; satellite data; a
                number of astronomical electronic journals; and astronomical computer programs.

Access: FTP host: `seds.lpl.arizona.edu`
                directory: `/pub`

Contact: e-mail: `ftpadmin@seds.lpl.arizona.edu`

■■

SIMBAD (Set of Identifications, Measurements, and Bibliography for Astronomical Data)

Contents: Data and bibliographic entries for stars and subsets of non-stellar objects.

Comments: Currently, this service is for use by astronomers with NASA or NSF funding. This service may become available via a mail server in the future.

Access: Accessible through Telnet, but one must have an account.

Contact: e-mail: `simbad@cfa.harvard.edu`
SIMBAD c/o Computation Facility
Smithsonian Astrophysical Laboratory
60 Garden St., MS 39
Cambridge, MA 02138 USA
voice: (617) 495-7301

Spacelink

Contents: General purpose databases and interactive system containing information about NASA and NASA activities. A large number of possible curricular activities for elementary and secondary science classes.

Comments: A tremendously valuable resource for elementary and secondary science teachers. Very easy to use (but sometimes slow!). In your first Telnet session, you will be prompted to create a unique userid and password for subsequent sessions. Files of interest can be downloaded during an interactive Telnet session.

Access: Telnet: `spacelink.msfc.nasa.gov` or `xsl.msfc.nasa.gov`
login: `newuser`
password: `newuser`

FTP host: `ames.arc.nasa.gov`
directory: `/pub/SPACE`

Contact: Spacelink Administrator
Mail Code CA-21
Public Affairs Office
Marshall Space Flight Center
Huntsville, AL 35812 USA
voice: (205) 544-0038

Yale Bright Star Catalog

Contents: Machine-readable version of the 4th Edition of the Yale Bright Star Catalog
             including such variables as photoelectric magnitudes, MK spectral types,
             parallaxed and radial velocity, comments (indication and identification of
             spectroscopic and occulation binaries), projected rotational velocities, variability,
             spectral characteristics, duplicity, and group membership.

Access: FTP:
             MS-DOS version:
             FTP host: `pomona.claremont.edu`
             directory: `/yale_bsc.dir`
             filenames: (many or all)

             UNIX version:
             FTP host: `uxc.cso.uiuc.edu`
             directory: `/pub/star-data/yale`
             filenames: (all files in all subdirectories)

Contact: e-mail: `jdishaw@hmcvax.claremont.edu`

More Info: FTP host: `pomona.claremont.edu`
             directory: `/yale_bsc.dir`
             filenames: `read.me`
                             `yaleread.me`

BIOLOGY

Biology-related materials that focus specifically on human health and genetics are in
Chapter 24, while those that focus on general biology or non-human biology are located
here.

 ### ANU Bioinformatics Facility (Australian National University)

Contents: Combined Gopher, FTP, and WWW server offering information on biodiversity,
             complex systems, landscape ecology, medical information, molecular biology,
             neuroscience, viruses (biological), and weather and global monitoring. Also offers
             access to the archives of mailing lists.

∎∎∎

(Continued)

Access:	Gopher:	`life.anu.edu.au`
	FTP host:	`life.anu.edu.au`
	directory:	`/pub`
	WWW:	`http://life.anu.edu.au/home.html`
Contact:	e-mail: `David.Green@anu.edu.au`	

Dr. David G. Green
Research School of Biological Sciences &
Centre for Information Science Research
Australian National University
GPO Box 475
Canberra 2601 Australia

voice: +61 6 249 2490 (RABS) or +61 6 249 5031 (ANUSF)
fax: +61 6 249 4437 or +61 6 247 3425

Bibliography of Theoretical Population Genetics

Contents:	A comprehensive bibliographic listing of articles on theoretical population genetics up to 1980; a must for any serious population geneticist.
Comments:	The two letters at ends of filenames, as in "bible.ac", indicate the range of primary author's last names in citations contained in each file.

Access:	FTP host:	`evolution.genetics.washington.edu`
	directory:	`/pub/bible`
	filenames:	(many or all)
Contact:	e-mail: `joe@genetics.washington.edu`	

Biodiversity and Biological Collections Gopher

Contents:	Material largely of interest to systematists and organismal biologists. Includes access to catalogs of biological collections at Harvard and Cornell Universities, taxonomic authority files, directories of biologists, reports of standards bodies, the archive of the TAXACOM online discussion list, access to electronic journals (*Flora On-line, The Bean Bag,* and *Erin Newsletter*), information on biodiversity projects (MUSE, Neodata, and Smasch), and pointers to other biology-oriented Gophers.

Access:	Gopher:	`huh.harvard.edu`
	menus:	(many or all)

■■■

Contact: e-mail: `beach@huh.harvard.edu`

James H. Beach
Data Administrator
MCZ, Herbaria, Arnold Arboretum
22 Divinity Avenue
Cambridge, MA 02138 USA
voice: (617) 495-1912
fax: (617) 495-9484

 ## Herbarium Mail Data Server

Contents: Currently, three datasets: 1) type specimens of the mint family from the Harvard Herbaria, comprising 1100 records; 2) complete herbarium catalog of the Kellogg Biological Station Herbarium, consisting of 6000 specimen records; 3) the Flora of Mt. Kinabalu specimen database of 16,300 specimen records of all known vascular plant collections from the mountain. Key word queries can be based on family, genus, species, locality, dates, and collector's names.

Access: By mail servers, to separate sites for the three datasets:

Harvard Mint Types   `herbdata@huh.harvard.edu`
Kellogg Herbarium   `herbdata@kbs.msu.edu`
Mt. Kinabalu Flora   `herbdata@herbarium.bpp.msu.edu`

To get started, send the following message to one of the three mail servers above.

```
mail:      <mail-server-address>
subject:   (none needed)
message:   help
           replyaddress=<your.internet.address>
```

E-mail addresses for sending corrections and annotations to the specimens:

Harvard: David Boufford
                 `boufford@huh.harvard.edu`
Kellogg: Steve Tonsor
                 `tonsor@kbs.msu.edu`
Kinabalu: John Beaman
                 `beaman@ibm.cl.msu.edu`

(Continued)

Contact: e-mail: beach@huh.harvard.edu
                  James H. Beach
                  Data Administrator
                  MCZ, Herbaria, Arnold Arboretum
                  22 Divinity Avenue
                  Cambridge, MA 02138 USA
                  voice: (617) 495-1912
                  fax: (617) 495-9484

More Info: FTP host: huh.harvard.edu
                  directory: /pub
                  filenames: (all files in the directory deal with ongoing taxonomic database
                                projects)
                  LISTSERV list: taxacom@harvarda.harvard.edu (Biological Systematics)
                  Taxacom list archives at:
                  Gopher: huh.harvard.edu
                  menu: Taxacom Services/

IUBio Archive for Biology (Indiana University Archive for Chemical and General Biology)

Contents: Molecular biology and chemistry software for DOS, MAC, etc.

Comments: Although this is not a database strictly speaking, it contains many software tools
                  useful for working with chemistry and biology databases. Getting the document
                  "Archive.doc" via FTP will make it easier for you to use this service.

Access: FTP host: ftp.bio.indiana.edu
                  directory: /chemistry

Contact: e-mail: archive@bio.indiana.edu
                  Don Gilbert
                  BioComputing Office
                  Biology Department
                  Indiana University
                  Bloomington, IN 47405 USA

More Info: FTP host: ftp.bio.indiana.edu
                  filename: Archive.doc

Jackson Laboratory Gopher and WWW Servers

Contents: Information about the laboratory, mouse resources, mouse DNA catalog, information on the lab's training program, and research reports.

Access: Gopher: `gopher.jax.org`
          menus: `Information at The`
                     `Jackson Laboratory/`

          WWW: `http://www.jax.org/`

Contact: e-mail: `computing@jax.org`
          The Jackson Laboratory Computing Service
          600 Main Street
          Bar Harbor, ME 04609-0800 USA
          voice: (207) 288-3371

 ## QUEST Protein Database Center

Contents: Graphical 2-D gel database that allows users to select and magnify images of proteins

Access: WWW: `http://siva.cshl.org/index.html`

Contact: e-mail: `boutell@netcom.com`
          Thomas Boutell
          Scientific Programmer
          Quest Protein Database Center
          Cold Spring Harbor, NY 11724 USA
          voice: (516) 323-8735
          fax: (516) 367-8818

 ## The W. M. Keck Center for Genome Informatics

Contents: Software and data supporting various informatics projects on topics including *Aspergillus nidulans*, domestic animals, crops, and the Genome Topographer package (with a visual interface).

Access: WWW: `http://keck.tamu.edu/cgi.html`

■■

(Continued)

Contact: e-mail: `leland@straylight.tamu.edu`
                  Leland Ellis, Ph.D.
                  Director, W. M. Keck Center for Genome Informatics
                  Institute of Biosciences and Technology
                  Texas A&M University
                  2121 Holcombe
                  Houston, TX 77030 USA
                  voice: (713) 677-7612
                  fax: (713) 677-7963

BUSINESS AND ECONOMICS

■■

X   **Budget of the United States Government,
               Fiscal Year 1995**

Contents: A complete copy of President Clinton's 1995 budget, including: background
                  information and historical tables, and an index.

Access: Gopher: `gopher.esa.doc.gov`
                  menu: `Budget of the United States Government, Fiscal`
                               `Year 1995/`
                  items: (many or all)

Contact: e-mail: `awilliams@esa.doc.gov`
                  Amy Williams
                  Rm. 4885
                  Office of Business Analysis
                  U.S. Commerce Department
                  Washington, DC 20230 USA
                  voice: (202) 482-5371
                  fax: (202) 482-2164

Economic Bulletin Board (EBB)
U.S. Commerce Department

Contents: Current business statistics, Defense Conversion Subcommittee (DCS) information, EBB and agency information, East Europe trade leads, economic indicators, employment statistics, energy statistics, foreign trade, general information files, industry statistics, International Monetary Insight (IMI) reports, monetary statistics, national income and products accounts, press releases from the U.S. Trade representative, price and productivity statistics, regional economic statistics, social and environmental files, special studies reports, summaries of current economic conditions, Trade Opportunity Program (TOP), U.S. Treasury action results, USDA agricultural leads.

Comments: This is a free version of the government's bulletin board; updated daily. Files are in a format for loading into a Lotus 1-2-3 database.

Access: Gopher: `una.hh.lib.umich.edu`
              menu: `ebb/`
              items: (many or all)

Contacts: e-mail: `grace.york@um.cc.umich.edu` (Grace York) or
                      `awilliams@esa.doc.gov` (Amy Williams)
                      `dbarber@sansfoy.hh.lib.umich.edu` (David Barber - technical questions)

              Grace York
              313 Hatcher Graduate Library
              The University of Michigan
              Ann Arbor, MI 48109-1205 USA

              voice: (313) 764-0410
              fax: (313) 764-0259

              Amy Williams
              Rm. 4885
              Office of Business Analysis
              U.S. Commerce Department
              Washington, DC 20230

              voice: (202) 482-5371
              fax: (202) 482-2164

              David Barber
              205A Hatcher Graduate Library
              The University of Michigan
              Ann Arbor, MI 48109-1205 USA

              voice: (313) 936-2363
              fax: (313) 764-0259

■■■

 ## Economic Conversion Information Exchange (ECIX)

Contents: Information on the conversion of U.S. funds from military to civilian programs. Includes information on the economic and defense impacts, programs and laws, people and organizations involved in the conversion, economic and demographic information on affected areas, case studies and "best practices," technology issues, regional statistics, and an index of all the information.

Access: Gopher: `ecix.doc.gov` or `gopher.esa.doc.gov`
            menu: `Economic Conversion Information Exchange/`
            items: (many or all)

Contact: e-mail: `awilliams@esa.doc.gov`
            Amy Williams
            Rm. 4885
            Office of Business Analysis
            U.S. Commerce Department
            Washington, DC 20230
            voice: (202) 482-5371
            fax: (202) 482-2164

 ## Nasdaq Financial Executive Journal

Contents: Quarterly journal offering expert opinions of major issues on corporate finance and investor relations.

Comments: This is a joint project of the Legal Information Institute at Cornell Law School and the Nasdaq[SM] Stock Market.

Access: WWW: `http://www.law.cornell.edu/nasdaq/nasdaqtoc.html`

Contact: e-mail: `nasdaq@www.law.cornell.edu` (journal contact)
                   `Thomas_Bruce@cornell.edu` (server contact)

 ## NYSERNet Special Collections: Business and Economic Development

Contents: A collection of items from a number of sources. Includes: Asian business information, economic announcements, the "National Trade Databank's International Business Practices Guide" and its "U.S. Industrial Outlook," industry profiles from the Small Business Administration, and more.

Access: Gopher: `nysernet.org`
               menu: `Special Collections: Business and Economic`
                              `Development`
Contact: e-mail: `info@nysernet.org`
               NYSERNet, Inc.
               200 Elwood Davis Rd.
               Suite 103
               Liverpool, NY 13088-6147 USA
               voice: (315) 453-2912
               fax: (315) 453-3052

U.S. Department of Agriculture Economics and Statistics Service

Contents: Statistical and economic data on worldwide textile fiber production, farm
               production expenses, European Community wheat supply, milk and dairy
               product sales, food and spending in American households, U.S. meat supply and
               consumption, fertilizer use, land, water, conservation, and more!

Comments: This is a joint project of the Albert R. Mann Library, Cornell University and The
               U.S. Department of Agriculture Economic Research Service National Agricultural
               Statistics Service.

               The files are mostly stored in Lotus 1-2-3 format and must be downloaded to use.
               They can be opened by either Lotus 1-2-3 or Microsoft Excel, or other Lotus 1-2-3
               compatible software. Using your own Gopher is the recommended mode of
               access, as it makes downloading easier, and reduces the load on the server.

Access: Gopher: `usda.mannlib.cornell.edu`   (preferred method)

               Telnet: `usda.mannlib.cornell.edu`
               login: `usda`   (lower case)

               FTP host: `usda.mannlib.cornell.edu`
               directory: `/usda`

Contact: e-mail: `oyr1@cornell.edu`
               Oya Y. Rieger
               Numeric Files Librarian
               Mann Library
               Cornell University
               Ithaca, NY 14853 USA
               voice: (607) 255-7960

COMPUTER SOFTWARE

General Information about Computer Software Databases

There are countless archives of computer software available through the Internet. This section is not meant to be a comprehensive listing, just a sampling. In particular, you should examine the contents of WUARCHIVE, described in the *General Interest "Databases"* section of this chapter.

 COSMIC

Contents: A huge collection of computer software for a wide variety of applications and operating systems created under projects funded by NASA. The COSMIC staff can also perform searches through the COSMIC database to locate programs appropriate to your interests and needs.

Comments: Most of the software must be purchased. The intended users are U.S. citizens.

Access: FTP access to the catalog. The catalog is 5 megabytes in size. You might want to consider getting information via the e-mail contact before retrieving this file.

        FTP host: `cossack.cosmic.uga.edu`
        directory: `/catalog`
        filenames: (in separate directories for domestic and international users)

Contact: e-mail: `service@cossack.cosmic.uga.edu`
        COSMIC
        The University of Georgia
        382 East Broad Street
        Athens, GA 30602 USA
        voice: (404) 542-3265

 SUPERSFT (IBM Supercomputing Program Database)

Contents: Catalog of programs suitable for use on IBM supercomputers using vector or parallel processing. The actual programs are not available through this service. If you have written such programs, you can submit information for inclusion in the catalog.

Access: Via a LISTSERVer. Example:

```
mail:      listserv@uicvm.cc.uic.edu
subject:   (none needed)
message:   (sample messages shown below)
get supersft help      (to get supersft help)
get supersft index     (for an index of files)
get filename filetype  (to obtain a particular file of
                        interest from the supersft index
                        list)
```

Contact: e-mail: supersft@uicvm.cc.uic.edu
             Supercomputing Support Office
             University of Illinois at Chicago
             Computer Center (mail code 135)
             Box 6998
             Chicago, IL 60680 USA
             voice: (312) 996-2981

VxWorks Users Group Archives

Contents: VxWorks operating environment programs and information.

Access: Via FTP:
             FTP host: thor.atd.ucar.edu
             directories: /pub/vx
             Via mail server:

```
mail:      vxworks_archive@ncar.ucar.edu
subject:   (none needed)
message:   send index
```

Contact: e-mail: thor@thor.atd.ucar.edu
                     ftpmaster@thor.atd.ucar.edu (for problems with the server)
             Richard Neitzel
             National Center for Atmospheric Research
             Box 3000
             Marshall Field Site
             Boulder, CO 80307-3000 USA
             voice: (303) 497-2057 or (303) 497-2060

██

ECOLOGY AND ENVIRONMENT

██

General Information about Ecological and Environmental Databases

A printed periodical called "The Green Library Journal: Environmental Topics in the Information World" aims to disseminate information about environmental databases and international environmental information centers. For more information about "The Green Library Journal," contact:

e-mail: `anna@idui1.csrv.uidaho.edu`
Maria Jankowska, Editor
Green Library Journal
University of Idaho Library
Moscow, Idaho 83843-4198 USA
voice: (208) 885-6260
fax: (208) 885-6817

CEAM (Center for Exposure Assessment Modeling)

Contents:	Environmental simulation models for urban and rural non-point sources, conventional and toxic pollution of streams, lakes and estuaries, tidal hydrodynamics, geochemical equilibrium, and aquatic food chain bioaccumulation.
Comments:	All of the BBS materials are not represented on the FTP server, but only those that do not require special instructions. All files are for use on DOS computers and are in the public domain.

Access: FTP host: `dggis.rtpnc.epa.gov`
          directory: `/pub/athena/`   (help files)
                      `/pub/athena/DOS`   (simulation files)

          modem: (706) 546-3402
          settings: data=8, parity=N, stop=1   (1200-14,400 baud)

          WWW: `ftp://dggis.rtpnc.epa.gov/pub/athens/wwwhtml/`

Contact: e-mail: `catherine@athens.ath.epa.gov`
          Catherine Green
          Center for Exposure Assessment Modeling
          Environmental Research Laboratories
          U.S. Environmental Protection Agency
          960 College Station Road
          Athens, GA 30605-2720 USA
          voice: (706) 546-3549
          fax: (706) 546-3340
          David W. Disney (BBS Sysop)
          voice: (706) 546-3590

■■

✗ Energy and Climate Information Exchange (ECIX)

Contents: Archive of files on environmental issues including air and water quality, land-use, energy, waste, wildlife and environmental education programs. Provides ongoing communication between individuals and organizations active in these areas.

Comments: The EcoNet ECIX is supported by the Joyce Mertz-Gilmore Foundation and the Energy Foundation.

Access: FTP host: `igc.org`
              directories: `/pub/ECIX/`
                             `pub/ECIXfiles`

Contact: e-mail: `larris@igc.org`
              Lelani Arris, Project Director
              EcoNet Energy and Climate Information Exchange
              Box 1061
              Jasper, Alberta T0E 1E0 Canada
              voice: (403) 852-4057   fax:(403) 852-5173

✗ US EPA Online Library System (OLS) (U.S. Environmental Protection Agency)

Contents: The EPA OLS is an online bibliographic database composed of citations submitted by EPA librarians around the U.S. The citations cover many sources, including those not held by the EPA. The databases available are: The National Catalog Database (EPA report bibliographic data and abstracts from the National Technical Information Service (NTIS), and bibliographic information from the Online Computer Library Center (OCLC)); The Hazardous Waste Database (bibliographic information on hazardous waste materials in the EPA Library Network); Environmental Financing Information Network (information on financing opportunities for state and local environmental projects, includes abstracts and case studies); Clean Lakes Database (information on restoration techniques, water quality assessment, lake problems, modeling, lake ecology, and other related topics); regional databases for regions I (Boston), V (Chicago), and IX (San Francisco).

Access: Telnet: `epaibm.rtpnc.epa.gov`
              login: `public`
              choose: `1 (OLS)`

Contact: For information on searching OLS, contact the nearest EPA library.
               Jonda Byrd, Manager of the National Library Program
              voice: (513) 487-4650
              Technical assistance:
              John Knight   voice:(919) 541-2794

More Info: Copies of OLS documentation: Research Triangle Park Library
               voice: (919) 541-2777

EDUCATION

IETF/RARE Catalogue of Network Training Materials (Internet Engineering Task Force/Resaux Associes pour la Recherche Europeenne–The Association of European Networks)

Contents: Catalog of network training materials from trainers around the world. Materials are not limited to Internet training, but include other networks, such as BITNET.

Access:
Gopher: mailbase.ac.uk
menu: Mailbase Lists - F-J/itti-networks/Other Files/
item: tms-list.txt

Contact: e-mail: margaret.isaacs@ncl.ac.uk

MOLIS (Minority Online Information Service)

Contents: Up-to-date information on Black and Hispanic colleges and universities, fellowships and scholarships, and other announcements and information of interest. Institutional information includes contact information, data on faculty and students, and granting opportunities. Also see FEDIX in the Grants section of this chapter.

Comments: First time users will be asked to enter contact information.

Access:
Telnet: fedix.fie.com
userid: new
select: 2 Minority College & University Capability
            Information (MOLIS)
modem: (800) 626-6547
            (301) 975-0103
settings: data=8, parity=N, stop=1   (1200-9600 baud)

Contact: e-mail: comments@fedix.fie.com
Federal Information Exchange
555 Quince Orchard Rd.
Suite 200
Gaithersburg, MD 20878 USA
help line: (301) 975-0103

X   Online Database for Distance Education

Contents: Information about distance education courses run by institutions in the
Commonwealth, a worldwide directory of distance teaching institutions and a
bibliographic database of literature about distance education. Courses and
literature database offers a hierarchical subject classification for searching as well
as keyword entry. Institutions are searchable by world regions and countries.

Comments: Access is currently free.

Access: Telnet: `acsvax.open.ac.uk`
login: `<the_name_of_your_country>` [no spaces]
account code: `AAA`

Contact: e-mail: `n.ismail@open.ac.uk`   (Internet)
e-mail: `n.ismail@uk.ac.open`   (Janet)

International Centre for Distance Learning (ICDL)
c/o The Open University, Walton Hall
Milton Keynes, MK7 6AA United Kingdom

voice: + 44 908 653537
fax: + 44 908 654173

GENETICS AND MOLECULAR BIOLOGY

Materials in the fields of genetics and molecular biology have been moved to either
the biology section of this chapter, or Chapter 24. Only those materials that focus specifically on human health and genetics are in Chapter 24, while the remaining resources are
in the Biology section above.

GEOGRAPHY AND GEOLOGY

 Geographic Name Server

Contents: Currently contains geographic information for U.S. cities, counties, states, some natural features taken from the U.S. Geodetic Survey, and the U.S. Postal Service. There is some international information. Variables stored include names, elevation, latitude, longitude, population, telephone area code, and ZIP codes where appropriate; many other variables are in the works.

Comments: Please enter "help" and "info" before using this service for instructions, recent changes, and answers to commonly asked questions. The output from this program is most easily used as input for other software packages.

Access: Telnet: `martini.eecs.umich.edu 3000` (Don't forget port 3000!)

Contact: e-mail: `libert@citi.umich.edu` (Tom Libert)
voice: (313) 936-0827

GLIS (Global Land Information System)

Contents: A database of information about earth science datasets, containing online samples for evaluation.

Comments: Online requests can be made for datasets of interest.

Access: Telnet: `glis.cr.usgs.gov`

Contact: e-mail: `glis@glis.cr.usgs.gov`
voice: (800) 252-GLIS

GRANTS AND AWARDS

 American Philosophical Association

Contents: Grants, fellowships and academic positions, primarily of interest to philosophers, but also many of interest to scholars in the humanities generally. Sources of funding described include NEH, NSF, ACLS, listing of academic and non-academic jobs, and stipends for summer institutes.

Many other resources of interest, besides funding and jobs, are in this bulletin board.

Comments: Although some of this information is available elsewhere, this is a convenient central source for humanities scholars.

Access: Telnet: `atl.calstate.edu`
           login: `apa`

Contact: e-mail: `traiger@oxy.edu`
            Saul Traiger
            Department of Philosophy
            Cognitive Science Program
            Occidental College
            Los Angeles, CA 90041 USA
            voice: (213) 259-2901

 FEDIX (Federal Information Exchange)

Contents: Information on Federal education and research programs (including descriptions, eligibility, funding, deadlines); scholarships, fellowships, and grants; used government research equipment; new funding for specific research and education activities from the "Commerce Business Daily," "Federal Register," and other sources; and minority assistance research and education programs.

Comments: Comprehensive education and research related agency information comes from the Department of Energy, Office of Naval Research, National Aeronautics and Space Administration, Air Force Office of Scientific Research, and Federal Aviation Administration. The National Science Foundation, Department of Housing and Urban Development, Department of Commerce, Department of Education, and National Security Agency are providing minority assistance information exclusively.

(Continued)

Access:	Telnet:	`fedix.fie.com`
	userid:	`new`
	select:	`3 Federal Opportunities (FEDIX)`
	modem:	(800) 783-3349
	settings:	data=8, parity=N, stop=1	(1200-9600 baud)

Contact: e-mail: `comments@fedix.fie.com`

Federal Information Exchange
555 Quince Orchard Rd.
Suite 200
Gaithersburg, MD 20878 USA

More Info: help line: (301) 975-0103 (M-F, 8:30 - 4:30 ET)

SPIN (Sponsored Programs Information Network)

Contents: Database of funding opportunities from corporate, Federal, and other sources for educational researchers and institutions.

Access: Via tn3270. Account required.

Contact: Sponsored Programs Information Network
Research Foundation of the State University of New York
Box 9
Albany, NY 12201-0009 USA
voice: (518) 434-7150

STIS (Science and Technology Information System)

Contents: National Science Foundation publications, including NSF Bulletin, Guide to NSF Programs, grants booklet including application forms, grants program announcements, press releases, NSF telephone book, reports of National Science Board, abstracts and descriptions of research projects currently funded by NSF, and analytical reports and news from the International Programs division.

Comments: The Gopher, Telnet, and modem front ends are very good (even fun!) and feature prompts and full screen menus, online viewing of documents, database search utilities, provisions for downloading, and tutorials. It is well worth your while to work through the "30-Second User's Guide" offered in the help menu. Gopher access is probably the easiest to use, while FTP is the most difficult.

(Continued)

Access:	WAIS:	`nsf-awards` and `nsf-pubs`
	Gopher:	`gopher.nsf.gov`
	Telnet: login:	`stis.nsf.gov` `public`
	FTP host: directory: filename:	`stis.nsf.gov` (all directories) (all subdirectories and files)
	modem: settings:	(703) 306-0212 data=7, parity=E, stop=1 (1200-9600 baud)
Contact:	e-mail:	`stis-request@nsf.gov` (technical help) `stisinfo@nsf.gov` (information on STIS itself)

Dr. STIS
National Science Foundation
Office of Information Systems
Room 401
1800 G. Street, NW
Washington, D.C. 20550 USA

voice: (202) 357-7555
fax: (202) 357-7745

History

General Information about History Databases

The FTP host "ra.msstate.edu" is a great source to check periodically if you want to keep abreast of developments in history databases. The directory listed below also contains many online archives, articles, bibliographies, and other electronic documents. The archives are maintained by Don Mabry of Mississippi State University.

FTP host: `ra.msstate.edu`
directory: `/pub/docs/history`

1492: An Ongoing Voyage

Contents: Images (GIF) of textual and graphical primary documents describing events and
             cultures in the Americas in the 15th Century. The exhibit is divided into six
             sections: What Came to Be Called "America;" The Mediterranean World;
             Christopher Columbus: Man and Myth; Inventing America; Europe Claims
             America; and the Epilogue.

Comments: These materials may not be republished or used for a commercial purpose. The
             World Wide Web version offers a "guided tour" of the exhibit. Exhibit provided by
             the Library of Congress.

Access: FTP host: `ftp.loc.gov`
             directory: `/pub/exhibit.images/1492.exhibit`

             WWW: `http://sunsite.unc.edu/expo/1492.exhibit/Intro.html`

Contact: e-mail: `kell@seq1.loc.gov`
             K. D. Ellis
             Special Projects Office
             Library of Congress
             Washington, DC 20540-9100 USA

 MEMDB (Medieval and Early Modern Data Bank)

Contents: Data on western Europe between 800-1800 A.D. Information includes wages,
             prices, housing, mortality, property, charity, nutrition, etc.

Comments: Fee-based account must be set up to access MEMDB through the RLIN (Research
             Libraries Information Network) system.

Access: Telnet: `rlg.stanford.edu`

Contacts: MEMDB: The Medieval and Early Modern Data Bank
             Department of History CN 5059
             Rutgers, The State University of New Jersey
             New Brunswick, NJ 08903 USA

             voice: (201) 932-8335

             e-mail: `bl.ric@rlg.stanford.edu`

             RLIN Information Center
             Research Libraries Group, Inc.
             1200 Villa St.
             Mountain View, CA 94041-1100 USA

             voice: (800) 537-7546

Military History Databases

Contents:	Databases of the U.S. Army Military History Institute and the U.S. Army War College.
Comments:	If you are a frequent user of this service, you are encouraged to download the pertinent table of contents files semi-annually.
Access:	Use the mail server to get started with this database. Try the following messages:

```
mail:     info-request@carlisle-emh2.army.mil
subject:  index
message:  (none needed)
```

To view what is available from the U.S. Army War College:

```
mail:     info-request@carlisle-emh2.army.mil
subject:  USAWC
message:  (none needed)
```

To view what is available from the U.S. Army Military History Institute:

```
mail:     info-request@carlisle-emh2.army.mil
subject:  USAMHI
message:  (none needed)
```

Contact:	e-mail: vetockd@carlisle-emh2.army.mil
	voice: (717) 245-3611

 ## Rome Reborn:
The Vatican Library & Renaissance Culture

Contents:	Some 200 images (GIF) of manuscripts, books, and maps from the Vatican Library with accompanying text. The nine sections of the exhibit are: The Vatican Library; Archeology; Humanism; Mathematics; Music; Medicine & Biology; Nature Described; A Wider World I: How the Orient Came to Rome; A Wider World II: How Rome Went to China.

(Continued)

Comments: These materials may not be republished or used for a commercial purpose. Exhibit provided by the Library of Congress.

Access: FTP host: `ftp.loc.gov`
           directory: `/pub/exhibit.images/vatican.exhibit`
           WWW:
           `http://sunsite.unc.edu/expo/vatican.exhibit/Vatican.exhibit.html`

Contact: e-mail: `vatican@kell.loc.gov`   (for questions about the content of the exhibit)
                    `kell@seq1.loc.gov`   (for questions about the system)
           K. D. Ellis
           Special Projects Office
           Library of Congress
           Washington, DC 20540-9100 USA

Scrolls from the Dead Sea: The Ancient Library of Qumran and Modern Scholarship

Contents: Includes images (GIF) of scroll fragments, commentary, and information about scroll scholarship itself. The four sections are: Introduction–The World of the Scrolls; The Qumran Community; The Qumran Library; and Today–2,000 Years Later.

Comments: These materials may not be republished or used for a commercial purpose. Also included is a list of resource materials for teachers. Exhibit provided by the Library of Congress.

Access: FTP host: `ftp.loc.gov`
           directory: `/pub/exhibit.images/deadsea.scrolls.exhibit`
           WWW:
           `http://sunsite.unc.edu/expo/deadsea.scrolls.exhibit/intro.html`

Contact: e-mail: `kell@seq1.loc.gov`
           K. D. Ellis
           Special Projects Office
           Library of Congress
           Washington, DC 20540-9100 USA

K-12 EDUCATION

For materials designed for use with K-12 education, see Chapter 23.

Library and Information Science

FAXON

Contents:	Comprehensive databases of serials publications for use by libraries and academics for ordering and cataloging.
Comments:	FAXON also provides e-mail services to its subscribers.
Access:	Telnet, once an account is established.
Contact:	The Faxon Company 15 Southwood Park Westwood, MA 02090 USA voice: (617) 329-3350 fax: (617) 329-9875

LC Marvel (Library of Congress)

Contents:	Includes information about the Library of Congress, Federal government information, information on copyright, and a subject-based collection of online materials from around the world.	
Access:	Telnet: `marvel.loc.gov`	(limited to 15 users at a time)
	login: `marvel`	
	Gopher: `marvel.loc.gov`	
Contact:	e-mail: `lcmarvel@seq1.loc.gov`	

Library of Congress Cataloging Records

Contents:	Entries from the Library of Congress databases searchable by subject, keyword, author, title, ISBN (International Standard Book Number), ISSN (International Standard Series Number), LCCN (Library of Congress Card Number), and other fields. Covers books, serials, and maps.

(Continued)

Comments: The online catalog does not cover all materials in the Library of Congress' collection. The most complete coverage is for English language materials cataloged since 1968, and other language materials cataloged since the 1970's. Available during the following hours (Eastern Time): Monday-Friday 6:30am - 9:30pm; Saturday 8am - 5pm; Sunday 1pm - 5pm.

Access: Telnet: `locis.loc.gov`

Contact: e-mail: `lconline@seq1.loc.gov`

A guide to searching the catalog is available via anonymous FTP:

FTP host: `ftp.loc.gov`
directory: `/pub/lc.online`
filenames: (all subdirectories and files)

The guide is also available for purchase in print from the Catalog Distributions Service (CDS):

voice: (202) 707-6100
fax: (202) 707-1334

Library-Oriented Lists and Electronic Serials

Contents: Information on well over 100 LISTSERV and other mailing lists in Librarianship along with a list of over 20 library-oriented electronic serials.

Access: Gopher: `info.lib.uh.edu`
menu: `Looking for Other Sources/`
    `Information About the Internet`
item: `Library-Oriented Lists and Electronic Serials`

Contact: e-mail: `lib3@uhupvm1.uh.edu`

Charles W. Bailey, Jr.
Assistant Director for Systems
University Libraries
University of Houston
Houston, TX 77204-2091 USA

voice: (713) 743-9804
fax: (713) 743-9811

■■■

 ## OCLC FirstSearch (Online Computer Library Center, Inc.)

Contents: Bibliographic databases containing more than 20 million records using an interface designed for use by the general public; databases include Library of Congress, Dissertation Abstracts, ERIC, and many others.

Comments: Fee-based account must be set up with OCLC.

Access: Telnet: `fscat.oclc.org`

Contact: Online Computer Library Center, Inc.
             6565 Frantz Road
             Dublin, OH 43017-3395 USA
             voice: (800) 848-5878 or (614) 764-3000
                      (800) 848-8268 (OH only)
             fax: (614) 764-6096

 ## RLIN (Research Libraries Information Network)

Contents: Bibliographic databases covering most of the major research libraries in the U.S. Includes Library of Congress records, ABI/Inform, *Art and Architecture Thesaurus*, *Dissertation Abstracts*, *Hispanic American Periodicals Index*, *Newspaper Abstracts*, *Periodical Abstracts*. Many are available as full text databases.

Comments: Fee-based account must be set up with the Research Libraries Group.

Access: Telnet: `rlg.stanford.edu`

Contact: e-mail: `bl.ric@rlg.stanford.edu`
             RLIN Information Center
             Research Libraries Group, Inc.
             1200 Villa St.
             Mountain View, CA 94041-1100 USA
             voice: (800) 537-7546

■■ I

LITERATURE

■■ I

✗ ### ARTFL (American and French Research on the Treasury of the French Language)

Contents: A textual database of nearly 2,000 French language texts, written from the 17th to 20th centuries, containing about 150 million words. Includes a sophisticated but easy to use full text retrieval system designed for single word and contextual searches. There are several related philological analysis programs available for use with ARTFL.

Comments: A cooperative project of the Centre National de la Recherche Scientifique and the University of Chicago.

Access: Telnet or modem; payment of a small fee by an institution allows all scholars and students access to ARTFL. CD version of the dataset may be available by late 1992.

There is a guest account *for evaluation purposes only:*

Telnet: `artfl.uchicago.edu`
login: `guest`
password: `suggest`   (The password for the guest account is changed periodically.)

Contact: e-mail: `mark@gide.uchicago.edu`

American and French Research on the Treasury of the French Language
Department of Romance Languages and Literatures
University of Chicago
1050 East 59th Street
Chicago, IL 60637 USA
voice: (812) 702-8488

More Info: FTP host: `ra.msstate.edu`
directory: `/pub/docs/history/databases`
filename: `database.ARTFL`   (user's guide)
              `artfl.guide`   (guide to search software)
              `artfl.bib`   (listing of database contents)

Dartmouth Dante Project

Contents: A database containing the text of Dante's *Divina Commedia* and full texts of 600 years of scholarly commentary on the work. The database uses the BRS/Search program.

Comments: Note that many of the commentaries are copyrighted, so the database itself cannot be distributed. Available 24 hours a day, except for Mondays, 4:15-6:30am Eastern Time.

Access: Telnet: `library.dartmouth.edu`

At the "->" prompt, enter "connect dante".

modem: (603) 643-6300   (300 and 1200 baud)
            (603) 643-6310   (> 1200 baud)

At the "->" prompt, enter "connect dante".

Contact: e-mail: `dante@dartmouth.edu`

Dartmouth Dante Project
1 Reed Hall
HB 6087
Dartmouth College
Hanover, NH 03755 USA
voice: (603) 646-2633

More Info: Online help and printed user's manual for $4.00 are available.

 ## Gopheur LITTERATURES (University of Montreal)

Contents: Dedicated to the support of research, instruction, and publications on French, Quebecois, and Francophone literatures. The Gopher is organized according to the programs of study in the department of French studies. Currently included are bibliographies, reviews, archives of discussion lists.

Comments: The language of the Gopher is French. Currently the text is in ASCII, but there are plans to offer ISO-LATIN text which supports accents and other diacritical marks.

Access: Gopher: `gopher.litteratures.umontreal.ca 7070`

Contact: e-mail: `gophlitt@ere.umontreal.ca`

■·■■·■

Online Chaucer Bibliography

Contents:	While this database is still "under construction" it is already useful in locating materials on Chaucer. The citations are searchable using author, title, subject, and keyword, and include abstracts.
Comments:	The default emulation for this database server is VT100. To check keyboard emulation, type <esc><h>. To end a session, enter "stop". For help using the terminal server (not the database), call the UTSA Office of Information Technology at (210) 691-4555.
Access:	Telnet: `utsaibm.utsa.edu`
	At the "TS> ! VT100,3278" prompt, press <enter>.
	At the "UTSA" screen, enter "library". Select "local" and then "chau".
Contact:	e-mail: `mallen@lonestar.utsa.edu`
	Mark Allen
	Division of English,
	Classics, and Philosophy
	The University of Texas at San Antonio
	San Antonio, TX 78249 USA
	voice: (210) 691-5338

MATHEMATICS

■·■■■·■

e-MATH (American Mathematical Society)

Contents:	Database of reviews and abstracts on nearly 100 topics, including applied mathematics in fields such as astronomy, economics, biology, and other natural sciences. The WAIS database contains preprint abstracts from Duke University, Los Alamos Laboratory, Kyoto, Mathematical Reviews Abstracts, Current Mathematical Publications Citations, University of Nebraska Press Catalog, and the American Mathematical Society Catalog. Also includes some full-text preprints.	
Access:	Gopher:	`e-math.ams.com`
	Telnet:	`e-math.ams.com`
	login:	`e-math`
	password:	`e-math`
	WAIS	
	(Telnet):	`e-math.ams.com`
	login:	`waisdemo`
	password:	`waisdemo`
Contact:	e-mail: `support@e-math.ams.com`	

15 • Databases and Bibliographies

▪■■■▪

Instant Math Preprints

Contents: A fully searchable database of preprint abstracts, and instructions on how to access the full texts via FTP.

Access:
tn3270:	`yalevm.ycc.yale.edu`
userid:	`Math1 (or Math2, 3, 4, or 5)`
password:	`Math1 (or Math2, 3, 4, or 5)`
operator ID:	`Math1 (or Math2, 3, 4, or 5)`

Contact: e-mail: `victor@jezebel.wustl.edu` (Victor Wickerhauser)

Maple FTP Archives

Contents: Tools for Maple software.

Access:
FTP host:	`otter.stanford.edu`	Stanford University
	`daisy.waterloo.edu`	University of Waterloo, Canada
directory:	`/maple`	
filename:	(many or all)	

Contact: For technical help with Maple problems:

e-mail: `support@maplesoft.on.ca`

Waterloo Maple Software
450 Phillip Street
Waterloo, Ontario, N2L-5J2
Canada

voice: (519) 747-2505
fax: (519) 747-5284

MATLAB User Group Archive

Contents: Functions and utilities for the MATLAB numeric computation system.

Comments: These MATLAB files are also accessible from NETLIB. (See NETLIB entry.) If you choose not to use NETLIB, you are encouraged to subscribe to the MATLAB users digest by sending a subscription request, including your e-mail userid and address, to matlab-users-request@mcs.anl.gov.

▪▪▪

(Continued)

Access:	FTP host:	`ftp.mathworks.com`
	directory:	`/matlab`
	filename:	(many or all) (FAQ is in directory /matlab/doc)
	Via mail server:	

```
mail:      matlib@mathworks.com
subject:   (none needed)
message:   send index
```

Contact: e-mail: `bischof@mcs.anl.gov`

Christian Bischoff
Math and Computer Sciences Division
Argonne National Labs
Argonne, IL 60439 USA
voice: (708) 972-8875

More Info: To subscribe to the MATLAB user's digest, send a request (including your userid and e-mail address) to the following:

`matlab-users-request@mcs.anl.gov`

newsgroup: `comp.soft-sys.matlab`

Mathematica FTP Archives

Contents: Tools for Mathematica software.

Comments: Mathematica is a remarkable software system for symbolic mathematics, featuring high-quality graphical displays of functions as graphs, surfaces, and three dimensional objects. Mathematica software is available for operating systems from Macintoshes to Crays.

Access: Several anonymous FTP sites store files pertinent to Mathematica.

FTP hosts: `mathsource.wri.com`
`otter.stanford.edu`
`siam.unibe.ch`
`vax.eedsp.gatech.edu`

More Info: For advanced discussions of symbolic math and symbolic math software packages, including Mathematica, refer to the following:

newsgroup: `sci.math.symbolic`

Netlib Mathematical Software Distribution System

Contents: A huge variety of mathematical software and algorithms.

Comments: A tremendously valuable resource. The AT&T site also features a menu driven
                    service called "walk" which allows one to hone-in on literature citations for the
                    algorithm appropriate for a particular purpose.

Access: Accessible through FTP, mail server, Telnet, and modem. Please use the site
                    nearest you!

        FTP hosts: `netlib.att.com`   (U.S.)
                        `draci.cs.uow.edu.au`   (Australia)
        directory: `/netlib`

        Via mail server:
                  `netlib@ornl.gov`   (North America)
                  `netlib@research.att.com` (North America)
                  `netlib@ukc.ac.uk`   (United Kingdom)
                  `netlib@nac.no`   (Europe)
                  `netlib@draci.cs.uow.edu.au` (Australia)

```
mail:     <mail-server of your choice>
subject:  (none needed)
message:  send index
```

        Telnet: `research.att.com`
        login: `walk`

        modem: (908) 582-1238
        login: `walk`

Contact: e-mail: `ehg@research.att.com` (Eric Grosse)
                    AT&T Bell Labs
                    2t-504
                    Murray Hill, NJ 07974 USA

        voice: (908) 582-5828

MEDICAL

Databases in medicine have been combined with other medical resources and
moved to Chapter 24. That chapter includes a whole range of health science resources
available on the Internet.

METEOROLOGY

General Information about Meteorology Databases

Ilana Stern (ilana@ncar.ucar.edu) maintains an up-to-date listing of Internet resources in meteorology, including databases, which is posted twice monthly to the newsgroups "sci.geo.meteorology" and "news.answers". The file is also available via FTP.

FTP host: `rtfm.mit.edu`
directory: `/pub/usenet-by-group/news.answers/weather/data`
filename: `part1`
              `part2`

 University of Michigan Weather Underground

Contents: Weather information for U.S. and Canada. Specific information includes current conditions, forecasts, ski conditions, long range regional forecasts, earthquake reports, severe weather summaries (including floods, tornados, and severe thunderstorms), hurricane advisories, and national weather summaries.

Comments: For educational purposes only. Potential commercial users should contact Zephyr Weather Information Service (508-898-3511), the providers of the data feed to the Weather Underground.

Access: Telnet: `downwind.sprl.umich.edu 3000`   (Don't forget port 3000!)

Contact: e-mail: `sdm@madlab.sprl.umich.edu`
               College of Engineering
               University of Michigan
               Ann Arbor, MI 48109-2143 USA

 UofI Weather Machine

Contents: Includes current satellite images (nested grid model, model output statistics, medium range forecast, visual, water vapor); weather maps; weather FAQs; regional weather information for Canada, the Caribbean, and Illinois; surface map showing locations of warm and cold fronts; and strip charts showing yesterday's temperature and dewpoint, precipitation, cloud base, and pressure for the following cities: Boise, Champaign, Chicago, Denver, Des Moines, Los Angeles, Miami, Minneapolis/St. Paul, New Orleans, New York, Oklahoma City, Peoria, San Francisco, Springfield (IL), Seattle, and Washington (DC).

Access: Gopher: `wx.atmos.uiuc.edu`

Contact: e-mail: `gopher@wx.atmos.uiuc.edu`
John Kemp
University of Illinois
Dept. of Atmospheric Science
105 S. Gregory Ave.
Urbana, IL 61801 USA

Miscellaneous

Emergency Preparedness Information Exchange (EPIX)

Contents: Information on recent natural disasters, emergency and disaster management organizations, upcoming emergency disaster management conferences and events, as well as connections to other emergency and disaster management networks.

Access: Gopher: `hoshi.cic.sfu.ca 5555`

Contact: e-mail: `anderson@sfu.ca`
Peter Anderson
Centre for Policy Research on Science and Technology
Harbour Centre Campus
Simon Fraser University
515 West Hastings St.
Vancouver, BC V6B 5K3 Canada

Multicultural Bisexual Lesbian Gay Alliance (U.C. Berkeley) Gopher

Contents: Includes a wealth of information about bisexual, lesbian, and gay organizations and activities around the U.S. and the world. Also included is access to other Gophers covering issues of gender and sexuality. Includes information and press releases from the International Gay and Lesbian Human Rights Commission, the Gay and Lesbian Alliance Against Defamation, the National Gay and Lesbian Task Force, the Human Rights Campaign Fund and the Lambda Legal Defense and Education Fund.

Access: Gopher: `uclink.berkeley.edu 1901`
menu: `National and International LGB Information/`

■■■

Contact: e-mail: mblga@uclink.berkeley.edu

                Multicultural Bisexual Lesbian Gay Alliance
                411 Eshleman Hall
                University of California
                Berkeley, CA 94720 USA
                voice: (510) 642-6942
                fax: (510) 643-6396

Smithsonian Institution "Photo1.SI.Edu" FTP Server

Contents: A fairly large collection of photographic images from the Smithsonian's
                collections. Images are of a wide variety of items, including events, people, places,
                and science and technology. Captions and a catalog are included.

Comments: Image viewing software is also available at this archive site. Materials are for non-
                commercial use only.

Access: FTP host: photo1.si.edu
                directory: /images

Contact: e-mail: psdmx@sivm.si.edu

                Smithsonian Institution
                Office of Printing & Photographic Services
                MAH CB-054
                Washington, DC 20560 US

MUSIC

■■■

Music and Lyrics Archives

Contents: Lyrics and tablature for thousands of songs, discographies, commentary on the
                classical music repertoire, and a growing number of other music related files.

Comments: There is a directory, /pub/tmp/incoming, to receive contributions to the archive.

Access: FTP host: vacs.uwp.edu
                directory: /pub/music/lyrics
                filename: files.directory

Contact: e-mail: datta@vacs.uwp.edu

Music Research Information Service (MRIS)

Contents: Information on music education, music psychology, music therapy, and music medicine. Includes access to the CAIRSS bibliographic database on music.

Comments: MRIS is a project of the Institute for Music Research at the University of Texas at San Antonio.

Access: Telnet: `runner.utsa.edu`
             login: `imr`
             password: `<enter>`

Contact: e-mail: `kwalls@lonestar.utsa.edu`

             Dr. Kimberly C. Wallis
             Institute for Music Research
             University of Texas at San Antonio
             San Antonio, TX 78249 USA
             voice: (210) 691-5321

NetJam

Contents: MIDI sequences deposited and redistributed for collaborative compositions by Internet users. NetJam is also a real-time activity using a client-server Wide-Area MIDI Network.

Access: Information and repositories of sequences by FTP.

             FTP host: `xcf.berkeley.edu`
             directory: `/pub/misc/netjam`
             filenames: (many or all)

             Much of the information in the archives can also be obtained via mail server. Refer to /misc/netjam/docs/guide on the FTP server for more information.

Contact: e-mail: `latta@xcf.berkeley.edu` (Craig Latta)

More Info: Mailing list: netjam-users@xcf.berkeley.edu. Please send subscription requests to netjam-request@xcf.berkeley.edu.

             For more information on the real-time NetJam, send a message "request for info" to the same address.

■ ■

OCEANOGRAPHY

■ ■

OCEANIC (The Ocean Information Center)

Contents:	Information about oceanography research activities throughout the world, particularly the activities of the World Ocean Circulation Experiment (WOCE). This database contains descriptions of oceanographic and climatological datasets and ordering information, directory of oceanographers, and related materials.
Comments:	It is possible to view some graphical displays of oceanographic data with Tektronix 4010 terminal emulation. There is also information available at the site on an MS-DOS program to help view the graphical displays.

Access: Telnet: `delocn.udel.edu`
             username: `INFO`

             Gopher: `diu.cms.udel.edu`

             WWW: `http://diu.cms.udel.edu`

Contact: OCEANIC
             University of Delaware
             College of Marine Studies
             Lewes, DE 19958 USA

PALEONTOLOGY

■ ■

An Exhibition of Fossil Life (Paleontology Museum, The University of California, Berkeley)

Contents: Geared towards younger investigators, this exhibit includes images of fossils and reconstructions along with explanatory text. Users may browse the exhibit using a number of methods: the room metaphor, by phylogene, by geneological relationships, and by geological age.

Access: WWW: `http://sunsite.unc.edu/expo/paleo.exhibit/paleo.html`

Contact: e-mail: `robg@fossil.berkeley.edu`

             Museum of Paleontology
             University of California, Berkeley
             Berkeley, CA 94720 USA

             voice: (510) 642-9696
             fax: (510) 642-1822

HCC Dinosaurs (Honolulu Community College)

Contents:	Images of dinosaur fossil replicas along with a spoken guided tour by the one of the exhibit's founders.
Comment:	The fossils presented here are replicas of fossils at the Museum of Natural History in New York City.
Access:	WWW: `http://www.hcc.hawaii.edu/dinos/dinos.1.html`
Contact:	Rick Ziegler Honolulu Community College #874 Dillingham Blvd. Honolulu, HI 96817 USA

POLITICAL SCIENCE

Bibliography of Senate Hearings (U.S.)

Contents:	Bibliographies of U.S. Senate Committee hearings and publications for the 99th-103nd Congresses with a WAIS index available.
Comments:	Filenames in the FTP host archive have a precise format whose meanings you should understand before using the database. Explanations of filename formats are provided in the readme file. Files are also available on floppy disk to subscribers, and on paper to subscribers and requestors.

Access:

Gopher:	`gopher.ncsu.edu`
menu:	`Desk Reference Tools/NCSU's "Library Without Walls"/Study Carrels (organized by subject)/ Government and Law/`
item:	`Bibliography of Senate Hearings, McGeachy/`
FTP host:	`ftp.ncsu.edu`
directory:	`/pub/ncsu/senate`
filenames:	`README.TXTYYMM` (where YY is the year and MM is the month) (many others)

■■■

Contact: e-mail: `Jack_McGeachy@ncsu.edu`
                John A. McGeachy
                Documents Department
                D.H. Hill Library,
                North Carolina State University
                Raleigh, NC 27695-7111 USA
                voice: (919) 515-3280

 Soviet Archive Exhibit

Contents: Images (GIF) of documents recently released from Soviet archives along with
                English translations. Subjects include: Stalin, Kirov's murder, the secret police
                (ChEKA/NKVD/KGB), the gulags, the Ukrainian famine, collectivization and
                industrialization, anti-religious campaigns, attacks on the intelligentsia, the Jewish
                Antifascist Committee, cooperation between the United States and the Soviet
                Union, and the Cold War.

Comments: These materials may not be republished or used for a commercial purpose. The
                World Wide Web version offers a "guided tour" of the exhibit. Exhibit provided by
                the Library of Congress.

Access: FTP host: `ftp.loc.gov`
                directory: `/pub/exhibit.images/soviet.archive`

                WWW:
                `http://sunsite.unc.edu/expo/soviet.archive/soviet.archive.html`

Contact: e-mail: `kell@seq1.loc.gov`
                K. D. Ellis
                Special Projects Office
                Library of Congress
                Washington, DC 20540-9100 USA

 United Nations Gopher

Contents: United Nations press releases, information on various UN programs, UN
                directories (United Nations Development Programme; United Nations
                Educational, Scientific & Cultural Organization (UNESCO); World Bank), as well
                as access to other United Nations Gophers, and other information systems.

Access: Gopher: `gopher.undp.org`

(Continued)

Via mail server:

```
mail:     gopher.undp.org
subject:  (none needed)
message:  (none needed)
```

Contact: e-mail: malcolm@undp.org
              Malcolm G. Chapman
              United Nations Development Programme
              Division for Administrative and Information Services
              1 United Nations Plaza
              New York, NY 10016 USA
              voice: (212) 906-6585
              fax: (212) 906-6365

X White House Publications

Contents: Documents and text of U.S. legislation and speeches related to areas such as, the
              Health Security Act, the Internet, the National Performance Review, and the
              Federal budget.

Comments: Access available via anonymous FTP host and e-mail server. For assistance using
              the e-mail server, send for the help file as instructed below.

Access: FTP host: whitehouse.gov
              directory: /pub

              Via mail server:

```
mail:     publications@whitehouse.gov
subject:  (none needed)
message:  help
```

Contact: e-mail: publications-comments@whitehouse.gov

SOCIAL SCIENCES

BIRON Archive System

Contents: A database of more than 3,000 datasets covering most areas of social and economic life in the United Kingdom, searchable by names of persons or organizations associated with particular datasets, titles or part titles, dates, and geographical areas of data collection.

Access: Telnet: `dasun.essex.ac.uk`
            login: `biron`
            password: `norib`

Contact: e-mail: `sheil@essex.ack.uk`

Coombspapers Databank

Contents: Intended to be the world's leading depository of social science and humanities research papers and documents, including offprints, specialist bibliographies, directories, thesis abstracts, and datasets. Currently consists of close to 40 databases. Areas of primary focus are South and Northeastern Asia.

Comments: Scholars are encouraged to send documents and datasets to the Databank. A special directory in the FTP host, coombspapers/inboundpapers, has been set up to receive such files in ASCII format.

Access: FTP host: `coombs.anu.edu.au`
            directory: `/coombspapers`
            filenames: `INDEX`
                               (all other files and subdirectories)
            WAIS databases: `ANU-Asian-Religions`
                               `ANU-Pacific-Linguistics`
                               `ANU-Pacific-Manuscripts`
                               `ANU-SocSci-Netlore`
                               `ANU-SSDA-Catalogues`
                               `ANU-Thai-Yunnan`
                               etc.
            WWW:
            `http://info.cern.ch/hypertext/DataSources/Archives/CoombsPapers.html`

■■

(Continued)

Contact: e-mail: `coombspapers@coombs.anu.edu.au`

Dr. T. Matthew Ciolek
Coombspapers Administrator
Coombs Computing Unit, RSPacS/RSSS,
Australian National University
Canberra 2601 Australia

voice: + 61 6 249 2214

CULDAT
(Canadian Union List of Machine Readable Data Files)

Contents: Bibliographic and descriptive information about computer readable data files held by Canadian academic and governmental data libraries and archives. There are currently about 2,000 databases accessible. Sources of databases searched in a CULDAT session include:

CUSSDA:	Carleton University, Social Science Data Archive
ICPSR:	Inter-University Consortium for Political and Social Research
NAC:	National Archives of Canada
STC:	Statistics Canada
UADL:	University of Alberta, Data Library
UBCDL:	University of British Columbia, Data Library
UMISE:	University of Manitoba, Institute for Social and Economic Research
UWOSS:	University of Western Ontario, Social Science Computing Lab
WATLS:	University of Waterloo, Leisure Studies Data Bank
YUISR:	York University, Institute for Social Research

Access: Via a mail server which accepts Remote Spires (RMSPIRES) commands. To get started, try the following message:

```
mail:    rmspires@vm.ucs.ualberta.ca
subject: (none needed)
message: explain culdat
```

Contact: e-mail: `abombak@vm.ucs.ualberta.ca`

Anna Bombak, Data Librarian
4-15 Cameron Library
University of Alberta
Edmonton, Alberta T6G 2J8 Canada

voice: (403) 492-5212

ICPSR (Inter-University Consortium for Political and Social Research)

Contents: An immense array of datasets for research and instruction in the social sciences.

Comments: ICPSR members can work with datasets remotely or have materials transferred directly over the Internet by e-mail. The Consortium Data Network (CDNet—not to be confused with the Canadian Research and Education Network whose abbreviation is also CDNet) is used for direct access to ICPSR datasets and services by way of the Internet.

Access: Through the Internet or CDNet once you establish an account.

Contact: e-mail: `icpsr.netmail@um.cc.umich.edu`

Member Services
ICPSR
Box 1248
Ann Arbor, MI 48106 USA

voice: (313) 764-2570
fax: (313) 764-8041

More Info: Gopher: `gopher.icpsr.umich.edu`

IRSS (The Institute for Research in the Social Sciences)

Contents: Extensive archives of social science data, including IRSS datasets, and public opinion polls (Louis Harris, Atlanta Journal Constitution, Carolina Poll, USA Today). IRSS datasets come from a wide variety of sources; poll databases can be searched for poll questions containing specific words, study dates, or study numbers.

Comments: You must access this service with tn3270 or use Telnet from a VM/CMS mainframe. If you're not used to the CMS operating system, expect to be lost and confused at times. (In particular, note that "PF#" commands never mean "P-F-#" literally. Usually "esc3" or "F3" will do the job of "PF3". Once you learn to get around beginning problems, this is a very good resource.

Access: tn3270:   `uncvm1.oit.unc.edu`   (or telnet from a VM/CMS host)
login: `irss1` through `irss7`
password: `irss`

Contact: e-mail: `uirdss@uncvm1.oit.unc.edu`

David Sheaves
Institute for Research in the Social Sciences
University of North Carolina
Chapel Hill, NC 27599 USA

voice: (919) 966-3348
fax: (919) 962-4777

X   National Archives Center for Electronic Records

Contents: An archive of more than 14,000 datasets, with an emphasis on U.S. Federal government information. Very strong in the areas of health, demography, and social sciences.

Access: Currently, one must order copies of datasets of interest on magnetic tape (9 track reels or 3480 cartridges).

Contact: For more information, or a free list of over 4,400 title list of holdings, contact the following:

e-mail: `tif@cu.nih.gov`

Theodore J. Hull
Archives Specialist
Archival Service Branch
Center for Electronic Records
National Archives and Records Administration
Washington, DC 20408 USA

voice: (202) 501-5579

More Info: Information about the holdings of the Archive are available for anonymous FTP.

FTP host:	ftp.cu.nih.gov	
directory:	`/NARA_ELECTRONIC`	
filename:	`TITLE.LIST.DEC1793`	(current title list–filename will vary by date)
	`CENTER`	(brief description of the Center)
	`GIL36`	(information on the Center and its policies)
	`GIL37`	(information on services to the public)
	`SERVICES`	(specific information on fee-based services)

There are two LISTSERV discussion groups of relevance to this and related government holdings.

`fedsig-l@wvnvm.wvnet.edu`	Federal Electronic Data Special Interest Group
`govdoc-l@psuvm.psu.edu`	Government Documents

RAPID-ESRC Database of Research Abstracts and Products (Research Awards and Publications Database-Economic and Social Research Council)

Contents: A database in Scotland of the research results of the Economic and Social Research Council.

Access: Telnet: `ercvax.ed.ac.uk`
          username: `rapid`
          password: `rapid`

SSDA (Aleph/Hebrew University Social Science Data Archive Catalog)

Contents: A catalog of a very wide variety of social science datasets about Israel. You can search by author, title, subject, and variable names. Cataloged datasets cover the following topics: agriculture, attitudes, census, commerce, crime and violence, culture, demography, drugs, education, elderly, elections, environmental quality, finance, foreign countries, government, health, household behavior, housing, immigration and absorption, incomes and wages, industry, international accounting, Jerusalem, Jewish Diaspora, kibbutzim, labour, leisure, local authorities, migration, national accounting, national economy, political behavior, political attitudes, quality of life, religion, savings, social mobility, social stratification, social structure, technology, transportation, welfare, women, and youth.

Access: Telnet: `har1.huji.ac.il`
          username: `SSDA`
          select: `2`

Contact: Datasets of interest can be ordered from:
          e-mail: `magar1@vms.huji.ac.il`
          voice: (972) 2-883181
          fax: (972) 2-883004

STATISTICS

✗ Statlib Statistical Software and Data Distribution System

Contents: Datasets of special interest to statisticians for their historical or theoretical importance, statistical software and algorithms, and a directory of statisticians.

Access: Statlib is accessible via FTP and mail server. Note that for the FTP host, you use the login name "statlib", not "anonymous".

FTP host: `lib.stat.cmu.edu`
login: `statlib`

password: `<your-e-mail-address>`
directories: (many or all)

Via mail server:

```
mail:     statlib@lib.stat.cmu.edu
subject:  (none needed)
message:  send index
```

Statlib will send a file containing information about the contents of the archives and more detailed instructions on how to use the mail server.

Contact: e-mail: `mikem@stat.cmu.edu` (Michael Meyer)
Department of Statistics
Carnegie Mellon University
Pittsburgh, PA 15213 USA
voice: (412) 268-3108

FOR MORE INFORMATION

Fellow Internet Users and Peers

A great way to keep up with developments in specific areas is to join a discussion group in your area of specialty. This will put you in touch with other Internet users and your peers, allowing you to share information. Refer to Chapters 9 and 10 for more information on using Usenet and LISTSERV respectively and on selecting the groups most appropriate for your needs.

Database Maintainers

If there are databases in this chapter of special interest to you, do a bit of research, perhaps using veronica, then try communicating with the listed contact person(s) to see if other related databases exist or are being planned. In many cases, the databases listed in this chapter contain pointers to other related databases. For example, the history archives at Mississippi State University provide information on history-specific sources throughout the world.

Other Online Compendia of Internet Databases

Online information about databases within particular disciplines was provided at the beginning of several of the topical entries throughout this chapter and listed in the Clearinghouse for Subject-Oriented Internet Resource Guides noted at the beginning of this chapter. In general, these will be the most up-to-date and comprehensive sources of information about databases in those topics.

The InterNIC (the "Network Information Center of first and last resort") maintains an online directory of Internet resources. Entries are in a standard format and are submitted by the resource administrator. The database, organized and maintained by AT&T, is kept up-to-date with regular queries sent to the information providers verifying the data. Access to the Directory of Directories is available through WAIS, anonymous FTP, Gopher, and e-mail.

```
WAIS
(Telnet):    ds.internic.net
login:       wais
database:    dirofdirs              (default)

FTP host:    ds.internic.net
directory:   /dirofdirs             (subdirectories by category)

Gopher:      ds.internic.net
menu:        InterNIC Directory and Database Services
             (AT&T)/InterNIC Directory of Directories/

Telnet:      ds.internic.net
login:       gopher

menu:        InterNIC Directory and Database Services
             (AT&T)/InterNIC Directory of Directories/
```

You can also access the Directory using e-mail. Send the following message to the mail server to get instructions on its use:

```
mail:    mailserv@ds.internic.net
subject: (none needed)
message: help
```

■■■

Alternatively, the "SURAnet Guide to Selected Internet Resources" is a thorough and constantly updated source of information about online databases.

FTP host: `ftp.sura.net`
directory: `/pub/nic`
filename: `infoguide.mm-yy.txt`   (where "mm-yy" is the month and year of the most recent version)

Bibliography of Commercial Online Databases and Search Issues

The following bibliography emphasizes commercial databases in several fields that are currently under-represented in freely available Internet databases: Law, K-12, Engineering, and Journalism. The Gale Research Company book is particularly comprehensive. Some of the databases described in these references may be available through your local institution or library.

Atkinson, S. D., and J. Hudson (eds.). *Women Online: Research in Women's Studies Using Online Databases*. New York: Haworth Press, 1990.

Aumente, J. *New Electronic Pathways: Videotex, Teletext, and Online Databases*. Newbury Park, Ca: Sage Publications, 1987.

Bjelland, H. *Using Online Scientific and Engineering Databases*. Blue Ridge Summit, PA: Windcrest, 1992.

Chan, L. M., and. R. Pollard. *Thesauri Used in Online Databases: An Analytical Guide*. New York: Greenwood Press, 1988.

Gale Directory of Databases. Detroit: Gale Research, 1993-

Gale Research Company. *Encyclopedia of Information Systems and Services*. Ann Arbor, Mich: Edwards Bros, 1971-1992.

Jackson, K. M. and N. L. Buchanan. "Unlimited Access to FirstSearch: An Online Success Story." *Online* 17(5) (September 1993):34-43.

Kinsock, J. E. *Legal Databases Online: LEXIS and WESTLAW*. Littleton, CO: Libraries Unlimited, 1985.

Koch, T. *Journalism for the 21st Century: Online Information, Electronic Databases, and the News*. New York: Greenwood Press, 1991.

Lathrop, A. (ed.). *Online and CD-ROM Databases in School Libraries: Readings*. Englewood, CO: Libraries Unlimited, 1989.

LePoer, P. M. "Importing Downloaded Bibliographic Records into dBase III+ and dBase IV: Tools and Methods." *Database* (February 1990):44-49.

Parisi, L. and V.L. Jones. *Directory of Online Databases and CD-ROM Resources for High Schools*. Santa Barbara, CA: ABC-Clio, 1988.

Pfaffenberger, B. *Democratizing Information: Online Databases and the Rise of End-user Searching*. Boston, MA: G.K. Hall, 1990.

SECTION

V

Resource Discovery and Retrieval Tools

CHAPTER

16

Archie

The FTP Archive Guru

Once you've learned how to use FTP to obtain files from archives on the Internet, you're faced with some challenging tasks. How do you find out which FTP site has the file you're looking for? For that matter, how can you find the FTP site with the most up-to-date version of the file? Until recently, to keep track of such resources, you either had to be an FTP archive guru who stayed awake all night prowling through the Internet, or else be lucky enough to know one.

A program called "archie" is an anonymous FTP guru for everyone on the Internet, and is ready and able to help you find what you are looking for. Archie maintains a constantly updated catalog of many of the world's anonymous FTP archives. Currently, it keeps track of more than 2,000,000 files in about 1,500 FTP hosts totaling nearly 100 Gigabytes of information. So if you want to make the most of anonymous FTP, it's well worth your while to learn how to use this service.

HOW DOES ARCHIE DO IT?

Each month, the archie program establishes an anonymous FTP connection to all sites contained in its master list. From each site, archie collects a complete directory listing of anonymous FTP holdings (using the recursive directory listing command, "ls-lR") and adds this information to the central archie database. This update is performed on each server on a rotating basis, so that the data on any server is no more than one month old.

The part of archie you will use is designed to let you search through this master catalog of FTP files just like you might use a library catalog for a title word search.

Archie's search output includes the Internet domain name of the FTP host and the directory in which a file is located, the size of the file in bytes, and the date on which the file was placed in that FTP host. Once you've gotten this list of sources from archie, you can FTP to a site that has what you are looking for and copy the file to your own computer.

WHAT KINDS OF QUESTIONS CAN ARCHIE ANSWER?

Archie is currently designed to answer the following questions:

- Is there a file or directory with a certain name or a certain set of characters? This will be referred to as a "name search."
- What files are about <topic x>? This will be referred to as a "file description search."
- What FTP hosts are currently monitored by archie, where are they located, and what files does a particular FTP host contain? This will be referred to as a "site search."

Although archie was designed to help retrieve copies of software from servers on the Internet, it indexes all files located on the FTP archives. This means that text files, pictures, sounds, and programs can all be located using archie.

Name Searches

The most common use of archie is to determine if there is a file or directory containing a particular set of characters in its name on an FTP host. Say you wanted to find a copy of the spiffy new shareware program called "gecko-graf". You could ask archie where in the world of anonymous FTP archives a file with the characters "gecko-graf" might be located.

File Description Searches

You can also search through archie's "Public Domain Software Description Database. This database contains descriptive information about the actual contents of some FTP'able files.

It's a good thing that archie is set up to perform file description searches. You'd be amazed at the obscurity of the names that some people give their programs, files, or directories. Just as a hypothetical example, you might think that a "Computer Aided Design" program would have the letters "CAD" somewhere in its name; but more often than you'd like, a CAD program might have a name like "TLZWYQXP.DTU". In such a case, you just have to hope that the author(s) of this program had the foresight to send a message to the archie folks saying that "TLZWWQXP" was a CAD program.

But be forewarned that only a small percentage of files from FTP hosts have been cataloged into the software description database. In general, file description searches will work best for retrieving information about RFCs, technical Internet documents, and Unix utilities.

Site Searches

Archie also allows you to get information about the FTP hosts which it monitors. You can even search for FTP hosts based on parts of their Internet addresses, so you could search for FTP hosts in a particular geographic region (e.g., FTP hosts in Sweden, whose addresses end with "se"), or you could request a copy of the catalog of files from a particular FTP host. (Please note: not all of the site search functions are available in the current version of archie, version 3.0.2, but are planned to be in later revisions.)

USING ARCHIE

You can access archie in a number of ways: from client software installed on your local Internet host; by e-mail requests to remote archie servers; by a Telnet connection to a remote archie server; or by using Gopher (Chapter 17). More information about the first three access methods will be presented later in this chapter. But first, let's go over the basic commands that you'll need to use your archie session.

■■ ■

Basic Archie Command Syntax

File and Directory Name Searches: Prog

The basic archie search command for a name search is "prog <textstring>", where <textstring> is a set of characters you think would be in a file or directory you are seeking.

Different servers have different defaults, so before starting an archie search, you should specify what kind of search you want archie to do by issuing the "set search" command, followed by one of four options:

`set search exact`	Precise searches ("prog Pine" would find only files and directories named "Pine", not "pine.2.2.tar.Z", "Pineapples", or any other variant or extension.)
`set search subcase`	Case sensitive substring searches ("prog Pine" would find "Pine" and "Chicken.Pineapple", but not "pineapple.chicken.gumbo".)
`set search sub`	Case insensitive substring searches ("prog pine" would find anything with the string "pine", including "ALPINE.doc", "pursuit.of.happiness", and so forth.)
`set search regex`	Searches done with "regular expressions" (This is a very sophisticated technique that allows you to use wildcards, specify whether the string is at the beginning or end of the name, and many other nifty tricks. For a thorough description of regex, use "help regex".)
`set match_domain`	Returns only those matches within the specified domain (such as .edu, .com, etc.). (The Australian archie server defaults to "set match_domain au". For more information on match_domain, use "help set match_domain".)

As a general rule, if you know the exact name of a file you're looking for, then use "set search exact". If you're on a fishing expedition, sub or regex may be most appropriate. For example, if you wanted to find poems with the word "grass" in the title, you would probably want to do a case insensitive substring search.

```
set search sub
prog grass
```

In response to this command, archie will present a list containing the names and locations of files and directories containing the string "grass", regardless of case or the location of "grass" in the name. Below is an excerpt of the search results.

```
Search request for 'grass'

Host slopoke.mlb.semi.harris.com     (132.158.82.36)
Last updated 17:47  7 Feb 1994


Location: /pub/doc/Poetry/Yeats
  FILE    -rw-r--r--      634 bytes  23:00 21 Jul 1985
     AnAcreOfGrass


Host etext.archive.umich.edu    (192.131.22.7)
Last updated 14:20 22 Jan 1994

Location:/pub/Politics/Feminism/ReadingRoom/Poetry/Dickinson
  FILE    -rw-r--r--      413 bytes  08:24  6 Aug 1993
     a-narrow-fellow-in-the-grass.gz

Host vixen.cso.uiuc.edu    (128.174.5.50)
Last updated 21:24 28 Jan 1994

Location: /pub
  DIRECTORY    drwxr-xr-x     512 bytes  23:00 31 May 1992
     grass
```

These results from archie tell you the FTP host at which the information is located (e.g., "Host slopoke.mlib.semi.harris.com"), the date when archie obtained this information (e.g., "Last Updated 17:47 7 Feb 1994"), the directory path in the FTP host (e.g., "/pub/doc/Poetry/Yeats"), and the name of the file or directory containing the character string you have specified in your prog request (e.g., the file "AnAcreOfGrass"). To get a copy of the poem, "An Acre of Grass," you would need to FTP to slopoke.mlb.semi.harris.com and cd to /pub/doc/Poetry/Yeats.

Note that this sample archie result also includes information about a directory whose name contains "grass". (In this case, GRASS refers to a public domain raster/vector geographic information system and image processing system.)

There are many other ways to tailor your archie name searches, some of which are described later in this chapter. Before using archie for real searches, be sure to use the "help" command and read the most current archie documentation.

File Description Searches: Whatis

Now let's examine a typical file description search. Just type "whatis" followed by any word. Let's try looking for calendar software.

■■

```
whatis calendar

cal               Print calendar
cal-entries       Long list of entries for input to calendar
calen             Calendar program
calend-remind     A souped-up version of UNIX calendar(1)
calendar          Calendar program
calgen            Calendar generation program
do                A calendar-like utility
month             Visual calendar program
monthtool         Monthly apointment calendar, for Suns
pcal              Calendar program, 1 month per page
perpetual         The Last Perpetual Calendar
xcal              A calendar program (X11)
xcalendar         A personal schedule maintainer in X11
xdiary            X11 based calendar and diary
xkal              X11 appointment calendar
```

All lines in the PD Software Description Database containing the word "calendar" have been displayed. Notice that whatis does not tell where any one of these files are located, and not all of these descriptions indicate what operating system the files are for. So submit a prog search for the file of interest, say the perpetual calendar. (A perpetual calendar would allow you to make a date book for March 1654, BC or AD, if you were so inclined.)

```
set search sub
prog perpetual
```

Site Searches

There are two main commands involved with site searches: "list" and "site".

The list command by itself will produce a list of all FTP hosts currently monitored by archie. You can also follow the list command with "regular expressions" using wildcards, anchors, and other useful features. For example, "list \.tw$" would display all FTP hosts in archie's catalog which end with ".tw", the top level domain for Taiwan. For more on how to use regular expressions, use "help regex".

The site command will give you a listing of all files known to archie from a particular FTP host. But this command should be used sparingly as an FTP host may have thousands or tens of thousands of files! Remember, this command will not work with version 3.0.2 of the archie server, but it is expected to be implemented with a later version.

Locations of Archie Servers

Now that you understand the basic commands, you need to know how to access archie. Regardless of which access method you use, your questions will be handled by an archie server. Try to use the server nearest you but, depending on the time of day, a server in another time zone may not be as busy. On the other hand, although using a server in another time zone (perhaps a few time zones away) may well be easier, it will put a greater demand on the network since the data will be travelling over a greater distance to reach you.

From North or South America, you should access one of the following servers:

archie.uqam.ca	(Canada)
archie.sura.net	(Maryland, USA)
archie.rutgers.edu	(New Jersey, USA)
archie.ans.net	(New York, USA)
archie.internic.net	(New York, USA)
archie.unl.edu	(Nebraska, USA)

From Eurasia or Africa, try:

archie.edvz.uni-linz.ac.at	(Austria)
archie.univie.ac.at	(Austria)
archie.funet.fi	(Finland)
archie.th-darmstadt.de	(Germany)
archie.unipi.it	(Italy)
archie.rediris.es	(Spain)
archie.luth.se	(Sweden)
archie.switch.ch	(Switzerland)
archie.doc.ic.ac.uk	(United Kingdom)

And from Australia, East Asia, New Zealand, Oceania (or Antarctica!) try:

archie.au	(Australia)
archie.kuis.kyoto-u.ac.jp	(Japan)
archie.wide.ad.jp	(Japan)
archie.sogang.ac.kr	(Korea)
archie.nz	(New Zealand)
archie.ncu.edu.tw	(Taiwan)

Archie from a Local Client

The best way to use archie is from a locally installed archie client. Using a client is faster for you and puts less of a load on the archie servers. You'll be delighted to find that archie client software has been developed for most major operating systems.

There may already be client software installed on your Internet host. Ask your local computer support staff or check the online help. If there isn't an archie client installed at your Internet host, you are strongly encouraged to obtain the software by FTP from any of the archie servers, usually located in the directory /archie/clients or /pub/archie/clients.

∎■■∎∎

You can also use the Telnet access method described below, and the welcome screen may provide instructions about where you can find client software via FTP.

Archie by E-mail

Just as you can perform FTP via e-mail you can also access archie this way. First time users are encouraged to request a help file with the following message:

```
mail:       archie@<an.archie.server.address>
subject:    help
message:    (none needed)
```

Asking for help is especially important because not all archie commands are available through the e-mail interface. When you access archie by e-mail, you can put archie search requests, one per line, in your message; archie can also read requests placed in the subject line. Note that commands in the message body must begin in the first column to be understood by archie. For example, sending the following e-mail message to an archie server will search for files or directories containing the characters "Yeats" and "Shelley" in their names, and the results will be sent to you in an e-mail message. If the result set is large, it will be broken up and sent as more than one message, each one numbered and indicating the total number of messages sent.

```
mail:       archie@<an.archie.server.address>
subject:    set search sub
message:

prog Yeats
prog Shelley
```

Archie by Telnet

Finally, you can access archie via Telnet to the nearest archie server. Use the login name "archie". No password is required. You might see a short help screen giving some basic explanation on how to use the system, information about recent changes to archie, and an e-mail (e.g., archie-admin@archie.unl.edu) address for questions concerning the use of that particular archie server.

You can get additional help about archie at any time during an archie session. Typing "help" will give you a list of help files and currently valid commands. To obtain help on a particular command on list, type "help" followed by the command name. For example, to get help on the "prog" command, type the following:

```
help prog
```

Now you're ready to do a name search for materials in the archie file catalog. Let's look for documents containing the text string "medical" in its name, regardless of whether the name is upper case, lower case, or any mixture of upper and lower case. First set your search to "sub", and then type "prog medical".

```
set search sub
prog medical

# Search type: sub.
# Your queue position: 2
# Estimated time for completion: 00:13
working...
```

Before archie actually submits the search it will display the search type, your position in the queue of searches, and an estimate of the time it will take to complete the search. This particular search for occurrences of the string "medical" in file or directory names netted over 80 files and directories.

If a search seems to be taking a very long time or possibly resulting in many spurious occurrences or "hits," you can stop archie by pressing "control c". (Simultaneously press the control key, usually labeled "ctrl", and the "c" key.) When you abort a search this way, archie will display the results of the search as it has been completed up to the point it was aborted.

Once an archie search is done and displayed, it may take you awhile to determine which of the files from the search results you actually want to FTP. Or, you may need to think carefully about whether your search needs to be respecified, either by changing the search string or by setting a different search type. If you want to e-mail a copy of the results of this search back to your own Internet host so you can examine archie's output at your leisure, just type:

```
mail <you>@<your.internet.host>
```

This is an especially good idea since it means you can logout of archie as soon as you're done. Remember, like most Internet resources, archie can only serve a finite number of users at once! The more quickly and efficiently you use it, the more other people can use it too. Besides, by mailing search results to your computer account, you will now have a copy to refer to later.

To end an archie Telnet session, simply type "quit".

Any search results you mailed during your Telnet session should arrive in your mailbox within a few minutes.

CUSTOMIZING ARCHIE SESSIONS WITH "SET" COMMANDS

Depending upon how you access archie, you may be able to customize many aspects of your archie session by specifying certain variables with the "set" command.

autologout	The number of minutes archie will tolerate inactivity before it logs you out. (Telnet access only.)
mailto	E-mail address to which output should be automatically mailed.
maxhits	Number of specified matches after which "prog" will stop its search. (A maxhits value of 100 is often about right for most searches.)
pager	Display search results one page at a time. (Telnet access only.) ("unset pager" lets output scroll continuously.)
search	Specifies how "prog" searches the database: options include "exact", "sub", "subcase", and "regex".
sortby	Specifies how "prog" output is sorted: options include "hostname", "time", "size", "filename", and "none". Each of these can be preceded by an "r" for reversal, such as "rtime" for reverse time.
status	Display search progress, or don't display ("unset status"). (Telnet access only.)
term	Describes your terminal type, e.g., "vt100". (Telnet access only.)

For example, to specify that archie should stop searching its catalog after finding 50 matches from one of your prog requests, you would enter "set maxhits 50" before issuing your prog request. For more information about these set variables, type "help set" or "help set <command>", where <command> is one of the commands listed above. To determine what your set variables are while using archie, type "show".

FOR MORE INFORMATION

Anything written about archie (or any other Internet resource) may be out-of-date a few days after it is written. When you telnet to archie and before you start your search, read the news messages that appear on your screen. The developers of archie may have implemented a new feature in their program that will make it even easier to use.

Best of all, archie may change in response to your suggestions. Once you've used archie, its developers would appreciate your feedback and comments so they can continue to make improvements. Send comments, bug reports, contributions to the database

■■

file, reports of anonymous FTP sites that archie doesn't seem to maintain, or even much deserved notes of appreciation to the following:

`archie-group@bunyip.com`

The archie program was written and is maintained by Alan Emtage and Bill Heelan. Ideas and inspiration were (and still are!) provided by Peter Deutsch.

Contact: e-mail: `info@bunyip.com`

               Bunyip Information Systems, Inc.
               310 St. Catherine St. West
               Suite 202
               Montreal, QC
               CANADA H2X 2A1

               voice: (514) 875-8611
               fax: (514) 875-8143

Definitive Archie Documents

Definitive archie documentation can be gotten by FTP from most all archie servers:

FTP host: `<any.archie.server>`
directories   `/pub/archie/doc` or `/archie/doc`
filenames: `archie.man.txt`   (ASCII archie manual)
            `whatis.archie`   (brief overview)
            (and many other files!)

Bibliography

Dern, D. P. "Peter Deutsch,'archie,' and Bunyip Systems." *Internet World* 4(2) (March 1993):11-16.

Deutsch, P. "Resource Discovery in an Internet Environment: the Archie Approach." *Electronic Networking: Research, Applications, and Policy* 2(1) (Spring 1992): 45-51.

Deutsch, P. and A. Emtage. "Archie: An Internet Electronic Directory Service." *ConneXions—The Interoperability Report.* (Advanced Computing Environments, Mountain View, CA.) 6(2) (1992):2-9.

Ryan, J. "A Pathfinder to Core Resources for Network Users." *Internet Research* 3(2) (Summer 1993):69-87.

CHAPTER

17

Gopher, Veronica, and Jughead

The Internet on Your Desktop and Your Desktop on the Internet

With hundreds of thousands of connected computers and millions of users world-wide, the Internet presents challenges to Internet users looking for information and to the folks who provide the information.

The typical Internet user wonders, "How and where can I find the resources I need? How can I keep track of files whose names and locations are constantly changing? Why do I have to learn how to use so many kinds of services to answer even the simplest questions?" As the amount of information available on the Internet grows in leaps and bounds, these issues become increasingly important.

Information providers struggle with the same kinds of questions, from a different, but complementary perspective: "What's the most efficient way of ensuring that Internet users can locate our resources? What's the most appropriate vehicle for storing and distributing our information? If the Internet is based on standards, why does information need to be put into so many different formats and services?"

To meet the needs of both the average Internet user and Internet information providers, a team of inspired programmers at the University of Minnesota created "The Internet Gopher" and subsequently, others created Gopher assistants veronica and jughead.

To the Internet user, Gopher is a very easy-to-use resource discovery tool. It provides a user friendly front end to the Internet for a large number of varied resources located throughout the Internet and presents them in a single directory system.

For the Internet information provider, Gopher is a powerful tool to present, organize, and distribute many services from a single platform. It provides a convenient method for "publishing" files or resources on the network.

The name "Gopher" is strikingly appropriate in several ways. Just as a real world Gopher knows how to get around its hidden burrows beneath the prairie, the Internet Gopher can tunnel through the invisible and twisty paths of the Internet and find the information you want. "Go-fer" is also American slang for someone who fetches things or provides services for other people. And by happy coincidence, the Golden Gopher is the school mascot of the University of Minnesota. (It's a good thing for the Internet that their mascot isn't one of the other characteristically Minnesotan animals, the mosquito or the lutefisk. But other sites have had fun with their taxonomic opportunities. For example, the University of California at Santa Cruz has a Gopher called InfoSlug, named after its mascot, the banana slug.) Like other rodents, the Internet Gopher has also proliferated and there are over 1,400 Gophers around the world that are registered at the University of Minnesota (there are many Gophers that are not registered), and the number of Gopher items is in the millions. In other words, it's a full-fledged infestation!

WHAT DO GOPHERS HAVE IN THEIR BURROWS?

Although Gopher was originally developed in April 1991 for use as a local campus wide information system (or "CWIS"), it has proven so powerful that there are now thousands of "Gopher holes" throughout the world interconnected to form what is fondly referred to as "gopherspace."

What is in gopherspace? You name it!

RESOURCE TYPE	SPECIFIC EXAMPLES
Text and files:	Electronic books
	Electronic journals
	Archives of Usenet newsgroups, LISTSERV lists, and other mailing lists
	Files from FTP archives
Telnet resources:	Online library catalogs (OPACs)
	Directories of telephone numbers and e-mail addresses
	Campus wide information systems (CWIS–see Chapter 19)
Database searches:	Full-text searches of files stored in Gopher
	Searches of the archie FTP archive database
	Wide Area Information Servers (WAIS–see Chapter 18)
Miscellaneous:	Digitized sounds, graphics

Gopher allows you to see all of this information throughout the Internet as if it were in a single set of directories and menus on your computer. You don't need to know where the information is physically located or how to get there from here, because Gopher does most of the hard work for you behind the scenes. Furthermore, Gopher is intentionally designed to easily accommodate new kinds of resources and computers as they evolve, so expect this list to keep growing over the coming years.

Like no previous application, Gopher brings information from the Internet to your desktop—and it also allows you to put information from your desktop on the Internet! See Chapter 22 for more detailed description of how to use Gopher to distribute your own information.

Accessing Gopher

There are three primary ways to access Gopher: from a local client installed on a personal computer, workstation, or mainframe; through CWISs or similar services; and by Telnet to a public-access client.

Regardless of how you access Gopher, it is a client-server application. Because the client and server software are separate, developers find that it's easy to change the

■■■

appearance and features of the client without affecting the server software. Gopher client and server software for many Internet applications has been written for most major personal computer and mainframe operating systems.

In addition, Gopher uses what is called "stateless" communication. The client you use sends a single question to the server ("Could you please display the menu of campus directories?"), the server responds with the requested information, and the connection is closed. This happens almost instantaneously and is more economical and speedy than dedicated connections. A computer wrestling with a handful of simultaneous dedicated sessions in an hour might be able to support thousands of stateless requests in the same time period. This is good for you and for the overall productivity of the Internet.

Gopher via Client Software

Gopher client software may already be installed on your local computer system. If you are using a Unix, VMS, DOS, or VM/CMS computer, you may be able to type "gopher" to launch this service. If you have access to X-windows services, try "xgopher". And if you're using a Mac, a NeXT, or a computer running MS Windows, there may be a Gopher icon which you can double click and launch. Ask your computer support staff for help locating your local Gopher services.

If there are no Gophers at your site yet, Gopher client software is available via FTP.

FTP host:	`boombox.micro.umn.edu`
directory:	`/pub/gopher`
filenames:	(many or all)

Gopher via Other Internet Front Ends

There are a number of other services which allow you to access Gopher, including many CWISs and the World Wide Web. (See Chapters 19 and 20.)

Gopher via Telnet

If a Gopher client is not installed on your Internet host computer, you can try one of the following Internet accessible Gopher clients via Telnet:

Hostname	Login	Location
`info.anu.edu.au`	`info`	Australia
`finfo.tu-graz.ac.at`	`info`	Austria
`infopath.ucsd.edu`	`infopath`	California, USA
`infoslug.ucsc.edu`	`infoslug`	California, USA

(Continued)

Hostname	Login	Location
tolten.puc.cl	gopher	Chile
gopher.denet.dk	gopher	Denmark
ecnet.ec	gopher	Ecuador
gopher.sunet.se	gopher	Europe
gopher.th-darmstadt.de	gopher	Germany
ux1.cso.uiuc.edu	gopher	Illinois, USA
panda.uiowa.edu	panda	Iowa, USA
gan.ncc.go.jp	gopher	Japan
nicol.jvnc.net	nicol	John von Neumann Network, USA
inform.umd.edu	gopher	Maryland, USA
seymour.md.gov	gopher	Maryland, USA
gopher.mus.edu	gopher	Michigan, USA
consultant.micro.umn.edu	gopher	Minnesota, USA
sunsite.unc.edu	gopher	North Carolina, USA
gopher.ora.com	gopher	O'Reilly & Associates, USA
gopher.torun.edu.pl	gopher	Poland
gopher.uv.es	gopher	Spain
gopher.chalmers.se	gopher	Sweden
hugin.ub2.lu.se	gopher	Sweden
ecosys.drdr.virginia.edu	gopher	Virginia, USA
gopher.virginia.edu	gwis	Virginia, USA
wsuaix.csc.wsu.edu	wsuinfo	Washington, USA
telnet.wiscinfo.wisc.edu	wiscinfo	Wisconsin, USA
gopher.brad.ac.uk	info	United Kingdom

Each of these sites is set up differently and has its own personality. Some, like Panda at the University of Iowa may use a modified version of Gopher with different commands and a significantly different look and feel than standard Gopher clients. Other Gophers, like "ecosys" have specialized information on specific topics, in this case, the environment.

SAMPLE GOPHER SESSION: PUTTING THE INTERNET ON YOUR DESKTOP

This sample session demonstrates the use of the text-only, Unix Curses client-used via the public gopher client or the University of Minnesota. Many of the files and menus shown here will be available on other Gophers as well, though their exact positions in the menus will be different.

Although you might initially learn how to use Gopher via Telnet, you really should consider installing and using Gopher client software on your local Internet host. You'll be richly rewarded in terms of speed, efficiency, and compliance with your normal operating system's features.

Accessing a Gopher Client

Either start a Gopher client from your host, or telnet to one of the clients listed above. For example:

```
telnet infoslug.ucsc.edu
```

You will see a connection being established and then be asked to login (type "gopher") and to enter your terminal emulation. (If in doubt, try vt100.)

```
Trying 128.114.143.25...
Connected to mclib.UCSC.EDU.
Escape character is '^]'.

ULTRIX V4.3 (Rev. 44) (mclib.ucsc.edu)

TERM = (vt100) vt100
```

Gopher Menus

Once you have entered a Gopher client, you'll see a list of menu options.

```
┌──────────────────────────────────────────────────────────────────┐
│                                                                    │
│            Internet Gopher Information Client 2.0 pl10             │
│                                                                    │
│              Welcome to InfoSlug at UC Santa Cruz                 │
│                                                                    │
│   -->  1.   About UCSC InfoSlug/                                  │
│        2.   Index to the InfoSlug Menu Tree <?>                   │
│        3.   The Academic Divisions/                               │
│        4.   The Campus/                                           │
│        5.   The Classroom/                                        │
│        6.   The Community/                                        │
│        7.   The Computer Center/                                  │
│        8.   The Library/                                          │
│        9.   The Researcher/                                       │
│        10.  The Student Center/                                   │
│        11.  The World/                                            │
│                                                                    │
│ Press ? for Help, q to Quit                     Page: 1/1         │
│                                                                    │
└──────────────────────────────────────────────────────────────────┘
```

The Pointer

The numbered list in the middle of the page is the root directory of files and services offered by this Gopher client. The "-->" in the left column is called the pointer, and indicates which item would be selected if you pressed the return key.

The Command Line

The bottom of a Gopher screen will usually show a few available commands. The specific commands displayed will change depending upon the type of screen being displayed. The "1/1" at the far right of this line indicates that this is the first page of a menu which has only 1 page.

Types of Gopher Menu Items

At the end of each menu item is a symbol that tells you what sort of information or service you'll get when you select that line. Here are the primary supported Gopher services and the symbols that appear in a Gopher menu:

.	a text file
/	a directory
<?>	a searchable index which will prompt you for a keyword when selected (Gopher will do a "full text" search—every word in every document is treated as a keyword—of the documents linked to the index; a list of retrieved documents will be shown on your screen.)
<TEL>	an item that automatically launches a Telnet session to the indicated resource–don't forget to check the required login sequence and disconnect procedures when you select the item

17 • Gopher, Veronica, and Jughead

■■

\<3270\>	an item that automatically launches a tn3270 session to the indicated resource–don't forget to check the required login sequence and disconnect procedures when you select the item
\<CSO\>	a directory search service which displays names, phone numbers, e-mail, and physical addresses
\<Bin\>	a file which is in binary code (You cannot actually retrieve or view these documents while in Gopher unless you are using your own Gopher client rather than Telnet.)
\<GIF\>	an image file in the graphical interchange format (GIF) (It must be saved or downloaded to your local system to view.)
\<TIFF\>	an image file in the tagged image file format (TIFF) (It must be saved or downloaded to your local system to view.)
\<JPEG\>	an image in a compressed format designed by the Joint Photographic Experts Group (JPEG) (It must be saved or downloaded to your local system to view.)
\<)	a digitized sound (Not all clients can handle this sort of information. The symbol \<) is meant to look like a speaker.)

Asking Gopher for Help

You can usually type "?" to request a display of Gopher client commands. Here are the basic commands for getting around in a Gopher server menu and selecting items in a menu.

```
The following commands are available in the browsing mode.

<Return> or <Right>   View current item
0-9                   Move to a line #
k, ctl-p,or <Up>      Move pointer up
j, ctl-n, or <Down>   Move pointer down
u, or <Left>          Go up a level
m                     Go to the first screen
q                     Exit Internet Gopher
>                     Next Page
<                     Previous Page
=                     Display Tech. info. about current item
o                     change options

?                     This help screen

(followed by a brief definition of Gopher menu items...)

Press <RETURN> to continue, <m> mail, <s> save, <p> print
```

<Right>, <Left>, <Up>, and <Down> refer to the arrow keys which you may have on your keyboard.

Because this help file is a document, the command line at the bottom now displays commands for document handling. If you press the "m" key, you will be asked for your e-mail address and the Gopher server will send the document to you by e-mail. The "s" and "p" commands are only available if you are using a client installed on your local Internet host. To leave this or any other Gopher document, simply press the return key and your screen will return to the directory from which you came.

If you are using a Gopher+ client (version 2.0 or higher –either on your desktop or you are telnetting to one), you will see a somewhat different help screen:

```
Quick Gopher Help
-----------------
Moving around Gopherspace
-------------------------
Press return to view a document.

Use the Arrow Keys or vi/emacs equivalent to move around.

<Up> .................: Move to previous line.
<Down> ...............: Move to next line.
<Right> Return .......: "Enter"/Display current item.
<Left>, u ...........: "Exit" current item/Go up a level.

>, +, Pgdwn, space ..: View next page.
<, -, Pgup, b .......: View previous page.

0-9 .................: Go to a specific line.
m   .................: Go back to the main menu.

Bookmarks
---------
a : Add current item to the bookmark list.


A : Add current directory/search to bookmark list.
v : View bookmark list.
d : Delete a bookmark/directory entry.

Other commands
--------------
s : Save current item to a file.
D : Download a file.
```

(Continued)

```
q : Quit with prompt.
Q : Quit unconditionally.
= : Display Technical information about current item.
o : Open a new gopher server.
O : Change Options.
/ : Search for an item in the menu.
n : Find next search item.
!, $ : Shell Escape (Unix) or Spawn subprocess (VMS)
```

Moving Around within a Menu

Once you have pressed the return key, you should be back in the main menu. Try moving the pointer up and down the menu by using the pointer movement keys described in the help file. You may find that some don't work from your terminal. You can also type the number of a menu item (it will appear on the command line), press return, and the pointer will jump to that item. To actually select that item, you'll need to press return again.

Selecting a Directory

Well, now we're ready to do some browsing through the Gopher hole. The first step is to learn how to select a directory. All you have to do is move the pointer to a menu item and press the return key. Let's try the "World" directory.

```
Internet Gopher Information Client 2.0 pl10

Welcome to InfoSlug at UC Santa Cruz

 -->   1.   About UCSC InfoSlug/
       2.   Index to the InfoSlug Menu Tree <?>
       3.   The Academic Divisions/


       4.   The Campus/
       5.   The Classroom/
       6.   The Community/
       7.   The Computer Center/
       8.   The Library/
       9.   The Researcher/
      10. The Student Center/
      11. The World/

Press ? for Help, q to Quit                      Page: 1/1
```

■ ■

Selecting and Viewing Documents

The World directory contains information about the Internet, weather forecasts for the U.S. and Canada, and U.S. State Department Travel Advisories.

```
                 Internet Gopher Information Client 2.0 pl10

                                 The World

       1.   Internet Assistance--Collected Resources via U.C.I./
       2.   Other Internet Gopher Servers/
       3.   Other Internet Systems and Databases/
       4.   The Internet Hunt/
 --> 5.    US State Department Travel Advisories/
       6.   Weather and More/
       7.   Wide Area Information Server (WAIS) databases/
       8.   Worldwide Internet Phone & Address Directories/

 Press ? for Help, q to Quit, u to go up              Page: 1/1
```

Selecting this menu item takes you to another menu offering three choices: a searchable index of all the current travel advisories, a country-by-country listing of the advisories, and access to the FTP archive of old advisories and other related material. The Gopher retrieves this new menu by connecting to a remote computer where the actual data is held (in this case, located at St. Olaf's College); but this happens behind the scenes, and all you see is a document that has been retrieved. No muss, no fuss.

```
                 Internet Gopher Information Client 2.0 pl10

                     US State Department Travel Advisories

         1.   Search US-State-Department-Travel-Advisories <?>
  -->  2.   Current-Advisories/
         3.   FTP-Archive/


 Press ? for Help, q to Quit, u to go up              Page: 1/1
```

When you select this item (Current-Advisories), you get a list of countries:

```
Internet Gopher Information Client 2.0 pl10

Current-Advisories

 -->   1.   afghanistan.
       2.   albania.
       3.   algeria.
       4.   andorra.
       5.   angola.
       6.   antigua-&-barbuda.
       7.   argentina.
       8.   armenia.
       9.   australia.
      10.   austria.
      11.   azerbaijan.
      12.   bahamas.
      13.   bahrain.
      14.   bangladesh.
      15.   barbados.
      16.   belarus.
      17.   belgium.
      18.   belize.

Press ? for Help, q to Quit, u to go up a menu        Page: 1/13
```

The situation in Kabul has been somewhat dramatic lately. By hitting the return key, we see what the U.S. State Department advises...

```
afghanistan (18k)                                        4%
+-----------------------------------------------------------+
STATE DEPARTMENT TRAVEL INFORMATION - Afghanistan
===========================================================
Afghanistan - Travel Warning            January 12, 1994
```

(Continued)

```
The Department of State warns all U.S. citizens against travel to
Afghanistan.  Fighting continues between opposing factions in the civil
war and indiscriminate rocket attacks, aerial bombardments, and other
violence can occur without warning.  Land mines are prevalent throughout
the countryside.  Westerners are vulnerable to politically and criminally-
motivated attacks, including robbery, kidnapping and hostage-taking.  All
U.S. personnel at the U.S. Embassy in Kabul were evacuated on January 31,
1989, and no other diplomatic mission represents U.S. interests or
provides consular services.


 No. 94-002

This replaces the Department of State Travel Warning of February 12, 1993,
to add information on dangers due to fighting between
+---------------------------------------------------------+
[PageDown: <SPACE>] [Help: ?] [Exit: u]
```

Well, after reading only four percent of the document (see the upper right corner), I'm pretty sure I won't be headed to Kabul in the near future. Hopefully the situation will be improving for all involved.

Launching Telnet Sessions from Gopher

Gopher also serves as a launching pad to Telnet accessible services throughout the world. Here is an example of a directory containing common Telnet resources–the first of three pages of library catalogs.

```
             Internet Gopher Information Client 2.0 pl10

                    Library Catalogs via Telnet

   --->  1. Advanced Tech. Info. Network CSU Fresno <TEL>
         2. Air Force Institute of Technology <TEL>
         3. Arizona State University <TEL>



         4. Athabasca University <TEL>
         5. Australian Defence Force Academy <TEL>


            (etc.)

Press ? for Help, q to Quit, u to go up            Page: 1/3
```

17 • Gopher, Veronica, and Jughead

■■

As usual, you should move the pointer to the service you want and press the return key. You will see a screen that may contain useful instructions for accessing and quitting the remote Telnet service you have selected.

```
             Warning!!!!!, you are about to leave the Internet
                Gopher program and connect to another host.
        If you get stuck press the control key and the ] key,
                         and then type quit

             Now connecting to <the service you requested>
```

(Gopher will often display required login information, such as userid, password, and preferred terminal types and occasionally, when appropriate, information on how to quit the service so you can return to your Gopher menu.)

```
                  Press return to connect:
```

Now that you've read what access codes are needed to use the service you've requested, press the return key, and you will see the entry screen for that service.

You may be prompted for access information, so enter the information that Gopher has so thoughtfully supplied in the previous screen. During this session, you will be using commands native to the Telnet service you connect to–not Gopher.

When you finally return to the Gopher from which you started, you will recognize the directory as the one where you selected the Telnet resource.

Searchable Databases

Note that "?" has two meanings on a Gopher screen: as a line command for getting help (?), and as a symbol at the end of a menu item indicating that it is a searchable database (<?>).

Most information stored in Gopher databases is indexed using a program called "gindex". This index is accessible by search engines such as WAIS and NeXT Librarian. Most of the time you select a searchable index (<?>), you will be using the WAIS search engine. Since WAIS uses a keyword search, all you need to do is enter a few words that accurately describe the topic you are searching for. For more advanced help on using the WAIS search engine, see Chapter 18.

Gopher also supports WAIS and archie database searches of non-gindexed materials at remote hosts, but if you plan to use those services a great deal, direct access is sometimes preferable to going through Gopher. (See Chapter 16 for more on archie.)

Similarly, you can access Usenet newsgroups through Gopher. (You won't be able to post to the newsgroups using the Gopher gateway, just read the messages.) However, you will find it more efficient to use a Usenet newsreader. (See Chapter 9 on Usenet for a list of Gophers that offer access to newsgroups.)

Before you start a search, you should understand what sorts of information are contained in the index you are using. To help you out, many directories with searchable indexes will contain an informative file, usually with a name like "About <topic>" or something similar. Read these files so you can make the most effective use of the particular search index.

When you select a menu item ending with <?>, you will be prompted for the word(s) for which you want to search, and Gopher will send a search request to the server where the indexed materials are stored. Looking again at the InfoSlug Gopher, we've selected the "Journalism Periodicals Index." To get to this service, from the root directory, we selected The Library and then Indexes and Abstracts.

```
              Internet Gopher Information Client 2.0 pl10

                        Indexes and Abstracts

       1.  AIDS Book Review Journal/
       2.  American Mathematical Society e-MATH System <TEL>


       ...

 -->  12. Journalism Periodicals Index <?>
      13. Latino WAIS Index (UCLA-UCSB) <?>
      14. Law and Politics Book Review (via Northwestern)/
```

When you select Journalism Periodicals Index, you're prompted to enter the word or words you want to search for. We chose "sound bite" as the keywords.

```
            Internet Gopher Information Client 2.0 pl10

                     Indexes and Abstracts

        1.  AIDS Book Review Journal/
        2.  American Mathematical Society e-MATH System <TEL>
        3.  Astrophysics Abstracts - SISSA/
        4.  CARL UNCOVER Database <TEL>
        5.  California Agriculture - Contents/
        6.  Catalog of LBL Research Abstracts/
   +------------Journalism Periodicals Index-------------+
   |                                                     |
   | Words to search for                                 |
   |                                                     |
   |   sound bite                                        |
   |                                                     |
   |                                                     |
   |   [Cancel: ^G] [Erase: ^U] [Accept: Enter]          |
   +-----------------------------------------------------+
        15. Librarianship Professional Reading Service. Mich./
        16. Life Sciences Collection CDROM List of Journ. <?>
        17. Math Reviews 1991 Subject Classifications/
        18. Math Reviews 1991 Subject Class.(searchable) <?>

Press ? for Help, q to Quit, u to go up a menu     Page: 1/2
```

Gopher creates a list of the files containing these words in their titles or text. To retrieve the full citation of the article, move the pointer to the article you're interested in and press the return key.

```
Internet Gopher Information Client 2.0 pl10

                 Journalism Periodicals Index: sound bite

   --> 1.  Apr 1991: Facilities: Making a sound bet: Winfi...
       2.  Mar..of the sound bite (Value of investigative ...
       3.  Apr 1989: Quayle: This is no 'sound-bite' admin...
       4.  Sep 1990: Sound bite seeks expert: If you know ...
       5.  May 31 1993: Forum: Singer Tom Waits protects h...

   ...

       18. Nov 21 1988: Campaign '88: Assessing the media:...

Press ? for Help, q to Quit, u to go up a menu     Page: 1/3
```

Searching <CSO> Directories ("Phone Books")

A growing number of campus directory services are accessible through Gopher. Here's a typical menu of directory selections.

```
                 Internet Gopher Information Client 2.0 pl10

                               Phone Books

  -->   1.  University of Minnesota <CSO>
        2.  University of Minnesota Phone Book (new and improved)/
        3.  About changing information in the U of M directory.
        4.  Phone books at other institutions/
        5.  Internet-wide e-mail address searches/
        6.  X.500 Gateway/
        7.  WHOIS Searches/
  Press ? for Help, q to Quit, u to go up a menu      Page: 1/1
```

After selecting the phone book of your choice, you will be presented with a screen like the following:

```
+----------------University of Minnesota------------------+
|                                                         |
|  name                                                   |
|  alias                                                  |
|  dn                                                     |
|  email                                                  |
|  X.400_address                                          |
|  other_mailbox                                          |
|  phone                                                  |
|  office_phone                                           |
|  home_phone                                             |
|  mobile_phone                                           |
|  pager                                                  |
|  fax                                                    |
|  telex                                                  |
|  address                                                |
|                                                         |
|[Switch Fields: TAB][Cancel: ^G][Erase: ^U][Accept: Enter]
+---------------------------------------------------------+

Press ? for Help, q to Quit, u to go up a menu         ...
```

Typically, you would enter the person's name, press return, and then see a listing of contact information for people with that name at the site whose directory you have selected. You can also search for information by providing a phone number or e-mail address, or almost any other bit of information you can think of!

FIELD GUIDE TO THE GOPHERS OF THE WORLD

From the main menu of most Gopher servers, you have the option of locating other Gopher and information servers.

```
Internet Gopher Information Client 2.0 pl10

                   Other Internet Gopher Servers

      1.   Africa/
 --> 2.   All the Gopher Servers in the World/
      3.   California/
      4.   Europe/
      5.   International Organizations/
      6.   Jughead - Search High-Level Gopher Menus (W&L) <?>
      7.   Library Gopher Menus and Servers/
      8.   Middle East/
      9.   North America/
     10.   Pacific/
     11.   South America/
     12.   Veronica search (UNR) of much of GopherSpace/
     13.   Veronica search options and access (UMN)/

Press ? for Help, q to Quit, u to go up a menu     Page: 1/1
```

Selecting "2" from the menu above retrieves a directory of Gopher servers throughout the world. Now your gopherspace travels can take you to Gophers in the United Kingdom, Australia, Switzerland—and maybe you will even run across a neighbor Gopher in your own backyard!

```
Internet Gopher Information Client 2.0 pl10

All the Gopher Servers in the World

 -->  1.   Search Gopherspace using Veronica/
       2.   ACADEME THIS WEEK (Chronicle of Higher Education)/
       3.   ACM SIGDA/
       4.   ACM SIGGRAPH/
       5.   ACTLab (UT Austin, RTF Dept)/
       6.   AMI -- A Friendly Public Interface/
       7.   AREA Science Park, Trieste, (IT)/
       8.   Academic Position Network/
       9.   Academy of Sciences, Bratislava (Slovakia)/
      10.   Acadia University Gopher/
      11.   Action for Blind People/
      12.   AgResearch Wallaceville, Upper Hutt, New Zealand/
      13.   Agricultural Genome Gopher/
      14.   Alamo Community College District/
      15.   Albert Einstein College of Medicine/
      16.   Alpha Phi Omega/
      17.   American Chemical Society/
      18.   American Demographics/

Press ? for Help, q to Quit, u to go up a menu     Page: 1/74
```

This seventy-four page listing only shows the main burrows of gopherspace. Each of these servers may be representing many other Gopher servers at that site, each of which is maintained by information providers who have used the Gopher protocol to put their desktops on the Internet. Again, the beauty of the Gopher protocol is that you don't need to know where the servers are to use them.

VERONICA: SEARCHING THROUGH GOPHERSPACE

Now that you've had a chance to work with Gopher a bit, you may be wondering, "where's the catalog?" How do you figure out where in gopherspace a particular kind of resource might be hiding? Well, just as archie serves as a catalog for the names of files in anonymous FTP hosts, a service called "veronica" lets you search for items in the menus of gopherspace.

Veronica is used from within Gopher, so you don't need to learn another set of commands or a strange new interface. In addition, veronica presents the results of its search in

■■■

the form of a Gopher menu, so you can immediately examine files, work with searchable indexes, and dive into menus, using whatever Gopher software you know and love.

So what does the name veronica mean? Well, yes, it's true, a character named Veronica is a buddy of the comic strip character Archie, but like almost everything on the Internet, the name is also an acronym (and the archie service is *not* named after the comic book character anyway). Are you ready? It stands for "Very Easy Rodent-Oriented Net-wide Index to Computerized Archives."

Working with Veronica

From most Gopher servers, you can usually get to veronica through one of the main directories, for example "All the Gophers in the World" or "Other Gopher and Information Servers." Once you reach a menu in which veronica is available, you might see a screen like the following:

```
Internet Gopher Information Client 2.0 pl10

Other Gopher Servers

        1.   How to use Gopher (free course)/
        2.   Guides to Internet Resources/
        3.   Gophers by Subject/
        4.   Gophers by Location/
  -->   5.   Gophers by Keyword Search (Veronica)/
        6.   The Mother Gopher at Minnesota/


           ...

Press ? for Help, q to Quit, u to go up a menu    Page: 1/15
```

Select veronica (item 5 in this menu), and you will see one or more Gopher searchable database prompts:

```
Internet Gopher Information Client 2.0 pl10

Gophers by Keyword Search (Veronica)

 -->  1.   Search gopherspace by veronica at U. of Manitoba <?>
       2.   Search gopherspace by veronica at University of Cologne <?>
       3.   Search Gopher Directory Titles using U. of Manitoba <?>
       4.   Search Gopher Directory Titles using University of Cologne <?>
       5.   FAQ:  Frequently-Asked Questions about veronica  (1993/08/23).
       6.   How to compose veronica queries (NEW June 24) READ ME!!.

Press ? for Help, q to Quit, u to go up a menu              Page: 1/1
```

Simply select the search index you want and enter a keyword. In a short while, veronica will return a Gopher menu containing items from its catalog of Gopher servers.

Notice that you can perform two different kinds of veronica searches. By selecting a search of Gopher Directories, you will limit your search to Gopher menu items–you will not retrieve files, searchable indexes, etc., but only those items that end in a "/". Depending on the item you are searching, you will probably find that selecting a directory search will help narrow down the number of "hits" and give you the most useful results at the same time. But if you select a general gopherspace search, you can retrieve any sort of Gopher resource from directories, to files, to binary files, or even searchable databases. Enjoy!

Veronica's (Current) Limitations

As wonderful as veronica is, this service currently has a number of limitations of which you should be aware. Some of these problems are likely to be addressed in the near future, while others may simply be limitations imposed by the nature of gopherspace.

To illustrate, let's go through a search that seems tailor made for veronica. Let's look for all Gopher menu items containing the word "physics". Veronica returns the following Gopher menu:

```
Internet Gopher Information Client 2.0 pl10

Veronica server at SUNET: physics

  -->  1.   Physics Agreement.tex.
       2.   Physics Agreement (text).
       3.   Physics.
       4.   Physics.
       5.   physics-faq_part1.
       6.   physics-faq_part2.
       7.   puzzles_archive_physics.
       8.   Sci.physics FAQ - December 1993  - Part 1/2.
       9.   Sci.physics FAQ - December 1993  - Part 2/2.
      10.   Rec.puzzles Archive (physics), part 27 of 35.
      11.   Sci.physics FAQ - December 1993  - Part 1/2.
      12.   Sci.physics FAQ - December 1993  - Part 2/2.
      13.   Atmospheric Physics.
      14.   Condensed Matter Physics.
      15.   Laser Physics and Quantum Optics.
      16.   Nuclear Physics.
      17.   Particle Physics and Relativity.
      18.   Introduction to the Department of Physics.

Press ? for Help, q to Quit, u to go up a menu    Page: 1/12
```

At first blush, this seems like a mighty haul indeed! And this is just the first of 12 pages of Gopher menus; the whole result set contains more than 6,500 items, many of which are themselves directories containing even more items. But as you may recall, Gopher was developed (and is currently widely used) as a CWIS. Consequently, it should come as no surprise that a great deal of this haul is material which is only of interest to folks at a particular institution or even a small department. (A note of warning is in order here: by default, veronica will only display the first 200 items of your search retrieval set; if you want all possible "hits" add the "-m" option after your last keyword in the search with a space between the keyword and the "-m".)

As it turns out, many of the entries are simply descriptions of physics courses given at a number of universities. Entries such as "Phys 5371s. INTRODUCTION TO ELEMEN-TARY PARTICLE PHYSICS." listing the time, room number, and instructor for a course, are probably not what a person doing a search for physics materials wanted, unless they happened to attend the school that was offering the course. A better search strategy here would be to combine two or more words, to more quickly locate an item like, "Works on the Foundations of Statistical Physics." Using the two words, "statistical" and "physics," you retrieve a result set only two pages in length with 20 items.

■■■

Well, this still leaves hundreds of items that probably would be interesting to a wide range of users. But now you need to contend with another potential result in your search. Many entries are either obvious duplications from multiple Gopher holes or multiple copies of files with different names which, in this case, reduces the number of unique resources you actually retrieved. The veronica developers are currently wrestling with methods to reduce this redundancy.

Other types of items that are of little or no use to the general user are those that are very local in nature (like the St. Patrick's Day Parade in Peoria, Illinois–well, that is my birthday and a trip to Peoria would be fun! ;-), items that are out of date, and even items that no longer exist! But lest we forget, it might take days of crawling through gopherspace to pull out what veronica has found in about a minute.

Some items listed in veronica result sets are ones that are not available to the general public. Usually these are items from a fee-based or otherwise proprietary database and access to the material is limited to a specific community of users. When you select one of these items, you will get an error message to the effect of, "Sorry, this item is not available to off-site users." (Local administrators can change this message to whatever suits their needs and may include additional information.)

"Veronica, Where in Gopherspace ARE We??"

One of the values of veronica is that it offers a view of gopherspace by keyword rather than by Gopher server. But suppose there is a particularly rich cluster of Gopher resources in a veronica search result, yet neither the titles nor the contents of the Gopher menu items give clues as to where a particular resource is actually located. After all, you might want to explore the Gopher hole from which those materials came, step by step and directory by directory.

To determine where in gopherspace a particular Gopher item is located, use the "=" command. This will display technical information about a Gopher menu item. (Note that this is a Gopher command that you can use for any item on any Gopher menu.) For example, where do they teach "Physics and Psychophysics of Music" whose Gopher directory is shown in the display below?

```
Internet Gopher Information Client 2.0 pl10

Veronica server at University of Cologne: physics

      55.    MATHEMATICS AND PHYSICS (B.Sc.).
      56.    PHYSICS AND ASTRONOMY + See ASTRONOMY.
      57.    PHYSICS AND BIOLOGY + See BIOLOGY.
      58.    PHYSICS AND CHEMISTRY + See CHEMICAL PHYSICS.
 -->  59.    JPA300Y   Physics and Archaeology   52L, 26P.
      60.    PHYSICS AND COMPUTER SCIENCE + See COMPUTER...
      61.    PHYSICS AND ENVIRONMENT + See DIVISION OF T...
      62.    PHYSICS AND GEOLOGY + See GEOLOGY.
      63.    PHYSICS AND MATHEMATICS + See MATHEMATICS.
```

Simply type "=" and you'll find out:

```
#
Type=0
Name=    JPA300Y    Physics and Archaeology    52L, 26P
Path=R11084-11748 gopher_root70:[_student._fas._courses.
_anthropology]_fas_course_ant.;2
Host=robarts.library.utoronto.ca
Port=70
URL: gopher://robarts.library.utoronto.ca:70/0R11084-11748-
gopher_root70:[_student._fas._courses._anthropology]_fas_course_ant.;2
```

"robarts.library.utoronto.ca" is located at the University of Toronto–no surprise there! (Although, as you are probably aware by now, it's not always so easy to figure out an institution's name on the basis of a domain name.) So, in this case, if you did want to keep track of the courses that are taught at the University of Toronto, you could select the University of Toronto Gopher from the list of Gophers in the server of your choice or install this technical information into your client software. (Please note, if you don't have a Gopher+ client and server running, you won't see the last line of the display that includes the URL. For more information on URLs, see Appendix D.)

JUGHEAD: VERONICA'S BEST FRIEND

If there's one thing that's obvious about veronica, it's that it's an equal opportunity gopherspace searcher–it searches a lot of data and returns large result sets. Sometimes that's just what you need, but other times, it is a hinderance. The solution is jughead. (Warning: tortured acronym alert!) Jughead is an acronym for Jonzy's Universal Gopher Hierarchy Excavation and Display. (Jonzy is the nickname of the jughead developer, Rhett Jones at the University of Utah). What you really need to know is that jughead is a mini version of veronica, in that it only indexes small portions of gopherspace as defined by the administrator. Most often, it only indexes a single Gopher, but it can be used to index a part of a Gopher or a set of Gophers. In practice, you use it just like veronica, but its faster, and gives you results from a smaller index.

What's your best strategy? Well, if you've found a really good Gopher, and you want to find specific resources on it, use jughead (which often appears as a menu item like, "Search items in this Gopher <?>"). Even better, suppose you're looking for information on biology, and you find a jughead entry specifically for biology Gophers. This is perfect since you'll be searching a set of related Gophers. When you perform a search using this type of jughead server, you will receive aggregated results from all of the servers that are indexed. This means you won't need to go through a whole veronica search, or go traipsing from Gopher to Gopher using each jughead index separately.

On the other hand, if you are having trouble locating a specific piece of information using jughead, or you know that what you are looking for is pretty esoteric, a veronica search is probably what you should try. In addition, if you want to be sure that you are casting the widest net, use veronica to start.

Putting Your Desktop on the Internet

Gopher is an extraordinary tool for information providers: you can put a wide variety of information into a Gopher hole, it's easy to advertise your service to all the other Gophers in the world, and users will be able to access your information from a service providing document retrieval, text searches, Telnet sessions, and more.

The technical details of setting up a Gopher server are beyond the scope of *The Internet Passport*, but here's some general information to help you get started and a few things to keep in mind if you decide to burrow your own Gopher hole. (For more details on becoming an information provider using Gopher and/or other software, see Chapter 22.)

Getting the Software

Gopher client and server software has been written for many operating systems. You can obtain this software for free by FTP from the University of Minnesota and other sites. The software is free for noncommercial use, other uses require a fee. For more information on licensing, please see the file "gopher-software-licensing-policy" at the FTP site. There are now Gopher clients and servers available to run on the following platforms: Macintosh, NeXT, DOS, Unix, VMS, MS Windows, Amiga, MVS, OSF, and OS2. Client and server software is available from a server at the University of Minnesota, affectionately known as "boombox."

FTP host:	`boombox.micro.umn.edu`
directories:	`/pub/gopher`
filenames:	(many or all)

How to Care For and Feed Your Gopher

If you choose to start a Gopher server, keep the following points in mind.

Gophers Are Highly Social

While a solitary server is useful, you can take full advantage of the Gopher world by letting other users know about your services. Register your server by sending an e-mail message to gopher@boombox.micro.umn.edu.

Gophers Have Ravenous Appetites

A growing number of people are using Gopher to store and retrieve the information they would like to share with other users both locally or globally. Because Gopher sets up pointers to remote resources rather than storing the information on your own computer, you can construct menu structures that make sense to you and your users without having to worry about running out of disk space. The downside to this is that you have little or no control over information stored on someone else's server.

Gophers Are Playful

The Gopher protocol is still young and very flexible, and the original authors of Gopher encourage experimentation with and customization of the client software. Many new and exciting applications are being developed by users throughout the world: for example, the "Gopher in A Forest" client developed for the NeXT computers allows the clients, the servers, and directories of gopherspace to be displayed graphically. Such a visual image of the service is useful—and engaging! Experiment with putting novel services on your client, modify the software to work with different operating systems, and in general, feel free to be creative.

FOR MORE INFORMATION

Although Gopher has only been in existence since April, 1991, it is already a major Internet service. The diversity of resources which will be added to Gopher and the number of Gopher servers and clients in the world is likely to keep growing. A new version of Gopher called Gopher+ (version 2.0 and higher) has been released which it provides further extensions to the already remarkably useful Gopher protocol. With a Gopher+ client running on your local computer, you can retrieve files of all types from within Gopher.

 Gopher Contact:

e-mail: gopher@boombox.micro.umn.edu
Microcomputer & Workstation Networks Center
152 Shepherd Labs
100 Union St. SE
University of Minnesota
Minneapolis, MN 55455 USA
voice: (612) 625-1300
fax: (612) 625-6817

 Veronica Contact:

e-mail: veronica@veronica.scs.unr.edu
Veronica Development Team
SCS Computer Center Building, MS 270
University of Nevada, Reno
Reno, NV 89557-0023 USA
voice: (702) 784-4292 or (702) 784-6557
fax: (702) 784-1108

Gopher, Know Thyself

If you already have access to Gopher, you can get a great deal of information from within Gopher itself.

- Most Gopher servers include a directory called "Information About Gopher" in the root directory. This should be your first stop for information about Gopher itself.

- Many Gopher servers also include a directory called "Information About This Gopher". This will provide you with information about the server, who is responsible for it, and where to report trouble. It should also tell you something about the contents of the server.

- As an exercise in exploring Gopher and veronica, you might want to see how much of the following reference material you can get from within gopherspace!

Usenet Newsgroups

If you want to keep up with the latest breaking news about Gopher via Usenet, read the following newsgroups:

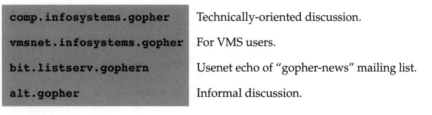

`comp.infosystems.gopher`	Technically-oriented discussion.
`vmsnet.infosystems.gopher`	For VMS users.
`bit.listserv.gophern`	Usenet echo of "gopher-news" mailing list.
`alt.gopher`	Informal discussion.

Internet Mailing List

To keep track of the evolution of Gopher, you can subscribe to the "gopher-news" mailing list by sending an e-mail subscription request to gopher-news-request@boombox.micro.umn.edu.

FTP Archive

Software for Gopher clients, servers, and some associated documentation can be found in the following FTP archive:

FTP host:	`boombox.micro.umn.edu`
directory:	`/pub/gopher`
filenames:	(many or all)

Bibliography

Anthes, G. H. "Tools Help Internet Users Discover Online Treasures." *Computerworld* 26(29) (July 20, 1992):51-52

■■

Brandt, D. S. "Accessing Electronic Journals." *Academic and Library Computing* 9(10) (November/December 1992):17-20.

Dern, D. P. "Leveraging the Internet: Counterpoint Uses Popular Internet Gopher, WAIS, and Internet Navigator/Search Tools for Value-Added Delivery and Access to Daily U.S. Government Federal Register, Commerce Business Daily Information." *Internet World* 4(3) (April 1993):4-5.

"Exploring Internet Gopher Space." *The Internet Society News* 1(2) (1992).

Kambitsch, T. et al. "Trip Notes From Internet Gopher 93 Conference" posted in two parts on PACS-L@UHUPVM1.UH.EDU (April 13, 1993). To obtain a copy of these postings, send the following e-mail message:

```
mail:        LISTSERV@UHUPVM1.UH.EDU
subject:     (none needed)
message:
Database Search DD=Rules
//Rules DD   *
Search kambitsch gopher in PACS-L from 93/04/20 to 93/04/22
Print all
/*
```

Notess, G. R. "Using Gophers to Burrow Throughout the Net." *Online* 17(3) (May 1993):100-102.

WAIS (Wide Area Information Server)

*Easy Access to
Internet Databases*

The Internet contains a vast amount of information stored in many different formats on computers with many different operating systems. To provide a single port of entry for searching diverse and large databases from a single, easy to use interface, a group of researchers have developed an innovative system called WAIS (the Wide Area Information Server). Although WAIS is used for accessing traditional databases, it is also adept at handling complex textual information, so in some ways it's more like an electronic librarian than a database service. Examples of materials currently accessible through WAIS include the following:

- books
- bibliographies
- network addresses
- traditional databases
- archie databases
- software catalogs
- library catalogs
- Internet information, such as lists of lists of Internet services
- archives of Usenet newsgroups, LISTSERV lists, and mailing lists

How WAIS Works

WAIS is based on the client-server model. You use a WAIS client that retrieves information from WAIS servers that may be located anywhere on the Internet. After selecting one or more databases (known as "sources" in the WAIS world) from the displayed list, you simply enter one or more keywords. Behind the scenes, WAIS makes connections to the remote servers where the information is actually stored. Materials containing your keywords are returned to your WAIS client and displayed on your screen.

Each retrieved document is assigned a score, up to 1000, for how well the document corresponds to what you want to find, with 1000 being deemed a perfect fit. The score is based on the frequency of the keywords within a document.

Like all information retrieval tools, how well WAIS works for you is largely a function of how well you specify your search. Unlike other database tools with which you may be familiar, WAIS features a special technique called "relevance feedback." You can select retrieved documents that closely match what you want and these texts will be used by WAIS as keyword sources for further searches.

One of the many exciting possibilities opened up by WAIS and related information servers is that you can create a personal electronic newspaper. You can have WAIS automatically pull all items of interest together into a single document monthly, weekly, or

■■

even daily. In fact, this was one of the main applications considered during the design of the software.

WAIS was originally created at the Thinking Machines Corporation by a group of developers headed by Brewster Kahle. In 1992, WAIS, Inc. was formed and the commercial, fully supported version of the software became available. At about the same time, the Clearinghouse for Networked Information Discovery and Retrieval (CNIDR–pronounced "snyder") took over the maintenance and development of the free version of WAIS, known as freeWAIS. Since that time, both WAIS, Inc. and CNIDR have continued development of the client and server programs as a coordinated effort.

Accessing WAIS

■■

WAIS Client Software

Because WAIS is a client-server application, it is best to use a locally installed WAIS client if you can. There are versions of WAIS available for the Mac, Unix computers, X-window terminals, and VMS. Ask your computer support staff if a local client is available.

If a local WAIS client is not yet installed, WAIS software can be obtained by anonymous FTP from one of the following sites:

FTP host:	`ftp.cnidr.org`	
directory:	`/pub/NIDR.tools/freewais`	
filenames:	`freeWAISXXX.tar.Z`	(Unix client; "XXX" denotes the version number)
directory:	`/pub/NIDR.tools/wais/pc/windows`	
filenames	`(many or all)`	(Windows clients and information)
FTP host:	`sunsite.unc.edu`	
directory:	`/pub/packages/infosystems/wais/clients`	
subdirectories:	`/macintosh`	
	`/ms-dos`	
	`/ms-windows`	
	`/NeXT`	
	`/os2`	(for use with X-windows)
	`/unix`	
	`/willow`	

■■■

Gopher, WWW, and CWISs

WAIS is easily accessed from a number of Internet information mediators, including Gopher, World Wide Web, and many CWISs. For more information on using these other services, please refer to Chapters 17, 20, and 19 respectively.

Telnet

You can use Telnet to directly access these WAIS clients which use Simple WAIS, or SWAIS, a basic text-only client available to anyone on the Internet.

sunsite.unc.edu (login as "swais")

wais.com (login as "wais")

Sample WAIS Session Using SWAIS

Even if you have access to WAIS via a local client or a Gopher, you are encouraged to work through this SWAIS example just to get a basic overview of how WAIS works. But once you have a grasp of the basic concepts, you will find the use of local client versions of WAIS to be much more powerful and satisfying.

Logging in to SWAIS

To get started with SWAIS, just telnet to wais.com or sunsite.unc.edu.

```
telnet wais.com
```

You will then be asked for a login name (enter "wais"), your e-mail address, and your terminal type. If you are unsure of the latter, try vt100.

```
login: wais

Welcome to swais.
Please type user identifier (user@host): <you>@<your.internet.host>

TERM = (vt100) wais
```

The Menu of WAIS Sources

In a short while, you should see a menu of WAIS databases, usually referred to as the sources.

```
SWAIS                    Source Selection            Sources: 490

 #            Server              Source                    Cost

001:   [            archie.au]   aarnet-resource-guide       Free
002:   [ndadsb.gsfc.nasa.gov]    AAS_jobs                    Free
003:   [ndadsb.gsfc.nasa.gov]    AAS_meeting                 Free
004:   [     munin.ub2.lu.se]    academic_email_conf         Free
005:   [     archive.orst.edu]   aeronautics                 Free
006:   [bruno.cs.colorado.ed]    aftp-cs-colorado-edu        Free
007:   [nostromo.oes.orst.ed]    agricultural-market-news    Free
008:   [     archive.orst.edu]   alt.drugs                   Free
009:   [     wais.oit.unc.edu]   alt.gopher                  Free
010:   [     sunsite.unc.edu]    alt.sys.sun                 Free
011:   [     wais.oit.unc.edu]   alt.wais                    Free
012:   [     munin.ub2.lu.se]    amiga_fish_contents         Free
013:   [    coombs.anu.edu.au]   ANU-Aboriginal-EconPolicies $0.00/min.
014:   [    coombs.anu.edu.au]   ANU-Aboriginal-Studies      $0.00/min.
015:   [    coombs.anu.edu.au]   ANU-Ancient-DNA-L           $0.00/min.
016:   [    coombs.anu.edu.au]   ANU-Ancient-DNA-Studies     $0.00/min.
017:   [    coombs.anu.edu.au]   ANU-Asian-Computing         $0.00/min.
018:   [    coombs.anu.edu.au]   ANU-Asian-Religions         $0.00/min.

Keywords:

<space> selects, w for keywords, arrows move, <return> searches
q quits, or ?
```

The column labeled "#" is a line number for the source; "server" is the Internet address of the server where the database is actually located; "source" is a brief description of the contents of the database; and "cost" is the cost to the user. (Currently, all databases in SWAIS are free.) In the upper right hand corner, "sources: 490" indicates that there are 490 sources known to this particular SWAIS client.

Source #1 should appear highlighted in some way on your screen. This indicates where your source selector is currently located.

At the bottom of most SWAIS screens, you will see a small selection of commands that you can use. To get started, let's use the "?" command.

Commands for Working with SWAIS Menus

After you've pressed the "?" key, you should see a list of commands that can be used with SWAIS to work with source menus. Notice that you've got several options for moving around within the menu of sources. So if your arrow keys don't work from your terminal, you can use letter commands, or you can type in a source's number. Just below we display the help file for menu commands, slightly edited to make it clearer:

```
SWAIS                    Source Selection Help              Page: 1


          1. Moving Around in the Source Menu

j, down arrow, ^N       Move Down one source
k, up arrow, ^P         Move Up one source
J, ^V, ^D               Move Down one screen
K, <esc> v, ^U          Move Up one screen
###                     Position to source number ###
/sss                    Search for source sss

          2. Selecting, Unselecting, and Getting Info About Sources

<space>, <period>       Select current source
=                       Deselect all sources
v, <comma>              View current source info

          3. Searching Sources

s                       Select new sources (refresh sources list)
w                       Select new keywords
<ret>                   Perform search

X, -                    Remove current source permanently
o                       Set and show swais options
h, ?                    Show this help display
H                       Get brief information about WAIS
q                       Leave WAIS
```

Press any key, and you will be back at the first page of the source menu.

Moving Around in the Source Menu

Now that you are back at the source menu, try the various commands for moving around in a menu that are listed in section 1 of the previous display. Find out which keys work (up and down arrow keys don't work from all terminal types) or are easiest for you to remember.

Selecting a Source

Now that you know how to move around in the menu, you're ready for the next steps: selecting and then searching a source.

Let's proceed by selecting and searching the ERIC (Educational Resources Information Center) Digests database which contains short reports of interest to educators. To get to this source you can move through the menu with the commands you've just learned, or you can press the "/" key, and then type "eric". This searches through the source names and puts the selector right on a source containing this word.

The part of the menu containing the ERIC sources should now be on your screen, and the line "ERIC archive" should be highlighted. If not, use your movement keys until it is highlighted.

```
110:  [        nic.sura.net]  ERIC-archive           Free
111:  [sun-wais.oit.unc.edu]  eric-digests           Free
112:  [    sun1.cr.usgs.gov]  eros-data-center       Free
```

To select this source, type "." or press the space bar. You should now see an asterisk in front of the number indicating that this source has been selected and is ready to be searched. (Note that you can select as many sources as you want for a keyword search. For this search, you might want to select the eric-digests as well.)

```
110: * [        nic.sura.net]  ERIC-archive           Free
111:   [sun-wais.oit.unc.edu]  eric-digests           Free
112:   [    sun1.cr.usgs.gov]  eros-data-center       Free
```

Searching Selected Sources

Keywords

To search a selected source, type "w", which stands for "keyword." Your cursor will appear in front of the "Keywords:" prompt. Since reform is a perennial topic in education, let's see what the ERIC database has to say on this topic. Type the word "reform" and press return.

```
110: * [        nic.sura.net]  ERIC-archive           Free
111:   [sun-wais.oit.unc.edu]  eric-digests           Free
112:   [        140.174.7.1]   fidonet-nodelist       Free

Keywords: reform
Searching ERIC-archive.src...
```

The SWAIS client is now establishing an Internet connection to the WAIS server at "nic.sura.net" and asking it to search through the ERIC database for any document containing the word "reform." In a few seconds, the search is done and the results are shown on your screen.

```
SWAIS                  Search Results                 Items: 40

  #    Score     Source                 Title               Lines

001: [1000] (ERIC-arch) Title: Social Studies Curriculum Reform  284
002: [ 945] (ERIC-arch) Title: Fiscal Policy Issues and School R  264
003: [ 834] (ERIC-arch) Title: The Impact of Educational Reform   254
004: [ 500] (ERIC-arch) Title: Trends and Directions in Career E  267
005: [ 500] (ERIC-arch) Title: The Old College Try. Balancing Ac  220
006: [ 500] (ERIC-arch) Title: The Influence of Reform on Inserv  212
007: [ 444] (ERIC-arch) Title: The 1983 Educational Reform Repor  219
008: [ 444] (ERIC-arch) Title: Education for Tomorrow's Vocation  292
009: [ 389] (ERIC-arch) Title: Restructuring the Schools. ERIC D  245
010: [ 333] (ERIC-arch) Title: At-Risk Students. ERIC Digest Ser  193
011: [ 333] (ERIC-arch) Title: Collaboration between Schools and  252
012: [ 333] (ERIC-arch) Title: Emerging Issues in State-Level Sc  237
013: [ 278] (ERIC-arch) Title: Foreign Language Teacher Educatio  230
014: [ 222] (ERIC-arch) Title: World History in the Secondary Sc  327
015: [ 222] (ERIC-arch) Title: Restructuring American Schools: T  339
016: [ 222] (ERIC-arch) Title: The Role of Business in Education  272
017: [ 222] (ERIC-arch) Title: Trends and Options in the Reorgan  284
018: [ 222] (ERIC-arch) Title: School-to-Work Transition: Its Ro  251

<space> selects, arrows move, w for keywords, s for sources,
? for help
```

SWAIS has retrieved 40 documents, which is the default maximum number of documents that SWAIS will allow. Most WAIS clients allow you to increase or decrease this maximum number of documents.

The "score" column indicates SWAIS's estimate as to how well that article fits your request, with 1000 being considered a "perfect fit" to your search request. This score is based on the density of keywords in the documents.

This "results" menu looks and works like the sources menu. Each document has a number in the left hand column and you can move up and down with position keys. To display a highlighted document, press the return key.

```
Title: Social Studies Curriculum Reform Reports. ERIC Digest.

Personal Author: Patrick, John J.

Clearinghouse Number: SO020890

Publication Date: Apr 90

Accession Number: ED322021

Descriptors: *Curriculum Development; Curriculum Problems;
*Educational Change; Educational Resources; *Elementary School
Curriculum; Elementary Secondary Education; Geography; History;
*Secondary School Curriculum; *Social Studies

Identifiers: 1980s; ERIC Digests

Abstract: The 1980s were years of concern about the curricula in
elementary and secondary schools. Throughout the decade educators in
the social studies, as well as in other fields of knowledge, formed
curriculum study groups to assess the status quo and to recommend
improvements in widely distributed reports. This ERIC Digest examines:-
More-
```

To leave a document you are viewing and return to the results menu, press the "q" key followed by the return key. To leave the results menu to return to the sources menu, press the "s" key.

Stopwords

When materials are WAIS indexed, certain words may be excluded from the indexing process, and therefore won't work as keywords. By default, any words that occur more than 20,000 times in the material are excluded. For example, a set of software description files containing 24,000 entries, each of which starts with the phrase "software name," would not contain the words "software" and "name" in the WAIS index you search. Similarly, WAIS indexed material will often exclude conjunctions ("but," "and," etc.), prepositions ("in," "around," etc.), articles ("a," "an," etc.), and a number of common verbs ("tell," "is," etc.). Such non-indexed words are called "stopwords."

Some of the words which are not included as WAIS keywords include the Boolean operators such as "not," "or," and "and," which you may be used to using in searches of databases or OPACs. Some versions of WAIS may include Boolean operators; try them to see if they work for you.

Although the fact that certain words, including Boolean operators, have not been indexed may be a disadvantage at times, it helps you use "natural language" queries more easily, if you are so inclined. The following two searches might yield exactly the same documents, depending upon the stopwords that had been used in creating the source.

```
keywords: Tell me where I can get french bread recipes
```

```
keywords: french bread
```

About Relevance Feedback

Humans take for granted their ability to synthesize many distinct impressions into an overall image, or "Gestalt." We can look at three objects and assert that object A is more like object B than it is like C, without necessarily being able to specify exactly why.

"Relevance feedback" is a feature of WAIS that allows you to involve your Gestalt impressions when searching databases. You can use part or all of a document you have retrieved in one search as input for further searches. This is, in some ways, equivalent to telling WAIS that, "sure enough, all the files you retrieved contain the keyword I have supplied, but this particular file is most like what I am looking for. Find more that are like it!"

As a trivial example, let's suppose that your keyword was "wing," and WAIS retrieved documents about airplane wings, wingtip shoes, and wing-nuts. By selecting one of the airplane wing documents as input for relevance feedback, words like "airplane," "aeronautics," and "fuselage" would become keywords in subsequent searches and should prevent spurious hits on gangster stories and hardware catalogs. As this point should make clear, a careful choice of keywords from the start probably would have worked as well, but the point of relevance feedback is to make database searches easy even for people who don't want to take the time to formulate a carefully specified search.

Using Relevance Feedback

How you invoke relevance feedback depends upon which client you are using. Typically, you select one or more articles from a previous WAIS search as being "relevant" to your question by putting it into a "similar to:" window. In some clients, you can copy portions of retrieved documents and place these passages into the relevance feedback hopper.

Although relevance feedback has a command in SWAIS ("r"), be forewarned! This feature does not currently work and is undocumented.

Determining Which Sources to Search

If you want to use WAIS to its fullest, you need to know which sources should be searched for a particular question.

■ I

Search the Directory of Servers

Say we want to identify which of the WAIS sources have information about agriculture. From the list of servers menu, select the source "directory of servers." (First be sure to unselect any other sources you may have been working with by typing the "=" command!) Start a keyword search and enter the word "agriculture."

```
...
098: * [      quake.think.com]  directory-of-servers            Free
...
Keywords: agriculture
```

SWAIS will respond with a list of source description files containing this term.

```
001:  [1000] (directory-of-se)   agricultural-market-news        23
002:  [ 834] (directory-of-se)   ANU-Thai-Yunnan                 44
003:  [ 834] (directory-of-se)   usda-rrdb                       28
```

If you select one of these documents, you'll see a source description file that begins with technical information used by WAIS client software followed by a brief description of what's in the source. If you select "agricultural-market-news," you will see the following information:

```
(:source
  :version  3
  :ip-address "128.193.124.4"
  :ip-name "nostromo.oes.orst.edu"
  :tcp-port 210
  :database-name "agricultural-market-news"
  :cost 0.00
  :cost-unit :free
  :maintainer "wais@nostromo.oes.orst.edu"
  :subjects "business marketing commodities agriculture agricultural"
  :description "Server created with WAIS release 8 b3.1 on Oct 5
                22:48:47 1991 by wais@nostromo.oes.orst.edu

This server contains the agricultural commodity market reports compiled
by the Agricultural Market News Service of the United States Department
of Agriculture. There are approximately 1200 reports from all over the
United States. Most of these reports are updated daily. Try searching for
'portland grain.'

For more information contact: wais@oes.orst.edu
```

■■■

To leave this technical description and return to the sources menu, press the "q" key followed by any other key.

Making Sense of the Source Titles

You could page through the menu of sources and identify likely sources by their names. Most names are fairly descriptive so you can pretty much guess what's in the source.

But how do you figure out what's in sources with names like "AAtDB," "uxc.cso.uiuc.edu," or "meval-bibtex-zenon-inria-fr?" To find out, enter the source number in the command line, press the return key, and enter "v", the view command. This will give you a brief descriptive file written by the person maintaining the source.

Ending an SWAIS Session

To leave SWAIS, simply type "q" from the sources menu.

FOR MORE INFORMATION

■■■

The FTP hosts at the Clearinghouse for Networked Information Discovery and Retrieval (CNIDR) and SunSITE at the University of North Carolina contain much of what you need to know to get started using or installing WAIS.

FTP host:	`ftp.cnidr.org`	
directory:	`/pub/NIDR.tools/freewais`	
filenames:	`freeWAISXXX.tar.Z`	(Unix client; "XXX" denotes the version number)
directory:	`/pub/NIDR.tools/wais/pc/windows`	
filenames:	(many or all)	(Windows clients and information)
FTP host:	`sunsite.unc.edu`	
directory:	`/pub/packages/infosystems/wais/clients`	
subdirectories:	`/macintosh`	
	`/ms-dos`	
	`/ms-windows`	
	`/NeXT`	
	`/os2`	
	`/unix`	
	`/willow`	(for use with X-windows)

■■

Mailing Lists

There are a number of Internet interest groups devoted to discussions about WAIS. To subscribe to one of the mailing lists, send the following message:

```
mail:    <listname>-request@<address>
subject: (none needed)
message: subscribe <listname> <Your-name>
```

Be sure to include the word "-request" with the list name, otherwise your request to be added to the list will be sent to the entire list!

`wais-discussion@think.com`	Moderated mailings every 2 weeks.
`wais-interest@think.com`	Major monthly announcements about WAIS.
`wais-flash@think.com`	WAIS, Inc. announcements.
`wais-talk@think.com`	Unmoderated and active discussion for WAIS users and implementors.

CNIDR maintains a listserver list devoted to FreeWAIS technical issues called "zip1." To subscribe, send the following message:

```
mail:    listserv@cnidr.org
subject: (none needed)
message: subscribe zip1 <Your-name>
```

Usenet Newsgroup

`comp.infosystems.wais`

Bibliography

A 1992 bibliography of written materials and resources is available via FTP.

FTP host:	`sunsite.unc.edu`
directory:	`/pub/packages/infosystems/wais/documents`
filename:	`bibliography.txt`

The original WAIS was developed as a joint project between Apple Computer, Dow Jones, KMPG Peat Marwick, and Thinking Machines Corporation. For basic information about WAIS, you can order hardcopies of documents from:

```
e-mail:        info@wais.com
```
Thinking Machines Corp.
1040 Noel Dr.
Menlo Park, CA 94025 USA
```
voice:         (415) 617-0444
fax:           (415) 327-6513
```

Other Materials

Brandt, D. S. "Accessing Electronic Journals." *Academic and Library Computing* 9(10) (November/December 1992):17-20.

Dern, D. P. "Leveraging the Internet: Counterpoint Uses Popular Internet Gopher, WAIS, and Internet Navigator/Search Tools for Value-Added Delivery and Access to Daily U.S. Government Federal Register, Commerce Business Daily Information." *Internet World* 4(3) (April 1993):4-5.

Kahle, B., et al. "Wide Area Information Servers: An Executive Information Systems for Unstructured Files." *Electronic Networking: Research, Applications, and Policy* 2(1) (Spring 1992): 59-68.

Lukanuski, M. "Help is on the WAIS." *American Libraries* 23(9) (October 1992):742-744.

Schwartz, M. F., et al. "A Comparison of Internet Resource Discovery Approaches." *Computing Systems* 5(4) (Fall 1992):461-493 [previously published in WAIS-discussion Digest 56 (October 22, 1992)].

Smith, J. "CNIDR: Coordinating Internet User Tools." *Internet World* 4(2) (March 1993): 8-10.

Stein, R. M. "Browsing Through Terabytes: Wide-Area Information Servers Open a New Frontier in Personal and Corporate Information Services." *BYTE* 16(5) (May 1991):157-164.

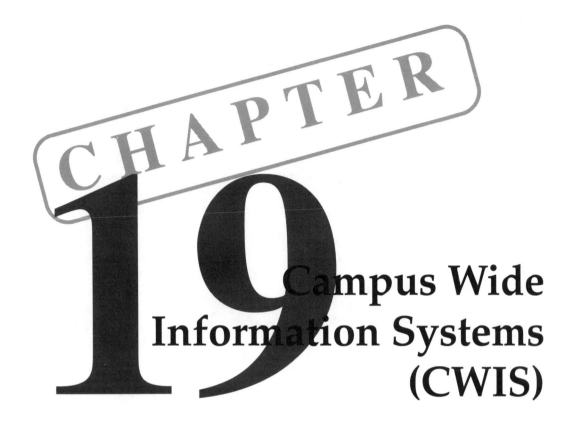

CHAPTER
19
Campus Wide Information Systems (CWIS)

■■■

A "campus wide information system" (CWIS) is an online service used as a central source of information at a college, university, institution, or company. The typical CWIS wears many hats: it might provide access to campus directories, newspapers, calendars of events, course descriptions, information about the surrounding community, reports from the local weather service, or potentially anything else that may be of interest to its users.

Typically, a CWIS is maintained on one or a few central computers and accessed from public terminals, networked personal computers, and workstations in people's workplaces, dorm-rooms, off-campus homes—or even by remote users throughout the Internet!

There are hundreds of Internet accessible CWISs installed around the world. Some CWIS services open doors to the Internet and are rapidly converging on what one might call "network wide information systems." A prime example of this is Gopher which fully integrates network resources in a campus or organizational setting. The fabric of online information is becoming more and more tightly knit, and CWISs are playing an increasingly important role in publishing and distributing local information globally, and global information locally.

THE BENEFITS OF CWISS

■■■

Information at Any Time

If you've ever tried to call campus information after working hours, you'll appreciate the value of a service which is alert and available 24 hours a day. A well maintained CWIS doesn't have to sleep.

One-Stop Information Shopping

How many documents would you need on your desk to keep track of campus phone numbers, the time and location of the Thespian Club's weekly meetings, which dining halls are serving sloppy joes ("again?!? yuck!"), and everything else you need to know about your campus? A good CWIS may be able to answer your most pressing (and maybe even some of your most frivolous) questions from the convenience of your personal computer.

Up-to-Date Information

Printed documents like directories, handbooks, and calendars are difficult to update or correct once they've been distributed. The economics of print as a medium means that such sources of information may be out of date for much of the time between reissues. But information on a CWIS may be updated much more frequently and be continuously available to the community.

Information for Remote Users

A CWIS connected to the Internet can enhance the accessibility of an institution. If you're a high school student comparing colleges, you might be able to obtain more information about a college's academics and extracurricular activities from a CWIS than the typical admissions office could fit into an envelope. If you're a nostalgic alumnus, you can stay in touch with your old *alma mater*. And if you're at an institution which does not yet have a CWIS installed, you can try out Internet-accessible CWIS's to determine the value of installing a CWIS at your own site.

Community (and Commonsense) in a Distributed (and Complicated) World

Keeping track of what's going on in a large campus can be daunting, especially for commuting students. A CWIS is like an informational student union for anyone at, or interested in, an institution.

Have you ever been unable to locate someone because you didn't know in which cubicle on which floor of which building of which sub-department of which school of which campus they were located? If your institution seems like an alphabet soup of departments and acronyms, a well organized CWIS can help people find who or what they need, quickly and easily.

A LIGHTHEARTED INTRODUCTION TO CWIS EXPLORATION: ALICE

To illustrate some of the common features of CWISs, consider the main menu (shown below) displayed by a CWIS named "ALICE" at the hypothetical "Wonderland University."

The main menu of a typical CWIS is like a book's table of contents and its index at the same time. You can move to "submenus" by selecting their numbers, and many CWIS also allow you to use a command to search through some or all of the CWIS for a particular word or phrase.

For example, by typing "2" in the main menu of ALICE, the screen would show the menu for the Admissions Office, which would probably include information about entrance requirements and related topics. Similarly, by typing "Find Red Queen" from the main menu you might retrieve information on courses she teaches in the Law School, what moves she made in the last Faculty-Student chess competition, or even when and why she declared "Off with their heads!" By selecting "11", ALICE would give you access to other information throughout the Internet. And if you became confused you could type

"Help", an option which Alice, the person, would have appreciated in her visit to Wonderland.

```
            Welcome to the Wonderland University CWIS
                              ALICE
           ("A Lighthearted Introduction to CWIS Exploration")
                            Main Menu
       Topic                 Partial Description of Contents
    ------------------        -----------------------------------
    1 About ALICE             Help, How to Answer Riddles
      ADMINISTRATIVE
    2 Admissions              Rabbit Hole, Mirrors; "Who are YOU?"
    3 Consulting              The Mad Hatter's Corner
    4 Courses                 Of Course a Catalog, Lessen Plans
    5 Policies                "Off With their Heads!"
      LIFE IN WONDERLAND
    6 Athletics               Croquet, Chess, Cards
    7 Calendar                Coming Events, When Will I Wake Up?
    8 Dining Halls            Eating, Drinking, How to Change Size
    9 Directory               Staff, Students, Animals
   10 Social Events           Lobster Quadrille, Tea Parties
      THROUGH THE LOOKING GLASS
   11 Internet                Resources Throughout the Internet
   Commands: Help, Backup, Find, Main_menu
   Enter # of Menu Choice, or First Letter of Command -->
```

So even the arbitrary and perplexing world on the other side of the Looking Glass might be rendered comprehensible and navigable by a CWIS.

CWIS ACCESS

If a remote CWIS is connected to the Internet, you can probably access it directly by Telnet, tn3270, or indirectly by going through a service like Gopher or Hytelnet that establishes the connection for you. You may be able to invoke a local CWIS at your institution by typing a simple command when you are connected to the campus network. Please contact your local user services staff for specific information on accessing a local CWIS.

CWIS Access via Telnet (or tn3270)

Most CWISs can be accessed through the Internet by Telnet or tn3270. To access a CWIS by this route, you will need to know the following:

- how to use Telnet or tn3270 (Chapter 6) and

- the Internet address of the CWIS. (See "Sample Table of CWISs" or one of the "Lists of CWISs" named at the end of this chapter.)

  In addition, you may also need to know some additional information:

- the login name, password, and possibly other access codes for the CWIS; and

- the type(s) of terminal emulation which can be used (e.g., vt100).

Once you've used CWISs and other Internet information systems for awhile, you can second-guess some of this access information based on subtle clues from the screen or the system's responses. But why waste time guessing? Consult one of the "CWIS Lists" named at the end of this chapter for a compendium of such information.

CWIS Access through "Network Wide Information Systems"

There are several network-wide information systems explicitly designed to automate and facilitate the use of services like CWISs throughout the world. Typically they contain a list of CWIS services and you can poke through the list, select a CWIS, and have a session launched without having to type in a lot of Internet addresses.

Gopher

Gopher was originally designed at the University of Minnesota as a local information system, but it has quickly proven to be a world-class, front end for a variety of Internet resources. Gopher presents lists of documents and services—even though they may be located elsewhere in the world—as menus on your screen. When you select a CWIS from a Gopher menu, Gopher supplies you with a screen containing up-to-date information about login names, passwords, or other quirks about the CWIS, and then launches a session. For more on Gopher, see Chapter 17.

Hytelnet

Hytelnet is an easy to use, customizable software package developed at the University of Saskatchewan. It contains a list of many Telnet accessible resources, and, when installed on an Internet host, it can automate logins to these sites. Hytelnet includes a great selection of CWISs, as well as exceptionally thorough coverage of OPACs, BBSs, and other Internet resources. You can try out the Hytelnet system via any of the Internet front ends described in the next section.

Hytelnet may already be installed at your local site. Try typing "hytelnet" at your system prompt; if this doesn't work, ask your local user services staff for assistance. Or, if you are feeling adventurous, you can obtain a copy of Hytelnet for your local computer. Installation is moderately difficult and may prove too challenging for the novice network user. There are currently versions of Hytelnet available for VMS, DOS, Mac, Amiga, and most Unix operating systems. You can get Hytelnet along with instructions on installation and customization via FTP.

```
                FTP host:           ftp.usask.ca
                directories:        /pub/hytelnet/amiga
                                    /pub/hytelnet/mac
                                    /pub/hytelnet/pc
                                    /pub/hytelnet/unix
                                    /pub/hytelnet/vms
```

Or you can access Hytelnet using Telnet.

```
                Telnet:             access.usask.ca
                login:              hytelnet
                select:             Other resources then_Campus-
                                    wide Information systems
```

Other Internet Front Ends

Several other Internet front ends can be used to access CWISs. For example, you can get to many CWISs by telnetting to the following multipurpose services:

Internet Address	Access	Location of CWIS info
bbs.oit.unc.edu	login as "bbs" and supply requested information	in the libtel menu
liberty.uc.wlu.edu	login as "lawlib"	main menu
wugate.wustl.edu	login as "services"	main menu

CWIS ETIQUETTE

Even if a CWIS is Internet accessible, it may not really be designed to support users from around the world. If messages on the screen indicate that there are restrictions for off-site users, respect those requests. For example, many CWISs feature databases that are licensed to a particular institution and cannot be used by remote users. And if you want to take a remote CWIS for a spin, try to restrict your use to that site's non-peak hours. Anytime after 5pm and before 9am their local time will help prevent undue congestion and degradation of service.

So what is true for all network services is sometimes even more true of CWISs: using or even exploring another institution's CWIS is a privilege, not a right.

SAMPLE CWIS SESSION

There are many different kinds of CWISs in operation, so there is no universal user interface. (As someone once sagely noted, "the problem with standards is that there are so many of them.") Furthermore, a single CWIS may be able to present different features

■■■

depending upon what kind of terminal emulation you are using. For example, you may be able to move around a full screen session with arrow and tab keys when using vt100 terminal emulation, but only access the command line when using dumb terminal emulation.

However, there are enough similarities among CWISs that a sample session to one robust site will be fairly representative. In this example, we will go through step-by-step instructions for using the University of North Carolina's CWIS, called "INFO." You can also try any of the CWISs listed in Gopher, Hytelnet, or one of the CWIS lists.

Accessing a CWIS

If you are using Telnet, type "telnet" followed by the Internet address of the CWIS. (If you are using a service such as Gopher or Hytelnet, the Telnet command may be executed for you.)

```
telnet info.oit.unc.edu
```

When the remote computer receives your connection request, you should see an acknowledgment of the connection, and possibly some useful information about how to exit from the CWIS.

Providing Login Information

Some CWISs may take you directly to a menu of options; others may request that you specify one or more of the following: a) a special username for the CWIS; b) a password; c) your terminal emulation. Screens prompting you for such information will sometimes tell you the magic words you need to get in. But to save yourself time and effort, obtain an up-to-date copy of one the CWIS lists or use Gopher or Hytelnet if they are available to you.

In the case of the University of North Carolina, we only need to supply the username "INFO" to get into the CWIS.

```
                    W E L C O M E    T O
                          U N C
              Office Of Information Technology
                    Computing Systems
                         UNCVX1
            Type INFO at the Username: prompt to
            access the Campus Information System
                           or
          Type LIBTEL to access Internet Library Services

                    Username: INFO
```

CWIS Main Menus

Once you've entered the correct access information, you will usually see a main menu for the CWIS. Such a screen will often contain a "Welcome" message of some sort, a list of topics available in the CWIS, and most importantly, how to get help.

```
                    Office of Information Technology
                           Information Center


1. About INFO                      8. Research

2. About UNC-Chapel Hill           9. Services and facilities

3. Academics                      10. Student life

4. Directories                    11. Transportation and parking

5. Events                         12. Other Information Systems

6. Faculty and staff information  13. Bicentennial Observance

7. Publications

Please type one of the numbers above or commands below and press return.
Commands:  Help  Quit  Find
     Enter menu choice number or command:
```

Commands

The basic commands available at a particular level are usually given at the bottom of your screen. When a word begins with an UPPERCASE or **BOLD** character (like "**Q**uit"), it generally means that you can use that single letter as an abbreviation for the whole command.

Selecting Items

In UNC INFO, we can select an item by typing its number in the "command area" following "command:" on the bottom line. Some CWISs allow you to use your arrow and tab keys to move around the screen and select items if you are using the correct terminal emulation. Those that can be accessed via a client (e.g., Gopher) may allow you to use application specific tools like a mouse or pull-down menus.

Obtaining Help in a CWIS

Be sure to take advantage of any online help. In addition to a concise list of commands at the bottom of the screen, you can usually get a more comprehensive explanation of commands available by typing "Help", "?", or something similar. Here's the first of many pages of expanded help available from UNC INFO.

```
------------------------------------------------------------------
Type | Command            | Command Description
------------------------------------------------------------------
 --> | Next Page          | Go to the next page in a document
 <-- | Previous Page      | Go to the previous page in a document
  B  | Backout            | Back out from the current page
 GM  | Go to Mark         | Return to a page where a book mark is
 GP  | Get PM             | Display your personalized menu
  H  | Help               | Display this help file
  L  | Local              | Save or print page or document, etc.
  M  | Main Menu          | Go to the Main Menu
 NC  | Next Choice        | Go to the next page of a menu range
 PC  | Previous Choice    | Go to the previous page of a menu range
  Q  | Quit               | Quit the UNC-CH INFO system
  R  | Reveal             | Display hidden information about a page
  S  | Search             | Search for page using predefined keyword
 SF  | Send Form          | Send a form after form is completed
 SM  | Set Mark           | Set a temporary book mark on a page
 SP  | Set PM             | Set up a personal frequent-use menu

------------------------------------------------------------------
|                  [HELP page 1 of 11]            Next page --> |
|   Commands:  Backout   Quit info                              |
------------------------------------------------------------------
    Enter command:
```

To exit from this help screen, enter "b" for Backout.

Exploring a CWIS: Diving into the Menus

Suppose you're a high school student looking for information about student life at UNC. By selecting item 10 (Student life) from the main menu of this CWIS, you'd get the following menu chock full of valuable information. It's almost like taking a tour of the campus without having to pay for the airfare.

```
Choose from the following topics about student life at UNC-Chapel Hill:
 1. Campus Code
 2. Campus Directory for Students (information current 2/23/94)
 3. Career Planning and Placement
 4. Counseling Center
 5. Extracurricular involvement
 6. Honor Code
 7. Housing
 8. Leadership
 9. Legal services
10. Orientation
11. Publications
12. Regulations and policies
13. The Source handbook
14. Student Affairs offices
15. Student Health Service
16. Student judicial governance
17. Student organizations (updated February 1994)
18. Veterans affairs

Commands: Help  Quit  Main  Backup  Find
    Enter menu choice number or command: 6
```

Let's see what the Honor Code is for UNC by selecting 6.

```
    Student Judicial Governance

For over a century, students at The University of North Carolina at Chapel
Hill have accepted responsibility for their own conduct and discipline in
academic and nonacademic affairs. Although the specific expectations with
regard to student behavior have varied over time, the faith in the individual
student's ability to conduct himself or herself in an honorable fashion has
not changed. The trust bestowed upon students has precluded the necessity of
any extensive system for monitoring student behavior inside or outside the
classroom. There is no need for active proctoring of exams by instructors, or
for oppressive supervision of student life outside the classroom. The honor
system has helped to cultivate the environment of relaxed pursuit of academic
and social activities which is enjoyed by the whole University community.
 (etc.)

                    The Undergraduate Bulletin, 1991-1993
Commands: Help  Quit  Main  Backup  Find  Next
    Enter command:
```

Exiting a CWIS

Since CWISs vary, so do the commands to end your session. Common exit commands are "Bye", "Quit", "Exit", "End", or "Logout". (Commands like "Let me out of

here!" or "Ecrassez l'infame!" usually don't work.) Refer to the online help if you are confused. If all else fails, you may have to terminate your Telnet session "ungracefully" by using the escape code specific to your software. For example, when using Telnet on a Unix system use "^]" (i.e., control right bracket) and then enter "quit" at the Telnet prompt.

CONCLUSION

For many people, the essence of the Internet has been the sharing of online information. Similarly, one of the goals of education is the dissemination of knowledge. A CWIS can be the union of these two visions and become an integral part of the give and take that is helping create a truly worldwide information environment.

If you are interested in starting a CWIS at your site, Chapter 22 explores options for providing information online and includes a section specifically on CWISs. In that overview, the focus is on the administrative and design issues associated with implementing and running a CWIS. You will also find information on obtaining CWIS software in that chapter.

FOR MORE INFORMATION

CWIS Usenet Groups and LISTSERV Mailing Lists

To keep up-to-date about CWISs, or to discuss CWISs with others, you can subscribe to the following LISTSERV mailing list, or read it as a Usenet newsgroup:

cwis-l@wuvmd.wustl.edu   (LISTSERV)

bit.listserv.cwis-l   (Usenet)

The archives of CWIS-L can be searched using the WAIS database "bit.listserv.cwis-l," or the LISTSERV LISTDB tool.

There are also several Usenet newsgroups for specific software platforms which can be used as, or as part of, CWIS services.

comp.infosystems.gis   (Usenet–Geographic Information Systems)

comp.infosystems.gopher   (Usenet–Gopher)

comp.infosystems.wais   (Usenet–WAIS)

comp.infosystems.www   (Usenet–World Wide Web)

For more information on using Usenet, LISTSERV along with LISTDB, and WAIS, please refer to Chapters 9, 10, and 18.

Master Lists of CWISs

Judy Hallman maintains an up-to-date list of CWISs. This list is periodically updated and posted to the CWIS-L LISTSERV mailing list described above.

Hallman's List:

```
FTP host:      sunsite.unc.edu
directory:     /pub/docs/about-the-net/cwis
filename:      cwis-l
```

The access files used by Hytelnet also provide good coverage of CWIS services. Refer back to the Hytelnet section of this chapter for accessing these files by FTP.

For more information about using FTP, refer to Chapter 7.

Bibliography

The following printed materials either deal with CWISs directly, or provide general information relevant to employing online information services in a campus setting.

Arms, C. R. (ed.). *Campus Strategies for Libraries and Electronic Information.* Bedford, MA: Digital Press, 1990.

Finnegan, G. A. "Wiring Information to a College Campus: A Port for Every Pillow." *Online* 14(2) (1990):37-40.

Hallman, J. (In press.) "Campus Wide Information Systems." *Advances in Library Automation and Networking.*

Hawkins, B. L. (ed.). *Organizing and Managing Information Resources on Campus.* McKinney, TX.: Academic Computing Publications, 1989.

Heterick, R. C., Jr. *A Single System Image: An Information Systems Strategy.* Professional Paper Series, #1. Maynard, MA: Digital Equipment Corp., 1988.

Kinney, T. "Toward Telecommunications Strategies" in: *Academic and Research Libraries: Ten Case Studies in Decision- Making and Implementation.* Washington, DC: Office of Management Services, 1988.

Waren, M. S. "How Much Paper Do You Need to Support an Electronic Information System?" *Proceedings, ACM SIGUCCS User Services Conference XVIII, 1990,* pp. 355-360. 1990.

20

World Wide Web

*A Hypertext-Based View
of the Internet*

World Wide Web—often abbreviated as WWW or W³—is an innovative front end to information located throughout the Internet. Like Gopher, it allows a single point of entry to many Internet sources, including WAIS, archie, Telnet accessible services, online databases, sounds, pictures, and text files.

The basic goal of WWW is (simply!) to make all online knowledge part of one "web" of interconnected documents and services, and to allow you to follow facts or texts in WWW anywhere they might lead, for as many steps as you care to travel. If you were reading this text in as a Web document, you could select a reference in this document—a word, a name, or a network service—and WWW might display definitions, contact information, or establish access to a network service. Each of these results could then be used as a jump-off point to other parts of the WWW universe, and so forth without end.

WWW is significantly different from most Internet services you've probably encountered so far because it uses a method called "hypertext" to organize, search, and present information. The unique approach of WWW is that it uses a combination of hypertext and full-text searching to allow you to view the information universe in any way that you might like. This has advantages, but it also creates unique challenges for the WWW user. So before you use WWW, you should have a basic understanding of the hypertext philosophy.

WHAT IS HYPERTEXT?

Hypertext is text that is accessed or stored, in part or in whole, in a non-hierarchical structure. Each piece of hypertext (or node) is connected to one or more other pieces of hypertext by "links." As more nodes and links are added to the structure, the nodes and links form a web. To help you visualize hypertext, think of something physical with a web-like structure: a piece of lace, or a spider's web glistening in the morning dew. You can get from place to place in the web by following many different paths and you don't have to return to where you started, unless you want to. There are no real ends in a web.

In contrast, directories are branching, hierarchical storage systems. To get to a certain document in a directory system, you start at the root, and then work your way down through a path of directories. Each step down the directory path leads to more and more specific subcategories, eventually leading you to a file (e.g., "/pub/documents/networks/a.file"). There is usually only one path to a particular file, and when you get to the end of a directory tree, your only options are to move backwards or exit.

Compare a bird flying from twig to twig in a tree to an ant climbing on branches and the difference between hypertext and hierarchical information should be clear. The methodical path of the ant represents an adherence to a tree's geometry, and the flights of the bird represent the hypertext links between any and all parts of a tree. Hypertext lets you "fly" from branch to branch (or node to node) in an information universe.

The Printed Word as Fossil Hypertext

The term hypertext sounds alien and futuristic, but in fact, we all use hypertext-like behavior. Consider an example from everyday life.

We usually think of sentences, paragraphs, and books as linear and hierarchical structures. This chapter has sections and subsections. This sentence had a beginning, and now it has an end. Maybe sometimes you'll jump around in a book, but it's usually to reread something you've forgotten in the linear presentation of the text, to jump to the materials cited in the text, to skip some information that you already know, or maybe to look at the pictures.

But no word, passage, or book exists in isolation. Whenever you go to a dictionary to define an unfamiliar word or refer to a book mentioned in a bibliography, you're using the hypertext model. In fact, there are many hypertext conventions in text, such as footnote numbers which point to text at the bottom of a page. Each footnote points to a citation elsewhere in the literature, a definition from a dictionary, or further explanatory text which would divert from the main expository purpose of the passage. To a specialist, hypertext links to other nodes are often the most valued part of a text. For more on hypertext, see the citations at the end of this chapter.   :–)

For example, you've probably seen (or maybe even written) essays which bristle with footnotes after almost every word. Consider a typical passage from a university term paper:

> In the summer of 1797, Samuel Taylor Coleridge had been prescribed an anodyne [1] by his doctor for an illness [2]. Drowsy from his medicine, he fell into a hypnagogic sleep [3] while reading the book "Purchas's Pilgrimage" [4]. In a dream, he composed a three hundred line poem named "Kubla Khan." Coleridge's friend and mentor, Lord George Byron, later read the poem, and encouraged Coleridge to publish the still incomplete piece. For the past 200 years, this poem, "Kubla Khan," about a mysterious locale, "Xanadu" [5], has inspired a voluminous discussion about the mysterious role of the unconscious in creativity [6]...

If the essay about Coleridge were in WWW format, each number would represent a node with a link to another hypertext node. By selecting "4", we might retrieve a citation for "Purchas's Pilgrimage" or possibly the entire document. By selecting "5", we might find out that Xanadu is the name of Ted Nelson's original hypertext system, or that it is a phonetic spelling of the old Chinese name for Beijing. And by selecting "6", we would expect to be led to something about creativity. If the entire essay is in WWW format, it could be broken up into multiple sections, so it would be arranged on the screen as a table of contents. Selecting a listing would then bring that section of the essay to the screen.

Hypertext, WWW, and the Internet

Hierarchical systems like library catalogs or file directories are very useful for storing and retrieving information that is static and/or easily classified. However they have weaknesses when dealing with information that is dynamic, multidisciplinary, difficult to classify, or chock-full of references to all sorts of seemingly unrelated things. (Sounds suspiciously like much of the Internet, doesn't it?)

The goal of WWW is to combine hypertext and full-text searches so that all information on the Internet can be linked according to a person's needs. This processed world converges in a global and dynamic web of information, memory, and imagination.

How Many Texts, Could a Hypertext Text, if a Hypertext Could Text Text?

With a universal hypertext system, a text no longer slumbers between its covers. Any part can leap out and be linked with passages from any other text. With hypertext a reader becomes an author, and this has been proclaimed as one of the great advantages of hypertext. But of course, not every reader is willing or able to take on the time and effort that authorship entails. This is one of the challenges of using hypertext systems.

Quite honestly, using WWW or other hypertext systems is sometimes frustrating. Although our own thoughts may be free-flowing links and associations, we usually count on an easy-to-understand order in our surroundings. When using someone else's WWW server, you might find yourself lost, going in circles through loops of texts, or unable to get to the document or service you're hoping to retrieve. Don't get discouraged! To become an effective, efficient hypertext voyager requires practice and perseverance.

WORLD WIDE WEB ACCESS

Client or "Browser" Software

WWW is at its best when used with locally installed client software. So if you plan to use WWW extensively, find out if there is a WWW client available at your site or ask your local computer support staff if they can help with installing a WWW client on your site's computers.

The "line browser" WWW client is a text-only version suitable for operating systems with character only displays, such as Unix, DOS, or VM/CMS. In WWW line browsers, you track hypertext links by typing their numbers. There are also a variety of WWW clients for operating systems with windowed environments, like X-windows, the NeXT, MS Windows, and the Macintosh. By far the most popular of these is NCSA Mosaic developed by the National Center for Supercomputer Applications. Mosaic is available via FTP and is free of charge to individual users. Information on obtaining NCSA Mosaic is available at the end of this chapter. Mosaic and other clients allow you to use the features of your local system that you know and love, such as using your mouse to click buttons, or playing sounds on your NeXT or Mac.

■ ■

Telnet Access

The following sites can be accessed directly via Telnet. The Swiss site (at the original home of the Web) and the Israeli site use the number-based method for selecting Web items, while the Dutch and American sites use a more graphical version with cursor control for item selection called Lynx. With the Lynx client at the University of North Carolina (www.unc.edu) you can use the "g" (for "go") command to access other documents and servers on the Web. All that is needed is the Uniform Resource Locator (URL). (For an explanation of URLs, see the section entitled *Seeing Hypertext Links in a List* in this chapter, and Appendix D.) All Web documents and servers in the Internet Passport are given with the appropriate URL, so you can just type them in beginning with "http://".

Domain Name	IP Address	Login	Country
info.cern.ch	(128.141.201.214)	(none)	(Switzerland)
dutiws.twi.tudelft.nl	(130.161.156.11)	lynx	(Netherlands)
ukanaix.cc.ukans.edu	(128.235.1.43)	kufacts	(USA)
www.unc.edu	(198.86.40.81)	lynx	(USA)
vms.huji.ac.il	(128.139.4.3)	www	(Israel)

Sample Session

■ ■

In this example, we will access the WWW line browser at CERN in Switzerland.

Because WWW uses a method for storing and displaying files different than you may be used to, this sample session is mainly a lesson in getting used to using the hypertext interface. Please take the time to learn the basic navigational tools before you dive into the web!

The WWW servers at ukanaix.cc.ukans.edu and vms.huji.ac.il allow access to many services which info.cern.ch displays, but won't let you access. However, the purpose of this sample session is to get you oriented with the WWW user interface, so CERN was chosen because it is the "authoritative" WWW site. If you want to use WWW for getting around the Internet, telnet to the ukanaix.cc.ukans.edu or vms.huji.ac.il sites listed in the table of Telnet accessible WWW sites or install a WWW client.

Entering the Web

To connect to the basic line browser at CERN, use Telnet from any Internet host.

■■

```
telnet info.cern.ch
```

Introductory Page

The first thing you'll see is an introductory page offering basic instructions on using this Web interface. The introduction also urges you to access the Web using a local client. Since many people do not have access to a local client, we will continue and select number 5, to get to the "home page" or CERN, the European Particle Physics Laboratory.

```
Welcome to the World-Wide Web
                    THE WORLD-WIDE WEB

   This is just one of many access points to the web, the universe of
information available over networks. To follow references, just type the
number then hit the return (enter) key.

   The features you have by connecting to this telnet server are very
primitive compared to the features you have when you run a W3 "client"
program on your own computer. If you possibly can, please pick up a client
for your platform to reduce the load on this service and  experience the
web in its full splendor.

   For more information, select by number:

 A list of available W3 client programs[1]
 Everything about the W3 project[2]
 Places to start exploring[3]
 The First International WWW Conference[4]

   This telnet service is provided by the WWW team at the European Particle
Physics Laboratory known as CERN[5]
 [End]
1-5, Up, Quit, or Help: 5
```

The Home Page

The home page gives you an overview of what this WWW site has to offer and the numbers you should enter to get to those items. In this case, the home page is several screens long. If you get lost in WWW, you can always return to the home page by typing "Home" at the command line.

■■

```
CERN Welcome
                                CERN

European Laboratory for Particle Physics

    Geneva, Switzerland,  (and birthplace of the World-Wide
    Web)
    _____
    ( don't forget the WWW'94[1]  Conference)

About the Laboratory:

        on CERN info[2] , whom to contact[3] , and about the
        World-Wide Web[4]

        General information[5],  divisions, groups and
        activities[6] , scientific committees[7]

        People  phone numbers, offices and e-mail
        addresses[8].

      "Yellow Pages[9]", or " Pages Jaunes[10]".

        CERN library[11] (Alice) , Preprint[12] Service

        HOT NEWS[13],  seminars[14],  from the Users'
        Office[15],  internal news groups[16],
        conferences[17],  other news[18].

Activities:
        ...
Other Laboratories:

        High-Energy Physics Laboratories[24] around the world.

Other Subjects:

        Other Subjects[25] and Types of Information
        Service[26].

1-28, Back, Up, <RETURN> for more, Quit, or Help:
```

The screen title information should help you figure out the purpose of any particular screen. The text and numbers in the body of the screen are information about current hypertext nodes and links or the results from searches when using WAIS or other services.

As long as you have not left WWW to access a remote service, you will see a command line at the bottom of the screen. The command line starts with a range of numbers corresponding to the numbers of the hypertext nodes to which you can link, and a subset of commands that are currently available to you from this screen. Finally, the input area at the lower right is where you actually enter your WWW requests.

If you have initiated a remote session from WWW, your screen will usually display the normal features of that remote service.

What Resources Are Available in the Web?

To find out what sorts of resources are in WWW, select the number for "server types" (26) or "other subjects" (25). This is the display from a request for server types.

```
RESOURCES CLASSIFIED BY TYPE OF SERVICE

   See also categorization exist by subject[1] .  If you know what sort
of a service you are looking for, look here:

World-Wide Web servers[2]
                          List of W3 native "HTTP" servers.
                          These are generally the most friendly.
                          See also: about the WWW initiative[3] .

WAIS servers[4]           Find WAIS index servers using the
                          directory of servers[5] , or lists
                          by name[6] or domain[7] . See also:
                          about WAIS[8] .

Network News[9]           Available directly in all www
                          browsers. See also this list of
                          FAQs[10] .

Gopher[11]                Campus-wide information systems,
                          etc, listed geographically. See
                          also: about Gopher[12] .

Telnet access[13]         Hypertext  catalogues by Peter
                          Scott. See also: list by Scott
                          Yanoff[14] . Also, Art St George's
                          index[15] (yet to be hyperized)
                          etc.
```

■■

(Continued)

```
...
X.500[23]                    Directory system originally
                             for electronic mail addresses. (Access:
                             Slightly uneven view through Gopher
                             gateway in Michigan[24], or telnet
                             to UC London service[25]).

WHOIS[26]                    A simple internet phonebook
                             system.

(etc.)

1-28, Back, Up, <RETURN> for more, Quit, or Help:
```

You could dive further into WWW by entering a bracketed number from the page. For example, entering "4" from the screen shown above allows you to search through the WAIS directory of servers. But, before you start weaving through the web, you should probably work through the following navigational lessons.

Getting Help

It's always a good idea to review the online help for any new Internet service you are exploring, and this is especially true of WWW. There are two main kinds of help available in this version of WWW: help on the actual underlying mechanics of WWW and help for commands that are available from any given screen.

Help for an Overview of World Wide Web

By typing "manual" on the command line you can get general help for WWW and much more detailed background information about the WWW project.

```
               User Guide for the WWW Line Mode Browser

               WWW LINE MODE BROWSER

The World Wide Web line-mode browser allows you to find
information by following references and/or by using
keywords.

References are numbers in [brackets] after particular
phrases. Type the number and RETURN for more information on
the phrase.
```

(Continued)

```
Some documents are indexes. These contain little text, but
allow you to search for information with keywords. Type
"find" or "f" (space) and the keywords. For example, "f
sgml examples" searches the index for items with keywords
SGML and EXAMPLE. You can only use the "find" command when
it is present in the prompt. You can omit the "f" if the
first keyword doesn't conflict with existing commands[1].

See also command line syntax[2], shortcuts[3],
installation[4], customization[5], deeper details[6].

Please send any bugs and suggestions to
www-bug@info.cern.ch.

1-7, Back, <RETURN> for more, Quit, or Help:
```

Help On Commands

Because WWW is a web instead of a tree, you have many ways of getting around. Again, from the command line, type "help" and you should get an up-to-date table of WWW commands.

Table of World Wide Web Commands

The following commands are available at the prompt within WWW. Some are disabled when not applicable. All commands (except "quit") may be abbreviated. Case is not significant.

```
COMMAND           DESCRIPTION

Help              List available commands

<Return>          Display next page of current document

<number>          Display a document referred to by the number

Find <keywords>   Search a current index for keywords

Back              Go back to the document you were reading

Home              Go back to the first document
```

■ ■

(Continued)

```
COMMAND            DESCRIPTION
Recall             List documents you have visited
Recall <#>         Select a document from the recall list

List               Display sources of documents
List <#>           Display source for a specified document

Next, Previous     Work through a list of documents, displayed
                   by the  "list" command

Go <address>       Go to the document represented by the given
                   hypertext address

Up, Down           Scroll up or down one page in the current
                   document

Top, Bottom        Go to the top or the bottom of the current
                   document

Verbose            Toggle verbose mode on or off

Quit               Leave WWW


Additional Commands for Unix versions of WWW

Print              Print the current document
> file             Save or append the current document to a
                   file
| command          Pipe current document to the given command,
                   without the numbered document references
! command          Execute a shell command without leaving WWW
CD (or LCD)        Changes the local working directory
```

The Recall Command

To keep track of where you are and have been in the web, you can use the "recall" command to display the screen names of the files that you have visited during your WWW session.

■■■

```
Documents you have visited:-

R  1)    in Welcome to the World-Wide Web
R  2)    The World Wide Web Initiative:   The Project
R  3)    User Guide for the WWW Line Mode Browser


1-3, Back, <RETURN> for more, Quit, or Help:
```

The recall command is really helpful if you've been wandering through the web for awhile and don't quite know where you are and how you got there. It works like a thread that is laid down while exploring—a tactic used by Theseus in the Greek myth of the Minotaur's labyrinth.

You can get back to any one of the displayed documents by entering "r" and its number. Pressing the return key from the recall screen without entering a request will return you to the most recently visited document.

Seeing Hypertext Links in a List

Another useful command when using WWW is "list". This displays the documents that are referenced on a particular screen. The list command also displays the actual locations and filenames of the links from a particular document.

First, be sure you are in the home directory by typing "home". Now type "list" and you should see a screen like the following:

```
    References from this document:-

[1] User Guide for the WWW Line Mode Browser
[2] The World Wide Web project
[3] CERN Entry Point
[4] High-Energy Physics Information
[5] http://info.cern.ch/hypertext/DataSources/bySubject/...
[6] http://info.cern.ch/hypertext/DataSources/ByAccess.html
[7] http://info.cern.ch/hypertext/WWW/LineMode/Defaults/Inst

1-7, Back, Up, Quit, or Help:
```

These are the seven documents linked to the home directory. They are shown in a list format instead of being embedded in text.

You can access any one of these documents directly from the list screen by selecting a document's number. When one of those documents is displayed, you can also work your way through the remaining documents from the list by using the "next" and "previous" commands. These commands allow you to step forward or backwards through the listed documents.

This display also shows where each document is actually located. Most document references have the following standard format:

`[#] protocol_type://Internet_host_address/directory_path/file_name`

This is the format of the Uniform Resource Locator (URL). URLs are use by Web clients to locate and display documents automatically, but a URL can also be used to navigate the Web manually. With the Lynx client, use the "g" command and with a graphical menu-based client use "Open URL" and then type in the desired URL in full and then hit the enter key. (Public-access Lynx clients may not have this feature enabled.) After entering a URL manually, the client will then make the connection to the designated server and display the requested document for you.

While URLs got their start in the World Wide Web, they have now made their way across the Internet, and should soon be an official Internet standard. For more on URLs, see Appendix D.

Using the Web as a Resource Discovery and Access Tool

Now that you've gone through a basic orientation of the intricacies of WWW, you are ready to use it as an informational resource. Because CERN restricts outgoing Telnet from WWW, you should try one of the other public-access sites for more extensive explorations. With a bit of searching, or from a local client, you can connect to the World Wide Web Meta Index of Internet resources.

`http://www.ncsa.uiuc.edu/SDG/Software/Mosaic/MetaIndex.html`

Like Gopher, WWW may be used as a resource discovery tool for the rest of the Internet. You can access remote Internet services such as Telnet, FTP, and Gopher (and Gopher's pals veronica and jughead) through WWW. When you use Telnet, the session will look the same as it did without using a Web client. FTP and Gopher, on the other hand, will look a bit different, depending on the client, but should be as easy or even easier to use than before.

To whet your appetite, the next page shows a partial listing of resources available in WWW organized by academic categories. (You'll find this listing by selecting "other subjects" from the home menu.)

```
The World-Wide Web Virtual Library: Subject Catalogue
              THE WWW VIRTUAL LIBRARY

    This is a distributed subject catalogue. See also arrangement  by
service type[1] ., and other subject catalogues of network information[2].
```

■■

(Continued)

Mail to maintainers[3] of the specified subject or www-
request@info.cern.ch to add pointers to this list, or if you would like
to contribute to administration of a subject area[4].

   See also how to put your data on the web[5]

   Aeronautics   Mailing list archive index[6] .
                                See also NASA LaRC[7]

   Agriculture   See Agricultural info[8] , Almanac
                                mail servers[9] ; the Agricultural
                                Genome[10] (National Agricultural
                                Library, part of the U.S.
                                Department of Agriculture) ; North
                                Carolina Cooperative Extension
                                Service Gopher[11]

Archaeology[12]   Separate list

Astronomy and Astrophysics[13]
                                Separate list.

Bio Sciences[14]   Separate list .

Chemistry[15]   Separate list

Climate research   The Deutsches Klimarechenzentrum[16]
                                (DKRZ, German Climate Computer
                                Centre)

Commercial Services[17]
                                Separate list

Computing[18]   Separate list.

Earth Science   US Geological Survey[19] ; McGill
                                University Department of Earth and
                                Planetary Sciences[20] . See also
                                geography[21] and bio sciences[22]

Economics   Newsgroups on economics[23] and
                                research[24] .

Education[25]   Separate list
(etc.)

Note that some displayed resources cannot be accessed when using the CERN WWW via a Telnet session; in such cases, you'll get a message saying something to the effect of "sorry, the service cannot be accessed; please install a WWW client to get full WWW services." If this is a problem, try the "ukanaix" or "huji" sites mentioned in the list of Telnet accessible WWW sites.

Exiting

From any screen, just type "q" or "quit".

WWW Indexes

A number of indexes to Web documents and servers have been created by various individuals and parties. Fortunately, these indexes have been collected in one location by the Centre Universitaire d'Informatique of the University of Geneva. This list of indexes, called "W3 Search Engines" is available to graphical and text browsers (Lynx).

WWW:`http://cui_www.unige.ch/meta-index.html`

Working with the World Wide Web Initiative

If you are excited by WWW and what it has to offer, install a local client. Using a local client allows you to construct a web that corresponds to your view of the world online.

Like WAIS and Gopher, the WWW Initiative will work best if there are many servers installed throughout the world. The WWW servers can store and distribute information in a wide variety of formats and have built-in gateways to archie, WAIS, Gopher, and most other kinds of Internet services. The master FTP source is info.cern.ch, directory /pub/WWW. Even if you don't install a WWW server, WWW server maintainers might be interested in including any datasets, text, or other machine accessible resources which you would like to share.

All aspects of WWW are still under development. Feel free to send your suggestions, comments, or contributions to www-bugs@info.cern.ch.

For More Information

LISTSERV Lists

There is only one BITNET LISTSERV list directly related to WWW, and that is one on hypertext in education. Remember to send your subscription request to LISTSERV@ITOC-SIVM using a BITNET gateway.

```
HYPEREDU@ITOCSIVM.BITNET     Hypertext in Education
```

Mailing Lists

There are two mailing lists for WWW. Note that these lists are maintained by Unix listserv software, which is not to be confused with BITNET LISTSERV software. (Subscription requests to listserv@info.cern.ch.)

`www-announce@info.cern.ch`	Major announcements of interest to the WWW community (This is intended to be a low volume, high subscription group.)
`www-talk@info.cern.ch`	Discussion among WWW developers (A good place for WWW users to share experiences and ask questions about WWW not addressed in the WWW online information.)

Usenet Newsgroups

`alt.hypertext`	Hypertext
`comp.infosystems.www`	WWW's own newsgroup (various subgroups)
`comp.text.sgml`	Technical discussion of Standard Generalized Markup Language

Software Archives

Servers

World Wide Web server software is available for Unix, Macintosh, VM/CMS, and VMS computers, and will run on reasonably modern versions of these computers. The WWW server is available from the developers at CERN:

> FTP host: `info.cern.ch`
> directory: `/pub/www/src`
> filenames: `www-server-guide.ps` (PostScript guide)
> `www-server-guide.txt`(ASCII text guide)
> (many or all)   (server software)
> WWW: `http://info.cern.ch/hypertext/WWW/Daemon/User/Guide.html`

Contact: e-mail: **`timbl@info.cern.ch`**
> Tim Berners-Lee
> WorldWideWeb project
> CERN
> 1211 Geneva 23 Switzerland
> voice: +41 22 767 3755
> fax: +41 22 767 7155

■■■

The GN server which accommodates both WWW and Gopher runs on Unix machines and is available for free from the developers at Northwestern University:

FTP host:	`ftp.acns.nwu.edu`
directory:	`/pub/gn`
filenames:	`README`
	`gn-X.X.tar.gz`

Contact: e-mail: **`john@math.nwu.edu`**

John Franks
Department of Mathematics
Northwestern University
Evanston, IL 60208-2730
USA
voice: (708) 491-5548
fax: (708) 491-8906

Clients

The Mosaic client requires a full connection to the Internet. While it should be possible to run one of these clients using a SLIP or PPP dialup connection, it is unlikely that the speed of data transfer will be satisfactory. Remember, graphics are large files and they can take substantial time to transfer. The client itself will run on reasonably modern versions of the following platforms: X-windows, Macintosh, and Microsoft Windows.

Mosaic client:

FTP host:	`ftp.ncsa.uiuc.edu`	
directory:	`/Mosaic`	(Mosaic for X)
	`/<systemname>/Mosaic`	(other platforms)
filenames:	(many or all)	
Contact:	e-mail:**`ebina@ncsa.uiuc.edu`**	

Eric Bina

Software Development Group

National Center for Supercomputing Applications

152 CAB

605 E. Springfield

Champaign, IL 61820 USA

voice: (217) 244-6133

fax: (217) 244-1987

Cello client:

FTP host:	`fatty.law.cornell.edu`
directory:	`/pub/LII/Cello`
files:	(many or all)
Contact:	e-mail: **tom@law.mail.cornell.edu**
	Thomas R. Bruce
	Research Associate
	Cornell Law School
	Myron Taylor Hall
	Ithaca, NY 14853 USA
	voice: (607) 255-1221
	fax: (607) 255-7193

Lynx browser:

The Lynx browser (a server with a public access client) has been compiled on the following platforms: DEC Ultrix, DEC Alpha OSF/1, Sun 4, NeXT, and VMS (Multinet). It has been rumored to run on these platforms: HP-UX (snake), Solaris 2, SVR4, VMS (UCX), LINUX, SGI, SUN 3, AIX 3.1, NeXTStep 3.x.

The server software itself is also available from the University of Kansas via anonymous FTP:

FTP host:	`kufacts.cc.ukans.edu`
directory:	`/pub/WWW/lynx`
files:	(many or all)
Contact:	e-mail: **rezac@kuhub.cc.ukans.edu**
	Charles Rezac
	University of Kansas
	Documentation Specialist
	Academic Computing Services
	208 Computer Facility
	Sunnyside and Illinois
	Lawrence, KS 66045 USA
	voice: (913) 864-0460

Bibliographies

WWW

Berners-Lee, T. J., et al. "World-Wide Web: The Information Universe." *Electronic Networking: Research, Applications, and Policy* 2(1) (Spring 1992): 52-58.

Berners-Lee, T. J., et al. "World Wide Web: An Information Infrastructure for High-Energy Physics." Presented at the Second International Workshop on Software Engineering, Artificial Intelligence and Expert Systems in High Energy and Nuclear Physics in La Londe-des-Maures, France, January 1992. Published in *New Computing Techniques in Physics Research II: Proceedings of the....* Singapore; River Edge, N.J.: World Scientific, 1992.

Berners-Lee, T. J. "Electronic publishing and visions of hypertext." *Physics World* 5(6) 1992.

Brandt, D. S. "Accessing Electronic Journals." *Academic and Library Computing* 9(10) (November/December 1992):17-20.

"The Fruitful, Tangled Trees of Knowledge." *The Economist* June 20, 1992.

Nickerson, G. "World Wide Web: Hypertext from CERN." *Computers in Libraries* 12(11) (December 1992):75-77.

Smith, J. "CNIDR: Coordinating Internet User Tools." *Internet World* 4(2) (March 1993): 8-10.

Hypertext

Atkinson, R. "Networks, Hypertext, and Academic Information Services: Some Longer-Range Implications." *College & Research Libraries* 54(3) (May 1993):199-215.

Barrett, E. (ed.). *The Society of Text: Hypertext, Hypermedia, and the Social Construction* of Information. Cambridge, MA: MIT Press, 1989.

Bolter, J. D. *The Writing Space: The Computer, Hypertext, and the History of Writing.* Hillsdale, NJ: L. Erlbaum Associates, 1991.

Horn, R. E. *Mapping Hypertext: The Analysis, Organization, and Display of Knowledge for the Next Generation of On-line Text and Graphics.* Lexington, MA: Lexington Institute, 1989.

Horton, W. K. *Designing and Writing Online Documentation: Help Files to Hypertext.* New York: Wiley, 1990.

Landow, G. P. *Hypertext: The Convergence of Contemporary Critical Theory and Technology.* Johns Hopkins University Press, 1992.

Nelson, T. *Computer Lib / Dream Machines.* Redmond, WA: Microsoft Press, 1987.

Nielsen, J. *Hypertext and Hypermedia.* Boston: Academic Press, 1990.

CHAPTER
21

A Big Black Book
Directories of Internet Users
and Hosts

INTERNET · PASSPORT

@

One of the most frequently asked Internet questions is, "how do I find someone's e-mail address?"

You can usually obtain a person's e-mail information with one or a few well-planned phone calls or postal letters. When you contact them, ask them directly for their e-mail address. But if you can't find a person's Internet address by these traditional methods, or if you are like a growing number of Internet users who want to do everything through the Internet, there are several Internet directory services that you can try. There are also a number of directories which can help you locate Internet services and their addresses, which will also be described in this chapter.

CHALLENGES TO INTERNET DIRECTORY SERVICES

It's easy to get information about telephone numbers: all we have to do is look in a phone book or call directory assistance. To provide analogous services for the Internet, there are many efforts to create resources that provide access to e-mail addresses of individuals and institutions, and contact information for Internet services. By loose analogy to the page colors of published telephone directories in the U.S., directories of Internet addresses for people and services indexed by name are often referred to as "white pages," while those directories that allow access to addresses of services by category are usually called "yellow pages."

But making directories of Internet users and services is a challenge for a number of reasons.

Volatility of Computer Information

E-mail addresses change more rapidly than postal addresses or people's names. Your town has probably been in the same state since it was established, the street you live on has probably had the same name for decades, and very few people change their first names. In contrast, the domain name of an Internet computer might change every couple of years, and your userid(s) can be changed at any time based on decisions made by you or systems administrators.

Local Information Services Are Still Embryonic

In order for an Internet-wide information directory system to be created, it would be useful for local sites to develop and perfect local directories, just like regional telephone companies keep track of phone numbers in their service areas. But unfortunately, many institutions still do not have a master list of local user-id's and services.

Privacy and Security Issues

Many sites are understandably reluctant to publicize some or all addresses or userids because of concerns about unauthorized access to sensitive data or costly computer resources, or the privacy of users at those sites.

Competing Paradigms

Standardized Internet protocols have already been established for transmitting data (TCP/IP) and resolving computer names (DNS), but there are still a number of competing approaches for providing Internet white pages and yellow pages services. Very likely, even more will be created in the next few years. On the bright side however, there are several protocols being developed to present a single user interface for querying distinct information databases.

Scalability

One of the biggest problems with creating a directory is the size of the problem itself. While there are currently about two to three times as many people on the Internet as there are people in New York, it is expected that that number should reach a billion(!) in the not-too-distant future. What kind of directory will remain usable with over a billion names in it? Consider those last names that have pages and pages of entries in a single city's phone book; now think globally. Hopefully, whatever systems are developed and deployed today will work for decades to come, or can be easily transformed into the directory services of tomorrow.

STRATEGIES FOR USING DIRECTORY SERVICES

As of 1994, there is no single directory service for all of the Internet. Services like Gopher and WAIS are including a growing number of the many bits and pieces of the directory world and may render documents such as this chapter obsolete at some time in the future. But it's still necessary to do a little poking around the net to find the directory service most appropriate for each search.

To find an Internet address, you should choose the directory which is most likely to have the information you are seeking. Before diving into the catalog of directory services, here's a quick review of possible strategies for some general classes of searches.

Finding Addresses of "Average Users"

There are several directory services of special interest in tracking down the average Internet user. Here's the order in which you might try these databases. (Complete information on using these resources is provided later in the chapter.)

▪▪

When You Don't Know Where They Are...

Most directory services will not be of much help unless you know where the person is located just as you can't get someone's telephone number unless you know what area code to call. However, a few directory services try to collect unique addresses from throughout the Internet.

The Usenet addresses database is a great place to start. It is created from the e-mail addresses in articles posted to Usenet newsgroups and currently contains hundreds of thousands of unique addresses.

Next, you might try the Knowbot Information Server which is a very powerful "one-stop shopping" service providing automatic access to several directory services from one front end.

For a command-line search, you can try "whois" which offers a keyword or string search of the three Whois directory databases.

Gopher and WAIS servers throughout the world are adding access to most of the directory services described in this chapter and may become the preferred interface for working with directory databases. (Please note, for directory databases, the public WAIS client of choice is the one maintained at the University of North Carolina: sun-site.unc.edu.) The University of Notre Dame Gopher is particularly strong with more than 300 directory services available as of March 1994.

The Usenet newsgroup "soc.net-people" is used specifically for tracking down people with whom you've lost contact. Typically, you would post a message with a subject line containing the person's name, a likely geographical region in which they are located, and a detailed message containing information that may help people figure out who you're talking about. This service should be considered a forum of last resort.

When You Do Know Where They Are...

If the person you are looking for is affiliated with an academic institution, the best first try is a campus Gopher or other Campus Wide Information System. These usually have directories of staff, and sometimes students, that include e-mail addresses. For more on Gophers and other Campus Wide Information Systems see Chapters 17 and 19, respectively.

InterNIC Directory Services offer access to three directory services, X.500, whois, and Netfind, via Telnet, Gopher, and e-mail. X.500 and Netfind work only if you have at least some idea of the organizational affiliation of the person for whom you are looking.

The command "finger" will often help you find e-mail addresses if you know the name of the Internet host where the person's home account is located. However, this will work only if finger is installed and active both on your Internet host and on the host you are querying.

Finding Addresses for Administrators

There are a number of directory services that are either intended solely as network administrative directories or are at early stages of development and have started with this restricted and structured set of information. Directions on using these services are provided later in the chapter.

Europe

"Paradise" is mainly an administrative directory service for the COSINE X.500 project in Europe. In the future it may contain a comprehensive directory of general users in Europe as well.

Japan

"whois@nic.ad.jp" is currently an experimental whois service for network administrators in Japan. At some point, it may become a general purpose directory service.

North America

"whois@ds.internic.net" is sort of the granddaddy of network directory services. It contains a great deal of contact information for network administrators. Some other Internet users are also in this database, but providing a general listing is not its primary focus.

The "PSI White Pages" contain contact information for network administrators and staff of participating institutions. This project might, in the future, become a general purpose directory service.

Worldwide

The section titled "Directories of Computer Addresses" describes databases which are primarily for finding addresses of Internet hosts, but many of these contain contact information for administrators and technical staff at the hosts as well.

GENERAL PURPOSE DIRECTORIES OF E-MAIL ADDRESSES

College E-mail

Overview: A very useful document for finding e-mail addresses at North American colleges and universities. Includes hints about which hosts are most likely to be used by certain sets of people, the conventions for the construction of user-ids, and local directory services at each site. Although focusing on students, the information is useful for finding administrators, faculty, and staff as well.

Access: FTP, WAIS, and as a periodic posting to the newsgroups "soc.college", "soc.net-people", and "news.answers".

WAIS: `college-email`
FTP host: `pit-manager.mit.edu`
directory: `/pub/usenet/soc.college`
filenames:
`FAQ:_College_Email_Addresses_1_3_[Monthly_posting]`
`FAQ:_College_Email_Addresses_2_3_[Monthly_posting]`
`FAQ:_College_Email_Addresses_3_3_[Monthly_posting]`

Contact: e-mail: **mkant@cs.cmu.edu** (Mark Kantrowitz)

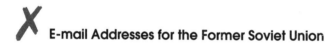

E-mail Addresses for the Former Soviet Union

Overview: A list of names, addresses, phone numbers, fax numbers, and some e-mail addresses for most organizations in the former Soviet Union which either have or plan to have e-mail connections.

Access: WAIS: `cissites`

Contact: e-mail: **cismap@dm.com**

Finger

Overview: Provides e-mail address, full name, telephone numbers, and other optional information about a particular user at a particular site. Although originally available only for Unix computers, there are now versions of finger for other operating systems as well.

Access: From your Internet host, try "finger <your-userid>". If you get a response containing contact information about yourself, finger is installed locally, and you can use it to obtain userids at remote hosts by typing "finger <userid>@<a.remote.internet.host>". Note that finger must be active and fully enabled at that other host for finger to work!

More Info: On Unix, "man finger", and on other operating systems, "help finger", may give you some information.

Gopher

Overview: A very easy to use interface for finding e-mail addresses—once you find which Gopher and which Gopher directory has the services you are looking for! Directory services from throughout the world can be accessed, including the following:

CSO nameservers (so called for the Computing Systems Office at University of Illinois, Champaign-Urbana) for several dozen institutions containing e-mail addresses and other contact information for staff and students;

access to many of the directory services listed in this chapter;

X.500 directory services; and

the University of Notre Dame has compiled a huge set of Gopher directories all in one place with well over 300 directories.

Access: Gopher: `gopher.nd.edu`
          menu: `Non-Notre-Dame Information Sources/`
          item: `Phone Books--Other Institutions`

Contact: e-mail: **cooper@utopia.cc.nd.edu** (Joel Cooper CSO nameservers)
                      mhpower@athena.mit.edu (Matt Power WHOIS servers)
                      tim@umich.edu (Tim Howes Gopher to X.500 gateway)

✗ InterNIC Directory Services ("White Pages")

Overview: The InterNIC Directory Service is a collection of searchable directories accessible through a number of methods run by AT&T. Access to X.500, Netfind, and whois, available via Telnet and Gopher and e-mail (not all services available through all methods).

Access

Gopher: `ds.internic.net`
menus: `InterNIC Directory and Database Services (AT&T)/InterNIC Directory Services ("White Pages")/`

WWW: `http://ds.internic.net/ds/dspgwp.html`

X.500 Service:

Telnet: `ds.internic.net`
login: `x.500`

Gopher: `ds.internic.net`
menus: `InterNIC Directory and Database Services (AT&T)/InterNIC Directory Services ("White Pages")/`
item: `X.500 Person/Organization Lookup (Gateway to X.500)/`

Via mail server: Send a message with one of the lines below, or just the word "help" for the full instructions.

```
mail:    mailserv@ds.internic.net
subject: (none needed)
message:
person <name, organization, country>    (person search)
institution <name, country>             (institution search)
```

....

Netfind:

Telnet:	`ds.internic.net`
login:	`netfind`
enter:	`<name keywords>` (where keywords are additional information about the person)

Gopher:	`ds.internic.net`
menus:	`InterNIC Directory and Database Services (AT&T)/InterNIC Directory Services ("White Pages")/`
item:	`Netfind Person/Organization Lookup (Gateway to Netfind)/`

Whois:

Gopher:	`ds.internic.net`
menus:	`InterNIC Directory and Database Services (AT&T)/InterNIC Directory Services ("White Pages")/`
item:	`WHOIS Person/Organization Lookup (Gateway to WHOIS)/`

You can also access the Whois from a Unix command-line with the command "whois -h ds.internic.net <lastname, firstname>".

Contact:	e-mail:	**admin@ds.internic.net**
	voice:	(800) 862-0677 or (908) 668-6587
	fax:	(908) 668-3763

X KIS (Knowbot Information Server)

Overview   The "Knowbot Information Server" retrieves e-mail addresses, postal addresses, telephone numbers, and institutional affiliation for users throughout the Internet. Knowbot is a resource that allows you to search through many directories at once. Some of the directory services currently accessible through Knowbot include the following:

```
finger@any.Unix.host
mcimail@nri.reston.va.us
mitwp@mit.edu
profile@gwen.cs.purdue.edu
profile@megaron.arizona.edu
profile@nri.reston.va.us
quipu
whois@nic.ddn.mil
X.500
```

Access   Via mail server: (multiple searches can also be sent in a single e-mail request as long as each user is placed on a separate line. Results will be mailed back to you)

```
mail:    kis@nri.reston.va.us
subject:
message:
query Sue Nimh
```

Telnet:
```
info.cnri.reston.va.us 185, or
regulus.cs.bucknell.edu 185
```

Example: This is a Telnet session in which we search for our dear hypothetical friend, Sue D. Nimh:

```
telnet info.cnri.reston.va.us
Trying 132.151.1.15...
Connected to info.cnri.reston.va.us.
Escape character is '^]'.
```

(Continued)

```
                 Knowbot Information Service
KIS Client (V2.0).    Copyright CNRI 1990.    All Rights Reserved.


The KIS system is undergoing some changes.
Type 'news' at the prompt for more information
Type 'help' for a quick reference to commands.

Backspace characters are '^H' or DEL

Please enter your email address in our guest book...
(Your email address?) > robison@nwnet.net

> query Sue Nimh
```

More Info:	Online help:	help, ?, and help <command> (e.g., help query)
	FTP host:	nri.reston.va.us
	directory:	/rdroms
	filenames:	KIS-id.PS
		KIS-id.txt
	Mailing list:	kis-users-request@nri.reston.va.edu

Comments: KIS can be installed locally and run on computers connected to the Internet using any version of Unix with Berkeley-style sockets. KIS currently has translation programs for whois (nic.ddn.mil), profile, mcimail, QUIPU, and finger. Any sites using these services can be added easily to a locally installed KIS.

JANET Directory

Overview: An online directory of individuals associated with JANET, the British Networking organization.

Access: Telnet: sun.nsf.ac.uk
             login: janet   (no password required)
             hostname: uk.ac.jnt.dir

Netfind

Overview: An Internet-wide directory service which can retrieve e-mail addresses and other contact information based on geographical, institutional, and host names.

Comments: This is a very powerful tool. Expect to have to choose between large numbers of possible domain nameservers and then hosts and be sure you have the ability to scroll backwards on your screen to see all the hosts from which you can choose.

Also, don't be surprised if you receive conflicting information, mainly due to old directory information on a person's previous host. Netfind uses information from Usenet news messages, the Domain Naming System, the Simple Mail Transfer Protocol, and the "finger" protocol. Select the Netfind server nearest you!

Access: Telnet

archie.au	Australia
bruno.cs.colorado.edu	Colorado
dino.conicit.ve	Venezuela
ds.internic.net	New Jersey (InterNIC)
eis.calstate.edu	California
hto-e.usc.edu	California
krnic.net	Korea
lincoln.technet.sg	Singapore
malloco.ing.puc.cl	Chile
monolith.cc.ic.ac.uk	United Kingdom
mudhoney.micro.umn.edu	Minnesota
netfind.anu.edu.au	Australia
netfind.ee.mcgill.ca	Canada
netfind.oc.com	Texas
nic.nm.kr	Korea
nic.uakom.sk	Slovakia
redmont.cis.uab.edu	Alabama

login: netfind

■■

Example: This is a sample session looking for our hypothetical friend, Sue D. Nimh. Let's assume that we have reason to believe that she's a software engineer in Corvallis, Oregon, and show you how to use this information to refine a Netfind search.

```
telnet bruno.cs.colorado.edu

login: netfind

(login messages deleted)

Top level choices:
        1. Help
        2. Search
        3. Seed database lookup
        4. Options
        5. Quit (exit server)
--> 2
Person & keys (blank exits)->nimh oregon corvallis

There are too many domains in the list.
Please select at most 3 of the following:

0. alborz.com (alborz systems, corvallis, oregon)
1. ch2m.com (ch2m hill, corvallis, oregon)
2. fenris.com (fenris computer services, inc, corvallis, oregon)
3. jasmic.com (jasmic systems, corvallis, oregon)
```

(...many other hosts listed)

```
40. phar.orst.edu (pharmacy school, oregon state university, corvallis,
oregon)
41. physics.orst.edu (physics department, oregon state university,
corvallis, oregon)
42. roguewave.com (rogue wave software, corvallis, oregon)
```

Example: Let's try one of the listed hosts by entering its number:

```
Enter selection (e.g., 3 1 2) --42


(0) check_name: checking domain roguewave.com. Level = 0
The domain 'roguewave.com' does not run its own name
servers.
        Skipping domain search phase for this domain.
```

This particular host does not have directory services enabled, so let's try another search including the word "computer" to see if we can have a narrower, more likely set of hosts from which to choose.

```
Enter person and keys --> nimh computer corvallis

There are too many domains in the list.

Please select at most 3 of the following:
0. cs.orst.edu (comp. sci. department, oregon state...)
1. ece.orst.edu (electrical and computer engineering...)
2. fenris.com (fenris computer services, inc, corvallis)
3. lynx.cs.orst.edu (comp. sci. department, oregon...)

Enter selection (e.g., 3 1 2) --> 1

( 0) check_name: checking domain ece.orst.edu.  Level = 0

SYSTEM: ece.orst.edu

Login name: sdn                In real life: Sue D. Nimh
Phone: 555-1958
Directory: /u1/user/sdn        Shell: /usr/local/bin/messg
Last login Tue Sep 29 12:09
No Plan
```

■■

Contact: e-mail: **netfind-dvl@cs.colorado.edu**

                    Mike Schwartz

                    Department of Computer Science

                    University of Colorado

                    Boulder, CO 80309-0430 USA

More Info: If Netfind is installed at your site, there may be online help. Try "help netfind" or "man netfind". Software and documentation is available at the following FTP host:

                    FTP host: `ftp.cs.colorado.edu`
                    directory: `/pub/distribs/netfind`
                    filenames: (many or all)

                    There are also two mailing lists for Netfind; to subscribe, send mail to the following addresses:

`netfind-users-` `request@cs.colorado.edu`	User changes and updates.
`netfind-servers-` `request@cs.colorado.edu`	For sites running Netfind servers.

PARADISE

Overview: E-mail address and telephone numbers of people and organizations participating in the COSINE Pilot Directory Service project.

Access: Telnet to one of two European sites:

United Kingdom
Telnet: `paradise.ulcc.ac.uk`
login: `dua`

Sweden:
Telnet: `hypatia.umdc.umu.se`
login: `de`

Contact: e-mail: `helpdesk@paradise.ulcc.ac.uk`

PARADISE Project
University College London
Computer Science Department
Gower St.
London WC1E 6BT UK
voice: + 44 71 405 8400 x432
fax: + 44 71 242 1845

More Info: Extensive online help and documents available via mail server.

```
mail:    info-server@paradise.ulcc.ac.uk
subject: (none needed)
message: PARADISE Project
```

soc.net-people (Usenet Newsgroup)

Overview: A newsgroup devoted to helping people find other people.

Access: You need access to Usenet newsreading software to make best use of this service. For more on using Usenet, refer to Chapter 9.

Example: When you post to this newsgroup, you should make the "subject" line as concise and informative as possible. The message should contain any relevant information that may spark the memory of a person reading the newsgroup.For example, an intelligent posting to find our hypothetical friend Sue D. Nimh might start like this:

```
subject: Oregon, Alaska, W. U.S.: Sue D. Nimh

I am attempting to locate a friend named Sue D. Nimh.

Sue grew up in Juneau Alaska, and studied computer
science at Oregon State University in Corvallis,
Oregon, from 1986-1990...

(Introductory sentence should be followed by other relevant
information, possibly including hobbies, physical
description, and so forth.)
```

Usenet Addresses

Overview   Searches through a catalog of e-mail addresses of people who have posted messages to Usenet newsgroups. This is a very useful service for finding Internet users who may not yet be in formal or administrative directories.

Access: WAIS: usenet-addresses
              Via mail server:

```
mail:     mail-server@pit-manager.mit.edu
subject:  (none needed)
message:  send usenet-addresses/<name>
```

whois

Overview: Many domains within the Internet have a "whois server" that provides
             directory information for the hosts within the domain.

Access: On most Unix hosts and some other Internet hosts, whois can often be used
             as a line command.

```
whois <-h server-name> <name>
```

The "<-h server-name>" is an option to specify a particular whois server. If
you do not include the "<-h server-name>", the whois command will default
to a whois server, very frequently, whois@nic.ddn.mil. (See entry in this
chapter.)

Sometimes, whois can be used via Telnet to a whois server through port 43, if
this service has been created for that domain. Enter the person's name once
the connection is established.

```
telnet <whois-server.address> 43
```

More Info: On Unix hosts, "man whois"; on other hosts, "help whois".

Matt Power (mhpower@athena.mit.edu) maintains a definitive list of whois
servers:

FTP host: `rtfm.mit.edu`
directory: `/pub/whois`
filename: `whois-servers.list`

■■■

X   whois@ds.internic.net

Overview: A database of names, e-mail and postal addresses, telephone numbers and
              other contact information for registered users, hosts, organizations,
              gateways, and networks throughout the Internet.

Access: Telnet, Gopher, or via command line query from many Internet hosts.

Examples: As a line command from most Internet hosts, just "whois -h ds.internic.net
              <name>" will query the whois server at ds.internic.net; or telnet directly to
              ds.internic.net.

              Telnet: `ds.internic.net`
              Gopher: `ds.internic.net`
              menus: `InterNIC Directory and Database Services`
                         `(AT&T)/InterNIC Directory Services ("White`
                         `Pages")/`
              item: `WHOIS Person/Organization Lookup (Gateway to`
                         `WHOIS)/`

Contact: `hostmaster@rs.internic.net`
              Network Solutions
              Attn: InterNIC Registration Services
              505 Huntmar Park Drive
              Herndon, VA USA 22070
              voice: (703) 742-4777

More Info: The Telnet accessible service has extensive online help. For help when using
              whois as a local Unix command, type "man whois".

■ ■

whois@nic.ddn.mil

Overview:	A database of names, e-mail and postal addresses, telephone numbers, and other contact information for registered users, hosts, organizations, and gateways. Most persons listed are network administrators or technical staff in MILNET (formerly ARPANET).
Comments:	For more general whois information, use the server at ds.internic.net.
Access:	Telnet or via command line query from many Internet hosts.
Examples:	As a line command from most Internet hosts, just "whois <name>" will query the whois server at nic.ddn.mil, or telnet directly to nic.ddn.mil.
	Telnet: `nic.ddn.mil`
More Info:	The Telnet accessible service has extensive online help. For help when using whois as a local Unix command, type "man whois".

whois@nic.ad.jp

Overview:	An experimental whois service for Japanese Internet networks. Responses can be given in English or in Japanese.
Access:	As a line command if the whois command is installed.
Example:	"whois -h nic.ad.jp <name>/e" for English queries; "whois -h nic.ad.jp <name>/j" responds in Japanese; the default is Japanese.
Contact:	e-mail: `hi@nic.ad.jp`

INSTITUTION-SPECIFIC DIRECTORIES OF E-MAIL ADDRESSES

■ ■

A growing number of institutions are putting their staff and student directories online in publicly accessible formats.

Although many of these are directly accessible via a Telnet connection and some using WAIS, by far the most common method is Gopher. Again, the easiest way to locate these is through the Gopher at the University of Notre Dame (gopher.nd.edu).

DISCIPLINE-SPECIFIC DIRECTORIES OF E-MAIL ADDRESSES

Review of LISTSERV Subscription Lists

Overview: Many LISTSERV discussion lists keep a record of their subscribers, that can be reviewed by sending a command to the LISTSERVer maintaining that list.

Comments: Keep in mind that not all LISTSERV subscribers realize that their contact information is automatically stored when they subscribe to a LISTSERV and not all subscribers to a list will be visible using the "rev" command.

Example: Suppose you have reason to believe that the person you are trying to contact subscribers to the (hypothetical) LISTSERV group, "AXOLOT-L@AMPHBIAN.BITNET". You would simply send the following e-mail message, and if the subscription list for AXOLOT-L is open to public viewing, you would receive a copy of all subscribers in an e-mail message.

```
mail:    listserv@amphbian.bitnet
subject: (none needed)
message: rev axolot-l
```

American Philosophical Association

Overview: Names and e-mail addresses of the membership of the American Philosophical Association.

Comments: There are many other services available when you log in.

Access: Gopher: `apa.oxy.edu`
item: `E-mail Address Books/`

Contact: e-mail: traiger@oxy.edu

Saul Traiger
Department of Philosophy
Cognitive Science Program
Occidental College
Los Angeles, CA 90041 USA
voice: (213) 259-2901

■■

X

Astronomers

Overview: A listing of the contact information for professional astronomers and astronomical facilities around the world.

Access: E-mail requests for this guide should be sent to: e-mail@srf.ro-greenwich.ac.uk.

X

Biologists

Overview: Access to directories of The American Society of Ichthyologists & Herpetologists, The American Society of Plant Taxonomists, Plant Taxonomists Online, The Natural History Museum, London, The Mycologists Online, and The American Museum of Natural History, New York.

Access: Gopher: huh.harvard.edu
item: Directories of Biologists/

Contact: e-mail: beach@huh.harvard.edu (Jim. H. Beach)
jmh3@cornell.edu (Julian Humphries)

X

Biology and Artificial Intelligence Researchers

Overview: Directory of molecular biologists working in artificial intelligence.

Access: WAIS: bionic-ai-researchers

Contact: e-mail: wais@nic.funet.fi (Rob Harper)

X

Bionet Users

Overview: Addresses of users of the bionet newsgroups.

Access: WAIS: biologists-addresses

Contact: e-mail: biosci@net.bio.net

Consortium for School Networking

Overview: A LISTSERV accessible directory of the full membership of the Consortium for School Networking (CoSN).

Access: E-mail messages to LISTSERV@BITNIC.CREN.NET

Example: Send the following e-mail message and you will receive the directory via e-mail:

```
mail:    LISTSERV@BITNIC.CREN.NET
subject: (none needed)
message: send cosnlist text
```

IEEE Directory

Overview: An aliasing directory of active IEEE volunteers, that allows you to search for e-mail addresses by supplying "i.lastname" where "i" is the person's first initial and "lastname" is their full last name. The main purpose of this service is for people to be able to send e-mail messages to IEEE members by their real names even if one doesn't know their e-mail address.

Access: You can obtain a list of all valid aliases in the five sections of the IEEE.ORG Directory Service by sending e-mail to each of the following addresses with the message "aliases". (No message will be larger than 32K.)

Volunteers	directory.vols@ieee.org
Staff	directory.staff@ieee.org
Sections	directory.sec@ieee.org
Student Branches	directory.sb@ieee.org
Societies	directory.soc@ieee.org

Oceanographers

Overview: E-mail and postal addresses, institutional affiliations, and names of oceanographers and related researchers.

Comment: Most first names are not included, just initials.

Access: Telnet: `delocn.udel.edu`
             login: `INFO`
             Once you are logged in, select the menu "Who's Who - electronic and mail addresses."

Vulcanologists

Overview: Names, e-mail addresses, institutional affiliations, and specializations of vulcanologists.

Access: E-mail requests to a LISTSERV to retrieve the entire directory.

```
mail:     listserv@asuvm.inre.asu.edu
subject: (none needed)
message: get vlist file
```

Contact: e-mail: `jordi@sc2a.unige.ch`

             Steve Jordi
             Department of Geophysics
             University of Geneva
             13, Rue des Maraichers
             1211 GENEVA 4
             Switzerland
             fax: + 41 22 320 5732

■■■

DIRECTORIES OF COMPUTER ADDRESSES

■■■

BITNET / EARN Nodes

Overview: A directory of authoritative information about BITNET and EARN hosts including administrative contacts and configuration of the hosts.

Access: FTP host: `vm.utdallas.edu`
                directory: `/bitnet`
                filename: `bitearn.nodes`

British Online Yellow Pages—British Telecom

Overview: A directory of British firms and organizations that can be searched by name of firm, location, and product.

Access: Telnet: `sun.nsf.ac.uk`
                login: `janet`   (no password required)
                hostname: `uk.ac.niss`
                NISS menu: select U
                UK menu: select E
                              Press the return key.

FidoNet Node List

Overview: A listing of the systems within FidoNet; contains FidoNet node number, geographic location, contact name, and title.

Access: WAIS: `fidonet-nodelist`

Contact: e-mail: `pozar@kumr.lns.com` or
                       `David.Dodell@f15.n114.z1.fidonet.org` (David Dodell)

                Fido Software
                Box 77731
                San Francisco, CA 94107 USA

▪▪

✗ Netinfo

Overview: A multi-purpose service with many commands for finding information about Internet hosts, and some information about BITNET and UUCP as well. Also contains great general online help for many aspects of network addressing. Although the help information has been collected specifically for users at Berkeley, much of the information is of value to any Internet users. For example "help mail net index" gives information on addressing e-mail messages to non-Internet networks.

Access: Telnet: `netinfo.berkeley.edu` 117 (Don't forget the port, 117!)
Online help: ? (use "?" for a quick display of available commands)

Contact: e-mail: `netinfo@netinfo.berkeley.edu` (Bill Wells)
voice: (510) 642-9801

✗ nslookup

Overview: A useful Unix command for finding an IP numeric address when you know the Fully Qualified Domain Name of a host. Has many additional features and options when run in interactive mode, such as listing hosts within a domain, using different name-servers, and using finger from within the nslookup session.

Access: From a Unix host enter "nslookup" followed by part or all of a Fully Qualified Domain Name (non-interactive mode). Entering "nslookup" by itself will launch an interactive nslookup session.

More Info: "man nslookup", or during an interactive session type "help" once you are at the ">" prompt.

✗ United Kingdom Name Registration Database

Overview: Contains hostnames and addresses of all hosts in the Janet network.

Access: WAIS: `uk-name-registration-service`

Contact: e-mail: `L.McLoughlin@doc.ic.ac.uk`

Administrative Directory Services

✗ Horton

Overview: A software package for the automatic updating of a site's whois database that operates by periodically fingering each host in a domain. If your company or university doesn't yet have an e-mail directory, Horton can help you get it started.

Access: The Horton source code is available via FTP from many Internet sites. Use archie to find the archive nearest you.

Contact: e-mail: `dank@blacks.jpl.nasa.gov` (Dan Kegel)

✗ RIPE (Reseaux IP Europeen) Network Management Database

Overview: E-mail and postal addresses, names, and phone numbers of administrators and managers of the RIPE network.

Access: WAIS: `ripe-database`

             FTP host: `ftp.ripe.net`
             directory: `/ripe/dbase`
             filename: `ripe.db`

Contact: e-mail: `Marten.Terpstra@ns.ripe.net`

             Marten Terpstra
             RIPE Network Coordination Centre (NCC)
             Kruislaan 409
             NL-1098 SJ Amsterdam Netherlands
             voice:+31 20 592 5064
             fax:+31 20 592 5090

Internet Directory Services: Where Do We Go from Here?

During the last few years there has been a tremendous change in the number and quality of Internet directory services. A lot of work has gone into the development of these services, as well as on standards for services of the future. It has taken years of development to attain the level of quality we have come to expect from traditional information systems such as telephone directory services, so it should not be surprising that

Internet directories are not yet as comprehensive, reliable, or easy to use as they could be. Rest assured though, there are many people and organizations working on this problem.

As the Internet evolves, available services respond to the needs and activities of its users. With strong demand from the user community and rapid response from service providers, more complete and reliable directory services should be at hand before the end of the decade.

FOR MORE INFORMATION

Most of the directory services described in this chapter have online help that may include pointers to technical references describing their inner workings.

The following RFCs contain some general discussion about directory services and specific information about the X.500 protocol:

RFC1107	Plan for Internet directory services
RFC1202	Directory Assistance service
RFC1295	User bill of rights for entries and listing in the Public Directory
RFC1308	Executive introduction to directory services using the X.500 protocol
RFC1309	Technical overview of directory services using the X.500 protocol
RFC1355	Privacy and Accuracy Issues in Network Information Center Databases
RFC1417	NADF Standing Documents: A Brief Overview (North American Directory Forum)
RFC1430	A Strategic Plan for Deploying an Internet X.500 Directory Service

Bibliography

Hill, J. M. "The X.500 Directory Service: A Discussion of the Concerns Raised by the Existence of a Global Directory." *Electronic Networking: Research, Applications, and Policy* 2(1) (Spring 1992): 24-29.

Kille, S. E. *Implementing X.400 and X.500: The PP and QUIPU Systems.* Boston, MA: Artech House, 1991.

Rose, M. T. *The Little Black Book: Mail Bonding With OSI Directory Services.* Englewood Cliffs, NJ: Prentice Hall, 1992.

Schwartz, M. "Applying an Information Gathering Architecture to Netfind: A White Pages Tool for a Changing and Growing Internet." December 1993. Available via anonymous FTP.

FTP host:	ftp.cs.colorado.edu
directory:	/pub/cs/techreports/schwartz/ASCII
filename:	Netfind.Gathering.txt.Z

SECTION VI

Targeted Interests

22
Becoming an Information Provider

Most Internet users actively pursue information that is provided by others. A typical user may be skilled at using several databases, a few favorite Gophers, and perhaps World Wide Web. Whatever your normal diet of information resources, a time will likely come when you want to share your own information in a setting more formal than an e-mail message or Usenet posting. This is especially likely if you are working in a library, school, business, research center, museum, or almost any other type of organization. In effect, you need to become a network publisher.

As a network reader, you can select electronic books, discussions, newsletters, annual reports, and more. As a network publisher, you might produce one or more of these products. Of course, publishing on the Internet involves certain considerations: copyrighting materials, supporting popular resources (e.g., 100 e-mail requests for a document you are offering), tracking the materials you distribute on the Net, charging for materials distributed (when can you? how can you?), etc. But it also offers great opportunities. You or your organization can offer information about yourselves, you can provide information resources to the public in an easily-accessible form, and generally, establish a new mode of communication with your clientele.

Please note: these methods of providing information to the Internet will require the use of special programs or functions located on a computer directly connected to the Internet (with the exception of e-mail aliases). This means that those of you with dialup or terminal connections can only use these functions with the cooperation of your system administrator. (Sound familiar?)

THE INTERNET PUBLISHING HOUSE

So, you want to be an Internet publisher. Excellent idea! What are your first steps? There are a number of issues that need to be considered before you start making your information formally available on the network.

- Who is your audience?
- What format best suits your needs?
- What materials should be included on your server?
- Who will provide the information?
- How is the work distributed?
- Who will be responsible for installing and maintaining the information?
- What information should be kept private?
- What kinds of equipment and software are available?
- What kinds of usage or readership statistics do you want or need?

You may want to go through this list of questions and think about them carefully; listed below is some background information on each of them. Furthermore, this chapter contains six sections devoted to specific applications that can be used for providing information to the Internet community and each of these sections focuses on issues related to that product that need to be considered. After you have evaluated these issues, note which ones are definite requirements, and what you can compromise on. Then use the list of requirements to evaluate the publication and distribution methods outlined in this chapter to decide how you want to distribute your work. While you can not plan for every contingency, you should design a system that is flexible and is likely to suit your needs for a couple years. Strategic planning for the longer term is a good idea, but remember that the Internet and its applications change quickly. Here and now, you may find that a combination of more than one method of electronic publication is best for your situation, such as offering your information through a mailing list, a Gopher, and an FTP archive.

Who Is Your Audience?

Consider your audience. Is it only people within your organization? Is it an external group? Or more likely, is it a combination of the two. Whatever the audience the more useful you make the system for them, the more people will use it. Don't be too parochial, but don't deluge people with too much information that is not directly related to their interests.

What Format Best Suits Your Needs?

Different methods of distribution often dictate the format of the document you distribute. E-mail, for instance, generally means you will be limited to ASCII text (though this is changing). The World Wide Web, on the other hand, offers the best method for distributing text along with graphics, movies, and sounds. But you also need to consider your audience: while e-mail is the most limited technically, it can reach the widest audience.

What Materials Should Be Included on Your Server?

If your archive will be storing more than just your own publications, you should consider creating a collection policy. The policy states what kinds of material are appropriate for your server, what person or group has the ultimate authority for deciding what should and should not be in the archive, who is responsible for adding material, and who is responsible for maintaining the site. Consider carefully whether materials copyrighted by others should be included on your server.

Who Will Provide the Information?

In the long run, providing and updating information on your system is likely to be the most time intensive and expensive task of running a computer-based publishing system, especially if your plans include the creation of a comprehensive information resource. The model that allows the most room for expansion is the one that distributes the information gathering and updating among the actual information providers. If you opt for this model, it would be useful to have well established procedures and templates for submitted materials. An additional time saver would be to have software that you can distribute to information providers for translating input directly into an approved format, ready for posting directly to the resource.

How Is the Work Distributed?

In many organizations it makes good sense to divide the work of electronic publication among a group of specialists. The work is usually distributed along functional lines rather than having one department responsible for all facets of the operation. It makes sense to have technically oriented people setting up and maintaining the equipment. If you have information being provided by a number of departments, it may make sense to have them funnel publications through a single person or small group before the materials are made publicly available. Explicit guidelines for the submission of material will save a lot of time and effort. Of course, the more work is decentralized, the more effort at coordination there needs to be. You will almost certainly want a single person who has oversight over the entire publishing operation to be sure that all the components are running smoothly and in concert.

Who Will Be Responsible for Installing and Maintaining the Information?

It's one thing to get the information onto the server, but who is responsible for the information once it's there? Who is responsible if the server crashes? At night? As with any computer service, you need to answer this question, and preferably *before* you open your service for business!

What Information Should Be Kept Private?

By what criteria should information in a publicly-accessible information system be considered sensitive or hidden? What sorts of concerns might staff, students, or clients have about online distribution of their contact information? While making the formula for fat free butter available online makes it easier for your collaborators to get to the materials, it also makes it easier for competitors to find it. Likewise, before putting information about individuals (for example a phone or e-mail directory) online, always contact the group at your site that maintains this information, or the individuals themselves. Discussing your needs and plans with the human resources office can help you to understand the privacy issues involved with making information about individuals publicly available.

What Kinds of Equipment and Software Are Available?

You will need to devote computer resources to your publishing effort. How much depends on a number of factors: the distribution method chosen, the amount of material being distributed, the size of the archives being stored, and the popularity of the resource. These variables are likely to change as time goes on and you learn to take the most advantage of this type of publication. Unlike the other variables, the popularity of your resource is something you can only try to predict. It has been known to happen that newly announced resources cause network traffic jams as word spreads and hundreds of users try to connect to a system all at once. (Remember the Holiday Gopher of 1993?)

What Kinds of Usage or Readership Statistics Do You Want or Need?

When most people log in to anonymous FTP servers, they assume that their use of the server is anonymous. On the contrary, it is possible to log each transaction and the user account that it is coming from. If you configure your FTP server to log transactions, you are obligated to announce this on your opening screen. You do run the risk of scaring people off, but you still ought to disclose what type of information you are collecting.

Conclusion

Becoming an information provider can be a lot of work. Be sure that you have the financial, hardware, and staff resources to devote to the endeavor before you start. It would be a shame to create a popular resource and then not be able to support it.

This chapter describes the ways that various Internet services can be used to deliver publications to your readers as well as the advantages and disadvantages of each method. For more general information about how to access and use each service, please refer to the chapter devoted to the service itself.

The applications described in this chapter are those that are available on the Internet today. But as we all know, the Internet is a shifting landscape and software development continues all the time. The choices you make today should not be considered permanent ones. Expect that you will probably be using a different publishing application within the next five years. While it is possible that you won't make such a shift in that time period, at least you won't be surprised if you do.

Using E-Mail to Distribute Information

E-mail distribution of information on the Internet is, for the reader, the method closest to traditional mail subscription in that the publication arrives in the reader's mailbox on a regular basis. For many publishers, it is the easiest way to get started in distributing their wares because just about all Internet-accessible computers have a mail feature that supports distribution lists. Furthermore, e-mail is the lowest common network denominator among readers. In other words, there are many people whose only access to the Internet is through e-mail. But there are problems and limitations involved with e-mail distribution, so it is not for everyone or every purpose.

This section describes both the advantages and disadvantages of e-mail distribution as a publishing method. After that there are descriptions of the various software packages available for managing e-mail distribution to a large number of people. The last part of

this section is a discussion of some special issues to consider when choosing e-mail as a distribution method.

Advantages of E-Mail Distribution

Simple Concept

Electronic mail distribution is very simple in concept. A list of subscribers is maintained manually or automatically, and when a publication is ready for publication, it is sent to everyone on the list. That's all there is to it. (Well, almost all there is to it).

Automatically Distribute Information Among a Group

One thing that some people love about e-mail distribution is that it requires no extra effort on the part of the reader. They just sit back and wait for the publication to appear in their mailbox. It's also possible to establish an e-mail distribution list that all of the subscribers can use to distribute information. While this may be efficient, be sure that your subscribers understand how the list works!

E-Mail Can Reach a Wider Audience

As we've said before, there are still many computer systems in the world that only have electronic mail access to the Internet. By using e-mail as one of your modes of distribution, you can reach the widest audience.

Low Cost

Most of the software necessary to offer e-mail distribution is free or is a part of a typical e-mail installation and will not require additional fees.

Disadvantages of E-Mail Distribution

Manual Maintenance Can Be Time Consuming (and Annoying)

Maintaining a mailing list manually, where people subscribe, unsubscribe, and go on vacation, can be an annoyance. If your list is large, say, over 500 entries, this can be a major drain on your time. If you expect your list to be larger than 500 entries, or if it ends up being fairly volatile, consider automating the subscribe/unsubscribe and "set nomail" processes. If you are performing manual additions and deletions, you may find that requests come in bursts. This is due to the organic nature of information propagation on the network and the yearly cycles of its academic users (still a large proportion of the network community). Try to keep up with the flow so that subscribers don't feel that their request is being ignored. People who have requested that they be unsubscribed and who continue receiving publications can get particularly upset. It is also a good idea to send confirmations for both subscribe and unsubscribe requests, whether they are handled manually or automatically. Programs like LISTSERV and ListProc will handle this process automatically.

Managing Bounced Mail

When your mailer sends a publication to one of your subscribers and it can't get through to them, the mail is "bounced" and returned to you with a terse explanation. Often enough, people subscribe to a publication, and some time later, their e-mail account is removed or changed. Sometimes mail is bounced because a server is temporarily down and at other times because the piece of mail sent out was too large for that local system to handle. In another scenario, mail does not bounce, but produces an automatic response from the subscriber's computer letting you know that the account owner is on vacation in Tahiti and that they are enjoying sun, surf, and sand and won't be reading their e-mail until they return in 3 months. :-) In all of these cases you need to have a way of dealing with these messages.

Automatically deleting all entries in your subscription list when mail bounces may be too Draconian. You can end up removing accounts that are only temporarily inaccessible or whose owners are really just on vacation. Returned mail will contain a message from the mailer explaining why the message bounced. Since this information is not always easy to understand and because the messages vary from system to system, human intervention is required to figure out what action, if any, should be taken.

Some People's Accounts Can Not Accept Large Files

Different mail systems have different limits on the maximum size of e-mail files. While the Internet itself has no maximum mail message size, some local mail systems, and BITNET, do. If the publication you send is too large for the mailer, the message will be bounced back to you. In this case, you may want to re-send the message in smaller pieces to the individuals who have a problem with file size. Then again, you may not want to go to that trouble. The other alternative is to limit the size of messages to all subscribers to 100K (a fairly safe size) by breaking up longer messages into multiple parts. If you do do this, be sure to label each part with the consecutive number and the total number (e.g., "part 1 of 3") in the subject line of the message.

A Large Number of E-Mail Systems Are Limited to Plain ASCII

Many e-mail systems connected to the Internet these days will only accept plain ASCII e-mail. This means: no font or style changes within the text, no color, no real illustrations, no hypertext buttons, no sound, and no special control sequences. For some publications this is not a limiting factor, for others it is detrimental, and for most it is an issue that needs to be handled carefully. For many readers, this limitation is a big turnoff, especially as more colorful, more interactive applications become more commonplace on the network.

Text Formatting

If you do publish with plain ASCII, you need to consider how to present the material so that it is friendly to the user: use short paragraphs with spaces between each one; use ALL CAPS very judiciously; keep the number of characters in a line to less than 70 (some mailers are limited to viewing 65 characters per line, so you may want to stick to that!);

■■ ■ ■

include a table of contents at the top of the message; and use headers appropriately throughout the text as they help the reader find their way.

Types of E-Mail Lists

LISTSERV (BITNET)

LISTERV lists on BITNET are a very common way of formally distributing mail to a large number of people. It has the distinct advantage of offering automated subscribe and unsubscribe functions (with or without notification to the list owner), automatic and searchable archiving, and a well-known and understood platform. LISTSERV version 1.7 is free to BITNET sites, but upgrades are not. One of the limitations of LISTSERV is that it currently only runs on IBM mainframes running the VM/CMS system. But changes are afoot, so do read on.

Contact: e-mail: `eric@searn.sunet.se`

L-Soft International
3509 Connecticut Ave., NW
Suite 300
Washington, DC 20008-2402 USA

voice: (301) 913-0390
fax: (301) 913-9849

LISTSERV for Unix, VMS, and MS Windows NT

It has been announced that L-Soft International will be developing versions of LIST-SERV for Unix, VMS, and MS Windows NT. Given the popularity of the original LIST-SERV program, and the popularity of Unix (and other) servers on the Internet, this development is fortuitous. Not surprisingly, there was much rejoicing on the Net when the announcement came out in the summer of 1993. Of course, the translation of the program from the original VM environment to these other three platforms will take some time. Current projections from L-Soft indicate that fully cross-compatible versions will be released by the end of 1995, or early 1996, and it is not expected to be free.

Contact: e-mail: `eric@searn.sunet.se`

L-Soft International
3509 Connecticut Ave., NW
Suite 300
Washington, DC 20008-2402 USA

voice: (301) 913-0390
fax: (301) 913-9849

The Unix Listserv Program (TULP), ListProcessor (ListProc), and Mailbase

There are a number of other programs used to automate mail processing. These include The Unix Listserv Program (TULP—*not* to be confused with LISTSERV for Unix), ListProcessor (ListProc—another Unix processor), and Mailbase (a British national mail processing program). These three programs may all be used without a fee, though certain restrictions may apply (e.g., you may not charge a fee to users of a list you create using one of these programs). For more information on these programs, please see the section, "For More Information" at the end of this chapter and/or contact those listed below.

Contacts:

Mailbase:

> e-mail: mailbase-helpline@mailbase.ac.uk
>
> NISP Team Computing Service
> The University of Newcastle upon Tyne
> NE1 7RU United Kingdom
>
> voice: +091 222 8080

ListProcessor (ListProc):

> e-mail: info@listproc.net
>
> CREN Information Center
> Suite 600, 1112 16th St., NW,
> Washington, DC 20036 USA

The Unix Listserv Program (TULP):

> e-mail: Christophe.Wolfhugel@univ-lyon1.fr
> (Christophe Wolfhugel) or
>
> Christophe Wolfhugel
> 9 Rue de Vaves
> 92130 Issy-les-Moulineaux France

Mailing List, Mail Reflector, or Mail Exploder

A mailing list, mail reflector, or mail exploder are the various names for a special account that is set up to automatically forward mail to a list of subscribers. Since all mail sent to that account name will be forwarded to all subscribers, you may want to use this judiciously. You can hide both the list of subscribers and the name of the account by using the "bcc" (blind carbon copy) function that is available on most mailers. The trick is to send the mail to yourself, as the publisher, and "blind cc" the account that forwards to the list. Information about the recipients of the "blind cc" is not shown in the message header, and the "To" field only includes the publisher. Cunning, yes?

It is usually easy to maintain a short list of subscribers yourself, and you maintain local control over the operation. On the other hand, this is a manual rather than automated system of maintenance, so it requires human involvement.

Aliases

A mail alias is similar to a reflector, but it is part of the your own account and no one else can use it. Aliases are often used to create nicknames for people you mail to often so that you can type in a short name in the "To" field and the program will substitute the full address. This can also be done with a list of people, so for instance, mail to

"working_group" will go out to all the members of the working group. The major problem with this method is that it is often limited to a certain number of people, depending on your mailer, and while you can send mail to the working group, the other members of the list cannot unless they create their own "working group" alias identical to yours.

Special Issues to Consider

Moderated Lists vs. Unmoderated Lists

Most listservers have the option of moderated or unmoderated service. To use the listserver as a publishing mechanism, it is pretty much required that you choose a moderated list. With a moderated list, nothing can go out to the list subscribers without the moderator's approval. Of course, this means that the moderator is also the monitor and editor. If you do indeed have a number of people contributing to your publication through a moderated list, the moderator will need to commit the time to check each message before it is sent to the subscribers. For more detailed information on this subject, see Chapter 10.

Technical Requirements

Most Services Are System Specific

As outlined above, LISTSERV (the original version) only works on IBM mainframes running VM/CMS, whereas the other programs are typically based on Unix. Things are changing, but right now choices are limited by the type of operating systems. The Unix-based mail processors can run on most Unix servers.

A Heavily Used List Will Produce Heavy E-Mail Traffic on the Server

While e-mail typically puts little demand on a system, it is conceivable that an active or large list on an already heavily-used server will cause problems. It may make sense to schedule large mailing jobs for the middle of the night, when your server is not likely to be doing much other work. The network in your part of the world is also likely to be less congested at night.

How Much Disk Space Is Required?

As a publisher, you will probably want to keep an archive of your material. Except for this archive, there is little disk space needed beyond that which the processor software itself takes up. (For example, ListProcessor version 6.0c weighs in at 1.3 Megabytes.)

ESTABLISHING YOUR OWN FTP ARCHIVE

Most Internet publishers will want to establish an FTP archive to both store and distribute their information. In most cases, the archive acts as just that–a place for people to access previously released materials. It can, however, be your primary mode of publication. Through various methods, you can "advertise" that your document or documents are available at your site and that people are welcome to retrieve copies. While the notices of availability will need to be distributed somehow, the distribution of the actual document is through FTP.

Advantages of Establishing Your Own FTP Archive

You Can Make Your Data Available to the Entire Internet Community

Offering your publications, current or previously released, through an FTP archive is very efficient. In fact, it is so easy and popular, that the largest single use of the Internet, in terms of bytes, is the transfer of files using FTP. While most of that data is made up of computer programs, this is still a form of electronic publication.

Little Maintenance Required

Most of the work of creating and maintaining an archive comes at the outset. You'll want to establish a collection policy and then organize the directories carefully so that users don't have trouble finding things. When new files are added, you will need to update your reference files to reflect the changes. To make this a successful service, keep all of your material current and properly documented. The amount of work this requires depends on the type of materials you are publishing. Providing an up-to-date listing of soccer scores from professional games worldwide will take more effort than listing the Oscar winners for the past decade. Remember, plan well and plan ahead and your maintenance will be reduced.

Files of Any Type Can Be Stored

While we typically think of electronic publishing as distributing text files, more and more electronic publications are including non-text material. These other formats include audio, graphics, and video. An FTP archive can store all of these types of files. To help your users, be sure to include file extensions, such as .au for audio files, .gif for GIF graphics files, and .mov for QuickTime movies, that let them know the format of each file. It's also a good idea to include meta-information on the server about the file types and how they can be used.

Low Cost

FTP server software is part of the basic Unix installation. For other platforms, FTP server software is usually a part of the networking package that supports TCP/IP so will not be an extra expense.

Disadvantages of Establishing Your Own FTP Archive

Archive Reorganization, or Spring Cleaning on Your FTP Host

As mentioned above, archives do grow. In fact, they often grow in an uneven, almost organic fashion. In order to avoid directory listings of over a hundred files, it may become necessary to reorganize the archive after a few years. With good planning and a fairly even flow of publication, however, it may be quite some time before this becomes necessary.

Some strategies to keep things under control: review all files and the directory structure on a regular basis—yearly if growth is slow and steady, or more frequently if growth is persistent or comes in spurts—and keep all informational files up to date.

Heavy Use of the Archive May Put Stress on the Server

Unlike mail, FTP puts a fair amount of demand on the server. If your site becomes popular, this may cause problems, especially if your server is doing more than just offering FTP'able archives. To reduce an overload problem, a site may limit the number of simultaneous FTP connections, offer "mirrored" archives, or, as a last resort for a publisher, remove their site from the archie index. (For more on this topic, see "Having Archie Help You Out" and "Mirrored Archives," below.)

Special Issues to Consider

Anonymous or Privileged FTP?

Your FTP archive can be set up so that any anonymous user can log in and read files in your FTP directory and its subdirectories. This type of archive offers the widest range of access: anyone with an Internet account can get your files through anonymous FTP or anonymous FTP through e-mail. If, however, you only want certain people to have access to the files (e.g., members of an organization, people who have paid a fee, etc.), you will need to set up privileged FTP using accounts with password protection. Be advised, though, that account and password maintenance will create a tremendous amount of overhead.

Security

Remember, when you establish a computer as an anonymous or even privileged FTP server, you are allowing strangers to use your computer. Typically, computers running FTP servers are performing double or triple duty, also serving e-mail and Gopher, for instance. This means that you must not only take care to protect the integrity of the material in the archive itself, but also to protect the files and directories in the other parts of the computer. Talk with your system administrator to establish proper security measures, and if you are using a Unix system, be sure to set the file permissions to prevent outside users from deleting or changing the files.

Having Archie Help You Out

One of the best ways to let the world know about your archive is to have its contents indexed by the archie service. However, archie will only index those anonymous FTP servers whose administrators have requested that they be indexed. If you do want archie to index your site, simply send e-mail to archie-admin@bunyip.com telling them that you want your site indexed. (Be sure to include the address of the site.) Conversely, if your site becomes overloaded with anonymous FTP sessions, or for some other reason you *don't* want the general public to know about your archive, then you can have the archie administrators remove your site from the index by sending mail to that effect to the same address.

Mirrored Archives

Another way to reduce the load on your FTP archive is to have other sites act as "mirror" archives for your site. A mirrored site is just that, another archive, or part of an archive, that holds a copy of the files in your archive. If you publicize the availability of the mirrored archive, and archie will help you do that, you will help spread the load of usage across more than one server. In addition, if people choose archives nearer their own site, they will reduce the load on the network when actually transferring files. Of course, you do need the cooperation of site administrators at remote locations, and many will be happy to help you out. It is crucial that mirrored sites be kept up-to-date either automatically or manually or else they quickly lose their value and frustrate users.

README

The best thing that you can do for your users besides putting the data in your archive is to offer them README, or other informational files, in every directory. README files are simply text files that explain what is in the directory, the dates of creation and last update, and who is responsible for it. Any other information about the files in the directory can be included, but this is the bare minimum. You may want to have multiple README files in a single directory, but be sure they are named in a helpful way, otherwise people don't know which one to start with, and may just ignore them all. As an example, you might have three files, README_FIRST, README_GIFs, README_PS, describing the contents of the directory in general, the GIF files and how they can be viewed, and the PostScript files and how they can be viewed, respectively.

There are two other types of files that let users know what materials are in the FTP archive: abstracts and ls-lR. Abstracts are listings of the archive contents along with a short description of each item in the archive. The ls-lR file is a copy of the Unix listing of files created by the command with the same name. The ls -lR command creates a recursive listing of all files and subdirectories from the current directory downward.

Technical Requirements

FTP Server Program

In order to offer an FTP archive, your server needs to be running an FTP server program. Most Unix hosts already have this available. Other computers can be set up as FTP servers with free or commercial software, as long as they are connected directly to the Internet. Unless the computer you are running is fairly powerful (especially when considering a PC-type computer), you may want to consider dedicating an entire computer to offering the FTP service.

Getting FTP Statistics

If usage statistics are important to you, consider using an FTP server program that will log the number of transactions on your server. A modified version of the standard

Unix FTP program called "wu-ftpd", was written by developers at Washington University in Saint Louis and is the best known of these. The software is available from the University's archive:

FTP host: `wuarchive.wustl.edu`
directory: `/packages/wuarchive-ftpd`
filenames: (many or all)

    Remember, you should notify your users that the transactions are being logged. Statistical information is very helpful in ascertaining which information in your archive is being used and by what type of user (local, remote, educational, etc.). With this information you can decide where to focus your resources, and if you need to weed your archive, you can target information that is never copied by others for removal from the server. If you are logging transactions, be aware that it is unethical to track the habits of particular users unless there is evidence that their FTP activities are criminal in some way.

JOINING THE GOPHER REVOLUTION

■■

    Over the past two years, the number of Gophers in the world has increased at an incredible rate. Current estimates are that there are well over 1500 Gophers in the world. Why such an increase? Gopher is a very efficient and dynamic way to publish information. For non-commercial use, the software is free. Since the Internet Gopher was originally designed as a Campus-Wide Information System (CWIS), you may also find it useful to check that section of this chapter for more information about establishing your own Gopher server.

Advantages of Having Your Own Gopher

Easy to Set Up

    Gopher client and server software are available via anonymous FTP. Most of it is self-configuring and requires little expert knowledge, although you will need help from a system administrator to install the server. If you decide to configure features for security or special handling of certain file types, installation can become more complicated. But Gopher is built from text files, so implementing changes does not require a degree in computer science.

    Server and client software are available for anonymous FTP from the developers:

FTP host: `boombox.micro.umn.edu`
directory: `/pub/gopher`
filenames: **(many or all)**
Contact: e-mail: `gopher@boombox.micro.umn.edu`
Microcomputer & Workstation Networks Center
152 Shepherd Labs
100 Union St. SE
University of Minnesota
Minneapolis, MN 55455 USA
voice: (612) 625-1300
fax: (612) 625-6817

■■■

Low Cost

Gopher server software and documentation are free to educational and other not-for-profit institutions who make their information available to the wider community. Commercial or private use requires that a licensing fee (sliding-scale) be paid to the University of Minnesota. For more detailed information, read the licensing agreement on the FTP server below:

	FTP host:	`boombox.micro.umn.edu`
	directory:	`/pub/gopher`
	filename:	`gopher-software-licensing-policy`
Contact:	e-mail:	`yen@boombox.micro.umn.edu`
	Shih Pau Yen	
	voice:	(612) 624-8865

Easy Way to Passively Distribute Your Information on a Wide Scale

Not only is a Gopher server easy to set up, but because Gophers are typically linked to one another, it is fairly easy for users to find your Gopher when browsing gopherspace or using the veronica index. In addition, other Gophers can point to specific data mounted on your server. Because Gopher is already so popular, presenting your information using this service will not force readers into unfamiliar territory.

Multiple File Types Available

For readers using a client to gain access to your Gopher, they may be able to access files of many types on your server, including graphics, sounds, and programs.

Easy to Add Large Amounts of Data from Other Sites

One of Gopher's main features is the ability to point to data and other Internet services (e.g., phone books, online catalogs, searchable indexes, pictures, etc.) both at your own site as well as at others. This means that you can create a local Gopher combining local resources with preferred remote resources. But read on to learn about the problems that can arise.

Disadvantages of Having Your Own Gopher

Maintenance Can Be Fairly Extensive

When your Gopher relies on a remote source for data or service, you have no control over how that data or service will be maintained, indeed, if it will be there at all. If a remote server or document disappears, the users of your Gopher will get an error message indicating that the server or item is unavailable when they try to select it. Pointers to resources that are no longer available are known as "dead links" and should be removed from your Gopher so as not to frustrate your readers. (Don't be too quick to remove a "dead" link, for it may be that it is only "asleep," that is, the remote server is only down temporarily.)

People Can Get Lost in a Gopher

Since most Gophers allow users to navigate freely through gopherspace, jumping from one Gopher to another as the inspiration moves them, people can get "lost in gopherspace" without realizing it. This is not to say that Gophers are too confusing to use, but this is something to consider when evaluating an information server. While the seamless nature of navigation in gopherspace has its advantages, some find it disorienting.

Special Issues to Consider

Registering Your Gopher

To let the Internet world know about your Gopher, register it with the official Gopher registry by sending e-mail to: gopher@boombox.micro.umn.edu mentioning the address of the Gopher and its geographical location. Once this is done, your Gopher will be listed among "All the Gopher Servers in the World" and the appropriate geographical section as well. You may also want to let others know about your Gopher by sending an announcement to the appropriate e-mail lists and newsgroups. Appropriate mailing lists and newsgroups are those that are specifically related to the subject or subjects represented in your Gopher or are designed to distribute information on new resources of all types.

Local Data vs. Remote Data

As mentioned earlier, relying on remote data can cause problems since you can't control information on someone else's server. If there is data that you want to be sure is available for your clientele, your best bet is to obtain a copy for yourselves and maintain it locally.

Gophers Are Addictive

You will probably find that once your Gopher is established, you and your colleagues will be overcome with zealous energy and will want to add and point to all sorts of data. Resist the temptation to add things wholesale! A Gopher crammed full of material is daunting and often overwhelms users. As with an FTP archive, it is wise to create a collection policy, outlining what is and is not appropriate for your Gopher, as well as who is responsible for deciding what should be added on an ongoing basis and who is responsible for maintenance. Even if you distribute the workload of adding new material, you should set an overall collection policy.

"About..." Files

Again, as with FTP, it is highly recommended that you include information about each menu in your Gopher. In Gopher these are called "About" files. Since they start with the letter "a" and Gopher menus default to an alphabetic listing, these conveniently live at the top of the menu. These files should include information on the contents of the menu, how the information got there, the dates of creation and last update, and who is responsible for it.

Should You Offer a Public-Access Client?

One of the biggest decisions you will need to make when setting up your Gopher server is whether or not you wish to offer a public-access client. Since Gopher is a client-server application, you have the option of setting up your server (offering your data in the Gopher format) without offering a public-access, or anonymous, client. In this case, each user that wants access to your Gopher must have their own client and use the gopher command, or its equivalent, to access your materials. In order to run a Gopher client, they need a full Internet connection, or dialup SLIP or PPP connection. If you do offer a public-access client, anyone with Internet access can telnet to your Gopher and use it that way.

Now, you may be asking, "Why shouldn't I offer a public-access client? Isn't it good netiquette to share what I have?" Well, you should not feel obligated to offer to the Net what you can not afford to, and there are two reasons why a public-access client may be more than you can afford. Even if you don't offer your own public-access client, users can get to your Gopher from someone else's public-access client. There may be items on your Gopher that you do not want to offer to the whole world but that you do want to offer to specific users. Establishing security so that external Gopher clients can not access these items is reasonably straightforward. Establishing security so that anonymous users telnetting to the public-access client is much more difficult.

The more compelling reason to avoid offering a public-access Gopher client is the fact that this service uses up significant computing resources. During a public-access session, your host is providing an ongoing connection to the outside user which means that there are fewer computing resources available to your other users. A regular client session, however, is "connectionless," that is, the client and server computers are only connected during the actual transmission of data. If you are fortunate enough to have the computing resources available to offer a public-access client, and the security concerns have been addressed, then by all means, offer your Gopher to the masses through a public-access client!

Limiting Access to Data

As mentioned before, you may wish to have some items on your Gopher limited to access by local users, while other parts are available to all. In this case, all menu items will appear on the screen, but outside users would receive an error message if they try to access the materials that are off limits to them. Without going into the technical details of how this is done, suffice it to say that gopher items can be limited by the IP address of the client that is accessing your server. This feature can be tricky, so when planning your Gopher, be sure to meet with your technical staff to discuss how this will work. If you do create menu items that are not accessible to all, try to make this clear in the text of the menu item itself so that outside users know that they can not access the items before they attempt to select them.

Using WAIS to Assist Your Gopher

One of the keen features of Gopher is its ability to incorporate other applications in a seamless interface. One of these applications is WAIS. (For more detailed information, see

Chapter 18.) WAIS can index the text of documents on your Gopher and offer key-word searching to your users. When a WAIS item is selected from a Gopher menu, and the search terms are entered, the search results are displayed as a new Gopher menu, with the items listed in order of relevance. Your users probably won't know they're using WAIS, but that's one of the advantages of the Gopher interface.

Organizing the Gopher (Plan, Plan, Plan)

Keeping a Gopher's contents stable enough that users are not disoriented by changes is tough. Since it's so easy to add things, there is a tendency to overload a Gopher. Providing access to lots of files and resources will only work if your Gopher is well organized. Ascertain what will be on your Gopher and set up a menu structure that is general enough to accept new materials, but specific enough that users can find their way. Keep the menu screens short at the top of the structure with only one screen (up to 18 items) for the first menu. It's not a good idea to change the first few menu layers very much as this will confuse your users; so planning these menus carefully will save you and them lots of grief.

Another design trap can be having too many layers of menus. Having to dig through more than 3 layers of menus to get to their item of interest can often frustrate users. The key, then, is to balance the length of menus with the depth of them.

Veronica and Jughead

Veronica and jughead are the pair that index Gopherspace. Veronica indexes most of Gopherspace as a whole, while jughead only indexes those parts of Gopherspace that you select. They allow users to use keywords to search for and then display Gopher items and menus. In many ways, veronica is the key to Gopher's ongoing success as an Internet-wide application.

Since the public-access veronica servers are typically overloaded, you may want to offer your own veronica server, though it will require additional maintenance and a large amount of disk space. If you do offer a local veronica server on your Gopher, you need to decide if it will be publicly accessible, or only available to your local users. (See Chapter 17 for more information on veronica and jughead.) To obtain veronica server software and installation information, use the FTP site below:

	FTP host:	`veronica.scs.unr.edu`
	directory:	`/`
	filenames:	**(many or all)**
Contact:	e-mail	`foster@unr.edu` (Steve Foster) or
		`barrie@unr.edu` (Fred F. Barrie)

Jughead uses fewer resources than veronica since jughead only indexes a small portion of Gopherspace. Jughead is customizable to your specifications and is loaded on the same computer as your Gopher. You can have jughead index your own Gopher, or a whole set of Gophers. This second option is especially helpful for subject-oriented

■■■

Gophers. (For instance, you could have a jughead index of all known medical Gophers.) To obtain jughead software and installation information use the FTP site below:

	FTP host:	`boombox.micro.umn.edu`
	directory:	`/pub/gopher/Unix/GopherTools/jughead`
	filenames:	**(many or all)**
Contact:	e-mail	`jonzy@cc.utah.edu` (Rhett "Jonzy" Jones)

Asking Others to Point to, Rather than Copy, Your Data

The ease of transferring materials electronically means that an electronic publisher can lose control of their publication. If other Gopher administrators copy your data to their system, you can no longer control what the viewer sees when they look at the materials on that system. While you may hope that the other Gopher administrator will update their copy of your publication regularly, there is no guarantee that they will.

As an example, suppose you publish a weekly newsletter on gardening. Your January issue talks about winter pruning. An avid gardener and Gopher administrator elsewhere likes this topic and copies it to their local system. Five months later, if the administrator has not updated the file, the summertime users of this Gopher are looking at a document on winter pruning. They may even assume that the newsletter is terribly behind the times, or went "out of business" completely! The electronic publications a user finds online are assumed to be the most current available, unless it is explicitly stated otherwise. This assumption is very different from walking into a doctor's office where magazines might be eight months old. In this case you don't presume that these are the most current issues.

Although it would be difficult to enforce, you may want to ask other Gopher administrators not to copy your data for mounting on their Gophers. Rather, ask them to point to the copy on your server, whereby you will have greater control over what the users see and you will also be able to keep more accurate statistics on the use of your data. To effect this, you should include this request in the README files and at the top of each data file as part of a copyright statement. Follow up by doing an occasional veronica search to see if anyone is storing a copy of your data. (A veronica search will also list those places that point to your server, so this type of enforcement may prove too inefficient.) If you do locate a *copy* of your data, check the Gopher in question and locate the contact person and ask them kindly to remove the data, reminding them that they are welcome to point to your own copy. Be aware though, that by asking others to rely on you for the data, you are giving yourself the responsibility of making sure that the data are available reliably. One downside to consider is that if your server goes down or is inaccessible, no one can get to your data. Another option is to establish a relationship with an administrator at a remote site and agree to keep an up-to-date copy of each other's data.

Technical Requirements

Gopher Servers (and Clients) Run on All Major Computer Platforms

There are now Gopher servers available to run on the following platforms: Macintosh, NeXT, DOS, Unix, VMS, MS Windows, Amiga, MVS, OSF, and OS2. It will run (as a server) on most relatively modern machines with these operating systems. In other words, you don't need a top-of-the-line computer to offer a Gopher server.

Usage Load

Offering a public-access client to a popular Gopher may drag your system down. Even if your own Gopher is not so popular, some users may telnet to your client, just to use your system to get to other Gophers. Remember, during a public-access client session, your host mediates every action.

WAIS AND MEANS

The Wide Area Information Server, or WAIS, is a full-text indexing system that provides access to large databases of unstructured data. WAIS retrieval results are ranked according to the density of keywords found in the documents and individual results can be returned to the server as a new search, thereby requesting "more documents like this one." Since WAIS is different from other types of search engines, or search mechanisms, you will need to consider whether your data are appropriate for use with WAIS. It is also recommended that you prepare a test database before you decide to use WAIS.

Advantages of Using a WAIS Database

Search a Large, Flat Database

The biggest advantage of WAIS is its ability to search a database that has no structure other than paragraphs or other small units. In other words, it is "flat." This means that a company could enter all of its correspondence, for instance, and then quickly find all related letters on a particular topic using a keyword search without specialized commands. Since no fields (e.g., author, title, date) are used in WAIS, most documents do not need special treatment to be indexed by WAIS. It's possible to designate whole files or single paragraphs (text separated by two carriage returns) of a file as the individual "records" of the database.

Search Multiple Databases at Once

WAIS clients allow users to select and search multiple databases, even if they are on different servers and offer aggregated results. As a provider of a server, it means that your data can be used in conjunction with data that others (or you yourself) have provided in a different database.

WAIS Can Search and Display Graphical Images and Sounds

While most people use WAIS to search through text databases, it can be used to search catalogs of images and sounds, then display or play the results on demand. (This assumes, of course, that your computer has the hardware and software capability to handle the playing or viewing of these file formats.)

Future Versions Expected to Comply with Z39.50

WAIS was originally based on the first version of the National Information Standards Organization Z39.50 (1988), a standard that has been incorporated into the International Standards Organization Search and Retrieval Protocol (ISO-SR). While Z39.50 and WAIS diverged somewhat in the last few years, it has been announced that the next major version of WAIS will be compliant with the next version of Z39.50. Why should you care about this? A system that is compliant with the international search and retrieval protocol means that it is likely to be compatible with other systems that you and your clients might use, and it is less likely to become obsolete in the near future.

WAIS Is Available for Free

There are currently two versions of the WAIS software both for Unix systems. One version, available for free, is known as FreeWAIS and is available from the Clearinghouse for Network Information Discovery and Retrieval (CNIDR) via FTP:

	FTP host:	`ftp.cnidr.org`
	directory:	`/pub/NIDR.tools`
	filename:	`freeWAIS-X.tar.Z`
		(where X is the version number)
Contact:	e-mail:	`freewais@cnidr.org`
		(general information)
		`Kevin.Gamiel@cnidr.org`
		(technical questions)

Kevin Gamiel
CNIDR/MCNC Center for Communications
3021 Cornwallis Road
Research Triangle Park, NC 27709 USA
voice: (919) 248-1911

The commercial version is fully supported and available for a fee from WAIS, Inc. a company founded by the original developers of WAIS.

Contact:	e-mail:	`info@wais.com`

WAIS Inc.
1040 Noel Drive, Suite 102
Menlo Park, CA 94025 USA
voice: (415) 617-0444

Little Maintenance Required

There is very little maintenance required to support a WAIS server. It is a good idea to keep the server software up-to-date, but new versions do not come out very often.

Other than that, all that needs to happen is to re-execute the indexing program each time new data are added or changed; depending on how data are added, you may be able to automate this procedure.

Disadvantages of Using a WAIS Database

Some Types of Data Are Difficult to Search Successfully

Since the database has no structure, no delimited fields, it is not possible to create searches for specific types of data in the database. For instance, you could not find documents written by a specific person, only those documents that include that person's name, no matter in what context. For some types of data, this search mechanism will not prove very successful. However, in the example above, if the database held documents that never mentioned personal names except as authors, then a name search would work just fine.

Ranking Algorithm May Not Produce Rankings with Much Meaning

The WAIS ranking algorithm ranks the hits returned from a search by evaluating the number of times the keyword search terms appear in the document and comparing this with the total number of words in the document and the total number of words in the database. The major failing of this method is that in a very short document, the appearance of a keyword a few times pushes that document up very high in the relevance rankings. Unfortunately, too often, a very short document may not have much useful information in it at all, while a longer and more helpful document with an equal number of keyword hits will rank much lower. Here again, consider your data to see if this will present a problem, try a test database, and take the rankings with a grain of salt.

Terminal Client Is Clumsy

If you expect that a large portion of your users will not have the ability to use a WAIS client (i.e., they do not have a direct network connection), you may want to reconsider using WAIS as a method of distributing your information. The terminal client, called Simple WAIS (SWAIS), that people can telnet to is difficult to use. (See Chapter 18.) If WAIS is used through Gopher, as described earlier, or is offered as an alternative to another method of access to your data, then this needn't be such a concern.

Special Issues to Consider

Is Your Data Appropriate for a WAIS Database?

Not all data are suitable for use with the WAIS search engine. Data that are highly structured and rely on that structure for "searchablility," or databases that have widely variant record sizes, probably won't work very well here. Data that use a variety of terms for the same concepts may also be difficult to search since WAIS does not currently have a thesaurus feature.

■■

Technical Requirements

A WAIS server will run on most Unix computers, but only on Unix computers. On the other hand, clients are currently available for the following platforms: DOS, Macintosh, NeXT, Unix, VMS, MS Windows, MS Windows NT, and X-windows, though the quality of the interface can vary quite a bit among them.

WHAT TANGLED WEBS WE CAN WEAVE

■■

A World Wide Web server puts your own data into an international web of data which, in turn, is part of the Internet. The Web is created by the documents and their hypertext and hypermedia links. On a more conceptual level, the World Wide Web integrates access to multiple documents and document types from multiple locations through a single, seamless interface.

Advantages of Establishing a World Wide Web Server

Ability to Store Information as Hypertext and Hypermedia

Hypertext is a feature that allows a user to browse through the concepts of a document or set of documents in a nonlinear fashion. In the hypertext format, various parts of the screen, including text, act as "buttons." When selected (clicked with a mouse, usually), a button activates a "link" that leads the user to another place in that document, to another document on that server, or to another document on another server halfway around the world. These other documents can be texts, sounds, or pictures (moving or otherwise)–hence, hypermedia.

Escaping the ASCII Prison

The texts in the Web are stored in a format that allows for the inclusion of formatting codes. This means that documents can employ different fonts and text styles. This ability makes publishing in this medium very attractive–literally!

Store Local Information in a Wider Web of International Knowledge

With the ability to add hypertext and hypermedia links to your data, you can include "live" references to items on other servers, whether they are Web servers or not. For instance, on your server there might be a document that is a scholarly paper that includes references. Any of the references to sources that are available electronically on the Internet can be made into buttons that take the reader directly to the sources. Or, as another example, your local server might have a lesson for your basic science class on meteorology, then, one click of the mouse away is the current satellite photo of the United States, Europe, or Africa.

410

⌒THE INTERNET PASSPORT⌒
■ ■

Disadvantages of Establishing a World Wide Web Server

Hypertext and Hypermedia Links Must Be Added to Documents Manually

While it is technically fairly simple to add hypertext and hypermedia links to Web documents, it does need to be done manually for each item in each document. People are working on ways to automate at least parts of the process, but it is likely to be some time before it is fully automated. There is also a fair amount of overhead in the process of deciding what to link and to where. Again, a lot of planning will help you implement this more smoothly. For more information on creating hypertext documents, see the following item:

WWW: `http://info.cern.ch/hypertext/WWW/Tools/Overview.html`

When No Direct Internet Connection Is Available

One of the biggest obstacles to wide-spread adoption of the World Wide Web is the poor performance of terminal clients that can't, because of their design, use a graphical display or mouse. With a desktop client (usually NCSA Mosaic) running over a direct network connection (versus a standard dialup connection) users can use their mouse to select buttons, view pictures and movies, and play sounds. With a terminal client, the interface is completely text-based and users must select buttons by typing the number of the labeled button. One recent development that helps alleviate this problem is the Lynx Web browser that runs using a VT100 emulation. With this client running, textual buttons are in bold-face and they are selected using the cursor keys, though the interface is still limited to text. You can try this public-access client out at the University of Kansas by using Telnet:

Telnet: `kufacts.cc.ukans.edu` (use VT100 emulation)
login: `kufacts`

Special Issues to Consider

WWW Clients

The most common client, or browser, used to access the World Wide Web is called NCSA Mosaic, developed by the National Center for Supercomputing Applications. There are currently versions of Mosaic for X-windows, Macintosh, and MS Windows. There is another browser called Cello, that was developed at the Legal Information Institute of the Cornell Law School for use on MS Windows computers. Cello works a bit differently than Mosaic for Windows, so you may want to try them both out and see which you prefer. If you are working in a mixed platform environment, Mosaic is probably your better choice. Both clients are available free of charge. For information on obtaining copies of the software, see the technical requirements section.

Graphical Displays

If you have data that you want to offer to your clients or the general public over the Internet, and your data includes graphics, then a World Wide Web server is probably the best way to publish it. This does not obviate the possibility of also offering your data via Gopher or FTP (and with the client problem, FTP access is a good idea), but it really does provide the best presentation of graphics with text. One note of caution: graphical images take much longer than text to transfer, so there is a trade-off between including graphics that are pleasing to the eye versus the time needed to wait for it to appear on the screen. This can be especially frustrating with "in-line" images–those that appear in the middle of text documents. To view the graphics, the user will need to have the appropriate viewer software program on their computer. Copies of the viewers used with the WWW clients are available at the same FTP sites as the clients themselves.

Peaceful Coexistence: FTP, Gopher, Telnet, WAIS, and WWW

Happily, choosing the World Wide Web as a server does not mean that you or your users must give up other Internet services. On the server side, there is a program called "GN" developed at Northwestern University that works much like Gopher, but allows you to serve a single document as either a hypertext document or a Gopher text document depending on the type of client that is connected: one set of files, two ways to access them. A GN server will not, unfortunately, offer the full functionality of a standard WWW server. Information on obtaining this server is provided in the technical requirements section (next).

Just as in Gopher, you can use WAIS to index documents and directories that reside on your WWW server. These indexes then become buttons on the screen. On the client side, the two graphical WWW browsers, Mosaic and Cello, both support FTP, Gopher, Telnet, and e-mail within the same interface. For this reason, many people consider them to be good front-ends to the many diverse services and resources of the Internet.

Technical Requirements

Servers

World Wide Web server software is available for Unix, Macintosh, VM/CMS, and VMS computers, and will run on reasonably modern versions of these computers. The WWW server is available from the developers at CERN:

	FTP host:	`info.cern.ch`	
	directory:	`/pub/www/src`	
	filenames:	`www-server-guide.ps`	(PostScript guide)
		`www-server-guide.txt`	(ASCII text guide)
		`(many or all)`	(server software)
WWW:		`http://info.cern.ch/hypertext/WWW/Daemon/User/Guide.html`	
Contact:	e-mail:	`timbl@info.cern.ch`	
	Tim Berners-Lee		
	WorldWideWeb project		
	CERN		
	1211 Geneva 23 Switzerland		
	voice:	+41 22 767 3755	
	fax:	+41 22 767 7155	

■■

The GN server runs on Unix machines and is available for free from the developers at Northwestern University:

	FTP host:	`ftp.acns.nwu.edu`
	directory:	`/pub/gn`
	filenames:	`README`
		`gn-X.X.tar.gz`
Contact:	e-mail:	`john@math.nwu.edu`

John Franks
Department of Mathematics
Northwestern University
Evanston, IL 60208-2730 USA
voice: (708) 491-5548
fax: (708) 491-8906

Clients

The Mosaic client requires a full connection to the Internet. While it should be possible to run one of these clients using a SLIP or PPP dialup connection, it is unlikely that the speed of data transfer will be satisfactory. Remember, graphics are large files and they can take substantial time to transfer. The client itself will run on reasonably modern versions of the following platforms: X-windows, Macintosh, and MS Windows.

Mosaic client:

	FTP host:	`ftp.ncsa.uiuc.edu`	
	directory:	`/Mosaic`	(Mosaic for X)
		`/<systemname>/Mosaic`	(other platforms)
	filenames:	**(many or all)**	
Contact:	e-mail:	`ebina@ncsa.uiuc.edu`	

Eric Bina
Software Development Group
National Center for Supercomputing Applications
152 CAB
605 E. Springfield
Champaign, IL 61820 USA
voice: (217) 244-6133
fax: (217) 244-1987

Cello client:

	FTP host:	`fatty.law.cornell.edu`
	directory:	`/pub/LII/Cello`
	files:	**(many or all)**
Contact:	e-mail:	`tom@law.mail.cornell.edu`

Thomas R. Bruce
Research Associate
Cornell Law School
Myron Taylor Hall
Ithaca, NY 14853 USA
voice: (607) 255-1221
fax: (607) 255-7193

Lynx browser:

The Lynx browser (a server with a public access client) has been compiled on the following platforms: DEC Ultrix, DEC Alpha OSF/1, Sun 4, NeXT, and VMS (Multinet). It has been rumored to run on these platforms: HP-UX (snake), Solaris 2, SVR4, VMS (UCX), LINUX, SGI, SUN 3, AIX 3.1, NeXTStep 3.x.

The server software itself is also available from the University of Kansas via anonymous FTP:

	FTP host:	`kufacts.cc.ukans.edu`
	directory:	`/pub/WWW/lynx`
	files:	**(many or all)**
Contact:	e-mail:	`rezac@kuhub.cc.ukans.edu`
	Charles Rezac	
	University of Kansas	
	Documentation Specialist	
	Academic Computing Services	
	208 Computer Facility	
	Sunnyside and Illinois	
	Lawrence, KS 66045 USA	
	voice:	(913) 864-0460

YOU DON'T HAVE TO BE A CAMPUS TO HAVE A CWIS

While the acronym CWIS stands for Campus Wide Information System, its utility is not limited to a college or university campus. Any organization that has information it would like to make available to either a local audience or an Internet-wide audience can benefit from having a CWIS.

But setting up a CWIS is not a matter of "plug and play." You should anticipate spending considerable organizational effort and resources (including plenty of staff time) to start and maintain a CWIS. As with a Gopher (which began its life as a CWIS and can still be used as one), the well-planned CWIS reaps the greatest rewards and will require less future maintenance overhauls and overhead.

Some of the information in this section is derived from Judy Hallman's 1992 CWIS article, cited in the bibliography of Chapter 19, and articles posted to the CWIS-L LIST-SERV mailing list. You are encouraged to read those sources for a much more thorough discussion of these issues.

Advantages of Running Your Own CWIS

Menu-Based Access to Your Data

CWISs offer the ability to mount your local data in a menu-based system. This is often the best way to offer a large amount of data to a diverse community because it requires little or no training. The best CWISs combine menu-based access using cursor controls, as well as bold-face characters (that will work with most, but not all terminal emulations) to help the user find the right information on the screen.

Information Available 24 Hours a Day at Every Computer

Having your organization's information online means that you don't have to wait for someone to arrive in the morning, make telephone calls (just so you can leave voice-mail), walk to another office, or wait for the information to arrive in your mail box. It's there for you, when and where you want it.

Disadvantages of Running Your Own CWIS

As we've seen with Gopher, this type of information distribution raises a number of issues. These include maintenance of the data and navigational difficulties on the part of the user. Be sure to read the Gopher section in this chapter for detailed information on these topics. There are a couple of problems that are more likely to appear with non-Gopher CWISs.

Control Issues (Well, We All Have Those ;–)

Most non-Gopher CWISs require substantial inter-departmental cooperation to get materials put into the CWIS. Often, the department that produces the data is not the department that runs the information systems and likewise, the CWIS software. In this case, the information providers must rely on the cooperation of the information systems staff to publish their data in a way that suits them. This means that final control over the information no longer rests with the information provider, but with the publisher. With a Gopher, on the other hand, many departments operate their own server as opposed to having the central information systems support staff do it.

Support for Your CWIS Software

You may find that as more and more people use Gophers and other, more common applications (World-Wide Web, WAIS), support for and development of other types of CWIS software dwindles. If you have your own computer staff that is ready to support your CWIS, then this will not be a problem. If you don't, you may end up needing to switch systems sooner than you planned.

CWIS Software

There is a variety of CWIS software packages and it's a good idea to explore the various services to see how well they would address the needs of your community.

Gopher vs. CWIS, or Gopher = CWIS?

One question arises quickly when deciding on a CWIS: why not use Gopher? And it's a good question. In fact, Gopher was originally designed as a CWIS (and is still frequently used this way), though Gopher seems to be running all other CWISs out of town! The biggest difference between Gopher and earlier versions of CWISs is that each Gopher server is typically a part of the larger gopherspace and the Internet as a whole. Most

CWISs tend to be more inwardly focused, offering mostly local information and few, if any, connections to the outside world. While the Internet may be used to get *to* a traditional CWIS, there are typically few opportunities to step out *from* the CWIS onto the Internet. While a Gopher can be configured for local use of local resources, you'll want to explore the features of other CWIS software too.

Other CWIS Software

Some of the "traditional" software platforms for CWIS include DEC VTX and AIE (for VAX computers). MUSIC/SP (for IBM mainframes and PS/2 machines), and CUINFO (for IBM mainframes) As was already mentioned, a rapidly growing number of sites are using Gopher for their CWISs. WAIS and World Wide Web are also beginning to appear in the CWIS world as well. For more information on these programs, see "For More Information" at the end of this chapter.

While exploring possible CWIS software options you should keep the following questions in mind:

- Will this software run on my system?
- How much, if anything, does it cost?
- Who, if anyone, supports it? Will upgrades be available?
- Is it easy to use or will our users need training?
- Is it easy to contribute information or will our information providers need training?
- How easy would it be to customize various features of the software if necessary?
- And if you don't find CWIS software that meets all of your needs, would the in-house development of a new system or modification of already available software be a cost effective route to consider?

Software Contacts

Academic Information Environment (AIE):

        e-mail: `percival@indiana.edu`
        Pete Percival
        University Computing Services
        Indiana University
        750 St. Rd. 46 Bypass
        Bloomington, IN 47405 USA
        phone: (812) 855-9146
        fax: (812) 855-8299

CUINFO:

        e-mail: `CUINFO-Admin@cornell.edu`
        Lynne Personius
        201 Olin Library
        Cornell University
        Ithaca, NY 14853 USA
        voice: (607) 255-3393
        fax: (607) 255-9346

■■■

DEC VTX:

> e-mail: `linda.braun@zko.dec.com`
> Linda Braun
> Digital Equipment Corporation
> 110 Spitbrook Rd.
> Nashua, NH 03060 USA
> voice: (603) 881-0260
> fax: (603) 881-0927

MUSIC/SP:

> e-mail: `roy@musicm.mcgill.ca`
> Roy Miller
> General Manager
> McGill University Systems, Inc.
> West Tower, Suite 1650
> 550 Sherbrooke St. W
> Montreal, QC, H3A 1B9 Canada
> voice: (514) 398-4477 or (514) 398-4480
> fax: (514) 398-4488

Special Issues to Consider

Organizing the CWIS (Plan, Plan, Plan)

As with Gopher, the best way to be sure your CWIS is user-friendly is to plan ahead. Figure out what types of materials will be on your CWIS and set up a menu structure that is general enough to accept new materials, but specific enough that users can find their way. Some CWIS programs will allow you to design menus and on-screen help. Be sure to keep things simple for your users, and don't try to pack too much onto each screen. Remember, planning menus carefully will save lots of grief for everyone.

How topics are organized will depend on the audience and how the system will be used. What categories should be included in the main menu? In what order should these items appear? Should the information be divided by administrative categories or by information type? Should entries be listed alphabetically, conceptually, or in some combination of the two?

As an example, the Comparative Literature Department and the Student Activity Center may both offer movie listings. If you list information by department, and users are looking for movie listings, they may not find all the information available. On the other hand, if you organize the information by category, in this case, "Movie Listings," those people who are interested in comparative literature may miss the opportunity to see a series offered by their department. As you can see, compromises sometimes have to be made. Listing the same data in more than one place may be the best answer.

Logical classification of diverse information is an area in which librarians have a great deal of expertise; but keep in mind that in addition to the purely informational role of the CWIS organization, there may be political or ideological implications to various set-

■■

ups. Such subtleties as the order in which items appear in the main menu or how many menus down one must go to obtain a certain class of information could have unexpected consequences that you should try to anticipate in discussions with your information providers.

Will Use of the System Strain the Computer Resources?

This answer depends partly on how popular the CWIS becomes. Just who are you trying to serve? Will the use of the system by users outside your organization be too much of a strain? Will it create a security risk? You may want to consider limiting the use of your CWIS to local users only.

"About" Files

Again, as with FTP and Gopher, it is highly recommended that you include information about each menu in your CWIS. These "About" files should include information on the contents of the menu, dates of creation and last update, and who is responsible for it.

CWIS Security

You should make sure that the CWIS software you install does not have security holes which could be broached by computer crackers. For example, some early CWIS systems allowed a user to "break out" of the CWIS shell and then gain anonymous access to your system and, potentially from there to the rest of the Internet. Or someone could get in and change the information on your CWIS. Such situations could be very embarrassing for your institution. Ask the vendor, developer, and other users of a particular CWIS software package direct questions about what security problems are known or suspected to exist.

Management: Who Will Operate the CWIS?

At different institutions, CWISs are operated by the staff of the computer center, library, administration, or any combination of these and other entities. Which organization(s) at your institution is most willing and able to operate and maintain a CWIS? You might find that portions of the task could be allocated to different departments. For example, CWIS software and hardware maintenance could be the responsibility of computer support staff, while various departments could contribute data.

However, the more distributed the handling of a CWIS, the more important it is to delineate roles and responsibilities. For example, if erroneous information is posted, who is responsible? If the system crashes in the middle of the night, who will set things right? If you plan to make your CWIS available to the Internet community at large, who will handle the request for assistance from remote users?

Technical Requirements

This depends on the CWIS software you select, the number of users who will be accessing the system, and the amount of information being made available. Likewise, these factors may also affect how much the software costs, if it is not free.

COPYRIGHT AND OTHER LEGAL ISSUES

■■■

Publishing on the Internet has engendered quite a bit of legal and ethical discussion, but so far, little case law. The most obvious issue is how to protect copyright in the digital world. But there are other problems that have yet to be fully addressed: what happens to a document that has left your hands? What if someone alters it? Who's liable for material you publish electronically written by someone else? What if you just "distribute" it?

Copyright

According to the terms of the Berne Convention (The Universal Copyright Code) and U.S. Law, most things that appear on the network are copyrighted automatically as they are published in a fixed form (the server) in a way that is perceivable to others. There are, of course, limitations on copyright, such as fair use (Sect. 107 of the U.S. Copyright Act) and the fact that short phrases or words can not be subject to copyright, though they can be trademarked.

What Copyright Protects

Copyright guarantees to the copyright holder, usually the author or publisher, the right to:
* reproduce the work;
* produce derivative works;
* distribute the work;
* perform the work publicly;
* display the work publicly;
* attribute the work to the author and prevent the work of others being attributed to the author;
* prevent others from creating altered versions of the work under the author's name and prevent destruction of the work.

In the case of items published in the U.S. today, the first five rights above last for the duration of the authors life plus 50 years; the last two rights only last for the lifetime of the author. However, for works for hire, copyright lasts until 100 years after creation or 75 years after first publication, whichever comes first.

For more detailed information on copyright law itself, you may wish to consult the following network resources:

"Frequently Asked Questions About Copyright":

Gopher:	gopher.uwo.ca
menu:	General Interest (Weather, On-line Info & more)/Frequently Asked Questions/FAQ directory (LARGE!)/Copyright-FAQ/
item:	**(many or all)**

■■■

```
FTP host:    rtfm.mit.edu
directory:   /pub/usenet-by-group/comp.answers/
             Copyright-FAQ/
filenames:   (many or all)
```

Copyright information, including the full text of the U.S. code, is available from the Legal Information Institute:

```
WWW:           http://fatty.law.cornell.edu
Telnet (WWW):  www.law.cornell.edu 8210
login:         www
```

General copyright information at the Library of Congress:

```
Gopher:   marvel.loc.gov
menu:     Copyright/
items:    (many or all)
Telnet:   marvel.loc.gov
login:    marvel
menu:     Copyright/
items:    (many or all)
```

A bibliography of print sources on copyright and other issues pertaining to electronic publishing appears at the end of this chapter.

The Copyright Statement

In terms of materials on the network, it is a good idea to include a copyright statement on all materials you are formally publishing (i.e., not your e-mail). This statement should outline what types of use and or copying are allowed. Remember, however, you can not place limits on the terms of the Fair Use clause of the U.S. copyright code. You may find it helpful to use the copyright statements of other information providers when the wording suits your purpose. Consulting a lawyer is also a good idea.

Maintaining Control After the Document Has Left Your Hands

As mentioned above, copyright includes the restriction against others creating derivative works from your own. This is something that electronic publication can make temptingly easy. To help protect yourself, it is a good idea to include mention of this protection in your copyright statement. You could also use a digital signature to technically inhibit others from distributing corrupted copies of your work. For more in digital signatures, see Appendix C on Internet security.

Liability

As a publisher, you are likely to be held liable for damaging materials that might be published on your system. This liability stems from the same liability that traditional publishers have. The only exception that might leave you, the administrator of the system,

■■■

exempt, is the situation where you do not and perhaps can not review all the material that is added to your system. Case law in this area is particularly slim, but it appears that system administrators that do not exercise editorial control over the material on their system are not considered publishers in the eyes of tort law. If you are not editing or reviewing the materials you make available, you probably should not call yourself a publisher. If you do want to be a publisher, then you need to take on the responsibilities of one. You would do well to ask your lawyer about this issue also.

COMMERCIAL ACTIVITIES ON THE INTERNET
■■■

One of the hottest topics and rapidly expanding areas on the Internet is commercial traffic. While there are some doomsayers predicting that the Internet will be ruined by commercial traffic, most understand that the continued growth and development of the network depends on such activity. While the research and education sector is still the largest group of users of the Internet, the rate at which commercial networks are being connected to the Internet is three times that of research and education networks.

Traditionally, there was no commercial traffic on the Internet due primarily to a prohibition of commercial traffic over the National Science Foundation Network (NSFNET) Backbone which specifically prohibits commercial traffic. (See Appendix F for the complete text of the current NSFNET Backbone Services Acceptable Use Policy (AUP).) Subsequently, many of the regional, or mid-level, networks also prohibited such traffic as they relied on the NSFNET Backbone for long-haul service. This situation has, however, changed rather rapidly in the last few years. With the establishment of a parallel backbone network called the Commercial Internet eXchange (CIX), mid-level service providers have been able to offer service to users that is free of the restriction on commercial traffic and commercial traffic has become somewhat commonplace.

The Rules

Among the rules for acceptable use of the NSFNET Backbone from the current NSFNET AUP are the following:

General Principle

(1) NSFNET Backbone services are provided to support open research and education in and among U.S. research and instructional institutions, plus research arms of for-profit firms when engaged in open scholarly communication and research. Use for other purposes is not acceptable.

Specifically Acceptable Uses

(6) Any other administrative communications or activities in direct support of research and instruction.

(7) Announcements of new products or services for use in research or instruction, but not advertising of any kind.

Item number 6 is important because it has been used to justify the availability of commercial services that are used primarily in "direct support of research and instruction" on the NSFNET Backbone. Item number 7, on the other hand, is a rule that clearly leaves room for interpretation. For a better understanding of how this rule might be applied, see the section on "Internet Culture" and advertising.

Listed in the NSFNET Backbone Service AUP is the following unacceptable use:

(10) Use for for-profit activities, unless covered by the General Principle or as a specifically acceptable use.

This is the overall NSFNET AUP prohibition on commercial traffic. It says that commercial traffic is not allowed unless it is specifically exempted from the prohibition as outlined above (numbers 6 and 7). Again, do read the entire text of the AUP that is included as Appendix F (it's only 1 page), or read it online at the InterNIC Gopher:

```
Gopher:    gopher.internic.net
menu:      InterNIC Information Services (General
           Atomics)/NSF, NREN, National Information
           Infrastructure Information/NSFNET Information/
item:      NSFNET Backbone Services Acceptable Use Policy.

Telnet:    gopher.internic.net
login:     gopher
menu:      InterNIC Information Services (General
           Atomics)/NSF, NREN, National Information
           Infrastructure Information/NSFNET Information/
item:      NSFNET Backbone Services Acceptable Use Policy.
```

As initiatives for the National Information Infrastructure (NII) and the national information superhighway gather steam, the overall nature of online information transfer–including commercial activities–will change. As a part of the larger information infrastructure, the Internet will likely be a part of these changes.

Internet Culture

One of the most prevalent fears with respect to the commercialization of the Internet is the fear that advertising will become commonplace, and our e-mail boxes will be deluged with one of the more actively despised products of modern society–junk mail. Considering the relative ease of such a venture, it is easy to see why there is such concern. But given the long-standing NSFNET AUP and cultural tradition of the Internet that discourages advertising and supports free and open access, it is not surprising that advertisers, where technically acceptable, are moving tentatively. After all, alienating your customer base is not considered a sound business move.

Here are some unofficial guidelines for advertising on the Internet:

- be sure the information you distribute is relevant to the individual(s) or group(s) you send it to;
- include useful information, not just hype—hype is easily spotted in ASCII;
- before posting to a list, check with the moderator or list owner;
- send only a brief summary with information on where more information is available if the reader chooses to get it.

Net culture tends to look more kindly on information that does not smack of a hard-sell and is being forwarded by someone without a personal financial interest in the product or service. Another way to look at creating an ad, or offering a commercial service over the Net, is to be sure it is something you think someone in your client community would feel comfortable passing on to others.

These traditional, accepted Internet advertising tactics are finding new company in advertisements accessible from several services on the CIX portion of the Internet. The new breed of advertisements share a common approach: they want the reader to come to them, rather than appearing as unsolicited mail in the reader's mailbox.

Examples of Commercial Activity on the Internet

For some examples of popular and unobtrusive, or network-polite, commercially-oriented services, you may want to sample the Electronic Newsstand offered by a commercial firm called The Internet Company:

```
Gopher:        gopher.internet.com
menu:          Electronic Newsstand (tm)/
```

and the Global Network Navigator offered by O'Reilly & Associates press:

```
WWW:           http://nearnet.gnn.com/gnn.html
```

For a large and well organized listing of many commercial servers on the Internet maintained by Henry Houh (hhh@mit.edu), connect to "Commercial Services on the Web." (Both Gopher and Web servers are listed here.) This list is kept up-to-date and new servers are added quite frequently.

```
WWW:           http://tns-www.lcs.mit.edu/commerce.html
```

Charging for Materials on the Internet

Assuming that you are not violating an AUP (local, regional, or backbone), you can offer fee-based publication distribution on the Internet, but it's not easy. Billing people for their use of services on the Internet is a difficult problem. Do you charge the user to connect? Do you charge for connect time? For the amount of material they access? A flat fee? Or some combination of these? Beyond price structure, how is the financial transaction accomplished? There are a number of schemes being proposed for conducting commerce on the Internet, but none of them has become standard nor is any one scheme likely to be suitable for all purposes. Regardless of the pricing structure and billing methods, charging for access is likely to require a fair amount of overhead.

■■

Credit Cards

So, you're offering a for-fee service on the Internet. Doesn't it sound convenient to accept credit card information over the Net as well? Yes, it is certainly convenient, but also imprudent. The danger is that, unencrypted, someone else could gather the credit card information from the network and use it for fraudulent purposes. There are efforts under-way to establish reliable and secure electronic money exchange systems that put neither party at risk for fraud or other types of monitoring.

Accounts

Another option is to require users to establish accounts in order to access your mate-rials. The drawback here is the administrative overhead on your part and the loss of spon-taneity for the reader. However, if they plan to use your service on a regular basis, it would be possible to get their credit card information on paper, or by phone and have them in your database for automatic charges, much the way a newspaper might charge your account on a regular basis. Once the initial account is established, the user can be given easy access to your service.

Successes

Despite these challenges, there are a number of companies that have successfully offered their services over the Internet for a number of years. These companies include: Mead Data (NEXIS/LEXIS), ClariNet (ClariNet News), and Colorado Association of Research Libraries (CARL UnCover).

FOR MORE INFORMATION

■■

Mailing Lists on Internet Publishing

There is a low volume mailing list devoted to publishing scholarly electronic jour-nals called, VPIEJ-L. To subscribe, send e-mail:

```
mail:    listserv@vtvm1.cc.vt.edu
subject: (none needed)
message: subscribe VPIEJ-L <your-full-name>
```

The archives of this list are searchable via WAIS as vpiej-l.src.
Another list that might be helpful is the GO4LIB-L list:

```
mail:    listserv@ucsbvm.ucsb.edu
subject: (none needed)
message: subscribe GO4LIB-L <your-full-name>
```

Although the list is devoted to the issues surrounding offering Gophers in libraries, a bit of lurking here might give you some ideas about what problems come up, and how they might be solved.

Yet one more list that might be helpful is the CWIS-L list devoted to issues related to providing a Campus Wide Information Service:

```
mail:    listserv@wuvmd.wustl.edu
subject: (none needed)
message: subscribe CWIS-L <your-full-name>
```

There is a discussion list for TULP, and Unix listservers in general:

```
mail:    listserv@graspl.univ-lyon1.fr
subject: (none needed)
message: subscribe LISTNIX <last_name-first_name>
```

More Information on CWISs and Listservers

Hallman, Judy. "Campus-Wide Information Systems (CWIS)." University of North Carolina at Chapel Hill. Last updated August 20, 1993. This master list of CWISs is available via anonymous FTP:

```
FTP host:  sunsite.unc.edu
directory: /pub/docs/about-the-net
filename:  cwis-l
```

"ListProcessor version 6.0: Preliminary User's Guide." July 1993. Available via Gopher.

```
Gopher: coral.bucknell.edu
menu:   Network Services (Local and Remote)/Bucknell Listserv
        lists and message archives/Listserv Help directory/
item:   listproc.
```

"Mailbase On-Line Service Reference Card (short)." November 1993. Available via Gopher.

```
Gopher: nisp.ncl.ac.uk
menu:   Mailbase Documents /
item:   Mailbase On-line Service Reference Card (short).
```

"Statement of Intent: L-Soft to Develop LISTSERV for Unix" August 22, 1993. Available via e-mail. For the plain text version, send the following message:

```
mail:    listserv@searn.sunet.se
subject: (none needed)
message: GET GM9309-1.MEMO
```

For the PostScript version, send this:

```
mail:    listserv@searn.sunet.se
subject: (none needed)
message: GET GM9308-1.PS
```

Thomas, Eric. "LISTSERV for the Non-Technical User" September 18, 1993. A PostScript version is available via e-mail.

```
mail:    listserv@searn.sunet.se
subject: (none needed)
message: GET GA9305-2.PS
```

Usenet Newsgroups on Publishing Systems

```
comp.infosystems.gopher

vmsnet.infosystems.gopher

bit.listserv.gopher

comp.infosystems.wais

comp.infosystems.www

cern.www.announce

alt.hypertext
```

Bibliography

Andorka, F. H. *A Practical Guide to Copyrights and Trademarks*. New York: Pharos Books, 1989.

Godwin, M. "The Law of the Net: Problems and Prospects." *Internet World* 4(8) (September/October 1993):52-54.

Hallman, J. "Campus-Wide Information Systems." University of North Carolina at Chapel Hill. May 19, 1992. Available via anonymous FTP:

>FTP host: `sunsite.unc.edu`
>directory: `/pub/docs/about-the-net`
>filename: `hallman.txt`

Jensen, M. B. "Making Copyright Work in Electronic Publishing Models." *Serials Review* 18(1-2) (1992):62-65.

Long, C. and C. Neesham. "Whose Copyright Is it Anyway?" *New Scientist* 139(1883) (July 24, 1993):21-22.

Medvinsky, G. and B. C. Neuman. "NetCash: A Design for Practical Electronic Currency on the Internet." Proceedings of the First ACM Conference on Computer Communications Security (November 1993). Available in compressed PostScript format via anonymous FTP:

>FTP host: `prospero.isi.edu`
>directory: `/pub/papers/security`
>filename: `netcash-cccs93.ps.Z`

Robison, D. F. W. "The Changing States of *Current Cites*: The Evolution of an Electronic Journal." *Computers in Libraries* 13(6) (June 1993):21-25.

Rosenberg, J. "Prototype for a National Info Highway?" *Editor & Publisher* 126(41) (October 9, 1993):26-29, 34-35.

Schwartz, E. I. "Like a Book on a Wire." *Publishers Weekly* 240(7) (November 22, 1993):33-35, 38.

Van Bergen, M. A. "Copyright Law, Fair Use, and Multimedia." *EDUCOM Review* 27(4) (July/August 1992):31-34. Also available electronically via Gopher, FTP, and WAIS:

>Gopher: `gopher.cni.org`
>menu: `Educom Services/EDUCOM Review 1992`
>item: `EDUCOM-Review-July-Van-Bergen-CopyrightFairUseMultimedia`
>FTP host: `educom.edu`
>directory: `/pub/EDUCOM-Review-1992/`
>filename `:EDUCOM-Review-July-Van-Bergen-CopyrightFairUseMultimedia`
>WAIS: `educom.src`

A Writer's Guide to Copyright. 2nd ed. New York: Poet & Writers, c1990.

CHAPTER 23

A Schoolhouse for the World

Using the Global Internet in K-12 Education

Until recently, computer networks have been used almost exclusively in universities, corporations, and governments. But in the past few years, there has been exponential growth in the use of local, national, and even international networks in pre-college, or "K-12," education.

Consider the possibilities: a global, pre-college school would have classrooms spanning continents. Although the plans of this global schoolhouse are still being drawn, its halls are already beginning to ring with the voices and activities of enthusiastic students and teachers.

The aim of this chapter is to provide the information you need to help you use the Internet in a way that is appropriate for you, your students—and your students' futures. You will get a quick tour of this rapidly growing global school. You'll be introduced to its classes, conference rooms, libraries, field trips, and science labs, and given some ideas about how the Internet is currently incorporated into the K-12 curriculum.

WHY USE GLOBAL NETWORKS IN K-12 SCHOOLS?

Computer networks might seem to be just another classroom gadget like film projectors or televisions. At first glance, a networked computer looks like a computer with some wires running into the wall. But the tiny hole in the wall through which those wires pass is actually a window to the world.

The many benefits offered by networked computers can be grouped into three categories: educational opportunities for the students, resource sharing, and in-service training for the teachers.

Educational Opportunities for the Students

For decades, visionaries have talked about how telecommunications could create a global village in which it is as easy to communicate with someone on the other side of the world as it is to visit a next-door neighbor. Computer networks are currently making this abstract global village a reality for students. From a humble classroom computer connected to networks like the Internet, your students can:

* engage in global dialogue with students and instructors using electronic mail;
* practice foreign language writing skills with native speakers in online discussion groups;
* participate in, or even initiate, meaningful projects based on collaboration and cooperation of thousands of students throughout the world;
* obtain supplemental instructions from online tutorials or enroll in distance education courses in your national or even foreign institutions; and
* gain "information literacy," a basic understanding of how to navigate in and take full advantage of the networked world into which they will be graduating.

Unlike outdated filmstrips of life in Hong Kong or Patagonia, a global network allows your students to communicate directly with fellow students from these and many other places.

Resource Sharing

When a school invests in the hardware and software to connect to a full-service, worldwide network like the Internet, it immediately gains access to billions of dollars of resources. Even the smallest and most isolated rural school can use the same services enjoyed by the largest and best endowed urban universities. These resources include:

- the catalogs of hundreds of the world's best libraries;
- free educational software and documents from file archives containing thousands of Megabytes of files;
- databases of real research data containing information from agricultural markets, global climate simulations, or even space missions to other planets; and
- supercomputer training programs which give students access to the world's most powerful computers.

Networks can be a powerful democratizer of educational resources. While not every school will use all of these resources, they are available if needed.

In-Service Education and Teacher Enrichment

The Internet and the global schoolhouse it creates can also address the needs of teachers and other educators. The staff of primary and secondary schools sometimes feel isolated from their peers or have difficulty maintaining contact with the professors and facilities they depended on throughout their training in colleges and universities. By using computer networks, K-12 educators can:

- increase the number and diversity of educational resources they use while teaching;
- participate in continued education by enrolling in universities and colleges that offer distance education programs via networks;
- continue professional contacts formed during their college or university education; and, of course,
- use the extraordinary informational resources of the Internet for any professional or personal development they might desire.

To What Network Should a K-12 School Connect?

K-12 schools can obtain network connectivity from a wide variety of providers, including government sponsored educational networks, not-for-profit cooperative networks, and commercial networks. How does one choose which network service is best? A wise decision will take, minimally, the following factors into account:

- How much computer experience do your teachers and students already have?
- What sort of computer equipment does your school already have?
- What are the costs of obtaining the hardware and software required for connectivity?
- What sorts of fees must you pay the service provider?
- What services are provided in exchange for the fees paid—technical support? Users support? Training? Documentation? Manuals and guides?
- Are there any legislative restrictions which make certain options difficult?
- How well will a particular option scale as more demands are placed on it by newly enthusiastic students and teachers?

If your school hasn't yet been connected to an external network, you might think that the most basic network services would be adequate. But judging from the experiences of universities and research institutions, it is likely that once you've made a connection to a global network, the use of computer networks by students and teachers at your school will grow rapidly.

Like universities, K-12 schools have many choices for network connectivity, including:

- Internet networks, such as NSF sponsored regional networks in the U.S.;
- statewide or provincial networks;
- not-for-profit cooperative networks; or
- commercial network providers.

Listed below are some of the types of networks that schools can connect to to gain access both direct and indirect, to the Internet. For an excellent listing of Internet service providers and assistance in choosing the best service and connection type for your situation, see Estrada (1993).

Internet Networks

In terms of comprehensive networking capabilities, the Internet has no match. In fact, most every kind of resource that is available through computer networks is available through the Internet.

It should be noted that Internet connectivity does not have to be high-tech nor high investment. Many school districts find that modem dialup access to the Internet initially provides ample service with only a small investment.

National Internet Networks

Of particular interest to K-12 educators in the U.S. is the National Science Foundation Network (NSFNET) and its successor, the National Research and Education Network (NREN). This high speed network was created specifically to support the use of computer networks in education and research. Analogous government sponsored networks have been or are being developed in many other nations.

In December of 1991, the High Performance Computing Act, authorizing the creation of a permanent NREN, was signed into law. The bill authorized the expenditure of

$2.9 billion over the next five years to enhance the U.S.'s high performance computing and communications infrastructure. At this time, the development of the NREN continues along with the development of the U.S. National Information Infrastructure (NII).

Regional Internet Networks

The NSFNET is a framework or "backbone" network currently linking NSF-sponsored regional networks in the U.S. Each regional network serves many sites throughout its specific geographic region.

Some regional networks, such as BARRNet in the San Francisco and Silicon Valley area, service a geographically small but densely computerized portion of a single state. Others help bring large, sparsely populated regions together into the network world. For example, NorthWestNet serves over 29% of the U.S. land mass, including Alaska, Idaho, Montana, North Dakota, Oregon, and Washington.

A growing number of K-12 schools are reaping the many benefits of direct connections to regional Internet networks.

Statewide or Provincial Networks

Another promising source of network connectivity for K-12 schools are statewide or provincial networks. Many of these networks are part of the Internet.

For example, within the U.S. a survey of statewide networks released in April, 1991, reported that most all 50 states either had established or were about to initiate state networks that would include K-12 connectivity as a central goal (Kurshan, 1991). Similar intranational networking is taking place in Canada and European nations.

Every state network is different. The technical sophistication of statewide networks varies tremendously between and within states. In some states, connections from K-12 schools are made through dialup modems, while other states use technologies such as high speed (T1) lines, fiber optics, point-to-point microwave, and satellite links. Some statewide networks feature direct K-12 Internet access. Most statewide networks offer electronic mail, though in some cases this is still restricted to administrative use.

Comprehensive overviews of state networks can be found in Kurshan (1990b, 1991).

Not-for-Profit Cooperative Networks

There are many national and even international not-for-profit, cooperative computer networks which may be appropriate for K-12 educational networking. These networks are particularly valuable for K-12 sites which cannot, or choose not, to connect directly to the Internet or whose state networks are still embryonic.

FidoNet

FidoNet is an international network with more than 10,000 electronic "bulletin board systems" (BBSs) in more than 50 countries. It is a grassroots, decentralized, not-for-profit network operated entirely through volunteer effort. FidoNet offers full e-mail access to the Internet via a gateway service. (See Chapter 5.)

A FidoNet BBS can be run with minimal hardware and software requirements. All you need is a telephone, a modem, a personal computer, a hard disk, and free FidoNet software. A good file backup system is a wise investment as well.

K12Net

Another particularly promising and widespread not-for-profit network for K-12 education is K12Net, an offshoot of FidoNet. The goal of K12Net is to create a demand for networking services within the K-12 education community by making it as easy as possible for K-12 schools to start networking. If you have access to a telephone, modem, and computer, you can dial up a FidoNet or K12Net BBS and start exploring the world of K-12 networking immediately. K12Net is an accessible, hands-on, network-based technology simple enough for students to learn and even operate.

K12Net offers the following services:

- global electronic mail, which can be sent to and received from the Internet;
- K-12 discussion groups;
- rich archives of K-12 oriented educational software (currently for MS-DOS computers only), documents, and other information available at 19 major K12Net BBSs.

In many ways the strengths of K12Net and FidoNet are derived from their simplicity, but this is also their limitation. They cannot offer the tremendous range of resources provided by the Internet. Contact information for several K12Net coordinators can be found at the end of this chapter.

National Public Telecomputing Network

The National Public Telecomputing Network (NPTN) is a not-for-profit organization dedicated to establishing and developing free computerized information and communication services for the general public, including the K-12 community. Current NPTN services are based on locally oriented bulletin board systems called Free-Nets. They provide information of interest to the general public, usually concentrating on serving a restricted geographic region. Please see Chapter 15 for more information on accessing Free-Nets.

NPTN sites are operating or are planned in many cities including Buffalo; Chicago; Cincinnati, OH; Cleveland; Columbia, MO; Denver; Dillon, MT; Helsinki, Finland; Lorain County, OH; Los Angeles; Medina County, OH; Minneapolis/St. Paul; Ottawa, Ontario; Peoria, IL; Philadelphia; Portland, OR; Singapore; Summit, NJ; Tallahassee, FL; Trail, British Columbia; Victoria, British Columbia; Washington, D.C.; Wellington, New Zealand; and Youngstown, OH.

GETTING STARTED WITH K-12 NETWORKING

Because K-12 networking began in earnest only a few years ago and because the networking world is evolving so rapidly, there are no definitive answers to even some of the most basic questions about how to use the Internet in K-12 education. In fact, there may never be definitive answers, and that may be a good thing!

Unlike many national, federally sponsored networks which have centralized authority and administration, each K-12 school district serves a distinct and unique constituency. This diversity and plurality will be reflected in the strategies adopted by each K-12 school district, from the technical to the pedagogical. No single solution can be right for everyone.

The rest of this chapter will present some specific examples of how the Internet is being used in K-12 education. What you learn in this chapter should help you make informed decisions about which Internet resources are best for your school.

Network Etiquette and Ethics

The current Internet community is mainly comprised of people from universities and research institutions who have developed unspoken rules of conduct in the networked world. Just as we unconsciously internalize standards of etiquette in our everyday behavior, the issue of network etiquette may not be apparent to new users of network services, especially among K-12 students. As Jack Crawford, one of the main forces behind K12Net has written, "the ability to keep our echoes animated, well behaved, and oriented toward K-12 curriculum increasingly depends upon the zealousness, energy, and skill of moderators."

Before starting a K-12 networking project with students, it would be wise to read about network etiquette so you have an appreciation of these rules before you and your students begin Internetworking. Chapter 4 deals with some of the issues of etiquette involved in electronic mail communications.

COMMUNICATING IN THE GLOBAL SCHOOLHOUSE

There are several discussion groups which act as the assembly halls and bulletin boards for teachers to announce projects requiring the cooperation of fellow K-12 classes, to share ideas, and in general, shape the future of K-12 use of the Internet.

Online discussion groups can put you in immediate communication with people throughout the world who share any interest you might have. Specific instructions on how to use Usenet, LISTSERV, and mailing lists are given in Chapters 9, 10, and 11 respectively. Just follow the examples in those chapters, and you can probably access any of the groups described below.

Usenet and K-12 Education

Among the thousands of Usenet newsgroups are a number of special interest to K-12 educators.

■ ■

The "k12" Hierarchy

As described in Chapter 9, there are several top level hierarchies within Usenet. The "k12" hierarchy contains newsgroups distributed to Internet and K12Net users and are geared directly towards K-12 education.

Newsgroup Address	Topic Areas
k12.chat.elementary	Informal discussion, elementary students, K-5
k12.chat.junior	Informal discussion, students in grades 6-8
k12.chat.senior	Informal discussion, high school students
k12.chat.teacher	Informal discussion, K-12 teachers
k12.ed.art	Art curriculum in K-12 education
k12.ed.business	Business education curriculum in grades K-12
k12.ed.comp.literacy	Teaching computer literacy in grades K-12
k12.ed.health-pe	Health and physical education in grades K-12
k12.ed.life-skills	Home economics and career education, grades K-12
k12.ed.math	Mathematics curriculum in K-12 education
k12.ed.music	Music and performing arts curriculum in K-12
k12.ed.science	Science curriculum in K-12 education
k12.ed.soc-studies	Social studies and history curriculum in K-12
k12.ed.special	Education for students with handicaps or special needs
k12.ed.tag	Education for talented and gifted students
k12.ed.tech	Industrial arts and vocational education in K-12
k12.lang.art	Language arts curriculum in K-12 education
k12.lang.deutsch-eng	Bilingual German/English with native speakers
k12.lang.esp-eng	Bilingual Spanish/English with native speakers
k12.lang.francais	Bilingual French/English with native speakers
k12.lang.russian	Bilingual Russian/English with native speakers
k12.library	Discussion of K-12 library use on the Internet

■ ■

The "k12.sys" Newsgroups

When you use the k12 Usenet hierarchy, you will notice newsgroups with names beginning "k12.sys." The newsgroup "k12.sys.projects" is for the coordination of activities in the newsgroups "k12.sys.channelX," where "X" is currently a number between 0 and 12. Each of these "channels" may be devoted to the exclusive use of a project for up to two months. For example, someone may announce in "k12.ed.science" or "k12.sys.projects" that they want to set up a project for collecting rainfall data. After participants have been collected, a "k12.sys" channel may be assigned for this project.

For more information about using the "k12.sys" newsgroups, read "k12.sys.projects."

Usenet Echoes of LISTSERV Groups in K-12

The following newsgroups are echoes of LISTSERV lists related to K-12 education. There are many more LISTERV lists related to K-12 education that do not have Usenet echoes. For a list of these, see "A Sampler of K12 Related LISTSERV Discussion Groups". For more information on KIDLINK, see the description in "LISTSERV Discussion Groups and K-12 Education" below.

Newsgroup Address	Topic Areas
bit.listserv.biosph-1	Anything relevant to planetary ecology
bit.listserv.blindnws	Blind News Digest
bit.listserv.coco	Tandy Color Computer
bit.listserv.edpolyan	Education Policy Analysis Forum
bit.listserv.intercul	Study of Intercultural Communication
bit.listserv.kidleadr	KIDLINK Coordination
bit.listserv.kidleads	Spanish KIDLINK Coordination
bit.listserv.lhcap	Technology for handicapped, funding info, etc.
bit.listserv.media-1	Media in Education
bit.listserv.response	Response to KIDLINK Questions

Other Usenet Newsgroups of Potential Interest to K-12

There are many newsgroups which, although not set up specifically for the K-12 community, may nonetheless be of interest to both K-12 educators and students. Here is a small subset of such general interest newsgroups.

```
bionet.general                  misc.rural

comp.dcom.modems                misc.writing

misc.consumers                  news.announce.newusers

misc.consumers.house            news.answers

misc.education                  news.newusers.questions

misc.education.multimedia       news.software.readers

misc.kids                       sci.edu
```

Mailing Lists

Among the best places for Internet users from the K-12 community to get started are the mailing lists KIDSPHERE and KIDS.

KIDSPHERE Mailing List

KIDSPHERE, formerly KIDSNET, is an international discussion group used by K-12 educators throughout the world. Think of KIDSPHERE as an assembly hall for the global K-12 Internet school.

If you want to learn about the latest activities, share your ideas, or find collaborators from throughout the world, KIDSPHERE is the place for you! Everyone can have a seat in the audience or climb onto the stage to make an announcement. KIDSPHERE is consistently informative and the mood of the group is positively uplifting. In the best spirit of the Internet, everyone on KIDSPHERE seems to be genuinely interested in sharing and helping.

Subscribing to KIDSPHERE

You can subscribe to KIDNSET by sending an e-mail message containing your request as follows:

```
mail:    kidsphere-request@vms.cis.pitt.edu
subject: (none needed)
message: <your subscription request>
```

After you have subscribed, copies of all messages that are sent to KIDSPHERE by subscribers throughout the world will be sent to your electronic mailbox.

KIDSPHERE is very active so you should be ready to handle 25-50 messages every day. If you do not plan to use your Internet account for an extended period, you should send an "unsubscribe" or "set nomail" request to the above e-mail address so that your mailbox does not become flooded with messages!

New KIDSPHERE subscribers are encouraged to introduce themselves to the list. To send an introduction or any other message to the readers of KIDSPHERE, send an e-mail message as follows:

```
mail:    kidsphere@vms.cis.pitt.edu
subject: <an informative subject line>
message: <your message>
```

Searching KIDSPHERE via WAIS

You can also search the archives of the KIDSPHERE discussion via WAIS. This database is named "kidsphere" and is accessible through the WAIS servers as described in Chapter 18.

KIDSPHERE FTP Archives

If you want to retrieve a whole month's worth of KIDSPHERE discussion, you can use anonymous FTP to retrieve digests of KIDSPHERE discussion.

```
FTP host:   hamlet.phyast.pitt.edu
directory:  /pub/kidsphere
filename:   kidsphere.YYMM
```

For each of the filenames, YY is the year, and MM is the month, for example, kidsphere.8905 is the first KIDSPHERE archive from May, 1989. The files are very large, in fact some are more than 1 megabyte in size, so be sure you have room on your hard disk or diskette for any file(s) you want to retrieve.

KIDSPHERE Teacher Introductions

An archive of messages from teachers in which they introduce themselves and explain their interests is available for reading via e-mail and anonymous FTP.

```
FTP host:   ftp.vt.edu
directory:  /pub/k12
filename:   teacherX.contacts    (where "X" is the number of the file)
```

These files can also be obtained via LISTSERV by sending the following message:

```
mail:    listserv@unmvm.unm.edu
subject: (none needed)
message:
get teacher1 contacts
get teacher2 contacts
get teacher3 contacts
get teacher4 contacts
```

For a subscription to the updated versions, send this message:

```
mail:     listserv@unmvm.unm.edu
subject: (none needed)
message:
afd add teacher1 contacts
afd add teacher2 contacts
afd add teacher3 contacts
afd add teacher4 contacts
```

KIDS Mailing List

"KIDS" is a spin-off mailing list of KIDSPHERE for all pre-college students with fewer than ten messages per day. You can meet thousands of students your age, from all over the world, just by reading and typing messages on your classroom computer. You may still be too young to travel around the world, but you can start making friends to visit when you do!

Subscribing to KIDS

You subscribe to KIDS by sending an e-mail message:

```
mail:     joinkids@vms.cis.pitt.edu
subject: kids subscription request
message:
Please add me to the KIDS list.

Thanks
<your name>
<your.e-mail.address>
```

After you have subscribed, messages sent by other students throughout the world will be sent to your electronic mailbox. Be sure you know how to read and get rid of e-mail messages before subscribing.

To send a message to all the kids subscribed to KIDS, send an e-mail message like the following:

```
mail:     kids@vms.cis.pitt.edu
subject: <one line telling what your message is about>
message: <a message you would like to share with other kids
         throughout the world>
```

Cancelling a Subscription to KIDS

Before you go on vacation or if you are getting too many messages, you may want to cancel your subscription to KIDS by sending the following e-mail message:

```
mail:    joinkids@vms.cis.pitt.edu
subject: cancelling kids subscription
message: <your request to cancel your KIDS subscription>
```

LISTSERV Discussion Groups and K-12 Education

There are more than 3,000 BITNET LISTSERV discussion groups, so first time users are sometimes overwhelmed by the global list-of-lists. At the end of this chapter is a list of the names and addresses of about 100 discussion groups organized by topic that may be of interest to K-12 users. Here are just two of these groups.

KIDLINK / KIDS-95

KIDS-95 is the name of a project designed to foster communication among children 10-15 years old. (Each year the name changes, and KIDS-95 lasts from May 1994-May 1995). KIDLINK is the name of the organization that runs the project and the name of the LISTSERV list that handles distribution of KIDS-95 announcements. (It is not a general discussion.) There are currently approximately 6,000 children in 48 countries involved in KIDS-95. To begin, each participating child posts an e-mail message to RESPONSE@VM1.NODAK.EDU answering the following four questions before they can engage in the dialog:

1. Who am I?

2. What do I want to be when I grow up?

3. How do I want the world to be better when I grow up?

4. What can I do to make this happen?

After these answers have been submitted they are archived and distributed on the RESPONSE list and the child can then participate in the KIDCAFE LISTSERV discussion group. Teachers may want to subscribe to the RESPONSE list first and read the postings for a day or so to get a sense of the project and help the children formulate their messages. RESPONSE and KIDCAFE are "read only" for people outside the 10-15 year-old age group.

There are a number of other groups in the project, some for kids and others for the adults that work with the kids. All subscriptions should be sent to LISTSERV@VM1.NODAK.EDU.

Newsgroup Address	Topic Areas
KIDLINK	KIDS-95 announcements only.
RESPONSE	Mailing list for posting and reading answers to the four questions. (Those outside the 10-15 age range are only allowed to read messages, not post them.)

(Continued)

Newsgroup Address	Topic Areas
KIDCAFE	Open forum for children aged 10-15. (Those outside the 10-15 age range are only allowed to read messages, not post them.)
KIDCAFEP	Portuguese language KIDCAFE.
KIDCAFEJ	Japanese language KIDCAFE.
KIDCAFEN	Scandinavian (Nordic) language
KIDCAFE.KIDFORUM	Discussion of focused topics; classroom discussions.
KIDPROJ	Discussion of projects by teachers and youth group leaders.
KIDLEADR	Casual forum for teachers, coordinators, parents, social workers, and others interested in KIDS-95.
KIDLEADP	Portuguese language KIDLEADR.
KIDLEADS	Spanish language KIDLEADR.
KIDLEADN	Scandinavian (Nordic) language KIDLEADR.
KIDPLAN	Detailed planning for the project.
KIDS-ACT	Activities forum for kids. (Temporarily closed.)

A more detailed description of the project is available via e-mail.

```
mail:    LISTSERV@VM1.NODAK.EDU
subject: (none needed)
message: GET KIDLINK GENERAL
```

Many of the countries involved with the KIDS-95 project have a designated contact for educators in that country who need assistance or further information. A country-by-country list of the contacts is also available via e-mail.

```
mail:    LISTSERV@VM1.NODAK.EDU
subject: (none needed)
message: GET KIDLINK CONTACTS
```

Contact: e-mail: opresno@extern.uio.no
                  Odd de Presno
                  KIDLINK
                  4815 Saltro
                  Norway
                  voice: +47 370 31204
                  fax: +47 370 27111

■■■

Daily Report Card

This is a daily collection of news items about education. Although it deals specifi-cally with how schools in the U.S. are working towards meeting national education goals, there is plenty of material of interest to educators worldwide. The Report Card is available via e-mail subscription or via Gopher.

To be added to the e-mail distribution list, send the following e-mail message:

```
mail:     listserv@gwuvm.gwu.edu
subject: (none needed)
message: sub rptcrd <your-full-name> <your-organizations-name)
```

The list is owned by Karl Eisenhower (drc@gwuvm.gwu.edu). This report is also available by mail in paper form.

Access: Gopher: nysernet.org
             menu: Special Collections: k-12
             item: Daily Report Card News Service

Contact: Daily Report Card
             American Political Network, Inc.
             282 N. Washington St.

             Falls Church, VA 22046 USA
             voice:(703) 237-5130

K-12 Oriented Gophers

Briarwood Educational Network K-12 Gopher

Offers a collection of other K-12 Gophers and other Internet resources. Also included is a sample from Briarwood's fee-based multimedia curriculum database. Subscription information for the database is also available.

Access: Gopher: gopher.briarwood.com

Contact: e-mail: rrk@briarwood.com
             Robin Kinzy
             Briarwood Educational Network
             379 N. University Ave. #202
             Provo, UT 84601 USA

             voice:(801) 373-1765
             fax:(801) 375-1528

California Department of Education

While directed towards educators in the state of California, this Gopher is also inter-esting to those outside the state. These users may not only be interested in the educational programs in California but also in how a Gopher can be used to serve the needs of educators in general. The server includes information on state education finances, curricula, special education, publications, news and announcements, and technology planning.

Access:	Gopher:	`goldmine.cde.ca.gov`
Contact:	e-mail:	`sfergus@goldmine.cde.ca.gov`

Susan Ferguson
Goldmine System Administrator
Educational Technology Office
California State Department of Education
721 Capitol Mall, 3rd Floor
Sacramento, CA 95814 USA

voice: (916) 654-8975
fax: (916) 657-3707

CRESST/UCLA–Research on Evaluation and Testing (Center for Research on Evaluation, Standards, and Student Testing/University of California, Los Angeles)

Access to CSE (Center for the Study of Evaluation)/CRESST technical reports, newsletters, and alternative assessments. Available both for browsing and full-text indexed searching.

Access:	Gopher:	`cse.ucla.edu`
	item:	`CRESST/UCLA - Research on Evaluation and Testing/`
Contact:	e-mail:	`comments@cse.ucla.edu`

CRESST/UCLA
Graduate School of Education
405 Hilgard Ave.
Los Angeles, CA 90024-1522 USA

voice:(310) 825-1532
fax: (310) 825-3883

■■ ┃

Internet Resources for Education (Ontario Institute for Studies in Education)

A collection of numerous resources for students and educators. Includes such specialities as deaf education, language education and research (including bilingualism), law for educators, a science teacher's corner, and a section designed to make learning the Internet especially fun.

Access:	Gopher:	`porpoise.oise.on.ca`
	menu:	`Information Resources in Education/ Internet Resources for Use in Education/`
	item:	`Internet Resources for Education/`
Contact:	email:	`rmclean@oise.on.ca`

Robert S. McLean
Computer Applications Program
Curriculum Department
Ontario Institute for Studies in Education
252 Bloor St. West
Toronto, Ontario M5S 1V6 Canada

voice:(416) 923-6641 ext. 2254

K-12 on the Internet: Select Education Resources (CICNet)

Collections of resources and resource descriptions which should be useful to teachers, students, and administrators. Includes: other Gopher servers; FTP sites; Internet projects in the classroom; mailing lists; and education-related publications.

Access:	Gopher:	`gopher.cic.net`
	menu:	`Other CICNet Projects and Gopher Servers/`
	item:	`K-12 on the Internet: Select Education Resources/`
Contact:	e-mail:	`rjacot@cic.net`

Rhana Jacot
Information Services Coordinator
CICNet, Inc.
Upper Pod A
Ann Arbor, MI 48105-2467 USA

voice:(313) 998-6521
fax:(313) 998-6105

National School Network Testbed (Bolt Beranek and Newman, Inc.)

This project is designed to assist in the development of ubiquitous school networking in the United States and is partially funded by the National Science Foundation. The Testbed works to "make available to schools up-to-date information resources, to engage students and teachers in authentic problem-solving, and to support the implementation of advances in pedagogy and educational technology." In addition to the Testbed projects, the Gopher offers access to other K-12 educational servers and resources.

Access: Gopher: `copernicus.bbn.com`

Contact: e-mail: `mhuntley@bbn.com` (Martin Huntley) for questions about the Gopher.

                           `dnewman@bbn.com` (Denis Newman) for questions about the National School Network Testbed.

Martin Huntley
Educational Technologies Department
Bolt Beranek and Newman, Inc.
150 Cambridge Park Drive
Cambridge, MA 02138 USA

Denis Newman
Bolt Beranek and Newman, Inc.
150 Cambridge Park Drive
Cambridge, MA 02138 USA

voice: (617) 873-4277 (Cambridge) or (619) 942-3734 (San Diego)

New Horizons for Learning

New Horizons for Learning is a not-for-profit, international network of people, programs, and publications dedicated to successful, innovative learning. Although the organization was founded in 1980, it recently moved onto the Internet by establishing a Gopher through the Bellevue, WA school network (Belnet). Members of the New Horizons Network receive publications and participate in online conferences. The Gopher includes membership information and fee structure as well as sample publications.

Access: Gopher: `belnet.bellevue.k12.wa.us`
                item: `New Horizons for Learning/`

                Telnet: `belnet.bellevue.k12.wa.us`
                login: `gopher`
                item: `New Horizons for Learning/`

Contact: e-mail: `nh10001@belnet.bellevue.k12.wa.us`

Dee Dickinson, CEO/Founder
Teri Howatt, Network Coordinator
Micki McKission Evans, President, Board of Directors
New Horizons for Learning
P.O. Box 15329
Seattle WA 98115-0329 USA

voice:(206) 547-7936

NYSERNet K-12 Gopher

Includes access to the CNN classroom curriculum guides, AskERIC, the Consortium for School Networking (CoSN) Gopher, the keypals wanted list, Daily Report Card news service, and access to a number of K-12 library catalogs.

Access:	Gopher: `nysernet.org`	
	item:	`Special Collections: k-12/`
Contact:	e-mail:	`info@nysernet.org`
	NYSERNet, Inc.	
	200 Elwood Davis Rd.	
	Suite 103	
	Liverpool, NY 13088-6147 USA	
	voice: (315) 453-2912	
	fax: (315) 453-3052	

U.S. Department of Education

Includes: general information on Department of Education programs and initiatives; information on education research, improvement, and statistics; announcements, bulletins, and press releases; publications; Department of Education phone directory; and educational software.

Access:	Gopher	`:gopher.ed.gov`
Contact:	e-mail:	`gopheradm@inet.ed.gov`
	INet Project Manager	
	U.S. Department of Education	
	Office of Educational Research and	
	Improvement/EIRD	
	555 New Jersey Ave. N.W., Room 214b	
	Washington, DC 20208-5725 USA	
	voice:(202) 219-1547	
	fax:(202) 219-1817	

K-12 Oriented World Wide Web Servers

Grand River Elementary School

This is the first elementary school Web server in the world! It is a server from Brad Marshall's 5th grade class in Lansing, Michigan. The server includes photos of and biographical information about children in the class. The students also have e-mail addresses listed on the server.

Access:	WWW:	`http://web.cal.msu.edu/JSRI/GR/grintro.html`
Contact:	e-mail:	`gary@ah3.cal.msu.edu` (Gary J. LaPointe)

Hillside Elementary School

Hillside Elementary School in Cottage Grove, Minnesota. From two classes, Mrs. Collins' sixth grade class and Mrs. Reid's third grade class. The server includes photos of and biographical information about children in the classes. The students also have e-mail addresses listed on the server.

Access:	WWW:	`http://hillside.coled.umn.edu`
Contact:	e-mail:	`sec@boombox.micro.umn.edu`

Stephen E. Collins
Distributed Computing Services
192 Shepherd Laboratories
University of Minnesota
Minneapolis, MN 55455 USA

voice: (612) 625-1300   fax:(612) 626-7496

Illinois Mathematics and Science Academy

A high school server with student home pages and information about various activities at the school. Included are student publications, descriptions of clubs, and the beginnings of an educational home page.

Access:	WWW:	`http://imsasun.imsa.edu`
Contact:	e-mail:	`http@imsa.edu`

NASA Planetary Data System Infrared Subnode

Though not dedicated to K-12 students, this server contains a number of resources that are appropriate for that environment–and fun–including photographs of planets in the solar system and their moons.

Access:	WWW:	`http://esther.la.asu.edu/asu_tes`

U.S. Department of Education

Includes: general information on Department of Education programs and initiatives; information on education research, improvement, and statistics; announcements, bulletins and press releases; publications; Department of Education phone directory; and educational software.

Access:	WWW:	`http://www.ed.gov/`
Contact:	e-mail:	`wwwadmin@inet.ed.gov`

INet Project Manager
U.S. Department of Education
Office of Educational Research and Improvement/EIRD
555 New Jersey Ave. N.W., Room 214b
Washington, DC 20208-5725 USA

voice: (202) 219-1547
fax: (202) 219-1817

COLLABORATIVE PROJECTS

One of the most exciting uses of the Internet in K-12 education is for communication and collaboration between and among students and teachers at distant schools. Such collaborative projects have the potential to dramatically reshape the educational process. You will learn about many such activities by subscribing to KIDSPHERE and the many other Usenet and LISTSERV groups. But to get you started, here's a sampler of some notable projects with which you and your students could become involved.

Disabled Data Link Group and Chatback

DDLG and the Chatback Project for Children currently involves about 100 schools supporting the use of networks by disabled students in an effort to assist those with special needs. For more information, please contact:

> e-mail: `Cliff.Jones@f71.n254.z2.fidonet.org.`
>
> Cliff Jones

Earth Kids is a not-for-profit international organization devoted to using networking to promote hands-on, community based ecological projects among the children of the world. For more information, contact:

> e-mail: `Marshall.Gilmore@f606.n105.z1.fidonet.org`
>
> Marshall Gilmore

Global Schoolhouse Project

The Global Schoolhouse Project, coordinated by the Global SchoolNet/FrEdMail Foundation specializes in establishing innovative and educationally rewarding collaborative projects using the Internet for the international K-12 community.

One exciting project uses Cornell University's CU-SeeMe software which allows students to conduct live video conferences from sites around the country and around the world. The conferences are conducted using Macintosh and Intel-based (80386/80486) computers. Macintosh users with or without video equipment can use software called Maven to conduct the audio portion of the conference over the Internet.

The main objectives of the 1993-1994 Global Schoolhouse activities are to demonstrate how the Internet can be used effectively in the classroom; to teach students to become active learners and information mangers; to develop an online system of training and support for teachers; demonstrate the most current network technologies for classroom use; and to encourage business, government, school, higher education, and community partnerships to join in ongoing collaboration. Specific projects that the Global Schoolhouse has participated in have included the TeleOlympics, the Eratosthenes Experiment, earthquake data analysis, alternative waste disposal, and the Space Shuttle Simulation.

The Global Schoolhouse project provides a Gopher server that includes information about the project, curricular activities, and other K-12 information.

Access: Gopher: `gsh.cnidr.org`

For more information about the Global Schoolhouse generally, please contact:

> e-mail: `andresyv@cerf.net`
> Yvonne Marie Andres
> Director, Global Schoolhouse Project
> 7040 Avenidas Encinas 104-281
> Carlsbad, CA 92009 USA
>
> voice: (619) 439-0914 or (619) 757-6061
> voice mail: (619) 931-5934
> fax: (619) 931-5934

I*EARN (International Education and Research Network)

I*EARN is a collaborative project of almost 500 schools in 23 countries including the U.S., Argentina, Australia, Brazil, Canada, China, Costa Rica, England, Finland, Hungary, Israel, Japan, Jordan, Kenya, Korea, Mexico, Netherlands, New Zealand, Russia, Singapore, South Africa, Spain, and the West Bank. Nicaragua participates but does not currently have direct communications available. Negotiations are currently underway with educational institutions in Egypt, Senegal, and Indonesia. Projects in I*EARN are intended to make meaningful contributions to the health and welfare of the planet.

Students participate in projects that take place in various "rooms." Projects include: Clean Water for Nicaragua Project, First Peoples Project, Heroes Project, Holocaust/Genocide Project, Hurricane Andrew Relief Project, "Kids Can" an elementary school newsletter, Power of Mathematics Project, Planet Project, Rainforest Project, Somalia Relief Project, Status of Women Project, Ultra-Violet Measurement Project, Youth Violence Project, "The Contemporary" global news magazine, and "A Vision" international literary anthology. There are also conferences devoted to communication among teachers, youth, and trainers.

In addition to e-mail messages, I*EARN member schools use low cost video-speaker telephones. Although I*EARN is based on the APC Network (comprised of EcoNet, PeaceNet, GlasNet, and GreenNet), all I*EARN mailboxes are accessible through the Internet.

For more information about I*EARN, contact:

> e-mail: `ed1@copenfund.igc.apc.org`
> Ed Gragert
> Director of Programs
> Copen Family Fund/I*EARN
> 345 Kear St.
> Yorktown Heights, NY 10598 USA
> voice: (914) 962-5864
> fax: (914) 962-6472

TERC

TERC is a not-for-profit organization that concentrates on establishing and coordinating well-planned and scientifically meaningful network-based collaborative projects in the sciences. A representative TERC project is The Global Laboratory Project, an international, telecommunications based initiative supporting biological, chemical, and physical monitoring of the environment by K-12 students.

　　　e-mail:　　ken-mayer@terc.edu

　　　TERC
　　　2067 Massachusetts Ave.
　　　Cambridge, MA 02140 USA

　　　voice:　　(617) 547-0430
　　　fax:　　　(617) 349-3535

Independently Developed Projects

A growing number of K-12 teachers and students are developing collaborative activities. This section describes two representative projects that have been started by one or a few individuals and have become effective and useful network wide projects. They are very good examples of the simple but very effective use of e-mail in the K-12 curriculum.

Although you are of course encouraged to participate in these activities, the main point of these examples is to help you realize that you don't need to invest a great deal of money in hardware or software to become a contributing member of the global classroom. Once you are part of the Internet, you can help direct the ways in which it is used for education, not only at your own school, but potentially throughout the world.

Kids WeatherNet

In this project classes throughout the Internet share local weather and climate information, either from a class weather station or from information taken from local weather bureaus. Each Monday, students send their weather reports to all participating schools. For more information, contact:

　　　e-mail:　　echo@triton.unm.edu

　　　Bill Wallace
　　　1801 Central Ave. NW
　　　Manzana Day School
　　　Albuquerque, NM 87104-1197 USA

　　　voice:　　(505) 243-6659

Ask a Young Scientist

Kurt Grosshans of the Christiansburg High School in Christiansburg, Virginia, has set up a service called Ask a Young Scientist, formerly, Mr. Science. Advanced placement (AP) students at the high school respond to e-mail questions about science sent in by elementary students from throughout the world. To submit a question to Ask a Young Scientist, send your question to apscichs@radford.vak12ed.edu. If you want to learn more about the Ask a Young Scientist project, send e-mail to kgrossha@radford.vak12ed.edu. Please limit messages to five questions each and do not include research or thesis type questions.

THE LIBRARY

Are the libraries in your school or even your community adequate for the needs of your students and educators? If not, you can use worldwide library, electronic journal, and online document resources that are available through the Internet.

Online Public Access Catalogs (OPACs)

Online library catalogs (more precisely known as "online public access catalogs," or OPACs for short) are electronic versions of library card catalogs. OPACs have been created at hundreds of the world's libraries and are generally free of charge for anyone with an Internet connection. A more complete discussion of OPACs is provided in Chapter 14.

What Can OPACs Offer K-12 Education?

Most OPACs on the Internet are based at the libraries of large research institutions, so you can generally do anything that students or faculty at those institutions can do with their OPAC. In particular, OPACs provide the following services of special interest to K-12 education:

* searches by school librarians to help determine which materials to order for the school library;
* resources for staff doing active research;
* access to online catalogs of the libraries of schools or departments of Education;
* inter-library loan arrangements; and,
* full literature searches for teachers or students.

Electronic Books

A growing number of services are offering books in electronic format, including many texts typically used in high school literature classes, such as Shakespeare or the poems of W.B. Yeats. Many of these electronic books are in pure text format that can be read and printed using most any kind of computer and printer. Many of these text services are described in Chapter 13.

Electronic Journals

Electronic journals are like regular magazines. They feature submitted articles which are reviewed, edited, and placed in an organized format within a computer file. The following table lists a few of the many electronic journals which may be of interest to K-12 educators. For more on electronic journals refer to Chapter 12.

Distance Education Online Symposium (DEOS-L)	Distance education; many articles on K-12 issues. Subscription: send e-mail to listserv@psuvm.psu.edu. message: SUB DEOS-L <your-full-name>. To cancel a subscription, send mail to the same address, message: UNSUB DEOS-L. A discussion of the articles appears on DEOSNEWS on the same LISTSERV.
EFFector Online	Computer based communication, especially issues of freedom of speech, privacy, censorship, and policy. Subscription: send an e-mail message to eff-request@eff.org.
Ejournal	An electronic journal about electronic journals. Subscription: send e-mail message to listserv@albany.edu with the message: SUB EJRNL <your-full-name>. To cancel a subscription, e-mail to the same address, message: UNSUB EJRNL.
Handicap Digest	Issues dealing with the handicapped. Subscription: send e-mail message to listserv@vm1.nodak.edu with the message: SUB L-HCAP <your-full-name>. To cancel a subscription, e-mail to the same address, message: UNSUB L-HCAP. Also available as newsgroup: bit.listserv.l-hcap; via modem: Handicap News BBS (203) 337-1607 (300, 1200 and 2400 baud); Fidonet 1:/141/420; Compuserve 73170,1064.
Impact Online	Social and ethical concerns of information technology; read via newsgroup comp.society. Submissions and back issue requests to bcs-ss1@compass.com.

K-12 Oriented Databases

Through the Internet, K-12 schools have access to databases which previously could only be used at research institutions. Of the many databases described in Chapter 15, there are several of special interest to or designed specifically for K-12 education. In particular, you should refer to the entries for FEDIX, MOLIS, and QUERRI. The PENpages, Spacelink, and ERIC databases are described in this chapter since they are probably of the most interest to the K-12 community.

PENpages

PENpages is a very easy to use, general interest database of articles and brochures on agriculture, careers, consumer issues, health, weather, and other topics from The Pennsylvania State University. The materials are written in simple and straightforward language and should be suitable for use as class materials in most schools.

Access:　　　Telnet:　`psupen.psu.edu`
　　　　　　login:　`<your state's 2 letter code>` (within USA)
　　　　　　　　　　`world`　　　　　　　　　　(outside USA)
　　　　　　choose:　`(1) PENpages`

Contact:　　e-mail:　`ppmenu@psupen.psu.edu`

Spacelink

Spacelink contains information about NASA and NASA activities, including a large number of curricular activities for elementary and secondary science classes. The FTP server contains a single directory with many files.

Access:　　　Telnet:　`spacelink.msfc.nasa.gov`
　　　　　　username: `newuser`
　　　　　　password: `newuser`

　　　　　　FTP host: `spacelink.msfc.nasa.gov`
　　　　　　username: `anonymous`
　　　　　　password: `guest`

　　　　　　modem:　(205) 895-0028
　　　　　　settings:　data=8, parity=N, stop=1　　(1200-9600 baud)

ERIC (Educational Resources Information Center)

ERIC is a database of short abstracts and information on education-related topics of interest to teachers and administrators. This database is funded by the Office of Educational Research and Improvement (OERI) of the U.S. Department of Education (ED). In addition to these databases, ERIC offers ERIC Digests, short informative articles, and AskERIC, an e-mail-accessible information service for teachers, library media specialists, and administrators. Information created by the AskERIC service is collected and turned into tip sheets and guides which are also made available on the Internet.

Many local network service providers include ERIC in CWISs or other information systems; for example, NorthWestNet members can use ERIC through the UWIN service at the University of Washington. Users throughout the Internet should be able to access ERIC in the following ways.

ERIC Access via Gopher and World Wide Web at the Source

Access ERIC at its source using the ERIC Gopher at Syracuse University. Along with the ERIC databases are other educational materials including AskERIC guides, lesson plans, ERIC Digests, educational LISTSERV archives, bibliographies, and a list of educational conferences.

Access:	Gopher:	`ericir.syr.edu`
	Telnet:	`ericir.syr.edu`
	login:	`Gopher`
	select:	`1 (Gopher) or 2 (WWW)`
	WWW:	`http://eryx.syr.edu/Main.html`
Contact:	e-mail:	`askeric@ericir.syr.edu`

ERIC at the University of Saskatchewan, Canada

The University of Saskatchewan currently provides access to two of the ERIC databases, "Current Index to Journals in Education" and "Resources in Education."

Access:	Telnet:	`skdevel2.usask.ca` or
		`skdevel.usask.ca`
	request:	`sklib`
	username:	`sonia`

Once you are connected, you should select "Education Databases" from the main menu. The University of Saskatchewan service also features a tutorial for beginning ERIC users. Just type "beginner" after you have accessed ERIC.

ERIC Access via WAIS

ERIC can also be accessed through WAIS. Unless you have WAIS installed on your local computer, you will have to use Telnet to access one of the publicly accessible WAIS clients. A sample session using WAIS and accessing the ERIC database is given in Chapter 18.

Access:	WAIS:	`ERIC-archive`
		`AskERIC-Helpsheets`
		`AskERIC-Infoguides`
		`AskERIC-Minisearches`
		`AskERIC-Questions`

THE SUPPLY ROOM: TEACHING AIDS AND EDUCATIONAL TOOLS

Another immediately valuable service of the Internet for K-12 education is the diversity of educational software and teaching materials that can be obtained free of charge.

Anonymous FTP Hosts

There are thousands of computers in the world containing file archives whose contents can be transferred for your own use at no charge. These FTP archives contain millions of files including documents, courseware, and software for almost any kind of computer. Overviews of using anonymous FTP archives can be found in Chapters 7 and 8.

K12Net Libraries

File archives useful for K-12 education are maintained in the "K12Net Libraries" located throughout the world. These K12Net Libraries contain thousands of files including:
- educational software;
- course outlines and other material for curricular development; and
- documents relating to education generally, including distance education and government publications.

Document files can be used on most any kind of personal computer. Most of the software currently held in the K12Net Library is for MS DOS based machines, but there are plans to start adding materials for other personal computers such as the Macintosh, Apple IIs, and Amigas.

You can currently access the K12Net Library by modem calls to K12Net sites. To locate the K12Net Library nearest you, get in touch with one of the K12Net contacts listed at the end of this chapter.

Software and Courseware Online Review

This resource lists software and courseware organized by subject and computer platform. It also includes information on research activities in the area of computer-based learning.

Access:	WAIS:	`k-12-software`
	Gopher:	`info.curtin.edu.au`
	menus:	`Subject Information (from Curtin`
		`University)/Education/`
	item:	`Software Courseware Online Review at Curtin/`

Contributions to this database can be sent to:

> e-mail: `scor@info.curtin.edu.au`
>
> Computing Centre
> Curtin University of Technology
> GPO U1987
> Perth 6001 Western Australia
>
> voice: +61 9 351 2897
> fax: +61 9 351 2673

K-12 Oriented Information Systems

There are a number of Internet online information services that contain BBSs, curriculum guides, training materials, and other files for the K-12 community.

GC EduNET

GC EduNET is an information system set up for educators in Georgia, but may also be of interest to K-12 throughout the world. Access to GC EduNET is currently free, but you will be asked to register when you first log in.

> Access: Telnet: `gcedunet.peachnet.edu`

Technology Resources in Education (TRIE)

The California Technology Project (CTP), in cooperation with the California State University's Telecommunications and Networking Resources group, operates the Technology Resources in Education (TRIE) electronic information service. This service informs educators throughout California about educational technology programs.

> Access: Telnet: `eis.calstate.edu`
>   login: `ctp`
>
> Contact: e-mail: `kvogt@ctp.org`
>
> Keith D. Vogt, Director
> The California Technology Project
> P.O. Box 3842
> Seal Beach, CA 90740 USA
> voice:(310) 985-9631

FIELD TRIPS WITHOUT BUSES

Of the many resources available via Telnet, Gopher, and the World Wide Web that have been described throughout *The Internet Passport*, many are of potential interest to the K-12 community. Using these resources can, if handled well, be like electronic field trips to remote sites. The trick is finding which services are appropriate!

Easy to Use Internet Front Ends

"Liberty," "Services," and the University of North Carolina Extended Bulletin Board (UNC EBB) are comprehensive front ends to the Internet that allow you to access a large proportion of the commonly used Telnet sites.

■■■

Liberty:	Telnet:	`liberty.uc.wlu.edu`
	login:	`lawlib`
Services:	Telnet:	`wugate.wustl.edu`
	login:	`services`
	terminal:	`VT100`
UNC EBB:	Telnet:	`bbs.oit.unc.edu`
	login:	`bbs`

Some Fun Places on the World Wide Web

Just to give you an idea of some interesting and fun places to visit on the Web, check these servers out.

Current Weather Maps/Movies (Michigan State University)

Choose from a number of images of the weather over the U.S., North America, the Atlantic Ocean, Africa, Europe, Antarctica, or the entire world! Included here are satellite photos, infrared, radar and weather maps as well as some movies of the weather.

| Access: | WWW: | `http://rs560.cl.msu.edu/weather/` |
| Contact: | e-mail: | `henrich@crh.cl.msu.edu` |

Charles Henrich
301 Computer Center
Michigan State University
East Lansing, MI 48824 USA

voice: (517) 353-2999

An Exhibition of Fossil Life (Paleontology Museum, The University of California, Berkeley)

Geared towards younger investigators, this exhibit includes images of fossils and reconstructions along with explanatory text. Users may browse the exhibit using a number of methods: the room metaphor, by phylogene, by geneological relationships, and by geological age.

Access:	WWW:	`http://sunsite.unc.edu/expo/paleo.exhibit/paleo.html`
Contact:	e-mail:	`robg@fossil.berkeley.ed`
	Museum of Paleontology	
	University of California, Berkeley	
	Berkeley, CA 94720 USA	

voice: (510) 642-9696
fax: (510) 642-1822

■■■

HCC Dinosaurs (Honolulu Community College)

Images of dinosaur fossil replicas along with a spoken guided tour by one of the exhibit's founders. The fossils presented here are replicas of fossils at the Museum of Natural History in New York City.

Access:	WWW: `http://www.hcc.hawaii.edu/dinos/dinos.1.html`
Contact:	Rick Ziegle Honolulu Community College #874 Dillingham Blvd Honolulu, HI 96817 USA

Japanese Tourist Information

Japan's Nippon Telegraph and Telephone Corporation has collected a wealth of information directed toward travelers, but don't let that stop you from becoming a virtual tourist! You can find information on geography, culture and customs, famous sites, language lessons, sports, law, and more. *Kore o kudasai!*

Access:	WWW: `http://www.ntt.jp/japan/index.html`
Contact:	e-mail: `www-admin@seraph.ntt.jp` Takada Toshihiro Information Science Research Lab NTT Basic Research Labs 3-1 Morinosato Wakamiya, Atsugi Kanagawa 243-01 Japan voice:+81 462 40 3637 fax:+81 462 40 4730

Russian and East European Studies Home Pages

A collection of servers devoted to the history and culture of Russia and other East European countries: Armenia, Austria, Azerbaijan, Belarus, Bosnia-Herzegovina, Bulgaria, Croatia, the Czech Republic, Estonia, Finland, the Former Yugoslav Republic of Macedonia, Georgia, Latvia, Lithuania, Poland, Slovakia, Slovenia, Ukraine, Yugoslavia, and other countries of the former Soviet Union.

Access:	WWW:	`http://www.pitt.edu/~cjp/rees.html`
Contact:	e-mail:	`cjp+@pitt.edu` (Casey Palowitch)

More...

Beyond these, the number of servers is growing all the time. To locate a server related to a particular topic, use one of the indexes located on the server at the University of Geneva.

Access:	WWW:	`http://cui_www.unige.ch/meta-index.html`
Contact:	e-mail:	`webmaster@cui.unige.ch`

23 • A Schoolhouse for the World

SUPERCOMPUTER TRAINING

Several of the NSF-sponsored supercomputer sites have established programs for K-12 students and educators. Typically, these programs feature visits to the supercomputer site or allocation of time and access to the supercomputers. Here are the phone contacts for information on five such programs:

- Cornell Theory Center (607) 254-8686
- National Center for Supercomputer Applications (217) 244-1993
- National Energy Research Supercomputer Center (415) 422-1544
- Pittsburgh Supercomputer Center (412) 268-4960
- San Diego Supercomputer Center (619) 534-5124

For more detailed information about these and other supercomputer sites, please refer to Chapter 25.

DISTANCE EDUCATION PROGRAMS FOR K-12 EDUCATORS

There are numerous opportunities for K-12 educators and students to enroll in courses at other institutions around the world. Such "distance education" programs are the electronic equivalent of correspondence schools, but with a major difference. They often allow real time, interactive contact with instructors and other students via computer networks with electronic mail or two-way video.

Moore and Thomson (1990) and Moore et al. (1990) discuss distance education generally. Information on specific statewide programs for K-12 educators can be found in Kurshan (1990b). There are also a number of LISTSERV discussion groups dealing with distance education, such as deosnews@psuvm.psu.edu.

CONCLUSION

Used appropriately, the Internet and other computer networks have a great deal to offer K-12 education. Beyond all the static information students and teachers can find, they can learn about the lives of their peers around the country and around the world. But with all the ballyhoo surrounding computers in the modern world, it's crucial to remember that computer networks should be thought of as only a supplement to K-12 education.

The quality of human life on earth ultimately depends upon the nurturing of fundamental interpersonal skills: what we learn as children, we build upon as adults. Computers and computer networks are a blessing only insofar as they promote these skills.

Similarly, the most important assets of schools are skilled, dedicated teachers and parents who have a supportive enthusiasm for their children's education. Computers are a tool or a supplement, but can never be a replacement for the human resources of our schools.

Happily, most applications of computer networks in education are sensitive to these issues. If used intelligently and always with an eye towards students and teachers as people, networks can deliver substantial educational benefits. Every K-12 school should consider the many advantages of joining a computer network and becoming part of the global schoolhouse.

For More Information

The best information on K-12 networking can be obtained by diving headlong into the active and exciting discussions taking place on computer networks throughout the world. Several of these discussion groups have been described in this chapter. Subscribe to some of the K12Net, Usenet, and LISTSERV groups, and you will be able to keep posted on collaborative projects suited to your particular educational curriculum.

Admittedly, this strategy presents a bit of a "bootstrapping" problem for those of you who do not yet have network access, so here's a list of printed references, journals, and professional societies which are of special interest to K-12 educators.

Bibliography

Aponick, N. "Linking Teachers and Students Across Networks." *Computers in Libraries* 13(9) (October 1993):56-58.

Beals, D.E. "Computer Mediated Communication among Beginning Teachers." *T.H.E. Journal*, 18(9) (1991):74-77.

Berenfeld, B. "Global Lab Project Cultivates Young Scientists." *GNN Magazine* 2 (1994). Available on the World Wide Web.
WWW:
`http://nearnet.gnn.com/gnn/mag/1_94/articles/boris/boris.intro.html`

Blau, A. "CPF Airs Issues for K-12 Access to the Internet." *Networks & Policy* 1(1):3, 6 and *EFFector Online* 5(4) (March 19, 1993). *EFFector Online* is available via anonymous FTP:
```
FTP host:      ftp.eff.org
directory:     /pub/EFF/Newsletters/EFFector
filename:      effector5.04
```

Burns, T. "SchoolNet: Canada's Educational Networking Initiative." *GNN Magazine* 2 (1994). Available on the World Wide Web.
WWW:
`http://nearnet.gnn.com/gnn/mag/1_94/articles/tyler/tyler.intro.html`

Carlitz, R.D. "Common Knowledge: Networks for Kindergarten through College." *Educom Review* 26(2) (1991):25-28.

Clement, J. "Constructing the K-12 Collaboratory on the NREN." *EDUCOM Review* 27(3) (May/June 1992). Available via anonymous FTP and Gopher:

FTP host: `educom.edu`
directory: `/pub/educom.review/review.92`
filename: `EDUCOM-Review-May-Clement-K12collaborationOntheNREN`
Gopher: `educom.edu`
menu: `EDUCOM Review Magazine/EDUCOM Review 1992/`
item: `EDUCOM-Review-May-Clement-K12collaborationOntheNREN.`

Clement, J. "Networking for K-12 Education: Bringing Everyone Together." Available from EDUCOM: 1112 16th Street, NW, Suite 600, Washington, D.C. 20036. 1990.

Clement, J. "Statewide Network Connections for K-12 Educators." *EDUCOM Review* 27(2) (March/April 1992):17-18, 20. Available via anonymous FTP and Gopher:

FTP host: `educom.edu`
directory: `/pub/educom.review/review.92`
filename: `EDUCOM-Review-Mar-Clement-K12Networking`
Gopher: `educom.edu`
menu: `EDUCOM Review Magazine/EDUCOM Review 1992/`
item: `EDUCOM-Review-Mar-Clement-K12Networking.`

Clement, J. "Surveying K-12 and Postsecondary School Networking Partnerships." *EDUCOM Review* 27(4) (July/August 1992):44-46. Available via anonymous FTP and Gopher:

FTP host: `educom.edu`
directory: `/pub/educom.review/review.92`
filename: `EDUCOM-Review-July-Clement-K12PostSecondaryPartnerships`
Gopher: `educom.edu`
menu: `EDUCOM Review Magazine/EDUCOM Review 1992/`
item: `EDUCOM-Review-July-Clement-K12PostSecondaryPartnerships.`

Delzeit, L. "Academy One Introduces Classrooms to the Internet." *GNN Magazine* 2 (1994). Available on the World Wide Web.
WWW:
`http://nearnet.gnn.com/gnn/mag/1_94/articles/linda/linda.intro.html`

de Presno, O. "KIDLINK - Global Networking for Youth 10 - 15." *GNN Magazine* 2 (1994). Available on the World Wide Web.
WWW:
`http://nearnet.gnn.com/gnn/mag/1_94/articles/odd/odd.intro.html`

Donovan, D. "Teaching and Learning in a Networked World." *GNN Magazine* 2 (1994). Available on the World Wide Web.
WWW:
http://nearnet.gnn.com/gnn/mag/1_94/articles/donovan/donovan.intro.html

Estrada, S. *Connecting to the Internet: A Buyer's Guide.* Sebastopol, CA: O'Reilly & Associates, Inc., 1993.

Hunter, B. "Linking for Learning: Computer and Communications Network Support for Nationwide Innovation in Education." *Journal of Science Education and Technology* 1 (1992).

Kinnaman, D. E. "Technology Makes Choice Inevitable." *Technology & Learning* 14(4) (January 1994):74.

Kollasch, M. "Modem Operandi." *Wilson Library Bulletin* 67(9) (May 1993):65-66.

Kurshan, B. "Home Market for Educational OnLine Services: Growth of Market and Strategies for Expansion." Research Report. Educorp Consultants, 4940 Buckhorn Rd., Roanoke, VA. 1990a.

Kurshan, B. "Statewide Telecommunications Networks: An Overview of the Current State and the Growth Potential." Research Report. Educorp Consultants, 4940 Buckhorn Rd., Roanoke, VA. 1990b.

Kurshan, B. "Statewide Education Networks Survey Results." Research Report. Educorp Consultants, 4940 Buckhorn Rd., Roanoke, VA. 1991.

The Leonardo Almanac: International Resources in Art, Science and Technology, Craig Harris, editor. Cambridge, MA: MIT Press, 1993.

Lieberman, D.B. "Teens for Telnet: K-12 and the Internet." *Internet World* 5(1) (January/February 1994):38-42.

"Making Connections with Telecommunications." *Technology & Learning* 13(8) (May-June 1993):33-34, 36.

Melmed, A. and F.D. Fisher. "Towards a National Information Infrastructure for Selected Social Sectors and Education." Center for Educational Technology and Economic Productivity. New York: New York University. 1991.

Moore, M.G. and M.M. Thompson. *The Effects of Distance Learning: a Summary of Literature.* University Park, PA: Pennsylvania State University. 1990.

Moore, M.G., P. Cookson, J. Donaldson, and B.A. Quigley. *Contemporary Issues in American Distance Education.* NY: Pergamon Press. 1990.

Murray, J. "K12 Network: Global Education Through Telecommunications." *Communications of the ACM* 36(8) (August 1993):36-41.

Newman, D., S.L. Bernstein, and P.A. Reese. Local Infrastructure for School Networking: Current Models and Prospects. *BBN Report 7726.* Cambridge, MA: Bolt Beranek and Newman, Inc. 1992.

Phillips, G.M., G.M. Santoro, and S.A. Kuehn. "The Use of Computer-Mediated Communication in Training Students in Group Problem-Solving and Decision-Making Techniques." *American Journal of Distance Education,* 2(1) (1988): 38-51.

Ratzan, L. "Reading, Writing, and Networking." *Wilson Library Bulletin* 68(1) (September 1993):73-74.

Roberts, N., G. Blakeslee, M. Brown, and C. Lenk. *Integrating Telecommunications into Education.* Englewood Cliffs, NJ: Prentice-Hall. 1990.

Roerden, L.P. "Environmental Education on the Net." *GNN Magazine 2* (1994). Available on the World Wide Web.
WWW:
`http://nearnet.gnn.com/gnn/mag/1_94/articles/laura/laura.intro.html`

Sellers, J. "FYI on Questions and Answers: Answers to Commonly Asked Primary and Secondary School Internet User Questions." RFC1578/FYI22. February 1994. (For information on retrieving RFCs, please see Appendix A.)

Showalter, M. "K-12 Schools on the Internet: One School's Experience." *GNN Magazine 2* (1994). Available on the World Wide Web.
WWW:
`http://nearnet.gnn.com/gnn/mag/1_94/articles/mike/mike1.intro.html`

St. George, A. "A Voice for K-12 Networking." *Research and Education Networking* 3(1) (1992):10-12.

U.S. Congress Office of Technology Assessment. "Rural America at the Crossroads: Networking for the Future." (S/N 052 003 0122806; available in government document repositories or through your legislator.) April 1991.

Printed Journals

The following printed journals are particularly informative for K-12 educators using computer networks:

American Journal of Distance Education

Computing Teacher

Educational Technology

*EDUCOM Review**

Electronic Learning

Internet Research (formerly, *Electronic Networking*)

Internet World

Journal of Computers in Mathematics and Science Teaching

Technology & Learning (formerly, *Classroom Computer Learning*)

T.H.E. Journal

*Educom Review is also available via Gopher and FTP:

FTP host:	`educom.edu`
directory:	`/pub/`
filename:	`educom.review`
Gopher:	`educom.edu`
item:	`EDUCOM Review Magazine/`

Educational Conferences

The U.S. Department of Education Gopher includes a listing of education conferences from a number of sources. The largest of these lists is the ERIC Calendar of Education-Related Conferences listing approximately 500 conferences.

Gopher:	`gopher.ed.gov`
menu:	`Announcements, Bulletins, and Press Releases/`
item:	`Upcoming Events/`

Organizations

e-mail: `cosn@bitnic.cren.net`
Consortium for School Networking (CoSN)
P.O. Box 6519
Washington, DC 20035-5193 USA

voice:	(202) 466-6296
fax:	(202) 872-4318

Gopher: `cosn.org`

e-mail: `info@educom.edu`
EDUCOM
1112 16th Street, NW
Suite 600
Washington, DC 20036 USA

voice:	(202) 872-4200
fax:	(202) 872-4318

Gopher: `educom.edu`

A Sampler of K-12 Related LISTSERV Discussion Groups

The list of K-12-oriented LISTSERV lists below is divided into general categories. Most of the lists are intended for teachers and others in the education profession. Those in the "Student Oriented Lists," "Chatback International Project," and "Hobbies and Recreation" are mostly geared towards direct student use. For more information on any list, send the following e-mail message:

```
mail:     listserv@<host.address>
subject:  (none needed)
message:  rev <listname>
```

This message issues the "review" command. The LISTSERV will respond by sending you a copy of the list "header" which should include a short description of the list. You may also receive a listing of the current subscribers to the list.

To subscribe to a LISTSERV list, send the following message:

```
mail:     listserv@<host.address>
subject:  (none needed)
message:  subscribe <listname> <Your-name>
```

Although Internet addresses have been provided for most of the BITNET nodes, a few do not have them. In these cases, you will need to send your mail through a BITNET gateway if your own site does not support the ".BITNET" extension. (For more information on gateways, see Chapter 5.)

Listname	Address	Topical Area
Student-Oriented Lists		
KIDCAFE	VM1.NODAK.EDU	KIDCAFE Youth Dialog
KIDS-ACT	VM1.NODAK.EDU	KIDS-ACT What can I do now?
SCOUTS-L	TCUBVM.IS.TCU.EDU	Youth groups including Boy and Girl Scouts, etc.
SGANET	VTVM1.CC.VT.EDU	Student Government Global Mail Network
Chatback International Project		
KIDINTRO	SJUVM.STJOHNS.EDU	Students in pairs introduce each other.
MEMORIES	SJUVM.STJOHNS.EDU	Students record memories of people in Britain during WWII.
TALBACK	SJUVM.STJOHNS.EDU	Discussion group for the children in the project.
TIMECAP	SJUVM.STJOHNS.EDU	Time capsule project for the children in the project.
Education Oriented Lists		
ECENET-L	VMD.CSO.UIUC.EDU	Early Childhood Education/Young Children (0-8)
EDUCOM-W	BITNIC.EDUCOM.EDU	Women and Information Technology
INTERCUL	VM.ITS.RPI.EDU	Study of Intercultural Communication
KIDLEADR	VM1.NODAK.EDU	KIDLINK Coordination
KIDLEADS	VM1.NODAK.EDU	Spanish KIDLINK Coordination

(Continued)

Listname	Address	Topical Area
KIDLINK	VM1.NODAK.EDU	KIDLINK Project
KIDPLAN	VM1.NODAK.EDU	KIDLINK Planning
KIDPLAN2	VM1.NODAK.EDU	KIDLINK Work Group
KIDPROJ	VM1.NODAK.EDU	Special KIDLINK Projects
K12STCTE	BITNIC.CREN.NET	CoSN Officers, Board Members, and Ctte. Chairs
MIDDLE-L	VMD.CSO.UIUC.EDU	Middle Level Education/Early Adolescence (10-14)
MULTC-ED	UMDD.UMD.EDU	Multicultural Education
NEWEDU-L	UHCCVM.UHCC.HAWAII.EDU	Newer Patterns in Education
RESPONSE	VM1.NODAK.EDU	Response to KIDLINK Questions
VT-HSNET	VTVM1.CC.VT.EDU	VT K-12 School Network

Hobbies and Recreation

Listname	Address	Topical Area
CHESS-L	HEARN.NIC.SURFNET.NL	Chess discussion and organization of tournaments.
DJ-L	VM1.NODAK.EDU	Campus Radio Disk Jockey Discussion
EAT-L	VTVM2.BITNET	Exchange of international recipes.
GAMES-L	BROWNVM.BROWN.EDU	Computer games of any sort.

Subject-Specific Lists Relevant to K12 Education

Listname	Address	Topical Area
AQUIFER	IBACSATA.BITNET	Pollution and groundwater recharge.
BIOSPH-L	UBVM.CC.BUFFALO.EDU	Anything relevant to planetary ecology.
CHEMED-L	UWF.CC.UWF.EDU	Chemistry Education
DISARM-L	UACSC2.ALBANY.EDU	Discussion of global disarmament.
HISTORY	UBVM.CC.BUFFALO.EDU	History Discussion Forum
IAPADV	IUBVM.UCS.INDIANA.EDU	International Arctic Project Adventure
IAPPLAN	IUBVM.UCS.INDIANA.EDU	International Arctic Project Planning

(Continued)

Listname	Address	Topical Area
LITERARY	UCF1VM.CC.UCF.EDU	Discussions about literature.
LLTI	DARTCMS1.DARTMOUTH.EDU	Language Learning and International Technology
MULTI-L	VM.BIU.AC.IL	Language and Education in Multilingual Settings
MUSIC-ED	VM1.SPCS.UMN.EDU	Music Education
NATIVE-L	TAMVM1.TAMU.EDU	Issues pertaining to aboriginal people.
PHYSHARE	PSUVM.BITNET	Sharing resources for high school physics.
RURALDEV	KSUVM.BITNET	Community and rural economic development.
SAIS-L	UNBVM1.BITNET	Science awareness and promotion.
SCREEN-L	UA1VM.BITNET	Discussion of TV from a pedagogical perspective.
SHAKSPER	UTORONTO.BITNET	International electronic Shakespeare conference.
SPORTPSY	TEMPLEVM.BITNET	Exercise and sports psychology.
URBANET	MSU.EDU	Urban planning student network.
WILDADV	IUBVM.UCS.INDIANA.EDU	Wild Adventures

Special Education/Talented and Gifted Education

Listname	Address	Topical Area
ALTLEARN	SJUVM.STJOHNS.EDU	Alternative learning strategies, physically handicapped.
AUTISM	SJUVM.STJOHNS.EDU	Autism and Developmental Disabilities
BEHAVIOR	ASUVM.INRE.ASU.EDU	Behavioral and Emotional Disorders in Children
BLIND-L	UAFSYSB.UARK.EDU	Computer Use by and for the Blind
BLINDNWS	VM1.NODAK.EDU	Blind News Digest
BRAILLE	EARN.CVUT.CZ	Discussion group for the blind, in English and Czech.
COMMDIS	VM.ITS.RPI.EDU	Speech Disorders

(Continued)

Listname	Address	Topical Area
DEAF-L	SIUCVMB.BITNET	Deaf List
L-HCAP	VM1.NODAK.EDU	Technology for handicapped, funding info, etc.
TAG-L	VM1.NODAK.EDU	Talented and Gifted Education

Teacher Oriented Lists

Listname	Address	Topical Area
BIOPI-L	KSUVM.KSU.EDU	Secondary Biology Teacher Enhancement
CHILDLIT	RUTVM1.RUTGERS.EDU	Children's Literature: Criticism and Theory
CHILDMUS	RICEVM1.RICE.EDU	Forum for Children's Museum Professionals
FLTEACH	UBVM.CC.BUFFALO.EDU	Foreign Language Training Forum (New York State focus)
KIDLIT-L	BINGVMB.CC.BINGHAMTON.EDU	Children's and Youth Literature
SS435-L	VM.UCS.ALBERTA.CA	Elementary Teacher List for Social Studies
SSLING	YALEVM.YCC.YALE.EDU	Sign Language Linguistics
TOC-READ	UICVM.UIC.EDUUIC	Literacy Tables of Contents Service
TEACHEFT	WCU.BITNET	Teaching Effectiveness
TESL-L	CUNYVM.CUNY.EDU	Teachers of English as a second language.

Educational Uses of Computers and Networks

Listname	Address	Topical Area
CNEDUC-L	TAMVM1.TAMU.EDU	Computer networking and education, esp. K-12.
COSNDISC	YUKON.CREN.ORG	Consortium for School Networking
DEOS-L	PSUVM.PSU.EDU	The Distance Education Online Symposium
DEOSNEWS	PSUVM.PSU.EDU	The Distance Education Online Symposium (Periodical)
DISTED	UWAVM.U.WASHINGTON.EDU	Journal of Distance Ed. and Communication
EDPOLYAN	ASUVM.INRE.ASU.EDU	Education Policy Analysis Forum
EDUTEL	VM.ITS.RPI.EDU	Education and Information Technologies
JEI-L	UMDD.UMD.EDU	Technology in Education (K12)

(Continued)

Listname	Address	Topical Area
MEDIA-L	BINGVMB.CC.BINGHAMTON.EDU	Media in Education
SCIT-L	QUCDN.QUEENSU.CA	Studies in Communication and Information Technology

Software for Education

ACSOFT-L	WUVMD.WUSTL.EDU	Academic software development.
PCSERV-L	VM.UCS.UALBERTA.CA	Public domain software servers.

Hardware and Operating System Oriented Lists

APPLE2-L	BROWNVM.BROWN.EDU	Apple II
COCO	PUCC.PRINCETON.EDU	Tandy Color Computer
COMMODOR	UBVM.CC.BUFFALO.EDU	Commodore Computers
I-AMIGA	UTARLVM1.UTA.EDU	Info-Amiga
I-IBMPC	RICEVM1.RICE.EDU	IBM PC
IBMPC-L	VTVM1.VT.EDU	INFO-IBMPC Digest
INFO-APP	VM1.NODAK.EDU	Apple user's mailing list.
INFO-MAC	VMD.CSO.UIUC.EDU	INFO-MAC Digest
MAC-L	YALEVM.YCC.YALE.EDU	Macintosh News and Information
MACPROG	WUVMD.WUSTL.EDU	Macintosh Programming
MACSYSTM	DARTCMS1.DARTMOUTH.EDU	Advice about Macintosh operating system.
NEXT-L	BROWNVM.BROWN.EDU	NeXT Computer
PC-L	UFRJ.BITNET	IBM PC forum
PCSUPT-L	YALEVM.YCC.YALE.EDU	Discussion for MS DOS PC technical support staff.
PCTECH-L	TREARN.BITNET	MS DOS Compatibles Support Group
SHOPTALK	MCGILL1.BITNET	Microcomputer users' forum.
SOFTREVU	BROWNVM.BROWN.EDU	Small Computing Systems Software Issues

■■■

(Continued)

Listname	Address	Topical Area
SYS7-L	UAFSYSB.BITNET	Macintosh System 7.0
WIN3-L	UICVM.UIC.EDU	Microsoft Windows Version 3 Forum and related issues.

Cooperative Not-for-Profit K-12 Network Providers

K12Net

For more information about K12Net, contact any of the following members of the K12Net Council of Coordinators in Australia, Belgium, Canada, or the U.S.

Gordon Benedict
6733 2nd Ave. N.W.
Calgary, Alberta T2N 0E4 CANADA
Sysop of 1:134/49 (403/283-5261 and 403/283-5292)
K12Net North American Backbone

e-mail: `Gordon.Benedict@f49.n134.z1.fidonet.org`
voice: (403) 283-5214

Terry Bowden
IBM New Zealand Ltd.
P.O. Box 6840
Auckland 1000 New Zealand
Sysop of 3:772/20 (+64 9 358 8635)
K12Net New Zealand Coordinator

e-mail: `bowden@vnet.ibm.com`
fax: +64 9 358 8632

Robert Brault
Ecole Secondaire Leopold-Gravel
766 St-Paul
Terrebonne, Quebec J6W 1M8 CANADA
Sysop of 1:167/130 (514/661-1625)
K12Net Echo Moderator Coordinator

voice: (514) 471-6636 x234

Jack Crawford, W-FL Teacher Resource Center
703 E. Maple Ave.
10 Eisenhower Hall
Newark, NY 14513-1863 USA
Sysop of 1:260/620 (716/526-6495)
K12Net North American Backbone

e-mail: `jack@rochgte.fidonet.org`
voice: (315) 331-1584 (afternoons only EST)

John Feltham
Ignatius Park College
P.O. Box 121
Aitkenvale 4814, Queensland Australia
Sysop of 3:640/706 (61 77 79 2250)
K12Net Australian Coordinator

voice: +61 77 795 844
fax: +61 77 795 060
Janet Murray, Wilson High School
1151 S.W. Vermont St.
Portland, OR 97219 USA
Sysop of 1:105/23 (503/245-4961)
K12Net North American Backbone
K12Net Listkeeper

e-mail: `jmurray@psg.com`
voice: (503) 280-5280 x450

Rob Reilly, Lanesboro School
P.O. Box 1509
Lanesboro, MA 01237 USA
Sysop of 1:321/218 (413/443-6725)
K12Net North American Backbone
K12Net Files Library

e-mail: `rreilly@mit.edu`
voice: (413) 443-0027

Gleason Sackmann
Technical Coordinator
SENDIT Project
226 IACC
Fargo, ND 58105 USA
K12Net Internet Coordinator

e-mail: sackman@plains.nodak.edu
voice: (701) 237-8109
fax: (701) 237-8541

Helen Sternheim
K12Net Projects and Channels Coordinator
Sysop of 1:321/110 (413/256-1037)

e-mail: `hsternheim@phast.umass.edu`

Mort Sternheim, Dept. of Physics and Astronomy
University of Massachusetts
Amherst, MA 01003 USA
Sysop of 1:321/109 (413/543-4453)
K12Net North American Backbone

e-mail: `sternheim@phast.umass.edu`
voice: (413) 545-1908

■ ■

Louis VanGeel
Maria Gorettistraat 17
B-2640 Mortsel, Belgium
Sysop of 2:29/777 (+32 3 455 2073)
K12Net European Backbone

e-mail: `lvg@k12.be`
voice: + 32 3 455 16 53
fax: + 32 3 455 16 55

National Public Telecommunications Network (NPTN)

T.M. Grundner, Ed.D.
President, NPTN
Box 1987
Cleveland, OH 44106 USA

e-mail: `tmg@nptn.org`
voice: (216) 368-2733
fax: (216) 247-3328

CHAPTER

24

Minding the Body

*Through Health Care, Medical,
and Related Science Resources*

Most human interactions on the Internet involve no sounds or images, so the participants might be viewed as disembodied personalities devoid of gender, age, or physical capabilities. In fact, each participant has skin, blood, muscle, and emotions, and each is equally capable of succumbing to illness or suffering an accident. Even for those who are healthy now, the body and mind are not "optional accessories," so staying healthy should be a frequent focus of attention. In matters corporeal and psychological, the Internet has much to offer.

SOMETHING FOR EVERYONE

Three essential components of health care are supported on the Internet: basic research, the provision and gathering of information, and open lines of communication. There are opportunities for everyone to participate. Health care professionals, researchers, and medical librarians will find as much utility from the Internet on matters medical as will schoolteachers and baristas. Furthermore, the wide array of medical resources on the Internet have the advantage of being accessible across broad geographic areas.

Conducting Basic Research

The basic research of medical scientists and biologists continually produces clues about the underlying causes of intractable diseases. Any new knowledge gained in basic research may someday lead to clinical trials and approved treatments. For those in some way personally affected by an incurable disease—Alzheimer's, AIDS, multiple sclerosis—every new discovery is an opportunity to move closer to solutions and to change the future of these diseases. On the Internet, information in support of and resulting from basic research can be exchanged quickly and broadly.

Providing and Gathering Information

If you are a health care provider or health care agency, you may have important information that could serve your community, for example, a schedule of upcoming CPR classes or, in the event of a flu outbreak in your town, professional advice on home treatments for flu symptoms as well as determining when it is wise to see a physician.

Or suppose your sibling has been diagnosed with skin cancer. What can he expect from the disease? What are the treatment options? Where might he look for treatment and support? How does this affect your likelihood of getting skin cancer?

In both cases, the assumption is that more professional information about health and medical issues is good. As a health care provider or agency, you need to get information to the public. As a member of the public, you need quick, easy access to health care information. The scenarios described here are only two examples in which valuable information can be provided and retrieved from the Internet.

Open Lines of Communications, Personal and Professional

No medical professional can possibly be a specialist on all human ailments. Referrals and second opinions are well-accepted as important components of complete medical care. But what if the patient can't get to a second doctor? Suppose a patient experiencing multiple, ambiguous symptoms seeks help from a general practitioner in a rural village; initial tests don't confirm the suspected cause and access to more sophisticated tests is unlikely in the near future. By sharing information about the patient's condition on the Internet, the general practitioner has access to hundreds of medical professionals who may be able to help.

Open communication is as essential for patients as it is for caregivers. In fact, it's a natural human response to find comfort in sharing the details of personal medical ailments. This communication can elicit emotional support, including consolation from fellow sufferers. There is as well the off chance that by sharing this information, you will find a lead to a new treatment or a clinical trial that will offer new options, perhaps new hope. On the Internet, you have access to a whole community of sympathetic ears, professional and otherwise. Some of these people will offer emotional support and others may direct you to new treatment alternatives. (As with any treatment for an illness, discuss it fully with your doctor first.)

In the broadest medical analysis, everyone is a fellow "sufferer" of the human condition. Modern health care practices speak decisively of the personal responsibilities for achieving a healthy, long-lived life; for example, avoid foods with high fat content, exercise regularly, eat plenty of vegetables and fruit, and don't smoke. In response, many people look for ways to apply these strategies to their own lifestyles. What exercise might be a good option for a 45-year-old with a 60-hour-a-week desk job? How can I resist temptation to smoke when others around me do? Is there a low-fat recipe for cheesecake? (Will it be worth eating?) The Internet offers several forums in which information of this type can be shared.

Finally, everyone is in one way or another affected by policies that impact their access to health care. In the U.S., broad reforms of the cost structures and access to health care services have been proposed. In Bosnia, international relief agencies negotiate to get medical supplies to villagers in war-torn regions. Near Chernobyl in Ukraine, residents must face the potential future consequences of radiation exposure and the uncertainty of what medical services they can expect. Conversations and information covering these issues can also be found on the Internet.

Crossing Geographic Boundaries

Every rural and remote clinic around the world that is served by the Internet can multiply their medical resources by virtue of this electronic pipeline of information. Patients and physicians have new opportunities to diagnose illnesses and locate options for proper treatments. For those who lack the means to travel, additional information on a medical condition can be obtained without leaving their community. Health care givers in distant parts of the globe can share experiences and expertise.

Forums and Resources on the Internet

A wide array of health care and medical science resources can be found on the Internet including toxicity reports, gene databases, patient care data, and even images of specimens and medical scans. And, as with other subjects, the wealth and value of the information available on the Internet is increased many times by the existence of professionals participating in international online forums, contributing their knowledge and experience—becoming resources themselves.

Through the participation of such organizations as the World Health Organization, the National Library of Medicine, and the National Cancer Institute, the Internet user will find most medical information highly organized and accessible. Much of the information is additionally, if not directly, available via Gopher. Furthermore, there are over 200 medically related LISTSERVs and mailing-lists as well as a number of FTP servers housing large amounts of data. The color graphics and hypertext capabilities of World Wide Web are just beginning to be exploited in the transfer of medical information.

The list of resources presented here is by no means exhaustive. The Internet changes too quickly for any non-automated system to keep up. (On the other hand, automated systems lack the advantage of human evaluation.) This list does attempt to catalog the most prominent Gophers and databases in the fields of health care and medical sciences. If you can find a LISTSERV, mailing list, or well-designed Gopher or WWW server that caters to your specific interests, stick around, for you are likely to continue finding new and interesting resources there.

HEALTH CARE AND MEDICAL SCIENCE RESOURCES

Health Care and Medical Databases

Medically related databases may also be found in this chapter in the Genetics and Molecular Biology section. Databases with political or social science sections may also include information relevant to the health sciences. Listings of these databases will be found in Chapter 15.

An electronic document, *Internet/Bitnet Health Sciences Resources*, contains up-to-date information about online medical databases and many other Internet resources of interest to medical professionals and the general public. Included in the list are e-mail discussion groups, online databases, Usenet newsgroups, Gopher sites, FTP sites, electronic publications, e-mail addresses of health agencies, and online catalogs of medical libraries. The list is maintained by Lee Hancock, Educational Technologist at the University of Kansas Medical Center, Dykes Library and is updated 4-5 times a year. The list is available via anonymous FTP, Gopher, and WWW. A special mode of WWW access is available through the Lynx system at the University of Kansas. Lynx allows those using VT100 terminal emulation to use the hypertext features of WWW by telnetting to the University of Kansas site.

FTP host:	`ftp.sura.net`	
directory:	`/pub/nic`	
filename:	`medical.resources. MM-YY`	(where MM-YY indicate the month and year of the last update)
Telnet (WWW):	`ukanaix.cc.ukans.edu`	(use VT100 emulation)
login:	`kufacts`	
select:	`Reference Shelf/ Internet Health Science Resources`	(use cursor controls to move through the screen; press "?" for help)
WWW:	`http://kufacts.cc.ukans.edu/cwis/units/medcntr/menu.html`	
Gopher:	`sluava.slu.edu`	(St. Louis University)
menu:	`Library Services/SLU Health Sciences Center Library/Health Sciences Center Library/Guides to Internet Resources`	
item:	`Lee Hancock's Health Sciences Resources (Hancock List)`	

AIDS Related Information (National Institute of Allergy and Infectious Diseases (NIAID) Gopher)

Contents:	Numerous resources focused on AIDS treatment, research, education, and prevention. The resources gathered in this section of the NIAID Gopher are from a number of different sources.	
Gopher:	`odie.niaid.nih.gov`	
menu:	`AIDS Related Information/`	
items:	`AIDS Tx News/`	(AIDS Treatment News)
	`AIDS Info BBS/`	(independent BBS)
	`CDC Daily Summaries/`	(summaries of mainstream media AIDS coverage)
	`CDC Statistics/` `Morbidity and Mortality Weekly Reports/` `NIAID Press Releases/`	

■■

(Continued)

	National AIDS Info Clearinghouse/	(various government reports on AIDS and AIDS prevention)
	National Commission on AIDS/	(reports of the Commission)
	Study Recruitment Information/	(information on studies needing human volunteers)
	UCSF FOCUS: A Guide to Research and Counseling/	(newsletter from the University of California, San Francisco)
	Veteran's Administration AIDS Information Newsletter/	
Contact:	e-mail: `alg@nih.gov`	

Al Graeff
NIAID Technical Service Division

voice: (301) 496-0204

Alcoholism Research Database (Cork)

Contents:	A bibliographic database on alcoholism and substance abuse. Citations may be displayed in short, medium, long, EndNote, or ProCite formats. Some citations include abstracts.
Access:	Telnet:	`library.dartmouth.edu`
		At the "->" prompt, enter "`select file cork`".
Contact:	e-mail:	`Project.Cork@dartmouth.edu`
		Project Cork Resource Center
		Butler Building
		Dartmouth College
		Hanover, NH 03755 USA
	voice	(603) 650-1122

Austin Hospital Digital Image Library

Contents:	Among other medical research resources is a good-sized collection of high quality digital images from the PET Centre in JPEG format. Along with the images themselves are documents describing each image, including the scan type, location, scanner.
Access:	Gopher:	`gopher.austin.unimelb.edu.au`
	item:	`Digital Image Library/`

Contact:	e-mail:	gopher@austin.unimelb.edu.au
		Daniel O'Callaghan
		Network and Systems Administrator
		PET Centre
		Austin Hospital
		Heidelberg, Vic, 3084 Australia
	voice:	+61 3 496 3994
	fax:	+61 3 457 6605

Bioethics Online Service
(Medical College of Wisconsin)

Contents: Abstracts of bills, laws, court decisions, book chapters, and journal and newspaper articles related to recent issues in bioethics. In addition to this bibliographic information, there is a list of US Bioethics Committee Networks and Bioethics Centers with contact information and an index of all of the databases on this system. One section that has not yet been implemented (at least at the time of this writing), but on the list, is an area for discussion of bioethical issues by users.

Access: Gopher: `post.its.mcw.edu 72`

          Telnet: `min.lib.mcw.edu`   (choose item 7)

Contact: e-mail   `biohelp@its.mcw.edu`
                    Bioethics Online Service
                    c/o Information Technology Systems
                    Medical College of Wisconsin
                    8701 Waterton Plank Road
                    Milwaukee, WI 53226 USA
          voice: (414) 257-8700

Comments or questions about the content of the service may be sent to:

          e-mail: `aderse@its.mcw.edu`
                    Arthur R. Derse, M.D., J.D.
                    Bioethics Online Service Director
                    Center for the Study of Bioethics
                    Medical College of Wisconsin
                    8701 Waterton Plank Road
                    Milwaukee, WI 53226 USA
          voice: (414) 257-8498

■■■

 ## CancerNet

Contents:	Cancer treatment information from the National Cancer Institute's (NCI) Physician Data Query (PDQ) database. Offers fact sheets on specific cancers, clinical trials, clinical trial guidelines, drug information, and treatment information designed for both doctors and patients. Gopher access includes a searchable index of the full text. The database is updated on a monthly basis. The database is easy to use and has a lot of information specifically designed for general consumption.
Access:	Gopher: `gopher.nih.gov`
	menus: `Health and Clinical Information/CancerNet Information`
	Mail server: To get started with this service, send the following e-mail message and you will receive up-to-date Cancer-Net instructions and the contents list:

```
mail:    cancernet@icicb.nci.nih.gov
subject: (none needed)
message: help
```

Contact:	e-mail:	`minht@icicb.nci.nih.gov`
	voice:	(301) 496-8880

 ## Fam-Med E-Mail List and Archives

Contents:	E-Mail discussion list and archives on computers and telecommunications technologies in family medicine.
Comments:	The Gopher version includes a searchable index of the digests. The e-mail comes in a digest version (with spurious messages deleted), or unmoderated.
Mailing list:	To subscribe to the FAM-MED mailing list, send e-mail to the list owner (choose the digested or unmoderated version of the list):

```
mail:    Paul@gac.edu
subject: Fam-Med subscription request
message: Please add me to the digested/unmoderated [choose one]
list Fam-Med.

Thank you,
<your name>
```

List archives	The list archives include a large amount of information that has been discussed on the list in the past, but may very well be helpful to you now.
Access:	FTP host: `ftp.gac.edu`
	directory: `/pub/fam-med`
	filenames: `000read-me-fam-med.txt` (describes archives)
	`fam-med-intro.txt` (describes Fam-Med)
	(many others)

Gopher: `gopher.gac.edu`
menus: `E-Mail Archives/fam-med`
items: `000read-me-fam-med.txt`   (describes archives)
               `fam-med-intro.txt`   (describes Fam-Med)
               (many others)

Contact: e-mail: `Paul@gac.edu`
                          Paul Kleeberg, M.D.
                          604 North 3rd St.
                          Saint Peter, MN 56082 USA
               voice: (507) 931-6721
               fax: (507) 931-6752

FDA Bulletin Board
(Food and Drug Administration)

Contents: The FDA BBS has a wide range of helpful materials. The highlights of this system are: news releases; reports of FDA legal enforcement; monthly drug and device approval lists; announcements and bulletins from the Center for Devices and Radiological Health; text from *Medical Bulletin, FDA Today*, and *MedWatch*; AIDS press releases and current information on AIDS policies and speeches; the FDA *Consumer Magazine* index and selected articles; summaries of FDA information on specific topics; an index of news releases and information summaries; FDA *Federal Register* summaries by publication date; text of testimony at FDA congressional hearings; speeches given by FDA Commissioner and Deputy; *Veterinary Medicine News* from the Center for Veterinary Medicine; list of upcoming FDA meetings, including information on sending comments to the meetings; lists of import alerts on foods, medical devices, biological articles, cosmetics, radiological articles, and veterinary medicine; and last, but certainly not least, an online user's manual.

(Continued)

Comments: The user interface is fairly straightforward, but a few hints are helpful: the backspace key may not work, but since there is not a lot to type, this should not be a big problem; when prompted to continue a display ("yes or no?"), hitting the enter or return key will default to "yes," additionally, you can use "y" or "n" rather than typing the entire word. When you sign on the first time, you will need to register using your name, a password you choose, your place of work, work address and phone number. The BBS is provided by the FDA Office of Public Affairs.

Access: Telnet: `fdabbs.fda.gov`

     login: `bbs`
     modem: `800-222-0185`   2400 Baud
                    `301-594-6849/6857`   9600 Baud
     login: `bbs`

                    settings: data=7, parity=E, stop=1

Contact: Technical Support (7am - 7pm EST, Monday - Friday):
                    Parklawn Computer Center
     voice: (301) 443-7318
     Information about the database:
                    Karen Malone
                    FDA Press Office
                    5600 Fishers Lane, Room 15A11
                    Rockville, MD 20857 USA
     voice: (301) 443-3285
     fax: (301) 443-1388

More Info: Tomaiuolo, Nicholas G. "Internet Database Review: The FDA BBS." *Database* 16(6) (December 1993):82-84.

X International Food and Nutrition Database

Contents: Non-technical articles on nutrition designed to help people learn about good eating habits and health.

Access: Telnet: `psupen.psu.edu`
     login: `<your state's 2 letter code>`   (from within USA)
                    `world`   (from outside USA)
     choose: `(1) PENpages`
                    `(3) General information (Menu)`
     to search,
     choose: `(1) PENpages`
                    `(4) Keyword Search`

Contact: e-mail: ppmenu@psupen.psu.edu
                             PENpages Coordinator
                             405 Agricultural Administration Building
                             The Pennsylvania State University
                             University Park, PA 16802 USA
               voice: (814) 863-3449
More Info: PENpages *User Guide* available online or by request from above
               address.

X Medical Informatics Lab: Graphics, Visualization, and Usability Center

Contents: Research into the visualization of medical information. Includes moving models
               and scans of the human heart.
Access: WWW:
               http://www.gatech.edu/gvu/medical_informatics/medinfo_home_page.html
Contact: e-mail: norberto@cc.gatech.edu
                             (Norberto Ezquerra - questions about the   content)
                             obrienj@cc.gatech.edu
                             (James O'Brien - technical questions)
                             Norberto F. Ezquerra
                             Medical Informatics Group
                             Graphics, Visualization & Usability Center
                             College of Computing
                             Georgia Institute of Computing
                             Atlanta, GA 30332-0280 USA
               voice: (404) 853-9173 or (404) 853-0672
               fax: (404) 853-0673

X National Institute of Allergy and Infectious Diseases (NIAID) Gopher, National Institutes of Health

Contents: Offers a number of services including the NIH phone book, informa-
               tion on the National Toxicology Program (NTP), AIDS information
               (see prior section on AIDS Related Information for a full description),
               and access to other NIH Gophers.
Access: Gopher: odie.niaid.nih.edu
Contact: e-mail: alg@nih.gov
                             Al Graeff
                             NIAID Technical Service Division
               voice: (301) 496-0204

■■

X National Institutes of Health (NIH) Gopher

Contents:		Health and clinical information, NIH phone numbers, grants and research information, information on current studies at NIH, a connection to the National Library of Medicine Locator service, and more.
Comments:		This Gopher also provides access to other resources such as CancerNet and the NIAID AIDS Gopher.
Access:	Gopher:	`gopher.nih.gov`
	item:	`Health and Clinical Information/`
		`Grants and Research Information/`
Contact:	e-mail:	`gopher@gopher.nih.gov` (Gopher Team)
		`cpo@helix.nih.gov` (Charlene Osborn)
		`pcf@helix.nih.gov` (Peter FitzGerald)
	voice:	(301) 496-4823 (Charlene Osborn)
		(301) 402-1141 (Peter FitzGerald)

X National Library of Medicine (NLM) Gopher and Web Servers

Contents:		Includes information about the Library; access to NLM's Locator online catalog; the full text of NLM Clinical Alerts and NLM Fact Sheets; bibliographic files on AIDS and the *Current Bibliographies in Medicine*; and information on the National Center on Health Services Research and Health Care Technology and the NLM's FTP archive. For those with an NLM access code, MEDLARS and TOXNET are also available.
Access:	Gopher:	`gopher.nlm.nih.gov`
Contact:	e-mail:	`admin@gopher.nlm.nih.gov`
		For general information on the NLM's online services, contact:
	e-mail:	`Bob_Mehnert@occshost.nlm.nih.gov`
		Robert Mehnert
		National Library of Medicine
		Building 38, Room 2S10
		8600 Rockville Pike
		Bethesda, Md. 20894
	voice:	(301) 496-6308
Access:	WWW:	`http://www.nlm.nih.gov/`

Contact:	e-mail:	rodgers@nlm.nih.gov
		R. P. C. Rodgers, M.D.
		Computer Science Branch
		Lister Hill National Center for Biomedical
		Communications
		National Library of Medicine
		National Institutes of Health
		Building 38A, Room 9S-916
		8600 Rockville Pike
		Bethesda, MD 20894 USA
	voice:	(301) 496-9300
	fax:	(301) 496-0673

SEFAIN
(Southeast Florida AIDS Information Network)

Contents: A database of AIDS information and AIDS-related activities including treatment and support services in southeastern Florida. Includes detailed information on organizations providing physical and mental health services and education.

Comments: Sponsored in part by the National Library of Medicine.

Access: Telnet: callcat.med.miami.edu
                login: library
                main menu: select "P"
                next menu: select "1"

Contact: Southeast Florida AIDS Information Network
                1601 NW 10th Ave.
                Miami, FL 33136 USA

State University of New York (SUNY)—
Brooklyn Health Science Center

Contents: Of special interest on this Gopher is the availability of U.S. government nutrient data and bulletins from the U.S. Department of Agriculture, Human Nutrition Information Service and Nutrient Data Bank. Included are conference schedules, publications lists, contact information, and survey data.

Access: Gopher: gopher1.medlib.hscbklyn.edu
                menu: The Researcher/
                item: Nutrient Data/

Contact: e-mail: long@medlib.hscbklyn.edu
                              Phillip Long, Ph.D.
                              Assoc. Director for Systems, Medical Research Library,
                              Campus Internet Coordinator and Gophermeister
                voice: (718) 270-7428
                fax: (718) 270-7468

**State University of New York (SUNY)—
Syracuse Health Science Center**

Contents: Highlights of this Gopher include a section on nursing resources and disability information.

Access: Gopher: `micro.ec.hscsyr.edu`

items: `Medical Resources/Nursing Resources/`
`Disability Information/`

Contact: e-mail: `hscgopher@vax.cs.hscsyr.edu`

 USCgopher (University of Southern California)

Contents: Among other excellent medical resources, the USC Health Sciences Campus Gopher offers clinical alerts from NIH and NLM, national (U.S.) health care policy documents (including an indexed version of the full text of the "National Health Security Plan"), information on the Unified Medical Language System, and the full text of *The Scientist* newspaper, though this last item has not always been current.

Access: Gopher: `cwis.usc.edu`

menu: `The Health Sciences Campus/`

items: `Medical and Health Related Electronic`
`Periodicals/The_Scientist/`
`Health Policy Documents/`
`Clinical and Research Information/`
`Clinical Alerts from NIH and NLM /`
`Clinical and Research Information/Unified`
`Medical Language System/`

Contact: e-mail: `gopher-guts@usc.edu` (Gopher team)

`mark@usc.edu` (primary contact)
Mark A. Brown
Director of Research, Development and Systems
University Computing Services
University of Southern California
Los Angeles, CA 90089 USA

voice: (213) 740-2957

fax: (213) 740-2837

X The Virtual Hospital

Contents: A growing set of multimedia resources designed to assist physicians, medical
              students, and patients, offering up-to-date medical information regardless of
              time or location.

Comments: This resource is provided by the Department on Radiology, University of Iowa
              College of Medicine, Hospital Information Systems, University of Iowa, and
              Apple Computer, Inc. The available multimedia textbooks are impressive.

Access: WWW: `http://indy.radiology.uiowa.edu/VirtualHospital.html`

Contact: e-mail: `libarian@indy.radiology.uiowa.edu`

X World Health Organization Gopher

Contents: A wealth of information about the World Health Organization (WHO)
              and its activities. Included in this Gopher are WHO press releases,
              information on specific diseases (communicable, non-communicable,
              and tropical) and on specific WHO programs in the areas of food and
              nutrition, environmental health, human reproduction, as well as
              WHO's Library and Health Literature Services (HLT).

Access: Gopher: `gopher.who.ch`
              Telnet: `gopher.who.ch`
              login: `gopher`

Contact: e-mail: `gopher@who.ch`
                           WHO Internet Gopher Root Server Administrator
                           Information Technology Office (ITO)
                           World Health Organization (WHO) Headquarters
                           CH-1211 Geneva 27 Switzerland
              voice: +41 22 791 2434
              fax: +41 22 791 0746

LISTSERVs in Medicine

This list of lists is an extracted, revised version of the list compiled by Lee Hancock
in *Internet/Bitnet Health Sciences Resources*. To subscribe to a LISTSERV list, send the following message:

```
mail:      listserv@<host.address>
subject:   (none needed)
message:   subscribe <listname> <Your-name>
```

For more information on any LISTSERV list, send the following e-mail message:

```
mail:      listserv@<host.address>
subject:   (none needed)
message:   rev <listname>
```

This message issues the "review" command. The LISTSERV will respond by sending you a copy of the list "header" which should include a short description of the list. You may also receive a listing of the current subscribers to the list.

Although Internet addresses have been provided for most of the BITNET nodes, a few do not have them. In these cases, you will need to send your mail through a BITNET gateway if your own site does not support the ".BITNET" extension. (For more information on gateways, see Chapter 5.)

LISTSERVs in Medicine

Listname	Address	Topical Area
ABLE-JOB	SJUVM.STJOHNS.EDU	Disabilities in the workplace.
ABUSE-L	UBVM.CC.BUFFALO.EDU	Child abuse discussion for professionals.
ADA-LAW	VM1.NODAK.EDU	Discussion of the Americans with Disabilities Act (ADA) and other disability-related laws.
ADDICT-L	KENTVM.KENT.EDU	An electronic conference for mature discussion of many types of addictions.
AGEING	DARESBURY.AC.UK	BIOSCI Aging Bulletin Board
AHL	GWUVM.GWU.EDU	American Health Line News Service
AIDS	RUTVM1.RUTGERS.EDU	(Peered) Sci.Med.AIDS Newsgroup
AIDSNEWS	RUTVM1.RUTGERS.EDU	(Peered) AIDS/HIV News
ALCOHOL	LMUACAD.BITNET	Alcohol and Drug Studies
AMALGAM	VM.GMD.DE	Distributes information about chronic mercury poisoning from dental "silver" tooth fillings.
AMIA-37	UMAB.UMD.EDU	American Medical Informatics Association

LISTSERVs in Medicine (Continued)

Listname	Address	Topical Area
AMIED-L	VM1.MCGILL.CA	American Medical Informatics Association Education Professional Specialty Group (PSG)
ANEST-L	UBVM.CC.BUFFALO.EDU	Topics related to anesthesiology.
APASD-L	VTVM2.CC.VT.EDU	APA Research Psychology Network. Research and training funding sources for psychology.
APASPAN	GWUVM.GWU.EDU	APA Scientific Grassroots Network
ASLING-L	YALEVM.CIS.YALE.EDU	American Sign Language List
AUDITORY	VM1.MCGILL.CA	Research in auditory perception.
AUTISM	SJUVM.STJOHNS.EDU	Provides a forum for those who are developmentally disabled, their teachers, and others who are interested.
BACKS-L	UVMVM.UVM.EDU	Research on low back pain, disability.
BEHAVIOR	ASUVM.INRE.ASU.EDU	Behavioral and Emotional Disorders in Children
BIOCIS-L	SIVM.SI.EDU	Biology Curriculum Innovation Study
BIOMCH-L	HEARN.NIC.SURFNET.NL	Biomechanics and Movement Science
BIOMED-L	VM1.MCGILL.CA	Association of Biomedical Communication Directors
BIOMED-L	VM1.NODAK.EDU	Biomedical Ethics
BLIND-L	UAFSYSB.UARK.EDU	Computer Use by and for the Blind
BOSTON-RSI	WORLD.STD.COM	Repetitive Stress Injuries
BRAIN-L	VM1.MCGILL.CA	Mind-Brain Discussion Group
BRAINTMR	MITVMA.MIT.EDU	Discussion on all types of brain tumors. For patients, their supporters, professionals, and researchers.
BRCTR	ULKYVM.LOUISVILLE.EDU	Braille Research Center Forum
BRIT-L	KSUVM.KSU.EDU	Behavioral Research in Transplantation

LISTSERVs in Medicine (Continued)

Listname	Address	Topical Area
C+HEALTH	IUBVM.UCS.INDIANA.EDU	Promote sharing of information, experiences, concerns, advice about computers and health.
CADUCEUS	BEACH.UTMB.EDU	History of Medicine Collections Forum (moderated)
CANCER-L	WVNVM.WVNET.EDU	Cancer discussion list.
CANCHID	VM1.YORKU.CA	Canadian University Consortium on Health in International Development (CUCHID)
CEMS-L	VM.MARIST.EDU	Collegiate Emergency Medical Services
CDMAJOR	KENTVM.KENT.EDU	Communication Disorders
CFS-L	LIST.NIH.GOV	Chronic Fatigue Syndrome/CFIDS (patient list)
CFS-MED	LIST.NIH.GOV	Chronic Fatigue Syndrome/CFIDS (medical list)
CHMINF-L	IUBVM.UCS.INDIANA.EDU	Chemical Information Sources
CLAN	FRMOP11.CNUS.FR	Cancer Liaison and Action Network
CLINALRT	UMAB.UMD.EDU	Clinical Alerts from NIH
CMEDSSOC	UTORONTO.BITNET	Canadian Medical Student Societies
COCAMED	UTORONTO.BITNET	Computers in Canadian Medical Education
COGSCI-L	VM1.YORKU.CA	Cognitive Science
COMPMED	WUVMD.WUSTL.EDU	Comparative Medicine
COMPUMED	SJUVM.STJOHNS.EDU	Computers in medicine and medical curricula.
CONFLIST	UCSFVM.UCSF.EDU	School of Medicine Conference List
CONFOCAL	UBVM.CC.BUFFALO.EDU	Confocal Microscopy List
CONSLINK	SIVM.SI.EDU	Biological Conservation

LISTSERVs in Medicine (Continued)

Listname	Address	Topical Area
CPRI-L	UKANAIX.CC.UKANS.EDU	Telecommunications and healthcare discussion for professionals, patients, and researchers.
CUSSNET	STAT.COM	Computer Users in the Social Sciences (CUSS) is devoted to issues of interest to human service workers of all disciplines including clinical health care.
CYSTIC-L	YALEVM.CIS.YALE.EDU	Cystic fibrosis discussion for doctors, caregivers, and patients.
DBLIST	UMAB.UMD.EDU	Databases for Dentistry
DDFIND-L	GITVM1.GATECH.EDU	Information Networking on Disability
DEAF-L	SIUCVMB.BITNET	Deaf List
DENTAL	UMAB.UMD.EDU	Dental Test List
DENTAL-L	IRLEARN.UCD.IE	Cosine Project - Dental Research Unit
DENTALMA	UCF1VM.CC.UCF.EDU	Dentistry related articles reports and testing
DIABETES	IRLEARN.UCD.IE	International Research Project on Diabetes
DIABETIC	PCCVM.BITNET	Forum for diabetic patient counseling.
DIARIA	INFOMED.CU	Informacion Diaria (diarrhea list with discussion in Spanish)
DIARRHOE	SEARN.SUNET.SE	Related to diseases, disorders, and chemicals which cause diarrhea in humans and animals.
DIET	INDYCMS.IUPUI.EDU	Support and Discussion of Weight Loss
DRUGABUS	UMAB.UMD.EDU	Drug Abuse Education Information and Research
DSSHE-L	UBVM.CC.BUFFALO.EDU	Disabled Student Services in Higher Education
DISRES-L	RYEVM.RYERSON.CA	This is the disability research list covering any kind of disability-related research.

LISTSERVs in Medicine (Continued)

Listname	Address	Topical Area
D-ORAL-L	LIST.NIH.GOV	Problems facing scientists and clinicians that deal with human and mammalian oral microbiota.
D-PERIO	LIST.NIH.GOV	Periodontal Diseases Program Discussion
DRUGABUS	UMAB.UMD.EDU	Drug Abuse Education Information and Research
DRUGHIED	TAMVM1.TAMU.EDU	Drug Abatement Research Discussion
EGRET-L	DARTCMS1.DARTMOUTH.EDU	Discussion of EGRET epidemiological software.
EMERG-L	VM.MARIST.EDU	Collegiate Emergency Medical Services
EMFLDS-L	UBVM.CC.BUFFALO.EDU	Electromagnetics in Medicine, Science & Communications
ENVBEH-L	VM.POLY.EDU	Forum on Environment and Human Behavior
EXPER-L	EGE.EDU.TR	Experiences on Viral Attacks
EYEMOV-L	SPCVXA.SPC.EDU	Eye Movement Network
FAMCOMM	VM.ECS.RPI.EDU	Marital/family & relational communication.
FAMILY-L	MIZZOU1.MISSOURI.EDU	Academic family medicine discussion.
FAM-MED	GAC.EDU	Use of computer technology in the teaching and practice of Family Medicine.
FET-NET	HEARN.NIC.SURFNET.NL	Topics concerning research in fetal and perinatal care.
FIBROM-L	VMD.CSO.UIUC.EDU	Fibromyalgia
FINAN-HC	WUVMD.WUSTL.EDU	Health Care Financial Matters
FORENS-L	ACC.FAU.EDU	Forensic Medicine and Sciences Interest Group
FORENSIC	UNMVMA.UNM.EDU	Forensic medicine anthropology, death investigation, and mortality.

LISTSERVs in Medicine (Continued)

Listname	Address	Topical Area
FORUMBIO	SCF.FUNDP.AC.BE	Forum on molecular biology.
GERINET	UBVM.CC.BUFFALO.EDU	Geriatric Health Care Discussion Group
GFULMED	VM1.NODAK.EDU	This is for discussion of the Grateful Med software package issued by NIH.
GMRLIST	UICVM.UIC.EDU	Greater Midwest Region Health Science Libraries
GNOME-PR	DARESBURY.AC.UK	Human Genome Program Bulletin Board
GRADNRSE	KENTVM.KENT.EDU	The GradNrse is a discussion for practicing nurses.
GRANTS-L	JHUVM.HCF.JHU.EDU	NSF Grants & Contracts Bulletin Board
HEALTH-L	IRLEARN.UCD.IE	International Discussion on Health Research
HEALTHCO	VM.ECS.RPI.EDU	Communication in Health/Medical Context
HEALTHMGMT	CHIMERA.SPH.UMN.EDU	Issues pertaining to the management and administration of health care organizations.
HEALTHRE	UKCC.UKY.EDU	Health Care Reform
HIM-L	FIONA.UMSMED.EDU	Health Information Managers
HELPNET	VM1.NODAK.EDU	Network Emergency Response Planning
HERB	EGE.EDU.TR	Medicinal and Aromatic Plants
HGML-L	YALEVM.CIS.YALE.EDU	Human Gene Mapping Library
HMATRIX-L	UKANAIX.CC.UKANS.EDU	Online Health Science Resources
H-PROMO	RYEVM.RYERSON.CA	Health Promotion Research
HQ-L	PSUHMC.HMC.PSU.EDU	HealthQuest Products Discussion
HSPNET-L	ALBNYDH2.BITNET	Hospital Computer Network Discussion
HSPNET-D	ALBNYDH2.BITNET	Hospital Computer Network Discussion (digest)

LISTSERVs in Medicine (Continued)

Listname	Address	Topical Area
HUMAGE-L	ASUVM.INRE.ASU.EDU	Humanistic Effects of Aging
HYPBAR-L	TECHNION.TECHNION.AC.IL	HyperBaric & Diving Medicine
HYPERMED	UMAB.UMD.EDU	Biomedical Hypermedia Instructional Design
IAPSY-L	UACSC2.ALBANY.EDU	Interamerican Psychologists List (SIPNET)
ICECA	RUTVM1.RUTGERS.EDU	International Committee for Electronic Communication on AIDS (ICECA); subscriptions only open to Committee members, but anyone can contribute; for more information contact Michael Smith at MNSMITH@UMAECS.BITNET.
IMIA-L	UMAB.UMD.EDU	International Medical Informatics Association Board
IMMNET-L	DARTCMS1.DARTMOUTH.EDU	Medical Immunization Tracking Systems
INGEST	CUVMB.CC.COLUMBIA.EDU	Ingestive Disorders
INHEALTH	VM.ECS.RPI.EDU	International Health Communication
INTVIO-L	URIACC.URI.EDU	All aspects of family violence.
IOOB-L	UGA.UGA.EDU	Industrial Psychology
IOOBF-L	UGA.UGA.EDU	Industrial Psychology Forum
JMEDCLUB	BROWNVM.BROWN.EDU	Medical Journal Discussion Club
KINST-L	ULKYVM.LOUISVILLE.EDU	Hand Microsurgery Research
L-HCAP	VM1.NODAK.EDU	Technology for the Handicapped
LACTACID	SEARN.SUNET.SE	Lactic Acid Bacteria Forum
LASMED-L	VM.TAU.AC.IL	Laser Medicine
LIVE-EYE	VM1.YORKU.CA	Color and Vision
LYMENET-L	LEHIGH.EDU	Lyme Disease Electronic Mail Network
MEDFORUM	ARIZVM1.CCIT.ARIZONA.EDU	Med Student Organization/Policy Forum

LISTSERVs in Medicine (Continued)

Listname	Address	Topical Area
MEDIMAGEX	PAX.TPA.COM.AU	Processing of medical images, availability and usefulness of software, and other information.
MEDINF-L	VM.GMD.DE	Biomedical Informatics Discussion Group
MEDLAB-L	VM.UCS.UALBERTA.CA	Medical laboratory professionals and educators.
MEDLIB-L	UBVM.CC.BUFFALO.EDU	Medical Libraries Discussion List
MEDNETS	VM1.NODAK.EDU	Medical Telecommunications Networks
MEDNEWS	ASUVM.INRE.ASU.EDU	Health Info-Com Network Newsletter
MEDPHY-L	AWIIMC12.IMC.UNIVIE.AC.AT	EFOMP Medical Physics Information Services
MEDSUP-L	YALEVM.CIS.YALE.EDU	Medical Support List
MEDSTU-L	UNMVMA.UNM.EDU	Medical Student Discussion List
MENOPAUS	PSUHMC.HMC.PSU.EDU	Menopause
MHCARE-L	MIZZOU1.MISSOURI.EDU	Discussion of topics pertaining to managed health care and continuous quality improvement.
MICEE-L	LFMOTOL.CUNI.CZ	Medical Informatics (discussion is in English)
MICZ-L	LFMOTOL.CUNI.CZ	Medical Informatics (discussion is in Czech)
MINHLTH	DAWN.HAMPSHIRE.EDU	Minority Health Issues List
MPSYCH-L	BROWNVM.BROWN.EDU	Society for Mathematical Psychology
MORPHMET	CUNYVM.CUNY.EDU	Biological Morphometrics
MOTORDEV	UMDD.UMD.EDU	Human Motor Skill Development
MSLIST-L	NCSUVM.CC.NCSU.EDU	Multiple Sclerosis Discussion/Support
MUCO-FR	FRMOP11.CNUSC.FR	Cystic Fibrosis - France (MucoViscidose)

LISTSERVs in Medicine (Continued)

Listname	Address	Topical Area
NCE-RESP	VM1.MCGILL.CA	Network of Centers of Excellence in Respiratory Health
NCIW-L	YALEVM.CIS.YALE.EDU	Nutrient Cycling Issues
NEURL	UICVM.UIC.EDU	Neuroscience Strategic Planning
NEUR-SCI	DARESBURY.AC. UK	Neuroscience Bulletin Board
NEURO1-L	UICVM.UIC.EDU	Neuroscience Information Forum
NEURON	CATTELL. PSYCH.UPENN.EDU	Neural networks especially natural systems, neurobiology, neuroscience...etc. (digest)
NEUS582	UICVM.UIC.EDU	Methods in Modern Neuroscience
NIATRN-L	BROWNVM.BROWN.EDU	National Institute of Aging Population Researchers and Trainees List
NIHDIS-L	JHUVM.HCF.JHU.EDU	NIH Guide
NIHGUIDE	UMAB.UMD.EDU	NIH Listing of Available Grants and Contracts
NNLM-SEA	UMAB.UMD.EDU	National Network Library of Medicine SEA
NRSING-L	NIC.UMASS.EDU	Nursing Informatics
NURCENS	GIBBS.OIT.UNC.EDU	Nursing Centers
NURSE-L	EMUVM1.CC.EMORY.EDU	Nursing School Project
NURSERES	KENTVM.KENT.EDU	Nursing Research
NUTEPI	TUBVM.CS.TU-BERLIN.DE	Nutritional Epidemiology
ORADLIST	UCLACN1.BITNET	Oral Radiology
OXYGEN-L	UMCVMB.MISSOURI.EDU	Oxygen Free Radical Biology and Medicine
PANET-L	YALEVM.CIS.YALE.EDU	Medical Education and Health Information
PHYSL-TR	TRITU.BITNET	Physiology

LISTSERVs in Medicine (Continued)

Listname	Address	Topical Area
PRENAT-L	ALBNYDH2.BITNET	Perinatal Outcomes
PSYC	PUCC.PRINCETON.EDU	Psychology, neuroscience, and behavioral psychology.
PSYCHE-D	NKI.BITNET	Discussion for those interested in the subject of consciousness.
QML	TBONE.BIOL.SCAROLINA.EDU	Quantitative Morphology
QUALRS-L	UGA.UGA.EDU	Qualitative Research for the Human Sciences
RADSIG	UWAVM.U.WASHINGTON.EDU	Radiology Special Interest Group
REVES	FRMOP11.CNUSC.FR	Network on Health Expectancy
RHCFRP-L	ALBNYDH2.BITNET	Residential Health Care Facilities
RISK	UTXVM.CC.UTEXAS.EDU	Issues concerning the general topic of risk management and insurance.
SCHIZOPH	UTORONTO.BITNET	Schizophrenia
SCODAE	UMAB.UMD.EDU	Communications Network for Pharmacy Schools
SCR-L	UMCVMB.MISSOURI.EDU	Study of Cognitive Rehabilitation
SHS	UTKVM1.UTK.EDU	Student Health Services in higher education.
SLEEP-L	QUCDN.QUEENSU.CA	Sleep Disorders: membership is restricted to health care providers involved in academic or clinical pursuits related to sleep.
SMCDCME	CMS.CC.WAYNE.EDU	Continuing Medical Education
SMDM-L	DARTCMS1.DARTMOUTH.EDU	Members of The Society for Medical Decision Making and others.
SMOKE-FREE	RA.MSSTATE.EDU	Support list for people recovering from addiction to cigarettes.
SMS-SNUG	GIBBS.OIT.UNC.EDU	Shared Medical Systems (SMS) National User Group (SNUG)

LISTSERVs in Medicine (Continued)

Listname	Address	Topical Area
SNURSE-L	UBVM.CC.BUFFALO.EDU	Student nurse discussion list.
SOREHAND	UCSFVM.UCSF.EDU	Carpal Tunnel Syndrome and Tendonitis
SSSSTALK	TAMVM1.TAMU.EDU	Professional researchers, clinicians, educators and students in the field of sexuality.
SPORTPSY	VM.TEMPLE.EDU	Exercise and Sports Psychology
STROKE-L	UKCC.UKY.EDU	CerebroVascular Accident (stroke)
STUT-HLP	BGU.EDU	For people who stutter and their families. It is *not* intended to be an academic discussion.
STUTT-L	VM.TEMPLE.EDU	Stuttering: Research and Clinical Practice
STUTT-X	ASUVM.INRE.ASU.EDU	For those who study stuttering.
TBI-SPRT	MORIA.NFBCAL.ORG	Traumatic Brain Injury list is for the exchange of information by patients, supporters, and professionals.
TECGRP-L	PSUVM.PSU.EDU	Technology and Social Behavior Group
TELEMED	LEON.NRCPS.ARIADNE-T.GR	Discussion group for providing brief news on telemedicine and discussing related issues.
TIPS	FRE.FSU.UMD.EDU	Teaching in the Psychological Sciences
THPHYSIO	FRMOP11.CNUSC.FR	Thermal Physiology
TRNSPLNT	WUVMD.WUSTL.EDU	For organ transplant recipients and anyone else who is interested.
VISION-L	ADS.COM	Eye movement research.
WHSCL-L	EMUVM1.CC.EMORY.EDU	Health Sciences Library Discussion
WMN-HLTH	UWAVM.U.WASHINGTON.EDU	Women's Health Electronic News Line
WU-AIDS	WUVMD.WUSTL.EDU	Sci.Med.AIDS Newsgroup
WUNIHG-L	WUVMD.WUSTL.EDU	Washington University NIH Guide Distribution

Mailing Lists in Medicine

This list of lists is an extracted, revised version of the list compiled by Lee Hancock in *Internet/Bitnet Health Sciences Resources*. To subscribe to a mailing list, send the following message:

```
mail:     <listname>-request@<address>
subject:  (none needed)
message:  subscribe <listname> <Your-name>
```

Be sure to include the word "-request" with the list name, otherwise your request to be added to the list will be sent to the entire list!

Mailing Lists in Medicine

Listname	Address	Topical Area
AIDS-STAT	WUBIOS.WUSTL.EDU	AIDS Statistics
AI-MEDICINE	MED.STANFORD.EDU	Artificial intelligence (AI) in medicine.
AI-MEDICINE	VUSE.VANDERBILT.EDU	List for the parts of medical informatics that deal with AI, like Computer-Assisted Instruction (CAI) or decision support.
CBT-GENERAL	VIRGINIA.EDU	Biological timing and circadian rhythms.
IMMUNE	WEBER.UCSD.EDU	For discussion of Chronic Fatigue Syndrome, Epstein-Barr, Lupus, allergies, chemical sensitivities, etc.
MEDPHYS	RADONC.DUKE.EDU	An attempt to foster electronic communication between medical physicists.
NUCMED	UWOVAX.UWO.CA	A discussion of nuclear medicine and related issues. Of particular concern is the format of digital images.
PHARM	DMU.AC.UK	Pharmacy Mail Exchange is a list for pharmacists.
PRION	ACC.STOLAF.EDU	Prion (slow virus) Infection Digest
TDR-SCIENTISTS	WHO.CH	Tropical Diseases Research
WITSENDO	DARTCMS1.DARTMOUTH.EDU	Endometriosis discussion list using non-technical language.

MAILBASE Lists in Medicine

This list of lists is an extracted, revised version of the list compiled by Lee Hancock in *Internet/Bitnet Health Sciences Resources*. To subscribe to a MAILBASE list, send the following message:

```
mail:    MAILBASE@MAILBASE.AC.UK
subject: (none needed)
message: join <listname> <Your-name>
```

MAILBASE Lists in Medicine

Listname	Topic Areas
AROMA-TRIALS	Discussion on the scientific investigation of the claims of aromatherapy and related areas of olfaction.
DNH-PILOT	Diet, Nutrition, and Health Project (European Community)
PHYSIO	Physiotherapy Discussion
PSYCHIATRY	Psychiatry and abnormal psychology (unmoderated)
PUBLIC-HEALTH	Epidemiology and public health.
TRAUMATIC-STRESS	Aspects of Post-Traumatic Stress Disorder
WHOORAL-PILOT	World Health Organization oral health.

Other Types of Lists in Medicine

This list of lists is an extracted, revised version of the list compiled by Lee Hancock in *Internet/Bitnet Health Sciences Resources*.

Other Lists in Medicine

Listname	Address	Information
ALS	BRO@HUEY.MET.FSU.EDU	This list has been set up to serve the world-wide amyotrophic lateral sclerosis, or Lou Gehrig's disease, community. (Subscription request: send a message requesting a subscription.)
CB-Net	Listserv@UCSD.EDU	Chinese Biotechnology Network (Subscription request: "add CB-Net" as the first line of the message.)
COMMDIS	COMSERVE@VM.ECS.RPI.EDU	Speech Disorders (Subscription request: "join commdis <your name>" as the first line of the message.)
EHS-INFO	LISTPROC@AEMRC.ARIZONA.EDU	Emergency Health Services (Subscription request: "subscribe ehs-info <your name>" as the first line of the message.)
IBDlist	IBDLIST-REQUEST%MVAC23@UDEL.EDU	Inflammatory Bowel Diseases (Subscription request: send a message requesting a subscription.)
METHODS	COMSERVE@RPITSVM.BITNET	Research Methodology (Subscription request: "join methods <your name>" as the first line of the message.)
OCC-ENV-MED-L	MAILSERV@MC.DUKE.EDU	Clinical aspects of occupational and environmental health. (Subscription request: "subscribe OCC-ENV-MED-L <your name>" as the first line of the message.

■ ■

Other Lists in Medicine (Continued)

Listname	Address	Information
PEDIATRIC-PAIN	MAILSERV@AC.DAL.CA	Pediatric Pain. This is an international forum for discussion of any topic related to pain in children. (Subscription request: "subscribe PEDIATRIC-PAIN" as the first line of the message.)

Usenet Newsgroups in Medicine

The topics covered in these newsgroups are quite varied in both style and substance. Some will be more professionally oriented, while others are less formal, and most are a mix of the two.

Usenet Newsgroups in Medicine

Newsgroup	Topics
alt.education.disabled	Issues concerning the disabled
misc.emerg-services	Emergency services discussion group
misc.handicap	Covers all areas of disabilities
misc.health.alternative	Alternative health
misc.health.diabetes	Diabetes
sci.bio	Biology and related sciences
sci.bio.technology	Technology in biology
sci.engr.biomed	Biomedical Engineering
sci.med	Medicine and its related products and regulations
sci.med.aids	AIDS: treatment, pathology, HIV prevention
sci.med.dentistry	Dentistry
sci.med.nutrition	Nutrition
sci.med.occupational	Occupational health and therapy

Usenet Newsgroups in Medicine (Continued)

Newsgroup	Topics
`sci.med.pharmacy`	Pharmacology
`sci.med.physics`	Physics in medicine
`sci.med.psychobiology`	Psychiatry and psychobiology
`sci.med.radiology`	Radiology
`sci.med.telemedicine`	Medical networking issues
`sci.med.psychology`	Psychology issues
`sci.med.psychology.digest`	Psychology issues in digest form
`sci.psychology.research`	Research in psychology
`talk.abortion`	Abortion issues
`talk.politics.drugs`	Politics of drug issues
`talk.politics.medicine`	Politics of medicine

BITNET Listserv Echoes

As with all of the bit.listserv news groups, these echo the corresponding Bitnet mailing lists.

BITNET Listserv Echo in Medicine

Newsgroup	Topics
`bit.listserv.aidsnews`	AIDSNEWS: AIDS/HIV News
`bit.listserv.autism`	Provides a forum for those who are developmentally disabled, their teachers, and those interested.
`bit.listserv.deaf-l`	DEAF-L: Deaf List
`bit.listserv.emflds-l`	EMFLDS-L: Electromagnetic Fields in Medicine, Science & Communications
`bit.listserv.l-hcap`	L-HCAP: Technology for the Handicapped
`bit.listserv.medlib-l`	MEDLIB-L: Medical Librarians List

BITNET Listserv Echo in Medicine (Continued)

Newsgroup	Topics
`bit.listserv.medforum`	Medical students discussion.
`bit.listserv.mednews`	MEDNEWS: Health Info-Com Network Newsletter

Electronic Journals in Medicine

Most of these journals are available for free from a LISTSERV and many are also available via FTP and Gopher. Only a few of these journals charge for subscription. Often, those that are issued irregularly simply post articles as they are ready for publication, reducing further the publishing lead time of traditional journals that only publish when a whole issue has been gathered.

Electronic Journals in Medicine

Journal Name	General Information	Subscription Information
ALS Digest	Amyotrophic Lateral Sclerosis (Lou Gehrig's Disease)	Send e-mail to BRO@HUEY.MET.FSU.EDU asking for a subscription.
American Health Line	Non-partisan digest of national media coverage of health care reform; issued daily.	Call (703) 237-5130; fee-based; files available for downloading or via e-mail.
Blind News Digest	Digest of articles from various online groups; issued irregularly.	Send e-mail to LISTSERV@VM1.NODAK.EDU with the message: SUB BLINDNWS <your name>. To cancel your subscription, send mail to the LISTSERV with the message: UNSUB BLINDNWS.
Chronic Fatigue Syndrome Newsletter	Issued one to four times per month.	Send e-mail to LISTSERV@LIST.NIH.GOV with the message: SUB CFS-NEWS <your name>. To cancel your subscription, send mail to the LISTSERV with the message: UNSUB CFS-NEWS.
Electronic Journal of Intimate Violence	Covers research and treatment of family and other intimate abuse; issued monthly (approx.).	Send e-mail to LISTSERV@URIACC.URI.EDU with the message: SUB EJINTVIO <your name>. To cancel your subscription, send mail to the LISTSERV with the message: UNSUB EJINTVIO.

Electronic Journals in Medicine (Continued)

Journal Name	General Information	Subscription Information
Handicap Digest	Digest of articles from various online groups (articles on visual impairment in Blind News Digest); issued irregularly.	Send e-mail to LISTSERV@VM1.NODAK.EDU with the message: SUB L-HCAP <your name>. To cancel your subscription, send mail to the LISTSERV with the message: UNSUB L-HCAP.
HICnet Newsletter (The Health InfoCom Newsletter)	Issued weekly in multiple sections.	Send e-mail to LISTSERV@ASUACAD.BITNET with the message: SUB MEDNEWS <your name>. To cancel your subscription, send mail to the LISTSERV with the message: UNSUB MEDNEWS.
Laboratory Primate Newsletter	Quarterly.	Send e-mail to LISTSERV@BROWNVM.BROWN.EDU with the message: SUB LPN-L <your name>. To cancel your subscription, send mail to the LISTSERV with the message: UNSUB LPN-L.
Online Journal of Current Clinical Trials	Issued irregularly.	E-mail PUBSAAAS@gwuvm.gwu.edu or call (202) 326-6446; fee-based.
PSYCHE: An Interdisciplinary Journal of Research on Consciousness	Consciousness and its relation to the brain; refereed; PSYCHE discussion on PSYCHE-D at the same LISTSERV; issued irregularly.	Send e-mail to LISTSERV@NKI.BITNET with the message: SUB PSYCHE-L <your name>. To cancel your subscription, send mail to the LISTSERV with the message: UNSUB PSYCHE-L.
PSYCOLOQUY: A Refereed Journal of Peer Commentary in Psychology, Neuroscience and Cognitive Science	Psychology, neuroscience, behavioral biology; refereed; issued irregularly.	Send e-mail to LISTSERV@PUCC.PRINCETON.EDU with the message: SUB PSYC <your name>. To cancel your subscription, send mail to the LISTSERV with the message: UNSUB PSYC.
RSInet Newsletter	Repetitive stress injury; issued every other month.	Send e-mail to dadadata@world.std.com with the subject: RSI Newsletter.

GENETICS AND MOLECULAR BIOLOGY

General Information about Genetics and Molecular Biology Databases

If you intend to use any of the Genetics and Molecular Biology databases listed in this section, you are advised to get the Listing of Molecular Biology Databases (LiMB) for an overview of what is available. Most, but not all, of the databases in this section are described in LiMB which is updated very frequently.

You should also make a point of exploring the FTP archives of the National Center for Biotechnology Information (NCBI) described in this section, as it is the most important single archive in the field.

Genetics and Molecular Biology Databases

The databases in this section are focused on services that include information on research tools that may relate, either directly or indirectly, to human development, human conditions, or the human genome. For information on the genetics and molecular biology of other organisms, please consult the biology section of Chapter 15. For a general listing of molecular biology databases, the resources listed below are a good start.

LiMB (Listing of Molecular Biology Databases)

Contents: A comprehensive listing of molecular biology and related databases.
Comments: The *essential* resource for anyone using or thinking of using genetics and molecular biology databases. If you are creating such a database, these are the people to contact to be sure of broad notification in the molecular biology community.
Access: The preferred method of obtaining this document is by sending an e-mail request to a mail server. You will receive the LiMB database by e-mail in several parts.

```
mail:   bioserve@life.lanl.gov
subject: (none needed)
message: limb-data
```

Contact: e-mail: limb@life.lanl.gov
                             LiMB
                             Theoretical Biology and Biophysics Group
                             T-10, Mail Stop K710
                             Los Alamos National Laboratory
                             Los Alamos, NM 87545 USA
              voice: (505) 667-7510

Cooperative Human Linkage Center (CHLC)

Contents: Collection of data on the human genome including maps, markers, and genotype data.

Contact: e-mail: `help@chlc.org`
                           Frank Manion (technical assistance)
                           Dr. Kenneth H. Buetow (content assistance)
                           The Fox Chase Cancer Center
                           Research Computing Services
                           7701 Burholme Ave.
                           Philadelphia, PA 19111 USA
              voice: (215) 728-3660
              fax: (215) 728-2513

ENZYME

Contents: Dictionary of 3072 enzymes containing nomenclature, information about catalytic activity, co-factors, and diseases associated with each enzyme.

Access: Accessible through FTP and mail server.
              FTP host: `ncbi.nlm.nih.gov`
              directory: `/repository/enzyme`
              filenames: `enzyme.get`   (describes various options for obtaining ENZYME)

                           `enzuser.txt`   (user's guide)
                           `enzyme.dat`   (the data set)
                           `enzclass.txt`   (enzyme classification)

              directory: `/repository/enzyme/asn`
              filenames: `enzspec.asn`   (specification)
                           `enzyme.asn`   (ASN.1 version of ENZYME)

              FTP host: `expasy.hcuge.ch`

              directory: `/databases/enzyme`
              filenames: `enzyme.get`   (describes various options for obtaining ENZYME)

                           `enzuser.txt`   (user's guide)
                           `enzyme.dat`   (the data set)
                           `enzclass.txt`   (enzyme classification)

▪▪▪

directory:	/databases/enzyme/asn	
filenames:	enzspec.asn	(specification)
	enzyme.asn	(ASN.1 version of ENZYME)

To get started with the mail server, send the following message:

```
mail:     netserv@embl-heidelberg.de
subject:  (none needed)
message:
get ENZYME:ENZYME.DAT
get ENZYME:ENZCLASS.TXT
get ENZYME:ENZYME.GET
get ENZYME:ENZUSER.TXT
```

Contact:	e-mail:	bairoch@cmu.unige.ch
		Amos Bairoch
		Medical Biochemistry Department
		Centre Medical Universitaire
		University of Geneva
		1, Rue Michel Servet
		1211 Geneva 4 Switzerland
	voice:	+41 22 61 84 92
	fax:	+41 22 347 33 34

Gene-Server

Contents:	Repository of several databases including GenBank; PIR protein sequences; R. Roberts Restriction Enzyme Database; and Matrix of Biological Knowledge Archive Server files; also a huge number of software programs for molecular biologists and geneticists.
Access:	By mail server send the following message for an introduction:

```
mail:     gene-server@bchs.uh.edu
subject:  (none needed)
message: send help
```

Contact:	e-mail:	davison@uh.edu
		Dan Davison
		BCHS - 5500
		Dept. of Biochemical and Biophysical Sciences
		University of Houston
		4800 Calhoun
		Houston, TX 77204-5500 USA
	voice:	(713) 743-836

■■■

 ## The Genome Database (GDB)

Contents:	Genome database searchable as a whole, or in subsets: citations, polymorphisms, contacts (people), loci, map information, mutations, or probes.
Comments:	A Macintosh program for accessing GDB and related genetic databases on the Internet is available from this menu as is access to the Online Mendelian Inheritance in Man (OMIM).
Access:	Gopher: `gopher.gdb.org`
	menus: `Genome Project/The Genome Database (GDB)`
	item: `OMIM - Online Mendelian Inheritance in Man`
Contact:	e-mail: `danj@mail.gdp.org`
	(Dan Jacobson - technical questions)
	`help@gdb.org` (questions about the database)
	GDB User Support
	Genome Data Base
	Johns Hopkins University School of Medicine
	2024 E. Monument Street
	Baltimore, MD 21205 USA
	voice: (410) 955-7058
	fax: (410) 614-0434

 ## The Johns Hopkins University BioInformatics Web Server

Contents:	Includes, Prot-Web, a collection of protein databases (OWL, NRL_3D, PIR, EC-Enzyme) which contain internal as well as external links; The Mouse Locus Catalog; software and data from around the world; a list of 37 other biology related Web servers; and general information about the World Wide Web.
Access:	WWW: `http://www.gdb.org/hopkins.html`
Contact:	e-mail: `danj@mail.gdp.org`
	(Dan Jacobson - technical questions)
	`help@gdb.org` (questions about the database)
	user support: BioInformatics Web Server
	Johns Hopkins University School of Medicine
	2024 E. Monument Street
	Baltimore, MD 21205 USA
	voice: (410) 955-7058
	fax: (410) 614-0434

■■■

MBCRR (Molecular Biology Computer Research Resource)

Contents:	Source code and documentation for DNA and protein sequence analysis software for Unix systems.	
Access:	FTP host:	`mbcrr.harvard.edu`
	directory:	`MBCRR-Package`
	filenames:	**(many or all)**
Contact:	e-mail:	`tsmith@mbcrr.harvard.edu`
		MBCRR, LG-S127
		44 Binney St.
		Boston, MA 02115 USA
	voice:	(617) 732-3746
More Info:	FTP host:	`mbcrr.harvard.edu`
	directory:	`MBCRR-Package`
	filename:	`README`

National Cancer Center (Tokyo, Japan)

Contents:	Information on cell and gene banks, a Center phone book (incomplete), and some image files. As the README indicates, "It is always under construction. (It is expanding all the time.)"	
Comments:	You can also find information on Japanese culture here!	
Access:	Gopher:	`gopher.ncc.go.jp`
	Telnet:	`gopher.ncc.go.jp`
	login:	`gopher`
	items:	`Japanese Cancer` (cell and gene bank data)
		`Research Resources`
		`Bank/`
Contact:	e-mail:	`hmizushi@gan.ncc.go.jp`
		Hiroshi Mizushima
		Biophysics Division
		Cancer Center Research Institute
		5-1-1 Tsukiji
		Chuo-ku Tokyo 104 Japan
	voice:	+81 3 3542 2511 ex. 4126 or +81 3 5550 202
	fax:	+81 3 5550 2027
More Info:	There is a discussion and announcement list for the Gopher	

```
mail:      ncc-gopher-news-request@gan.ncc.go.jp
subject:   Subscription request
message:
Please add me to the English/Japanese version [choose one]  of the
ncc-gopher-news list.
Thank you,


<your name>
<your_e-mail_address>
```

Postings to the list should be sent to `ncc-gopher-news@gan.ncc.go.jp`.

National Institutes of Health GenoBase Server

Contents: Includes primary GenoBase index organized by genome and locus, a full-text GenBank search index, and other searchable indexes of GenBank data.

Access: WWW: `http://specter.dcrt.nih.gov:8004/`

Contact: e-mail: `rtaylor@alw.nih.gov`
                          Ronald Taylor
                          Building 12A, Room 2011
                          Division of Computer Research & Technology
                          National Institutes of Health
                          9000 Rockville Pike
                          Bethesda, MD 20892 USA
              voice: (301) 402-4064

NCBI
(National Center for Biotechnology Information)

Contents: Voluminous FTP and Gopher archives of databases and software tools for biotechnology. Specific databases currently stored include transcription factors, normalized gene designations, eukaryotic promoters, REBASE, SWISS-PROT, Enzyme Data Bank, SEQANALREF, tables of contents of molecular biology journals, *Drosophila* genetics (FlyBase), *Caenorhabditis elegans* database, expressed sequence tags, ECO2DBASE, pkinase, and The Reference Library DataBase.

Comments: The National Center for Biotechnology Information (NCBI) was created by an act of the U.S. Congress to support the development of biotechnology and medicine in the U.S. As mandated by this act, NCBI shall:

              1) create automated systems for knowledge about molecular biology, biochemistry, and genetics;

              2) perform research into advanced methods of analyzing and interpreting molecular biology data;

∎∎∎

(Continued)

           3) enable biotechnology researchers and medical care personnel to use the systems and methods developed; and

           4) coordinate efforts to gather biotechnology information worldwide

Access:	FTP host:	`ncbi.nlm.nih.gov`
	directory:	`/repository`
	filenames:	**(many or all)**

Most of the databases are in the repository directory. Be sure to obtain the README file for a current overview of its contents. There are many other directories of interest in this host and many useful software tools for practicing biotechnologists. For a complete overview, examine the ls-lR file in the root directory.

Contact:	e-mail:	`repository@ncbi.nlm.nih.gov`
		National Center for Biotechnology Information
		National Library of Medicine
		Building 38A
		National Institutes of Health
		8600 Rockville Pike
		Bethesda, MD 20894 USA
	voice:	(301) 496-2475

Online Mendelian Inheritance in Man (OMIM)

Contents:	Searchable version of the OMIM database with digests of articles on various genetic aspects of humans.	
Comments:	Access to the Genome Database (GDB) is also available at this menu.	
Access:	Gopher:	`gopher.gdb.org`
	menus:	`Genome Project/The Genome Database (GDB)`
	item:	`OMIM - Online Mendelian Inheritance in Man`
Contact:	e-mail:	`danj@mail.gdb.org`
		(Dan Jacobson - technical questions)
		`help@gdb.org` (questions about the database)
		OMIM User Support
		Online Mendelian Inheritance in Man
		Johns Hopkins University School of Medicine
		2024 E. Monument Street
		Baltimore, MD 21205 USA
	voice:	(410) 955-7058
	fax:	(410) 614-0434

PROSITE

Contents: Dictionary of protein sites and patterns.
Access: FTP host: `ncbi.nlm.nih.gov`
directory: `/repository/prosite`
filenames: `prosite.dat` (PROSITE data file)
`prosite.doc` (patterns documentation file)
`prosite.lis` (list of documentation chapters and patterns)

FTP host: `expasy.hcuge.ch`
directory: `/databases/prosite`
filenames: `prosite.dat` (PROSITE data file)
`prosite.doc` (patterns documentation file)
`prosite.lis` (list of documentation chapters and patterns)

Gopher: `ncbi.nlm.nih.gov`
menus: `repository/prosite/`
items: `prosite.dat` (PROSITE data file)
`prosite.doc` (patterns documentation file)

Contact: e-mail: `bairoch@cmu.unige.ch`
Amos Bairoch
Medical Biochemistry Department
Centre Medical Universitaire
University of Geneva
1, Rue Michel Servet
1211 Geneva 4 Switzerland
voice: +41 22 61 84 92
fax: +41 22 347 33 34
More Info: Bairoch, A. "PROSITE: A Dictionary of Sites and Patterns Proteins."
Nucleic Acids Research 20 (1992):2013-2018.

The handbook, user's manual, and options for obtaining PROSITE:

FTP host: **ncbi.nlm.nih.gov**
directory: `/repository/prosite`
filenames: `prosite.txt` (user's manual)
`prosite.prg` (list of programs that make use of PROSITE)
`prosite.get` (describes options for obtaining PROSITE)

■■■

(Continued)

FTP host:	`expasy.hcuge.ch`		
directory:	`/databases/prosite`		
filenames:	`prosite.txt`	(user's manual)	
	`prosite.prg`	(list of programs that make use of PROSITE)	
	`prosite.get`	(describes options for obtaining PROSITE)	
Gopher:	`ncbi.nlm.nih.gov`		
menus:	`repository/prosite/`		
items:	`prosite.txt`	(user's manual)	
	`prosite.prg`	(list of programs that make use of PROSITE)	
	`prosite.get`	(describes options for obtaining PROSITE)	

X SEQANALREF

Contents:	DNA sequence analysis bibliography containing 2,371 references and 1,193 abstracts.		
Access:	FTP host:	`ncbi.nlm.nih.gov`	
	directory:	`/repository/seqanalref`	
	filenames:	`seqanalr.dat`	(the bibliography)
		`seqanalr.abs`	(abstracts)
		`seqanalr.txt`	(help file)
	Gopher:	`ncbi.nlm.nih.gov`	
	menus:	`repository/seqanalref/`	
	items:	`seqanalr.dat`	(the bibliography)
		`seqanalr.abs`	(abstracts)
		`seqanalr.txt`	(help file)
Contact:	e-mail:	`bairoch@cmu.unige.ch`	
		Amos Bairoch	
		Medical Biochemistry Department	
		Centre Medical Universitaire	
		University of Geneva	
		1, Rue Michel Servet	
		1211 Geneva 4 Switzerland	
	voice:	+41 22 61 84 92	
	fax:	+41 22 347 33 34	
More Info:	Bairoch, A. "SEQANALREF: A Sequence Analysis Bibliographic Reference Data Bank." *CABIOS* 7 (1991): 268.1		

SWISS-PROT

Contents:	Protein sequence data bank containing 33,329 sequences and 32,314 references.
Comments:	Frequent updates; the ExPASy server includes graphical images of crystallized proteins along with GIF file viewers for Macintosh and Silicon Graphics computers (SGI).

Access:

FTP host:	`ncbi.nlm.nih.gov`	
directory:	`/repository/swiss-prot`	
filenames:	`userman.txt`	(user's manual)
	`shortdes.txt`	(short description of entries in SWISS-PROT)
	`sprot27.dat`	(SWISS-PROT data file)
	(many others)	
FTP host:	`expasy.hcuge.ch`	
directory:	`/databases/swiss-prot`	
filenames:	`userman.txt`	(user's manual)
	`shortdes.txt`	(short description of entries in SWISS-PROT)
	`sprot27.dat`	SWISS-PROT data file
	(many others)	
directory:	`/pub/Graphics`	(graphical image files)
filenames:	**(many others)**	
Gopher:	`ncbi.nlm.nih.gov 70`	
directory:	`repository/swiss-prot`	
items:	`userman.txt`	(user's manual)
	`shortdes.txt`	(short description of entries in SWISS-PROT)
	`sprot27.dat`	(SWISS-PROT data file)
	(many others)	
WWW:	`http://expasy.hcuge.ch`	

Contact:	e-mail: `bairoch@cmu.unige.ch`
	Amos Bairoch
	Medical Biochemistry Department
	Centre Medical Universitaire
	University of Geneva
	1, Rue Michel Servet
	1211 Geneva 4 Switzerland
	voice: +41 22 61 84 92
	fax: +41 22 347 33 34
More Info:	Bairoch, A., and B. Boeckmann. "The SWISS-PROTT Protein Sequence Databank." *Nucleic Acids Research* 20 (1991): 2019-2022.

X
The University of Washington, Pathology Department

Contents:	Standard idiogram albums of both human and mouse genomes. Files stored in both PostScript and GIF formats.
Comments:	From the README: "The Human set is based on the ISCN 1985 High Resolution Banding (ISCN 1985: An International System for Human Cytogenetic Nomenclature, Harden, D.G. and Klinger, H.P., eds., published in collaboration with Cytogenet. Cell Genet., Karger, Basel, 1985). Each human file contains idiograms for three resolutions of banding (400, 550, 850 total bands). The mouse set banding patterns are adapted from Nesbitt and Francke (Chromosoma 41:1 45-158, 1973) and Edward Evans' standard karyotype from Lyon & Searle 'Genetic variants & strains of the laboratory mouse' 2nd edition, OUP 1989.

"These files are provided for use by individuals only. Use for or by 'for profit' organizations is explicitly prohibited. You may not distribute the 'Albums'. 'Idiogram Album: Human' and 'Idiogram Album: Mouse' are copyrighted. You may copy the files for personal use only. You may use the files for research publication figures [and] meeting presentation slides."

Access:	Gopher:	`larry.pathology.washington.edu`
Contact:	e-mail:	`dadler@u.washington.edu`
		David Adler
		University of Washington
		Pathology SM-30
		Seattle, WA 98195 USA
	voice:	(206) 543-0716
	fax:	(206) 543-3644

LISTSERVs in Genetics and Molecular Biology

This list of lists is an extracted, revised version of the list compiled by Lee Hancock in *Internet/Bitnet Health Sciences Resources* and Una R. Smith's *A Biologist's Guide to Internet Resources*. To subscribe to a LISTSERV list, send the following message:

```
mail:      listserv@<host.address>
subject:   (none needed)
message:   subscribe <listname> <Your-name>
```

For more information on any LISTSERV list, send the following e-mail message:

```
mail:      listserv@<host.address>
subject:   (none needed)
message:   rev <listname>
```

This message issues the "review" command. The LISTSERV will respond by sending you a copy of the list "header" which should include a short description of the list. You may also receive a listing of the current subscribers to the list.

Although Internet addresses have been provided for most of the BITNET nodes, a few do not have them. In these cases, you will need to send your mail through a BITNET gateway if your own site does not support the ".BITNET" extension. (For more information on gateways, see Chapter 5.)

LISTSERVs in Genetics and Molecular Biology

Listname	Address	Topical Area
BIOTECH	UMDD.UMD.EDU	Biotechnology
EBCBBUL	HDETUD1. TUDELFT.NL	Computers in Biotechnology, Research, and Education
EBCBCAT	HDETUD1. TUDELFT.NL	Catalog of biotechnology software.
EMBINFO	IBACSATA. BITNET	EMBNet (European Molecular Biology Network)
FORUMBIO	SCF.FUNDP.AC.BE	Forum on Molecular Biology
RBMI	FRORS13. BITNET	Molecular Biology Research Group
GSA	IUBVM.UCS. INDIANA.EDU	Genetic Stock Administrators
MOLBIO-L	MIZZOU1. MISSOURI.EDU	Molecular Biology

Other Types of Lists in Medicine

Other types of lists in Medicine

Listname	Address	Topical Area
GENSTAT	LISTRAL@IB.RL.AC.UK	Genstat statistics package. (Subscription request: "subscribe genstat <your name>" as the first line of the message.)

Usenet Newsgroups in Genetics and Molecular Biology

General Biology-Related Newsgroups

General Biology-Related Newsgroups

Newsgroup	Topics
`sci.bio`	Biology and related sciences.
`sci.bio.technology`	Technology in Biology
`sci.engr.biomed`	Biomedical Engineering
`sci.engr.chem`	Chemical Engineering

Bionet Newsgroups

Unlike most Usenet newsgroups, the bionet newsgroups are all gatewayed to mailing lists. David Kristofferson is responsible for maintaining the mailing lists, as well as proposing the creation of the bionet domain of Usenet and starting many of the bionet newsgroups. Requests for e-mail subscriptions to bionet newsgroups should be sent to `biosci@net.bio.net` (for requests from the Americas) and `biosci@daresbury.ac.uk` (for all others). Bionet newsgroups are intended as a forum for professional discussions by biological researchers. This service is funded by the U.S. National Science Foundation.

There is a BIOSCI Information Sheet and a BIOSCI Newsgroups FAQ which provide details on the BIOSCI program and how to participate in BIOSCI forums. Both documents (as well as bioscience newsgroup archives) are available via anonymous FTP and gopher:

FTP host:	`net.bio.net`
directory:	`/pub/BIOSCI/doc`
filenames:	`biosci-us.infosheet`
	`biosci-uk.infosheet`
	`biosci.FAQ`
Gopher:	`net.bio.net`
menu:	`FAQs and Other`
	`Documents/`
items:	`(many or all)`

These documents (as well as infosheets for other parts of the world) may also be requested by e-mail to `biosci-help@net.bio.net` (use plain English–this is not a mail server address). The FAQ is also posted the first of each month to the bionet.announce newsgroup along with the BIOSCI information sheet and the list of changes to the newsgroups during the preceding month.

Bionet Newsgroups

Newsgroup	Topics
bionet.announce	Bionet Announcements
bionet.cellbio	Cell Biology
bionet.general	General BIOSCI discussion.
bionet.genome.chrom22	Chromosome 22
bionet.journals. contents	Biology Journals Contents
bionet.journals.note	Publication issues in biology.
bionet.immunology	Immunology research.
bionet.metabolic-reg	Metabolic regulation and thermodynamics.
bionet.molbio.ageing	Cellular and organismal aging.
bionet.molbio.bio-matrix	Computer applications to biological databases.
bionet.molbio.embldatabank	EMBL nucleic acid database.
bionet.molbio.evolution	Evolution, especially molecular.
bionet.molbio.gdb	GDB Database
bionet.molbio.genbank	Discussion with GenBank Nucleic Acid Sequence Database staff.
bionet.molbio.genbank.updates	GenBank Updates (moderated)
bionet.molbio.gene-linkage	Genetic linkage analysis.
bionet.molbio.genome-program	Human Genome Project tissues.
bionet.molbio.hiv	Molecular biology of HIV.
bionet.molbio.methds-reagnts	Laboratory methods and reagents.
bionet.molbio.proteins	Research on proteins and protein databases.
bionet.molbio.rapd	Randomly Amplified Polymorphic DNA
bionet.neuroscience	Research issues in the neurosciences.
bionet.sci-resources	Information about funding agencies.

Bionet Newsgroups (Continued)

Newsgroup	Topics
`bionet.virology`	Research in Virology
`bionet.xtallography`	Protein Crystallography

EMBNet Newsgroups

The European Molecular Biology Network (EMBNet) has established a number of newsgroups that are only distributed in Europe. E-mail subscriptions are available from nethelp@embl-heidelberg.de. General questions about EMBNet newsgroups can be sent to embnet@comp.bioz.unibas. The newsgroups can also be read via Gopher:

Gopher: `nic.switch.ch`

EMBNet Newsgroups

Newsgroup	Topic
`embnet.general`	General EMBNet discussion.
`embnet.net-dev`	EMBNet Development
`embnet.rpc`	Technical discussion of data transfers.

FOR MORE INFORMATION

Mailing Lists

Lee Hancock has founded a discussion list concerning online health science resources. The intent of the list is to share location and access information as well as guidance on the use of particular resources. To subscribe, send the following e-mail message:

```
mail:      listserv@ukanaix.cc.ukans.edu
subject:   (none needed)
message:   subscribe HMATRIX-L <Your-name>
```

The archives of the list are available via Gopher:

Gopher:	selway.umt.edu 700
menu:	Internet Health-related Resources/Usenet News & Electronic Mail Discussion Groups on Health Issues
item:	HMATRIX-L: Discussion of Electronic Health Resources

Online Resources

Hancock, Lee. *Internet/Bitnet Health Sciences Resources.*

FTP host:	ftp.sura.net	
directory:	/pub/nicfilename:medical .resources.MM-YY	(where MM-YY indicate the month and year of the last update)
Telnet (WWW):	ukanaix.cc.ukans.edu	(use VT100 emulation)
login:	kufacts	
select:	Reference Shelf/ Internet Health Science Resources	(use cursor controls to move through the screen; press "?" for help)
Gopher:	sluava.slu.edu	(St. Louis University)
menu:	Library Services/SLU Health Sciences Center Library/Health Sciences Center Library/Guides to Internet Resources	
item:	Lee Hancock's Health Sciences Resources (Hancock List)	

Smith, Una R. *A Biologists Guide to Internet Resources. 1993-*

Usenet:	sci.answers	
Gopher:	sunsite.unc.edu	
menus:	Worlds of SunSITE -- by Subject/Ecology and Evolution	
item:	A Biologist's Guide to Internet Resources (Read me online)/	(Designed for reading online)
	A Biologist's Guide to Internet Resources (Retrieve me).	(A single file to mail or download)

```
(Continued)
FTP host:      rtfm.mit.edu
directory:     /pub/usenet/news.
               answers/biology/guide
items:         part1
               part2
               part3
               part4
               part5
               part6
```
Mail server: (File sent as six messages)

```
mail:      mail-server@rtfm.mit.edu
subject:   (none needed)
message:   send usenet/news.answers/biology/guide/*
```

Biology Servers is an online list of biology WWW and Gopher servers compiled and updated by the United States Geological Survey.

WWW: `http://info.er.usgs.gov/network/science/biology/index.html`

Medical Oriented Gophers.

```
Gopher:   sluava.slu.edu          (St. Louis University)
menus:    Library Services/SLU
          Health Sciences
          Center
          Library/Health
          Sciences Center
          Library/
item:     Medical Oriented
          Gophers
```

Bibliography

Anthes, G.H. "A Step Beyond a Database: Johns Hopkins' Networked Databases Benefit Genetic Research." *Computerworld* 25(9) (March 4, 1991):28.

Broering, N.C. "Georgetown University: the Virtual Medical Library." *Computers in Libraries* 13(2) (February 1993):13.

Martin, N.J., T. Primich, and R.A. Riley. "Accessing Genetics Databases." *Database* 17(1) (February 1994):51-58.

McKinney, W.P. and G. Bunton. "Exploring the Medical Applications of the Internet - A Guide for Beginning Users." *American Journal of the Medical Sciences* 306(3) (September 1993):141-144.

Smith, J.M. and K. Power. "Task Force Mulls Health Data Sharing." *Government Computer News* 12(8) (April 12, 1993):1, 120.

CHAPTER

25

Using
Supercomputers

One of the original purposes of many parts of the Internet within the U.S. (particularly NSFNET) was to provide researchers easy access to supercomputing resources at a number of centralized supercomputer sites. This chapter provides an introduction to the basic principles of supercomputer use and includes detailed site descriptions for a number of the NSF-sponsored supercomputer facilities accessible through the Internet.

SUPERCOMPUTERS: GROWTH AND FUTURE

One of the most amazing phenomena of recent times has been the growth of the computer industry from a laboratory curiosity at the end of World War II to a major player in the economies of the world today, followed by rapid penetration into nearly all areas of life. The growth has been accomplished through extraordinary reductions in size and cost, and improvements in speed, reliability, and usability.

Not long ago a new class of computers has emerged: supercomputers. By one definition supercomputers are "At any given time, that class of general-purpose computers that are both faster than their commercial competitors and have sufficient central memory to store the problem sets for which they are designed" [1]. By this definition, it might appear that supercomputers have been with us from the start, and differ only quantitatively from other computers. In fact, supercomputers are qualitatively different in that they employ different architectures which result in major differences in programming and use.

According to the report "A National Computing Initiative" [2] the American research community will require a thousandfold increase in computational power over the next few years. This growth is propelled by factors which are likely to exist for a long time to come.

One reason is the dramatic change in international economic competition. Since World War II many countries, especially in Eastern Asia, have entered into the economic mainstream armed with a powerful combination of Western technology and indigenous cultural backgrounds. These countries are redefining many economic and industrial roles and are putting severe pressure on the American economy. Technological innovation, especially in leading-edge fields such as computers, is viewed as a major way to help our competitive stature.

Another reason is that computers are assuming new roles. Computation is now recognized as the third mode of science, coequal with theory and laboratory research [2]. Simulation of complex real world phenomena is increasingly possible and indeed necessary for future advance: investigations of very large (galaxies), very small (electron orbits), very fast, very slow, very complex, dangerous, or highly energetic phenomena are often possible only through simulation. Computers can also provide "impossible views" of objects under conditions which can never be obtained physically.

Finally, human activities are causing changes in the natural world: developments such as pollution, the destruction of rain forests, ozone depletion, and the greenhouse effect, require extensive monitoring and modeling which would be impossible without the computational and data management capabilities of supercomputers.

Supercomputers—Always a Need

The enormous progress in computer hardware will result in a "desk-top-CRAY" in the near future. With such powerful personal computers will we still need supercomputers? The answer appears to be yes. However powerful PC's become, there will always be problems which strain the leading edge of whatever computational powers we develop. The objects of study of disciplines such as mathematics (especially combinatorial problems), and the physical, biological and social sciences are infinitely complex, and computer simulations can never exhaust analytical possibilities. Many simulations today scrape by with the coarsest possible resolution in the hope that important details are not neglected. Increased resolution can come only at great computational cost: for example, a tenfold increase in spatial resolution in each of 3 dimensions translates into a thousand-fold increase in computational operations. Naturally, many-dimensional problems would require much greater increases. The combined requirements of computational power, data storage, and data flow should insure the continued need for supercomputer sites.

Supercomputer Sites

By their very nature, supercomputers are expensive and require extensive hardware, software, documentation, and personnel support in order to function. Vast computational performance must be matched by massive data storage capacities, large data flows, high resolution output devices, an extensive communications interface, as well as a wealth of software applications, libraries, documentation, and expert consulting.

A number of supercomputer sites are currently promoted as national research centers. They are focal points for the collection and distribution of software, documentation, and extensive sets of examples; for training programs, seminars, and symposiums for high-performance graphics laboratories for visualization; and communication facilities in the form of e-mail, lists, and bulletin boards for specialized user groups.

The wealth of different services available at supercomputer sites implies that you should shop carefully in order to locate a site which best matches your needs. The types of software (editors, languages, packages, and operating systems), hardware (memory size and structure, vector and parallel hardware), and services (graphic output, type of consulting) affect the appropriateness of a site to your intended uses. For example, some systems couple high performance vectorization with somewhat limited memories, others feature very large memories with limited vectorization capabilities, whereas others specialize in massively parallel systems.

The National MetaCenter for Computational Science and Engineering

The National MetaCenter for Computational Science and Engineering is a cooperative effort between the supercomputer centers funded by the National Science Foundation. Researchers use the diverse high performance and scalable parallel architectures available at the centers to attack Grand Challenge problems. Grand Challenge problems are those that deal with the interaction of large systems, such as the earth's oceanic and surface biospheres. MetaCenter proposals are reviewed by a joint panel, the MetaCenter Allocation Committee (MAC). The MAC meets annually and provides allocations across all NSF supercomputing centers.

The NSF Backbone

Supercomputers were born in the U.S. but were generally unavailable to university scientists because of their high costs. Some American scientists actually went to Europe to obtain time on U.S.-built supercomputers. Recognizing the importance of computing access, the NSF established five supercomputer centers across the nation in 1984. Time on these machines is obtained mainly through several grant mechanisms and is otherwise free of charge.

The NSF also helped establish a communications network, called the NSF backbone, which connects these centers and links them to regional networks.

Originally, the centers were deliberately designed to differ from one another in order to make more options available to researchers, and to test out a variety of novel machine architectures, operating systems, and support strategies under real-life conditions. Recently, however, the systems have converged around several models of CRAY computers and the new massively parallel Connection Machines, mostly running slight variants of Unix.

SUPERCOMPUTER HARDWARE

Supercomputers are not just big, fast machines that use state-of-the-art hardware; they also feature special architectures. While these architectures can greatly boost performance, their full power can only be exploited under certain conditions and often require that the program and/or problem itself be restructured by someone who understands how these architectures function.

The most common supercomputer architectures include special memory organization, such as independent memory banks in the CRAYs, vector hardware (also called pipeline hardware) present in nearly all supercomputers, and parallel hardware, usually in the form of multiple processors. All of these features have recently started to appear on non-supercomputers, but their implementation and support are especially well developed on supercomputers.

Cache Memories

For a given price, memory can either be big and slow or small and fast. A cache is a small and very fast memory which serves as a buffer to a large slow memory; therefore, cache memories can, under certain conditions, improve overall performance by reducing the time to access main memory. When an operand is fetched from main memory, both it and a number of its nearest neighbors are placed in the high speed cache. If the next reference is to a neighbor, it will be taken from the cache instead of the main memory. If memory usage in the program tends to be highly clustered, then the program operates mainly out of the cache and performance increases greatly. On the other hand, if memory usage is highly scattered, then the cache memory can actually degrade performance.

Independent Memory Banks

Independent memory banks are another method for speeding memory access and storage. A reference to a given bank of memory cells ties up the bank for a number of machine cycles, and no further access is possible until the bank is free. Some computers arrange memory into a number (64 on the CRAY) of independent banks so that most memory references address different banks and do not interfere with one another.

Typically the banks are arranged so that adjacent words, such as X(1), X(2), X(3), reside in different banks. For example, the loop

```
DO 10 I=1,N
```

runs faster with an independent memory bank architecture since the storage times for X(1), X(2), X(3), X(4) etc., are overlapped. However, array structures or patterns of array access which are discordant with the memory architecture can defeat the architecture and slow execution considerably. For example, on a 64 bank memory the code

```
       DIMENSION X(64,50)
       DO 10 J = 1,50
10     X(1,J) = 0.0
```

would nail the same bank each and every time through the "J" loop, since X(1,1), X(1,2), X(1,3) etc. reside in the same bank. In this case the problem can easily be solved by redimensioning X as X(65,50) in order to change the memory layout.

Vector Hardware

Vector hardware is currently the most widespread and mature of the special architectures found in supercomputers. Vector units consist of CPU components such as add or multiply units which are divided into a number of sequential stages or segments. The units typically accept two vectors of numbers which proceed through the segments and

■■■

emerge out the other end as a vector of results. As long as the vectors continue to flow, the process is efficient, and speedups by a factor of 5 or 10 are not uncommon, but starting and stopping the units for short vectors can actually increase execution time. Efficient vector operation often requires some restructuring of code by the programmer as well as the use of compiler directives to monitor and control the process. A more complete description of vector operations appears later in this chapter.

Parallel Hardware

Parallel architecture distributes the processing of a single program over a number of different physical processing units. It offers the greatest potential for vast increases in performance of any known architectural layout. For example, a machine with 10,000 processors might solve some problems almost 10,000 times more quickly than a single processor machine. However, most programs cannot be partitioned so completely into independent units, and many difficult hardware and software issues remain unsolved and are the subject of intense research. At present, limited parallelism can be exploited on the CRAYs, and massive parallelism is possible with the Connection Machine. The effort needed to restructure code ranges from about the same as for vectorization to considerably more. A more complete description of parallel operations appears later in this chapter.

Impact on Debugging and Graphics

Supercomputers are so powerful and generate such vast amounts of information that they force major changes in both debugging techniques and in the presentation of output. Ad hoc debugging techniques are woefully inadequate for dealing with, say, an error in the 471,000-th iteration of a 500 variable program operating on 18 million separate values. Special debugging software is required which lets you examine values, restart code at various points, observe the effects of changes in values, run controlled experiments, etc.

Similarly, traditional printed and even standard graphical output is often inadequate to represent the millions or even billions of separate data values that can be provided by a supercomputer run. The term "visualization" is used to describe the sets of advanced graphical techniques which address this problem. Visualization often involves high resolution displays, extensive use of color, 3D representations, and extensive interactive control of the image in order to control the viewing angle, collapse dimensions in a multi-dimensional data set, or perform image processing functions in order to extract or highlight desired information. Existing graphics packages are often insufficient for the task as they emphasize the display of 2- and 3-dimensional XY, XYZ, or contour plots, whereas the representations of complex simulated phenomena require some combination of image processing approaches along with more standard graphic techniques. In addition, graphics rendering, especially when combined with real time interaction, can place severe demands on data transmission paths.

Other Hardware Issues

Other hardware issues include memory size and use of high speed peripherals, such as the Solid State Disk (SSD) available on some CRAYs.

The hardware available at different supercomputer sites should be a major consideration in your selection. For example, a CRAY Y-MP is extremely good for highly optimized vector operations, but is somewhat limited in terms of memory, and a Connection Machine is much superior for highly parallel problems.

Supercomputer Software

Supercomputer sites are often endowed with a rich collection of applications software in the areas of chemistry, physics, engineering, mathematics, and graphics. Computer languages, however, are confined mainly to FORTRAN, Pascal, and C, and FORTRAN is often the only language that is extensively optimized for vector/parallel operations at all sites.

Operating Systems

While the early sites featured a variety of operating systems, most have converted to variants of Unix (UNICOS on the CRAYs and ULTRIX on some front ends).

Workstation Support

Some sites provide extensive support for workstation and PC software to be used in conjunction with the supercomputer or its front end. NCSA at Illinois, for example, provides free downloadable graphics and communications software for PCs, SUNs, and Macintoshes.

Software is probably the single most important consideration in site selection. Unfamiliar languages or editors can greatly increase learning time; programs, data files, and data formats may have to be restructured to move to a particular environment, and future portability must be kept in mind; non-FORTRAN programs may have to be rewritten or run in a non- or sub-optimized mode; and major applications programs, libraries, or graphics libraries may be unavailable or at different revision levels.

Supercomputer Performance Gains

Despite the many "fringe" benefits of supercomputer sites, such as access to software, training, graphics, and collaborative research, the main purpose in using supercomputers is to exploit their size and speed in order to handle otherwise intractable problems. The performance of supercomputers is due mainly to two factors.

- Supercomputers are generally big, fast machines which employ high performance technology. As a result, all computer programs automatically benefit.
- Hardware architectures, such as cache memory, independent banks, instruction stacks, high speed I/O, vector, and parallel operations which, although not unique to supercomputers, are usually more highly developed. The exploitation of these features is partly automatic but can also benefit significantly from modifications by the programmer.

Vector and parallel architectures are most often emphasized in optimization, but attention to the other architectures mentioned above can bring about major performance gains as well. One should also note that (a) extensive optimization should only be done in conjunction with special timing tools which locate those portions of the program which can benefit most, and (b) optimization should only be carried to a certain degree—smarter compilers in the near future will be able to optimize well structured code much better than the "spaghetti" code that often results from overzealous hand optimization.

PERFORMANCE GAINS THROUGH SPECIALIZED HARDWARE

The most significant performance gains are obtainable through vector processing and parallel processing hardware.

Vector Processing

Vector processing can best be explained through analogy. Imagine a factory that assembles 6-bladed airplane propellers. It has 6 people, p1 through p6, at 6 workstations who attach each blade in turn to the hub. Person p1 receives a tray with the parts and assembles the first blade to the hub. When done, he passes the tray along with his partial assembly to p2. P2 attaches the 2nd blade and when done passes the tray and his partial assembly to p3, and so on.

Of course, when p1 has passed his partial assembly to p2 he does not just quit for the day. Instead he immediately gets a new tray and starts a new assembly. Similarly, p2 no sooner finishes his assembly when he gets the tray and the partial assembly from p1 and begins attaching the second blade.

After 6 time periods, the pipeline is filled with 6 different stages of assembly. The important point to note is that while it still takes 6 time periods to assemble any given propeller, a new finished propeller emerges from the assembly pipeline each and every time period. We have speeded up the assembly process by a factor of 6 by using 6 people in a quasi-parallel manner. Note that even if a product required 10,000 stages to assemble, the products would still emerge at the rate of 1 per time period. In other words, production speed is independent of the complexity or length of the assembly process. On the other hand, if the pipeline is interrupted for any reason, a very long pipeline (or assembly process) will take much longer to restart than a short one.

In supercomputers, the vector or pipeline process is usually applied to arithmetic units, such as add, multiply, or divide units which "assemble" new numbers from the vectors of input numbers.

For example, a multiply unit on the CRAY contains 7 stages. The FORTRAN code

```
DO 10 I = 1,60
10  C(I) = A(I)*B(I)
```

is converted to vector instructions which start loading the vectors A(1), A(2),... and B(1), B(2),... into special vector registers. As soon as the first pair is available, A(1) and B(1) enter the multiply unit to begin the first stage of multiplication.

At the end of one clock cycle, the partial multiplication of A(1)*B(1) moves to the 2nd stage in the multiply unit, and A(2), B(2) enter stage 1; at the end of the 2nd cycle, A(1)*B(1) moves to stage 3, A(2)*B(2) moves to stage 2, and A(3), B(3) enter stage 1. This process continues and at cycle 7 all seven stages are being utilized, the fully multiplied value of A(1)*B(1) emerges and is stored in C(1), and A(8), B(8) get ready to enter stage 1. From then on, a new multiply is finished every clock cycle, even though it takes 7 cycles to complete one multiply. We have increased the speed almost by a factor of 7 (except for initiating the pipeline).

Vectorization only applies to explicit DO-loops in FORTRAN and their equivalents in other languages. Only one loop within a nest of loops can be vectorized, but the software automatically selects the loop unless that choice is overridden by directives from the programmer.

There exist many obstacles to vectorization, some of which are easily overcome (for example, changing the order of statements), some which require use of compiler directives to modify the vectorization process, and some which require major restructuring of the code. On high performance vector machines, such as the CRAY, speedups of a factor of 5 or 10 for that portion of the code that can be vectorized are not uncommon.

Parallel Processing

The basic idea of parallel processing is easier to grasp than vector processing, but the usage, implementation, and many of the concepts are more difficult. On the other hand, the rewards may be much greater since the potential speedup is proportional to the number of processors available, whereas vector speedup can never be much more than a factor of 10.

Parallel systems distribute the work of a program or subroutine among a number of processors. In some implementations, such as CRAY Macrotasking, the number and operation of parallel processors must be predetermined; in other implementations, such as CRAY Microtasking, the number, identity, or order of execution of the processors is unknown and variable (this has many consequences which influence the structure of a parallel program and hence the modifications needed to convert an existing program to parallel operation). Most of the following discussion applies to CRAY Microtasking.

Some of the concepts of parallel processing are illustrated by the execution profile of subroutine ABC.

SUBROUTINE ABC

(Block B1)   a block of code executed by one processor

(Block B2)   another block executed by a processor

(Block B3)   another block executed by a processor

RETURN

END

The subroutine is entered at the top under the control of a single processor, after which control is transferred to one, two, or three other processors for blocks B1, B2, and B3. When all of the blocks are finished, control is returned to a single processor which terminates the subroutine. The execution profile might look like this:

Time	Processor 1	Processor 6	Processor 4
1	Start ABC	x	x
2	Run B2	Run B1	Run B3
3	x	x	Exit ABC

where "x" means the processor is idle or engaged with another program. The profile is generally unpredictable and the actual number and identity of processors depends on many factors. Because of this unpredictability, the parallel operation is often referred to as a "fray."

A DO-loop is a special case of the above structure:

SUBROUTINE ABC

DO 10 I = 1,3   (the i-th iteration of the loop is block B(i))

10   CONTINUE

RETURN

END

in which some iterations of the loop may be handled by different processors.

Some obvious and not-so-obvious consequences derive from such an implementation. The different code blocks must be totally independent of the sequence in which they are processed: Block 3, for example, cannot depend on the results of, say, Block 1. It is less obvious that local variables assigned values inside a block can have no validity outside the block, that values associated with loop iterations must be explicitly tied to the loop index, and that global variables which are not indexed by a loop index must be "guarded" from simultaneous access. Consider the following section of code:

```
K = 0
DO 10 I = 1, 1000
K = K + 1
10  CONTINUE
```

The operation of the above loop depends on whether K is local or global. Local variables in a parallel block of code are replicated for each processor that joins in the "fray" whereas global variables occupy a single location which is accessed by all processors.

Suppose that K is a local variable and the 1000 iterations of the loop are randomly distributed among, say, 64 processors. Then processor 17 might handle 23 iterations of the loop, processor 39 might handle 11 iterations, and so on. At the end of the loop, if control is assigned solely to processor 17 then K=23, if assigned to processor 39 then K=11, whereas in a nonparallel environment K always equals 1000.

Inside the loop, if K is used as a substitute for the loop index, then its value depends only on how many times that processor has handled the loop and so will generally have little relation to the value of the loop index itself. Thus A(K) rarely is the same as A(I), whereas in a nonparallel environment it is always so.

If K is a global variable then it must be guarded from simultaneous access by more than 1 processor. For example, suppose that K=0 and processors 13 and 19 begin execution of RK=K+1S at slightly different times. If 19 accesses the expression before 13 has finished, then K will be reset to 1 instead of being set to 2 as it should be.

This type of code is called a "critical section" and must be guarded by explicit directives which guarantee that another processor can only enter that section of code when the current processor has finished.

Parallel and vector processing are quite compatible and can be used not only in the same program but often in the same nest of loops. For example, some compilers analyze a DO-loop nest and select one loop for vectorization and another for parallel processing. On the CRAY, a single loop can be partitioned into vectorized and parallelized sections.

Interaction with Optimizing Compilers

The goal of an optimizing compiler is to speed the execution of a program without changing the results. It scans the user's source code and identifies structures which can utilize the special hardware found in supercomputers. Since the conditions under which these structures can be safely optimized are very limited, it must analyze much of the surrounding code to determine if, and to what degree, the code can be optimized.

The compiler is subject to several important constraints which limit its effectiveness. Since the optimization is done at compile time, it can have no knowledge of the run-time structure of the job. Thus, input data values which may change the flow of execution and the degree of optimization cannot be considered, so the compiler has to assume the worst case and do the least amount of optimization. Another constraint is that optimization is often limited to the scope of a single routine, and interactions between routines which might affect optimization cannot be taken into account. In addition, the technology of optimizing compilers is continually advancing, and any given compiler may be unable to optimize code which later versions can handle.

Because of these limitations it is often necessary for the programmer to supply auxiliary information which eliminates ambiguity and resolves problems which the compiler cannot handle. This is especially important in parallel processing, but is also often required in vectorization. The programmer supplies global directives on the compile statement or embeds local directives in the source code, or both, which guide the optimization process. For example, the following loop would be rejected by any vectorizing FORTRAN because of a "recurrence" relation in the loop:

```
      K = IVAL
      DO 10 I = 1,N
10    A(I) = A(I-K) + 1.0
```

While recurrence and other inhibitors of vectorization are beyond the scope of this report (see [4] and [5] for more information), the above code can be vectorized on a CRAY provided that (a) K is negative, or (b) K is greater than 64. If the programmer knows this he can insert compiler directives which force the compiler to vectorize. Thus the code

```
      CDIR$ IVDEP          ("ignore vector dependency")
      DO 10 I = 1,N
10    A(I) = A(I-K) + 1.0
```

in effect, tells the compiler that "I know more than you, so forget your inhibitions and vectorize anyway."

Parallel optimization usually requires more embedded directives than vectorization. It is frequently necessary to explicitly prevent multiple processors from accessing code until all processors have finished operating on a previous section. For example, the CRAY compiler directives

```
CMIC$ DO GLOBAL
      DO 10 J = 1,N      (operation on the J-th column of A)
10    CONTINUE
      CMIC$ DO GLOBAL
      DO 20 I = 1,M      (operation on the I-th row of A)
20    CONTINUE
```

would distribute the operations of the N columns of A and the M rows of A to different processors, but would assure that all columns were finished before any rows were processed. The directives are signaled by "CMIC$" (for Microtasking) in columns 1-5 and apply to the next DO-loop. Thus the start of the second "CMIC$" terminates the first "CMIC$" and tells the compiler that the two loops are to be processed in sequence.

MIGRATING PROGRAMS TO SUPERCOMPUTERS

The main point in using supercomputers is to achieve dramatic increases in processing speeds. The increases are partially due to the fact that supercomputers are simply big and fast computers, but much of the increase comes from the special architectures that supercomputers employ. Achieving a high degree of optimization on supercomputers requires a well thought-out strategy as well as realistic expectations as to what can actually be achieved.

The maximum gains that can be obtained through parallel processing or vectorization are controlled by "Amdahl's" law [1]: $P = 1/(1-X+X/a)$ where P is the performance gain, X is that ratio of the code which can be optimized (vectorized or processed in parallel), and "a" is the speedup ratio for vector or parallel code. The important part of the law is that the performance is much more controlled by X, the proportion of the code that can be optimized, than by "a." For example, suppose that $X = 0.80$, so that 80% of the code can be vectorized or processed in parallel. Then the absolute maximum speedup possible is a factor of 5, even if vector or parallel operations are infinitely fast (that is, even if "a" is infinity, then $P = 1/(1-0.8 + 0.8/\text{infinity}) = 1/(0.2) = 5$).

Note that it is rare for X to exceed 0.8 (factor of 5 speedup) for vector processing applications, whereas X may often exceed 0.99 (factor of 100 speedup) for parallel processing applications.

The first step in migrating code to a supercomputer (after making any adjustments to insure that the FORTRAN code will actually compile and run), is to instrument the program in order to identify "hotspots," that is, code which is extremely CPU intensive. A good candidate program for optimization should have an execution profile such that nearly all of the CPU time is spent in just a few percent of the code. (If the execution profile is fairly uniform, then hand optimization may be a waste of time.) Most supercomputer sites provide easily used compiler directives or other tools which will show you a histogram of CPU time spent versus source code.

If the program has identifiable hotspots, the next step is to read and understand the compiler messages which identify obstacles to optimization. Some compilers provide an in depth analysis of each loop, which identifies not only the obstacles to vectorization, but also the results of an "economic" analysis to determine which loop in a nest of loops yields the best results.

At this point you should analyze the loops highlighted by the compiler to see if any can be replaced by routines from existing optimized libraries. Many such routines are coded in assembly language and are optimized to a very high degree. After this, you should attempt to remove inhibitors to optimization by making local modifications to loops. In many cases this can be done simply by reordering statements, splitting loops, or adding compiler directives. For example, the loops on the left will not vectorize, while the loops on the right (which produce exactly the same results) will:

```
      DO 10 I=2,N             DO 10 I=2,N
      B(I) = A(I-1)           A(I)=C(I)
10    A(I) = C(I)        10   B(I) = A(I-1)


      DO 10 I=1,N             DO 10 J=1,N
      DO 10 J=1,N             DO 10 I=1,N
10    A(I,J)=A(I,J-1)*B(I,J)  10  A(I,J)=A(I,J-1)*B(I,J)
```

In the above examples, a recurrence relation existed which prevented vectorization. In the following example, the recurrence relation could not be avoided for one expression, but by splitting the loop into two parts, one of the two expressions on the right can be vectorized:

```
      DO 10 I=1,60            DO 10 I=1,60
      A(I)=B(I)*C(I)     10   A(I)=B(I)*C(I)
10    D(I)=D(I-1)*E(I)   20   D(I)=D(I-1)*E(I)
```

When these steps have been taken, further optimization can be achieved by paying careful attention to memory layout or by restructuring the program to obtain the best match between program structure and the architecture of the machine. The latter is, of course, a very time consuming operation and should only be undertaken when the benefits and the costs are fully considered.

SUPERCOMPUTER ACCESS

Resources on all of the NSF sites and some of the other sites are mainly allocated on the basis of grants, rather than by money. Three main grant types are commonly available.

* Large allocations which are subject to formal peer review boards which meet at scheduled times during the year. These boards are comprised of personnel which may be from the site, jointly from several sites, or from NSF.

* Small allocations for startup or familiarization purposes. These are usually available at any time throughout a year.

* Block grants awarded to universities. The universities allocate sub-blocks of time through their own review boards.

■■■

SUPERCOMPUTER REFERENCES

■■■

[1]   "Supercomputing: An Informal Glossary of Terms." IEEE Washington Office, 1111 Nineteenth Street, NW, Washington, D.C. 20036. 1987.

[2]   H.J. Raveche, D.H. Lawrie, and A. Despain. "A National Computing Initiative—An Agenda for Leadership." Society of Industrial and Applied Mathematics, 1400 Architects Building, 117 So. 17th Street, Philadelphia, PA, 19103-5052. 1987.

[3]   N.P. Smith. "Of Supers and Minisupers." *Computer Graphics World*, August 1988.

[4]   H.M. Doerr and F. Verdier. "Improving Vector Performance" and "Introduction to Vectorization." Cornell National Supercomputer Facility, Cornell University, Ithaca, New York. September 1987.

[5]   D.D. Soll. "Vectorization and Vector Migration Techniques." *IBM Technical Bulletin*, SR20-4966-0.

SUPERCOMPUTER SITE DESCRIPTIONS

■■■

The remainder of this chapter provides detailed information about a number of supercomputer sites in the U.S. The purpose of these site descriptions is to allow you to do some preliminary comparisons of each site's hardware, software, and training programs so you can select the supercomputer site which would be most appropriate for your particular research needs.

All of these site descriptions were reviewed or contributed to by representatives of each site's user services staff in February and March of 1994. We'd like to thank the following individuals for their participation:

Supercomputer Site	Reviewed By
Cornell Theory Center	Dan Dwyer
National Center for Atmospheric Research	Juliana Rew
National Center for Supercomputer Applications (NCSA)	Jarrett S. Cohen
National Energy Research Supercomputer Center	Emily Yim
Ohio Supercomputer Center	Frankie Harris
Pittsburgh Supercomputer Center	Deb Nigra
San Diego Supercomputer Center	Andrea Alvarado

■■■

CORNELL THEORY CENTER (CTC)

■■■

Hardware

IBM ES/9000-900
- 6 processors each with a peak performance of 444 Mflops
- 2.66 Gflops peak aggregate performance
- 9 Gbytes shared memory
- Each user process may access up to 2 Gbytes virtual memory
- 250 Gbytes disk space
- Parallelism through shared memory

Kendall Square Research KSR1
- 128 processors each with a peak performance of 40 Mflops
- 5.12 Gflops peak aggregate performance
- 32 Mbytes local processor memory (cache)
- 4 Gbytes shared memory
- 1000 Gbyte address space per processor
- 50 Gbytes disk space
- Parallelism through ALLCACHE

IBM PVS
- 32 processors each with a peak performance of 78 Mflops
- 2.50 Gflops aggregate performance
- 16 Mbytes local processor memory
- 0.5 Gbytes shared memory
- 32 Mbytes address space per processor
- 22.2 Gbytes disk space
- Parallelism through shared memory

Parallel RS/6000 Cluster
- 12 processors with a peak performance of 84 Mflops
- 1.01 Gflops aggregate peak performance
- 128 Mbytes local processor memory
- 4 Gbytes address space per processor
- Disk space provided through afs
- Parallelism through message passing

Serial RS/6000 Cluster
- 8 processors with a peak performance of 84 Mflops
- 0.67 Gflops aggregate peak performance
- 256 Mbytes local processor memory
- 4 Gbytes address space per processor

- Disk space provided through afs
- Parallelism through message passing

IBM SP1

- 64 processors with a peak performance of 120 Mflops
- 7.68 Gflops aggregate peak performance
- 128 Mbytes local processor memory
- 4 Gbytes address space per processor
- Disk space provided through afs
- Parallelism through message passing

For the most up-to-date information on CTC's hardware, see "Hardware Platforms: Documentation for Using Each."

Gopher:	gopher.tc.cornell.edu
item:	Hardware Platforms: Documentation for Using Each
WWW:	http://www.tc.cornell.edu/UserDoc/hardware.html

Software

Since the software available at the CTC changes with some frequency, it is recommended that you use the CTC Gopher to check on specific programs.

Gopher:	gopher.tc.cornell.edu
item:	Software

- AIX operating system
- Software support for vectorization and parallelization
- Interactive and batch modes
- Editors: vi, emacs, aXe, jove
- Text Processor: TeX
- FORTRAN: apf, fvs, xlf
- Other languages: C, C++

Computational Chemistry

ALCHEMY II	AMBER	AMPAC	CAR-PARINELLO
CHARMm	CORNING	DISCOVER	DMOL
GAMESS	GAUSSIAN	HONDO	MELDF
MOPAC			

Computational Fluid Dynamics

FIDAP

Graphics

AVS	DATA EXPLORER	CONTOUR	DISSPLA
GNUPLOT	PV-WAVE	SAS/GRAPH	WAVEFRONT

Numerical Libraries and Mathematics

ACMALG	BSPLINE	EISPACK	ELLPACK
ESSL	FAUX	FFTPACK	FISHPACK
FUNPACK	IMSL	IMSLCMATH	ITPACKV
LAPACK	LINPACK	MINPACK	NAG
ODEPACK	OSL	PCGPAK	QUADPACK
RECIPES	SAS	SLATEC	SMPAK
SPARSPAK	SPLUS	TOEPLITZ	

Mechanics

ABAQUS	ANSYS

Parallel Tools

FVS	EXPRESS	FORGE90	GIST
HENCE	PAT	PDD	PG
PVM	XAB	PROFVIEW	TCGMSG
UDB			

Statistics

GLIM	NTSYS	SAS	SAS/ETS
SAS/IML	SAS/STAT		

Symbolic Algebra

AXIOM	MAPLE	MATHEMATICA

Utilities

CLOGIN	CMSTAPE	CMSUNF	COLLAGE
DIRED	emacs	FPDIFF	GDIFF
GMAKE	Gopher/XGopher	LESS	RCS
ReelLibrarian	tex	Mosaic	Lynx
VAST2			

Training

- Local and remote workshops
- Introduction to systems, access, languages, and optimization tools for new users

- Summer institutes for researchers working on code
- Undergraduate/Faculty workshops
- Workshops on parallel processing and vectorization
- Discipline specific workshops (e.g. computational chemistry)
- Smart Node regional and consultant workshops
- Visualization and remote graphics workshops

SuperQuest

Ambitious and creative high school students and their teachers are immersed in science and supercomputing through SuperQuest, the only national computational competition of its kind, sponsored by the Cornell Theory Center. Sixteen of twenty teams, chosen on a competitive basis, spend several weeks of intensive training during the summer at the Cornell Theory Center or one of four other supercomputing institutes. Their high-performance computing education includes sessions on vectorization, parallel processing, and visualization techniques. The teams begin projects on the supercomputer that are continued at their home school with the use of computer equipment awarded through the competition.

To bridge the gap between high school and undergraduate use of computational resources, the Theory Center also provides training in computational science technique for high school teachers, so they too can move into the future of scientific experimentation. Since early 1990, more than 57 high school teachers from throughout New York State have received supercomputer training at the Center. This helps to increase the number of college-bound students ready to explore modern methods of scientific analysis and discovery.

For the most up-to-date information see the SuperQuest document at the National Center for Supercomputing Applications:

WWW: `http://www.ncsa.uiuc.edu/Edu/SuperQuest/new/SQ93.html`

SPUR

The Supercomputing Program for Undergraduate Research (SPUR) provides talented undergraduates with the opportunity to become an integral part of current computational research by involving them in a 10-week session of intensive training and scientific inquiry using computational tools. Students work with a research advisor on projects in the fields ranging from geology to chemistry and electrical engineering to biology.

For more information and application materials, see the document entitled, "SPUR: Supercomputing Program for Undergraduate Research," available on the World Wide Web as follows.

WWW: `http://www.tc.cornell.edu/Edu/SPUR/SPUROverview.html`

Collaborative Research

- User groups and Research Interest Groups (Computational Chemistry and Statistics)
- Interdisciplinary research groups open to all researchers
- Corporate Research Institute

Documentation

- Theory center on-line information is accessible through the World Wide Web at http://www.tc.cornell.edu/; Gopher at gopher.tc.cornell.edu; WAIS at wais.tc.cornell.edu as source cnsinfo.src; and anonymous FTP from ftp.tc.cornell.edu
- On-line documentation: CTCINFO
- Vendor documentation: IBM InfoExplorer, IBM Bookmanager, KSR Online Manuals
- Newsletter: ForeFronts
- Training notebooks of presentations from classes and lab exercises
- Online instruction: tutorials through CTCINFO
- Online help program and man pages

Consulting

- Consulting via e-mail
- Large scale computing consulting
- Computational research associate staff in agricultural and biological engineering, astrophysics, chemistry, engineering, mathematics, operations research, and statistics
- Visualization consulting
- Strategic user program for those using parallel computing in production work
- Corporate research consulting

Graphics Support

- Support for remote X-Windows (including xim with WaveFront), Tektronix 4105, 4010; Versaterm for Mac; GRAF for PC; VT100 emulators; gnuPLOT and a version of xmovie
- Power Visualization Server running IBM ImageExplorer
- An extensive graphics lab with high speed fiber optic links, an image processing system, facilities for videotape production, a digital camera for 35 mm slides, printers for producing camera ready copy, plotters and color PostScript printers, and a number of Unix workstations

For more information on graphics support at CTC, see the document entitled, "Visualization at the Cornell Theory Center," as follows.

    WWW: `http://www.tc.cornell.edu/Visualization/vis.html`

■■■ ı

Administration

All proposals for time on the Theory Center's resources are subject to peer review through the Theory Center's National Allocations Committee; researchers must submit an application for supercomputer time directly to the Theory Center to allocations coordinator, Pat Colasurdo. Corporations interested in using the Theory Center through the Center's Corporate Research Institute may contact Linda Callahan.

Contact Summaries

Consulting:	(607) 254-8686 consult@tc.cornell.edu
Visualization:	Bruce Land land@tc.cornell.edu (607) 254-8686
Allocations:	Pat Colasurdo pat@tc.cornell.edu (607) 254-8686
Training:	Susan Mehringer susan@tc.cornell.edu (607) 254-8686
System Status:	(607) 255-7138
Network help:	Network Management Center (24 hrs/day, 7 days/week) (607) 255-9900
IBM ES/9000:	eagle.tc.cornell.edu
RS/6000 cluster:	cluster.tc.cornell.edu
IBM SP1:	pps1 - pps8.tc.cornell.edu
KSR1:	homer.tc.cornell.edu

Login Script

The following script shows how to connect to the CTC ES/9000, login, compile, load and run a program, and then logout. It assumes that you connect from some local machine which supports the TCP/IP Telnet program. Prompts are represented by "local>" for your local system prompt, "Eagle" for the ES/9000, and "EagUs" for user commands supplied to the ES/9000. Comments are enclosed in parentheses.

Prompt	Dialog	Comments
local>	telnet eagle.tc.cornell.edu	(Telnet to eagle)
	...	(Telnet messages)
EagUs>	login: <your userid>	
EagUs>	password: <your password>	

(Continued)

```
Eagle>  ...                          (Login messages from eagle)
EagUs>  fvs -o hello hello.f         (Compile FORTRAN program)
EagUs>  hello                        (Run Program)
Eagle>  HELLO WORLD
EagUs>  logout                       (Log out)
```

NATIONAL CENTER FOR ATMOSPHERIC RESEARCH (NCAR)

Hardware

- CRAY Y-MP8/864 with 8 processors; CRAY Y-MP2D with 2 processors; CRAY EL92 with 2 processors
- 64 Mwords of main memory for the Y-MP8; 16 Mwords for the Y-MP2; 64 Mwords for the EL92
- 48 Mword maximum memory per job for batch; 32 Mwords for interactive; for some dedicated job queues, 62 Mwords maximum
- Vector processing hardware for both CRAYs
- 256 million word SSD for Y-MP8 (1000 Mbyte/sec channel), 128 million word SSD for Y-MP2
- 100 Gbytes of local storage for the Y-MP8, 20 Gbytes of local storage for the Y-MP2
- Unix front end
- NCAR Mass Storage System (MSS): hierarchical file storage system with no limit per user (The MSS has a 120 Gbyte disk farm and over 82,000 tape cartridges. It features a StorageTek 4400 Automated Cartridge System capable of holding 6,000 cartridges, or 2 terabytes of information. Currently, MSS stores over 40 terabytes of data and offers extremely high data transfer to the CRAYs; is accessible from front end and from the Internet through a gateway system.)
- Connection Machine CM-5 with 32 processors, 128 Mwords of main memory, a 2.08 ns clock cycles and 20 Gbytes disk storage
- A cluster of 4 IBM RISC System/6000 590 and 550 workstations, an IBM SP1 (scalable parallel) system 8 RS/6000 370 processors; both clusters are controlled by an IBM RS/6000 980 system; the clusters provide interactive single- and multiprocessor floating-point operations
- CRAY-3 with 4 processors, 128 Mwords of main memory, a 2.08 ns clock cycle, and 20 Gbytes of disk storage
- Gateway for NCAR's Internet Remote Job Entry System (IRJE): create and submit CRAY jobs from local hosts connected to the Internet with output automatically shipped back to the remote host

■ I

Planned Hardware Additions (Summer 1994)

- CRAY Y-MP8I/564 with 5 processor and 64 Mwords of memory, 256 Mword SSD (upgrading to 8 processors in October 1994)
- CRAY T3D with 32 nodes, each with 2 processors; each processor has a local memory of 8 Mwords for a total of 512 Mwords; processors are DECchip 21064 64-bit IEEE microprocessors with a 6.6 ns clock cycle
- IBM SP2 with 16 Power 2 processors will replace the SP1

Software

- UNICOS operating system on Crays
- FORTRAN: CFT 77 F90
- Other languages: vectorizing C and Pascal compilers

Application Libraries

Application libraries and documentation are available via the Distributed Software Libraries (dsl) utility. To access dsl, telnet to dsl.ucar.edu and login as "dsl". When prompted for the password, type "software".

ALFPACK	AMOSLIB	CRAYFISH	ECMFFT
EDA	EISPACK	EISPKD	FFTPACK
FISHPAK	FITPACK	FUNPACK	IMSL
LINPACK	MINPACK	MUDPACK	NAG
NCARM	NCARO	ODEPACK	SPHERE
SLATEC	SSDLIN	STARPAC	

Graphics

NCAR/GKS Version 3.1.3a

Training

- UNICOS orientation: a one-day class introducing Unix/UNICOS programming tools and the NCAR computing environment
- Unix Basics Class: Two-day hands-on introduction to the basics of Unix
- Remote site visits for sites with a significant number of users
- User conference held every two years: updates users on new developments and new directions in computing at NCAR
- NCAR Graphics on and off site workshops and Fortran optimization workshops

Collaborative Research

- User groups
- Real-time computing during field programs
- Classroom grants of computer time

Documentation

Documentation and User Documentation Catalog referencing both the SCD-supported and vendor documentation available via anonymous FTP and Gopher:

FTP host: `ftp.ucar.edu`
directory: `/docs`
items: **(many or all)**

Gopher: `gopher.ucar.edu`
menu: `NCAR/UCAR Gophers/`
item: `Scientific Computing Division`
`Publications & Documents/`

- Online documentation for most of the utilities in the supported libraries via the Distributed Software Libraries (dsl) utility

- Scientific Computing Division (SCD) hard copy documentation (free except for the NCAR Graphics manual)

- NCAR UNICOS Primer: basic information to begin computing at NCAR with step by step examples to create, submit, and receive output from the CRAYs

- Daily Bulletin: Online source of up-to-date information on the computing systems

- Newsletter: SCD Computing News (free)

- Annual planning report: "Supercomputing: The View From NCAR"; the current report is available on the World Wide Web:

    WWW: `http://http.ucar.edu/docs/94DevPlan/dp94toc.html`

- NCAR Annual Report

- NCAR Annual Scientific Report

Consulting

- Phone, 8-5 MST weekdays; walk-in consulting for visitors and local users and extended consulting by appointment

- E-mail consulting available from the Internet and BITNET

- Specialized consulting for software libraries, networking and data communications, optimization, multitasking, CRAY I/O optimization, segmentation (overlaying) of large applications, math algorithms, NCAR Graphics, IBM PC/AT and Macintosh terminal emulations, and Unix and UNICOS operating systems

- Visitor assistance: access 24 hrs/day, 7 days/week; IBM PCs, Macintoshes, and Sun Workstations for terminal or stand-alone use, color graphics terminals

Graphics Support

- Text and graphics system for both on-site and off-site users providing 16mm film, 35mm color slides, 4" x 5" color film, microfiche, and videotape (VHS, SVHS, Betacam, Umatic-SP)
- Xerox 4050 laser printers for paper graphical output
- Color and black and white hard copy output
- CGM metafile support
- Remote graphics support with an NCAR graphics translator (ctrans) on the front end
- Output mailings to users at remote sites

Strengths and Limitations

Strengths

- High performance vector processing
- Extensive user support services
- SSD for large I/O applications
- Extensive data archives for atmospheric and oceanographic research
- High volume fast access mass storage system
- Extremely high volume graphics output capabilities
- Video support and movie-making
- Remote job entry system via the Internet

Limitations

- Few applications outside atmospheric, oceanographic, and related geosciences

Administration

- Allocations for university researchers with NSF grants in atmospheric, oceanographic, and related sciences; grant requests reviewed by a peer review board composed of NCAR staff and university researchers
- Allocations for research organizations on a cost recovery basis

Contact Summaries

Consulting:	consult1@ncar.ucar.edu (303) 497-1278
Visitor/User Information:	scdinfo@ncar.ucar.edu (303) 497-1225
Allocations:	allocations@ncar.ucar.edu (303) 497-1207
Classroom Use:	cal@ncar.ucar.edu (303) 497-1229
Documentation Orders:	docorder@ncar.ucar.edu (303) 497-1232
IRJE (remote job entry):	rje@migs.ucar.edu

NATIONAL CENTER FOR SUPERCOMPUTING APPLICATIONS (NCSA)

Hardware

- CRAY Y-MP4/464 with 4 processors; Connection Machine Model 5 (CM-5) with 512 nodes; Connection Machine Model 2 (CM-2) with 32,000 nodes and 64 bit floating point hardware; and Convex C3880 (C3) with 8 processors
- 64 Mwords of main memory for the Y-MP; the CM-5 has 100 Gbytes parallel disk; 1 Gbyte main memory for the CM-2; 4 Gbyte of physical memory for the Convex C3880
- 6.0 ns clock speed for the CRAY Y-MP; 4.1 ns clock speed for the CRAY-2; 7.0 MHZ clock on the CM-2
- Vector, scalar, and parallel processing
- High speed 128 Mword Solid State Disk (SSD) for the CRAY Y-MP
- 16 Gbytes temporary storage for CRAY; 30 GByte DataVault for the CM-5 and CM-2
- Mass storage on UniTree running on a CONVEX C220 system with 220 Gbytes of disk and magnetic storage
- Large datasets (10+ Gbytes) stored using DD-2 helical scan tape
- Three IBM RISC System 6000 model 550's (high-end superscalar machines for predominantly scalar applications); a total six of 550's and one RS/6000 model 950 front end / file server
- Three Sun 4/490 front ends running SunOS for the CM-2
- Numerous high end machines from Silicon Graphics, Apple, IBM, and SUN in the Numerical Laboratory, accessible over the Internet
- Testbed research project (BLANCA) underway at 622 Mbps to prepare for the national gigabyte transcontinental network (NREN); 45 Mbit/sec links to Berkeley and Bell labs and to University of Wisconsin are in place

■■■

Software

- All production systems run a version of Unix
- Multitasking is supported on the CRAYS; dedicated time is available to allow access to all 4 CPUs
- Editors: vi and emacs on the CRAYs
- FORTRAN: CF77; cdbx is the debugger on both CRAYs
- Other languages: vectorizing C compiler on both CRAYs
- cfs utility to move files between CFS and the CRAYs and many example programs for vectorization and graphics on CFS
- CM-2: CM Fortran (CMF) supports Fortran 90 and FORTRAN77 constructs; C* programming language with data parallel extensions; *Lisp, and extension of common Lisp
- In-house software development applications staff

NCSA Developed Workstation Software

Public domain software for workstations is available via anonymous FTP from ftp.ncsa.uiuc.edu or 141.142.20.50. (Get the file "README.FIRST" for an informative overview of current holdings and FTP instructions. Each directory, including the root, contains a file named "INDEX" which contains a recursive listing of the files of that directory and of all subdirectories within it.)

Software may also be purchased; contact orders@ncsa.uiuc.edu for additional information and a copy of the current Technical Resources Catalog.

Utility	IBM PC	Mac	SGI	Other Unix
NCSA ALVIS			•	•
NCSA Audible Collage	•			
NCSA Brick			•	•
NCSA Collage	•	•	•	•
NCSA GelReader		•		
NCSA HDF	•	•	•	•
NCSA Height-Color Visualizer			•	
NCSA Import2HDF		•		
NCSA Isosurface Visualizer			•	
NCSA Mesher		•		
NCSA MinMaxer			•	•
NCSA Mosaic	•	•	•	•

(Continued)

Utility	IBM PC	Mac	SGI	Other Unix
NCSA PC Show	•			
NCSA Poly View			•	
NCSA Reformat/ XReformat			•	•
NCSA Telnet	•	•		
NCSA UIFlow		•		
NCSA X DataSlice			•	•
NCSA X Image			•	•

Software On the CRAYs

Astronomy

MIRIAD

Chemical Engineering

ASPEN PLUS

Chemistry

AMBER	AMPAC	BROOKHAVEN PDb	CADPAC
CHARMm	DISCO	GAMESS	GAUSSIAN92
GPRLSA	MINP	MM2	MOLECULE-SWEDEN
MOPAC	NCSAdisco	RANFOLD	RNAFOLD
RPAC	SYBYL	XPLOR	

Computational Fluid Dynamics

FIDAP	FLOW3D	KIVA II	PHOENICS

Electrical Engineering

CAzM	HSPICE	MSC/EMAS	PISCES
SIGVIEW	SPICE	SUPREM 4	

Graphics

Blaze	GNUPLOT	GPLOT	MPG
NCAR (GKS)	NCSA Viewit	PVI Contouring	PVI DI-3000
PVI GK-2000	PVI GRAFMAKER	PVI Metafile System	PVI TEXTPRO
Zetavu			

Mathematics and Statistics

ACM Algorithms	ACSL	ALFPACK	BCS
BCSEXT	CALMATH	DASSL	ECMFFT
EDA	EISPACK3	ELLPACK	FFT
FITPACK	GLIM	HSML	IMSL
ITPACK	KMN	LAPACK	LASO2
MARK14	MINOS	MINPACK	MUDPACK
NAG	NUMERICAL RECIPES	ODEPACK	PCGPAK
PCGPAK2	PORT	POSSOL	SCILIB
SLAM II	SLATEC	SMPAK	SPARSE
SPECFUN	SPSS-X	SSDLIN	TOEPLITZ
XLP	XML2	ZOOM	

Solid Mechanics and General Engineering

ABAQUS	ADINA	ADINAT	ADINA-IN
ADINAPLOT	ANSYS	DADS	DYNA2D
DYNA3D	INGRID	MAZE	MSC/NASTRAN
NIKE2D	ORION	TAURUS	TOPAZ2D

Systems and Utilities

AS	BENCHLIB	CDBX	CF77
CFT	CFT77	GNU Emacs	HDF
KAP/Cray	NCSAHDF	NCSA X IMAGE	PASCAL
PCC	SCC		

Training

- Education program featuring supercomputer use for users from kindergarteners to advanced researchers; strong emphasis on incorporating scientific visualization techniques into education
- Academic Affiliates Program with members at more than 100 institutions; features special training and block grants of computer time for members
- Visitor program for faculty, postdoctoral, and student researchers to support working visits to NCSA
- Renaissance Experimental Laboratory for teaching visualization skills and efforts to incorporate scientific visualization into course curricula
- Workshops and seminars on specialized topics in various disciplines
- Summer institutes and workshops
- Many training video tapes: vectorization, CRAY architecture, multitasking, etc.

■■■

Collaborative Research

- Association with the Beckman Institute, an interdisciplinary program for artists, computer scientists, and researchers in many intellectual disciplines
- NCSA Collage (Collaborative Analysis and Graphics Environment) (Lets researchers conduct real-time collaborative work sessions across a wide variety of hardware platforms. Collage software and documentation are available without charge by downloading from NCSA's anonymous FTP host; see Software.)
- Unix mail on the CRAYs (Users are encouraged to forward mail to their home systems.)
- The Industrial Program offers partnerships between NCSA and industrial partners to produce business solutions.

Documentation

- Unix man pages for technical information
- Documentation system (originally from CTSS) ported to UNICOS for access to complete manuals
- NCSA Technical Resources Catalog lists documentation available from NCSA or third parties
- Many documents available through anonymous FTP in the /ncsapubs directory (see Software)
- Innovative video magazine (NCSA RealTime)
- New users provided with an extensive startup kit and kept informed via frequent distribution of online and printed materials
- Many documents free or for purchase
- Online help available through the new information system called "ncsainfo," based on the BNU Texinfo documentation system (An NCSA gopher server is being established as well.)
- Extensive sets of example programs are available on CFS
- Bimonthly technical newsletter: "datalink" (online)
- Quarterly general information newsletter: "access"

Consulting

- Consulting available via e-mail (24 hours a day) and phone (8am to 5pm central time) (See Contact Summaries below.)
- On-line information system (ncsainfo) as well as specific information resources on each system

Graphics Support

- Strong emphasis on local and remote use for scientific visualization
- Workstation tools for graphics analysis

- CGM metafile support

- Support for remote graphics terminals including Tektronix 4014, 4105, 4113, 4115/4125, PostScript, HPGL, Macintosh

- Media facility features video and audio resources, including Silicon Graphics Inc. frame buffers, Abekas digital disk recorders, D1 format digital VCRs, Macintosh-based digital audio recording, Betacam SP format analog VCRs, computer-controlled editing and routing, and over 150 other components. Activities supported include transfer of images from computers to video, audio, hard copy, and film, as well as between the different formats within each of these media; media processing such as video editing, text generation, electronic paintbox, digital effects, and compositing; audio recording and editing to further supplement basic imagery; and video field production for documentary programming and special projects

- Consulting on media systems ranging from desktop through digital HDTV

Strengths

- Massively parallel processor systems

- High performance vector processing

- Solid State Disk for fast internal I/O

- Scientific visualization

- State-of-the-art graphics laboratories

Administration

- Requests for 100 or more service units of CPU time are reviewed by a joint NCSA/Pittsburgh Peer Review Board quarterly.

- Requests for fewer than 100 service units are processed eight times a year.

- Applications for less than six service units are reviewed internally by NCSA in the Small Allocations Committee.

- Researchers at academic affiliate institutions may apply for start-up grants for 1-5 hours on the CRAY Y-MP4/464 through their campus affiliate representatives.

- Education projects are available on the Cray systems and Connection Machines. Only a limited number of projects can be allocated on the CMs. For additional information on applying for an education account, send e-mail to uadmin@ncsa.uiuc.edu

  (Note: service units are CPU or wall clock hours weighted by different factors for the various computers.)

∎∎∎

Contact Summaries

Accounts / Affiliates Program / Client Administration:	Judy Olson `uadmin@ncsa.uiuc.edu` (217) 244-1986
Allocations:	Radha Nandkumar `radha@ncsa.uiuc.edu` (207) 244-0650
Applications:	Melanie Loots `mloots@ncsa.uiuc.edu` (207) 244-2921
Central Facilities:	Sue Lewis `slewis@ncsa.uiuc.edu` (217) 244-0708 For services/help: (217) 244-0710
Chemistry Users Group:	Balaji Veerarghavan `balajiv@ncsa.uiuc.edu` (217) 333-2754
Computing and Communications:	Charles Catlett `catlett@ncsa.uiuc.edu` (217) 333-1163
Consulting:	`consult@ncsa.uiuc.edu` (217) 244-1144
Educational Outreach:	Scott Lathrop `slathrop@ncsa.uiuc.edu` (217) 244-1099
Faculty Program:	Melanie Loots `mloots@ncsa.uiuc.edu` (217) 244-2921
Industrial Program:	John Stevenson (217) 244-0474
Media Relations:	Jarrett Cohen `jcohen@ncsa.uiuc.edu` (217) 244-3049

Media Services:	Vincent Jurgens
	`vjurgens@ncsa.uiuc.edu`
	`media@ncsa.uiuc.edu`
	(217) 244-1543

MetaCenter Allocations:	Susan Zukofsky `allocations@ncsa.uiuc.edu` (217) 333-2754
Networking:	`network@ncsa.uiuc.edu`

Orders for Publications and Multimedia:	Debbie Shirley `orders@ncsa.uiuc.edu` (217) 244-4130
Publications Group:	Melisa Johnson `melissaj@ncsa.uiuc.edu` (217) 244-0645
Software Development Group:	Joseph Hardin `jhardin@ncsa.uiuc.edu` (217) 244-6095
Software Tools Technical Support:	Jennie File `jfile@ncsa.uiuc.edu` (217) 244-0638
Systems Software:	Curt Canada `canada@ncsa.uiuc.edu` (217) 333-3480
Training:	Alan Craig (information) `acraig@ncsa.uiuc.edu` (217) 244-1988
	Deanna Walker (registration) `dwalker@ncsa.uiuc.edu` (217) 244-1996
User Services:	Jim Bottum (acting) `bottum@ncsa.uiuc.edu` (217) 244-0633
Visitors Program:	Jean Soliday `jsoliday@ncsa.uiuc.edu` (217) 244-1972
Hardware Status:	(217) 244-0710
NSFNET Problems:	(617) 873-3400
CRAY Operations:	(217) 244-0710
CRAY Y-MP address:	`uy.ncsa.uiuc.edu`
CRAY-2 address:	`u2.ncsa.uiuc.edu`

CM Sun Front Ends:	`cmsun1.ncsa.uiuc.edu`
	`cmsun2.ncsa.uiuc.edu`
	`cmsun3.ncsa.uiuc.edu`

Dial-up Access:	(217) 244-0664 (217) 244-0662
Anonymous FTP:	`ftp.ncsa.uiuc.edu` (141.142.20.50)

Login Script

The following script shows how to Telnet to the NCSA CRAY, list files, compile and run a job, and logout. The script assumes that you connect to the CRAY from a local machine which supports the TCP/IP program Telnet. Prompts are represented by "user>"

for you, "CRAY>" for the CRAY, "Teln>" for Telnet, and "CRus>" for CRAY responses followed by user entries on the same line. Most CRAY responses are abbreviated. Comments are enclosed in parentheses.

Prompt	Dialog	Comments
user>	`telnet u2.ncsa.uiuc.edu`	(Telnet to the CRAY-2)
Teln>	`...`	(Telnet messages)
CRAY>	`CRAY-2 UNICOS 5.0.7 (u2)`	
CRAY>	`National Center for Supercomputing Applications`	
CRus>	`login: <your CRAY userid>`	(login to the CRAY)
CRus>	`Password:<your password>`	
CRus>	`account:<your account>`	
CRAY>	`...`	(CRAY login messages)
CRus>	`u2 1% ls -la`	(ask to list your files)
CRAY>	`.         ..            .cshrc` `.login    .profile   hello.f`	
CRus>	`u2 2% cft77 hello.f`	(compile program called "hello.f", generate a binary object file called "hello.o")
CRus>	`u2 3% segldr -o hello hello.o`	(load the object file and create an executable file called "hello")
CRus>	`u2 4% hello`	(submit executable file)
CRus>	`u2 5% cat fort.6`	(display contents of output file)
CRAY>	`Hello world, goodbye world`	
CRus>	`u2 6% logout`	(logoff CRAY and return to local machine)

NATIONAL ENERGY RESEARCH SUPERCOMPUTER CENTER (NERSC)

Hardware

- One CRAY 2/8, one CRAY 2/4, one CRAY Y-MP C90, and a YMPEL 4-512 for High School Supercomputer Honors Program
- Memory sizes are 128 Mwords memory on the CRAY 2's, 256 Mwords on the C90, and 64 Mwords on the YMPEL
- Vector and parallel hardware; 2 processors on the YMPEL 4-512, 8 processors on one of the CRAY 2's, and 4 on the other, and 16 processors on the C90
- Permanent storage on the IBM-based CFS storage system
- 15 terabytes total mass storage
- Auxiliary computers: VAXs, HPs, and other networked computers

Software

- UNICOS 7.0 on the CRAY 2's and the CRAY YMPEL 4-512; UNICOS 7.C. on the C90 developed by Cray Research, Inc.
- Auxiliary VAXs with VMS operating system
- Editors on the CRAYs: vi, emacs, and standard Unix editors
- FORTRAN compilers: CF77, CF90
- Other languages: C, C++, Pascal, and LISP compilers, and CRAY Assembler
- Afs distributed file system
- CFS software for mass storage
- Example sets, sample programs, and extensive documentation available through the online DOCVIEW program

Math

Libraries:

ACM Algorithms	BCSLIB	BCSLIB-EXT	HARWELL
IMSL	LAPACK	NAG	SCILIB
SLATEC			

Applications:

IMSLIDL	MACYMA	MAPLE	MATHCAD
MATHEMATICA	MATLAB	PDE2D	

Graphics

Libraries:

DISSPLA	GKS	GRAFLIB	IMSLEXP
NCARGKS	TV80LIB		

Applications:

AGX Tool Master	AVS	Explorer	KHORDS
PVWAVE			

Training

- New user workshops available both on site and for export
- Classes on supercomputer related topics
- A high school Supercomputing Honors Program each summer

Collaborative Research

- E-mail via MAIL, MAILX
- Bulletin Board Server with rn, xrn, trn

- ESNET supported by NERSC networks and providing remote logins, e-mail, and file transfers to and from nodes on these networks and the Internet

Documentation

- Monthly newsletter, "The BUFFER"
- On-line packages: document, docview, and man pages
- WWW server in development

Consulting

- Phone consulting Mondays through Fridays, 8:00-11:45am, 12:45-4:45pm
- Online e-mail consulting via mail to consultants@nersc.gov

Graphics Support

- Fiche output; available to remote users
- Support for remote graphics terminals including most Tektronix and X-windows displays
- Output mailings free of charge to users at remote sites
- Videotapes of HDF movie files

Strengths

- Highly optimized vector processing
- Large memory machines
- A network connecting energy research sites supporting collaboration and exchange of information between researchers

Administration

- Most allocations made by applying to the Department of Energy (DOE)

Contact Summaries

Consulting:	(510) 422-1544
	(800) 66NERSC
Accounts (passwords and ID's):	(510) 422-2888
Allocations:	(510) 422-1544
Training:	(510) 422-1544
Hardware status:	(510) 422-4283

Network status:		(510) 422-4283
Direct CRAY connection:		`f.nersc.gov`
		`c.nersc.gov`
		`a.nersc.gov`

Login Script

The following script shows how to telnet to the NERSC CRAYs, login, transfer files from a local account to the CRAY using FTP, list files, compile/load/execute a program, and then logout. It assumes that you connect to the CRAY from some local machine which supports the TCP/IP Telnet program.

Prompts are represented by "user>" for you, "Teln>" for Telnet, "CRAY>" for the CRAY, and "CRus>" for CRAY responses followed by user entries on the same line. Comments are enclosed in parentheses. Most CRAY responses are abbreviated using the "..." ellipsis notation.

Prompt	Dialog	Comments
user>	`telnet f.nersc.gov`	(Telnet to the CRAY)
Teln>	`...`	(Telnet messages)
CRus>	`login: <your usernumber>`	(enter CRAY usernumber)
CRus>	`password: <your password>`	(enter CRAY password)
CRAY>	`...`	(CRAY login messages)
user>	`ftp`	(start FTP)
CRus>	`FTP> connect 128.95.137.4`	(make connection with FTP to your local account)
CRAY>	`...`	(FTP messages)
CRus>	`...`	(login to your local account)
CRus>	`MAX.U.WASHINGTON.EDU> get hello.for hello.f`	
		(get your program with FTP from your local account and send to the CRAY)
CRAY>	`...`	(file transfer messages from FTP)
CRus>	`MAX.U.WASHINGTON.EDU> quit`	(quit FTP and return to CRAY session)
CRAY>	`...`	(more FTP messages)
user>	`ls`	(ask to list your files)
CRAY>	`hello.f`	
user>	`CF77 hello`	(compile and load your FORTRAN program)
user>	`logout`	(logout from the CRAY)

Ohio Supercomputer Center (OSC)

The Ohio Supercomputer Center provides state-of-the-art computing to Ohio colleges, universities, and companies. In July 1989, a CRAY Y-MP8/864, the most powerful supercomputer available, was installed. In 1994, a Computational Quantum Chemistry

Engine and a Massively Parallel Processing (MPP) system both became newly available to OSC users.

Computer Hardware

CRAY Y-MP8/864

- UNICOS operating system
- Eight CPU processors, six nanosecond cycle time
- 64 million words (512 Mbytes) of memory
- 128 Mw Solid-state Device
- 80 Gbytes of primary storage on DS-41 and DS-42 disk drives
- Four I/O processors (MIOP, BIOP, DIOP, XIOP)
- Communications interfaces: VAX/VMS, TCP/IP, FDDI, HIPPI
- StorageTek Robotic Tape Silo with one terabyte storage capacity (connected to Y-MP8 and EL) and six drives
- CRAY Y-MP EL File Server System
- 256 Mbytes (32 Mws) of main memory
- 3 CPUs
- UNICOS and Data Migration software
- 80 Gbytes of data on DAS-2 units and DD-4 disk drives
- HIPPI interface connection to the Y-MP8 at 100 Mbytes/sec
- Ethernet interface
- FDDI interface

T3D Massively Parallel Processing (MPP) System

- UNICOS operating system
- 32 DEC Alpha 21064 processors
- 8 megawords of memory per processor
- CRI-designed memory logic
- Torus topology
- 6.67 nanosecond clock cycle

CRAY Y-MP 2E

- Model EIOS
- 32 Megawords
- 2 CPU processors
- HIPPI interface
- TCP/IP network
- 65 Gbytes of data on DD-301 disk drives

DEC 3000/300 CPU Entry-Level Computational Quantum Chemistry Engine

- 256 Mbytes
- 10 Gbytes of disk
- 4 millimeter DAT tape

- CD-ROM reader
- FDDI and Ethernet interfaces
- Local workstations

Software (on Y-MP8 only)

Chemistry

AMBER	AMPAC	BIGSTRN3	CADPAC 4.0
CHARMm21	COORD	DMOL	GAMESS
Gaussian 90	Gaussian 92	HONDO7	MOPAC5
SYBYL			

Computational Fluid Dynamics

ARC2D	ARC3D	DSMC	EAGLE
FIDAP 5.02	FIDAP 6.02	FDL3D	FLOW3D

Graphics

ABAPLOT	ABAPOST	apE	DISSPLA
DI-3000	NCAR	PLOT3D	

Mathematics and Statistics

BCSLIB	BCSEXT	BNCHLIB	GISPACK
IMSL	ITPACK	LAPACK	LINPACK
MINPACK	NAGhelp	NAGlib	SPARSE

Programming Languages

C	Fortran	LISP	Pascal
PROLOG	PSL	REDUCE	SISAL

Solid Mechanics and General Engineering

ABAQUS	ABAQUS/EXPLICIT	ANSYS	ASTROS
DYNA2D	DYNA3D	INGRID	NASTRAN
NIKE2D	NIKE3D	SPICE2	TAURUS
TOPAZ2D	TOPAZ3D		

Systems and Utilities

ABQNQS	ANSNQS	BNCHUTL	F2C

Training

- Training for beginning and advanced CRAY users
- Special programs for computational mechanics and computational chemistry

- Workshops on UNICOS, Cray Fortran, C programming, vectorization and optimization, performance analysis tools, job control, and network use
- Summer classroom programs for high school and undergraduate students
- Summer internships for high school students

Collaborative Research

- Program for Computational Reactive Mechanics
- Online information archive and mailing list for computational chemistry
- Software porting program providing blocks of time for software developers
- Trollius multicomputer operating system development and distribution
- Visiting collaboration with University of Florida Quantum Theory Project
- Local Area Multicomputer (LAM), a distributed memory MIMD programming and operating environment for heterogeneous Unix computers on a network

Documentation

- Quarterly Visions general purpose and SuperBits user newsletters
- Monthly "oscbits" e-mail newsletter for up-to-date user information
- World Wide Web and Gopher servers providing online access to OSC documents and information
- Online mailings: "oscupub" for reporting publications by users; "oscalloc" for reporting allocations of CRAY resources from the Statewide Users Group
- Online e-mail archive for computational chemistry, academic grant application, electronic mailings and newsletters
- Local and CRAY documentation on docview information system
- Documentation directory on CRAY containing software and general publications and user documentation
- OSC Program Book gives "one-stop" source of information for users on programs, account charges, software, etc.
- Local quick-start manual, EZGUIDE to supercomputing
- UNICOS online manual pages
- Manuals from Cray Research available on order from Kinko's copies in Columbus by U.S. mail or pickup

Consulting

- Resident consulting at Ohio universities and colleges on most aspects of supercomputer use and access
- By e-mail to oschelp@osca.osc.edu anytime
- By telephone (toll-free inside Ohio) M-F, 1-5pm
- Emergencies after hours or network access problems: contact OARnet Network Operations Center at (800) 627-6623

■■■

Graphics Support

- Ohio Visualization Laboratory with state-of-the-art graphics equipment and output services for computer graphics and animation

- Systems: 7 SPARCstation with an aggregate of 7.5 Gbytes of disk space, Macintosh II, Sun 3/60, Sun 3/110 workstations, NeXT 68040 processor, Silicon Graphics Personal Iris (4D/70GT), NeXT Dimension, Stellar GS2000

- Output media: 2 Texas Instruments OmniLaser 2115 Printers, 2 Tektronix 4693D Thermal Transfer Color Printers, Apple Laserwriter II Printer

- Video equipment: Sony 3/4" Video Editing Suite, Ampex 1" Video Editing Suite, Solitare Film Recorder, Slide Scanner, Abekas Still Storer

Strengths

- Vector, parallel processing on CRAY Y-MP8/864

- Computational chemistry and computational mechanics software support

- Strong user group involvement

- Availability of CRAY for university classes

Administration

- Active user group, with committees for allocations, hardware and operations, and software and activities

- Grant applications accepted by e-mail; 10 resource unit (10 CRAY Y-MP hours, approximately) awards available on demand to Ohio academic researchers; 100 resource unit awards depending on committee review; and larger awards depending on peer review

- Dedicated CRAY Y-MP time available for challenging parallel applications

- Availability of CRAY for classroom educational activities

- Industrial program for U.S. companies: CRAY time, consulting, and code development services

Contact Summaries

The Ohio Supercomputer Center (OSC) staff supplies a variety of administrative and consulting services to aid use of the supercomputer. Special efforts to help users include site consultants located at colleges and universities across the state, graphics consulting, and advanced optimization assistance.

■■■

Accounts/Allocations:	Michele Erlenwein `michele@osc.edu`
Address/Investigator Changes:	Michele Erlenwein `michele@osc.edu`
Consulting:	M-F 1-5pm, (614) 292-1800 or (800) 686-6472 `oschelp@osca.osc.edu`
Cray R&D Grants:	Larry Cooperc `lc@osc.edu`
CRAY Manuals:	Al Stutz `al@osc.edu`
CRAY System Administration:	Paul Buerger and Sam Bair `paul@osc.edu` and `sam@osc.edu`
Graphics Support/Development:	Al Stutz and Leslie Southern `al@osc.edu`
Industrial Program:	Charlie Bender, Marty Lobdell, and Al Stutz `marty@osc.edu` and `al@osc.edu`
Newsletters:	Barbara Woodall `woodall@osc.edu`
Numerical Analysis Assistance:	Steve Koehl and Moti Mittal `steve@osc.edu` and `moti@osc.edu`
Ohio Visualization Laboratory:	Barb Helfer `barb@ovl.osc.edu`
OSC Documents:	Frankie Harris `frankie@osc.edu`
Service Programs:	Elaine Hamilton `elaine@osc.edu`
Visitors:	Elaine Hamilton `elaine@osc.edu`
Workshops:	Dave Ennis `dje@osc.edu`
Workstation Administration and Staff Networking:	Brian Powell and Sam Bair `bpowell@osc.edu` and `sam@osc.edu`
WWW/Gopher Administration:	Stacy Coil `coil@osc.edu`

■■■

PITTSBURGH SUPERCOMPUTING CENTER (PSC)
■■■

Hardware

Cray Y-MP/C90

- 16 connected processors
- 512 million 64-bit words of memory (two Gbytes)
- High speed (156 Mword/second) 512 million word Solid-state Storage Device (SSD) serving as an extension of memory
- Each processor capable of performing a billion calculations per second
- High performance parallel and vector hardware
- Coupled to massively parallel T3D
- Very large temporary storage per user
- Permanent storage in both the Andrew File System (afs) and the file archiver (far) (See later sections on afs and far.)
- Dedicated time available through request

Cray T3D

- MPP machine with 256 processors
- Each processor has a peak theoretical performance of 150 Mflops
- Three-dimensional torus topography
- 16 Mbytes of memory per processor
- Tightly coupled to C90

Alpha SuperCluster

- 12 clustered workstations which are used as compute nodes
- 4 DEC Alpha AXP 3000/400 with 64 Mbytes of memory each
- 8 DEC Alpha AXP 3000/500 with 256 Mbytes of memory each
- 2 DEC Alpha AXP 3000/400 for use as front ends for the cluster
- Available in parallel mode with the Parallel Virtual Machine (PVM) library software
- Limited temporary storage available; permanent storage available in afs

Front End Machines

- Two VAX 6420s (CPWSCA and CPWSCB) running VMS from which you can reach either the C90; 10,000 blocks of permanent storage and a large amount of temporary storage for users
- Two Vaxstation 5100s (PSCUXA and PSCUXB) running ULTRIX from which the C90 can be reached; these front ends running afs as their file system; 10,000 1024-byte blocks of permanent storage on afs and a limited amount of temporary space for users

- Two DEC Alpha AXP 3000/400 systems which act as front ends to the Alpha Cluster; the front ends, axpfea and axpfeb, are used for compiling programs to be run on the Cluster and for submitting batch jobs to the Cluster's compute nodes

System Software

C90

- UNICOS
- Editors include emacs, vi, ed
- FORTRAN CF77 compiling system includes CFT77, automatic parallel processing, automatic vectorization and scalar optimization
- Cray standard C with automatic vectorization, scalar optimization, and automatic parallel processing
- Mass storage: afs and far
- A large examples system: sample jobs, data, and the resulting output available to public
- Downloadable public domain software

T3D

- Cray Research Adaptive Fortran (CRAFT)
- C, and soon, C++
- Apprentice, a performance tuning tool
- TotalView, a parallel debugger

Alpha Cluster

- Front ends to run OSF/1
- Editors on front ends include emacs, vi, and ed
- C89 ANSI-compliant C compiler, cc, DEC OSF/1 C compiler, GNU C compiler
- f77 DEC Fortran compiler
- Mass storage: afs

Application Software

The software lists below are not comprehensive. No utilities, benchmarking software, or similar packages have been included.

Not every package is available on every platform.

General Biomedical

CLUSTER	CONSORT	FIBERDRAW	IB_TO_GB
MAKSEQ	PICKEMBL	PICKGEN	SPIDER

■■■ı

Biomedical Databases

BROOKHAVEN	CAMBRIDGE	CONDENSE	ECD
EMBL	ENZYME	EPD	GENBANK
PROSITE	REBASE	NBRF-PIR	SWISS-PROT

Fluid Dynamics

FIDAP	FLOW3D	KIVA II	NEKTON

Gene Sequencing

AMPS	COMPAR	CONSENSUS	GCG
HELIXNET	MALFORM	MALIGNED	MAXSEGS
MSA	MSC	NWGAP	PATSER
PROFILESS	RNAFOLD	SN	SP
ST			

Molecular Mechanics

AMBER	AMPAC	CHARMM	DISCOVER
GROMOS	MOPAC		

Molecular Structure Determination

CORMA	DISTAN	IRMA	MARDIGRAS
VEMBED	VIEWIT		

Quantum Chemistry

AMSOL	CADPAC	GAMESS	GAUSSIAN
MOLPRO	SWEDEN		

Structural Analysis

ABAQUS	ADINA	ANSYS	DYNA2D
DYNA3D	INGRID	MAZE	NIKE2D
NIKE3D	SUPERWHAMS	TOPAZ2D	TOPAZ3D

X-ray Crystallography

GPRLSA	HKSCAT	PROTIN	XPLOR
XRFORM			

Image Analysis

MDPP

Graphics and Animation Software

ANIMATOR	CODEBOOK	DI3000	DISPLAY-P3D
DISSPLA	DRAW	DRAWCGM	DRAWP3D
GEODATA	GPLOT	GRAPHX	IMAGETOOL
LVR	MARCHP3D	MOVIE	MP3D
MPEG-PLAY	NAVIEW	NCARGKS2	ORION
PDBMODEL	PLOT3D	PLT2	RENDER-P3D
REQUESTAPE	SMONGO	TAURUS	TEXTMAKER
TITLEMAKER	TURB3D	XMGR	

Mathematical and Statistical Software

AMOS	AMOSLIB	APML	APSTAT
AUTO	BAILEY	BCSLIB	BISON
BLAS	CADSOL	CFTLIB	CGLIB
CYCLE	DVERK	ECMFFT	EISPACK
FFTPACK	FFTPACKT	FIDISOL	FISHPACK
GAMS	HARWELL	HBSMC	IMSL
IMSL IDL	INSITE	ITPACK	LAPACK
LASO	LINPACK	MAPLE	MATLAB
MUDPACK	NAG	NSPCG	ODEPACK
RANPACK	REDUCE	S	SGEFAC
SLAP	SLATEC	STEAM	SUBSET
TESTMAT	VECFEM	VFFTPK	YSMP

Andrew File System

The Andrew File System (afs) is a distributed network file system. Afs is the mass storage file system used on the C90, the Alpha Cluster, and the Ultrix front ends. Users, therefore, maintain one set of files, accessible from all machines, so it is not necessary to keep multiple copies of files. Automatic daily backups are performed. PSC maintains documentation, examples, libraries, executables and source code on afs in a single location which is accessible from all machines. Each user has a quota of 10,000 1024-byte blocks of permanent storage. A limited amount of temporary storage is also available.

File ARchiver (FAR)

Permanent file space on the Cray C90 is very limited. PSC has developed a new mass storage system using the Cray Data Migration Facility (DMF). DMF runs on far.psc.edu, a Cray YMP/EL running UNICOS. Every C90 user has a home directory on far.psc.edu. Any file created on the C90 which is to be kept indefinitely must be archived on far.psc.edu. Once stored on far.psc.edu, DMF will automatically migrate files to tape and retrieve them on request. Archived files can be accessed either through the far program, an interface to far.psc.edu, or FTP.

The Biomedical Initiative

PSC received a grant from the National Institutes of Health's (NIH) Division of Research Resources Biomedical Research Technology program to provide the biomedical community with supercomputing resources, training, and user support. The staff of the Biomedical Initiative includes four PhD's and two programmers with large-scale computational backgrounds to support the supercomputing activities of the biomedical community.

The High School Initiative

The PSC, with support from the NSF, has developed a High School Initiative program which is designed to create excitement about science among high school teachers and their students. Now concluding its third year, the program provides training, supercomputing time, user consulting, and a scientific mentor from a local university or industry to ten student/teacher teams. The teams are selected nationally on the basis of a science project they propose. A proposal is judged on scientific merit, suitability to the computational approach, feasibility, and how well it lends itself to cross-cultural study. The size and the aid ratio of the school district are taken into consideration also, as are indications of minority, female, and underserved populations.

Applications and project proposals are due in the spring for the program beginning the following fall. For more information, contact the Secondary Education Outreach Coordinator at (412) 268-4960.

Training

New User Workshops
- Supercomputer Techniques: Cray C90 workshop (5 days) including two days of advanced topics: Code Optimization, Multitasking, and Advanced Graphics
- Supercomputing Techniques: Parallel Processing/Cray T3D (5 days)
- PVM and Heterogeneous Computing (5 days)
- Summer Institute (2 weeks)

Discipline-Specific Workshops
- Introduction to Gaussian Theory and Practice (4 days)
- National Institutes of Health Workshops

Through grants from the National Institutes of Health, the PSC offers a series of workshops dedicated to the biomedical research community, including an overview of biomedical software and databases available at PSC. Topics presented have included molecular mechanics/dynamics, nucleic acid and protein sequence analysis, macromolecular structure refinement, fluid dynamics with immersed flexible structures, and image reconstruction from electron microscopy. Topic-specific workshops are provided on an "as needed" basis and new workshops are under continual development (e.g., biomechanics and neural nets).

Documentation

- Many vendor and hundreds of PSC publications, including policy, allocations, and user guides, are available online through WWW:

  WWW: `http://pscinfo.psc.edu`

- Hot tips and news in BULLETIN and rn on the VMS front ends and the ULTRIX front ends, respectively; also notices posted on 'news' on the C90
- Online help includes man pages on every PSC system
- PSC Users Guide mailed to all users
- Online EXAMPLES system with complete job setups, also on WWW server
- PSC NEWS, the PSC newsletter is available online on the WWW server and by (free) subscription
- An annual report, "Projects in Scientific Computing," highlights the scientific projects completed at PSC

Consulting

- Phone consulting available M-F 9am to 8pm, Saturday 9am to 4pm (Eastern time)
- E-mail consulting via userid REMARKS
- Online man pages
- Discipline-specific consulting
- "Life-cycle" consulting: starting with algorithm selection through data layout, programming, and program optimization for T3D users

Graphics Support

- CGM metafile support
- CGM-based video animation system for VHS tape and videodisk
- Support for remote graphics terminals includes many devices (Also PSC is willing to acquire or develop drivers for nearly any modern device on request.)
- VHS tape output mailed to remote users
- On-site graphics labs with Silicon Graphics Crimson with Reality Engine, Silicon Graphics Indigo II, SUN Sparcstation, and DECStation 5000
- Capability to make 35mm color slides using Matrix Instruments SlideWriter
- Color output from Cannon CLC-500 color copier/printer (Prints color PostScript files as well as makes color copies.)

▗■■■▗

Administration

- All proposals to PSC are screened by the Internal Review Committee (IRC) for scientific merit and computational efficiency. The IRC meets on the first and third Mondays of each month and may award up to 99 service units. Larger grant requests are referred by the IRC to an independent Peer Review Board (PRB). The PRB meets quarterly. Final consensus on awards is arrived at by group caucus of all PRB members. Any decision of the IRC or PRB may be appealed in writing. Awards initially last one year, but may be renewed to complete the research project.

- Starter grants are available for any researcher who wishes to explore the use of the PSC.

Contact summaries:	Consulting	(412) 268-4960
	Accounts	(412) 268-4960
	Allocations	(412)268-4960
	Training	(412) 268-4960
	High School Initiative	(412) 268-4960
	Hardware status	(412) 268-4960
	Network status	(412) 268-4960
Internet Addresses:	VMS front ends	`a.psc.edub.psc.edu`
		`b.psc.edu`
	Ultrix front ends	`cuxa.psc.edu`
		`pscuxb.psc.edu`
	Alpha Cluster front ends	`axpfea.psc.edu`
		`axpfeb.psc.edu`

Login Script

The following script shows how to connect to the front end VMS VAX, login, create a job which submits 'hello.f' to the CRAY, and then logout. It assumes that you connect to the front end from some local machine which supports the TCP/IP Telnet program.

Prompts are represented by "user>" for you, "PSC>" for the front end, "Teln>" for Telnet, and "PSCus>" for front end responses followed by user entries on the same line. Most responses are abbreviated. Comments are enclosed in parentheses.

■■■ ■

Prompt	Dialog	Comments
user>	telnet a.psc.edu	(telnet to the front end)
Tel>	...	(Telnet messages)
PSCus>	Username: <your userid>	
PSCus>	Password: <your password>	
PSC>	...	(PSC login messages)
user>	emacs hello.job	(create the following job to be submitted to the CRAY)
	#USER=<userid> PW=<password>	
	#QSUB -r hello	(name the job "hello")
	#QSUB -lM 0.8 Mw	(specify 0.8 Mw limit)
	#QSUB -lT 5	(specify 5 second limit)
	ja	(start accounting log)
	date	
	set -x	(echo commands to output)
	cd $TMP	(move to temp space)
	fetch hello.f -t 'usr$root0:[userid]hello.f	(fetch hello.f from CPWSCA)
	cf77 hello.f limsl11	(compile hello.f; include the IMSL library)
	mv a.out hello.exe	(rename the executable "hello.exe")
	hello.exe > results	(run "hello"; store answers in file "results")
	far store results results	(store results in far)
	rm hello.exe hello.f	(delete code and executable)
	ja -st	(stop accounting and print an accounting record for yourself)
	(At this point, you save your job and exit from EMACS.)	
user>	cray	
PSC>	The Cray Station is available	
user>	csubmit hello.job	
PSC>	%CX-S-SUB_OK, Job: Hello queued for submission	
PSC>	VAX TO CRAY:%SYSTEM-S-NORMAL, normal successful completion	
PSC>	VAX TO CRAY: FILE=HELLO	
PSC>	VAX TO CRAY: 1215 BYTES TRANSFERRED	
PSC>	CRAY TO VAX: %RMS-S-NORMAL, normal successful completion	
PSC>	CRAY TO VAX: FILE = 1DUA102: [USR2.USERID]HELLO.CPR;1	("hello.cpr" is the log of the Cray job "hello.job")
PSC>	CRAY TO VAX: 34 BYTES TRANSFERRED	
user>	logout	

San Diego Supercomputer Center (SDSC)

Hardware

- 8-processor Cray C90 running UNICOS
- 128 Mwords (1 Gbyte) main memory
- 4.167 ns clock; 7.8 peak Gflop rating (for full 64 bit arithmetic)
- Vector processing hardware
- 188 directly attached disk space
- 1024 MWord SSD (8 Gbytes)
- Intel Paragon, 416 nodes
- 64 nodes with 32 Megabytes of memory; all others with 16 Mbytes
- Peak speed of 40 Gflops (for 32-bit arithmetic)
- DataTree for file storage on an Amdahl 5860

Software Available on the Cray C90

- UNICOS
- Editors: vi, emacs, and standard Unix line editors
- FORTRAN: CF77 vectorizing compiler
- ANSI C: CC vectorizing compiler, AS (CRAY Assembly language)
- Extensive example programs available

Biology

FASTA	FOLD	GENBANK	PIR
PIR			

Chemistry

AMBER	BIGSTRN	CADPAC	CAMBRIDGE DB
CHELP	CORMA	DGEOM	DISCOVER
DMOL	GAMESS	GAUSSIAN	MM2
MM3	MMX	MOPAC	MP
NETCDF	PROLSQ	PSI77	QCFF/PI
X-PLOR			

Graphics

CGMUTILS	GKSNCAR	GKSUL	GNUPLOT
GPLOT	GRIDGEN	HDF	IMTOOLS
KHOROS	NCARGRAPHICS	VPR	XDATASLICE
XIMAGE	XMANDEL	XV	

Mechanics

ABAQUS	ADINA	ANSYS	DYNA2D
DYNA3D	EAGLE	FIDAP	FLOW-3D
INGRID	INS3D	MARC	MAZE
MSC/NASTRAN	NIKE2D	NIKE3D	ORION
SINDA85	TAURUS	TOPAZ2D	TOPAZ3D
VSAERO			

Math

BCS	DRMATHLIB	HARWELL	HOMPACK
IMSL	LAPACK	LASO	NAG
ODEPACK	SLAP	SLATEC	SMPAK
SPARSPAK	TOEPLITZ	VECTFFT	

Nuclear Engineering

DIF3D	DOS	NEKTON	REBUS
SABRINA	SCALE	TAD	TWODANT-SYS

Training

- Two-day workshops for new users at the beginning of each quarter and at remote sites when requested
- Advanced workshops on specialized topics (e.g., vectorization, visualization, and parallel computing); both on-site and for export
- Summer Institute applications reviewed by an SDSC committee and open to faculty, graduate students, undergraduates, and industry

Education

- SDSC field trip
- HPCC half-day in-service
- SDSC road show

Collaborative Research

- Visiting scientists program
- Research Fellows program for undergrads, postdoctoral, and senior staff

Documentation

- Over 150 complete user documents online for viewing and/or printing
- Over 3,000 man pages online, including over 300 developed locally
- Hot tips and news in news

- The bimonthly newsletter "Gather/Scatter"
- User's Guide for Cray and Paragon
- Extensive examples and instructions available online
- Annual report, "Science at the San Diego Supercomputer Center 19xx"
- An overview brochure with application for computing resources

Consulting

- Phone consulting 8am-5pm, Monday–Friday (Pacific time)
- Online consulting through e-mail to consult@sdsc.edu
- Discipline-specific consulting in most applications

Graphics Support

- Canon CLC-500 color laser copier/printer/scanner
- A Management Graphics Solitaire-8 digital film recorder
- Matrix 6264 analog film recorder
- Lasergraphics LFR Macintosh film recorder
- Hewlett-Packard Paintwriter color Macintosh printer
- Complete audio and video post-production facility for animations
- Complete set of image manipulation and conversion software
- Rendering software including Alias, AVS, Explorer, Renderman, and Wavefront
- Output mailings to your site

Strengths

- MIMD parallel computing
- Networking—infrastructure and research
- Visualization
- Large collection of applications and math software
- High performance vectorization

Administration

- Allocations for large blocks of time are reviewed by allocation committee and must be submitted 60 days prior to each quarter.
- Small allocations (1-50 hours) may be submitted at any time.

■■■

Contact Summaries

Consulting:	consult@sdsc.edu
	(619) 534-5100
Accounts:	(619) 534-5100
Allocations:	Bob Leary
	leary@sdsc.edu
	(619) 534-5123
Training:	Ms. Jayne Keller
	jaynek@sdsc.edu
	(619) 534-5124
Hardware status:	(619) 534-5100
Network status:	(619) 534-5100
CRAY Internet address:	c90.sdsc.edu (132.249.10.1)

Login Script

The following script shows how to telnet to the San Diego CRAY, login, list files, compile and execute a simple FORTRAN program, and then logout.

Prompts are represented by "user>" for you, "Teln>" for Telnet, "CRAY>" for the CRAY, and "CRus>" for CRAY responses followed by user entries on the same line. Comments are enclosed in parentheses. Most CRAY responses are abbreviated using the "..." ellipsis notation. Note that the system prompts on the SDSC CRAY Y-MP currently have the form "y1-n%" where "n" is the line number.

Prompt	Dialog	Comments
user>	*telnet y1.sdsc.edu*	(telnet to the CRAY)
Teln>	**...**	(Telnet messages)
CRus>	**login:** *<your CRAY userid>*	(login to the CRAY)
CRus>	**Password:** *<your password>*	
CRAY>	**...**	(CRAY login messages)
CRus>	y1-1% *ls*	(ask to list your files)
CRAY>	*hello.f*	
CRus>	y1-2% *cf77 -o hello hello.f*	(compile "hello.f" code and generate executable file called "hello")
CRus>	y1-3% *hello*	(execute "hello" program)
CRus>	y1-4% *logout*	(logoff CRAY, return to your local machine)

FOR MORE INFORMATION

Supercomputer Information on the Web

For more information on supercomputer centers in the U.S., the Coalition of Academic Supercomputing Centers (CASC) has made a World Wide Web server available. It includes information on the supercomputer program as well as access to the home pages of other supercomputer Web servers.

WWW: `http://www.osc.edu/casc.html`

LISTERV Lists on Supercomputing

There are a couple LISTSERV lists related to supercomputing.

`SUPER-L@VM1.MCGILL.CA`	Super Computer Users Forum
`CNSF-L@UBVM.CC.BUFFALO.EDU`	Cornell National Supercomputer Facility Announcements List (solely announcements, not discussion)

Newsgroups on Supercomputing

There are a number of newsgroups related to supercomputing and its applications.

`bit.listserv.cnsf-l`	CNSF LISTSERV list echo.
`comp.sys.super`	Supercomputing systems.
`comp.graphics.visualization`	Visualization techniques.
`comp.parallel`	Parallel processing.
`comp.simulation`	Computer simulations.

APPENDIX

A

Learning More About the Internet

To a large degree, the Internet is self documented. Pointers to online information specific to particular Internet applications are provided in each of the chapters of *The Internet Passport*. But there are thousands of online documents dealing with both general and technical issues in far more detail than is possible in any introductory Internet book. The purpose of this appendix is to familiarize you with general purpose online or organizational resources not specific to particular Internet applications.

REQUESTS FOR COMMENTS (RFCs)

Requests For Comments, or "RFCs", are documents created by and distributed among members of the Internet community to help define the nuts and bolts of the Internet. As of April 1994, there were more than 1,500 RFCs containing general information, technical specifications, and occasional general essays of interest to Internet users. In particular, all the components of the TCP/IP protocol suite are specified in many of the RFCs.

RFCs are available as online documents which you can retrieve from many of the services described throughout this book, such as mail servers, anonymous FTP hosts, or information systems such as Gopher, WAIS, campus wide information systems, or World Wide Web.

Here are three of the many current RFC repositories:

FTP host:	`ds.internic.net`
directory:	`/rfc`
filenames:	`rfcxxxx.txt` (where "xxxx" is the RFC number, e.g., rfc1000.txt or rfc822.txt)

Telnet:	`ds.internic.net`
login:	`gopher`
menus:	`InterNIC Information Services (General Atomics)/Internet Information for Everybody/All About Request for Comments (RFCs) Documents & Retrieval/`
item:	(many or all)

Gopher:	`is.internic.net`
menus:	`InterNIC Information Services (General Atomics)/Internet Information for Everybody/All About Request for Comments (RFCs) Documents & Retrieval/`
items:	(many or all)

```
FTP host:    nis.nsf.net
directory:   /internet/documents/rfc
filenames:   rfcxxxx.txt
```
(where "xxxx" is the RFC number, e.g., rfc1000.txt or rfc0822.txt)

```
FTP host:    src.doc.ic.ac.uc
directory:   /rfc
filenames:   rfcxxxx.txt.Z
```
(where "xxxx" is the RFC number, e.g., rfc1000.txt.Z or rfc822.txt.Z)

For the most up-to-date information on obtaining RFCs via FTP or e-mail send the following mail message:

```
mail:    rfc-info@isi.edu
subject: (none needed)
message: help: ways_to_get_rfcs
```

In response to this request, you should receive a file named "rfc-retrieval.txt," containing detailed information about all primary and secondary FTP repositories of RFCs.

If you want to receive new RFCs as they are released, you can subscribe to the RFC distribution list by sending a subscription request to rfc-request@nic.ddn.mil. (Note that this is not a discussion list, but rather a list from which you will receive materials.)

Here are some introductory RFCs which are useful as an overview of the Internet:

RFC1087	Ethics and the Internet
RFC1118	Hitchhiker's guide to the Internet
RFC1150	F.Y.I. On F.Y.I.: Introduction to the F.Y.I. notes
RFC1175	FYI on where to start: A bibliography of Internetworking information
RFC1206	FYI on questions and answers: Answers to commonly asked "new Internet user" questions
RFC1207	FYI on questions and answers: Answers to commonly asked "experienced Internet user" questions
RFC1208	Glossary of networking terms
RFC1402	There's gold in them thar networks! or searching for treasure in all the wrong places
RFC 1359	Connecting to the Internet: What connecting institutions should anticipate

If you do not yet have access to the Internet, many of the RFCs have been collected and organized topically into a multi-volume printed series called *The Internet Technology Handbook*, available from:

■■

SRI International
Network Information Systems Center
333 Ravenswood Ave., Room EJ291
Menlo Park, CA 94015 USA

e-mail: `nisc@nisc.sri.com`
voice: (415) 859-6387
fax: (415) 859-6028

The FYI (For Your Information) Notes

A subset of the RFC series, called the FYI (For Your Information) notes, is of particular interest to new Internet users. The numbers in the left column are the FYI series numbers.

1	RFC1150	F.Y.I. on F.Y.I.: Introduction to the F.Y.I. notes
2	RFC1147	FYI on a network management tool catalog: Tools for monitoring and debugging TCP/IP internets and interconnected devices
3	RFC1175	FYI on where to start: A bibliography of internetworking information
4	RFC1325	FYI on questions and answers: Answers to commonly asked "new Internet user" questions
5	RFC1178	Choosing a name for your computer
6	RFC1198	FYI on the X window system
7	RFC1207	FYI on Questions and Answers: Answers to commonly asked "experienced Internet user" questions
8	RFC1244	Site Security Handbook
9	RFC1336	Who's who in the Internet: Biographies of IAB, IESG and IRSG members.
10	RFC1402	There's gold in them thar networks! or searching for treasure in all the wrong places
11	RFC1292	Catalog of available X.500 implementations
12	RFC1302	Building a network information services infrastructure
13	RFC1308	Executive introduction to directory services using the X.500 protocol
14	RFC1309	Technical overview of directory services using the X.500 protocol
15	RFC1355	Privacy and accuracy issues in network information center databases
16	RFC1359	Connecting to the Internet: What connecting institutions should anticipate
17	RFC1391	The Tao of IETF: A guide for new attendees of the Internet Engineering Task Force

These documents can be obtained by any of the methods described for RFCs; they are also often stored and available with the filenames "fyixx.txt," where "xx" is their number within the FYI series. For a current list of FYIs, look for a file called "fyi-index."

FYIs may also be ordered via e-mail by sending a message to mail-server@nisc.sri.com. In the body of the message, write "send fyixx". To obtain the FYI index, your message should read "send fyi-index".

If you do not yet have an Internet connection, you can obtain printed copies of any FYI from SRI, either individually or as part of an RFC subscription. For more information about this service contact nisc@nisc.sri.com or call (415) 859-6387.

The National Research and Education Network (NREN)

The National Research and Education Network (NREN) is an emerging national network in the U.S. that is part of the global Internet and designed to promote greater collaboration among educational institutions, government, and federal research laboratories, industry, and high-performance computing centers. Congress has enacted a number of laws ("The High Performance Computing Act" and other laws) allocating billions of dollars for development of the NREN through testbed projects and grants. More legislation is under consideration.

Information on the NREN is available from the following servers:

FTP host: `nis.nsf.net`
directory: `/nren`
filenames: (many or all)

Gopher: `nis.nsf.net`
menu: `Internet Documents/`
item: `nren`

FTP host: `farnet.org`
directory: `/farnet/nren`
filenames: (many or all)

Gopher: `farnet.org`
menu: `FARNET Information/`
item: `NREN Information/`

The following mailing lists deal with the NREN, and the commercialization and privatization of the Internet:

Mailing List name:	To subscribe, send e-mail to:
nren-discuss@psi.com	ren-discuss-request@psi.com
com-priv@psi.com	com-priv-request@uu.psi.com

Some Organizations and Conferences for Internet Users

As a new or prospective member of the Internet, you may be interested in joining one of the many organizations devoted to the future of Internetworking. Many of these organizations also sponsor periodic meetings or conferences. Although the following list is not comprehensive, it should serve as a good starting point for learning what organizations or conferences may be of interest to you.

Association for Computing Machinery (ACM)

"The Association for Computing Machinery is dedicated to the development of information processing as a discipline, and to the responsible use of computers in an increasing diversity of applications..."

"ACM's Special Interest Groups (SIGs), devoted to the technical activities of its members, offer the individual ACM member all the advantages of a homogeneous, narrower-purpose group within a large professional society The SIGs operate as semiautonomous bodies within ACM for the advancement of activities in varying subject areas. ACM members are eligible to join as many special interest groups as they wish..."

[Of particular interest to Internet users is SIGCOMM:] "This special interest group is devoted to encouraging and reporting scholarly research and developments in the field of computer communication systems. The scope of SIGCOMM interests include design, analysis, measurement, maintenance, standards, applications, and social impacts of computer networking. Regulatory matters and the transfer of technology into the marketplace are also of great interest."

—From the *Communications of the ACM*

The Association for Computing Machinery
1515 Broadway
New York, NY 10036 USA

e-mail:	`acmhelp@acm.org`
voice:	(212) 869-7440
fax:	(212) 869-0481

FTP host:	`acm.org`	
directories:	(many or all)	(note that this is a VMS based FTP host, so refer to Chapter 7 if you need help)

Gopher:	`acm.org`
items:	(many or all)

Coalition for Networked Information (CNI)

"The Coalition for Networked Information, a joint project of the Association of Research Libraries, CAUSE, and EDUCOM, promotes the creation of and access to information resources in networked environments in order to enrich scholarship and to enhance intellectual productivity. Roughly 175 organizations and institutions are members of the Coalition Task Force."

—From the CNI mission statement in the file
"About the Coalition for Networked Information"
available on the CNI Gopher server.

■■I

Joan K. Lippincott
Assistant Executive Director
Coalition for Networked Information
21 Dupont Circle, N.W.
Washington, DC 20036 USA

e-mail:	`joan@cni.org`
voice:	(202) 290-5098

FTP host:	`ftp.cni.org`
directory:	`/CNI`
directories:	(many or all)

Gopher:	`gopher.cni.org`
items:	(many or all)

Computer Professionals for Social Responsibility (CPSR)

"The mission of CPSR is to provide the public and policymakers with realistic assessments of the power, promise, and problems of information technology. As concerned citizens, CPSR members work to direct public attention to critical choices concerning the applications of information technology and how those choices affect society."

—From the file "cpsr brochure" available on
the FTP and Gopher servers.

CPSR National Office
Box 717
Palo Alto, CA 94301 USA

e-mail:	`cpsr@cpsr.org`
voice:	(415) 322-3778
fax:	(415) 322-4748

FTP host:	`ftp.cpsr.org`
directory:	`/pub`
filenames:	(many or all)

Gopher:	`gopher.cpsr.org`
menu:	`Computer Professionals for Social Responsibility` `Main Directory/`
items:	(many or all)

EDUCOM

"Educom serves the leaders who manage information technology in higher education. For more than 25 years, Educom has been leading the nation's educational community in integrating information technology into classrooms, curricula and research. Today,

■■

Educom's membership encompasses a broad range of institutions–from large, technologically sophisticated universities to small liberal arts and community colleges."

—From the file "EDUCOM-what-is-EDUCOM" in the FTP and Gopher servers.

EDUCOM
1112 16th Street, NW
Suite 600
Washington, DC 20036 USA

e-mail: `info@educom.edu`
voice: (202) 872-4200
fax: (202) 872-4318

FTP host: `educom.edu`
directory: `/pub`
filenames: (many or all)

Gopher: `educom.edu`
items: (many or all)

Electronic Frontier Foundation (EFF)

"Since its inception, EFF has worked to shape our nation's communications infrastructure and the policies that govern it in order to maintain and enhance First Amendment, privacy and other democratic values. We believe that our overriding public goal must be the creation of Electronic Democracy, so our work focuses on the establishment of:

- new laws that protect citizens' basic Constitutional rights as they use new communications technologies,
- a policy of common carriage requirements for all network providers so that all speech, no matter how controversial, will be carried without discrimination,
- a National Public Network where voice, data and video services are accessible to all citizens on an equitable and affordable basis, and
- a diversity of communities that enable all citizens to have a voice in the information age."

—From the file "About the Electronic Frontier Foundation" in the Gopher host.

The Electronic Frontier Foundation
1001 G Street N.W., Suite 950 E
Washington DC 20001 USA

e-mail: `ask@eff.org`
voice: (202) 347-5400
fax: (202) 393-5509

■■■ ।

FTP host:	`ftp.eff.org`	
directory:	`/pub/EFF`	
filenames:	(many or all)	
Gopher:	`gopher.eff.org`	
items:	(many or all)	
WWW:	`http://www.eff.org/`	
modem:	(202) 638-6120	
settings	:data=8, parity=N, stop=1	(300-14,400 baud V.32/V42bis)

FARNET (Federation of American Research Networks)

"FARNET is a non-profit corporation whose mission is to advance the use of computer networks to improve research and education. ...FARNET offers frequent educational programs for its members; works with other national and international organizations to improve the quality of information and services available to network users; provides information about networking to interested consumers, the media, and decision-makers; negotiates discounts on products and services for its members; provides a forum for the discussion of key technical and policy issues; publishes a monthly online newsletter and regular proceedings of its meetings. ...Membership in FARNET is open to any organization that supports its mission."

—From the file "what-is-farnet"
in the FTP and Gopher servers.

FARNET
1511 K. Street N.W.
Suite 1165
Washington, D.C. 20005

e-mail:	`jimw@farnet.org`
voice:	(202) 637-9557
fax:	(202) 637-9363
FTP host:	`ftp.cerf.net`
directory:	`/farnet`
filenames:	(many or all)
Gopher:	`farnet.org`
menu:	`FARNET Information/`
items:	(many or all)

Internet Engineering Task Force (IETF)

"The Internet Engineering Task Force is a loosely self-organized group of people who make technical and other contributions to the engineering and evolution of the Internet and its technologies. It is the principal body engaged in the development of new Internet Standard specifications. Its mission includes:

- Identifying, and proposing solutions to, pressing operational and technical problems in the Internet;
- Specifying the development or usage of protocols and the near-term architecture to solve such technical problems for the Internet;
- Making recommendations to the Internet Engineering Steering Group (IESG) regarding the standardization of protocols and protocol usage in the Internet;
- Facilitating technology transfer from the Internet Research Task Force (IRTF) to the wider Internet community; and
- Providing a forum for the exchange of information within the Internet community between vendors, users, researchers, agency contractors, and network managers.

"The IETF Plenary meeting is not a conference, although there are technical presentations. The IETF is not a traditional standards organization, although many standards are produced. The IETF is the volunteers who meet three times a year to fulfill the IETF mission.

"There is no membership in the IETF. Anyone may register for and attend any meeting. The closest thing there is to being an IETF member is being on the IETF or Working Group mailing lists (see the IETF Mailing Lists section [of the Gopher]). This is where the best information about current IETF activities and focus can be found."

> —From the file "The Tao of IETF"
> (RFC1539 and FYI17) on the FTP
> and Gopher servers.

Internet Society
Attn: IETF Secretariat
12020 Sunrise Valley Drive, suite 270
Reston, VA 22091 USA

e-mail: `ietf-info@cnri.reston.va.us`
voice: (703) 648-9888
            (800) 468-9707 (USA only)
fax: (703) 648-9887

FTP host: `ftp.isoc.org`
directory: `/ietf`
filenames: (many or all)

Gopher: `gopher.isoc.org`
menus: `Internet Society (includes IETF)/ IETF - Internet Engineering Task Force/`
items: (many or all)

Internet Society

The Internet Society is a not-for-profit organization whose "principal purpose is to maintain and extend the development and availability of the Internet and its associated technologies and applications–both as ends in themselves, and as a means of enabling organizations, professions, and individuals world-wide to more effectively collaborate, cooperate, and innovate in their respective fields and interests. Its specific goals and purposes include:

- development, maintenance, evolution, and dissemination of standards for the Internet and its internetworking technologies and applications;
- growth and evolution of the Internet architecture;
- maintenance and evolution of effective administrative processes necessary for operation of the global Internet and internets;
- education and research related to the Internet and internetworking;
- harmonization of actions and activities at international levels to facilitate the development and availability of the Internet;
- collection and dissemination of information related to the Internet and internetworking, including histories and archives;
- assisting technologically developing countries, areas, and peoples in implementing and evolving their Internet infrastructure and use;
- liaison with other organizations, governments, and the general public for coordination, collaboration, and education in effecting the above purposes."

—From the file
"what-is-ISOC.txt" on
the FTP host ftp.isoc.org

Internet Society
12020 Sunrise Valley Drive, suite 270
Reston, VA 22091 USA

e-mail:	`isoc@isoc.org`
voice:	(703) 648-9888
	(800) 468-9707 (USA only)
fax:	(703) 648-9887
FTP host:	`ftp.isoc.org`
directory:	`/isoc`
filenames:	(many or all)
Gopher:	`gopher.isoc.org`
menus:	`Internet Society (includes IETF)/`
items:	(many or all)

The InterNIC

The InterNIC is known as the Network Information Center (NIC) of first and last resort. It provides network information, name registration and directory services for the NSFNET community. Funded largely by the National Science Foundation, the InterNIC is composed of three sections, each provided by a different company: Information Services (provided by General Atomics); Directory and Database Services (provided by AT&T); and Registration Services (provided by Network Solutions, Inc.).

■■■

The InterNIC
General Atomics (GA)
P.O. Box 85608
San Diego, CA 92186-9784 USA

voice: (800) 444-4345
              (619) 455-4600
fax: (619) 455-4640

FTP hosts: `is.internic.net`   (Information Services)
              `ds.internic.net`   (Directory Services)
              `rs.internic.net`   (Registration Services)

Gopher: `internic.net`

WWW: `http://internic.net`

APPENDIX

B

Connecting to the Internet

Even if you don't think you have access to the Internet, you might! If you are in school or are employed, your organization may already have Internet access. So before spending a great deal of time and effort examining Internet access options, ask around. If your organization is not connected to the Internet, suggest that they consider the many benefits of the Internet to their activities. Organizations located in Alaska, Idaho, Montana, North Dakota, Oregon, or Washington, are encouraged to call NorthWestNet for information.

If you are certain that your organization lacks Internet connectivity, or if you want a private account, there are a growing number of Internet service providers who would be happy to help you.

In general, there are two classes of Internet connections: connectivity for sites such as schools or companies that will support many users, and access for individuals. The former is most often achieved by obtaining "dedicated access," i.e., direct IP connections to the Internet. Individuals usually obtain a "dialup" account which is reached through a modem connected to your personal computer.

There are also varying degrees of Internet service. Your options range from e-mail-only access, to full-service connectivity with optional access to commercial databases thrown in. You'll want to consider a number of factors other than price and pricing structure:

- How many people at your site will want to use the Internet?
- What applications will users at your site want to use (e-mail, Telnet, Gopher, Mosaic, etc.)?
- What hardware and software is available to you locally? from the service provider?
- How fast a connection will be needed to support the needs of you and your users?
- How much technical and user assistance will you require? after business hours?
- What reliability rate do you require of the service?
- What can you predict about your needs for the future and will the service provider be able to grow with you?

So be sure to shop around, compare prices, and consider what options are most appropriate to your needs.

The following are directions on how to get frequently updated lists of Internet service providers.

▪▪▪

OBTAINING CURRENT LISTS OF U.S. INTERNET SERVICE PROVIDERS

▪▪▪

Multi-User Service Providers

An up-to-date list of organizations that provide Internet access to schools or companies can be obtained from the InterNIC. This list contains basic location and contact information for the providers covering both the U.S. and Canada.

FTP host:	`is.internic.net`
directory:	`/infoguide/getting-connected/us-dedicated`
filename:	`internic-provider-list`
Gopher:	`is.internic.net`
menus:	`InterNIC Information Services (General Atomics)/Getting Connected to the Internet/`
	`U.S. Dedicated Line Providers/`
item:	`InterNIC Internet Service Providers List`

Public-Access Internet Hosts

A growing number of entrepreneurs are providing Internet access from Bulletin Board Systems which you can call from your personal computer via modem.

Peter Kaminski maintains a list of such services, which is distributed as a periodic posting to several Usenet newsgroups ("alt.bbs.lists" and "news.answers") and via e-mail requests:

```
mail:    info-deli-server@netcom.com
subject: Send PDIAL
message: (none needed)
```

You can also subscribe to the PDIAL distribution so that you will receive updates as they are released.

```
mail:    info-deli-server@netcom.com
subject: Subscribe PDIAL
message: (none needed)
```

PDIAL is also available via Gopher and anonymous FTP at many sites. The FTP site listed below is the authoritative site (Kaminsky's home site), and the Gopher provides access to the very same file using the Gopher protocol.

```
FTP host:   ftp.netcom.com
directory:  pub/info-deli/public-access
filename:   pdial

Gopher:     gopher.gsfc.nasa.gov
menus:      Networking/Internet stuff/Dialup Internet access providers/
item:       PDIAL list (Peter Kaminski)/
```

Another list of this sort is known as the "nixpub" (uNIX PUBlic access systems) list. These are typically Unix-based BBSs providing access to Usenet newsgroups and e-mail access to the Internet. Short and long versions of the nixpub list are distributed as a periodic posting to the Usenet newsgroups "comp.misc" and the various "alt.bbs" newsgroups, or you can request a copy by sending one of the following e-mail messages:

```
mail:     nixpub@digex.com
subject:  (none needed)
message:  (none needed)
```

```
mail:     archive-server@cs.widener.edu
subject:  (none needed)
message:  (one of the following messages)

send nixpub long
send nixpub short
send nixpub long short
index nixpub
```

Or by connecting to the following Gopher server (of many that offer access to this list).

```
Gopher:   gopher.sbu.edu
menu:     Finding Your Way Around the Internet/
items:    Public/Open Access UNIX Sites (nixpub long)
          Public/Open Access UNIX Sites (nixpub short)
```

The InterNIC has collected these files and placed them in a single directory accessible via Gopher and FTP.

```
FTP host:   is.internic.net
directory:  /infoguide/getting-connected/us-dialup
filenames:  (many or all)

Gopher:     is.internic.net
menus:      InterNIC Information Services (General Atomics)/Getting
            Connected to the Internet/
            U.S. Dial-up Service Providers/
item: (many or all)
```

■■

Obtaining Current Lists of Non-U.S. Internet Service Providers

A list of Internet service providers worldwide is currently maintained by SRI, International and is available in their printed book, *Internet: Getting Started*, listed in the bibliography.

The InterNIC also maintains lists of international providers organized by geographic area.

```
FTP host:    is.internic.net
directory:   /infoguide/getting-connected/international
filenames:   (many or all)

Gopher:      is.internic.net
menus:       InterNIC Information Services (General Atomics)/Getting
             Connected to the Internet/International Providers/
items:       (many or all)
```

Bibliography

The following printed books are particularly thorough in their coverage of Internet service providers. An excellent title to help located providers and analyze various offerings is *Connecting to the Internet* by Estrada. Frey and Adams, Marine et al., and Quarterman also provide great coverage of network service providers outside the U.S. Notess focuses on dialup providers rather than direct connections. Be aware, however, that printed materials about the Internet become outdated very quickly, and you are encouraged to obtain one of the lists mentioned earlier in this appendix for the most up-to-date information.

Estrada, S. *Connecting to the Internet: An O'Reilly Buyer's Guide*. Sebastapol, CA: O'Reilly and Associates, 1993.

Frey, D. and R. Adams. *!%@:: A Directory of Electronic Mail Addressing and Networks*. Sebastapol, CA: O'Reilly and Associates, 1993.

LaQuey, T. *The User's Directory of Computer Networks*. Bedford, MA: Digital Press, 1990.

Marine, A., S. Kirkpatrick, V. Neou, and C. Ward. *Internet: Getting Started*. Englewood Cliffs, NJ: Prentice Hall, 1993.

Notess, G. *Internet Access Providers: An International Resource Directory*. Westport: Meckler, 1994.

Quarterman, J. S. *The Matrix: Computer Networks and Conferencing Systems Worldwide*. Bedford, MA: Digital Press, 1990.

The User's Perspective on Internet Security

■■

The old adage, "a chain is only as strong as its weakest link," is an appropriate meta-phor for computer and network security. From the privacy of e-mail messages to a company's trade secrets to protection against viruses and other vandalism, people should be concerned about the security of their computer systems. This is not to say that the Internet has been a hotbed of illicit and unethical behavior, quite the contrary! Most Internet users respect the privacy of others on the Net and many Internet services maintain secure facilities and have some security procedures built in. A few simple precautions will help you maintain a secure system today. In the coming years, more and more options will become common.

Passwords: Your First Line of Defense

Just as you lock your front door when you leave your home to protect its contents, a password is the key to locking your network account. Both the lock on the front door of your home and the password protection provide the first line of defense for protecting your property. But the lock on a front door can only prevent people from easily entering and if someone has a copy of your key the security is compromised. The same is true for the password to your account. If someone breaks into the system where your account resides, they may have access to your files without ever knowing your password. Alternatively, if someone finds out your password, they then have the key to get to your files, read them, change them, or delete them.

The most important aspect of choosing a password is to choose one that is difficult for humans and computers to figure out. Don't use real words or names, don't use your birthdate, license plate, or similar obvious number. On the other hand, you don't want to pick something that is impossible to remember because you won't be writing it down, right? One easy way to come up with a safe password is to make up a saying or word that either combines text with numbers or symbols or combines two words together. This way a program that tries all the words in the dictionary won't match your password. Some examples of these are:

* coffee4u   (a bit long, but tasty!)
* Te@for2   (romantic, but I like coffee better)
* Do11ar$ (those are "one's" in the middle)
* p@perw8   (OK, it's a bit tortured)
* stonesoup   (literary gourmet)

In general, passwords should follow these guidelines:

* At least 6-8 characters long
* Include a symbol or combine two words together
* Use mixed case (many systems are case sensitive)

C • The User's Perspective on Internet Security

The importance of difficult-to-break passwords can not be stressed enough. If someone guesses your password, they have access to the data on your system. And on no account should you write your password down or share it with others!

Watch the login reports on your account. Upon login, many systems will display the date, time, and location of the last login (location being the modem or machine from which you last connected). Check this information and be sure that it reflects the last time you remember logging in. If you think someone else has logged in, change your password immediately! As a matter of fact, it is recommended that you change your password regularly anyway (every three to six months is a good rule of thumb). Just don't forget that you did. ;-)

fjz*l;)9S: Using Encryption to Scramble Your Data

Encryption of data both traveling across the Internet and located on Internet-connected computers is a hot topic these days. In the past, when the data was owned mostly by research institutions and few people other than researchers were using the network, there was not as much concern with data security. (A large and noticeable exception has always been the military.) With the recent growth of commercial businesses joining the network, along with the incredible increase in the number of users overall, there has been a strong push for increased security using data encryption using either a public or private key.

Data encryption may be necessary during transmission of data because the Internet is a shared network, and data packets flow over common carrier media. Just as it is possible to tap into phone calls if you have both the right equipment and physical access to the phone circuit, it is also possible to "tap" the Net and gather packets addressed to certain parties and either steal or copy the data. However, considering the amount of data that flows on the network, the complex network topology (usually over circuits provided by a phone company), and the fact that messages or files are broken up into packets which may not all flow along the same route, tapping the Internet is not an easy task. But to be sure your secrets remain just that, you may want to consider encrypting your most sensitive data before sending it out on the network.

Encrypting data stored on an Internet-connected computer may also be prudent. Some users who have sensitive information to store, choose not to store it on a computer that is directly connected to the Internet. (Read about Firewalls below.) However, if you choose to store such information on a connected computer, consider encrypting the information on it, or at least the sensitive information.

The world of encryption can change rather suddenly and these changes occur for two reasons. As was mentioned earlier, encryption is a hot topic and a lot of software developers are working hard on creating new algorithms and types of encryption. On the other hand, due to national security and law enforcement concerns, the U.S. government has placed some restrictions on encryption and may be issuing new rules or voluntary guidelines regarding the use of encryption technology within the U.S. For details on specific types of encryption that might be available to you on your system, contact your technical staff.

Using a Digital Signature

A digital signature attaches a code to the end of a message that acts as verification that you are the original sender and that no changes have been made to the message during its transmission. The message itself may or may not be encrypted using this technique, so readers without the signature software may be able to read the message with no trouble. However, without digital signature software on their own computer that verifies the integrity of the message, the reader can not be sure that the message is free from alteration or forgery. Again, to see if you have digital signatures available to you, contact your technical staff.

What is a Firewall?

A firewall is a means of protecting a private network that is attached to the Internet from unauthorized intrusion. Often, this is handled through the combined use of routers and computers that prevent outside traffic from entering your network. Firewalls are typically designed and installed by network technical staff.

APPENDIX

D

Uniform Resource Locator

■■■

Uniform Resource Locators (URL) are becoming the call numbers of the Internet. They help both humans and computers locate documents, images, sounds, and applications on the Internet. Tim Berners-Lee designed the original URL in 1989 for use on the World Wide Web (WWW). At the time, it was called a "WWW address" and very little of the original specification has been modified since then, but rather new items have been added. Although only WWW clients such as Mosaic and Lynx are currently capable of using URLs for navigation, many people are using them as a shorthand way of describing how to find a resource on the Internet.

The Uniform Resource Identifier Working Group (URI-WG) of the Internet Engineering Task Force (IETF) is updating the URL specification and working to bring it to the level of an Internet standard. Once the specification is accepted as a standard, an Internet Request for Comments (RFC) will be issued. Other Internet resource and discovery tools, such as Gopher, may also eventually be able to use URLs.

In practice, a URL is simply the concatenation of the scheme for accessing a particular resource. It identifies the name of the computer that holds that particular copy of the document or other type of resource, the location of the resource on the computer and the specific Internet tool of protocol needed for access. The generic URL for most objects looks like this: <URL:protocol://computer.domain.name/object.name>. There are different URL formats for different access protocols. Some examples of real-life URLs are listed in the table below, along with an explanation of each one. (The angle brackets and "URL:" label are only needed when the URL appears in free text.)

Uniform Resource Locator	Resource it Describes
`ftp://ftp.nwnet.net/nodenews/1293.nodenews`	Make an FTP connection to the host ftp.nwnet.net and retrieve a copy of the 12/93 issue of NorthWestNet's NodeNews in directory /nodenews
`telnet://fedix@fedix.fie.com`	Make a telnet connection to fedix.fie.com and login as "fedix"
`telnet://martini.eecs.umich.edu:3000`	Make a telnet connection to martini.eecs.umich.edu port 3000

■ ■

(Continued)

`telnet://guest:visitor@cap.gwu.edu`	Make a telnet connection to cap.gwu.edu login as "guest" with the password "visitor"
`gopher://marvel.loc.gov:70/1`	Make a Gopher connection to the Library of Congress Gopher
`http://indy.radiology.uiowa.edu/VirtualHospital.html`	Make a hypertext connection to the host indy.radiology.uiowa.edu and read the hypertext mark-up language (HTML) file VirtualHospital.html
`gopher://veronica.uni-koeln.de:2347/7?recycling`	Make a Gopher connection to the veronica server at the University of Cologne and search the word "recycling"

A WWW client can use the above URLs to go directly to the specified resource using the appropriate protocol. For resources available through Telnet, WWW clients spawn a separate Telnet client to make the connection to the remote computer, while the Gopher and FTP resources are accessed from within the WWW client itself. WWW also has its own protocol, the Hypertext Transport Protocol (HTTP). HTTP allows you to access Hypertext Mark-Up Language (HTML) documents which contain embedded codes for seamlessly linking documents, sounds, graphics, and other resources together, regardless of their location on the Internet.

When you are using a WWW client, you can simply type (or paste) the URL of a document you want into an "Open URL" dialog box (selected from the "File" menu), and it will be retrieved for you. Within the Lynx WWW client, the "g" command allows you to enter the URL for the desired document. If you don't have a WWW client, you can extract the basic information your need from a URL for use with other Internet tools, such as Gopher or FTP. (A public Lynx client is available via Telnet at ukanaix.cc.ukans.edu.)

URLs are not the only tools being developed by the IETF to assist in the discovery and retrieval of networked resources. Still to come are Uniform Resource Names (URNs) and Uniform Resource Citations or Characteristics (URCs). These two resource identifiers, along with URLs are all Uniform Resource Identifiers (URI). With the acronyms out of the way, we can look at what these tools provide. The URL, as stated above, describes the location of a specific instance of a networked object and is akin to a call number. The URN is the name given to a specific object no matter where the copy or copies of the object reside and is akin to an international standard book number (ISBN), which are found on the back of the title page in books. The URC contains information about the resource (known as meta-information), possibly including such items as publication date, version number, file type information, price, etc.

The developers of these standards realize that the terms and acronyms are more technical than most people feel comfortable with. The plan is that most users will not have to use the URIs directly in the near future, that is, computers will handle the messy parts and present a clear and coherent set of information to the user. A major part of this automation is the translation of a URN to a list of URLs. In plain English, this means, "I've heard of this document (URN). Where can I find a copy (URL)?"

URLs, URNs, and URCs are under development and not yet standards. The URL specifications are the furthest along, and URLs have been in use for quite some time.

The URI Working Group spent several hours discussing the specifications and the overall architecture of the URIs at the 29th IETF held in Seattle in late March 1994. Further discussion continues to be carried out on the URI mailing list.

For more information and papers covering the architecture, specifications, and requirements of URIs, connect to the Web using your favorite client (Mosaic, Lynx, or Cello), and view "WWW Names and Addresses, URIs, URLs, URNs."

Access: WWW: **http://info.cern.ch/hypertext/WWW/Addressing/Addressing.html**

APPENDIX

E

NorthWestNet Acceptable Use Policies

NorthWestNet Acceptable Use Policy for Research and Education

NorthWestNet is a regional data communications network serving a consortium of universities, colleges, industrial research groups, libraries, hospitals, government agencies, primary and secondary schools and school districts, and commercial enterprises in the northwestern United States. NorthWestNet is wholly owned, managed, and operated by the Northwest Academic Computing Consortium, Inc. (NWACC).

NorthWestNet embraces the mission to promote research, education, and economic development by providing access to network communications, computing, and electronic information systems and services. This document describes certain research and education uses which are consistent with the objectives of NorthWestNet, but does not exhaustively enumerate all such possible acceptable uses. Membership in NorthWestNet conveys the right to access NorthWestNet facilities and network services for research and educational purposes. A companion document, "NorthWestNet Acceptable Use Policy for Commercial Enterprise," describes access and usage policies for business enterprise.

Some Acceptable Uses of NorthWestNet Facilities Include:

1. All use of NorthWestNet network services and facilities shall be consistent with the mission of NorthWestNet and NWACC. All use shall be intended to facilitate the exchange of information, intellectual property, and services to promote research, education, and technology diffusion, and otherwise be consistent with the broad objectives of NorthWestNet.

2. Use of NorthWestNet facilities and services for research, education, instruction, and as a vehicle for scholarly communications by member institutions through the provision of a high-speed data communications and computing, and electronic information resources and services is encouraged.

3. Use as a means for members to access remote computing and information resources for the purpose of research, education, or instruction is encouraged. Notable examples of such resources are the NSF supercomputing centers.

4. Use necessary to support other acceptable uses is itself acceptable. For example, administrative communications which are part of the support infrastructure needed for research, education, instruction, and development are acceptable.

5. Use required by agreements with NSF, a primary funding agency for NorthWestNet, is acceptable.

6. Use by member institutions as a laboratory for research and experimentation in computer communications is permitted where such use does not interfere with production usage. However, any experimental use requiring modification to router software or protocol layers below ISO layer 4 requires prior review and approval from the Director of Technical Services.

Some Unacceptable Uses:

7. Use of NorthWestNet facilities and network services for any illegal purpose, or to achieve unauthorized access to systems, software, or data is prohibited.

8. NorthWestNet shall not be used to transmit any communication where the meaning of the message, or its transmission or distribution, is intended to be highly abusive to the recipient or recipients thereof.

9. NorthWestNet is a production communications network on which many users depend. Users of NorthWestNet network services and facilities should promote efficient use of the networks and thereby attempt to minimize and, if possible, avoid unnecessary network traffic which might interfere or otherwise impact negatively with the work of other users of NorthWestNet or connected networks. Uses that significantly interfere with the ability of others to make effective use of the network or which disrupt NorthWestNet or any connected networks, systems, services, or equipment are prohibited.

10. Use for business or commercial enterprise is prohibited under this policy. However, access to NorthWestNet facilities and network services for commercial use is available as a value-added service to NorthWestNet member organizations for an additional service fee.

Interpretation, application, and modification of this Acceptable Use Policy shall be within the sole discretion of NorthWestNet and NWACC. Questions about any issue related to this Policy should be directed to NorthWestNet by member organizations when an issue first arises.

NorthWestNet and NWACC make no warranty of any kind, expressed or implied, regarding Internet resources or services, or the contents of resources or electronic messages over the Internet, nor shall NorthWestNet or NWACC be liable in any event for incidental or consequential damages, direct or indirect, resulting from the use of either NorthWestNet or the resources and services available through NorthWestNet Internet facilities or network services.

Version 3.1
February 12, 1993

NorthWestNet Acceptable Use Policy for Commercial Enterprise

NorthWestNet is a regional data communications network serving a consortium of universities, colleges, industrial research groups, libraries, hospitals, government agencies, primary and secondary schools and school districts, and commercial enterprises in the northwestern United States. NorthWestNet is wholly owned, managed, and operated by the Northwest Academic Computing Consortium, Inc. (NWACC). NorthWestNet embraces the mission to promote research, education, and economic development by providing access to network communications, computing, and electronic information systems and services.

This document describes certain commercial enterprise uses which are consistent with the objectives of NorthWestNet, but does not exhaustively enumerate all such possible acceptable uses. Membership in NorthWestNet conveys the right to access NorthWestNet facilities and network services for research and educational purposes as defined in a companion document, "NorthWestNet Acceptable Use Policy for Research and Education." Access to NorthWestNet facilities and network services for commercial use as described in this Policy is available as a value-added service to NorthWestNet member organizations for an additional service fee.

Some Acceptable Uses of NorthWestNet Facilities Include:

1. All use of NorthWestNet network services and facilities shall be consistent with the mission of NorthWestNet and NWACC. All use shall be intended to facilitate the exchange of information, intellectual property, and services to promote research, education, technology diffusion, economic development, and commerce and otherwise be consistent with the broad objectives of NorthWestNet.

2. All uses defined as acceptable under the companion policy, "NorthWestNet Acceptable Use Policy for Research and Education" are acceptable.

3. When requested by a user of NorthWestNet or any connected network, transmission of product information and commercial messages is permitted. Discussion of a product's relative advantages and disadvantages by users of the product, and vendors' responses to those who pose questions about their products, is permitted.

Some Unacceptable Uses:

4. Use of NorthWestNet facilities and network services for any illegal purpose, or to achieve unauthorized access to systems, software, or data is prohibited.

5. NorthWestNet shall not be used to transmit any communication where the meaning of the message, or its transmission or distribution, is intended to be highly offensive to the recipient or recipients thereof.

6. Intrusive or unsolicited advertising (or other commercial information) may not be "broadcast" or be otherwise sent to any user of NorthWestNet or any connected network.

7. NorthWestNet is a production communications network on which many users depend. Users of NorthWestNet network services and facilities should promote efficient use of the networks and thereby attempt to minimize and, if possible, avoid unnecessary network traffic which might interfere or otherwise impact negatively with the work of other users of NorthWestNet or connected networks. Uses that significantly interfere with the ability of others to make effective use of the network or which disrupt NorthWestNet or any connected networks, systems, services, or equipment are prohibited.

Interpretation, application, and modification of this Acceptable Use Policy shall be within the sole discretion of NorthWestNet and NWACC. Questions about any issue related to this Policy should be directed to NorthWestNet by member organizations when an issue first arises.

NorthWestNet and NWACC make no warranty of any kind, expressed or implied, regarding Internet resources or services, or the contents of resources or electronic messages over the Internet, nor shall NorthWestNet or NWACC be liable in any event for incidental or consequential damages, direct or indirect, resulting from the use of either NorthWestNet or the resources and services available through NorthWestNet.

Version 1.1
February 12, 1993

F

NSFNET
Backbone Services

Acceptable Use Policies

GENERAL PRINCIPLE:

1. NSFNET Backbone services are provided to support open research and education in and among US research and instructional institutions, plus research arms of for-profit firms when engaged in open scholarly communication and research. Use for other purposes is not acceptable.

Specifically Acceptable Uses:

2. Communication with foreign researchers and educators in connection with research or instruction, as long as any network that the foreign user employs for such communication provides reciprocal access to US researchers and educators.

3. Communication and exchange for professional development, to maintain currency, or to debate issues in a field or subfield of knowledge.

4. Use for disciplinary-society, university-association, government-advisory, or standards activities related to the user's research and instructional activities.

5. Use in applying for or administering grants or contracts for research or instruction, but not for other fund-raising or public relations activities.

6. Any other administrative communications or activities in direct support of research and instruction.

7. Announcements of new products or services for use in research or instruction, but not advertising of any kind.

8. Any traffic originating from a network of another member agency of the Federal Networking Council if the traffic meets the acceptable use policy of that agency.

9. Communication incidental to otherwise acceptable use, except for illegal or specifically unacceptable use.

Unacceptable Uses:

10. Use for-profit activities, unless covered by the General Principle or as a specifically acceptable use.

11. Extensive use for private or personal business.

This statement applies to use of the NSFNET Backbone only. NSF expects that connecting networks will formulate their own use policies. The NSF Division of Networking and Communications Research and Infrastructure will resolve any questions about this Policy or its interpretation.

June 1992

Glossary

INTERNET SYMBOLS, TERMS, AND ACRONYMS

This glossary covers some of the symbols, terms, and acronyms you may need to have defined in your excursions through the Internet. It is a potpourri of standard Internet terminology and a few terms from general telecommunications and computer science meant to complement the materials covered in *The Internet Passport*.

Many of the terms in this glossary have additional meanings outside of the context of the Internet; but the definitions provided here are meant to cover only those meanings relevant to the Internet. In many cases, there are a variety of definitions or shades of meaning for a term even in the context of the Internet. The definitions given are usually for the most frequently encountered uses of the terms.

While using the Internet, you are bound to encounter many terms and acronyms which have not been included in this glossary. For additional materials you may want to obtain the "Glossary of Networking Terms" currently available as RFC1208 (recently updated and soon to be assigned a new RFC number).

Letters, Symbols, and Numbers

C
The programming language of choice in the Unix operating system and much of the Internet.

K
Abbreviation for kilo. "K" is used to denote 1000 (kilogram = 1000 grams, kilometer = 1000 meters, etc.) In the computing vernacular, K often refers to a kilobyte, or 1024 bytes. Why 1024? Because, as with many useful numbers in the computing sciences, 1024 is a power of 2 (2 to the 10th to be exact). To help make K concrete, one K of text is a little less than a standard screen of text.

.Z

Suffix added to the names of files which have been compressed with the Unix compress program; for example, the file "passport.txt.Z" is very likely a compressed version of the file "passport.txt."

:-)

A smiley. Looks like a smiling face when viewed sideways. Used in electronic messages to indicate that the preceding text was meant in a humorous or lighthearted way. There are many variants on the basic smiley to indicate subtleties of tone. See Chapter 4 for a compact bestiary of smilies.

::

Part of the notation typically found in DECNet addresses which separates a userid and a DECNet address (decnet_host::userid).

@

"At." the symbol separating a userid from an Internet host name in a user's e-mail address. Indicates that a given userid is "at" (i.e., has a mailbox at) a certain Internet address; for example, userid@an.internet.address. This symbol is also used in the same role in the addressing syntaxes of many other networks, such as BITNET.

!

"Bang." Part of bang path notation within the UUCP network separating host names along the route a message is to take in UUCP's store and forward delivery paradigm. (See "bang path.")

%

A symbol typically used to make an alien network's addressing syntax pass through the Internet unscathed so it can be processed by an e-mail gateway. For example, an Internet user can send a message to a user on a BITNET host by sending an e-mail message to the e-mail gateway cunyvm.cuny.edu with the following syntax:

userid%host.bitnet@cunyvm.cuny.edu

The gateway at cunyvm converts the "userid%host.bitnet" to "userid@host," and forwards the message onto the BITNET network for delivery. Mixing "%" and "!" in an address should be avoided.

/

In Unix notation the forward slash is a separator between directory, subdirectory, and file names; e.g., "directory/subdirectory/filename". DOS uses "\" (backslash) for the same purpose. By itself, "/" represents the root directory of the Unix system.

*

A wildcard. Many operating systems and software packages allow you to use this symbol to indicate that any possible character(s) or value(s) might be in it's place. For example, in Unix you might use this to move all files beginning with the word "passport" into an appropriate directory:

mv passport.* /essential.internet.documents

56Kbps

56 thousand bits per second; a common speed for dedicated access lines to the Internet.

Words and Acronyms

Acceptable Use Policy (AUP)

Conditions or restrictions that apply to the use of a network. For example, some portions of the Internet explicitly restrict commercial communications, or an institution may prohibit the playing of computer games on an Internet host during certain hours.

acknowledgment

A message returned to its sender to indicate that data has successfully arrived at a destination; a feature found in some e-mail software packages.

address

Loosely used to refer to either an e-mail address (see "e-mail address") or an internet address (see "internet address" and "domain name").

address resolution

The conversion of an Internet address to its corresponding physical address.

alias

A short and easy to remember name or command that substitutes for a longer, harder to remember name or command. Aliases are often used for e-mail addresses, e.g., "sue" could be an alias for the full e-mail address sra@idacrk.hs.idaho.edu.

Andrew File System (afs)

A distributed file system developed at Carnegie Mellon University allowing files on one computer to be used as if they were files on the user's computer, even if these computers are thousands of miles apart.

anonymous FTP

An Internet application which allows one to gain access to a remote Internet host through the userid "anonymous" and to copy files from the remote host to one's local computer.

anonymous FTP host

A computer on the Internet that allows anonymous FTP access for remote file retrieval, and sometimes storage, by remote users. There are more than 1,000 substantial anonymous FTP hosts throughout the world that collectively contain millions of files.

ANSI (American National Standards Institute)

U.S. organization which, among other things, approves computer communications standards. ANSI is also sometime used, in context, for specific ANSI standards (e.g., ANSI terminal emulation).

application

A software program designed to perform a specific task for a user.

archie

A software program developed at McGill University that maintains a frequently updated central catalog of files contained in many of the world's anonymous FTP hosts.

archive

1) An organized holding of computer files stored for later retrieval, for example, an anonymous FTP archive, or collections of messages from mailing lists or discussion groups;

2) a set of files which are stored as a single file to simplify handling and processing; an archived file must be "unpacked" before it can be used. (See "tar" and "self-extracting archive.")

ARPANET (Advanced Research Projects Agency Network)

A network sponsored by the Advanced Research Projects Agency which served as a testbed for many of the communications protocols used in today's Internet.

■■■

ASCII (American Standard Code for Information Interchange)

A method of representing the alphabetic, numeric, and control characters used in computer communications and coded in hexadecimal notation. "ASCII file" is used to indicate a file that is stored in clear text (i.e., readable by humans). Also see "EBCDIC."

authentication

Verification of the "true" identity of an individual or process, usually in the context of systems security and access.

backbone

A portion of an internet that acts as a main connection for the interconnection of other networks. The top structural level of many internets. In some cases, the backbone of an internet is built with higher capacity lines to accommodate the aggregation of traffic from the other "tributary" networks.

bandwidth

1) The amount of digital information that a circuit is capable of transmitting in a given amount of time; e.g., a 56Kbps circuit can, under optimal conditions, transmit 56 kilobits (56,000 bits) of information per second.

2) The specific electromagnetic frequency or range of frequencies (usually measured in hertz) that a given medium is designed to carry.

bang path

A sequential list of the names of computer hosts, each separated by "!", through which a message must be routed for transmission through the UUCP network; for example "next_host!intermediate_host!destination_host". Bang paths may soon be a thing of the past.

baud

A unit of communications speed measured as the number of distinguishable events per second. If each event is a bit, then baud is equivalent to bits per second (BPS). Used most often to describe the speed of modems; e.g., a 9600 baud modem can transmit data 4 times as fast as a 2400 baud modem.

BBS (Bulletin Board System)

A computer and associated software that typically provides electronic messaging services, archives of files, and any other services or activities of interest to the bulletin board system's operator (SYSOP). Although BBSs have traditionally been the domain of hobbyists, an increasing number of BBSs are connected directly to the Internet, and many BBSs are currently operated by government, educational, and research institutions.

binary

Representation of information in the form of "0" and "1" (base 2 notation). In terms of electrical circuits, 0 and 1 correspond to "off" and "on." Humans, having ten fingers, like to use base 10; computers, who don't have fingers, prefer base 2.   :-)

binary file

Used to denote a non-ASCII file, often an executable program or a file used by application software.

bit

Abbreviation for "binary element." The smallest possible unit of information: "yes" or "no," "on" or "off," "1" or "0."

BITNET (Because It's Time Network)

1) An e-mail and file sharing network used by a large number of academic and research institutions, based on a proprietary store and forward transport protocol. Now gatewayed in many places to the Internet.

2) The specific BITNET network coordinated by the Corporation for Research and Educational Networks. (See "CREN.")

Boolean search

A method of searching for information, often used in databases and online library catalogs, using the Boolean operators, "AND," "OR," "NAND" (not and), and "NOR" (not or).

bounce

The network equivalent of the famous Elvis Presley song, "Return to Sender, Address Unknown." The return of an e-mail message because of an error in it's addressing or delivery.

bps (bits per second)

The number of bits of information transmitted per second through a transmission medium.

BTW (By The Way)

A "three letter acronym" (TLA) frequently used in e-mail messages.

cache

Area in volatile memory where information is retained for rapid access. In contrast, when information is written to disk, tape or other permanent storage media, access time is longer.

CAUSE (Association for the Management of Information Technology in Higher Education)

An association for the management of information technology in colleges and universities.

CCIRN (Coordinating Committee for Intercontinental Research Networks)

An international organization responsible for planning and coordinating the research and implementation of international networking activities.

CCITT (Comité Consultatif International de Télégraphique et Téléphonique)

A branch of the United Nations International Telecommunications Union that makes recommendations about protocols for data communications systems.

checksum

A value computed from the entire contents of a message before and after transmission. A receiving host compares the transmitted checksum with a calculated checksum; if the two match, it is likely that the message was transmitted without error.

CIX (Commercial Internet Exchange)

U.S. backbone network parallel to the NSFNET that permits the transfer of commercial traffic. Free of the Acceptable Use Restrictions (AUP) of the NSFNET. (Pronounced "kicks.")

client

A computer or process that relies on the resources of another computer or process (the server).

CMC (Computer Mediated Communication)

Systems like e-mail, mailing lists, and discussion groups, that allow people to exchange messages using computers.

■■■ ı

CNI (Coalition for Networked Information)
A working group established jointly by EDUCOM, ARL (Association of Research Libraries) and CAUSE that focuses on implementation of and access to network information services and resources.

CNIDR (Clearinghouse for Networked Information Discovery and Retrieval)
An NSF-funded clearinghouse for information on and development of network communication tools such as WAIS, veronica, etc. (Pronounced "snyder.")

Community Net
Similar to the Free-Nets, these are local networking initiatives that offer access to community resources and Internet-accessible accounts for use by the general public. These sometimes involve "civic networking" projects where citizens may participate in public-interest discussions. A Community Net may charge fees to recover costs.

compression
Methods of reducing the amount of storage or bandwidth that information occupies without altering the informational content. Files on anonymous FTP hosts are often stored in various compressed formats. As a trivial example of one compression technique, the many blank spaces that frequently occur at the ends of lines of computer files can be stored as the symbol for blank space plus the number of blank spaces that follow.

connectionless communication
Networking communications in which information is transmitted without prior establishment of a connection. Each packet of data contains enough information to reach its destination.

cracker
IMHO, an individual who willfully and sometimes maliciously attempts to breach the integrity and security of other's computer resources and data. Not to be confused with hacker!

CREN (Corporation for Research and Educational Networking)
An umbrella organization formerly responsible for two national U.S. networks, BITNET and CSNET. Although CSNET is now defunct and BITNET is losing some of its popularity to the Internet, CREN continues to focus on network access and tools.

crossposting
Submitting a message to two or more discussion groups or newsgroups.

CWIS (Campus Wide Information System)
A software system for electronically providing information of interest to the members of a particular community, most frequently a college or university.

cyberpunk
A popular literature dealing with a (hypothetical?) computer based society or a person who embraces the cyberpunk vision.

cyberspace
Loosely used to describe the indeterminate location of one's mind when using computer networks; for example, "I had a Telnet connection to Switzerland, from which I launched an FTP session to Singapore, and I forgot where *I* was: I think I was sort of lost in cyberspace." A term coined by William Gibson in his cyberpunk novel *Neuromancer*, to describe a "space," partly visual, partly conceptual, in which human minds and networks meet through brain-computer interfaces.

DARPA (Defense Advanced Research Projects Agency)
An agency of the U.S. Department of Defense which (among other activities) funded the research that led to communications protocols that have in turn made today's Internet possible.

DDN (Defense Data Network)
A network of networks used by the U.S. Department of Defense (DARPANET, MILNET, etc.).

DDN NIC (Defense Data Network Network Information Center)
Formerly the authoritative repository of many of the core documents for the Internet (RFCs, FYI's, Internet Drafts, etc.), as well as the central database for Internet IP addresses and domain names. These services are now provided by the InterNIC. The DDN NIC now provides directory and other services for MILNET only.

/dev/null
A place to which information goes, never to be seen again. The term is based on the Unix data sink of the same name and is equivalent to the old fashioned "circular file" or the Orwellian "memory hole." As a particularly brutal example that captures the pathos of the slang usage of this term, if you've broken up with your boyfriend via e-mail, you might write in closing, "send any responses to /dev/null."

dialup
Connection between computers via a telephone line, usually by way of a modem. Unlike dedicated connections, dialup connections are established only for the duration of the session.

digital signature
A method of "signing" an e-mail message that uses an encrypted signature. This signature, which looks like gibberish, can then be unencrypted to verify the sender.

directory service
A service which may provide network addresses and/or userids of individuals, hosts, and services; also see "yellow pages" and "white pages."

discussion group
A forum for communication about a topic by e-mail. Each discussion group has a network address to which messages are sent and from which messages are distributed to all discussion group members. Examples of discussion groups include LISTSERV and MAILBASE.

distribution
In Usenet, the geographical region to which a message will be sent. Typically, one can choose institutional, local, regional, continental, or global distribution.

distribution list
A list of e-mail addresses for people who receive periodic messages from a person or a software program. Unlike a mailing list, which acts as a "many-to-many" service, a distribution list is primarily a "one-to-many" service.

DNS (Domain Name System)
The online distributed database that translates human-readable domain names into numeric IP addresses. DNS servers are located throughout the Internet, and no one DNS server contains information for all Internet hosts.

domain name

The Internet convention of constructing an address by using userid@domain_name. That is, everything to the right of the @ sign is the domain name. Domain names are an administrative tool and a convenience to human beings; they are not a physical description of the network.

"dot"

The separator between elements of a host computer name, for example, "marvel.loc.gov" is pronounced, "marvel-dot-el-oh-see-dot-guv". The designation is distinguished since the mark is neither a period nor a decimal point.

dumb terminal

A terminal which only has the capacity to connect to another computer on which the actual application software and storage reside. Prior to the personal computer revolution, almost all terminals used were dumb terminals connected to mainframe computers at data processing centers. (I still keep a dumb terminal on my desk to boost the morale of my aging Macintosh SE.)

duplex

Simultaneous transmission of signals in both directions through a transmission medium.

EBCDIC (Extended Binary Coded Decimal Interchange Code)

A method of representing alphabetic, numeric, and control characters, used by most IBM computers. Also see "ASCII."

EDUCOM

A not-for-profit consortium of higher education institutions in the USA that facilitates the introduction, use, and management of information resources in the educational and research communities.

EFF (Electronic Frontier Foundation)

An organization established to serve as a clearinghouse and forum for discussion of the many legal and social issues associated with computer communications in the U.S. and the world.

e-mail address

A userid + a domain name (e.g., info@nwnet.net) designating a person or service at a particular network host. By analogy to regular postal mail, an e-mail address contains a "name" and a "location."

emoticon

A non verbal symbol used to express emotional nuances in electronic communication. "!," "?" and so forth are already well-established, traditional emoticons. In computer mediated communications, symbols such as "*" for *emphasis,* smilies, and other special symbols are also used.

encryption

The process of translating data into a more or less secret code. Encrypted data requires a "key" to translate the code back to the original state. Encryption is used when storing or transmitting valuable information: for example, files containing passwords should be encrypted, and sensitive or private e-mail messages might be encrypted.

Ethernet

A popular local area network technology. Ethernet allows for transmission speeds of 10 Mbps (10 million bits per second), and is typically found running over passive coaxial cable or shielded twisted pair wiring as the transmission medium.

FAQ (Frequently Asked Question)
Questions that are often posed to a particular discussion or newsgroup. To keep such questions from overwhelming discussion, these questions along with their answers are compiled and distributed in files called FAQs. Most groups routinely post the FAQ or directions on how to obtain it.

FARNET (Federation of American Research Networks)
A not-for-profit organization whose mission is to advance the use of computer networks and to improve research and education. Its members include Internet service providers, telecommunications companies, and network equipment manufacturers (e.g., NorthWestNet, ANS, Bellcore, Merit, Sprint, CERFnet, PSINet, CICNet, and NYSERNet).

FDDI (Fiber Distributed Data Interface)
A high-speed networking standard using fiber optics as a transmission medium and a Token Ring topology.

fiber optics
Technology that allows high speed data transmission using light though a flexible bundle of glass fibers.

file server
A computer that shares its file storage media with other computers; also see "mail server" and "archive."

file transfer
Moving a file from one computer to another.

firewall
A configuration of local computers or networks that protects local systems and information from intruders coming from the external network.

finger
A program that displays information about one or more users on a particular Unix host.

flame
An intentionally polemical, inflammatory, or argumentative statement in an electronic message, or to send a message containing such a statement. When two or more people flame each other in a discussion or newsgroup you have a "flame war"— not a good thing to get involved with and an annoyance to everyone subjected to the heat. "Flame bait" is a statement in a posting to a Usenet newsgroup or other discussion group that is meant to provoke others into a flame war. Resist the temptation to take such bait.

FNC (Federal Networking Council)
A group of representatives from U.S. federal agencies who coordinate networking activities of these agencies.

FQDN (Fully Qualified Domain Name)
The complete domain name by which an Internet host is uniquely identified within the Internet. For example, at your site you may be able to login to an Internet host by typing "solaris", but the FQDN might be solaris.brasilia.br.

Free-Net
A site using the "Free-Net" software developed at Case Western Reserve University; designed to provide community based, public access networking services to the general public.

freeware
Software which can be used and copied without charge.

FTP (File Transfer Protocol)
A machine and operating system independent method of transferring files between computers connected to the Internet.

full duplex
A circuit which allows simultaneous, two way transmission of information.

FYI (For Your Information)
A collection of introductory documents for Internet users within the RFC series distributed by the InterNIC.

gateway
A computer that connects networks using different communications protocols or applications and that can translate the formats in which data are packaged in the different networks. For example, there are several gateways that allow e-mail messages to be transmitted between Internet and BIT-NET hosts even though these networks use very different formats for addresses.

GIF (Graphical Interchange Format)
A format for encoding high resolution graphics in computer files. Developed originally in the CompuServe network, but now widely used throughout the Internet.

Gopher
A document delivery system that allows information from all over the Internet to be presented to a user in a hierarchically organized front end. A Gopher user can search through remote documents for texts of interest and can retrieve remote documents to their local system.

the great renaming
The day when the current hierarchical, multilevel Usenet naming scheme was developed (comp, misc, sci, etc., with multilevel subnames). Prior to this time, Usenet newsgroup names had the format "net.newsgroupname," but this became unwieldy with the proliferation of Usenet beyond it's originator's wildest dreams.

GOSIP (Government OSI Profile)
A subset of OSI standards which are intended to become the de facto networking standards for U.S. government networking.

GSI (Government System Inc.)
The current manager of the DDN NIC.

GUI (Graphical User Interface)
A type of full screen software that employs on-screen images of any combination of windows, menus, icons, scroll bars, and other images for manipulating information, and uses peripheral devices such as mice, trackballs, wired gloves, light pens, or eye-trackers to manipulate these on-screen images.

hacker
A person who delights in having an intimate understanding of the internal workings of a system, in particular, computers or networks. For hackers, this understanding leads to an obsession with elegant solutions that extend the capabilities and functionality of the system in question. The popular press has used the word "hacker" for people who break into computers and networks, but such individuals should be referred to as "crackers." Confusing the terms "hacker" and "cracker" is

bound to raise a hacker's hackles. (For a wonderful tour through the language and culture of hackers, read *The New Hacker's Dictionary,* by Eric Raymond.)

half duplex
A circuit which can transmit data only in one direction at a time.

header
Information at the beginning of an Internet packet, e-mail message, or Usenet article, that contains information about source and destination addresses, and other information useful for ensuring that the data is transmitted through the network.

heterogeneous network
A network comprised of computers using a variety of operating systems and/or communications protocols.

hexadecimal notation
Numerical notation in base 16 (a.k.a. "hex"), with the numbers 10 through 15 having the values "A" through "F." Thus, in hex, 16 would be written as "10," and 31 as "1F." Much computer code is stored and represented in hex notation.

hierarchical file system
A method of storing files in directories and sub-directories in a hierarchical fashion. A hierarchical file system can be represented as a tree, with a root (directory), branches (sub-directories), and branches off of branches. The leaves (or fruits!) at the ends of the branches of this tree are the files.

host
As used within *The Internet Passport*, a specific computer or computer system connected to the Internet. For example, "YALEVM" refers to an IBM mainframe host at Yale University, whose fully qualified domain name is yalevm.ycc.yale.edu. While we typically think of a host as a computer on the Internet that offers services to users (i.e., acts as a literal host to guests), all computers connected to the Internet can act as a host and can be thus designated.

host name
The portion of the fully qualified domain name that refers to the host itself. For example, in milton.u.washington.edu, "milton" is a host name within the "u.washington.edu" domain.

hypermedia
The inclusion of multiple media within a single format. For example, it is now possible to include digitized sounds and images in e-mail messages by using MIME inclusions.

IESG (Internet Engineering Steering Group)
A group of IETF area leaders concerned with facilitating the progress of the IETF working groups.

IETF (Internet Engineering Task Force)
A volunteer task force consisting of engineers and scientists from academia, government, and industry, which aids in the development, deployment, and maintenance of new Internet technologies. The IETF is subdivided into many working groups, each addressing specific Internet engineering and operating issues.

IMHO (In My Humble Opinion)
A way of indicating that the writer is aware that others may be offended by a controversial statement; e.g., "IMHO, baseball is vastly inferior to chess in exercising the upper arms."

interest group

A forum for the discussion of a topic via e-mail. The term "interest groups" is traditionally used to describe mailing lists on the Internet. There is usually a network address to which messages are sent and from which messages are distributed to all group members.

internet

(with a lower case "i") A set of heterogeneous networks that can intercommunicate by virtue of applications, gateways, routers, and bridges. Note that an "internet" may include networks which do not use TCP/IP. (See "Internet.")

Internet

(with an upper case "I") Historically, the network of networks throughout the world that intercommunicate by virtue of the IP suite of protocols.

Internet address

A numeric address of the format "www.xxx.yyy.zzz" that is assigned to devices on a TCP/IP network: for example, 128.95.112.1 is the Internet address of the Internet host ftphost.nwnet.net, stored internally as four binary "octets" of 8 bits each.

Internet draft

A preliminary version of an RFC distributed within the Internet community for suggestions and feedback.

Internet Society

see "ISOC (Internet Society)."

InterNIC

The InterNIC is the Network Information Center (NIC) "of first and last resort." It provides three sets of services: registration services for computers on the Internet, directory services for people and resources on the Internet, and information services devoted to information on networking itself.

IP (Internet Protocol)

A protocol specifying how packets of information are sent across a connectionless network. IP (sometimes referred to as TCP/IP) defines a general set of rules for formatting and routing packets from one network device to another.

ISDN (Integrated Services Digital Network)

A traditional telephone system upgraded with digital switches offering users with specialized equipment the ability to simultaneously send and receive both voice and data over a single standard telephone line.

ISOC (Internet Society)

A not-for-profit organization devoted to furthering the interconnecting of networks into a global communications and information infrastructure.

Kermit

A file transfer and terminal emulation program developed at Columbia University; available for a wide variety of operating systems.

Kilobyte

1,024 bytes of data.

knowbot

An application that carries a user's request for information to multiple locations on the network. At each service contacted, the user query is implemented in commands specific to that service. All search results are then collected and returned to the user.

LAN (Local Area Network)

A network connecting computers in a relatively small area, usually within a room, building, or set of buildings. Because of the short distances between computers in a LAN, these are often high-speed networks despite the use of low-cost transmission media such as coaxial cables or twisted pair wiring.

LISTSERV

A software program for efficient setup and maintenance of discussion groups. Although originally developed for use in the BITNET network, LISTSERV groups can be subscribed to by Internet users and many LISTSERV discussion groups are gatewayed to Usenet newsgroups.

mailbox

A file or directory on a user's host computer into which incoming e-mail messages are stored.

mail exploder

Software which allows e-mail sent to one e-mail address to be automatically distributed ("exploded") to many e-mail addresses.

mail gateway

A host which transfers e-mail messages between distinct networks and performs reformatting of mail addresses and headers needed for successful handling in the destination network.

mailing list

A list of the e-mail addresses of people interested in a particular topic. Typically, one sends a message to a mailbox associated with the mailing list, and the message will be distributed to all members of the mailing list.

mail server

A software program that distributes files or information in response to requests sent via e-mail. Internet examples include Almanac and netlib. Mail servers have also been used in BITNET to provide FTP-like services.

MAN (Metropolitan Area Network)

A network servicing a metropolitan area; in terms of geographic area serviced, midway between a LAN and a WAN.

MILNET

DDN network restricted to non-classified data. A part of the original ARPANET.

MIME (Multipurpose Internet Mail Extension)

An extension to Internet e-mail that allows transmission of non-textual data such as graphics, audio, video, and applications data (e.g., spreadsheets and word processing documents).

modem

A device which facilitates transmissions between digital devices (such as computers) over analog circuits (such as voice telephone lines).

Mosaic
A graphical interface (client) for the World Wide Web developed by the National Center for Super-computer Applications (NCSA). Currently runs on X-windows, MS Windows, and Macintosh computers.

name resolution
Conversion of a domain name to a numeric IP address.

NCSA Telnet
A freeware version of the Telnet software developed by the National Center for Supercomputer Applications for a variety of PC operating systems.

netiquette
"Network etiquette" or socially acceptable actions and communications on a network.

network
Two or more devices connected together in such a way that they can exchange data with each other.

newbie
A usually derogatory (but sometimes affectionate) term for someone new to a network and/or specific network services.

newsfeed
The host from which one receives Usenet news.

newsgroup
A topical discussion group within Usenet propagated via newsfeeds to a loosely defined, world-wide network of computers, including many on the Internet. One may submit messages to a news-group and read other's messages with newsreader software.

NIC (Network Information Center)
An organization that provides documentation, training, and related services for users of a particular network.

NII (National Information Infrastructure)
The combined national data, voice, and video communications infrastructure of the future. As part of a global information infrastructure, the NII is envisioned to offer computer, telephone, and video services to the majority of the U.S. population. Often referred to with the popular term "information superhighway."

NNTP (Network News Transfer Protocol)
A protocol that allows Usenet news stored on one Internet host to be selectively copied to or read by newsreaders on other Internet hosts.

NOC (Network Operations Center)
An organization responsible for the day-to-day monitoring, maintenance, and technical trouble-shooting of a particular network.

node
1) In the context of the Internet, a particular computer or computer system connected to the Internet.
2) In the context of hypertext, an individual piece of text; each node is connected by one or more links to one or more hypertext nodes.

NPTN (National Public Telecomputing Network)
A not-for-profit U.S. organization dedicated to establishing and developing free computerized information and communication services for the general public. Loosely modeled on the U.S. National Public Broadcasting systems for radio and television.

NREN (National Research and Education Network)
An emerging national network in the U.S. designed to promote greater collaboration among educational institutions, government, and federal research laboratories, industry, and high-performance computing centers.

NSF (National Science Foundation)
U.S. government agency that provides funds for research and education in many areas, including computer networking.

NSFNET (National Science Foundation Network)
A high-speed TCP/IP backbone in the U.S. connecting midlevel networks. Originally created to provide high speed access to NSF sponsored supercomputer sites, NSFNET has broadened its focus to provide general network connectivity to research and education communities throughout the U.S.

NTIA (National Telecommunications and Information Administration)
A division of the U.S. Department of Commerce that functions as the principle advisor to president on telecommunications issues; develops and presents plans and policies in telecommunications; serves as the principle federal telecommunications research and engineering laboratory

NTP (Network Time Protocol)
An IP protocol that synchronizes clocks on hosts throughout the Internet.

octet
Generally, a set of eight. In the context of IP addresses, this term refers to the eight digits in binary (base 2) notation needed to represent the possible values from 0 to 255 ("00000000" to "11111111"). In classical music, an ensemble of eight instruments, or a piece of music written for eight instruments (e.g., Stravinsky's "L'Histoire du Soldat," one of my favorite pieces of music).

OPAC (Online Public Access Catalog)
Electronic databases of library holdings often accessible via a network. OPACs facilitate retrieval of information on library holdings by allowing users to search on such variables as author, title, keyword, and subject.

operating system (OS)
Software that controls the operation of a computer, installed software, and communications with attached devices. The operating system handles such tasks as input/output control, assignment of storage locations for data, control of peripheral devices like disk drives, scheduling of events within the computer, and much much much much much more.

OTOH (On the Other Hand)
Another example of e-mail shorthand.

packet
A unit of data sent through a packet switching network.

packet switching network
A network which can transmit data as packets in a connectionless mode.

■■

ping (Packet InterNet Groper)
A program used to determine if a remote Internet host is currently reachable from a local host; also used as a verb, e.g., "to ping a host."

poll
To periodically check a remote host for files, e-mail, or other information. Archie is an example of a software program which polls remote hosts.

POP (Post Office Protocol)
Mail server protocol required by some electronic mail programs.

port
1) Real or virtual access points to a computer, often times with distinct functions.
2) To modify a program so that it will run on a system for which it was not originally designed.

post
1) To send a message to a newsgroup.
2) An individual item in a newsgroup. Also called a "posting" or an "article."

postmaster
A person responsible for the installation, maintenance, and debugging of e-mail software at a given site. Often, but not always, reachable by the userid "postmaster" (or "postmast" on BITNET hosts).

PostScript
A programming language with powerful graphics and page-markup capabilities developed by Adobe Systems Incorporated. Many Internet documents are distributed in PostScript format and can be printed on PostScript capable laser printers yielding near publication quality output. On the Internet, files in PostScript format conventionally have filenames which end with ".ps", for example, "rfc1125.ps".

PPP (Point-to-Point Protocol)
A communications protocol that allows IP communications over serial lines. Also see, SLIP (Serial Line Internet Protocol).

protocol
Like "protocol" in human diplomacy, a set of previously agreed upon rules of communication within a network. Formal specification of the means of formatting, encoding, transmitting, receiving data, and recovering from communications faux pas.

RARE (Réseaux Associés pour la Recherche Européenne)
A European association of research networks.

relevance feedback
A method for finding information in which the contents of a search result is itself used as input for another search. A major feature of WAIS, relevance feedback is an attempt to allow computer searches to use a method that human beings seem to find natural ("this is like what I'm looking for but I can't tell you exactly how") but which is difficult to specify with standard Boolean logic.

resolver
A software program that provides name resolution services.

RFCs (Request For Comments)
Formal documents which are created by and distributed among members of the Internet community to help define the nuts and bolts of the Internet. The Internet would not exist without the core

documentation contained in RFCs. In the grand Internet tradition, RFCs range from documents proposing, formalizing, or modifying standard Internet protocols which must be used by all computers connected to the Internet (the bolts) to frivolous doggerel for the amusement of Internet users (the nuts).

root
1) In operating systems with hierarchical file systems, the directory from which all other directories branch.
2) In Unix, a special account set aside for use by the system manager, who has "root privileges," e.g., they can do almost anything.

route
The path which information takes in its passage through a network.

router
Network communications device that reads the header of each data packet and either directs it to the local network or sends it on down the line as appropriate. Physically, it's about the size of a large briefcase.

RTFM
A mildly sarcastic way of suggesting that someone asking a question should "Read The Friendly Manual" first. Or is it "Read The FAQ, Matey?"

self extracting archive
An archive of files which will automatically unpack to its component files when executed. Sometimes designated with the file extension ".sea".

server
A computer or device which provides a service to other computers or devices in a network. This is a real catch-all term: for example, name servers provide information about Internet hosts; terminal servers allow terminals to access computers, modem pools, or networks; and mail servers distribute files in response to e-mail requests.

shareware
Software that a person obtains for free with the understanding that if it is found to be of value, some small fee should be paid to the shareware author.

shell
A program usually accessed immediately upon login to a Unix account that interprets and executes whatever other programs the user requests. From the shell the user can change their password, look at their file listing, or start another program such as an editor. Common Unix shells include the C, Bourne, and Korn shells.

sig, or signature
The several lines of text which people often add to the end of their outgoing e-mail messages or Usenet postings; it usually includes contact information and, depending on preference, nuggets of personal philosophy, standard disclaimers, or whatever. If you use a signature, keep it short (< 5 lines, ideally).

SLIP (Serial Line Internet Protocol)
A communications protocol used over serial lines (such as computers connected via modem to dialup phone circuits) to support IP connectivity. Also see, PPP (Point-to-Point Protocol).

SMTP (Simple Mail Transfer Protocol)

A protocol used on the Internet that defines the format, packaging, and commands for the transmission and receipt of e-mail messages.

snail mail

The derogatory term for regular postal mail used by those of us who have become spoiled by the immediacy of e-mail. Still useful for whatever we can't cram into our terminals, like chocolates or care packages.

SNMP (Simple Network Management Protocol)

The protocol that includes management of an internet, and network entities such as hosts and terminal servers.

standard disclaimer

A phrase at the end of an electronic message which is supposed to dissociate an individual's statement from the organization with which they are affiliated.

store and forward

A stepping-stone version of networking used by BITNET, FidoNet, and their related networks. Although the details vary among these networks, the basic method is that a transmitted message is received and held in an intermediate host until a circuit to the destination or other intermediate host becomes available.

systems administrator

The person(s) responsible for the day-to-day maintenance of an Internet host; sometimes abbreviated as "sysadmin" or "admin." Usually a sysadmin is working for an institution and does not technically "own" the host, but nonetheless is vested with responsibilities and privileges associated with ownership.

SYSOP (Systems Operator)

The person responsible for the day-to-day maintenance of a BBS (Bulletin Board System). With the notable exceptions of government and corporate BBSs, a sysop is frequently the owner of the BBS.

T1

Telecommunications at speeds of approximately 1.5 megabits/second.

T3

Telecommunications at speeds of approximately 45 megabits/second.

tar

1) A Unix program that combines two or more separate files into one file; often used to simplify the handling and transferring of files.

2) The suffix conventionally appended to the filename of an archive made by the tar program.

TCP (Transmission Control Protocol)

A major protocol used over the Internet Protocol (IP) providing reliable, ordered, end-to-end transmission of byte streams.

TCP/IP (Transmission Control Protocol over Internet Protocol)

A set of protocols which make Telnet, FTP, electronic mail and other services possible among the computers within a heterogeneous network.

■■■I

TELENET
Not to be confused with Telnet! A commercial e-mail service packet switched network using the CCITT X.25 protocols.

Telnet
The Internet standard protocol allowing logins to remote hosts. With Telnet, one has access to the commands, services, and central processing unit of the remote host.

terminal emulation
A process by which a computer acts like a specific kind of terminal when connected to another computer. This is necessary because of the wide variety of proprietary methods used by different computers for encoding and sending information: for example, IBM developed "3270" terminals, and DEC developed "VT" series terminals (such as VT100) for use with their mainframes. Terminal emulation software typically allows emulation of a variety of terminal types.

thread
A topic that is being discussed in a successive exchange of messages by two or more participants within a newsgroup or discussion group.

tn3270
A version of Telnet used for remote logins to IBM mainframes that uses 3270 terminal type emulation.

Unix
A multi-user, multitasking operating system which includes numerous utilities that can be linked together for greater effect. Developed at Bell Laboratories, modified by the University of California at Berkeley, and used extensively in the early development of the IP protocols, Unix is a common operating system used throughout the Internet. "*nix" refers to the various versions and dialects (also known as "flavors") of Unix that have been developed, including Dynix, Ultrix, and AIX.

URL (Uniform Resource Locator)
A URL is a method for describing the location and access method of a resource on the Internet. Designed originally for use on the World Wide Web, URLs are being used in more and more situations.

Usenet
A collection of thousands of topically named newsgroups, the set of computers which exchange some or all of these newsgroups, and the community of people who read or submit Usenet news. Not all Internet hosts subscribe to Usenet newsgroups, and Usenet newsgroups may be received by non-Internet hosts.

userid
User Identification. The name by which one has authorized access to a computer system, and the part of an Internet address by which a person or service is known in an Internet address.

UUCP (Unix to Unix CoPy)
1) A method of sending files and e-mail via dialup lines that was originally developed for use between Unix computers.
2) A network which currently uses the UUCP program for transmitting Usenet news and e-mail.

uuencode / uudecode
Unix commands for modifying binary files in order to be sent via Internet e-mail or UUCP.

■■

vaporware

Software which has been promised (and often described in glowing terms) but which has not yet been (and may never be) released.

VT100

A common form of terminal emulation using communications protocols developed for the VT100 terminal from Digital Equipment Corporation. Most communications software includes VT100 emulation, and emulation for other members of the VT family (VT52, VT102, etc.).

WAIS (Wide Area Information Server)

A client-server information system based on the Z39.50 protocol which allows users to search through heterogeneous databases with a single user interface.

WAN (Wide Area Network)

A network designed to cover large geographic areas.

white pages

By analogy to telephone directories, a listing of e-mail addresses and other information pertaining to network users and usually available over the network.

whois

An Internet directory service program that allows users to obtain information about other users, domains, networks, and hosts. Whois is commonly used to query a central database maintained by the DDN NIC, but may also be used to search databases maintained for smaller portions of the Internet.

WWW (World Wide Web)

An increasingly popular client-server software package which uses hypertext to organize and present information and services throughout the Internet.

X-windows or X11

A windowed graphical user interface developed at MIT. X-windows allows information from multiple hosts to be displayed in separate windows on a single screen.

X.400

A CCITT and ISO e-mail standard.

X.500

A CCITT and ISO standard for directory services.

yellow pages

By analogy to telephone directories, a listing of Internet services and/or service providers, ideally including the type(s) of service(s) offered and access information.

Z39.50

An ANSI information searching and retrieval protocol which allows the searching of multiple databases using a common protocol. Currently employed by WAIS and some online library systems.

Index

■■■

■■

■ I

■■■

■■■

■■■

■■